CHRIST AND SPIRIT
IN THE NEW TESTAMENT

CHRIST AND SPIRIT
IN THE
NEW TESTAMENT

EDITED BY

BARNABAS LINDARS, s.s.f.

Lecturer in Old Testament Studies in the University of Cambridge

AND

STEPHEN S. SMALLEY

Lecturer in New Testament Studies in the University of Manchester

IN HONOUR OF

CHARLES FRANCIS DIGBY MOULE

M.A., HON. D.D., F.B.A.

Lady Margaret's Professor of Divinity in the University of Cambridge

CAMBRIDGE
AT THE UNIVERSITY PRESS
1973

Published by the Syndics of the Cambridge University Press
Bentley House, 200 Euston Road, London NW1 DB2
American Branch: 32 East 57th Street, New York, N.Y.10022

© Cambridge University Press 1973

Library of Congress Catalogue Card Number: 72-91367

ISBN: 0 521 20148 9

Printed in Great Britain
at the University Printing House, Cambridge
(Brooke Crutchley, University Printer)

CONTENTS

Contents

PART TWO

THE SPIRIT IN THE NEW TESTAMENT

Contents

PART THREE
CHRIST AND SPIRIT TODAY

OPEN LETTER

Dear Professor Moule,

This volume of essays is presented to you as a token of the affection and esteem of your many friends. We have chosen 'Christ and Spirit' as the themes of this book, because it is in these two theological areas that you have yourself shown most interest and written most. But the application of your special gifts of teaching and research has never been restricted, and your unique contribution to New Testament scholarship in general, associated particularly with the Lady Margaret's chair of Divinity in Cambridge which you have occupied for several years with such distinction, is one for which very many will always remain in your debt.

The essays gathered in this volume represent the high regard for you of many people throughout the world, who in company with the editors and contributors speak for your wide range of contacts and wish to honour you as a Christian and a scholar. Your personal example of selfless humility and interest in others we shall always cherish. Above all, we shall continue to be grateful for the way in which you have taught us that faith and scholarship can belong together and become mutually illuminating.

Our hope is that by your written and spoken words, as well as by your life of dedication, you will long continue to be an inspiration to us.

With our grateful thanks,

BARNABAS LINDARS, S.S.F.
STEPHEN SMALLEY

C. F. D. MOULE

CURRICULUM VITAE

Born: 3 December 1908 in Hangchow, China.

Classical scholar, Emmanuel College, Cambridge, 1927 (Classical Tripos, Part i, first class, 1929; Part ii, first class, 1931, B.A., 1931; M.A., 1934. Evans Prize, 1931; Jeremie Septuagint Prize, 1932; Crosse Scholarship, 1933.

Theological training, Ridley Hall, Cambridge, 1931–3. Ordained deacon, 1933; priest, 1934.

Curate of St Mark's Church and Tutor of Ridley Hall, Cambridge, 1933–4.

Curate of St Andrew's Church, Rugby, 1934–6.

Vice-Principal of Ridley Hall, Cambridge, 1936–44.

Curate of the University Church of St Mary the Great, Cambridge, 1936–40.

Fellow of Clare College, Cambridge, 1944–; Dean, 1944–51.

Assistant Lecturer in Divinity, University of Cambridge, 1944–7; Lecturer, 1947–51.

Lady Margaret's Professor of Divinity, University of Cambridge, 1951–.

Canon Theologian of Leicester Cathedral, 1955–.

Hon. D.D., St Andrews, 1958.

Fellow of the British Academy, 1966–.

President of Studiorum Novi Testamenti Societas, 1967–8.

Burkitt Medal of the British Academy, 1970.

Honorary Fellow of Emmanuel College, Cambridge, 1972–.

Honorary Member of the Society for Biblical Literature (U.S.A.).

Special lectures: The Ethel M. Wood Lecture in the University of London, 1964; the Manson Memorial Lecture in the University of Manchester, 1964; the first David S. Schaff Lectures at Pittsburgh Theological Seminary, Pennsylvania, 1966; the Purdy Lectures of the Hartford Seminary Foundation, Connecticut, 1970.

BIBLIOGRAPHY OF THE WORKS OF
C. F. D. MOULE

1939

'Matthew 5: 21, 22', *Exp. T.* l (1938–9), pp. 189f.

1944

'Revelation and the Bible', *The Churchman* lviii (1944), pp. 110ff.

1945

'Baptism with Water and with the Holy Ghost', *Theology* xlviii (1945), pp. 246ff.

'A Note on Gal. 2: 17, 18', *Exp. T.* lvi (1944–5), p. 223.

1948

'The Origins of the Christian Ministry', *The Churchman* lxii (1948), pp. 71ff.

'A Note on ὀφθαλμοδουλία', *Exp. T.* lix (1947–8), p. 250.

'A Note on Eph. 1: 22, 23', *Exp. T.* lx (1948–9), p. 53.

1951

'"Fullness" and "Fill" in the New Testament', *Scottish Journal of Theology* iv (1951), pp. 79ff.

1952

The Language of the New Testament: Inaugural Lecture (Cambridge: University Press, 1952).

'The Use of Parables and Sayings as Illustrative Material in Early Christian Catechesis', *JTS* n.s. iii (1952), pp. 75ff.

'From Defendant to Judge – and Deliverer: an Inquiry into the Use and Limitations of the Theme of Vindication in the New Testament', *Bulletin of* Studiorum Novi Testamenti Societas iii (Cambridge: University Press, 1952; reprinted 1963), pp. 40ff. Reprinted in *The Phenomenon of the New Testament* (London: SCM, 1967), pp. 82ff.

1953

An Idiom Book of New Testament Greek (Cambridge: University Press, 1953).

The Meaning of Hope (London: Highway Press, 1953). Reprinted, with introduction by J. Reumann, as Facet Book, Biblical Series no. 5 (Philadelphia: Fortress Press, 1963).

1954

'H. W. Moule on Acts 4: 25', *Exp. T.* lxv (1953–4), pp. 220f.

'A Note on "Under the fig tree" in John 1: 48, 50', *JTS* n.s. v (1954), pp. 210f.

1955

'A Note on *Didache* 9: 4', *JTS* n.s. vi (1955), pp. 240ff.

'Deacons in the New Testament', *Theology* lviii (1955), pp. 405ff.

'Some Reflections on the "Stone" *Testimonia* in Relation to the Name Peter', *NTS* ii (1955–6), pp. 56ff.

'St Mark 16: 8 Once More', *NTS* ii (1955–6), pp. 58f.

1956

The Sacrifice of Christ (London: Hodder & Stoughton, 1956). Reprinted, with introduction by J. Reumann, as Facet Book, Biblical Series no. 12 (Philadelphia: Fortress Press, 1964).

'The Judgment Theme in the Sacraments', in *The Background of the New Testament and its Eschatology: Studies in Honour of C. H. Dodd*, edd. W. D. Davies and D. Daube (Cambridge: University Press, 1956), pp. 464ff.

(With A. M. G. Stephenson), 'R. G. Heard on Q and Mark', *NTS* ii (1955–6), pp. 114ff.

'Read and Grasp', *Theology Today* xii (1955–6), pp. 484ff.

'The Nature and Purpose of 1 Peter', *NTS* iii (1956–7), pp. 1ff.

1957

The Epistles of Paul the Apostle to the Colossians and to Philemon, The Cambridge Greek Testament Commentary (Cambridge: University Press, 1957).

Christ's Messengers, World Christian Books no. 19 (London: Lutterworth, 1957).

'The Biblical Conception of "Faith"', *Exp. T.* lxviii (1956–7), pp. 157, 221f.

'The Ascension – Acts 1:9', in series, 'Expository Problems', *Exp. T.* lxviii (1956–7), pp. 205 ff.

'The Post-Resurrection Appearances in the Light of Festival Pilgrimages', *NTS* iv (1957–8), pp. 58ff.

1958

'Form Criticism and Philological Studies', *The London Quarterly and Holborn Review* clxxxiii (1958), pp. 87ff.

'Commentaries on the Epistle to the Hebrews', *Theology* lxi (1958), pp. 228ff.

1959

An Idiom-Book of New Testament Greek, 2nd edition (Cambridge: University Press, 1959).

'The Intention of the Evangelists', in *New Testament Essays: Studies in Memory of T. W. Manson*, ed. A. J. B. Higgins (Manchester: University Press, 1959), pp. 165ff. Reprinted in *The Phenomenon of the New Testament* (London: SCM, 1967), pp. 100ff.

'Once More, Who Were the Hellenists?', *Exp. T.* lxx (1958–9), pp. 100ff.

'The Influence of Circumstances on the Use of Christological Terms', *JTS* n.s. x (1959), pp. 247ff.

1960

'A Reconsideration of the Context of *Maranatha*', *NTS* vi (1959–60), pp. 307ff.

Worship in the New Testament, Ecumenical Studies in Worship, edd. J. G. Davies and A. R. George, no. 9 (London: Lutterworth, 1961).

A Chosen Vessel, World Christian Books, no. 37 (London: Lutterworth, 1961).

'The Parables of the Jesus of History and the Lord of Faith', in *Religion in Education* xxviii (1961), pp. 60ff.

'Problems in Translating the Bible', *The Listener* lxv (23 March 1961), pp. 527, 530.

'Revised Reviews: Hoskyns and Davey, *The Riddle of the New Testament*', *Theology* lxiv (1961), pp. 144ff.

1962

The Birth of the New Testament (London: A. & C. Black, 1962).

A Commentary on the Acts of the Apostles (Colombo: C.P.C.L., 1962)

– a single version in Sinhalese of *Christ's Messengers* and *A Chosen Vessel*.

'Colossians and Philemon', in *Peake's Commentary on the Bible*, revised by M. Black and H. H. Rowley (London: Nelson, 1962).

Articles: 'Adoption', 'Children of God', 'Fulfil', 'God, N.T.', 'Mystery', 'Pleroma', 'Providence', in *The Interpreter's Dictionary of the Bible*, ed. G. A. Buttrick (New York: Abingdon Press, 1962).

'The Sacrifice of the People of God (1)', in *The Parish Communion Today*, ed. D. M. Paton (London: S.P.C.K., 1962), pp. 78ff.

'The Individualism of the Fourth Gospel', *Nov. T.* v (1962), pp. 171ff.

'Funk–Debrunner, 1961: an Epoch', *Exp. T.* lxxiii (1961–2), pp. 336ff.

1963

'Commentaries on Matthew', *Theology* lxvi (1963), pp. 140ff.

'Prolegomena: the New Testament and Moral Decisions', in series, 'Important Moral Issues', *Exp. T.* lxxiv (1962–3), pp. 370ff. Reprinted in *Important Moral Issues*, edd. A. W. and E. Hastings (Edinburgh: T. & T. Clark, 1966), pp. 9ff.

1964

Man and Nature in the New Testament, Ethel M. Wood Lecture (London: Athlone Press, 1964). Reprinted, with introduction by J. Reumann, Facet Book, Biblical Series no. 17 (Philadelphia: Fortress Press, 1967).

'The Influence of Circumstances on the Use of Eschatological Terms' (Presidential Address to the Oxford Society of Historical Theology, October 1962), *JTS* n.s. xv (1964), pp. 1ff.

Articles: 'Colossians, Epistle to the', 'Ephesians, Epistle to the', 'Philemon, Epistle to', in *Encyclopaedia Britannica* (London: 1964 edition).

'St Matthew: Some Neglected Features', *Studia Evangelica II = Texte und Untersuchungen zur Geschichte der altchristlichen Literatur*, lxxxvii (Berlin: Akademie-Verlag, 1964), pp. 91ff.

'Is Christ Unique?', in *Faith, Fact and Fantasy* (London: Collins, Fontana, 1964), pp. 101ff.

1965

Editor: *Miracles: Cambridge Studies in their Philosophy and History* (London: Mowbray, 1965).

'The Vocabulary of Miracles', *Miracles*, pp. 235ff.

'The Classification of Miracle Stories', *Miracles*, pp. 239ff.

The Gospel according to Mark, The Cambridge Bible Commentary (Cambridge: University Press, 1965).

'How the New Testament Came into Being', in *Understanding the New Testament*, The Cambridge Bible Commentary, Introductory Volume, ed. O. J. Lace (Cambridge: University Press, 1965), pp. 64ff.

'Punishment and Retribution: an Attempt to Delimit their Scope in New Testament Thought', *Svensk Exegetisk Årsbok* xxx (1965), pp. 21ff.

'The Problem of the Pastoral Epistles: a Reappraisal', Manson Memorial Lecture, 1964, *Bulletin of the John Rylands Library* xlvii (1965), pp. 430ff.

1966

The Birth of the New Testament, 2nd edition (London: A. & C. Black, 1966).

Het Nieuwe Testament in de Oude Kerk = Birth, translated by L. A. Rood (Utrecht: Het Spectrum 1966).

'The Christology of Acts', in *Studies in Luke–Acts: Essays Presented in Honour of Paul Schubert*, edd. L. E. Keck and J. L. Martyn (Nashville, Tennessee: Abingdon, 1966), pp. 159ff.

'St Paul and "Dualism": the Pauline Conception of Resurrection', *NTS* xii (1965–6), pp. 106ff.

1967

Joint editor: *Christian History and Interpretation: Studies Presented to John Knox* (Cambridge: University Press, 1967).

'Obligation in the Ethic of Paul', in *Christian History and Interpretation*, edd. W. R. Farmer, C. F. D. Moule and R. R. Niebuhr (Cambridge: University Press, 1967), pp. 389ff.

The Phenomenon of the New Testament, Studies in Biblical Theology, Second Series 1 (London: S.C.M., 1967).

1968

'Fulfilment-Words in the New Testament: Use and Abuse' (Presidential Address to Studiorum Novi Testamenti Societas, 1967), *NTS* xiv (1967–8), pp. 293ff.

Introduction to *The Significance of the Message of the Resurrection for*

Faith in Jesus Christ, Studies in Biblical Theology, Second Series 8 (London: SCM, 1968).

'Some Fresh Considerations on St Paul's "Dualism"', *Studia Evangelica IV = Texte und Untersuchungen zur Geschichte der altchristlichen Literatur* cii (Berlin: Akademie-Verlag, 1968), pp. 340ff.

'The Christian Understanding of Forgiveness', *Theology* lxxi (1968), pp. 435ff.

1969

The Letters of Paul the Apostle to the 1960s, Drawbridge Memorial Lecture, 1969 (London: Christian Evidence Society, 1969).

The Gospel according to Mark, The Cambridge Bible Commentary, 2nd edition (Cambridge: University Press, 1969).

Articles: 'Epaphras', 'Epaphroditus', 'Epheserbrief', 'Gefangenschaftsbriefe', 'Kolossä', 'Kolosserbrief', 'Laodicenerbrief', 'Schuldbrief', in *Biblisch-Historisches Handwörterbuch*, hrsg. von B. Reicke und L. Rost (Göttingen: Vandenhoeck u. Ruprecht, 1969).

'Mark 4: 1–20 Yet Once More', in *Neotestamentica et Semitica: Studies in Honour of Principal Matthew Black*, edd. E. E. Ellis and M. Wilcox (Edinburgh: T. & T. Clark, 1969), pp. 95ff.

'The Angry Word (Matt. 5: 21)', in series, 'Uncomfortable Words', *Exp. T.* lxxxi (1969–70), pp. 10ff.

1970

'Further Reflections on Philippians 2: 5–11', in *Apostolic History and the Gospel: Biblical and Historical Essays presented to F. F. Bruce on his 60th Birthday*, edd. W. W. Gasque and R. P. Martin (Exeter: Paternoster Press, 1970), pp. 264ff.

'Death "to Sin", "to Law", and "to the World": a Note on certain Datives', in *Mélanges Bibliques en hommage au Révérend Père Béda Rigaux*, edd. A. Descamps and A. de Halleux (Gembloux: Duculot, 1970), pp. 367ff.

'A Neglected Factor in the Interpretation of Johannine Eschatology', in *Studies in John presented to Professor Dr J. N. Sevenster on the occasion of his Seventieth Birthday* (Leiden: Brill, 1970), pp. 155ff.

'Jesus in the New Testament Kerygma', in *Verborum Veritas: Festschrift für Gustav Stählin zur 70. Geburtstag*, hrsg. von O. Böcher und K. Haacker (Wuppertal: Brockhaus, 1970), pp. 15ff.

1971

La Genèse du Nouveau Testament = *Birth*, translated by R. Mazerand (Delachaux et Niestlé, 1971).

El Fenomeno del Nuevo Testamento = *Phenomenon*, translated by J. M. Cortés (Desclée de Brouwer, 1971).

Le origini del Nuovo Testamento = *Birth*, Studi Biblici 15, translated by P. Spanu, revised by F. Ronchi (Brescia: Paideia Editrice, 1971).

'The Techniques of New Testament Research: A Critical Survey', in *Jesus and Man's Hope*, vol. ii (Pittsburgh Theological Seminary, 1971), pp. 29ff.

'The New Testament', in *Preface to Christian Studies*, ed. F. G. Healey (London: Lutterworth, 1971), pp. 33ff.

'The Theory of Forgiveness', in *From Fear to Faith: Studies of Suffering and Wholeness*, ed. N. Autton (London: S.P.C.K., 1971), pp. 61ff.

'The Holy Spirit in the Scriptures', *The Church Quarterly* iii (1971), pp. 279ff.

1972

'2 Cor. 3: 18b, καθάπερ ἀπὸ κυρίου πνεύματος', in *Neues Testament und Geschichte: historisches Geschehen und Deutung im Neuen Testament, Oscar Cullmann zum 70. Geburtstag*, hrsg. von H. Baltensweiler und B. Reicke (Zürich: Theologischer Verlag/Tübingen: J. C. B. Mohr, 1972), pp. 231ff.

'The Manhood of Jesus in the New Testament', in *Christ, Faith and History, Cambridge Studies in Christology*, ed. S. W. Sykes and J. P. Clayton (Cambridge University Press, 1972), pp. 95ff.

ABBREVIATIONS

Series and Periodicals

An. Bibl.	*Analecta Biblica*
B. ev. Th.	*Beiträge zur evangelischen Theologie*
BJRL	*Bulletin of the John Rylands Library*
BZ	*Biblische Zeitschrift*
BZNW	*Beihefte zur Zeitschrift für die Neutestamentliche Wissenschaft*
CB	*The New Century Bible*
CBQ	*Catholic Biblical Quarterly*
CNT	*Commentaire du Nouveau Testament*
CQR	*Church Quarterly Review*
CSEL	*Corpus Scriptorum Ecclesiasticorum Latinorum*
Ét. Bibl.	*Études bibliques*
EKK	*Evangelisch-Katholischer Kommentar*
Ev. Th.	*Evangelische Theologie*
Exp. T.	*Expository Times*
HNT	*Handbuch zum Neuen Testament*
ICC	*The International Critical Commentary*
IDB	*The Interpreter's Dictionary of the Bible*
Int. B.	*The Interpreter's Bible*
JBL	*Journal of Biblical Literature*
JEH	*Journal of Ecclesiastical History*
JTS (n.s.)	*Journal of Theological Studies* (new series)
MNTC	*Moffatt New Testament Commentary*
NIC	*The New International Commentary on the New Testament* (= *The New London Commentary*)
Nov. T.	*Novum Testamentum*
NTD	*Das Neue Testament Deutsch*
NTS	*New Testament Studies*
OTS	*Oudtestamentische Studiën*
Pr.–Bauer	Erwin Preuschen, *Griechisch-deutsches Wörterbuch zu den Schriften des NT und der übrigen urchristlichen Literatur, bearbeitet von Walter Bauer*, Berlin, ⁵1958 (1971).

RAC	*Reallexikon für Antike und Christentum*
RB	*Revue Biblique*
RGG	*Die Religion in Geschichte und Gegenwart*
RHPR	*Revue d'Histoire et de Philosophie Religieuses*
RQ	*Revue de Qumran*
RSR	*Recherches de Science Religieuse*
TDNT	*A Theological Dictionary of the New Testament (= TWNT)*
Th. BL.	*Theologisches Begriffslexikon zum Neuen Testament*
Th. E.	*Theologische Existenz heute*
Th. HK.	*Theologischer Hand-Kommentar zum Neuen Testament*
Th. Z.	*Theologische Zeitschrift*
TLZ	*Theologische Literaturzeitung*
TNTC	*The Tyndale New Testament Commentary*
TU	*Texte und Untersuchungen zur Geschichte der altchristlichen Literatur*
TWNT	*Theologisches Wörterbuch zum Neuen Testament*
ZKG	*Zeitschrift für Kirchengeschichte*
ZNW	*Zeitschrift für die neutestamentliche Wissenschaft und die Kunde der älteren Kirche*
ZTK	*Zeitschrift für Theologie und Kirche*

PART ONE

CHRIST IN THE NEW TESTAMENT

Is there a Markan Christology?

E. TROCMÉ

There was a time when the Gospel of Mark was considered by a majority among New Testament scholars as a naïve and straight-forward Life of Jesus, which for the most part remained undistorted by 'later' christological ideas. No sensible person would dream to-day of going back to a non-christological interpretation of this fascinating little book. But it may be doubted whether enough thought has been given to the relationship between the evangelist's own christology and that (or those, as we shall see) of the various layers of tradition used by him. Did 'Mark', as W. Wrede and his followers claim, emphasize strongly a christological trend which had only begun to appear in an originally non-christological, Palestinian tradition? Or did he write with a view to reconciling the diverging christologies which he found in the various strands of tradition he brought together? Did he perhaps also tone down some of the wildest christological claims made on behalf of Jesus in these traditions and try to call the attention of his readers to what really mattered – their own attitude towards the Master and his call to follow him? There are some good reasons to opt for the latter hypothesis.

But before I go into that, a few basic assumptions of this essay may be simply stated, as space forbids any discussion on those points:[1]

(1) The Markan Gospel, as we have it to-day, may not be the earliest of the canonical Gospels; Luke could be slightly earlier (A.D. 80?). But there was an 'Urmarkus', which differed only slightly from the canonical Gospel except for its ending and was a good deal older than any other Gospel. In fact, it was with this *Urmarkus* that the literary *genre* had its origin.

(2) The raw material which went into the making of Mark, both in its original and in its canonical forms, consisted mostly of Palestinian traditions about Jesus, many of which had grown in the early Church,

---

[1] I stated my reasons to opt for these views in E. Trocmé, *La formation de l'Évangile selon Marc* (Paris, 1963).

while others came from other Palestinian circles where an interest in Jesus had developed at an early date.

(3) The writer of the original Gospel of Mark must have been strongly motivated to write such a book as his in spite of his very limited literary abilities. His motives and his purpose, as well as his own ideas on a number of topics, can certainly be detected if we look carefully at the selection and arrangement of traditions he achieved, and also at the editorial additions he made, whenever these can be traced.

There is no denying that the person of Jesus stands at the centre of the whole Markan Gospel. The narratives in which others play the main part are few and far apart: John the Baptist in 1: 1–8 and 6: 14–29; Peter in 14: 66–72; some women in 16: 1–8. The summaries which the evangelist uses as connecting links between small groups of anecdotes all report about Jesus or the reaction of other people to his teaching or his actions.

It is equally evident that the person of Jesus as he appears in the Gospel is quite out of the usual. As a teacher, as a healer, as a debater, as a leader of men, Jesus is described as radically different from the man in the street and greatly superior to the most prominent people (1: 7–8, 22, 27; 2: 12, 27–8; 3: 11, 27). These facts provide a wide and firm basis for a far-reaching christology.

But this striking emphasis on the person of Jesus was not the evangelist's own creation. It is almost universally accepted that early *Christian* tradition, in all its forms, was centred around Jesus and depicted him as having been vastly superior to any man. In the other stories used by Mark – miracle stories, for instance – Jesus usually played the main part and behaved in a most extraordinary way. In other words, the evangelist cannot be credited with the intention to turn an average rabbi or healer into a supernatural being. He started from Jesus-centred sayings and narratives and, even if he altered the image of the Master he found there, wrote an equally Jesus-centred book.

Many scholars belonging to various schools of thought accept this, but insist that Mark's own contribution was to superimpose a new conception of the person of Jesus on traditions which had so far made use of other categories when speaking about him. A very common brand of this approach is the assertion that the evangelist tried to build the christology of the Hellenistic church into a Palestinian tradition

4

which had so far nothing to do with the kerygma of Greek-speaking Christians. By so doing, this writer wanted – so we are told – to reinterpret the life of the Jesus of history as a Christ-event. This well-known theory is often taken for granted. It is based mostly on the penetrating exegetical remarks made by W. Wrede at the beginning of the century and has been carefully restated by well-known scholars on a number of occasions since then.[2] In other words, it cannot be treated lightly.

It is nonetheless difficult to avoid having second thoughts about it. Wrede's theory looks rather too much like an over-simplification to be wholly convincing. The traditions used in Mark were in part Hellenistic and quite a few, as for instance many of the miracle stories, had christological features from the start. As for Palestinian, Semitic traditions, it would be bold indeed to claim that they were utterly non-christological. The Son-of-Man sayings cannot all be struck out as late outgrowths, *pace* Ph. Vielhauer,[3] nor can every single saying about the Kingdom of God in which Jesus' ministry plays a part. Moreover, the Dead Sea Scrolls and cognate literature are there to remind us that Messianic undertones of all kinds were quite common in the Palestinian writings of those days.

Thus, it seems wiser to say that the evangelist made use of traditions which were all agreed on the fact that Jesus was an extraordinary man, but interpreted it in different ways: some christologically and some not; some with the help of Hellenistic ideas and some without. His literary endeavour was not aimed at 'kerygmatizing' the image of Jesus found in tradition, but at synthesizing the various images of the Master that existed earlier into a reasonably coherent whole.

This being said, one further mistake should be avoided. The evangelist is often thought to have had as his main purpose the building of a christology. But this might well be one aspect only of a wider design. Since all the traditions available to the evangelist were centred on Jesus, their combination was bound to give the impression of an exclusive interest in this person. Under close scrutiny, though, the structure of

---

[2] W. Wrede, *Das Messiasgeheimnis in den Evangelien, zugleich ein Beitrag zum Verständnis des Markusevangeliums*, Göttingen, 1901; M. Dibelius, *Die Formgeschichte des Evangeliums* (Tübingen, 1919; fifth edition 1966, cited here), pp. 230–4; R. Bultmann, *Die Geschichte der synoptischen Tradition* (Göttingen, 1921; 6th edition 1964, cited here), pp. 370–6; J. Schreiber, 'Die Christologie des Markusevangeliums', *ZTK*, lviii (1961), pp. 154–83.
[3] See his *Aufsätze zum Neuen Testament* (Munich, 1965), pp. 55–140.

the Markan Gospel and its redactional seams show a somewhat different picture.

Each one of the main sections concentrates on the relationship between Jesus and this or that group of people: the Galilean crowd in 1: 14 to 3: 12; the chosen disciples in 3: 13 to 6: 13; the crowd and the disciples in 6: 14 to 8: 29; the disciples as suffering servants in 8: 30 to 10: 52; the disciples and the Jerusalem crowd in 11: 1 to 13: 37. The Passion narrative is a case of its own, which may be left aside at this point. As each of these main sections is a combination of various strands of tradition, one gains the impression of a persistent effort made by the evangelist to turn Jesus-centred traditions into larger literary units in which men are confronted with the Master.

In the same way, the connecting remarks added by the evangelist put the stress on the relationship between Jesus and people around him, either crowd (1: 22, 32–4, 45; 2: 13; 3: 7–12; 4: 1; etc.) or disciples (3: 34; 5: 18–20; 6: 1, 30–2; 8: 17–21, 30; 9: 28–9) or even opponents (3: 6, 30; 7: 1–2; 11: 18). It is therefore a fair statement to say that the Gospel of Mark centres around the person of Jesus *and the behaviour of those who come face to face with him*. In its earliest form, this was an ecclesiological Gospel, if by ecclesiology we mean the doctrine of the gathering of men around Jesus. Its christological side was important, but less so than its constant emphasis on the call to follow the Master, learn from him and become the church-for-the-world. This should be borne in mind as we now turn to the Markan teaching about Jesus.

To begin with, let us try and discover which means the evangelist used in order to give his readers a new image of the Master.

The first of these is the blending of various types of tradition. It is most unlikely, for instance, that the miracle stories and the sayings of Jesus found side by side in the Markan Gospel should have come from the same circles. As a matter of fact, Jesus behaves so much like a magician in some of the roughest narratives of that book that these cannot possibly have originated in Church tradition, whether Palestinian or Hellenistic (5: 1–18; 5: 25–34; 7: 32–7; 8: 22–6; 11: 12–14, 20–1). Those stories were gathered by the evangelist and left unedited although they were put next to more edifying narratives and sayings, where the Master played the part of a rabbi. By choosing to depict the Lord as a preacher one minute, as a sorcerer the next moment, the writer was bound to give a shock to all his readers and to arouse their attention. They were led to expect something quite out of the usual and to realize that Mark's christology went beyond that of any of the Churches they knew.

Many scholars consider that the earliest evangelist expressed his bold new ideas about Jesus through his use of christological titles.[4] But opinions differ as to the titles favoured by Mark. Neither προφήτης nor the name Elijah, both rejected in 8: 27–9, nor κύριος, used almost exclusively as an address or with the meaning 'owner' or 'master', have any christological significance in Mark. 'Christ' – and the cognate titles 'Son of David' and 'King of the Jews' – is to say the least ambiguous in the eyes of the evangelist (see 8: 29ff.; 12: 35–7; 14: 61–2). It carries no special stress, even though it is not as drastically rejected as some think.[5]

'Son of God', 'Son of Man' and διδάσκαλος (with its cognates *rabbi* and *rabbouni*) are somewhat more common in the Gospel and do not seem to raise any objection on the part of the writer. But can it be said that those three titles, or one of them, are used by Mark to give expression to a new image of Jesus? 'Son of God' occurs six times only in the Gospel (1: 11; 3: 11; 5: 7; 9: 7; 14: 61; 15: 39), to which 13: 32 may perhaps be added, but not 1: 1, where textual evidence favours the omission of this phrase. The two occurrences in the Passion narrative (14: 61 and 15: 39) stand rather apart and did not belong to the original Gospel; even thus, the use of the title is limited to outsiders and plays no great part in chapters 14 to 16. Elsewhere in Mark, 'Son of God' is accepted only as a divine utterance (1: 11; 9: 7) which men have no right to imitate (3: 11–12; 5: 7–8); the evangelist objects to its use as a confession of christological faith.

'Son of Man' is somewhat more common in Mark: fourteen occurrences, concentrated mostly in the fourth main section of the Gospel (8: 31, 38; 9: 9, 12, 31; 10: 33, 45), as well as in chapter 14 (verses 21 – twice – 41 and 62), to which 2: 10, 28 and 13: 26 should be added. Although the phrase comes to the evangelist from tradition in a

---

[4] To take but a few recent examples, see E. Best, *The Temptation and the Passion: the Markan Soteriology* (Cambridge, 1965), pp. 160–77; B. Rigaux, *Témoignage de l'Évangile de Marc* (Bruges/Paris, 1965), pp. 118–20, 139–52; M. D. Hooker, *The Son of Man in Mark* (London, 1967), pp. 174–82; Ch. Masson, *L'Évangile de Marc et l'Église de Rome* (Neuchâtel, 1968), pp. 51–76; G. Minette de Tillesse, *Le secret messianique dans l'Évangile de Marc* (Paris, 1968), pp. 327–88.

[5] J. Héring, *Le Royaume de Dieu et sa venue* (2nd ed., Neuchâtel, 1959), pp. 111–43.

majority of cases, he may have inserted it himself here or there (10: 45?). But he is so careless about identifying this mysterious figure with Jesus that it cannot be claimed as part of a christological structure built by him on top of what various layers of tradition said about the Master. As a matter of fact, one may even wonder whether Mark has not left out 'Son of Man' occasionally in sayings offered by tradition, either by omitting part of the saying (3: 28; cf. Matt. 12: 32 and Luke 12: 10)[6] or by leaving aside the whole *logion* (cf. Matt. 8: 20 and Luke 9: 58; Matt. 11: 19 and Luke 7: 34; Matt. 12: 40 and Luke 11: 30). In other words, the use of 'Son of Man' in Mark reflects a very early christology which the evangelist found somewhat unsatisfactory and did not really make his own.

As to διδάσκαλος, it occurs twelve times in Mark (4: 38; 5: 35; 9: 17, 38; 10: 17, 20, 35; 12: 14, 19, 32; 13: 1; 14: 14), while *rabbi* is used three times (9: 5; 11: 21; 14: 45) and *rabbouni* once (10: 51). Interestingly enough, these figures are higher than the corresponding ones in Matthew (twelve times) and Luke (thirteen times), although the other two Synoptics are a good deal longer than Mark and devote much more space to recording the teaching of Jesus. Could that mean that the oldest Gospel favours a christology of the Master, which could be compared with the emphasis put in Qumran on the divine mission entrusted to the Teacher of Righteousness? It is not likely. In most of their occurrences, διδάσκαλος, *rabbi* and *rabbouni* are simply forms of address into which it would be quite wrong to read a deep christological meaning.

Thus, none of the titles applied to Jesus in the Gospel of Mark appears to be used by the evangelist as a vehicle for his own christology.

Another hypothesis was put forward by W. Wrede seventy years ago:[7] in order to superimpose the christological doctrine of his church on traditions to which it was foreign, Mark made use, it is suggested, of the literary device of the Messianic Secret; in other words, he re-arranged all the sayings and narratives which he started from in such a way as to show that the real nature of Jesus was revealed only to the privileged few in the Master's life-time, but carefully hidden from most

---

[6] H. E. Tödt, *Der Menschensohn in der synoptischen Überlieferung* (Gütersloh, 1959), pp. 111–12.

[7] W. Wrede, *op. cit.* Among recent treatments of this theory, see T. A. Burkill, *Mysterious Revelation, an Examination of the Philosophy of St Mark's Gospel* (Ithaca, 1963); G. Minette de Tillesse, *op. cit.*, with a very full bibliography.

people. Many of the literary features of the Gospel were mentioned as evidence for this bold theory: the secrecy that surrounded many of the healings, the silencing of demons, of witnesses and of disciples, the lack of understanding on the part of the disciples. This sounded so convincing that even those scholars who could not bring themselves to thinking of the evangelist as such a clever schemer concentrated their efforts on finding the origin of the Messianic Secret in the behaviour of Jesus himself or in tradition and forgot to ask whether that Secret really existed in the Markan Gospel.

In actual fact, there is every reason to doubt that existence. Wrede was so eager to give evidence for this theory that he brought together a number of features of Mark which have nothing to do with one another. The fact that some healings are achieved secretly (5: 40; 7: 33; 8: 23) is part of the pre-Markan narratives themselves; in spite of what is often said, it is not a common feature at all in Mark; there is no sign of an effort of the evangelist to generalize what remains the exception. Some patients, once they have been healed, are warned by Jesus against spreading the news of their recovery (1: 44; 5: 43; 7: 36; cf. 8: 26), but again this is the exception; there is every reason to think that this warning comes from pre-Markan tradition, notably since it is contradicted in two of those stories by the redactional ending added by the evangelist himself (1: 45; 7: 36–7); even if the warning is Mark's creation in this or that case, it is meant to emphasize the moral greatness of Jesus, not to hide his powers from the masses (5: 43; 8: 26). The silencing of demons is mentioned only three times (1: 24, 34; 3: 11–12), once in a pre-Markan narrative (1: 24) where it has no christological implication, but twice in summaries due to the evangelist in which the order is directly related to his christology; it is not an attempt at keeping secret what should not be known, as the context shows; it is rather the rejection of efforts made to stifle Jesus' action under words of praise spoken by those who cannot become disciples (cf. 8: 30ff.).

This polemical aspect of the Markan Gospel accounts also for part of what the writer has to say about the lack of understanding shown by the disciples – another feature of his work which is all too often taken as evidence of the Messianic Secret. Polemics against the wrong type of disciples mixes here with exhortations aimed at those who can still be made to understand what discipleship really means. To take but a few instances, polemics are central in 4: 10–13, which should be read as a reprimand addressed to 'those who surrounded him with the Twelve':

9

although the secret of the parables is theirs, they do not even understand the simplest of them; there is no sign whatever of a *Messianic Secret* here, but scorn is poured on those who claim to be initiates and are in fact dumb. The exhortatory aspect is more visible in 4: 35–41, even though the disciples are blamed for lack of faith (verse 40); no secret of any sort is alluded to here and the final question is nothing but a confession of faith. The obtuseness of the disciples is underscored by Mark in connection with the miraculous feedings (6: 35–7, 52; 8: 4, 15–21), the main theme being here an exhortation for the church to share its spiritual wealth with the crowd; it is hardly necessary to say that all this has nothing to do with a secret – except perhaps to repudiate the very idea of it. If the disciples seem particularly stupid in 9: 32, this is not evidence for a Messianic Secret, but for their foolish ambition and pride, their narrow-mindedness and heartlessness (9: 33–48).

Another feature of the Markan Gospel might seem to come to the rescue of the theory of the Messianic Secret, especially as it is a result of the literary activity of the evangelist; the private teaching given by Jesus to his disciples once the crowd has been offered what it can take (1: 38; 4: 33–4; 7: 17–23; 8: 15–21; 9: 28–9). But the additional information granted to the companions of the Master on those occasions is not christological in most cases. It concerns numerous aspects of the life of the Christian church and of Christians individually. As a matter of fact, it is simply a literary device meant to attract the attention of the readers of the Gospel to some consequences of the teaching and action of Jesus for their own lives.

In other words, under close scrutiny, the theory of the Messianic Secret simply vanishes for lack of evidence. We must look elsewhere to find out how Mark tried to convey to his readers a new image of Jesus.

Two examples will be enough if we keep in mind some of the remarks made earlier. The story of the day in Capernaum (1: 21–38) is based on two miracle stories (verses 23–7 and 29–31) and a saying (verse 38) which may have been part of a brief apophthegm (verses 35–8). The exorcism in verses 23–7 certainly comes from tradition which originated outside of the Christian church, whereas the other two units look like ecclesiastical tradition: this bold blending of widely diverging elements makes it necessary for Mark to suggest a christological synthesis. This is done in the first place by the emphasis put on the teaching of the Master (verses 21–2 and a few words in verse 27). It is the unique combination of teaching and healing which achieves momentous success (verse 28), so that, when healing claims exclusive rights on the time of Jesus (verses 29–34), a balance has to be restored (verse 39). Christ is thus both a peerless teacher and an immensely powerful lord of nature, whose ministry is urgently needed. No one can tie him down, least of all the disciples, whose task it is to follow him, not to make impressive statements about him (cf. verses 24 and 34).

The confession of Peter at Caesarea Philippi and the stern discourse that follows (8: 27 to 9: 1) is even more centred on the person of Jesus than the day in Capernaum. Mark combines here an apophthegm which he seems to have shortened (verses 27–9) and a number of isolated sayings, built into a dialogue followed by a speech where the hand of the evangelist is visible everywhere. Several imperfect christologies are set aside as popular and the title 'Christ' preferred: Mark has nothing to object to that classification, but goes into no ecstasy about it – rather to the contrary since, according to him, Jesus orders his disciples to keep silent about him instead of telling them whether they are right to call him 'Christ'. This sharp remark (verse 30) must be read in conjunction with what follows: the prophecy of the Passion (verses 31–2a), the rebuke to Peter (verses 32b–33), the menacing speech about cowards who hope to save their lives (8: 34 to 9: 1). The evangelist is reacting against some Christians, whose spokesman is Peter, who know too well who Jesus is and like saying it, but dare not risk too much to spread the Gospel. To his mind, the right christology is primarily an acceptance of suffering for the sake of Christ. It is easy to see here how the blending of traditions is used by Mark as the starting point of a new christology.

Can we also go one step further and gain an idea of the inner structure and balance of this Markan christology? Where lies the main emphasis in that rather bitty whole? As we saw, none of the christological titles can help us there. Neither can the average christology of the Hellenistic churches, nor, for that matter, that of the Palestinian churches, provided we were able to reconstruct it.

As a matter of fact, Mark seems to object to any christology which to his mind would pin down Jesus and bring him under the control of men. Are we then to assume that he replaced christology by a mere call to action, in the steps of Jesus? But that is not sufficient to account for the passionate interest he takes in the person of the Master. There is undoubtedly something more to his thinking about this Master.

We must remember that Mark was responsible for combining the sacred tradition of the early church with the roughest, queerest type of folk-tales about Jesus: the miracle stories. He must have been keenly interested in them to make that bold move and his interest may well have been aroused in the first place by the image of Jesus he found in these strange anecdotes. It was that of a θεῖος ἀνήρ, of course,[8] but too varied and too vague to become the direct basis for a christology.

But the evangelist was impressed in a special way by the ending of many of these stories: a sentence reporting on the astonishment and the fear felt by the crowd that had seen the miracle or heard about it (1: 27; 2: 12; 4: 41; 5: 15, 20; 5: 42; 7: 37; 9: 6). This expression of religious fear is in most cases part of the original stories. What is striking is that Mark borrowed it there and applied it to the teaching of Jesus (1: 22; 6: 2; 12: 17), suggesting thus that the right attitude towards all the activities of the Master was the stupefaction and fear aroused by miracles.[9]

If these feelings were in his eyes the proper confession of the faith, one may perhaps understand a little better why he felt he could cut short Peter's orthodox confession at Caesarea Philippi. It was too verbose for his taste and brought with itself an inability to grasp fundamental truths and a temptation to order the Lord about (verse 32b). It may also be easier to see why to the evangelist the question in 4: 41, asked in fear and trembling by the disciples, was a better expression of genuine christological faith than the solemn statement in 8: 29.

Mark's choice of a christology of awe based on the θεῖος ἀνήρ image of Jesus found in the miracle stories might be considered an option for Hellenism as opposed to Palestinian, Jewish thinking. The first evangelist would thus appear as a forerunner, if not of Paul, whose contemporary he was, at least of later first-century exponents of the christologies of the κύριος or the λόγος. There is an element of truth in this, but the idea should not be made to bear too much weight. First of all, as was said before, the contrast between Palestinian and Hellenistic ways of thinking and speaking should not be overemphasized: Hellenism was present in Jewish Palestine under many forms, Jewish

---

[8] U. Luz made some interesting points on this use of miracle stories by Mark in his article 'Das Geheimnismotiv und die markinische Christologie', *ZNW* lvi (1965), pp. 9–29.

[9] This was conclusively shown by K. Tagawa in his excellent book *Miracles et Évangile: la pensée personnelle de l'Évangéliste Marc* (Paris, 1966), pp. 92–122.

ideas and words had spread afar with the growth of the *diaspora*. As a matter of fact, Mark comes from Palestine, as well as the miracle stories he took over.

The main reason why the first evangelist ought not to pass for a conscious Hellenizer of early christology is that in his eyes the miracles mattered not as half-pagan narratives, but as the memories of Jesus cherished by the country folk of the area around the Sea of Galilee. Whether Jews, Syrians or Greeks, the plain people of that district remembered an unbelievably powerful and kind healer who had passed through their hard lives and left them in amazement and fear. According to Mark, they had a fuller understanding of Jesus than the sophisticated church leaders of Jerusalem. They were ready to accept the Gospel, if only someone cared to bring it to them.

In order to make it possible, the first evangelist tried to awaken the church of his time to its evangelizing responsibility. A fairly elaborate christology was, he felt, one of the obstacles he met among the church leaders. By pointing to a simpler, more religious type of christology such as existed among the people he wanted to evangelize, he hoped to convince his readers that discipleship meant more than giving first-class lip-service to Christ: giving up one's life for Jesus' sake and that of the Gospel (8: 35).

Mark's christology, plain though it is, is thus a perfect example of *pensée engagée*, a phrase which would also be an apt description of Professor Moule's theological work. May this coincidence appear to our esteemed Cambridge colleague as a slight recommendation for this essay, which I am happy to present to him as a token of our gratitude for all he has given us.

2

Mit wem identifiziert sich Jesus?
Eine exegetische Rekonstruktion ad
Matt. 25: 31–46

JINDŘICH MÁNEK

Das gewaltige Bild vom Weltgericht (Matt. 25: 31–46), das sich unmittelbar vor dem Anfang der Passionsgeschichte befindet, wurde mehr als irgendein anderes besonders von Malern und Bildhauern des Mittelalters dargestellt. Auf dem Mosaik des letzten Gerichtes über der 'Porta aurea' der Prager St. Veitskathedrale befinden sich symbolisch Gestalten der Seligen zur Rechten und Gestalten der Verdammten zur Linken und über ihnen der Weltenrichter. Das Bild bringt die Botschaft, daß am Ende aller unserer Wege uns der Menschensohn als der Richter erwartet, bei dem die Scheidung stattfindet. Der Grund für die Aufstellung zur Rechten oder zur Linken scheint ganz klar zu sein: Ob wir barmherzig oder unbarmherzig gegen die Hungrigen, Durstigen, Fremden, Nackten, Kranken und Eingekerkerten gewesen sind. Es kommt also alles nur auf die Werke der Barmherzigkeit an. Der Heiland setzt alles auf Liebeswerke.

Es gibt nur wenige Abschnitte der Bibel, die so oft zitiert werden, wie dieser. Und wir lieben die Botschaft, die der Abschnitt enthält, besonders in der anziehenden Bearbeitung und Darbietung von L. N. Tolstoj (*Die Erzählung von dem Schuhmacher Martin Avdějič*).

Enthält aber der Abschnitt jene Botschaft, die man ihm gewöhnlich und in der Regel ganz selbstverständlich zuschreibt? Wer steht eigentlich vor dem Gericht des Menschensohnes, wer ist der Menschensohn, wer der König, wer sind die Seligen und die Verdammten, wer die Hungrigen, Durstigen, Fremden, Nackten, Kranken und Eingekerkerten?

Das Bild bezieht sich auf die Zeit, wann der Menschensohn in seiner Herrlichkeit mit den Engeln kommen wird, um sich auf den Thron zu setzen (25, 31). Engel kommen in den Evangelien in Verbindung mit den wichtigen Ereignissen des Lebens Jesu und darum auch in Verbindung mit seinem Wiederkommen und Gericht vor (Matt. 13:

39, 41, 49; 16: 27; 24: 31; Mark 8: 38; 13: 27). Ist Jesus in diesem Bild mit dem Menschensohn identisch?

In der Erzählung treten drei wichtige Gestalten auf: Vater, Menschensohn und König. Es ist bemerkenswert, daß das Gericht nicht durch den Vater, sondern durch den König, das bedeutet durch Jesus Christus, durchgeführt wird (vgl. Matt. 21: 5). Es ist die Frage, ob die Bezeichnung 'König' ein Synonym für den Menschensohn ist. Auf den ersten Blick scheint es so zu sein. Warum spricht aber Matthäus (25: 31) von dem Menschensohn und ein paar Verse weiter (25: 34) von dem König? Ist dies deshalb so, weil die Einleitung der Geschichte von Matthäus stilisiert wurde, während der Evangelist die folgenden Verse aus der Tradition übernommen hat?[1] Im Lichte dessen, was in dem Abschnitt folgt, läßt sich dies bezweifeln.

Der Schlüssel zur Bestimmung des Unterschiedes zwischen dem Menschensohn und dem König stellt das Erkennen dar, daß in dem Abschnitt außer denen, die sich der Schwachen angenommen haben und denen, die sich ihrer nicht angenommen haben, in der Erzählung noch jene Leidenden vorkommen, die als 'Brüder' bezeichnet werden (25: 40). Diese sind verschieden von jenen, die sich zur Rechten und zur Linken befinden. Die einzige klare Lösung ist, daß sie im Begriff des Menschensohnes einbezogen sind und das dieser Begriff das danielische Volk der Heiligen des Höchsten (Dan. 7: 27) darstellt, dessen Haupt Christus ist. Diese Meinung, die T. W. Manson[2] prägte, ist für das Verständnis der Geschichte anregend: Christus als Weltenrichter kommt nicht zur Übernahme der Macht über die Welt allein, sondern mit seinen Treuen. Das bestätigen auch andere neutestamentliche Texte, wie zum Beispiel Matt. 19: 28 und 1. Thess. 3: 13. Auch Didache weiß davon, daß der Herr mit allen seinen Heiligen kommt (16: 7).

Der Menschensohn in unserem Abschnitt ist also nicht Christus allein; zu dem Menschensohn gehören auch jene, die ihm treue Anhänglichkeit beweisen, die ihm in Treue zugetan sind. Wie ist es dann aber möglich, daß der Terminus 'Menschensohn' in den Evangelien oft nur für Jesus benutzt wird? T. W. Manson[3] beantwortet diese Frage derart, daß Jesus allein als Menschensohn in die Welt eingetreten ist, daß es aber seine Aufgabe war, nicht allein zu bleiben,

---

[1] J. Jeremias, *Die Gleichnisse Jesu* (Göttingen, 1965), S. 204.
[2] T. W. Manson, *The Teaching of Jesus* (Cambridge, 1945), S. 265.
[3] Siehe Manson (Anm. 2), S. 227.

sondern das Volk der Heiligen des Höchsten zu schaffen. Christus und alle seine Treuen bilden ein Ganzes, einen Leib, dessen Haupt Christus ist. Was immer mit einem Teil des Leibes passiert, betrifft alle Glieder des Leibes. In der Lehre des Apostels Paulus von dem Leib Christi kann man dieselbe Konzeption finden, nur mit dem Unterschied, daß der Apostel den Ausdruck 'Menschensohn' meidet. C. F. D. Moule[4] sagt, daß 'the term (Son of Man) is to this extent a collective one, that the person of Jesus is representative, inclusive, incorporative'.

Die Erzählung spricht von dem Völkergericht – also nicht von dem Gericht über die Einzelpersönlichkeiten; das ist schon unsere Individualisierung! Dieses Gericht findet nicht nur vor Jesus Christus, sondern auch vor denen statt, die zu ihm gehören und mit ihm eine Gemeinschaft bilden, die also 'Menschensohn' bezeichnet wird. Schon das Alte Testament kennt die Vorstellung des göttlichen Gerichtes, des Tages Jahve, der den eschatologischen Schlußakt der Geschichte darstellt. In irgendwelchen Büchern des Alten Testaments betrifft dieses Gericht nur die heidnischen Völker, wie zum Beispiel bei Joel. Der Botschaft von großen Propheten gemäß gipfelt aber das Ethos des Gerichtsgedankens darin, daß auch Israel von Gott gerichtet wird. Dann umfaßt der Gerichtsgedanke die ganze Welt. Alle Völker der Erde werden vor dem Weltenrichter versammelt. 'Die großen Propheten sind sowohl gegen Israel wie gegen die Völkerwelt.'[5]

In unserem Abschnitt wird von dem Gericht über alle Völker gesprochen (25:32). In der Regel bedeutet der Terminus ἔθνη (Völker) im Neuen Testament nur heidnische Völker. Es ist sozusagen ein Terminus technicus, der im Gegensatz zu Israel benutzt wird. Aber da, wo von 'allen Völkern' gesprochen wird, ist Israel einbezogen, wie es besonders klar aus Luk. 24:47 hervorgeht: '... und daß auf seinen Namen hin Buße zur Vergebung der Sünden gepredigt werden solle unter allen Völkern, beginnend mit Jerusalem'. K. L. Schmidt[6] teilt das Vorkommen des Terminus ἔθνη im Neuen Testament in drei Gruppen ein: (1) Wo alle Völker einschließlich Israel gemeint sind. In diese Gruppe reiht Schmidt auch unsere Stelle ein – das ergibt sich aus dem Zusatz πάντα. (2) Wo die Einreihung unsicher ist. (3) Wo es

[4] C. F. D. Moule, *The Phenomenon of the New Testament* (London, 1967), S. 90.
[5] O. Proksch, *Theologie des Alten Testaments* (Gütersloh, 1950), S. 579.
[6] K. L. Schmidt, Artikel ἔθνος im *TWNT* (Stuttgart, 1957), II/366.

klar ist, daß die heidnischen Völker gemeint sind. Die gleiche Ansicht
wie Schmidt hat auch W. G. Kümmel.[7]

Das herrliche Bild des Endgerichtes konzentriert sich hier nicht auf
Individuen, sondern auf Völker. Vor dem Menschensohn, d. h. vor
Christus und seinen Treuen werden alle Völker der Welt versammelt.
Schuld oder Unschuld werden hier in Verbindung mit den Völker-
Kollektiven angesehen. Für die heutigen Menschen ist diese Ansicht
wenig begreiflich. Wir sind einseitig auf den Einzelnen konzentriert
und sind nicht geneigt die Existenz der kollektiven Schuld anzuer-
kennen. In der Bibel wird aber keine so scharfe Grenze zwischen dem
Einzelnen und der Gemeinschaft gezogen, wie dies in unserem Denken
der Fall ist. In der Bibel kann die ganze Gemeinschaft gerettet oder
verdammt werden, wie es auch aus dem Wort Jesu offenbar ist: 'Wehe
dir, Chorazin, wehe dir Bethsaida! Denn wenn in Tyrus und Sidon die
machtvollen Taten geschehen wären, die bei euch geschehen sind, so
hätten sie längst in Sack und Asche Buße getan' (Matt. 11: 21 = Luk.
10: 13). Auch hier wird die Bewohnerschaft der erwähnten Städte als
ein verantwortliches Ganzes angesehen.

Die versammelten Völker werden im Endgericht von dem Menschensohn zur Rechten und zur Linken geschieden, ähnlich wie der
palästinische Hirt Schafe und Ziegen scheidet. Die weiße Farbe der
Schafe macht sie im Unterschied zum Schwarz der Ziegen zum Symbol
der Gerechten. Nach der Scheidung der Völker, die die Ouvertüre zum
Gericht ist, wendet sich der König (d. h. Christus, vgl. Matt. 2: 2; 21:
5; 27: 11) zuerst zu denen, die zu seiner Rechten sind und verheißt
ihnen das Reich, das für sie von Grundlegung der Welt bereitet ist
(25: 34).

Der Grund warum einigen Völkern der Platz zur Rechten des
Menschensohnes gegeben wird, besteht darin, daß sie dem König
geholfen haben, als er Hilfe brauchte: Als er hungrig war, haben sie
ihm zum Essen gegeben; als er durstig war, haben sie ihn getränkt; als
er fremd war, haben sie ihn beherbergt; als er nackt war, haben sie ihn
besucht; als er im Gefängnis war, sind sie zu ihm gekommen. Wer sind
aber jene Menschen, die in solchem Maß den Schwierigkeiten
ausgesetzt worden sind? Hunger, Durst, kein schützendes Obdach,
Mangel an Kleidern, Krankheit, Gefängnis – wer ist damit betroffen?
Meint hier Jesus jeden Menschen ohne Unterschied, der ein bitteres,

---

[7] Feine–Behm–Kümmel, *Einleitung in das Neue Testament* (Heidelberg, 1969),
S. 68.

hartes Los hat? In der Regel wird der Abschnitt im folgenden Sinn erklärt: Es handelt sich um die Hilfe den Notleidenden, Bedrängten. Wer ihnen geholfen hat, hat Christi geholfen. Die Gerechten sind diejenigen, die allen Elenden gedient haben. Christus identifiziert sich mit allen Schwachen, mit allen Hilfsbedürftigen, mit allen Eingekerkerten auf der Welt. Man soll Jesus in jedem Menschen sehen, der Nahrung, Kleidung und Freundschaft nötig hat. Es wurde schon gesagt: Diese Erklärung gefällt uns. Ist dies aber wirklich die Botschaft des Absatzes?

Fragen wir nun, für wen die Schwierigkeiten typisch sind, die dieser Absatz erwähnt. Besonders auffallend ist es, daß sich zwischen dem Durstigen und dem Nackten ein Fremder befindet: Für das ewige Schicksal ist es entscheidend, ob ein Volk den Fremdling gastlich aufnimmt. Wenn man das 11. Kapitel des 2. Korintherbriefes öffnet, in dem der Apostel von seinen Missionsbeschwerden spricht, findet man hier alle jene Schwierigkeiten, die unser Abschnitt erwähnt. Paulus 'rühmt sich' hier des Hungers und des Durstes, spricht von vielen Reisen, von Gefahren aus dem eignen Volk, von Gefahren von Heiden, von Kälte und Blöße, von Mühsal und Beschwerde, von Schlagen, Todesgefahren und Gefangenschaften. Der Ausdruck ξένος, den Matthäus verwendet (25:35) und der sich auch in 3. Joh. 5 befindet oder die Umschreibung dieses Termins in 2. Kor. 11:26, kommt im Kontext der Mission vor. Die christlichen Missionäre sollen beherbergt werden. Auch dies bestimmt den Wert des Volkes, ob es die Boten Christi aufnimmt oder nicht. Im Hintergrund der Worte Jesu über die Scheidung im Endgericht steht die christliche Mission.

Das bestätigt auch der weitere Kontext in dem sich die Schilderung des Weltgerichts befindet. Im Vordergrund des 24. und 25. Kapitels des Matthäusevangeliums befindet sich die Erwartung des Menschensohnes, sein Kommen vom Himmel. Die Parusie hängt eng mit dem Gericht, der Vollendung des Weltlaufs und dem Ende der Welt zusammen. In dieser Zeit der Erwartung ist das Wachen und die Ausnützung der Zeit sehr wichtig. Wie der Abschluß des Matthäusevangeliums besonders betont, spielt die Aufgabe der Mission in dieser gespannten Erwartung eine wichtige Rolle: Die Apostel werden von dem Auferstandenen gesandt alle Völker zu Jüngern zu machen. Wenn sie dies tun, ist Christus mit ihnen. Im 10. Kapitel des Matthäusevangeliums, wo von der Aussendung der Jünger gesprochen wird, hört man folgende Worte Jesu: 'Wer euch aufnimmt, der nimmt mich auf; und wer mich aufnimmt, der nimmt den auf, der mich gesandt hat' (10: 40). Wer die Boten Jesu aufnimmt, nimmt auch Jesus auf. Wer aber die Boten Jesu verwirft, der verwirft auch Jesus (Luk. 10: 16).

Auf diese Weise wird auch in der Apostellehre (Didache) von den aus der Fremde kommenden Lehrern des göttlichen Wortes, den Aposteln und Propheten und von den zureisenden christlichen Brüdern, sowie von dem Verhalten gegen sie geredet: 'Kommt einer und lehrt euch alles das, was bisher hier gesagt ist, so nehmt ihn auf. Lehrt aber der Lehrer selbst, davon abgewandt, eine andre Lehre, die zur Auflösung führt, so hört nicht auf ihn. Lehrt er aber zur Mehrung der Gerechtigkeit und Erkenntnis des Herrn, so nehmt ihn auf wie den Herrn. Was aber die Apostel und Propheten betrifft, so handelt nach der Bestimmung des Evangeliums also: Jeder Apostel, der zu euch kommt, soll aufgenommen werden wie der Herr' (11: 1–3).

Den Evangelien und der Apostellehre (Didache) nach verkörpert der Gesandte denjenigen, der ihn selbst mit seiner Vertretung beglaubigte. Dies ist im Einklang mit dem semitischen Botenrecht, wie dies auch im Alten Testament vorausgesetzt wird. 'Dort repräsentiert der Bote völlig den, der ihn sendet, in der Regel den König, und das ist ja auch der ursprüngliche Sinn der Sendung eines Bevollmächtigten. Die schmachvolle Behandlung eines Gesandten trifft weniger ihn als seinen Herrn und kann darum nicht ohne Folge bleiben. So wird 2. Sam. 10: 1ff. die Schändung der Boten Davids durch die Ammoniter der Anlaß zum vernichtenden Kriege gegen sie.'[8] Die Rabbiner haben diese Tatsache in dem bekannten Satz ausgedrückt: 'Der Abgesandte eines Menschen ist wie er selbst.' Der Gebrauch von ἀπόστολος im Neuen Testament hat zu dieser Auffassung des Botenrechtes sehr nahe, besonders bei Joh. 13: 16: 'Ein Knecht ist nicht größer als sein Herr, noch ein Gesandter größer als der, welcher ihn gesandt hat.'

Die Frage, wie ein Bote Jesu behandelt werden soll, mußte in der Zeit der ersten Missionsschritte sehr aktuell sein. Aller Wahrscheinlichkeit nach bearbeitet Matt. 25: 31–46 diese Frage. Wenn diese Annahme richtig ist, handelt es sich in diesem Abschnitt nicht um die Beziehung zu wem auch immer, sondern um die Beziehung zu den Boten Jesu. Die Ethik hängt hier am engsten mit der Christologie zusammen. Die folgenden Verse unseres Textes werden uns davon vielleicht etwas mehr sagen.

Die Völker (es handelt sich doch um das Völkergericht!), die zur

---

[8] K. H. Rengstorf, Artikel ἀπόστολος, *TWNT* I/415.

Rechten sind, verstehen nicht, wann sie dem König Liebe erweisen sollten. Sie wissen nichts davon. Sie sind dem hungernden und kranken König gar nicht begegnet. Sie verstehen nicht, was der König meint. Gerade dies ist ein überraschender Charakterzug der Erzählung: Daß der in den hungernden und eingekerkerten Boten verborgene Christus den Völkern gegenübertrat. Die Urkirche in der Missionssituation sah Jesus Christus in jedem Boten, welcher Nahrung, Kleidung und Freundschaft nötig hatte. Es handelte sich um die Fürsorge für auswärtige Boten, um Missionäre, die bei ihrer Arbeit auf die Aufnahme seitens der Völker angewiesen waren. In jedem Boten wird Jesus selbst geliebt. Jesus stellt sich selbst mit seinen Boten gleich. Die Qualität der Völker, die zur Rechten sind, zeigt sich auch darin, daß sie jedes Verdienst zurückweisen. Sie sind überzeugt, daß es nicht ihnen gehört. Christus aber gibt ihnen diese Erklärung: 'Wahrlich ich sage euch: Wiefern ihr es einem dieser meiner geringsten Brüder getan habt, habt ihr es mir getan.'

Wer ist aber mit den Brüdern im Vers 40 gemeint? Sind es alle Bedrängten ohne Unterschied? Wird hier das Wort 'Bruder' im Sinne 'Nächster' verstanden? Joachim Jeremias meint, daß der Vergleich mit Vers 45 (wo das Wort fehlt) zeigt, daß mit den ἀδελφοί an dieser Stelle nicht die Jünger gemeint sind.[9] Diese Meinung wird gewöhnlich vertreten. J. Schniewind schreibt in seinem Matthäuskommentar: 'Dabei darf nicht vergessen werden, daß das im Vers 40 gebrauchte Wort "Brüder" (in Vers 45 fehlt es) sich nicht ausschließlich auf die Christen beziehen muß, sondern – entsprechend der Universalität des alle Heiden einschließenden Weltgerichtes ebenso allgemein die Hungernden, Dürstenden, Fremden, Kranken meinen kann, die der Hilfe bedürfen, ohne nach der ausdrücklichen Beziehung zu Christus zu fragen.'[10] J. C. Fenton ist nicht so einseitig. Obwohl er meint, daß mit den Brüdern ohne Unterschied die Bedrängten gemeint sind,[11] bemerkt er jedoch, daß 'Matthew probably thought of the brethren here as the disciples of Jesus, but in the original parable it may have referred to anyone who was in distress'.[12]

Die Frage, wer 'die Brüder' sind, kann nur mit Bezug auf das gesamte Matthäusevangelium beurteilt werden. Wenn wir dieses Wort

---

[9] Siehe Jeremias (Anm. 1), S. 205.
[10] J. Schniewind, *Das Evangelium nach Matthäus* (Göttingen, 1962), S. 253.
[11] J. C. Fenton, *Saint Matthew* (Harmondsworth, 1963), S. 403.
[12] Siehe Fenton (Anm. 11), S. 402.

bei Matthäus verfolgen (vgl. 5: 47; 12: 48; 18: 15; 23: 8; 28: 10 – und schon bei Mark. 3: 33–5), kann man nicht bestreiten, daß es ganz klar christlichen Charakter hat. Das gesteht auch Joachim Jeremias ein, wenn er von der Neigung des Matthäus spricht, das Wort ἀδελφός zu verchristlichen.[13] Bruder ist für Matthäus nicht jeder Mensch, sondern nur derjenige, der Jesus als seinen Meister und Herrn anerkennt: 'Denn einer ist euer Meister, ihr alle aber seid Brüder' (23: 8). 'Bruder' ist bei Matthäus ein Synonym für Jünger. Wer einem Durstigen nur einen Becher kalten Wassers zu trinken gibt, weil er ein Jünger ist, der tut es in Wirklichkeit dem Herrn (Matt. 10: 40–2).

'Die Brüder' im Vers 40 sind also höchstwahrscheinlich nicht alle Bedrängte und Notleidende ohne Unterschied, sondern die Jünger Jesu. Das bestätigt auch die nähere adjektive Qualifikation des Hauptwortes. Der Abschnitt spricht von den 'geringsten' Brüdern: 'Wiefern ihr es einem dieser meiner geringsten Brüder getan habt, habt ihr es mir getan' (Vers 40). Das Semitische hat keinen Superlativ. Es besteht kein Unterschied zwischen μικροί und ἐλάχιστοι (vgl. Matt. 10: 42, wo das Manuskript D ἐλάχιστος hat, wohingegen andere Manuskripte μικρός anführen. Lateinische Übersetzungen lesen: unus ex minimis istis). Wenn Matthäus von den 'Kleinen' oder sogar von den 'Geringsten' spricht, meint er damit nicht unwichtige, mittelmäßige Gemeindeglieder. Matthäus arbeitet mit einer paradoxen Hierarchie, nach der der Höchste jener ist, der am meisten dient (23: 11; 20: 26f.). Die 'Kleinen' sind die wichtigsten Gemeindeglieder.[14] Jesu Wort ruft die Jünger zum Kleinsein, zum Leiden und Sterben. Die Matthäusgemeinde soll die Schar der Kleinen sein, die in der Nachfolge des demütigen Königs der Niedrigkeit ihren Weg gehen. Die 'geringsten Brüder' ist bei Matthäus ein besonders hoher Titel, der höchste Titel für die treuen Jünger, für diejenigen, die dem Herrn am meisten dienen, die in der Kirche eine wichtige Aufgabe haben. Kleinsein in diesem Sinn ist die Bedingung zur Größe in der Zukunft. Es ist also fraglich, ob Matthäus mit den geringsten Brüdern alle Bedrängten und Notleidenden in der Welt meint, wie dies die Exegese geläufig behauptet.

Auf die Tatsache, daß Matthäus mit den geringsten Brüdern die Jünger meint, zeigt auch das Demonstrativum τούτων. Joachim

---

[13] Siehe Jeremias (Anm. 1), S. 102 Anm. 2.

[14] E. Schweizer, *Gemeinde und Gemeindeordnung im Neuen Testament* (Zürich, 1959), S. 53.

Jeremias glaubt im Geiste seiner Konzeption, daß es sich um ein überflüssiges Demonstrativum handelt, das im Deutschen unübersetzt bleiben soll.[15] Dieses Demonstrativum ist aber höchst funktional, wenn man in Betracht zieht, daß die geringsten Brüder im Endgericht anwesend sind und daß sie sich weder zur Rechten noch zur Linken des Königs befinden, sondern zu dem König gehören und mit ihm eine Gesamtheit bilden, die den Namen 'Menschensohn' trägt. T. W. Manson[16] hat recht, wenn er sagt: 'The "Son of Man" is a corporate body and the rest of mankind are judged by their treatment of that body.' Auch Mansons Hinweis auf Matt. 19: 28 und Luk. 22: 30 ist wertvoll, wo den Jüngern die Funktion der Richter zugesprochen wird. (Vgl. auch 1. Kor. 6: 2: 'Oder wißt ihr nicht, daß die Heiligen die Welt richten werden? Und wenn durch euch die Welt gerichtet wird, seid ihr dann nicht würdig, über ganz geringe Sachen zu richten?')

In dem Abschnitt 25: 34–40 handelt es sich um die Anrede deren, die sich zur Rechten des Königs befinden. In den folgenden Versen (41–5) wendet sich der König zu den Völkern, die sich zur Linken befinden. Sie werden als Verfluchte bezeichnet und in das ewige Feuer gesandt. Als Jesus hungrig war, haben sie ihm nicht zu Essen gegeben, als er durstig war, haben sie ihn nicht getränkt, als er fremd war, haben sie ihn nicht beherbergt, als er nackt war, haben sie ihn nicht bekleidet, als er krank und im Gefängnis war, haben sie ihn nicht besucht. Diese Vorwürfe beantworten die Völker, die sich zur Linken des Königs befinden, mit der Frage: 'Herr, wann sahen wir dich hungrig oder durstig oder als Fremden oder nackt oder krank oder im Gefängnis und haben dir nicht gedient?' Sie haben den König nie in Not gesehen, so daß sie zur Hilfe angerufen worden wären. Sie haben Jesus nie in einer solchen Situation getroffen. Jesus aber erklärt, daß wiefern sie es einem seiner Geringsten nicht getan haben, das heißt denen, die in seiner Begleitung sind, haben sie es auch ihm nicht getan. Die Schuld der verurteilten Völker besteht nicht in grausamen Taten, sondern in der Versäumnis guter Taten (vgl. Luk. 16: 19–31). Vor dem Gericht wird nach den Werken gefragt. Jedes Volk wird als Täter in seinen Werken ernstgenommen und geprüft.

Die Geschichte der Exegese des Abschnittes Matt. 25: 31–46 bringt im Grunde dreierlei Antwort auf die Frage, wer die 'geringsten Brüder' (Vers 40) sind:

(1) Die Antwort, die am öftesten – und man kann sagen fast

---

[15] Siehe Jeremias (Anm. 1), S. 36 und 205.   [16] Siehe Manson (Anm. 2), S. 270.

ausschließlich – gegeben wird: Jesus meint allgemein die Hungernden, Dürstenden, Fremden, Kranken, Gefangenen, die der Hilfe bedürfen, ohne nach der ausdrücklichen Beziehung zu Christus zu fragen. Wie R. Bultmann[17] sagt: 'Die Moral des Stückes ist nicht spezifisch christlich. Wie Gott die Nackten bekleidete, also bekleide auch die Nackten, wie Gott die Kranken besuchte, also besuche auch du die Kranken usw.' H. Braun[18] drückt dieselbe Meinung auf diese Weise aus: 'So kann man das große Gleichnis vom Weltgericht direkt als ein Denkmal bezeichnen, welches die Gemeindetradition dem Anwalt der schrankenlosen Nächstenliebe errichtet: man dient Jesus in der Weise, daß man Hungernde, Dürstende, Herberglose, Frierende, Kranke und Gefangene betreut, und dann merkt man es nicht einmal, daß man Jesus dient; man verfehlt den Dienst an Jesus in der Weise, daß man sich um solche Hilfsbedürftigen nicht kümmert, und dabei wird einem nicht einmal klar, daß es Jesus ist, den man verfehlt hat.' Der Abschnitt in dieser üblichen Auffassung verkündigt, daß Jesus in allen Bedrängten und in Not Befindlichen incognito anwesend ist. 'Es handelt sich hier um die Liebe als Liebe zu den Armen, Elenden und Notleidenden aller Art.'[19]

(2) Eine andere Antwort auf die Frage, wer die 'geringsten Brüder' sind, gibt z. B. E. Schlink,[20] der ganz eindeutig sagt: 'Die geringsten Brüder sind diejenigen, die in der Nachfolge Christi arm, obdachlos gebunden werden gleich ihrem Herrn.' In dieser Auffassung handelt es sich hier nicht mehr um die 'common humanity'. Jesus und seine Nachfolger, Jesus und die Kirche sind eins (vgl. Apg. 9: 5). Kann man aber voraussetzen, daß in der Zeit, als Matthäus dies schrieb, die Christen unter allen Völkern lebten? Und weiter: Jesus spricht nicht nur von den Brüdern, sondern von den geringsten Brüdern, d. h. von den seiner Sache am besten dienenden Brüdern.

(3) Die dritte mögliche Antwort, die dieser Aufsatz zu unterstützen versucht, identifiziert die geringsten Brüder mit den Boten Christi. Die gerechten Völker sind diejenigen, die die hungernden Boten Christi gespeist, dürstende getränkt, nackte bekleidet und gefangene besucht haben. Damit haben sie – nach dem Wort des Weltrichters – Christus selbst gedient. Verschiedenen Völkern ist Jesus nicht

---

[17] R. Bultmann, *Geschichte der synoptischen Tradition* (Göttingen, 1931), S. 130–1.
[18] H. Braun, *Jesus* (Stuttgart, 1969), S. 127.
[19] H. D. Wendland, *Ethik des Neuen Testaments* (Göttingen, 1970), S. 35.
[20] E. Schlink, zitiert von H. J. Iwand in *Predigt-Meditationen* (Göttingen, 1964), S. 244f.

persönlich, sondern in seinen Boten begegnet. Wer ihnen Liebe erwies, erwies sie ihm. Das Verhalten, das seine Motivierung im Mitleid hat, ist sicher wertvoll, aber es ist noch wertvoller, wenn es mit Hilfe der Verkündigung Christi verbunden ist.

Die Weltmission, die im Hintergrund unseres Abschnittes steht, ist eine notwendige eschatologische Aufgabe (Matt. 28: 19–20). Die Völker, die bisher durch Gewalt und Gehorsam zusammengehalten waren, sollen zu 'Jüngern' werden, verbunden in dem gleichen Glauben und Dienst. Das Leben der Völker an sich war ohnedies nicht gut. Christi Boten, die das Wort des Herrn weitertrugen, brachten den Völkern das Wichtigste, das Entscheidende und Christus ging mit ihnen. Sie haben ihn selbst bei sich bis zum Ende der Welt. Deswegen, was die Völker für die Boten Christi getan haben, haben sie auch für Jesus getan.

Mit wem identifiziert sich Jesus?

JINDŘICH MÁNEK

The Parable of the Great Assize (Matt. 25: 31–46) has always been interpreted in a way that makes works of mercy the decisive factor for salvation. Christ is identified with the poor and needy, whoever they may be. Close attention to the details of the parable suggests, however, that this is not the true interpretation.

The Son of Man (verse 31) is not the King (who is Jesus Christ, verses 34ff.), since the expression 'Son of Man' here denotes the body of which Jesus is the head, and includes the 'brethren' (verse 40). The setting of this story is one of collective judgement, including that of Israel. The crucial point is that those whom the righteous have helped (verses 35–9) are not sufferers in general, but the messengers of Jesus, for whom the hardships described here are typical (cf. 2 Cor. 11). The missionary activity of the early church has in fact shaped this narrative, so that hospitality to the missionary, whose work has been vital during the interval before the parousia, is now seen to be the determining factor of a nation's worth; for the messenger is identified with the Master (cf. Matt. 10: 40; Luke 10: 16; *Didache* 11). Ethics and christology belong closely together in this part of Matthew.

The 'brethren' (verse 40) are specifically Christians. They are more narrowly defined as ἐλάχιστοι, a title of high honour in the paradoxical Matthean system of values, denoting those who have served most. They belong to the King, and with him form the totality called the Son of Man (note the use of τούτων in verses 40, 45). So at the end of the world Christ confronts the nations in the messengers who are his own representatives; and what the nations have done for them, they have done for him.

3

On the christology of Q*

GRAHAM N. STANTON

The Q material in the Gospels has exerted a powerful fascination on
New Testament scholars for a long time. So many diverse and even
contradictory estimates of the nature of Q have been made that it is
not surprising that opponents of the Q hypothesis have been quick to
point a ridiculing finger at the lack of any kind of scholarly consensus.[1]
But the Q hypothesis cannot be rejected quite so easily. The cumulative
case for the existence of Q remains compelling.[2]

Not surprisingly, Q has recently attracted renewed interest in the
wake of redaction criticism. What distinctive christological emphases
are found in Q? What was its original purpose? Have Matthew and
Luke, by subsuming Q into Mark's 'Gospel' *Gattung*, all but
obliterated an early christology – a christology quite different from
their own?

The most recent answers to such questions have been rather less
diverse than earlier phases in the study of Q would lead one to expect.[3]
There is now general agreement that Q was not intended primarily to
provide catechetical or hortatory material for Christian believers;[4]
christology belongs not merely to a preface[5] or to a few isolated

---

* A modified version of this article was delivered in Cambridge in July 1972 as
  the Tyndale New Testament Lecture for 1972.
[1] Cf. S. Petrie, '"Q" is only what you make it', *Nov. T.* iii (1959), pp. 28–33.
[2] For a recent careful defence of the Q hypothesis, see J. A. Fitzmyer, 'The
  Priority of Mark and the "Q" Source in Luke', in *Jesus and Man's Hope* I
  (Pittsburgh, 1970), pp. 131–70. In this essay Q is assumed to have been a written
  document. But I regard the distinction between Q as a written document and
  Q as a layer of oral tradition with a fairly fixed order as comparatively unimportant.
[3] For surveys of earlier studies of Q, see H. E. Tödt, *The Son of Man in the Synoptic
  Tradition* (E.T. London, 1965), pp. 235–46; W. D. Davies, *The Setting of the
  Sermon on the Mount* (Cambridge, 1964), pp. 366ff.
[4] See H. E. Tödt, *Son of Man*, pp. 243ff.; W. D. Davies, *Sermon*, pp. 370–86;
  D. Lührmann, *Die Redaktion der Logienquelle* (Neukirchen, 1969), p. 95.
[5] A. Harnack argued that Q contained a christological introduction (the baptism
  and temptation narratives), but that the rest of the Q material reflected a very
  different understanding of Jesus. *The Sayings of Jesus* (E.T. London, 1908),
  pp. 243ff.

sections, but is so much part and parcel of the document that the original purpose of Q can be clarified only by laying bare its main christological emphases. Several recent writers have taken a further step and have argued that it is possible, from a discovery of important christological innovations made by the Q community to the traditions at its disposal, to underline the extent to which the christology of Q is distinctive – indeed, unique, within primitive Christianity.

H. E. Tödt's discussion of Q's Son-of-Man christology is proving to be as influential on current study of Q as A. Harnack's work was over fifty years earlier. In his study of Q, Tödt concentrates on the title Son of Man, arguing that the purpose of the Q material can be un- covered by elucidating the Q community's use and development of Son-of-Man sayings. Tödt concludes that the Q community was deliberately continuing Jesus' proclamation of the imminence of God's kingdom. The community did not develop a passion kerygma, but was convinced that Jesus, who has re-established fellowship with his followers as the risen one, is also the one who, as the coming Son of Man, will be the eschatological guarantor of that fellowship.[6] Similar conclusions about the purpose of Q have been defended by D. Lührmann and R. A. Edwards.[7] Both scholars modify the details of Tödt's interpretation at a number of points, but both agree that the dominant theme of Q is a strong expectation of coming judgement in which Jesus will appear as Son of Man.

A Son-of-Man christology and an expectation of coming judgement are both prominent in Q. But are they so central to the theological understanding of the Q community that they provide the key to the purpose of Q? In spite of a web of carefully developed arguments, there are a number of weak threads on which a good deal of weight hangs. Before taking up some of them, other important and very different christological themes in Q will be discussed – themes which have been

---

[6] H. E. Tödt, *Son of Man*, p. 273.

[7] D. Lührmann attempts to drive a thin wedge between tradition and redaction by applying the methods used in recent redaction critical studies. For the Q community, 'Jesus is not the One who is proclaimed, but the content of the proclamation of the coming judgement, in which Jesus, as Son of Man, will save his community.' *Logienquelle*, pp. 96f. R. A. Edwards also underlines (by a rather different approach) the importance of the Q community's identification of Jesus with the Son of Man who was expected to appear soon to bring God's judgement. *The Sign of Jonah in the Theology of the Evangelists and Q* (London, 1971), pp. 54f. See also, M. J. Suggs, *Wisdom, Christology and Law in Matthew's Gospel* (Harvard, 1970), p. 94.

given insufficient attention in recent studies of Q and which suggest a rather different understanding of the purpose of Q.

Scant attention has been paid to the opening sections of Q in recent discussions of its christology and purpose.[8] This is a little surprising in view of the obvious importance of the opening sections of documents which might be seen as offering a rough parallel to Q: the Old Testament prophetic writings and *Pirke Aboth*, to say nothing of the opening verses of Mark's Gospel. It is not easy to reconstruct the opening sections of Q with precision. But on the widely held view that Luke preserves fairly faithfully the order of Q, some important theological emphases can be located in the opening sections of Q.[9] In the discussion which follows, Matt. 11: 2–6 = Luke 7: 18–23 is taken as the starting point; we shall then seek to demonstrate that the main themes of this passage are also prominent in the preceding opening sections of Q, as well as elsewhere in Q.

Matt. 11: 2–6 = Luke 7: 18–23 stands at the beginning of a comparatively lengthy section of material about Jesus and John which has been linked together loosely in Q. Although both Matthew and Luke have introduced some important modifications,[10] the 'core' of the pericope is found almost *verbatim* in both Gospels and is undoubtedly Q material.

John's question σὺ εἶ ὁ ἐρχόμενος; and the reply of Jesus which utilises phrases from Isaiah both contain important christological implications. Jesus neither denies nor explicitly affirms that he is ὁ ἐρχόμενος and this is a weighty argument in favour of the authenticity of Jesus' answer.[11] But how did the Q community interpret these words?

The words of Jesus allude to Isa. 29: 18f.; 35: 5 and 61: 1f. The first two passages provide the general theme of an eschatological time when

---

[8] Cf. E. Bammel, 'Das Ende von Q', in *Verborum Veritas* (Festschrift for G. Stählin), eds. O. Böcher and K. Haacker (Wuppertal, 1970), pp. 39–50.

[9] It is just conceivable that the Marcan order has influenced both Matthew and Luke to place Q traditions about John near the beginning of their Gospels. But it is difficult to envisage baptism and temptation narratives in any position other than at or near the beginning of Q.

[10] I take τὰ ἔργα τοῦ χριστοῦ (Matt. 11: 2) to be a Matthaean addition and Luke 7: 21 to be a Lucan addition. The longer Lucan introduction may well be original in view of Matthew's tendency to abbreviate his sources. Cf. Matt. 8: 5–13 = Luke 7: 1–10.

[11] Cf. W. G. Kümmel, *Promise and Fulfilment* (E.T. London, 1957), pp. 109ff.

the deaf will hear, the blind see and the lame walk. But the climax clearly comes with the allusion to Isa. 61: 1, πτωχοὶ εὐαγγελίζονται.[11a] Only with these words do we have a hint of a more specific answer to John's question about the person of Jesus: it is not God himself but the one anointed with God's spirit who announces good tidings to the poor – Jesus. For the Q community this was the point of Jesus' reply; this is not the only Q passage for which Isa. 61: 1f. provides the background – πτωχοὶ εὐαγγελίζονται is followed immediately by a μακάριος logion which also has its background in Isa. 61: 1.[12]

Was Jesus understood to be hinting that he was an eschatological prophetic figure, or even that he was Messiah? There is now clear evidence that at the time of Jesus Isa. 61: 1 was being interpreted in a quite specific way as referring to *the* eschatological prophet.[13] The recently discovered 11Q Melchizedek,[14] although fragmentary and difficult to interpret in detail, contains a cluster of allusions to Isa. 61: 1f.[15] Line 18 reads והמבשר הו[א]ה מ[שיח הרו[ח] [אשר אמר.[16] In the context Isa. 52: 7 is quoted in full – המבשר is the eschatological herald of good tidings. The line can be translated 'And he that brings good tidings, he is the one anointed by the spirit, about whom he says...'[17]

11a In a few mss. νεκροὶ ἐγείρονται is seen as the climax and is placed at the end of the list.

12 Cf. P. Stuhlmacher, *Das paulinische Evangelium* I (Göttingen, 1968), p. 219. In addition to the references cited in n. 3 and n. 4, note A. Finkel, *The Pharisees and the Teacher of Nazareth* (Leiden, 1964), pp. 155–8. Finkel suggests that the Beatitudes are a kind of *pesher* interpretation of Isa. 61: 1ff.

13 P. Stuhlmacher, *Das paulinische Evangelium*, pp. 142ff. with reference to 1QH 18: 14. לבשר ענוים is cited from Isa. 61: 1 – cf. Q, πτωχοὶ εὐαγγελίζονται.

14 See the *editio princeps*, A. S. van der Woude 'Melchisedek als himmlische Erlösergestalt in den neugefundenen eschatologischen Midraschim aus Qumran Höhle 11, *OTS* xiv (Leiden, 1965), pp. 354–73; also, A. S. van der Woude and M. de Jonge, '11Q Melchizedek and the New Testament', *NTS* xii (1965–6), pp. 310–26.

15 See M. P. Miller, 'The Function of Isa. 61: 1–2 in 11Q Melchizedek', *JBL* lxxxviii (1969), pp. 467–9. Miller argues convincingly that Isa. 61: 1–2 stands behind the unfolding *pesher* material in 11Q Melch.; he shows that the three major texts quoted (Lev. 23: 13; Isa. 52: 7; Ps. 82: 1–2) 'unfold their inner relation and meaning for the community with reference to Isa. 61: 1–2' (p. 469).

16 At line 18 the *editio princeps* read והמבשר הו[א]ה המ[שיח הוא]ה [אשר אמר. The emendation quoted has now been accepted by several scholars. M. de Jonge and A. S. van der Woude note the remarkable parallel to CD 2, 12 which speaks of משיחי רוח קדשו with reference to prophets; the term 'anointed ones' is also used in the plural to denote prophets in CD 6: 1 and 1QM 11, but 11Q Melch. line 18 is the first instance in the Qumran literature of a singular use of that expression to denote a prophet; '11Q Melchizedek', *NTS* xii (1965–6), pp. 306f.

17 *Ibid.* p. 302.

The herald of good tidings of Isa. 52: 7 is closely linked with Isa. 61: 1 and is identified as '*the* anointed one'.[18]

Although it has frequently been assumed that the reply of Jesus to John would be understood as an indirect claim to be Messiah,[19] there are some grounds for caution, even in spite of 11Q Melch. For it is difficult to find clear-cut evidence that Isa. 61: 1 was referred to the Messiah in late Judaism.[20]

On the other hand, the 'herald of good tidings' of Isa. 52: 7 was often identified as the Messiah – although other identifications were also suggested.[21] Both Matthew and Luke interpret the pericope in this way. Matthew links the reply of Jesus to τὰ ἔργα τοῦ Χριστοῦ – a phrase which he adds to the Q pericope (Matt. 11: 2). Luke almost certainly understood ὁ ἐρχόμενος as the Messiah, especially in the light of Luke 4: 17f.[22]

While in this passage ὁ ἐρχόμενος could well be taken as a reference to the eschatological prophet, the related Q passage Matt. 3: 11f. = Luke 3: 16f. (where ὁ δὲ ὀπίσω μου ἐρχόμενος Matt. 3: 11 is probably from Q) does not fit the prophet, but does fit the Messiah.[23] In the very next closely related Q pericope (Matt. 11: 9ff. = Luke 7: 26ff.)

---

[18] Cf. Acts 10: 36 where Isa. 61: 1 and Isa. 52: 7 are both alluded to, but not linked closely together.

In addition to the literature noted above, see P. Stuhlmacher, *Das paulinische Evangelium*, pp. 142ff. and 218ff. More recently, J. A. Fitzmyer, 'Further Light on Melchizedek from Qumran Cave 11', *JBL* lxxxvi (1967), pp. 24–41; J. Carmignac, 'Le Document de Qumrân sur Melkisédeq', *RQ* vii (1970), pp. 343–78. Fitzmyer accepts that line 18 refers to 'the Anointed One' and translates 'And the herald is that Anointed One (about) whom Daniel said...'. Fitzmyer notes that this definite use of 'Messiah' is paralleled also in 1Q Sa 2: 13, and 4Q Patr. Bless. 3; art. cit. p. 40.

[19] E.g. C. K. Barrett, *The Holy Spirit and the Gospel Tradition* (London, 1947), p. 118; W. G. Kümmel, *Heilsgeschehen und Geschichte* (Marburg, 1965), p. 434; D. Lührmann, *Logienquelle*, p. 26.

[20] See P. Stuhlmacher, *Das paulinische Evangelium*, p. 145 n. 4 and p. 219 n. 2; A. S. van der Woude and M. de Jonge, *NTS* xii, p. 308; M. de Jonge, 'The Word "Anointed" in the Time of Jesus', *Nov. T.* viii (1966), pp. 132–48, esp. pp. 141ff.

[21] See the references cited by J. A. Fitzmyer, *JBL* lxxxvi, p. 30, and P. Stuhlmacher, *Das paulinische Evangelium*, pp. 148f.

[22] At Luke 19: 38 Luke defines ὁ ἐρχόμενος as ὁ βασιλεύς (cf. Mark 11: 10).

[23] D. R. Catchpole, 'The "Triumphal" Entry', *The Zealots and Jesus*, eds. C. F. D. Moule and E. Bammel (Cambridge, forthcoming). See also D. R. Catchpole, *The Trial of Jesus* (Leiden, 1971), p. 164 n. 1; M. A. Chevallier, *L'Esprit et le Messie* (Paris, 1958), pp. 53f.; W. G. Kümmel, *Promise*, p. 110.

Jesus indicates that John is greater than a prophet; indeed, he is the greatest of those born of women; for the Q community, not Jesus, but John is *the* eschatological prophet, since John is certainly not ὁ ἐρχόμενος.[24]

The reply of Jesus to John stands at the beginning of a very important section of Q which revolves around the questions, 'Who is Jesus?' and 'What is John's relationship to him?' The Q community interpreted this passage christologically: Jesus claimed that the prophetic eschatological promises were being fulfilled in his actions *and* words. This Q passage lays less emphasis on the person through whom God is acting than on the evidence of God's actions (as is also the case in 11Q Melch.). But in the light of John's initial question, σὺ εἶ ὁ ἐρχόμενος;, it is difficult to resist the conclusion that for the Q community the actions and words of Jesus were those of the Messiah.

The ἐν ἐμοί of the concluding logion indicates that the signs of the dawn of the new age and the proclamation of Jesus are linked inseparably to the person of Jesus. The logion also stresses that some have taken offence at Jesus. As we shall note below, the rejection of Jesus is a theme which runs through a good deal of the Q material.

These conclusions would be strengthened considerably if we could be sure that Luke 4: 16–30 stemmed from Q, for there the main themes of Jesus' reply to John are all stated more explicitly and fully. The similar way Isa. 61 is used in both passages has often been noted as particularly striking and as not a little puzzling.[25] A few scholars have suggested that Luke 4: 16–30 stems from Q, but this possibility has not been taken seriously in research on Q. However, H. Schürmann has recently defended this hypothesis with such skill and learning that it cannot be neglected.[26] Schürmann argues that Luke 4: 17–21 and 25–7 are later

---

24 Cf. G. Friedrich, art. προφήτης, *TDNT* vi, p. 839. The Q form of Matt. 11: 12f. = Luke 16: 16 is probably to be taken as an indication that the appearance of John marks the dawn of the new age.

25 See, for example, R. H. Fuller, *The Foundations of New Testament Christology* (London, 1965), p. 170; P. Stuhlmacher, *Das paulinische Evangelium*, p. 227.

26 H. Schürmann, 'Zur Nazareth-Perikope Lk. 4: 16–30', in *Mélanges Bibliques en hommage au R.P. Béda Rigaux*, ed. A. Descamps and A. de Halleux (Gembloux, 1970), pp. 187–205. Schürmann notes several earlier attempts to assign parts of Luke 4: 16–30 to Q and includes J. V. Bartlet. But Bartlet was arguing *against* the standard two document hypothesis! 'The Sources of St Luke's Gospel', in *Studies in the Synoptic Gospels*, ed. W. Sanday (Oxford, 1911), pp. 315–63.

additions to the original pericope and do not come from Luke's own hand; he then attempts to show that the original pericope is not merely a Lucan rewriting of Mark 6: 1–6. Up to this point Schürmann's argument is well-grounded.

In the concluding section of his article Schürmann suggests that the original pericope and the two later additions (verses 17–21 and 25–7) all stem from Q. This is an attractive suggestion, but the evidence offered in support is not completely convincing.[27] Schürmann has shown that some of the emphases of Luke 4: 16–30 can be related to Q themes, but he has not demonstrated that this material cannot stem from L. Schürmann argues that an Old Testament citation comparable to Luke 4: 17f. would be quite unusual for L, but not for Q. But is there any other passage in Q comparable to Luke 4: 16–30 which, on Schürmann's view, consisted of three originally separate traditions not merely placed side by side but woven together closely in Q? Schürmann suggests that since Isa. 61: 1f. is used in a similar way in Luke 6: 20f., Luke 7: 18–23 and Luke 4: 17ff., all three passages would seem to stem from Q. But Isa. 61: 1 is also used in Acts 10: 38; here Isa. 61: 1 forms part of a section of pre-Lucan (but not Q!) tradition revised and reshaped by Luke himself. On Schürmann's view, Luke 4: 16–30 would have stood near the beginning of Q, and may possibly have arisen within the Q tradition as a further development of Matt. 11: 2–6 = Luke 7: 18–23.[28] But if so, then Q would have begun with a clear and explicit christological understanding of the nature and purpose of the ministry of Jesus, to be followed by John's question σὺ εἶ ὁ ἐρχόμενος; and the indirect and somewhat enigmatic reply of Jesus. If Luke 4: 16ff. is a development from Luke 7: 18ff., would the latter passage have been retained in its present form?[29]

There is insufficient evidence to enable us to appeal to Luke 4: 16–30 as Q material. However, several passages which undoubtedly do come from Q support the conclusions drawn from the reply of Jesus to John. Matt. 13: 16f. = Luke 10: 23f. also emphasises that God's new age is dawning and is to be seen in both the actions and words of Jesus.

---

[27] Schürmann readily admits that many of the individual points he makes are not conclusive; he rests his case on the force of a cumulative argument.

[28] *Op. cit.* pp. 203f.

[29] In addition, it is not easy (in spite of the explanations Schürmann offers) to understand why Matthew would have by-passed this Q material in favour of other traditions.

Those who see the actions of Jesus and hear his words are μακάριοι, for they are witnessing the long hoped for fulfilment of God's promises.[30]

In the opening Beatitude ἡ βασιλεία τοῦ θεοῦ is promised (Matt. 5: 3 = Luke 6: 20b). But in the light of the two closely related Beatitudes which follow in Luke, who stands closer to Q, this must be taken as referring to the future, in spite of ἐστιν. However, μακάριοι οἱ πτωχοί undoubtedly refers to the present. Once again Isa. 61: 1f. is in view – in fact this passage lies behind the first three Lucan (Q) Beatitudes.[31] In the Q Beatitudes which stand at the head of a lengthy section of Q material, Jesus announces that the eschatological promises are now being fulfilled.

In Matt. 12: 28 = Luke 11: 20 Jesus claims that his exorcisms provide evidence of the presence of God's kingdom. Jesus' insistence that his actions and words mark the dawn of God's new age is deeply rooted in the Q material; Matt. 11: 2–6 = Luke 7: 18–23 is no isolated phenomenon.

Matt. 12: 28 = Luke 11: 20 also emphasises that it is because of his relationship to God that Jesus exorcises demons. Here, as in Jesus' reply to John, we have an implied christology. Jesus' relationship to God and the grounds of his authority are also firmly underlined in two closely related passages which stood near the beginning of Q: the temptation and baptism narratives.

Most scholars accept that the temptation narratives, Matt. 4: 1–11 = Luke 4: 1–13, stood in Q.[32] If we accept the Matthaean order as original,[33] the first two temptations are introduced by εἰ υἱὸς εἶ τοῦ θεοῦ. Whatever may have been the origin of these verses, in their present form they are christological: Jesus' authority as God's Son is challenged but vindicated. υἱὸς τοῦ θεοῦ is very probably a Messianic title here – especially in view of 4Q flor, and the hints in this passage

---

[30] W. G. Kümmel notes that the juxtaposition of seeing and hearing, as evidence of the time of fulfilment, does not correspond to Jewish parallels, but to Matt. 11: 5f.; *Promise*, p. 112.

[31] See J. Dupont, *Les Béatitudes* ii (Paris, 1970), pp. 92–9; A. Finkel, *The Pharisees*, pp. 155–8.

[32] D. Lührmann suggests that Matthew and Luke have had access to independent traditions as this material differs markedly from the rest of Q. But the verbal agreement is much closer than in many other passages which Lührmann accepts as Q material. *Logienquelle*, p. 56.

[33] This is the usual view, but H. Schürmann argues that Matthew has altered the Q order. *Das Lukasevangelium* i (Freiburg, 1969), p. 218.

of polemic against false understandings of Messiahship.[34] Matt. 11: 25–7 = Luke 10: 21f. also contains an important 'Son' christology, but the two passages do not seem to have been related to each other by the Q community: in the temptation narratives υἱός is anarthrous and linked with τοῦ θεοῦ in both cases. A 'Son' or 'Son of God' christology is not developed into a central theme in Q; christological titles are of less interest to Q than the grounds of the authority of Jesus.

Q almost certainly contained an account of the baptism of Jesus.[35] The temptation narratives indicate a prior appointment as God's Son and also Jesus' reception of the Spirit.[36] Hence the Q version of the baptism of Jesus was probably very similar to the Marcan account; this is not the only point at which Mark and Q seem to have overlapped closely. If this is so, it is not rash to suggest that Q's account of the baptism contained three themes: the new age is dawning in which God again speaks, and in which his Spirit is again active; Jesus enters upon his eschatological task as God's Son (or, perhaps originally, God's servant); and, having received the Spirit, Jesus can accomplish his word and work with real authority.[37]

The baptism and temptation narratives cannot be considered merely as a christological preface which can be removed leaving a very different kind of document.[38] For the themes prominent in these verses are also found in a number of Q passages. Or, to put our point another way, even if it could be proved that Q did not contain baptism and temptation narratives, there is plenty of evidence to confirm that for the Q community the actions and proclamation of Jesus marked the

---

[34] See P. Hoffmann, 'Die Versuchungsgeschichte in der Logienquelle', *BZ* xiii–xiv (1969–70), pp. 207–23; also F. Hahn, *The Titles of Jesus in Christology* (E.T. London, 1969), p. 158 and p. 208.

[35] See B. H. Streeter, *The Four Gospels* (London, 1924), pp. 186ff.; H. Schürmann, *Lukasevangelium*, p. 197. D. Lührmann does not accept that Q contained an account of the baptism of Jesus. He notes that there is no evidence of Q material in the baptism narratives and adds, 'überhaupt ist Q ja kein Evangelium!' But one suspects that here, as in his discussion of Matt. 4: 1–11 = Luke 4: 1–13, Lührmann's source-critical conclusions are determined partly by preconceived notions about the nature of Q. *Logienquelle*, p. 56 n. 2.

[36] The Marcan account of the temptation seems to have influenced Matthew and Luke's versions only very slightly, if at all.

[37] F. Hahn, *Titles*, p. 338.

[38] Cf. H. E. Tödt, 'In the narratives about the baptism and temptation, Jesus is seen as the Son of God; but Harnack is right in insisting that the Q material must be interpreted independently of this prefixed introduction', *Son of Man*, p. 264.

dawn of the new age, for Jesus was claiming to fulfil the prophetic promises. The opening Beatitudes and Jesus' reply to John are to be read against the backdrop of Isa. 61: 1f. – Jesus is the one anointed with the Spirit of God who has been sent to bring good news to the poor. The 'past' of Jesus, as well as his soon-expected parousia, is important to the Q community.

Jesus' reply to John's question is followed by two closely related pericopae. Together they form an important central section in Q. At the end of the third pericope two christological themes emerge in Q for the first time: Jesus as Son of Man and Jesus (and John) as Wisdom's representative(s).[39] Both have attracted considerable attention in recent studies of the Q material. Can either be claimed to be so central in Q as to provide an answer to the puzzle of the purpose of Q?

While a number of Q logia may be said to be wisdom sayings, there are four passages in which Jesus may possibly stand in a definite relationship to personified Wisdom, Sophia. The parable of the children in the market place concludes with the logion καὶ ἐδικαιώθη ἡ σοφία ἀπὸ (πάντων) τῶν τέκνων αὐτῆς (Luke 7: 35).[40] Matthew's version reads καὶ ἐδικαιώθη ἡ σοφία ἀπὸ τῶν ἔργων αὐτῆς, and represents his secondary modification of the logion. At the very beginning of this section of three pericopae Matthew interprets the miraculous actions of Jesus as τὰ ἔργα τοῦ Χριστοῦ (Matt. 11: 2); right at the end of this section ἔργα are emphasised – Jesus' messianic deeds are again in view, but now Jesus is explicitly identified as Sophia.[41] In the Q logion Jesus and Sophia are not identified; Jesus and John are Sophia's representatives. An alternative interpretation would identify Jesus as Sophia who is rejected by 'the men of this generation', but justified by a particular group, in this context the tax collectors and sinners.[42] But this is unlikely to be the meaning of the Q logion, as it concludes three pericopae in which John is very closely associated with Jesus. In addition, in order to identify Jesus with Sophia in this logion, it is

---

[39] Son of Man may possibly have occurred earlier in Q. Cf. Luke 6: 22 ἕνεκα τοῦ υἱοῦ τοῦ ἀνθρώπου and Matthew's equivalent logion ἕνεκεν ἐμοῦ, 5: 11.

[40] πάντων in Luke 7: 35 may stem from the evangelist's interpretation of the logion. F. Christ, *Jesus Sophia, Die Sophia-Christologie bei den Synoptikern* (Zürich, 1970), p. 79.

[41] M. J. Suggs, *Wisdom, Christology and Law in Matthew's Gospel* (Harvard, 1970), pp. 33ff.; F. Christ, *Jesus Sophia*, p. 76.

[42] F. Christ, *Jesus Sophia*, p. 73.

necessary to read it against the background of a fully-fledged tradition about Sophia who is scorned by the majority, but received by only a few.

Whether or not this logion is interpreted as part of an explicit Widsom christology in Q, it is the present earthly ministry of Jesus to 'this generation' which is in view: at the end of this section of Q material the rejection of Jesus (and John) is underlined.[43]

There is no doubt that the *Jubelruf* (Matt. 11: 25–7 = Luke 10: 21f.) comes from Q and that it is to be interpreted almost in its entirety against the background of Wisdom motifs.[44] But need the corollary be that Jesus is here identified as Sophia?[45] It is possible to read Matt. 11: 28–30 δεῦτε πρός με ... as the invitation of Sophia,[46] but it is much less easy to read the preceding verses in this way, unless one accepts as a presupposition that a Wisdom christology lies at the heart of Q.

The third so-called Wisdom passage in Q, Matt. 23: 34–6 = Luke 11: 49–51, also bristles with difficulties. Luke's introduction reads διὰ τοῦτο καὶ ἡ σοφία τοῦ θεοῦ εἶπεν ἀποστελῶ εἰς αὐτοὺς προφήτας .... Matthew has dropped the reference to σοφία, making the passage into words of Jesus, and has changed the tense of the verb into the present: διὰ τοῦτο ἰδοὺ ἐγὼ ἀποστέλλω πρὸς ὑμᾶς προφήτας .... Luke's version is closer to Q; Matthew seems to remove some of the difficulties and to identify Jesus with Sophia by placing the words in the mouth of Jesus.[47] But does Jesus speak as the Wisdom of God in the original Q passage? This is unlikely, especially in view of the aorist εἶπεν; the words are probably an oracle of Wisdom given as a quotation from a now lost document. Once again there is more than a hint of the rejection of Jesus.

The logia which follow in Matthew (Matt. 23: 37–9 = Luke 13: 34–5), Ἰερουσαλήμ, Ἰερουσαλήμ, ἡ ἀποκτείνουσα τοὺς προφήτας ..., also contain a number of wisdom motifs. It is quite possible that

---

43 Cf. D. Lührmann, *Logienquelle*, pp. 30f.
44 Although one might suspect that revelation to babes rather than to the wise would run counter to the Wisdom tradition, denial of wisdom to the wise and its revelation to the humble is a firmly established theme found in a number of passages. F. Christ, *Jesus Sophia*, pp. 83f.
45 Cf. F. Christ, 'Die Sohn-Christologie ist also zugleich auch Weisheitschristologie', *Jesus Sophia*, p. 87.
46 It is now widely accepted that Matt. 11: 28–30 did not follow Matt. 11: 25–7 in Q.
47 M. J. Suggs, *Wisdom*, pp. 13ff.

Matthew has linked two separate Q passages; if he does identify Jesus as Sophia in the preceding verses, the identification may well continue into this passage.[48] But it is not necessary to assume that Jesus is identified with Wisdom in the original Q tradition. As W. G. Kümmel notes, 'Jesus could very well use of himself the traditional picture of a mother hen; besides there is no authority anywhere for connecting the wisdom myth with the expectation of the coming Messiah (Matt. 23: 39)'.[49]

The extent to which Wisdom motifs are present in all four passages is striking; in other parts of the Synoptic traditions, with the exception of Matt. 11: 28–30, they are much less conspicuous.[50] The Q community seems to have been interested in Wisdom traditions, but Q does not contain a fully developed Wisdom christology.[51] If there is one theme which is common to all four Wisdom passages (though it is not always equally prominent), then surely it is that Jesus has been sent by God (perhaps as Sophia's representative) but has been rejected by many of those to whom he has been sent.

As there is little or no evidence to suggest that the Q community has developed or extended a Wisdom christology beyond the traditions to which it had access, it would be hazardous to draw conclusions about the purpose of Q from the christology of these four passages.[52]

Conclusions about the christology – and purpose – of Q have been drawn by H. E. Tödt and other recent writers from the Son-of-Man logia in Q. If one assumes that the Son of Man of Jewish apocalyptic, to

---

48 Cf. M. J. Suggs, *Wisdom*, pp. 63ff.   49 W. G. Kümmel, *Promise*, pp. 8of.

50 F. Christ lists Luke 2: 40–52; Matt. 2: 1–12; Mark 6: 2; Matt. 12: 38 = Luke 11: 31. *Jesus Sophia*, pp. 61f.

51 M. J. Suggs argues that Sophia is a christological title in Matt. and Paul, but not in Q or among Paul's opponents. *Wisdom*, p. 58 and p. 130; cf. D. Lührmann, *Logienquelle*, p. 99. The opposite view is taken by F. Christ who reads a fully developed Sophia tradition into each of the Q passages discussed above. Cf. also U. Wilckens, art. σοφία in *TWNT* vii, pp. 515ff.

52 J. M. Robinson has attempted to do this from a rather different angle. He argues that Q belongs to a particular *Gattung, Logoi Sophōn*, 'Sayings of the Sages', which can be traced in Jewish, Christian and gnostic literature; Q belongs to the same *Gattung* as *Pirke Aboth* and the Gospel of Thomas. There are striking similarities between the various collections of sayings Robinson discusses, but their content and form both differ so markedly that clarification of the *Gattung* of Q seems to tell us little about its theological stance and purpose. '*Logoi Sophōn*: on the *Gattung* of Q', in *The Future of our Religious Past* (Bultmann Festschrift), ed. J. M. Robinson (E.T. London, 1971), pp. 84–130.

which the Synoptic logia must be related, is a transcendent figure with 'traditional attributes',[53] and that it is on the basis of a few authentic 'future' Son-of-Man sayings that the Q community developed a Son-of-Man christology, then it is not surprising that the theology of Q is considered to have been dominated completely by expectations of an imminent parousia. On this view, the Son-of-Man sayings in Q which refer to the earthly ministry of Jesus are generally considered to have been created by the Q community as a secondary development of its convictions about Jesus as the coming Son of Man.

I do not propose to rehearse the now familiar arguments in favour of a very different approach, which, taking Dan. 7 as the primary background of Son of Man, accepts as authentic some Son-of-Man sayings in all three of the groups into which the Son-of-Man traditions are usually (but misleadingly) divided. The Son of Man is not simply an apocalyptic figure who appears at the end of time to act as judge; 'rather it is because he is Son of Man now – i.e. elect, obedient, faithful and therefore suffering – that he will be vindicated as Son of Man in the future: the eschatological rôle of the Son of Man is based upon his obedient response to God now'.[54] On this view it is the 'present' Son-of-Man sayings, rather than the 'future' sayings, which may be seen as the central element in a Son-of-Man christology. And if this is a plausible approach to the whole Son-of-Man question, a very different understanding of the purpose of Q becomes possible.

This is not the only aspect of Tödt's discussion of Q against which a firm question mark must be placed. Tödt argues that the Q community resumed Jesus' preaching concerning the soon expected coming of the Kingdom, but deliberately by-passed the passion and resurrection of Jesus. 'The passion and resurrection were not what had to be preached, but what enabled them to preach.'[55] Tödt suggests that the Q community had come into existence thanks to the risen one's once more turning towards them in love – only on this basis could the preaching of Jesus be taken up again.[56] Is it possible to accept that the resurrection

53 H. E. Tödt, *Son of Man*, pp. 22ff.
54 M. D. Hooker, *The Son of Man in Mark* (1967), p. 190. See also (with differences) O. Betz, *What do we Know about Jesus?* (E.T. London, 1968), pp. 109ff.; F. H. Borsch, *The Son of Man in Myth and History* (London, 1967), pp. 43ff.; C. F. D. Moule's review of H. E. Tödt's *Son of Man*, in *Theology* lxix (1966), pp. 172ff.; R. Leivestad, 'Exit the Apocalyptic Son of Man', *NTS* xviii (1972), pp. 243–67.
55 H. E. Tödt, *Son of Man*, p. 250. 56 *Ibid.*, also p. 273.

was crucial – indeed axiomatic – for the Q community, but to argue that it did not form part of its proclamation? And if the resurrection was axiomatic, then surely the community must have asked itself the awkward question, 'Why did Jesus die?' – however unsophisticated the answer may have been. Tödt assumes that the community quite deliberately failed to face up to this question: 'The events of Jesus' being executed, laid under the curse of the cross and turned out of Israel could not fail to cast doubt upon the authority of his teaching.'[57]

But a number of Q sayings, some of which have been noted above, suggest that the scandal of the rejection of Jesus during his ministry, if not his ultimate rejection, was not obliterated or by-passed, and was not understood as undermining the authority of Jesus.

In Matt. 11: 19 = Luke 7: 34 Jesus states that critics of his conduct have written him off as a glutton and a winebibber, a friend of tax collectors and sinners. In Matt. 8: 20 = Luke 9: 59 Jesus states that while foxes have holes and the birds of the air have nests, the Son of Man has nowhere to lay his head: the logion speaks of the homelessness of Jesus – to be understood as his alienation from his family or his rejection by those among whom he moved. In short, if the Q community was able to accept the notion that the earthly Jesus was rejected by 'this generation', then some kind of answer to the question, 'Why did Jesus die?', must have been possible. The eschatological expectations of the Q community are hardly likely to have smothered all interest in the 'past' of Jesus. Once one concedes that the resurrection was axiomatic for the Q community, even though it is not mentioned explicitly in Q, then it is most unlikely that the Q community did not have any kind of theological understanding of the death of Jesus. There are, then, good reasons for hesitating to accept that a 'future' Son-of-Man christology is the central christological theme in Q and that the proclamation of the Q community was concerned solely or even primarily with impending judgement.

Recent attempts to grapple with christological themes in the New Testament have concentrated rather too rigidly on christological titles. This is particularly noticeable in recent studies of Q. There is one important christological title, Son of Man, in Q, but Q contains such a variety of other christological themes which are rarely related closely

[57] H. E. Tödt, *Son of Man*, p. 250.

to each other that Q can be called a christological document only with cautious qualification.[58]

The relationship between Q and passion material has always puzzled scholars. If Q is not merely catechetical or hortatory material which supplemented a passion and resurrection kerygma,[59] and if the Q community was not so concerned with the future coming of Jesus as Son of Man that we need conclude that it deliberately by-passed the passion and resurrection of Jesus in its proclamation, is there a plausible alternative?

The Q material answers the questions, 'Who was Jesus? With what authority did he act and speak?'[60] In other words it does contain christological material – in the broadest sense of the term. But it was also concerned with the question, 'What demands did Jesus make on those who would follow him?' In addition Q contains a number of traditions about John – not because the Q community was involved in polemics with John's disciples, but because of the deep conviction that the Christian story started with John; the relationship of Jesus to John was bound to be of interest and significance.

Q contains such varied material that it is impossible to locate *one* specific purpose for which it was used. Q traditions would surely have been useful both for instruction of those within the community and in an evangelistic context. The clear warning note of impending judgement, as well as Q's strong interest in the 'past' of Jesus, would have been appropriate in both contexts. There is no reason to regard Q either as solely kerygmatic material or solely didactic material – for the customary division is often both artificial and misleading.

Since the Q community accepted that the one anointed with God's Spirit, whose words and actions marked the dawn of God's age of salvation, was rejected by those to whom he was sent, passion material would not have been incongruous alongside, but separate from Q.

---

[58] Cf. P. Stuhlmacher, *Das paulinische Evangelium*, p. 218.

[59] See the references given in note 4 on p. 25 above.

[60] Cf. A. P. Polag, 'Zu den Stufen der Christologie in Q', *Studia Evangelica* iv/i (1968), pp. 72–5. Polag also draws attention to Jesus' reply to John. His brief but perceptive article seems to summarise the results of his research on Q. Unfortunately I have not had access to his two unpublished dissertations, *Der Ursprung der Logienquelle* (Trier, 1966), and *Die Christologie der Logienquelle* (Trier, 1968).

See also K. Berger, 'Zum traditionsgeschichtlichen Hintergrund christologischer Hoheitstitel', *NTS* xvii (1971), pp. 391–425, esp. pp. 396ff.

There is no reason to assume that Q contains all the theological convictions of the Q community.

There is good Old Testament and late Jewish precedent for a document like Q – but not for Mark. Hence it is not surprising that at first passion material was not linked explicitly with Q. And in view of the fact that both Matthew and Luke (and presumably also their communities) had access to two very different and originally separate kinds of material about Jesus (Q and Mark), is it not at least possible that the Q community also had two different kinds of material? If so, we might envisage traditions which set out the teaching of Jesus, but underlined the grounds of his authoritative words and actions, being used in instruction of those within the community and also in an evangelistic context. And, alongside Q, traditions which told the story of the ultimate rejection of Jesus by men, but proclaimed his vindication by God – such traditions being used primarily in the worship of the community.

4

The Son of Man
in the Johannine christology

BARNABAS LINDARS

The perennial debate on the figure of the Son of Man tends to leave the Fourth Gospel on one side. Interest centres on the problem of Jesus and the Son of Man, how far the Synoptic sayings may be accepted as authentic, whether Jesus used the title as a self-designation, and how far he is indebted to a distinct concept of the Son-of-Man figure in contemporary Jewish apocalyptic. For all these questions the Fourth Gospel is dismissed as providing no help.[1] When the Fourth Gospel itself is considered, the questions asked are whether the Son of Man truly belongs to John's christological thought or represents an alien element in the later editing of the gospel;[2] or, if it is conceded that the references come from his hand, whether he is influenced byHellenistic or incipient gnostic speculations.[3]

Attempts have been made to rehabilitate John's use of the Son-of-Man figure by finding a traditional basis in the words of Jesus for all the places where the title occurs.[4] But this scarcely does justice to the Johannine cast of the great majority of the sayings. Nor does it take into account the larger context in each case. The subtle interplay of John's use of different titles within a single context goes largely unrecognised.

[1] Thus H. E. Tödt, *The Son of Man in the Synoptic Tradition* (London, 1965), does not find it necessary to use the evidence of the Fourth Gospel; A. J. B. Higgins, *Jesus and the Son of Man* (London, 1964) thinks that the Johannine sayings are partly derived from earlier tradition, but discounts them for his main purpose; F. H. Borsch, *The Son of Man in Myth and History* (London, 1967), is more positive, in that he sees in them evidence for an early Christian debate which points to the fact that Jesus *did* apply the Son of Man to himself in some sense. For a full survey of work on the Son of Man in John, see E. Ruckstuhl, 'Die johanneische Menschensohnforschung 1957–1969', in *Theologische Berichte* i, ed. J. Pfammatter und F. Furger (Zürich, 1972), pp. 171–284.

[2] Bultmann ascribes the sayings to the Evangelist, or (in the case of 5: 27) to the ecclesiastical redactor.

[3] For the debate on this issue see R. Schnackenburg, 'Der Menschensohn im Johannesevangelium', *NTS* xi (1964–5), pp. 123–37.

[4] The case is well presented by S. S. Smalley, 'The Johannine Son of Man Sayings', *NTS* xv (1968–9), pp. 278–301.

In fact John's variation between 'the Son of God', 'the Son', and 'the Son of man' is never accidental, but is carefully chosen in accordance with the needs of his argument.[5]

It will be argued in this essay that the concept of the Son of Man holds a key place in John's thought. Whatever may be the origin of the designation and the source of his ideas, John makes use of the concept because it provides him with the means to express the relationship of Jesus to God, which is his major concern. His use of it is not simply a kind of local colour, derived from the tradition of the words of Jesus, without much bearing on his real thought. It is essential to his task as a creative thinker, an indispensable element in the constructive christology which is his unique contribution to Christianity. Whether other Son-of-Man christologies existed in the early church is a question which cannot be answered without first taking into account the fact that such a christology exists at least in the Fourth Gospel. This also has a bearing on the problem of the Son-of-Man figure in first century Judaism.

The title first occurs in John 1: 51. Thereafter it occurs in 3: 13, 14; 5: 27; 6: 27, 53, 62; 8: 28; 9: 35; 12: 23, 34 (twice); 13: 31. It thus belongs to the first half of the gospel, in which traditions of the ministry of Jesus are employed for the unfolding of John's christological argument. It never occurs in the passion narrative, except for 13: 31, which picks up the theme of 12: 23 to provide the link between the two halves of the gospel.

Any attempt to analyse the argument of the first twelve chapters inevitably encounters the vexed question of the composition of the book. The question is too large to be treated within the confines of a short study. So I must content myself with briefly summarising what I have written elsewhere on this subject.[6] I hold that the division of the gospel into two major sources, the *Semeia-Quelle* and the *Offenbarungs-reden-Quelle*, with the elaborate redactional theory which this entails, is mistaken. Also the case for accidental displacements has not been made out. But the gospel cannot have been written straight off just as it stands, because of the glaring breaks in the continuity and abrupt

---

5 The argument of E. D. Freed, 'The Son of Man in the Fourth Gospel', *JBL* lxxxvi (1967), that John uses these titles indifferently for stylistic variation, is wholly unconvincing.

6 *Behind the Fourth Gospel* (London, 1971); *The Gospel of John* (*The Century Bible: Revised Edition*, London, 1972). For a similar theory, see R. E. Brown, *The Gospel according to John* (*The Anchor Bible*, Garden City, N.Y., 1966; London, 1971), vol. i, pp. xxxiv–xxxix.

changes of theme. I believe that John wrote the gospel in two principal stages, making use of a number of shorter pieces which he had composed earlier, possibly as self-contained homilies. The first edition did not include the Prologue (1: 1–18), the Discourse on the Bread of Life (chapter 6), the Raising of Lazarus (11: 1–44), the second Supper Discourse (chapters 15 and 16), and the Prayer of Jesus (chapter 17). All these items were added at the second stage. At the same time some further adjustments were made, the most important being the transference of the Cleansing of the Temple from its original position in chapter 12 to its present position in chapter 2.

One observation can be made at once on the basis of this theory. The Son-of-Man title is confined to material which belongs to the first edition of the gospel, with the notable exception of chapter 6. This is important, because the christological argument of that chapter, and the special use of the Son-of-Man figure within it, interfere with the main argument of the rest of the book. This argument is complete, and stands out more clearly, when attention is confined to the sections which belong to the first edition. On the other hand the argument in chapter 6 presupposes the total argument of the rest and confirms it.

The christological argument of John begins with a series of scenes (1: 19–51), in which the various titles of Jesus are introduced. The reader's interest is engaged at the outset by the questioning of the Baptist, which may be an adaptation of the questioning about Jesus preserved in the Synoptic tradition.[7] Here 'the Christ', 'Elijah', and 'the prophet' are mentioned. Though repudiated by the Baptist, the possibility that they could be applied to Jesus is not excluded. Then the first title actually applied to Jesus is 'the Lamb of God' (1: 29, 36).[8] This introduces a reminiscence of the baptism of Jesus, including a traditional reference to him as one who 'baptizes with Holy Spirit' (1: 33). This in its turns leads to the affirmation that Jesus is 'the Son of God' or 'the Elect of God' (1: 34).[9] Then follow 'the Messiah' (1: 41), the one 'of whom Moses in the law and of whom the prophets wrote' (1: 45), and 'the Son of God . . . the king of Israel' (1: 49). All

---

[7] Cf. Mark 6: 14f.; 8: 28f. The Synoptic tradition also contains questioning about the Baptist, cf. Matt. 11: 7–15; Mark 11: 29–32; Luke 3: 15.

[8] The interpretation of this title remains uncertain. For the principal views see R. E. Brown *ad loc*. In any case it plays no further part in John's argument.

[9] Read probably ὁ ἐκλεκτός with 𝔓5 א* e ff² sy^sc sa, as the harder reading. Then ὁ υἱὸς τοῦ θεοῦ is reserved until the climax of the sequence at verse 49.

these titles have been spoken by others. Finally Jesus himself promises a sight more compelling than any that has evoked the preceding confessions of faith: 'Amen, amen, I say to you, you will see the heaven opened and the angels of God ascending and descending on the Son of man' (1: 51).

Several points about this saying are highly important for the present discussion. In the first place it has long been recognised that it is an addition to the original composition of 1: 19–49, linked to it by means of verse 50. Thus the underlying homily, which John has used as the first section of his gospel, originally ended with the climax of Nathanael's confession in verse 49. The Son of Man was not mentioned in this homily. But when John set about composing a complete gospel, he added this saying as a further climax, so as to introduce the argument which will follow. As such it anticipates what is to be unfolded in the ensuing chapters. Of the numerous interpretations offered for the meaning of the saying,[10] there is much to be said for the contention that this is a symbolic description of the baptismal experience of Jesus (for τὸν οὐρανὸν ἀνεῳγότα cf. Matt. 3: 16 and parallels), in which Jesus' future glory as the Son of Man is disclosed, and the link between his earthly ministry and his heavenly status is established (here represented by the ascending and descending angels).[11] But as it refers to a future event, and the baptism has already taken place (verses 32–4), John's thought cannot be confined to this. In fact the saying will be fulfilled in a deeper and fuller sense in the passion of Jesus, which is the hour when the Son of Man is glorified (12: 23). The saying thus points forward to the conclusion of the whole of the argument which John is about to expound.

In the second place it is noteworthy that John uses the arthrous form of the phrase (τὸν υἱὸν τοῦ ἀνθρώπου) in common with the Synoptic tradition. This is sufficient to establish the fact that it is a title, and not the common Aramaic בר אנשא. The significance of this will appear when we reach 5: 27, the only place where John uses the anarthrous

---

[10] Cf. Higgins, pp. 157–71; Borsch, pp. 278–80.

[11] As Borsch, p. 280 n. 5, points out, the glorification of the Son of Man is not mentioned as such. He remains on earth, and the opening of the heavens allows the passage of the angels upon him, just as in the baptismal vision the Spirit comes down upon Jesus. That this is the correct interpretation, so that it is wrong to suppose that the Son of Man is at this point seen in heaven, is indicated by the biblical allusion to Gen. 28: 12. John's text follows the Hebrew of this verse exactly.

form. As the form with the article occurs only in the words of Jesus (and Acts 7: 56), the conclusion is inevitable that John derives it from the Jesus-tradition, rather than from Jewish or Hellenistic sources.

Thirdly the Amen-formula is an indication that John is drawing on the sayings of Jesus.[12] He not only derives the title from this tradition, but has formed the verse by adapting a traditional saying, such as Mark 14: 62 (which may also lie behind Acts 7: 56). The christological argument in John constantly draws on traditional sayings in this way.

After the symbolic tale of the Marriage at Cana, in which the new dimension of the coming of Jesus is expressed, John resumes the christological argument in the discourse with Nicodemus in chapter 3. Starting from another Amen saying (verse 3),[13] Jesus insists on the necessity of rebirth, which is nothing less than birth from above.[14] Nicodemus is nonplussed. His rabbinic training has not prepared him for this. Jesus then explains that he is himself the source of divine knowledge (verse 11, again an Amen saying).[15] It will appear subsequently that Jesus is also the giver of the spiritual life which comes through the birth from above. But for the moment attention is confined to the question of the divine knowledge. Jesus asserts that it is only accessible through the Son of Man (verse 13). To those who have pondered the implications of 1: 51 this should occasion no surprise. For if there is a link between earth and heaven through the earthly ministry of him who is to be glorified as Son of man, then it is through Jesus that the divine knowledge is mediated to men.

It is the aim of John at this point to state that Jesus is the sole mediator of eternal life. It is tempting to see the influence of Hellenistic

---

[12] The Amen-formula probably does not go back to Jesus himself, but is rather a very early form of asseveration to guarantee an apocalyptic statement, extended in Mark and John to denote the legitimation of the Jesus-tradition. It is thus a sure sign that the words which it introduces are based on authentic logia of Jesus. Cf. K. Berger, *Die Amen-Wörter Jesu: eine Untersuchung zum Problem der Legitimation in apokalyptischer Rede* (*BZNW* xxxix, 1970).

[13] The saying is a variant of Matt. 18: 3.

[14] Following Schnackenburg, I take ἄνωθεν to mean 'from above' each time it occurs (verses 3, 7, 31). Verse 4a shows that it is the kind of birth which is the point at issue. It is only at 4b that Nicodemus points out that Jesus' statement entails rebirth of some kind. As the birth from above is not the same thing as physical birth, it is not strictly rebirth at all.

[15] There is no Synoptic parallel, but the proverbial character of the verse, with the sudden change to plural verbs and parallelism of the first two clauses, suggests a traditional saying.

religion here, but this is probably a mistake. In fact man gains eternal life not through gnosis, but through belief in Jesus crucified and exalted (verse 14). The divine secret is nothing else than the vindication and glorification of Jesus. The 'heavenly things' which Nicodemus is not ready to believe are precisely this vindication and glorification. They are accessible now, because he who is to be the Son of man has come down in the incarnation of Jesus. The background to this idea is probably not the myth of the descent of a heavenly revealer, but the Wisdom christology presupposed by John elsewhere, and developed by him in the Prologue.[16] Jewish seers may claim to have been admitted to the divine secrets, and indeed they have been so admitted inasmuch as they have seen the future glory of the Son of Man (cf. 12: 41). But they cannot reveal God's plan with such clarity as the Son of man himself, by whom it is accomplished.

Before going further, it will be worth while to consider why John found it necessary to use the Son-of-Man theme at this point. It is because this theme, as already implied in 1: 51, enabled him to express the relation between the earthly ministry of Jesus and his heavenly glory in which God's purpose for mankind is achieved. And the crucial act in this process is the cross. John states this fact immediately (verse 14), though it will have to be worked out in detail in the ensuing chapters. It is not at once obvious why the cross should most fully reveal the future glory of the Son of Man. For the moment John is content to express it by a play on words, using the double meaning of ὑψωθῆναι, reinforced with the typology of the serpent in the wilderness. It will appear in the end, however, that the glory of Jesus as the Son of Man consists in his union with the Father, and the cross most fully reveals this because it is the ultimate expression of the union of his will with the Father's. This is to anticipate matters, for it is the climax of John's argument. But it is important to see that John is using the Son-of-Man theme in chapter 3 in order to lay out the terms in which his argument is to be expressed.

16 It is important to notice that John never says that the Son of Man has come down from heaven. All he does here is to identify the one who has come down from heaven with the Son of Man. In other words, *descent is not part of the Johannine Son-of-Man myth, though it is an essential feature of his christology.* Normally he uses the idea of sending to express this, in line with Paul (cf. Rom. 8: 3; Gal. 4: 4) and some Synoptic sayings (e.g. Mark 9: 37). Apart from 3: 13, καταβαίνω is only used of the incarnation in the discourse of chapter 6, where it is probably dependent on the typology of the manna miracle. See further the article of Schnackenburg cited above.

Even if the serpent typology is taken to be an original contribution of John himself, there can be little doubt that he is indebted to the important work of apologetic in early Christianity with regard to the passion of Jesus. John's δεῖ is reminiscent of the first prediction of the passion (Mark 8: 31 and parallels). It was necessary that Jesus should suffer, because it was written in scripture. John is familiar with this argument from scriptural fulfilment, and shares the predestinarian outlook which it implies (cf. 19: 28–30), and indeed the allusion here to Num. 21: 9 is the fruit of further biblical work along the same line. But the necessity of the passion is much greater than this. It is indispensable for the salvation of men, because they cannot reach the level of faith required for eternal life without it (verse 15). And the irony of this is that John knows only too well that it is at the cross that the faith of the Jews stumbles (12: 31–6; cf. 1 Cor. 1: 23).

Direct reference to the Son of Man in the discourse is now concluded. But there are two supplementary pieces (verses 16–20 and 31–6) which add further features to John's argument.[17] These two paragraphs are important for two reasons. (*a*) They introduce two new themes, which will play a major part later on. These are the themes of *judging* and of *giving life*. The judgment is not a judicial verdict in the literal sense, but the inevitable consequence of belief or unbelief. Belief leads to life, whereas unbelief renders a man self-condemned (verse 18). Belief is necessary in order to appropriate life, because Jesus gives life by conveying the *words* of God unstintingly, being himself fully endowed with the Spirit (verse 34).[18] (*b*) These paragraphs also introduce new descriptions of Jesus, which have not been used before in the first edition of the gospel. These are τὸν υἱὸν τὸν μονογενῆ, τὸν υἱόν, and τοῦ μονογενοῦς υἱοῦ τοῦ θεοῦ (verses 16–18). Moreover in verse 35 ὁ πατήρ is correlated with ὁ υἱός for the first time. Although it is natural to regard these titles as variants of ὁ υἱὸς τοῦ θεοῦ, and it may well be legitimate to do so in the light of the full spectrum of John's christology, in the present context the thematic connection with verses 11–15 strongly suggests that they are alternatives to ὁ υἱὸς τοῦ ἀνθρώπου.

[17] The use of material of a very different type between these two paragraphs presents a difficult problem. Theories of transposition (Bernard, Bultmann) or subsequent addition (Schnackenburg) have been suggested. But it can be accounted for equally well on the theory that John first composed this discourse as a self-contained homily, which he then broke up in the making of the first edition of his gospel (see my commentary *ad loc.*).

[18] Taking God to be the subject of δίδωσιν (so Bernard, Bultmann, Barrett).

The adjective μονογενής emphasises the uniqueness of Jesus in his capacity as God's agent of salvation.[19] The simple ὁ υἱός expresses his personal relationship with God, but in an open way, without tying down the meaning to the special implications of either ὁ υἱὸς τοῦ θεοῦ or ὁ υἱὸς τοῦ ἀνθρώπου. It has often been observed that John regularly uses 'the Son' in correlation with 'the Father'. It has not always been noticed that John does this deliberately, in order to leave the further implications open. In the present context it is virtually an abbreviation of 'the Son of Man'. But the subject of the discourse has run out into more general considerations, for which it is desirable to keep open the full range of meaning implied by *both* titles. The significance of this observation will appear when we turn to the argument in chapter 5.

The discourse with the Samaritan woman in chapter 4 has figured prominently in recent work on the Fourth Gospel, because of the interest among scholars in early Christian contacts with the Samaritans.[20] The chapter stands apart from the main christological argument nevertheless. The themes already adumbrated are developed further, it is true. The function of Jesus as the giver of life is expounded in the conversation on the water of life, and is demonstrated in the healing of the officer's son at the end of the chapter. Jesus' capacity to reveal the divine knowledge is also represented in the second part of the conversation, where the woman recognises in him the Prophet-Messiah of Samaritan expectation. This is given wider significance in the people's affirmation that he is 'the saviour of the world' (verse 42). But these thoughts are not resumed in the sequel. The chapter gives impressive testimony to the results of belief in Jesus, but does not bring any new insight into the nature of the relationship between Jesus and God, which is the real issue in the Johannine christology.

When we turn to chapter 5, however, the idea of 'the Son' becomes prominent once more. The argument begins with the Parable of the Apprenticed Son (verses 19–20a),[21] where the words 'father' and

---

19 Cf. D. Moody, 'God's Only Son: the Translation of John 3: 16 in the Revised Standard Version', *JBL* lxxii (1953), pp. 213–19.

20 Among recent studies see especially W. A. Meeks, *The Prophet-King: Moses Traditions and Johannine Christology* (Supplements to Nov. T. xiv, Leiden, 1967).

21 Cf. C. H. Dodd, 'Une parabole cachée dans le quatrième évangile', *RHPR* xlii (1962), pp. 46–50 (= 'A Hidden Parable in the Fourth Gospel', *More New Testament Studies* (Manchester, 1968), pp. 30–40); P. Gächter, 'Zur Form

'son' are ambiguous. They might refer to any father and son. But they could be intended to refer specifically to God and Jesus. The ambiguity remains unresolved in the verses which immediately follow. But as the craft which the father teaches turns out to be the eschatological functions of giving life and performing judgment, it is (at least) clear that the father is God. It is only at verse 24, when Jesus suddenly adopts the first person, that we are made aware that he is himself the son.

We are already familiar with the functions of giving life and judging. But there is also here a new theme, which has not been mentioned before, and which will have profound consequences for the progress of the christological argument. This is the idea, already hinted at in verse 18, and explicitly stated in verse 23, that the Son has the right to equal 'honour' with the Father, so that those who withhold honour from him *ipso facto* withhold it from the Father himself.

It is only in the second paragraph of the discourse (verses 25–9) that the Son is identified as the Son of Man, though this is the natural conclusion to which the argument has been leading. To begin with there is a surprise. Verse 25 reads: 'The dead shall hear the voice of the Son of God...' In view of what follows, we should naturally expect 'the Son of man' (it is actually read by KS 28 *al.*). But that can hardly be right, as it would spoil the climax in verse 27. 'Son of God' must either be retained as an intentional variation in the styling of the argument, designed to hold back the climax at the same time as giving a hint of it; or, more probably in my opinion, it should be regarded as a very early corruption of the text due to the influence of the Lazarus story in chapter 11.[22] It must be admitted that 'the Son' alone best fits the flow of the argument. Then in the next verse the Father and Son correlation is employed, recalling the Father's delegation of his prerogative of giving life. Finally, in verse 27, the other function of judging is mentioned, and at last the reason for the delegation of these powers is given. It is because the Son is υἱὸς ἀνθρώπου. The anarthrous form, unique in the New Testament, can only be intended to be a

von Joh. 5: 19–30', in *Neutestamentliche Aufsätze*, edited by J. Blinzler, O. Kuss and F. Mussner (Regensburg, 1963), pp. 65–8.

[22] To overcome the difficulty, Wendt conjectured the omission of ἀνθρώπου in verse 27. But this makes nonsense of the verse. Variants for αὐτοῦ at the end of verse 28 attest confusion at an early date. Thus sy^c reads *da'lāhā'*, Origen τοῦ υἱοῦ τοῦ θεοῦ, and Irenaeus *filii hominis*. The latter reading is probably influenced by verse 25 (hence the addition of *mortui* in the same verse). It thus seems likely that both τοῦ θεοῦ and τοῦ ἀνθρώπου are attempts to elucidate an original τοῦ υἱοῦ.

direct allusion to the foundation text, Dan. 7: 13. Notice also the unmistakable allusion to Dan. 12: 2 in the next two verses. The conclusion can now be drawn that the acts of Jesus in his earthly life anticipate his functions at the End of the Age, when he will be glorified as the Son of Man. The rest of the discourse does not take this point further, as it is taken up with the testimony to this claim.

One further feature of this passage should not be missed. The biblical allusion to Dan. 7: 13 is the clue to the argument, but it is not the origin of John's use of the Son-of-Man title. That comes, as we have seen, from the tradition of the sayings of Jesus. But of course John knows perfectly well that the title comes in the first instance from Daniel. So here he takes the title from the tradition, and builds his argument on it with conscious reference to the biblical passage from which it is ultimately derived. We shall see a comparable literary feature in connection with the phrase ἐγώ εἰμι.

Passing over chapter 6, we come to the composite assemblage of teachings at the Feast of Tabernacles in chapters 7 and 8. The problem of Jesus' credentials is still the main topic in chapter 7. Doubts are expressed whether he fulfils the conditions for a genuine messianic claimant. In chapter 8, however, the thought fastens once more on the subject of Jesus' relationship to God. In other words, the argument passes from consideration of the physical origin of Jesus to the question of his heavenly origin.

To begin with, Jesus does not use a title to refer to himself, but speaks in the first person. First he announces the theme: 'I am the light of the world' (8: 12). It quickly becomes clear that the reference of τὸ φῶς is not to revelation of esoteric knowledge, but to the Jewish concept of exposing good and bad, truth and falsehood, by illuminating the mind. The argument in verses 13–19 is taken up with Jesus' claim to do this. His ἐγώ εἰμι is refuted on the grounds that it is self-witness. Jesus counters this on the grounds that he knows his own origin and destiny, which the Jews do not know (verse 14). Jesus here adds a disclaimer. He does not pass this sort of earthly, ill-informed judgment. This rather artificial disclaimer acts as a bridge to the next point in the argument, that the *content* of what Jesus claims to be, the judge (or light) of the world, cannot be denied, because it has the twofold witness required by the canons of Jewish legal practice. For his own judgment is confirmed by the Father who has delegated this function to him.

So far no title for Jesus has been used. But at verse 21 the discussion is reopened on a fresh occasion, and now the issue is brought to a head. In covert language Jesus forecasts the passion, which, as we have already seen, is a crucial item in the Son-of-Man themes. This in fact will be the decisive act, whereby Jesus' heavenly origin is revealed and the unbelieving world is judged (verse 23f.). The thought is moving in the categories of the Son-of-Man christology, as may be seen by comparison with 3: 11–15, where the heavenly origin of the Son of Man and the passion are both referred to. The language of the present passage keeps harping on the ἐγώ εἰμι of verse 12. It has been taken up in verse 18, where the self-witness which it implies (verse 13f.) is given formal justification. Now it comes again in verse 23 to express Jesus' heavenly origin in contrast with all other men. At the same time the predicate (τὸ φῶς) is not forgotten. It is implied in the phrase 'you will die in your sins' (verses 21 and 24 twice), which is the consequence of exposure to the light of judgment, as explained in 3: 18–21. This, Jesus asserts, is inevitable, *unless* the Jews believe that ἐγώ εἰμι. The predicate is not expressed. But it is clear from the whole tenor of the argument that it is all that Jesus has been claiming about himself. And this is at least what he has claimed in the immediate context, that he is the light of the world, the one who judges, the one who comes from above, the one who must mysteriously 'go away'. But all these are things that can be said of the Son of Man, according to John's use of this title. With his customary skill, John leaves the matter open for the moment. Naturally the lack of a predicate in verse 24 draws the question 'Who are you?' Jesus' reply is indirect, and may seem evasive.[23] But it becomes unmistakably clear that the predicate should be the Son of Man, when Jesus magnificently concludes the argument with a further allusion to 3: 14 in verse 28: 'When you have lifted up the Son of man, then you will know that ἐγώ εἰμι . . .' The allusion to the argument in 5: 19–30 in the remainder of the verse should also be noted.

It is at this point that we may observe how John's technique has a certain similarity to his use of scripture in 5: 27. There a title from the tradition was elucidated by reference to the actual biblical passage from which it was derived. Here a phrase which John is using christologically

[23] For the problems of this verse see commentaries. The translation turns on the meaning of the idiomatic τὴν ἀρχήν. The lack of classical style elsewhere in the gospel scarcely favours the meaning 'at all', cf. F. N. Davey in E. C. Hoskyns, *The Fourth Gospel* (London, ²1947), pp. 335f.

is treated in a similar way. Whether ἐγώ εἰμι was already in use as a title is disputed.[24] But John's very special use of it does not require a prior history in the tradition. In fact, if it arises simply from ἐγώ εἰμι τὸ φῶς τοῦ κόσμου at the beginning of the section,[25] we can see how it has come into being from John's adaptation of a quite different saying in the tradition.[26] But when John reaches the climax of the argument he introduces a striking allusion to a biblical passage in which ἐγώ εἰμι occurs, Isa. 43: 10: γένεσθέ μοι μάρτυρες, κἀγώ μάρτυς, λέγει κύριος ὁ θεός, καὶ ὁ παῖς, ὃν ἐξελεξάμην, ἵνα γνῶτε καὶ πιστεύσητε καὶ συνῆτε ὅτι ἐγώ εἰμι ... We may notice how this also includes the theme of joint witness (cf. verses 13–20), and how the context may account for the troublesome τὴν ἀρχήν of verse 25 (cf. Isa. 43: 9, 13). The force of this allusion is to deepen immeasurably the awe-inspiring implications of Jesus' claim to be the Son of Man. It lays stress on his relationship to the God of incomparable majesty, who is to accomplish salvation. This prepares the way for the breath-taking climax of the whole section in 8: 58, where once more the ἐγώ εἰμι is used.

The rest of the chapter is concerned with paternity. It answers the question Who is Jesus' Father? Though it begins with another parable, comparable to 5: 19f., in which a 'son' figures,[27] the sonship titles are not actually employed. That Jesus is the Son is presupposed throughout. The argument is consistent with his claim to be the Son of Man, for it is concerned with his heavenly origins, in this case especially with the aspect of pre-existence. But the special themes associated with the Son of Man – judging, giving life, the passion and exaltation – are not

---

24 See Bultmann's valuable note on 6: 35, and the discussion in Appendix IV of the commentary by R. E. Brown, vol. i, pp. 533–8.

25 ἐγώ εἰμι has occurred previously at 6: 20, 35, 51, but if this chapter is taken to belong to the second edition of John, 8: 12 must be regarded as the first use of the formula. The absolute ἐγώ εἰμι is found eight times in John. 6: 20 comes from John's source (cf. Mark 6: 50), and it is not certain that he intends deeper overtones to be read into it. 8: 24, 28 acquire these overtones from the allusion to Isa. 43: 10. 13: 19 is a cross-reference to 8: 28, and 18: 5, 6, 8, by the unnecessary reference to Judas in 5b, probably intends an allusion to 13: 19 to explain the awe-inspiring effect of the phrase on those who have come to arrest Jesus. 8: 58 cannot be regarded as a title, because it requires the meaning 'I am in existence'. Again, although the nuance is different, the awesome effect of the words has been prepared for by the allusion to Isa. 43: 10 in 8: 28.

26 Cf. Matt. 5: 14. It is not to be supposed that John has created the saying on the basis of this or a similar logion without taking into account the vast ramifications of the theme of light in late Judaism and the ancient world.

27 Cf. C. H. Dodd, *Historical Tradition in the Fourth Gospel* (Cambridge, 1963), pp. 379–82.

under consideration. The theme of life, or rather of escaping death, appears, it is true, in verse 51f.,[28] but only as a lead-in to the climax in verse 58. It is thus not surprising that the Son-of-Man title does not occur in this discourse. John only uses it when the special themes are present. True to his aim, he pursues the grand unfolding of the relation of Jesus to God, for which he has indeed employed the Son-of-Man title at crucial points, but for which he is never dominated by the various titles at his disposal.

The christological argument reaches its conclusion in the discourse of 10: 22–39. In order to pave the way for his final statement, John uses two originally independent sequences, the Man Born Blind in chapter 9 and the Allegory of the Shepherd in 10: 1–18. The first of these reverts once more to the theme of judgment. The blind man, illuminated by the creative hand of Jesus, is capable of recognising him as the one who is to perform the eschatological judgment. The Pharisees, on the other hand, are self-condemned by their unbelief. It is thus no accident that 'the Son of man' is used in 9: 35.[29] The man now has the evidence that Jesus is the Son of Man, and only needs to make his act of allegiance. His illumination has prefigured the devastating clarity of the day of judgment, and has been done with that precise intention. Hence the assertion that his blindness from birth was ἵνα φανερωθῇ τὰ ἔργα τοῦ θεοῦ ἐν αὐτῷ (verse 3). It is no accident that there is a cross-reference to 8: 12 in verse 5: ὅταν ἐν τῷ κόσμῳ ὦ, φῶς εἰμι τοῦ κόσμου (note the avoidance of ἐγώ εἰμι here). The man's profession of faith is not just the reaction to a miracle-worker, but the acknowledgment of the true meaning of what has been done.

The Allegory of the Shepherd has a passing allusion to the judgment theme in the figure of the thief, but all the emphasis goes on to the other main function of the Son of Man, that of giving life. The title itself is not used. When Jesus abandons the allegory, he uses the first person. John is leading up to the climax that Jesus is the Son of God (10: 36). The allegory brings to expression what is to John the essential point of his christology, i.e. the perfect unity of will between Jesus and the Father, which justifies the use of the various titles. So, when the question of Jesus' identity is raised (verse 24), the allegory is resumed

[28] An Amen saying, which may well be a variant tradition of Mark 9: 1.
[29] The reading of the best manuscripts. The majority reading 'the Son of God' is probably due to the influence of the baptismal confession of faith.

so as to prepare the way for the most concise expression of exactly this point: 'I and the Father are one' (verse 30).[30]

In what follows, John uses once more the feature which has been observed at 5: 27 and 8: 28. A biblical quotation provides explication and confirmation of what has been argued. Jesus 'makes himself God' (verse 33) in the sense that, as the one 'whom the Father consecrated and sent into the world', he is 'the Son of God' (verse 36). This accords with scripture (Ps. 82: 6, quoted in verse 34). But even this title is not to be taken as exhausting the meaning of his relationship to the Father. No title by itself is sufficient to express this. But the point is that this and all the other titles contribute to the full understanding of the grand affirmation to which the whole work of Jesus has been directed, 'that you may come to know and continue to know that the Father is in me and I am in the Father' (verse 38).[31]

The main argument is now finished. But it remains to describe the final act whereby the work of Jesus in obedience to the Father is accomplished. This is the Passion, as we know already from 3: 14 and 8: 28. So, in preparation for the Passion narrative, to ensure that it is understood correctly, John is at pains to show that it is the moment, the hour, when the Son of Man is glorified (12: 20–36). All the Son-of-Man themes are now drawn together. The glorification takes the form of a death which is fruitful for eternal life, and so fulfils the Son of Man's function of giving life (verses 24–6, based on traditional sayings). The cross is inevitable, and indeed is the Father's will. It is the decisive act, whereby 'the ruler of this world' is judged, but 'all men' are attracted. It can only be understood when it is recognised that Jesus is the Son of Man. To the people's puzzled question on this point, Jesus replies with a challenge to walk in the light while it is still with them (verse 35f.). The allusion to 8: 12 is obvious, and so warns the reader to ensure that he has grasped the argument which followed from it. If he will only accept now, while he has the light, that Jesus is the Son of Man, who is destined to be glorified, but must first be lifted up, who is the giver of life and the judge of the world, then he will have the faith which will

---

30 Verses 27–9 certainly belong to the allegory in its original form as an independent homily, but John has reserved them deliberately for their present position in writing the gospel. Transposition theories miss the point. See my commentary *ad loc.*

31 Reading γνῶτε καὶ γινώσκητε. The repetition of the same verb adds a note of urgent appeal to the reader to accept this crucial statement.

make him one of the sons of light, those who escape the judgment of the world.

It is only after this full explanation of his meaning that John can speak of Jesus' death as his glorification, without further discussion, in the setting of the Last Supper at 13: 31f. But the idea is now laden with the whole range of the Son-of-Man christology, which has been unfolded since the first mention of this theme in 1: 51. And it is not without significance that, in this last mention of the Son of Man, Jesus speaks of the reciprocal glorifying of the Son of Man and God. For the Son-of-Man christology has always been at the service of John's most treasured idea of the unity that subsists between the Father and the Son.

It is not the object of this paper to discuss in detail the origin of John's thought about the Son of Man. He takes over the title from the sayings of Jesus. But the picture which immediately springs to his mind when he uses it is the glorification of the Son of Man in Dan. 7 (cf. the allusion in 5: 27). This is a vision in which the Son of Man is given royal power and honour. John accordingly regards the exalted Jesus as worthy of such honour, indeed of equal honour with the Father. John also holds that the exaltation of Jesus as the Son of Man follows his passion. This idea has its precedent in the Synoptic passion predictions. John does not give evidence for solving the problem of the origin of this idea, though it remains possible that it was deduced in the first place from the explanation of the vision in Dan. 7: 15–27.[32] But it is clear that he is indebted to the scriptural exegesis of the early church, in which the necessity of the Passion was worked out. In this connection it is possible that his use of ὑψοῦν in 3: 14; 8: 28; 12: 32, 34 depends on the employment of Isa. 52: 13 in the course of this work.

It is more difficult to see how John arrived at the idea that the Son of Man has the delegated functions of God's prerogatives of giving life and performing the eschatological judgment. But for the latter at least he had precedents in the Synoptic tradition,[33] and redaction criticism

[32] This is not to deny the correctness of H. H. Rowley's observation that only the people suffer, and the Son-of-Man figure is exclusively concerned with the subsequent stage of glory (*The Servant of the Lord*, Oxford, ²1965, p. 64 n. 3). But the equation Son of Man = Saints of the Most High could lead to this interpretation. See A. J. B. Higgins, 'Son of Man-*Forschung* since "The Teaching of Jesus"', *New Testament Essays*, edited by A. J. B. Higgins (Manchester, 1959), pp. 119–35.

[33] In Mark only at 8: 38. But the Q variant (Matt. 10: 32f. = Luke 12: 8f.) shows the wide diffusion of sayings of this type.

points to the conclusion that the idea became increasingly important in at any rate some circles of early Christianity.[34] And once the notion of the Son of Man's activity in performing the judgment has been reached, it is only a short step to the idea that he is actively concerned in the general resurrection that precedes it. That this is how some thought about the Son of Man is indicated by the Similitudes of Enoch, which is probably neither a direct influence on the New Testament nor on the other hand directly dependent on the New Testament, but an independent example of the development of Son-of-Man mythology.[35] It has to be remembered that the Son of Man was not primarily thought to be a man in the strict, earthly sense. He was 'one like a son of man', a heavenly being. As he was superior to the angels, it was inevitable that the description of his glory and his activity should be borrowed from those of God himself. The real difficulty is, then, not to see how the Son of Man should do these acts at the End of the Age, but how he can be a man on earth, whose acts already anticipate them. But here again there are precedents for John's ideas in the Synoptic Gospels (Mark 2: 10, 28, etc.). However we explain these sayings, John did not doubt either their authenticity or their truth. What he did was to take the idea that Jesus' miracles are works of the Son of Man and transform it into a systematic doctrine. The earthly ministry of Jesus declares in advance, to those who have eyes to see it, what is to be at the End of the Age, and so provides the means whereby men may already pass from death to life through faith.

It is against this full background of John's thought that we must consider the discourse on the Bread of Life in chapter 6, the only place where he uses the Son-of-Man figure in the additions for the second edition of his work. It is well known that the idea of the renewal of the manna miracle was current in Jewish eschatological thought, but that there is no precedent for the idea that the Son of Man will actually perform it. In fact this is only stated in verse 27. In the rest of the discourse Jesus is the bread himself, and the giver of it is God to begin with (verse 32f.). When the Son of Man is mentioned again (verses 40 –

---

34 Strenuously denied by Borsch, who regards Matthew as preserving the more primitive form of the relevant logia. But Borsch's thesis, that the Son of Man is original in the Jesus-tradition and progressively disappears from it, is not spoilt by the possibility that there was some development of the Son-of-Man christology for a while in the Matthaean circle, just as in the case of John.

35 This is the thesis of Morna D. Hooker, *The Son of Man in Mark* (London, 1967).

on which see below – and 53), the idea of the eschatological renewal of the manna is not the point at issue. It is probable that the original form of the discourse, before John reworked it for inclusion in the gospel, began with the people's question in verse 28, as they are not aware that Jesus has already given a sign (verse 30). Verse 27, then, belongs to an artificial dialogue, contrived to link the opening narrative with the ensuing discourse. The purpose of mentioning the Son of Man in this verse is to set the eschatological perspective for it (hence Jesus adds τοῦτον γὰρ ὁ πατὴρ ἐσφράγισεν ὁ θεός).

The other references to the Son of Man are completely consistent with John's use of the idea elsewhere. The discourse is really an exposition of the manna text in verse 31. The purpose of the eschatological bread is to 'give life to the world' (verse 33). This is expressed in terms of the consistent eschatology of resurrection on the last day. And those who recognise the Son now, and believe in him, already have eternal life, which anticipates this future resurrection (verse 40). The idea is quite similar to 5 : 24, where the present activity of Jesus as 'the Son' anticipates the final work of the Son of Man. But John will not allow that this is possible without acceptance of the necessity of the passion. It is for this reason that he adds verses 51b–58, which should not be deleted as an interpolation. The Son of Man must suffer before he is glorified, and so also the believers must receive his flesh and blood before they can participate in the life he gives (verse 53). This is the scandal of the cross (61b), which is only resolved when men see the Son of Man rise to glory (62).[36]

The central aim of the Johannine christology is to expound the intimate relationship of Jesus and God. For this purpose John takes over the idea of the Son of Man, already current in the gospel tradition. He works creatively on this basis, in full view of the primary text in Dan. 7, and in the light of developments from it in Jewish apocalyptic. His use of the term keeps strictly within the categories of Jewish apocalyptic, and does not show any influence of the syncretistic mythology of the Primal Man. John has no hint of Paul's Adam christology. When forced to expound his cosmology, he drops the theme of the Son of Man in favour of a Wisdom christology, which appears as the Logos in the Prologue.

John's constructive use of the Son-of-Man figure is unique in early

---

[36] Following the interpretation of Bauer and Odeberg, against Bultmann.

Christian literature.[37] Elsewhere, with the possible exception of Matthew, there is a tendency to drop the title, even where the concepts associated with the Son of Man are used and developed. Thus Paul never uses the title, nor does it appear as a title in the Book of Revelation, in spite of its large debt to Daniel and Jewish apocalyptic and actual allusions to Dan. 7: 13 in 1: 13; 14: 14. Justin uses it, but only to prove that Jesus fulfils the vision of Dan. 7, just as he fulfils all the other Old Testament types. Other writers use the phrase sparingly, but their purpose is to express the humanity of Jesus, following a Jewish usage derived from the Psalms. The Son of Man appears much more frequently in the Gnostic literature, sometimes in dependence on John. But here there is no interest in apocalyptic, and the thought is wholly dominated by cosmological speculations. As so often in Gnostic writings, we are faced here with a complex amalgam of ideas and literary influences, including Jewish cosmological speculations and apocalyptic ideas, compounded with reminiscences of Synoptic and Johannine sayings in which the Son of Man figures. These works scarcely provide evidence for a constructive Son-of-Man christology within more orthodox Christian circles, to which the writers might have been indebted. John's work remains without parallel.

The Son of Man is not a title in the true sense, like the Messiah or the High Priest. In so far as it is to be distinguished from the Aramaic בר אנשא, it is the designation of a particular figure, first described in Dan. 7. He is a mythological figure, capable of expansion and contraction in the hands of different practitioners. This myth may have been a fundamental influence on Jesus himself, inspiring him with his sense of mission and destiny.[38] Consequently Son-of-Man sayings have been preserved in the most primitive gospel strands. John, with his unerring capacity to pierce through to the inner meaning of the primitive logia, has the unique distinction of bringing to expression on the basis of them the deepest and most compelling interpretation of Jesus' self-understanding before God.

In conclusion, it is a pleasure to record how much this essay owes to discussion of the tantalising problems of the Son of Man with Professor C. F. D. Moule, to whom it is dedicated with admiration and affection.

---

37 For what follows in this paragraph, see the full discussion in F. H. Borsch, *The Christian and Gnostic Son of Man* (*Studies in Biblical Theology*, second series xiv, London, 1970).

38 Cf. Borsch, *The Son of Man in Myth and History*, pp. 402ff.

5

The use of the
Fourth Gospel for christology today[1]

JOHN A. T. ROBINSON

Nothing colours the presuppositions lying behind the christology of an age or an author more than the position given to the evidence of the Fourth Gospel. In the patristic age it was taken for granted that texts from this Gospel were to be regarded as primary data of the problem which had to be solved.[2] No christology which did not do justice, for instance, to both the sayings 'I and the Father are one' and 'my Father is greater than I' or which failed to posit in Jesus both genuine human limitations and a consciousness of pre-existent glory could satisfy the 'facts'. It was material from St John which more than any other compelled, and tested, the doctrine of the Two Natures in its various forms. (Most of the illustrations, for instance, in the *Tome* of Leo of what it meant for Jesus to do some things as God and some things as man are drawn from this Gospel.) Still a century ago so liberal a theologian as Schleiermacher regarded the Fourth Gospel as having priority in date and authority,[3] and his picture of the absolute, changeless, sinless perfection of One who did not have his origin in this world clearly reflects this – though ironically the Fourth Gospel really gives remarkably little basis for the sinlessness of Christ.[4] Even up to the First

---

[1] As the title implies, this question raised itself for me in the course of preparing my Hulsean Lectures on a Christology for today. I have therefore myself 'used' certain sections of it, with permission, in the published version of these lectures, *The Human Face of God* (London, 1973).

[2] Cf. M. F. Wiles, *The Spiritual Gospel* (Cambridge, 1960); T. E. Pollard, *Johannine Christology and the Early Church* (Cambridge, 1970).

[3] Cf. A. Schweitzer, *The Quest of the Historical Jesus* (E.T., 3rd ed. London, 1954), pp. 66–7: 'It is, according to him, only in this Gospel that the consciousness of Jesus is truly reflected', since it alone has behind it the authority of an eye-witness. 'The contradictions could not be explained if all our Gospels stood equally close to Jesus. But if John stands closer than the others....'.

[4] The key text, John 8: 46, classically translated 'Which of you convicteth me of sin?', is much more likely in the context to have the limited reference given it in the New English Bible: 'Which of you can prove me in the wrong?' In fact, nowhere more than in this Gospel is the opinion canvassed that Jesus is bad (7: 12; 9: 16, 24; 10: 21, 33) quite apart from the more frequent suggestions that he is mad or unbalanced (2: 17; 6: 42; 7: 20; 8: 48, 52; 10: 20).

World War it was possible for a person like Bishop Frank Weston to write his great book *The One Christ* as though the data for the problem of the self-consciousness of Christ were still basically set, largely by the Fourth Gospel, in the way that they had been for Cyril of Alexandria. What Weston claimed, with some success, was to produce a more adequate hypothesis to account for the same evidence: he did not question, let alone set aside, the evidence of John. 'The most important evidence', he wrote, 'to the divine nature of the Christ is that which is based upon the revelation of His self-consciousness, His knowledge of His pre-existence, and His memory of the state of eternal glory.'[5]

The swing away from this position, which of course had set in in liberal circles long before Weston,[6] has been almost total. It hardly needs illustration to show that the prevailing assumption in recent christological writing is that the only secure foundation (if indeed there is *any* secure foundation) for the kind of way Jesus thought, spoke or acted is the Synoptic material. Among dozens of judgements that might be quoted I cite two from theologians who are far from extreme. The first is W. R. Matthews in *The Problem of Christ in the Twentieth Century*:

There are still eminent authorities who hold that the Gospel of John is a primary historical source for the life and words of Jesus. And yet I must express my clear view that they are advocating a lost cause...No: the supreme value of the Fourth Gospel lies elsewhere...It is the primary document for all Christian mysticism and it is the noblest landmark in the course of the development of Christian doctrine.[7]

The second is Hugh Montefiore writing in *Soundings*:

The testimony of Jesus himself is far more important than the interpretation that the early Church put on his person and status, for, if his claims about himself are true, he alone would have been in a position to know his relationship to his Father. Here the challenge of higher criticism must be accepted, and attempt made to distinguish the words of Jesus from the logia of the

---

[5] *Op. cit.* (2nd ed., London, 1914), p. 38.
[6] Cf. P. W. Schmiedel, *The Johannine Writings* (E.T., London, 1908), whose conclusion is that the Gospel 'is dominated by complete indifference as to the faithfulness of a record; that importance is attached only to giving as impressive a representation as possible of certain ideas; and that the whole is sustained by a reverence for Jesus which has lost every standard for measuring what can really happen' (p. 139).
[7] *Op. cit.* (London, 1950), pp. 7–8.

Gospels; and, although the case cannot be argued in this essay, the synoptic gospels must be set apart from the Fourth Gospel: only the former may confidently be used for this purpose.[8]

On the Continent the swing away has, of course, been still more pronounced, but even so relatively conservative a scholar as Günter Bornkamm says at the beginning of his *Jesus of Nazareth*:

The gospel according to John has so different a character in comparison with the other three, and is to such a degree the product of a developed theological reflection, that we can only treat it as a secondary source.[9]

And it has so far largely been ignored in the 'new quest' of the historical Jesus.[10]

There is another equally powerful school which would take the line that since *all* the Gospels contain practically no history worth mentioning John and the Synoptists can for doctrinal purposes be used more or less indifferently. Of this Paul Tillich is representative:

It was the desire of the so-called *liberal theology* to go behind the biblical records of Jesus as the Christ. In such an attempt the first three Gospels emerge as by far the most important part of the New Testament, and this is what they became in the estimation of many modern theologians. But the moment when one realises that the Christian faith cannot be built on such a foundation, the Fourth Gospel and the Epistles become equally important with the Synoptics.[11]

As is well known, a considerable critical reaction has more recently set in in New Testament circles against writing off the historical value of the Johannine tradition – a reaction with which I have long been in

---

[8] 'Towards a Christology for Today', *op. cit.* (ed. A. R. Vidler, Cambridge, 1962), pp. 157–8.

[9] *Op. cit.* (E.T., London, 1960), p. 14.

[10] It is characteristic that R. S. Barbour's excellent little survey and critique should be called *Traditio-Historical Criticism of the Gospels* (London, 1972) and then confine itself, without explanation, entirely to the Synoptic Gospels. Of the one book mentioned by Norman Perrin in his *What is Redaction Criticism?* (Philadelphia and London, 1970) as applying this method, so far, to the Gospel of John, J. Louis Martyn's *History and Theology in the Fourth Gospel* (New York, 1968), he writes, almost in commendation (!), that 'both the history and the theology mentioned in the title are those of the evangelist and his church, not of Jesus' (p. 84).

[11] *Systematic Theology* ii (London, 1957), p. 135.

sympathy.[12] It is conveniently summarized in A. M. Hunter's *According to John*[13] and documented in a masterly way in C. H. Dodd's *Historical Tradition in the Fourth Gospel*,[14] which is the more impressive because he came to his conclusions from a very different position. At all sorts of points, from the broadest outline of the ministry to the minutest topographical detail, the Fourth Gospel is coming to be seen as preserving tradition not only in regard to the events of Jesus' life but also in regard to his teaching which has claim to go back at least as far as and sometimes further than anything in the Synoptic Gospels. Nevertheless, when it comes to the central issue of all, the picture which John gives us of Jesus and the use that we can make of it for doctrine, the criteria have not, I think, been adequately reassessed. Clearly the clock cannot be put back to the pre-critical position, but do the recent emphases make no difference? What is the proper, as opposed to the improper, use of the Johannine material today? This seems to me to depend upon clarifying what the author's own concerns really were and what they were not.

We may fairly take as representative his key christological text from the climax of the prologue: 'The word became flesh: he came to dwell among us, and we saw his glory, such glory as befits the Father's only Son, full of grace and truth.'[15] Though it is only in the prologue, which I believe the author to have added later,[16] that the λόγος terminology is used, the theme of the whole Gospel is the interrelation of the two levels of reality—λόγος, spirit, the eternal glory of the divine, on the one hand, and flesh, this world of space and time, on the other. The great affirmation of this writer is that they coincide in Christ: the Word becomes flesh and the glory of the invisible God is seen and heard and handled. Both the spirit and the flesh are of equal importance and must be taken with equal seriousness. Flesh without

---

12 See my lecture 'The New Look on the Fourth Gospel' given to the international conference on 'The Four Gospels' at Oxford in 1957, reprinted in my *Twelve New Testament Studies* (London, 1962), pp. 94–106, and my essay 'The Place of the Fourth Gospel' in *The Roads Converge* (ed. P. Gardner-Smith, London, 1963).

13 London, 1968; cf. A. J. B. Higgins, *The Historicity of the Fourth Gospel* (London, 1960), and R. E. Brown, 'The Problem of Historicity in John', *New Testament Essays* (Milwaukee, 1965), pp. 143–67.

14 Cambridge, 1963.

15 1: 14 (NEB). On the proper translation of this see below.

16 'The Relation of the Prologue to the Gospel of St John', *NTS* ix (1962–3), pp. 120–9.

spirit is of no significance,[17] but the flesh is utterly indispensable as the locus of the revelation. The over-riding purpose of the Gospel is to show these coinciding and coinhering in Jesus as the Christ, the Son of God.[18]

Beside the truth of this nothing else matters. John is content to hold them together, to allow one to shine through the other, to let the flesh be 'diaphanous' of the spirit (to use Teilhard de Chardin's word), so that the glory is visible in and through it. About the verity of this he cares intensely. That in the process verisimilitude suffers he cares little. For flesh that is diaphanous does not look like flesh: the shining through of the divine gives a docetic appearance. Hence the sense that many have felt, like John Knox[19] and still more Ernst Käsemann,[20] that John does not give us a genuinely human Christ at all. And this indeed was clearly the earliest reaction. John was adopted by the Gnostics as 'their' Gospel and the stress in the Johannine Epistles on Jesus come in the flesh[21] must be seen as reaction to the docetic impression his teaching evidently provoked. But the very fact that the reaction was so vehement suggests that this is genuinely a *misinterpretation* of his intention: indeed for him it is very 'antichrist'.[22]

Perhaps the balance can best be held by saying that John is insistent, with equal emphasis, on the Word and the flesh, but is ready by comparison to sit light to the mediating connections involved in the

---

[17] 3: 6; 6: 63.

[18] 20: 31.

[19] *The Humanity and the Divinity of Christ* (Cambridge, 1967), p. 62: 'One may affirm the humanity as a formal fact and then proceed so to define or portray it as to deny its reality in any ordinarily accepted sense.' Cf. E. L. Titus, 'The Fourth Gospel and the Historical Jesus', in *Jesus and the Historian: Written in Honor of Ernest Cadman Colwell* (ed. F. T. Trotter, Philadelphia, 1968), pp. 98–113.

[20] *The Testament of Jesus* (E.T., London, 1968). He sees in this Gospel an unashamedly 'naive docetism' (p. 26), 'the consistent presentation of Jesus as God walking on the face of the earth' (p. 73). 'The Church committed an error when it declared the Gospel to be orthodox' (p. 76): 'neither apostolic authorship nor apostolic content can be affirmed for it' (p. 74). See the reply by G. Bornkamm, 'Zur Interpretation des Johannes-Evangeliums', *Geschichte und Glaube*, erster Teil, *Gesammelte Aufsätze*, Band iii (Munich, 1968), pp. 104–21; cf. S. S. Smalley, 'Diversity and Development in John', *NTS* xvii (1970–1), pp. 278–81.   [21] 1 John 1: 1; 4: 2; 2 John 7.

[22] This reaction in the Johannine Epistles is, as Bornkamm points out, completely ignored by Käsemann, who now, I understand, regards them as composed by a different writer as a corrective. But the Epistles read as a recall to teaching given, not as an attack upon it.

'becoming'. He is prepared to treat freely all the questions of 'how', the processes of coming into being and coming to know, the lines of temporal and psychological development. In this Gospel there is little interest if any in the progression by which men reach the truth about Jesus. He is acknowledged as Christ from the beginning,[23] and is prepared to declare himself such.[24] There is no 'Messianic secret' in the Markan sense. As Jesus says to the High Priest at the end, 'I have spoken openly to all the world . . ., I have said nothing in secret'.[25] The fact nevertheless that the truth about him has been veiled and, in contrast with Mark,[26] must remain so even to the disciples till the Spirit brings to clarity what has hitherto come in riddles,[27] does not mean that all along the light has not been shining in its fulness of grace and truth. Nor is there any sign of growth in Jesus' own awareness. There is no suggestion that he 'learned' from the things he suffered[28] – merely a waiting for his 'hour' to come and his 'time' to ripen.[29] Whereas in Hebrews it is he who is subject to τελείωσις or maturation,[30] there is no hint of this in the τετέλεσται of John:[31] he never develops. All that we moderns are naturally interested in from the scientific and historical point of view, and in particular from the psychological point of view, is fundamentally uninteresting to this evangelist. He is consumed with the one need to present the truth of Jesus as he has come to know it. And this truth Jesus himself cannot help but express in every word he speaks and every deed he does. They are all 'signs', sacramental of the reality which shines through him. By comparison *how* he thought or spoke is entirely subordinate. He speaks 'Johannine' language – in the same way as the Italian painter paints him as an Italian.[32] John is interested in verity not verisimilitude, in the real not the realistic, in history not historicism. And he is not worried by anachronisms. Indeed the whole Gospel is deliberately ana-chronistic: it is an attempt see Jesus *from* the end, from the age of the Spirit who alone clarifies,

[23] John 1: 29, 34, 41, 45, 49. [24] John 4: 25–6; 9: 36–7.

[25] John 18: 20.

[26] Mark 4: 11. I take ἐν παραβολαῖς here to mean originally the same as ἐν παροι-μίαις still means in John 16: 25.

[27] John 16: 12–15, 25–32. [28] Heb. 5: 8.

[29] John 2: 4; 7: 6, 8, 30; 8: 20; 12: 23; 13: 1; 17: 1.

[30] Heb. 2: 10; 5: 9; 7: 28.

[31] John 19: 30.

[32] It is notoriously difficult to know in chapter 3, for instance, where the speech of Jesus ends and the comment of the Evangelist begins. See the footnotes in the RSV at John 3: 15 and 30.

declares and brings to remembrance[33] what was the truth all along. And if it was the truth all along, then that is what it is important to present, even if no one recognized it at the time.

It is no wonder therefore that by all the standards of verisimilitude the Gospel *looks* docetic, static and unhistorical. Indeed, taken literally, as a biography, it *is* docetic, and it is not in the least surprising that this has been the charge it has invited from the beginning. Yet we should do the author the justice of accepting that such a judgement is in his eyes a fearful misunderstanding. For this point of view is not the point of view from which it should be assessed. For that is to judge things 'superficially',[34] 'by worldly standards',[35] rather than with true discernment.

Yet, with all this said, this does not mean that John is unconcerned with historicity. Nor is to 'remember', however creatively, to invent. Rather, it is, in the power and truth and freedom of the Spirit, to take the things of Jesus and hold them up to the light, so that the light can transfigure them and show them in their true glory. It is *not* to make up things about Jesus in order to illustrate timeless truths. For John has a profound reverence for history, for happenedness. As the locus of incarnation it cannot be treated lightly or wantonly: it is holy ground. I am not persuaded that he is simply prepared to play ducks and drakes with the history, as many commentators suppose, in the interests of theology.[36] Indeed, so many of the details, especially of location and topography, which have been verified in enrect study, have apparently no conceivable theological point or motivation. He has occasion to mention them simply because they were 'there'. At points where he differs from the Synoptists (of whom I believe, with an increasing weight of scholarship, his tradition is fundamentally independent) his evidence is to be taken very seriously – e.g. on the early Judaean ministry, the duration of the ministry as a whole, the political significance of the desert feeding, the timing of the cleansing of the temple, the date of the crucifixion, and even, I believe, with Jeremias,[37] the empty tomb tradition. This does not, of course, mean that John is always to be preferred, let alone that every historical statement he makes is correct. But I am convinced he has every claim to be heard as history and not simply as theology.

---

[33] John 14: 25–6; 15: 26; 16: 12–15, 23–30; cf. 2: 22; 20: 9.
[34] John 7: 24.   [35] John 8: 15.
[36] As a test of his method, see my article 'The "Others" of John 4: 38', *Twelve New Testament Studies* (London, 1962), pp. 61–6.
[37] *New Testament Theology* i (E.T., London, 1971), pp. 304–5.

How then does this comport with his admitted disinterest in empirical realism or historical reconstruction? The lines of demarcation may in practice be thin and difficult to draw and the kind of judgement involved is not the sort that makes easily for objective consensus. But what we can say, straight away, is that John is not evidence, and does not set out to be evidence, of how things looked to Jesus or the disciples or for that matter to anyone else before the Resurrection. Nor does John supply material for any kind of reconstruction of Jesus's self-consciousness.[38] The fact that Jesus speaks in this Gospel of his eternal existence or his pre-incarnate glory or of his heavenly origin and destination, and indeed the whole impression he gives of spiritual aloofness and superiority, not to say of arrogance and megalomania – all this is to be judged not as data for psychological analysis but as declaring the truth that, while unquestionably *a man* in the fullest sense of both words (and no other Gospel uses ἄνθρωπος anything like as much of Jesus),[39] he was veridical also of another entire world of being. Like almost every incident and indeed phrase in the Fourth Gospel, Jesus' whole life speaks at two levels of meaning. But the 'how' of the signs and the lines of connection or causation between the flesh and the spirit, the history and the theology, are of utterly subordinate interest. They can therefore be written up (in every sense of the word) freely and are not to be estimated by the canons of historicism. But equally the events described are not just fiction nor is the Fourth Evangelist a novel-writer, even a historical novel-writer.

Where in particular the line is to be drawn is bound, as I said, to differ from one assessment to another. But I am sure there is all the difference between saying that a line *is* there, however difficult to determine, and saying that there is no line at all. And, greatly daring, I should like to try to indicate where I would come down, not on subordinate incidents, but on the total impression given by the Johannine portrait of Jesus.

Reading the Gospel through at a sitting, one is left with the overwhelming impression of a man whose life was lived in *absolutely intimate dependence*[40] (stressing all three words) upon God as his Father. Everything Jesus was and said and did has its source in this

---

[38] Here I would agree with Montefiore's comment quoted above from *Soundings*.

[39] The figures are Matt. 1; Mark 1; Luke 6 (the Matthaean and Markan parallels, plus four times on the lips of Pilate); John 16 (plus ἀνήρ once).

[40] For the stress on the dependence of Christ in this Gospel, cf. J. E. Davey, *The Jesus of St John* (London, 1958).

utter closeness of spiritual relationship which he describes as sonship or 'sent-ness'.[41] Now clearly, as I have said, the *way* this is described is governed not by psychological realism but by theological reality – though this is *not* the same as saying that it is to be interpreted (as we tend instinctively to do with this vocabulary of 'the Father' and 'the Son') in terms of Nicene ontology. Indeed, even in regard to language we are coming to recognize that John is nearer to source than we should recently have dared to think, and that he is drawing out the remembered tradition rather than simply imposing upon Jesus categories of his own. Particularly is this proving to be so where the vocabulary is most theological, and on the face of it most 'Johannine'.

Nothing is more characteristic of John's style than such sayings as:

The Father loves the Son and has entrusted him with all authority;

I know him because I come from him and he it is who sent me;

The Father knows me and I know the Father;

Jesus, well aware that the Father had entrusted everything to him;

O righteous Father, although the world does not know thee, I know thee, and these men know that thou didst send me.[42]

Yet these are all variations and meditations upon the theme represented in the Q saying of Matt. 11: 27 (= Luke 10: 22):

Everything is entrusted to me by my Father;
and no one knows the Son but the Father,
and no one knows the Father but the Son
and those to whom the Son may choose to reveal him.

Now Jeremias has convincingly shown[43] that, so far from this being a metaphysical 'bolt from the Johannine sky',[44] that has dropped unaccountably into the Synoptic tradition, it is in origin parabolic language, the 'the' before father and son being not ontological but generic – as in 'the sower went forth to sow'[45] or (in John) 'the grain of wheat remains solitary',[46] where English idiom requires an 'a'. The

---

[41] John 3: 17, 34; 4: 34; 5: 23–4, 30, 36–8; 6: 29, 38, 44, 57; 7: 16, 18, 28–9, 33; 8: 16, 18, 26, 29, 42; 9: 4; 10: 36; 11: 42; 12: 44–5, 49; 13: 20; 14: 24; 15: 21; 16: 5; 17: 3, 8, 18, 21, 23, 25; 20: 21.

[42] John 3: 35; 7: 29; 10: 15; 13: 3; 17: 25.

[43] *The Central Message of the New Testament* (E.T., London, 1965), pp. 23–6.

[44] K. von Hase, *Die Geschichte Jesu* (2nd ed., Leipzig, 1876), p. 422.

[45] Mark 4: 3.   [46] John 12: 24.

Q saying is a parable of the intimate knowledge that only a father and a son have of each other (this was before the generation gap!), which Jesus is using to describe the *abba*-relationship to God that he is claiming for himself, and ideally for every child of man. Of course this parabolic language is interpreted or allegorized – and correctly so – by the Evangelists to designate Jesus in his unique relationship to God – just as, in the parable of the Wicked Husbandmen,[47] the son who is heir to the estate in contrast with the servants clearly stands for Jesus. Indeed, I believe it is inconceivable that Jesus did not intend it to be taken thus – the story having no point unless in some sense it is a picture of God's dealings with Israel through the prophets and now through himself.[48] 'The Father' and 'the Son' thus come to stand in Mark[49] and Q[50] as in John simply as proper names for God and Christ. But it is in John that the original parabolic foundation of this language is still most clearly visible beneath the theological surface.

In fact where he first introduces it, at the climax of the prologue, it is specifically in the form of a simile from human relationships: 'glory *as* of a father's only son' (δόξαν ὡς μονογενοῦς παρὰ πατρός).[51] There are no articles in the Greek, and yet they are constantly supplied by translators and interpreters (Moffatt's 'glory such as an only son enjoys from his father' being a rare exception). The simile was already a familiar one in describing Israel in relation to God: 'Thy chastisement is upon us as upon a first-born, only son.'[52] I have not been able yet to find a precise parallel for an only son being called his father's glory.[53]

---

[47] Mark 12: 1–9.
[48] Cf. Dodd, *The Parables of the Kingdom* (London, 1935), pp. 124–32. This is not, of course, to say that there is not pointing up and elaboration in the transmission. Indeed, Dodd's reconstruction of the original form of the story as telling of two servants followed by a son (Mark 12: 5 being later expansion to fit the history of Israel) has been strikingly vindicated by the version in the *Gospel of Thomas* 66.
[49] Mark 13: 42.
[50] Matt. 11: 27 = Luke 10: 22.
[51] John 1: 14; cf. the ὡς υἱός of Heb. 3: 6.
[52] Ps. Sol. 18: 4; cf. 13: 8. For the metaphor applied to Israel, cf. 2 Esdras 6: 58, 'We thy people whom thou hast called thy first-born, thy only-begotten, thy beloved', and, earlier, Exod. 4: 22; Ps. 89: 27; Jer. 31: 9.
[53] Prov. 17: 6 has 'the glory of sons is their father', but here 'glory' means 'pride', as in Sir Walter Scott's 'his mother's pride, his father's glory'. The nearest parallel I know to what I believe to be the *sense* is Ecclus. 30: 4, where it is said of a son, 'When the father dies it is as if he were still alive, for he has left a copy of himself (ὅμοιον γὰρ αὐτῷ) behind him'.

But δόξα and εἰκών were used as equivalents in late Judaism to mean 'reflection',[54] as in 1 Cor. 11: 7: 'Man is the image and glory of God; but the woman is the glory of man.'[55] The idea behind John 1:14 is therefore almost certainly that the incarnate Christ is the exact counterpart or reflection of God, his spit and image, as we should say, like an only son of his father. Indeed, words used by Montefiore in exegesis of Heb. 1: 3[56] get precisely what I believe John is here saying: 'As a son may be said to reflect his father's character, so the Son is the refulgence of his Father's glory, and so the exact representation of God's being.' But what is introduced as a simile in verse 14 is already fully allegorized by verse 18, especially if the astonishing μονογενὴς θεός, 'the only one who is himself God', is indeed the right reading.

At other points too in the Gospel the parabolic basis of this father–son language still shows through. Dodd has argued this of John 5: 19–20,[57] where, again transposing from the definite to the English indefinite article, we have what he calls the parable of the Apprentice:

A son can do nothing on his own;
he does only what he sees his father doing:
what father does, son does;
For a father loves his son and shows him all his trade.[58]

---

[54] See J. Jervell, *Imago Dei* (Göttingen, 1960), especially pp. 174–5, 180, 299–300, 325–6. He takes this to be the meaning in John 1: 14, but does not notice it as a simile from human relationships. I am grateful to Professor Moule for putting me on to this reference, and indeed for supplying, and gently correcting, so much else. See also L. H. Brockington, 'The Septuagintal Background to the New Testament Use of δόξα', *Studies in the Gospels: Essays in Memory of R. H. Lightfoot* (ed. D. E. Nineham, Oxford, 1955), pp. 7–8, and the extensive literature cited by R. P. Martin, *Carmen Christi: Philippians 2: 5–11 in Recent Interpretation and in the Setting of Early Christian Worship* (Cambridge, 1967), pp. 102–19.

[55] Cf. 2 Cor. 3: 18, 'We all reflect as in a mirror the glory of the Lord; thus we are transfigured into his image, from glory to glory', and 8: 23 (as rendered in NEB margin), 'They are delegates of our congregations: they reflect Christ (δόξα Χριστοῦ)'. For the association of εἰκών and δόξα: Rom. 1: 23; 1 Cor. 11: 7; 15: 43, 49; 2 Cor. 3: 18; 4: 4; of εἰκών and πρωτότοκος: Col. 1: 15; of δόξα and υἱός: John 14: 13; 17: 1; Rom. 8: 14–23; 9: 4; Eph. 1: 5–6; Heb. 2: 10; and of all four words: Rom. 8: 29–30 and Heb. 1: 2–6 (where χαρακτήρ replaces εἰκών).

[56] *The Epistle to the Hebrews* (Black's New Testament Commentaries, London, 1964), *ad loc.*

[57] 'Une parabole cachée dans le quatrième Évangile', *RHPR*, 1962, nos. 2–3, pp. 107–15; *Historical Tradition in the Fourth Gospel*, p. 386.

[58] Cf. Phil. 2: 22, 'He has been at my side...like a son working under his father'.

There is also what must be recognized[59] as the parable of the Servant and the Son in 8: 35:

> A servant has no permanent standing in the household,[60]
> but a son belongs to it always.[61]

Moreover, nowhere in the New Testament are we closer than in the Fourth Gospel to the fundamental Hebraic use of sonship to designate not an absolute status or title but a functional relationship marked by character. This comes out very plainly in the dialogue that follows in 8: 37–47. To be a son is to show the character, to reproduce the thought and action, of another, whether it be Abraham, or the Devil, or God. To claim therefore to be a son of God is not blasphemy, as the Jews suppose. Their Bible should have taught them better. This is made explicit in Jesus's reply in 10: 34–8:

Is it not written in your Law, 'I said: You are gods'? Those are called gods to whom the word of God was delivered – and Scripture cannot be set aside.[62] Then why do you charge me with blasphemy because I, conse-crated and sent into the world by the Father, said 'I am a son of God'?[63]

[59] Dodd, *Historical Tradition in the Fourth Gospel*, pp. 380–2.

[60] Cf. 15: 15, 'A servant does not know what his master is about', which is clearly parabolic.

[61] The same contrasts occur in the Synoptic parables of the Prodigal Son (Luke 15: 19, 'I am no longer fit to be called your son; treat me as one of your paid servants'; 15: 31, 'My boy, you are always with me, and everything I have is yours') and the Wicked Husbandmen (Mark 12: 1–9, where the son is the heir while the servants are thrown out). The Johannine point of the freedom enjoyed by the son of the house (8: 36) is reflected in the parable of Jesus's other great figure for God, the king, in Matt. 17: 25–6: '"What do you think, Simon? From whom do kings of the earth take toll or tribute? From their sons or from others?" And when he said, "From others", Jesus said to him: "Then the sons are free".'

[62] This is not such an artificial argument as it sounds to us. Those who are called 'gods' in Ps. 82: 6, which Jesus quotes, are judges. (The interpretation of them as angels by J. A. Emerton, *JTS*, n.s. xi (1960), pp. 329–32, and xvii (1966), pp. 399–401, even if made in late Judaism, fits the context neither of the Psalm (cf. vv. 2–4) nor of John (cf. 10: 33, 'a mere man').) And the judges are called 'God' (cf. Exod. 21: 6; 22: 8–9, 28) because they 'represent' him, just as Jesus is claiming to do. Indeed H. Odeberg, *The Fourth Gospel* (Chicago, 1928; Uppsala, 1929), p. 292, argues that in using the phrase 'your law' (10: 34; cf. 8: 17; 15: 25) Jesus is not saying something un-Jewish (as is often supposed) but is claiming to stand in the same relation to the *Torah* as his Father (cf. 7: 16–22). While the Jews say 'our law' (7: 51; cf. 18: 31; 19: 7), God says 'my law' or 'your law'.

[63] Again no articles, except in MS readings that are evidently secondary. Their absence would not in itself be decisive for the sense, for 'definite predicate

If I am not acting as my Father would, do not believe me. But if I am, accept the evidence of my deeds, even if you do not believe me, so that you may recognize and know that the Father is in me, and I in the Father.

This argument which places Jesus on exactly the same metaphysical level as every other son of God yet attests him functionally unique, because he alone 'always does what is acceptable to him',[64] could not have been invented later,[65] nor even, I believe, in a Greek-thinking milieu.[66] It carries us back as near to source as we are likely to get – to very early Jewish-Christian controversy in Palestine, if not to Jesus himself. Historically we cannot say more, nor, I think, less.[67]

nouns which precede the verb usually lack the article' (C. F. D. Moule, *An Idiom Book of New Testament Greek* (Cambridge, 1953), p. 115, citing E. C. Colwell's rule). But the logic of the passage would be destroyed if Jesus were here claiming to be *the* son of God in a sense that could not be true of the men of the Old Testament.

[64] John 8: 29.

[65] So too Hunter, *op. cit.* p. 94.

[66] Cf. J. H. Bernard, *St John (ICC,* Edinburgh, 1928), *ad loc*: 'The argument is one which would never have occurred to a Greek Christian, and its presence here reveals behind the narrative a genuine reminiscence of one who remembered how Jesus argued with the Rabbis on their own principles.'

[67] Cf. Dodd on the relation between John 10: 15, 'The Father knows me and I know the Father', and Matt. 11: 27 = Luke 10: 22: 'The saying we are now considering belongs to the earliest strain of tradition to which we can hope to penetrate, since it can be traced to the period before the formation of the common source (whether oral or written) of Matthew and Luke (Q), and the evidence suggests that before any written record of it appeared it had developed variant forms, three of which appear independently in Matthew, Luke and John, while others appear in ancient versions and patristic citations', *Historical Tradition in the Fourth Gospel,* p. 361. It would be tempting to pursue the implications of this for the origins of the Johannine linguistic tradition. Jeremias makes the comment: 'Matt. 11: 27 is not a Johannine verse amidst the synoptic material, but rather one of those sayings from which Johannine theology developed. Without such points of departure within the synoptic tradition it would be an eternal puzzle how Johannine theology could have originated at all' (*The Central Message of the New Testament,* p. 25). But if this is so, what comes through John's style cannot merely reflect the coloration of his glass: there must have been something of it in the light itself. The Johannine sayings with close verbal parallels in the other traditions, analysed by Dodd (*op. cit.* pp. 335–65) as going back at least as far as their Synoptic counterparts, raise the question whether their 'Johannine' tinting is any further from the original style of Jesus than, say, the increasingly apocalyptic tone given to it, as I believe, by Mark and Matthew (cf. my *Jesus and His Coming* (London, 1957), pp. 94–102). I discussed this, all too briefly, in my essay, 'The Place of the Fourth Gospel', *op. cit.* pp. 63–7. To the evidence I assembled there I would add the question raised by W. H. Brownlee, 'Jesus and Qumran', in *Jesus and the Historian* (ed. F. T. Trotter), p. 76: 'The really serious question posed by the

This does not mean, of course, that in theological reflection John does not see Christ as *also* being metaphysically unique – a distinction he recognizes by reserving the word 'son' for Jesus and 'children of God' for Christians.[68] But, unlike later dogmaticians, he shows no awareness of a contradiction or even of a tension at this point. Indeed it is of the essence of his insight into the incarnation that moral affinity and metaphysical union should not be seen as the alternatives they so disastrously were in the subsequent disputes between Antioch and Alexandria. Jesus can say in the same discourse that 'the Father is in me, and I in the Father'[69] and 'my Father and I are one'[70] *because* he is acting as his Father would[71] and his deeds are done in his name.[72] Again he says in a later discourse,[73] 'Anyone who has seen me has seen the Father' because 'I am *not* myself the source of the words I speak to you: it is the Father who dwells in me doing his own work'. He is 'God's only son', the very 'exegesis' of the Father,[74] indeed himself θεός, 'what God is',[75] because as a mere man[76] he is utterly transparent to *another*, who is greater than himself[77] and indeed than all.[78] The paradox is staggering, and it is no wonder that this christology later fell apart at the seams. But for John there is no antithesis, any more than there is for the author to the Hebrews, between the humanity and the divinity, the historical and the theological.

Scrolls is whether the two types of vocabulary belonged authentically to Jesus, with a polarization of the two elements taking place in different Gospel traditions: the Synoptics preserving and emphasizing Jesus' ethical teaching in an apocalyptic context and the Fourth Gospel preserving and elaborating his mystical teaching in a dualistic context. Palestinian Judaism contained both elements, not simply in different communities but also in the same community. More than this, apocalypticism and light–darkness dualism were blended together in the same passages.' *Of course*, in John we are still not reading the *ipsissima verba*, but may we not, in Jeremias' useful distinction, be hearing the *ipsissima vox*? At the end of his discussion of this distinction in his *New Testament Theology* (i, p. 37) he formulates the following 'principle of method': 'In the synoptic tradition it is the inauthenticity and not the authenticity of the sayings of Jesus that must be demonstrated.' With every proper regard for the differences of aim I mentioned before, I would ask why this methodological principle needs to be prefaced with the words 'in the synoptic tradition'. *As authenticity is understood in John* (which is certainly not literalistically), I believe it may be just as applicable to his material.

68 John 1: 12; 11: 52; 1 John 3: 1–2, 8–10; 5: 2.

69 John 10: 38.	70 John 10: 30.
71 John 10: 37.	72 John 10: 25.
73 John 14: 9–10.	74 John 1: 18.
75 John 1: 1.	76 John 10: 33.
77 John 14: 28.	78 John 10: 29.

Yet the question remains, Is this impression which John leaves us of Jesus fundamentally one that is invented or one that is 'remembered' in the pregnant sense in which the Evangelist uses that word, of *history really entered into*? I suggest that there is every reason to believe, from his whole theology of history, that the latter is what he intended, and that we should take his intention seriously. In other words, he is elucidating ('What first were guessed as points, I now knew stars')[79] the inexpungeable impression of a man whose entire life was lived 'from God',[80] and whose words and actions bespoke a relationship in which he was in the deepest sense 'at home' and where as a truly normal (and *for that reason* unique) human being he 'belonged'.

It is this sense of belonging elsewhere, this sense that the source and ground of his being and acting and speaking is not 'of himself',[81] nor 'of this world',[82] but 'from above',[83] that the Evangelist seeks to express, spatially and temporally, in the late-Jewish, Hellenistic myth of pre-existence. His being is 'with God'[84] 'in the bosom of the Father';[85] his home is 'in heaven',[86] from which he 'comes down'[87] and to which he will return in ascent.[88] Equally his ἀρχή or origin is not just the moment of his historical birth, but is before Abraham,[89] before the world,[90] and indeed at the beginning of all things.[91]

Take this language literally, whether as history or psychology, let alone the consciousness of it, and you have shattered the conditions of genuine humanity. As John A. Baker has said,[92]

It is simply not possible at one and the same time to share the common lot of humanity, and to be aware of oneself as one who has existed from

---

[79] R. Browning, 'A Death in the Desert', which from his early essay in *Foundations* (ed. B. H. Streeter, London, 1913), p. 216, to his *Readings in St John's Gospel* (London, 1939), p. xvii, William Temple called 'the most penetrating interpretation of St John that exists in the English language'.

[80] παρὰ τοῦ θεοῦ: John 6: 46; 7: 29; 8: 26, 40; 9: 33; 10: 18; 15: 15, 26; 16: 27; 17: 7–8; ἐκ τοῦ θεοῦ: 8: 42, 47; 10: 32; 16: 28; ἀπὸ τοῦ θεοῦ: 3: 2; 13: 3; 16: 30.

[81] John 5: 19, 30; 7: 16–18, 28; 12: 49.

[82] John 8: 23; 17: 14, 16; 18: 36. [83] John 3: 31; 8: 23.

[84] John 1: 1. [85] John 1: 18.

[86] John 3: 13. But the words ὁ ὢν ἐν τῷ οὐρανῷ, which might be taken to imply that the Son of Man is (really) still in heaven even during the Incarnation, are almost certainly not part of the original text (despite the NEB – against the RSV). [87] John 3: 13, 31; 6: 33–58.

[88] John 3: 13; 6: 62; 13: 1, 3; 20: 17. [89] John 8: 58.

[90] John 17: 5, 24. [91] John 1: 1–2.

[92] *The Foolishness of God* (London, 1970), p. 144.

everlasting with God and will continue to do so. . . You cannot have both the Jesus of John 8: 58 as a piece of accurate reporting and the doctrine of the Incarnation.

But the crux of the matter is what is meant by 'accurate reporting'. If this refers to the language of 'the flesh', to psychological description, to what can be seen and judged as the eyes see, then of course the conclusion follows. But it is precisely not accuracy of this kind, I submit, that the Evangelist is seeking to report. ἀκρίβεια (and its cognates) is characteristically the virtue extolled by Luke–Acts:[93] John's consuming interest is rather in ἀλήθεια and its cognates.[94] Yet as testimony to the impact Jesus made at the deepest spiritual level his report may be properly and profoundly accurate. In this sense we could concur with his own claim that 'his witness is true'.[95] But, as the context of this claim makes clear, truth at this level is not independent of history nor indifferent to it: for the claim proceeds from the statement, 'This is vouched for by an eye-witness'. It is the truth *of* the flesh.

Perhaps the 'feel' of such a man as John is seeking to depict, who is utterly human and yet whose entire life is lived from God as its centre and source, can be captured from a picture drawn from human experience, and with no reference to the Fourth Gospel, which has been given by Greville Norburn of the mysterious quality of the 'charismatic' man.[96]

Such a person, says Norburn, speaks with an authenticity and personal authority. He tells of what he has seen and known. He has been there. He lives, sometimes fitfully, in other cases more permanently, on intimate, confident and even confidential terms with the object of his vision. That with which he claims to be in touch is a mystery that lies too deep for words, of which he can only say 'Not this', 'Not that', and yet which he frequently speaks of in terms of 'I' and 'Thou'. There is about him a certain distance and remoteness

93 Especially Luke 1: 3; cf. Acts 18: 25–6; 22: 3; 23: 15, 20; 24: 22; 26: 5. Elsewhere in the New Testament it occurs only of Herod's anxious interrogations of the wise men (Matt. 2: 7–8, 16) and in Eph. 5: 15 and 1 Thess. 5: 2.
94 The Gospel and Epistles of John contain almost as many instances as the rest of the New Testament put together.
95 John 19: 35.
96 With permission and gratitude I paraphrase and then quote from an article, 'Kant's Philosophy of Religion', due to be published in the *Scottish Journal of Theology* in 1973.

from the rest of us – a quality of holiness which brings us up with a sense of uneasiness in his presence.[97] He is rejected, inevitably, by the majority, yet attracts the few who know they must learn of him. But he is fascinating to friend and foe alike. For he has achieved, or been given, emancipation from the anxiety of finitude which is the lot of ordinary mortals: he is whole, undivided, reconciled. He bears a quality of saintliness which transcends goodness as the expert transcends the amateur. He seems to be given to us unaccountably, even arbitrarily.

Such men, goes on Norburn, 'summon their contemporaries, by the fact of their numinous existence, to make the crucial choice as to whether they are right or whether they are wrong'. They serve as midwives of faith for the rest of us:

They do surrogate-duty in the sphere of religion for the empirical control which in its own sphere science requires for the confirmation of its hypotheses. They *certify* as true what we can only *think*. They authorize us to make the venture of faith for ourselves. For by the wholeness of their character, by the hidden source of their confidence and power, by their distance from the rest of us, by the self-authenticating hallmark of truth which they exemplify, they produce the indefeasible impression that they are just the sort of persons we should expect to occur, if a reality corresponding to our own inchoate idea of God really exists.

Of course, the Fourth Evangelist is saying *more* than this of Jesus. He is giving a theological interpretation of the impression Norburn is describing in purely human categories. But I suggest that at least something remarkably like that impression lies behind the picture John presents to us, and that it is not invented. Indeed, I am persuaded that it is as authentic historically of the impact left by Jesus as any we get in the New Testament (which include not only those in Mark, Luke and Matthew but, I increasingly think, the Epistle to the Hebrews).[98] And John's picture is the more whole. As long as we do not misuse the

---

97 Cf. the effect of the 'righteous man' in Wisd. 2: 12–20, a passage which seems to have been strangely neglected by early Christian apologetic, except *possibly* in Luke 23: 47, where 'righteous (or innocent) man' replaces 'God's son' of Mark 15: 39. The two are equated in Wisd. 2: 18: 'If the righteous man is God's son, God will stretch out a hand and save him.'

98 The picture of Jesus perfected out of temptation and suffering (especially in Heb. 5: 7–9) rests, I am convinced, on oral tradition independent of, and indeed, I believe with H. Montefiore, *The Epistle to the Hebrews* (Black's N.T. Commentaries, London, 1964), earlier than, that of the Gospels.

portrait by treating it as a photograph (either here or indeed in any of the other sources), then I believe it has a quite indispensable contribution to make to the total 'synoptic' material out of which an adequate christology has to be fashioned today.[99]

[99] Since writing this I have re-read the essay by Dodd, 'The Portrait of Jesus in John and in the Synoptics', in *Christian History and Interpretation: Studies Presented to John Knox* (edd. W. R. Farmer, C. F. D. Moule, R. R. Niebuhr, Cambridge, 1967), pp. 183–98. Concentrating on an aspect on which I have not touched (Christ as judge), he comes nevertheless to a very similar conclusion: 'John's rendering of the portrait of Jesus will be neither his own invention nor the re-colouring of another artist's sketch. He will have had, through memories or traditions available to him, access to the sitter, and the similarities we have noted will go far to assure us that behind the two renderings of the portrait [viz. of John and the Synoptics] there stands a real historical person' (p. 195).

In a comment on the draft of this essay Dodd has kindly written to me with regard to John 1:14: 'I think we should now agree that the true rendering is "a father's only son", the statement being, as in other similar passages, essentially a parable.'

6

The christology of Acts again

STEPHEN S. SMALLEY

I

In an earlier article on the subject of the christology of Acts,[1] I examined the major titles of Jesus which are used in the early speeches of Acts, in an attempt to discover how far, if at all, the writer of Luke–Acts (whom I take to be Luke himself) was in touch with the primitive christological traditions of the post-resurrection Christian community. For this purpose I first discussed the obviously relevant issue of the historicity of the speeches themselves, and suggested that they 'preserve an outline of the kerygma recognizably in line with a received New Testament substructure',[2] even if Luke's reporting technique has involved a certain amount of summarizing and redaction.[3]

---

[1] S. S. Smalley, 'The Christology of Acts', *Exp. T.* lxxiii (1961–2), pp. 358–62.
[2] *Ibid.* p. 359.
[3] So also, but more cautiously, E. Trocmé, *Le 'Livre des Actes' et L'Histoire* (Paris, 1957), esp. pp. 207–14. See also T. F. Glasson, 'The Speeches in Acts and Thucydides', *Exp. T.* lxxvi (1964–5), p. 165. For studies of the speeches in Acts which from a different angle lend support to their pre-Lucan character, see R. A. Martin, 'Syntactical Evidence of Aramaic Sources in Acts i–xv', *NTS* xi (1964–5), pp. 38–59; J. W. Bowker, 'Speeches in Acts: A study in Proem and Yelammedenu form', *NTS* xiv (1967–8), pp. 96–111; E. E. Ellis, 'Midrashic Features in the Speeches of Acts', in A. Descamps and A. de Halleux (ed.), *Mélanges Bibliques: en hommage au Béda Rigaux* (Gembloux, 1970), pp. 303–12. On the other side, see U. Wilckens, *Die Missionsreden der Apostelgeschichte: Form- und Traditionsgeschichtliche Untersuchungen* (Neukirchen, 1963²), and the discussion of this work by J. Dupont, 'Les Discours Missionnaires des Actes des Apôtres: d'après un ouvrage récent', in *R.B.* lxix (1962), pp. 37–60. Note also M. Dibelius, 'The Speeches in Acts and Ancient Historiography', in *Studies in the Acts of the Apostles*, ed. H. Greeven (E.T. London, 1956), pp. 138–85; E. Schweizer, 'Concerning the Speeches in Acts', in L. E. Keck and J. L. Martyn (ed.), *Studies in Luke–Acts* (London, 1968), pp. 208–16; and more recently, C. F. Evans, '"Speeches" in Acts', in A. Descamps and A. de Halleux (ed.), *op. cit.*, pp. 287–302. See further, on Luke's fidelity to his sources with reference to the third Gospel, F. C. Burkitt, 'The Use of Mark in the Gospel According to Luke', in F. J. Foakes Jackson and K. Lake (ed.), *The Beginnings of Christianity*, i. 2 (London, 1922), pp. 106–20, esp. p. 119.

A second introductory matter concerned what I called 'levels of christology' in Acts.[4] A certain degree of variation is evident in the christology (or christologies) of the speeches of Acts, of which we need to take account. There is, for example, an apparent tension between the use of the title Χριστός for Jesus in Acts 2 (cf. verse 36, the coronation of the Christ), and the use of the same title in Acts 3 (cf. verse 20, the expectation of the Christ). This has led J. A. T. Robinson, for one, to conclude that these chapters contain two different and inconsistent christologies. In Acts 3, he claims, we have the 'fossil' of a primitive christological formulation, surrounded by other embryonic titles, in which the messianic event is still hesitantly awaited. In Acts 2, the conviction has been reached that Jesus is already Lord and Christ, and that the age of the Spirit has already begun.[5] Robinson's conclusion is that the outworking of this unresolved christological tension eventually set the pattern for New Testament eschatology as a whole. My query, which still persists, is whether this tension is as great as Dr Robinson claims, in view of the desperate critical surgery that must go on (for example, the removal of Acts 3: 18, with its reference to the suffering of Christ in the present) if the life of this thesis is to be saved. I also wonder still how it is that Peter or Luke, or both, held together these 'inconsistent' christologies without detecting any contradiction between them. If we are going to say, as Robinson does say, that Luke's inventive genius has been at work at all in the speeches of Acts,[6] should we not expect in general rather more smoothing of the rough edges? In fact there is no basic inconsistency between the use of Χριστός in Acts 2 and 3, if Acts 3: 20 ('that he may send the Christ appointed for you') refers to the 'second' and not the 'first' parousia of Jesus. This is no doubt the case. In Acts 2: 36 the Christ, pre-existently destined to suffer (2: 23), is vindicated and crowned; in 3: 20 the return of the exalted Christ is awaited. The earliest stratum of Christian understanding included belief in the *present* messiahship of Jesus.[7]

---

[4] S. S. Smalley, *loc. cit.*, pp. 359f.

[5] J. A. T. Robinson, 'The Most Primitive Christology of All?', *JTS*, n.s. vii (1956), pp. 177–89; reprinted in *Twelve New Testament Studies* (London, 1962), pp. 139–53. See also J. A. T. Robinson, *Jesus and his Coming: The Emergence of a Doctrine* (London, 1957), pp. 142–55.

[6] J. A. T. Robinson, *Jesus and His Coming*, p. 146 (discussing Acts 3: 18).

[7] So R. N. Longenecker, *The Christology of Early Jewish Christianity* (London, 1970), p. 79; cf. also E. Haenchen, *Die Apostelgeschichte* (Göttingen, [15]1968),

There is one further preliminary issue to be mentioned at this point, which despite its relevance to any investigation of the christology of Acts only featured as an assumption in my article. This concerns the method to be adopted when conducting such an investigation. Do we consider the christology of the speeches of Acts independently, analyzing on their own the titles which are there applied to Jesus? Or do we examine the christology of the speeches in the context of the general understanding of Christ's person which prevails in Luke's writings?

Hans Conzelmann has rightly warned us of the dangers of determining the special elements in Luke's christology by 'a statistical analysis of the titles applied to Jesus'.[8] It is true that Luke's use of titles, especially in his Gospel, may be traditional, and that these titles do not by themselves form the basis of a distinctive and developed Lucan christology. Nevertheless, Luke cannot have been unaware of their significance, to judge from their spread and variety in the apostolic preaching he records. On the contrary, he seems to have taken them over from his sources with great care, conscious of their deep if growing content, and used them to illustrate different aspects of the person of Christ as he developed his chief theological themes. Clearly, then, it is impossible to estimate the christological content of the apostolic speeches in Acts by surveying the titles of Jesus in isolation. This does not mean that the titles themselves have no place in Luke's total christology; they provide a vital framework for it. But it does mean that they should ultimately be related to the christology of Luke–Acts and indeed of the New Testament as a whole.[9] And needless to say, we

---

in loc., p. 168; E.T. *The Acts of the Apostles* (Oxford, 1971), p. 208. A more pertinent example than the alleged conflict between Acts 2 and 3, is the apparent 'adoptionism' of Acts 2: 36 ('God has made him both Lord and Christ'), compared (say) with the more 'developed' christology of 2: 23, the foreordained suffering of the pre-existent Christ. But even this kind of diversity would have presented no real problem to the New Testament writers, who were not concerned to preserve a doctrinal balance such as now characterizes systematic theology. Cf. S. S. Smalley, 'Diversity and Development in John', *NTS* xvii (1970–1), pp. 276–92. In the end, the truth about the person of Jesus does not lie on one christological side (adoptionism) or the other (docetism); but between them both.

[8] H. Conzelmann, *Die Mitte der Zeit: Studien zur Theologie des Lukas* (Tübingen, 1954), p. 146; E.T. *The Theology of St Luke* (London, 1960), p. 170.

[9] Dr Vincent Taylor and I have both been accused of failing to do this. See C. H. Talbert, 'An Anti-Gnostic Tendency in Lucan Christology', *NTS* xiv (1967–8), p. 261 n. 1.

cannot make deductions about the nature of this christology on any kind of mathematical, computerized basis.[10]

However, critics such as C. H. Talbert[11] who argue for the importance of reckoning seriously with Luke's christology as a whole, too often assume that the christology of the speeches of Acts has been so redacted that it has become simply a reflection of the Lucan mind, out of contact with any historical basis at all. But to admit that redaction has taken place in the course of writing Acts does not necessarily mean that Luke was unaware of the differences in character and emphasis between the christology of the period of history about which he is writing and that of his own day. Professor C. F. D. Moule himself has shown us that in the case of Luke–Acts we are in a unique position to compare a New Testament writer with himself on both sides of the resurrection.[12] When we do, it becomes clear at once that Luke's christological presentation in his two volumes, as seen precisely from his use of titles for Jesus, accurately reflects the situation. He mostly avoids post-resurrection titles for Jesus in the Gospel, and pre-resurrection titles in Acts (7: 56 is a notable exception). If Luke is thus sensitive to the distinction between history and faith, and at the same time aware of the continuity between them, can we not expect him also to have been conscious of any differences in christological level characteristic of the apostolic kerygma, as well as of the difference between the primitive and more developed forms of that preaching? And can we not expect him to have reflected these variations accurately in his composition of Acts?

II

Since 1962 several important studies in New Testament christology have appeared, which of necessity impinge on such an essay as this. There is, for example, Ferdinand Hahn's magisterial book, *Christo-*

---

[10] But cf. A. Q. Morton and G. H. C. MacGregor, *The Structure of Luke and Acts* (London, 1964), esp. pp. 11–22.

[11] C. H. Talbert, *loc. cit.*, esp. pp. 259–61. See also C. H. Talbert, *Luke and the Gnostics: An Examination of the Lucan Purpose* (Nashville and New York, 1966), esp. pp. 17–22. This exercise in *Redaktionsgeschichte* claims that Luke–Acts was written 'to serve as a defence against Gnosticism' (p. 16). The speeches in Acts, Talbert suggests, assist this purpose; they 'reflect Luke's mind' in their treatment of the theme of apostolic witness (p. 19).

[12] C. F. D. Moule, *The Phenomenon of the New Testament: An Inquiry into the Implications of Certain Features of the New Testament* (London, 1967); see esp. pp. 56–61.

logische Hoheitstitel.[13] Professor Hahn in this volume applies the traditio-historical critical method to his study of the Gospels and Acts, and argues on this basis that the titles of Jesus in the New Testament have been subject in the history of their development to influence at three main stages of early Christian thought: Palestinian Judaism, Hellenistic Judaism and Gentilic Hellenism. His conclusion is that in the end New Testament christology, including Luke's, has more to do with the interpretation of the early Christians than with the historical Jesus himself.[14] This thesis depends, *inter alia*, on the sharp division of early Christianity into separate stages, and a clear demarcation between what is Jewish and what is Greek about them. But this presupposition is open to serious question. Judaism and Hellenism were nothing if not interactive in the Mediterranean world at all points in the New Testament period.[15]

A study which similarly concerns itself with New Testament christology as a whole is R. H. Fuller's monograph, *The Foundations of New Testament Christology.*[16] Fuller follows Hahn in believing that the christology of the early church is 'a response to its total encounter with Jesus, not only in his earthly history but also in its continuing life'.[17] He also discovers, with Hahn, a development of that christology in three distinct stages.

Our concern in this essay is inevitably more limited. We are dealing here only with the christology of Acts; and within this area we shall be chiefly concerned with the title Χριστός.[18] In this particular connection two further studies may be mentioned. The first is Professor C. F. D. Moule's article on the christology of Acts in the Paul Schubert *Festschrift.*[19] In this study Professor Moule examines the connection in Luke's writings between history and interpretation. He begins by comparing the christologies of Luke and Acts in order to test their

[13] F. Hahn, *Christologische Hoheitstitel: Ihre Geschichte im frühen Christentum* (Göttingen, 1963); E.T. *The Titles of Jesus in Christology* (London, 1969).
[14] *Ibid.*, esp. pp. 347–50 (E.T. pp. 347–51).
[15] Cf. S. S. Smalley, 'Diversity and Development in John', *loc. cit.*, pp. 277f.
[16] R. H. Fuller, *The Foundations of New Testament Christology* (London, 1965).
[17] *Ibid.*, p. 15.
[18] F. Hahn, *op. cit.*, pp. 133–241, esp. 189–218 (E.T. pp. 136–239, esp. 168–89), believes that the title Χριστός was originally applied to Jesus with reference to his parousia in glory. Only later, and in the light of the so-called 'delay' of the parousia, was the title related, under Hellenistic influence, to the present work and exaltation of Jesus. R. H. Fuller's argumentation on this point (*op. cit.*, pp. 158–62, *al.*) develops along similar lines.
[19] C. F. D. Moule, 'The Christology of Acts', in L. E. Keck and J. L. Martyn (ed.), *op. cit.*, pp. 159–85.

theological relationship, and reaches the conclusion that the main titles of Jesus used in Luke's two volumes reflect in their usage discontinuity, caused by the dividing-point of the resurrection, and yet also continuity. Professor Moule discovers variation but not discrepancy in the different christological levels; and this suggests to him the likelihood that Luke is following reliable sources for his material at this point. Finally, this essay compares the christology of Acts with that of other New Testament writings. The Lucan estimate of the person of Christ is shown to be traditional, if not uniform; but where Luke's own mentality can be discerned, it is found to differ from that of Paul and John in certain respects, and to be more 'averagely apostolic'.[20] In support of this claim Professor Moule offers a number of test cases for Luke's historical precision in the use of the title Χριστός.

The use of this title in Luke–Acts is considered by Donald L. Jones, in an essay which reaches very different conclusions from those just discussed, but provides a useful foil to them.[21] Jones believes that Luke was aware of the use and meaning of Χριστός in the earliest christological thinking of the church, when traditional, 'official' designations of Christ were current. But Luke's own use, he claims, reveals a late development in Christian thought in that it is 'dominated by his own theological emphases and suggested solutions to pressing problems in the late first century A.D.'[22] In other words, Luke has tinted his use of Χριστός by reflection on the messianic mission of Jesus, including his suffering and resurrection, and under the influence of such problems as the so-called 'delay' of the parousia.[23] Thus the appearance of this title in Lucan contexts tells us more about the christology of Luke's day than about that of the early Christian community.[24]

III

My purpose now is to suggest one further line along which the foundations of Luke's christology in Acts may be considered; namely, the relation between the Petrine speeches of Acts and 1 Peter. It is well known,

[20] *Ibid.*, pp. 181f.
[21] D. L. Jones, 'The Title *Christos* in Luke–Acts', *CBQ* xxxii (1970), pp. 69–76.
[22] *Ibid.*, p. 76.
[23] *Ibid.*, pp. 70f. But cf. S. S. Smalley, 'The Delay of the Parousia', *JBL* lxxxiii (1964), pp. 41–54.
[24] D. L. Jones, *loc. cit.*, p. 76. Similarly, R. P. C. Hanson, *The Acts* (Oxford, 1967), esp. pp. 35–48.

of course, that there are critical problems involved here, not least the question of the authorship of 1 Peter. But if that letter is allowed in some sense to be Petrine, whether or not it was actually written by the apostle Peter (and I do not find such a position impossible to hold),[25] then it seems reasonable to undertake this enquiry. Two issues will be discussed in this connection: (*a*) the use of Χριστός as a name in Acts and 1 Peter; (*b*) the association in Acts and 1 Peter between Χριστός and πάθημα.

(A) THE USE OF Χριστός AS A NAME

The term Χριστός is used in Acts as both a title and a name. H. J. Cadbury made three suggestions about the use of Χριστός in Acts: it is rarely used as a name; it is never used by itself as a name; and it usually carries a fully messianic meaning, apposite to an explanation of the messianic identity of Jesus.[26] But Cadbury's conclusions obscure the fact that the nominal use of Χριστός is as obvious as its titular use. Jesus is called the Christ, as a title, 13 times in Acts (discounting the dubious readings at 4: 33 and 8: 37). Seven of these occurrences are liturgical[27] or editorial,[28] and four of them appear in Pauline contexts. Of the remaining six titular uses in speeches, two are associated with Paul[29] and four with Peter.[30]

Χριστός used as a name also appears 13 times in Acts. Five of these occurrences are epistolary[31] or editorial.[32] Of the remaining eight nominal uses in speeches, two are (or possibly only one is) associated with Paul[33] and six (or five) with Peter.[34]

---

25 On the authorship of 1 Peter, see E. G. Selwyn, *The First Epistle of St Peter* (London, [2]1947), pp. 7–38 (Peter through Silvanus); A. M. Stibbs and A. F. Walls, *The First Epistle General of Peter* (London, 1959), pp. 15–30 (some form of the Silvanus hypothesis); R. H. Gundry, '"Verba Christi" in 1 Peter', *NTS* xiii (1966–7), pp. 336–50 (Peter); J. N. D. Kelly, *A Commentary on the Epistles of Peter and of Jude* (London, 1969), pp. 30–3 (some connection with Peter). On the other side, see F. W. Beare, *The First Epistle of Peter* (Oxford, [3]1970), pp. 43–50 (pseudonymous); E. Best, *1 Peter* (London, 1971), pp. 49–63 (pseudonymous, but from a Petrine school).
26 H. J. Cadbury, 'The Titles of Jesus in Acts', in *The Beginnings of Christianity*, i. 5 (London, 1933), pp. 357–9. See further, for both Acts and 1 Peter, R. H. Fuller, *op. cit.*, pp. 160–2.   27 Acts 4: 26.
28 Acts 5: 42; 8: 5; 9: 22; 17: 3a; 18: 5, 28.   29 Acts 17: 3b; 26: 23.
30 Acts 2: 31, 36; 3: 18, 20.   31 Acts 15: 26.
32 Acts 8: 12; 10: 48; 24: 24, using Χριστὸς Ἰησοῦς; 28: 31, ℵ* *al.* omit Χριστοῦ.
33 Acts 16: 18; 20: 21, *s.v.l.*
34 Acts 2: 38, syᵖ, Iren. omit Χριστοῦ; 3: 6; 4: 10; 9: 34; 10: 36; 11: 17.

Manifestly, any conclusions from evidence such as this must be carefully drawn. As Professor Moule suggests,[35] it might seem as if Luke himself used Χριστός as a proper name, and attributed a similar use to Peter; whereas in general he gave to Paul a titular, messianic usage, thus running counter to Paul's normal practice in his letters.[36] Professor Moule argues that on the contrary, the messianic use of Χριστός in Acts is confined to apologetic contexts which happen to be Pauline, while the other (mostly Petrine) uses are of a 'formula' kind in liturgical or quasi-liturgical settings.[37]

But in fact the position is even less straightforward than this. We cannot, for a start, simply dismiss the 13 titular and directly messianic uses of Χριστός in Acts, as Hans Conzelmann would have us do.[38] The fact remains that in speech and narrative associated with Peter and Paul (and Philip), Χριστός is used messianically. If with Professor Moule we regard the Pauline titular occurrences as coincidentally linked with the apostle (although this accounts for Acts 26: 23 only with difficulty), we are not able to argue for a primitive use of the term Χριστός in Acts on the grounds that it is untypical of Paul. But there still remain, to go no further, four titular uses of Χριστός in speeches by Peter which are not shaped as in Paul's case by the requirements of an apologetic formulation (such as Acts 9: 22, 'Saul confounded the Jews by proving that Jesus was the Christ'). This messianic usage in itself suggests a primitive stratum of christology. And in Peter's speeches it lies side by side with a nominal use. Luke makes no attempt to bring the two uses into line with each other. It is likely, then, that when the *nominal* use of Χριστός occurs in the speeches of Acts (rarely in those of Paul, five or six times in those of Peter), it reflects an early if developing tradition, and indicates that Luke is faithfully reproducing his sources at this point rather than freely redacting.

---

[35] C. F. D. Moule, 'The Christology of Acts', *loc. cit.*

[36] See further on the use of Χριστός in Paul, W. Kramer, *Christos, Kyrios, Gottessohn: Untersuchungen zu Gebrauch und Bedeutung der christologischen Bezeichnungen bei Paulus und den vorpaulinischen Gemeinden* (Zürich–Stuttgart, 1963), pp. 131–48, 203–14 (E.T. *Christ, Lord, Son of God*, London, 1966, pp. 133–50, 203–14). Kramer argues that there are no criteria for deciding whether 'Christ' was used as a messianic title by the Gentile church of the Pauline period, even if in Paul's own case there is an earlier linguistic tradition in the use of Χριστός which points in this direction (p. 213; E.T. pp. 213f.). See also W. C. van Unnik, 'Jesus the Christ', *NTS* viii (1961–2), pp. 101–16, esp. p. 105.

[37] C. F. D. Moule, 'The Christology of Acts', *loc. cit.*, p. 175.

[38] H. Conzelmann, *op. cit.*, p. 147 n. 2 (E.T. p. 171 n. 2), on the use of the title 'Christ' in Acts (at 2: 31, 36, *al.*), says: '...man diesen Gebrauch nicht auf Vorlagen zurückführen kann, sondern dem Lukas zuschreiben muß.'

In this connection it is perhaps significant that the use of Χριστός as a name occurs more frequently in the speeches of Peter than of Paul in Acts. The titular use of Χριστός by Peter is balanced by a nominal use which is stronger than that ascribed to Paul (six or five to two or one); although the nominal use of Χριστός is supposedly typical of a later theological tradition dependent on Paul (who broadly speaking uses Χριστός as a proper name in his letters).

I submit, then, that the use of Χριστός as both a title and a name in the speeches of Peter in Acts points to the primitive character of Luke's christology.[39] Let us now examine more closely Peter's use of Χριστός as a personal name for Jesus, and relate it to the occurrence of Χριστός in 1 Peter.

According to Acts, Peter was familiar with the nominal use of Χριστός. Even if, as Professor Moule claims, he is drawing on a formula-like tradition when he invokes the name of Jesus Christ for purposes of baptism, healing and so on, Peter identifies himself with the personal implications of this formula sufficiently closely to use it frequently and on his own account. This provides, as it happens, a point of contact with the use of Χριστός in 1 Peter. Of the 22 occurrences of Χριστός in that letter,[40] 12 involve the use of Χριστός by itself. In all 12, Χριστός is used as a personal name, even if (as at 4: 13 and 5: 1, where the article appears) an 'official' sense occasionally clings to it. On one occasion, 1 Peter 4: 14 (εἰ ὀνειδίζεσθε ἐν ὀνόματι Χριστοῦ), the usage has a formula-like ring about it which recalls some of the phrases of Peter in Acts (for example, 2: 38 and 10: 48, baptism in (using ἐπί or ἐν) the name of Jesus Christ; 3: 6 and 4: 10, healing in (ἐν) the name of Jesus Christ of Nazareth).[41] We may notice also the Pauline-flavoured use of ἐν Χριστῷ in 1 Peter 5: 10 (instrumental and incorporative)[42] and 5: 14

---

39 The Petrine confession of Mark 8: 29 (Σὺ εἶ ὁ Χριστός) par. probably has a place in this discussion. See, with reference to the Matthean version of the confession, O. Cullmann, *Petrus, Jünger – Apostel – Märtyrer: Das historische und das theologische Petrusproblem* (Zürich, 1952), pp. 176–238; E.T. *Peter: Disciple, Apostle, Martyr* (London, ²1962), pp. 164–217.

40 21 if with B Χριστοῦ is omitted from 1 Pet. 1: 11.

41 Cf. 1 Pet. 4: 16.

42 Too much cannot be made of the occurrence of ἐν Χριστῷ in this context, however. The whole wish-prayer of 1 Pet. 5: 10f. abounds in Semitisms, and is stylistically similar to other prayers used in Jewish and early Christian worship. Notice: the use of δέ (a regular feature of Pauline benedictions); the predicate with God's name in the nominative case; the associated use of the genitive with πάσης; the conjoint use of δόξα and αἰώνιος; the use of the future (or optative) of verbs of strengthening, common in contexts of prayer or paraenesis; and in

(incorporative), which is similarly formal and even liturgical, and thus corresponds to the Petrine usage of Χριστός in Acts.[43]

(B) THE ASSOCIATION BETWEEN Χριστός AND πάθημα

The second point in this discussion about possible contacts between the Petrine speeches of Acts and 1 Peter, in terms of their common use of Χριστός, concerns the marked association in 1 Peter between the name Χριστός and the concept of suffering. This link between Χριστός and πάθημα occurs six times in 1 Peter;[44] and there is a further indirect allusion to it at 1: 19 ('the precious blood of Christ, like that of a lamb').[45]

It could be argued that this connection in 1 Peter is striking, without being distinctively Petrine. Furthermore, it might be claimed, the

the doxology (verse 11), the use of the dative + αὐτῷ; the occurrence of κράτος; the eternity measure; the ἀμήν. However, some features of this passage in 1 Peter (notably the presence of ὀλίγον παθόντας) fit the actual situation of the letter. See further, E. Norden, *Agnostos Theos: Untersuchungen zur Formengeschichte Religiöser Rede* (Stuttgart, 1956), pp. 380–3, esp. p. 382. Thus, as Dr Peter O'Brien of Yeotmal has suggested to me, the use of ἐν Χριστῷ here need not be distinctively Petrine at all; it may have come from Paul into early church worship, and back into 1 Peter through Silvanus.

43 Liturgical, even baptismal influences on the content and structure of 1 Peter are very probable. But it is unlikely that on this basis we should regard the letter *tout court* as a baptismal (paschal) liturgy. So (*inter alios*) H. Windisch, ed. H. Preisker, *Die Katholischen Briefe* (Tübingen, ³1951), pp. 156–62. See also F. L. Cross, *1 Peter: A Paschal Liturgy* (London, 1954); and the reply by C. F. D. Moule, 'The Nature and Purpose of 1 Peter', *NTS* iii (1956–7), pp. 1–11. See further C. Spicq, *Les Épîtres de Saint Pierre* (Paris, 1966), pp. 14f., and the literature there cited.

44 1 Pet. 1: 11, B omits Χριστοῦ; 2: 21; 3: 18; 4: 1, 13; 5: 1.

45 In 1 Pet. 2: 21–4, a *locus classicus* for the theme of *imitatio Christi* in the New Testament, the vicarious suffering of Christ (Χριστὸς ἔπαθεν ὑπὲρ ὑμῶν, verse 21) is regarded as extending from his trial to the crucifixion. Its effects extend (to the Christian) beyond that point (ἵνα ταῖς ἁμαρτίαις ἀπογενόμενοι τῇ δικαιοσύνῃ ζήσωμεν, verse 24). See also the explication of the Christ–Christian relationship in the context of suffering in 1 Pet. (3: 18), 4: 1 and 13. The 'suffering in the flesh' of both Christ and the Christian referred to in 4: 1 is less likely to be a Pauline reference to spiritual death with Christ to sin in baptism (so C. E. B. Cranfield, *1 and 2 Peter and Jude*, London, 1960, *in loc.*, pp. 107f.), than a reference to the conquest of sin in flesh, the seat of sin (so R. Knopf, *Die Briefe Petri und Judä*, Göttingen, 1912, *in loc.*, pp. 160–3). See further E. Best, *op. cit.*, *in loc.*, pp. 151f. Thus there is a link here with both the πολλὰ παθεῖν theme of the Gospel tradition (e.g. Mark 8: 31 = Luke 9: 22) and the 'suffering and glory' formulation used, according to Luke alone, by the risen Christ (cf. Luke 24: 26, οὐχὶ ταῦτα ἔδει παθεῖν τὸν Χριστόν; ; note also 24: 46, using again παθεῖν τὸν Χριστόν).

background to this letter would have been sufficient by itself to prompt the thought of suffering and indeed glory as soon as the Christ was mentioned. The readers of 1 Peter were suffering already, or were about to suffer, through persecution;[46] and the figure of a suffering as well as triumphant Messiah was by now central to the primitive Christian confession. It would seem only logical to draw these two streams of thought together.

Nevertheless, the connection between Χριστός and πάθημα in 1 Peter is more distinctive than might at first appear. For it so happens that beyond 1 Peter the appearance of the 'suffering Christ' theme in the New Testament is remarkably restrained. The Petrine speeches of Acts maintain the link,[47] and so do a few other Lucan passages, including two which are attributed to Paul.[48] But apart from Luke–Acts and 1 Peter, only two New Testament verses connect Χριστός and πάθημα explicitly, and these are both Pauline.[49] There are, of course, frequent references to the death of Christ which do not openly mention suffering;

[46] Cf. F. L. Cross, *op. cit.*, *passim*; C. F. D. Moule, 'The Nature and Purpose of 1 Peter', *loc. cit.*; J. N. D. Kelly, *op. cit.*, pp. 5–11.

[47] Acts 3: 18, the suffering of God's Christ; 2: 31, the resurrection of the Christ; 2: 36, the coronation of Christ. Cf. also the parallel Petrine use of the λίθος testimonium of Ps. 118: 22 at Acts 4: 11 and 1 Pet. 2: 7. See further, B. Lindars, *New Testament Apologetic: The Doctrinal Significance of the Old Testament Quotations* (London, 1961), pp. 169–86; also J. H. Elliott, *The Elect and the Holy: An Exegetical Examination of 1 Peter 2: 4–10* (Leiden, 1966), pp. 26–38, 129–45. It is true that Acts, in contrast to 1 Peter, provides us with no developed theology of suffering as such. But the death of Christ is emphatically present in the early speeches of Peter in Acts, even if these treat the crucifixion of Jesus as a miscarriage of justice without dwelling on the thought of suffering *per se* (cf. Acts 2: 23; 3: 15; 4: 10). And that death is proclaimed, with the resurrection, in a context which makes it clear that Jesus is the Messiah (Acts 3: 18; cf. 17: 3) and also the suffering servant of God (Acts 3: 13, 26; 4: 26f.; cf. 8: 32–5). See on this last point S. S. Smalley, 'The Christology of Acts', *loc. cit.*, pp. 360f.; *contra* J. C. O'Neill, *The Theology of Acts in its Historical Setting* (London, 1961), pp. 133–9. Dr O'Neill has omitted the chapter on the titles given to Jesus in the second edition of his book (1970). C. H. Dodd, *According to the Scriptures: The Substructure of New Testament Theology* (London, 1952), pp. 88–96, finds the 'servant' concept of Isa. 52: 13 – 53: 12, *al.* (through Peter?) behind parts of both Acts (e.g. 2: 33, exaltation after suffering) and 1 Peter (e.g. 2: 22–5, healing through humiliation); see esp. pp. 92f.

[48] Cf. Acts 17: 3; 26: 23, *al.*

[49] 2 Cor. 1: 5 (τὰ παθήματα τοῦ Χριστοῦ); Phil. 3: 10 (ἡ κοινωνία παθημάτων αὐτοῦ). Both passages deal with the Christian's share of Christ's suffering. But cf. also 1 Cor. 5: 7 (using πάσχα with Χριστός) and Phil. 1: 29 (Christian suffering, using πάσχειν, for the sake of Christ). Manifestly, even the Pauline canvas is limited.

although again they are mostly Pauline.[50] These facts suggest that there is some common ground here, at least, between Peter in Acts and 1 Peter. Even if Luke and the writer of 1 Peter are simply sharing what has by now become a traditional motif,[51] it cannot be entirely insignificant that 'Peter' is so largely associated with its appearance in the New Testament.[52]

An important witness to this motif in Acts is provided by Acts 3: 18, a verse to which reference has already been made. J. A. T. Robinson claims that this passage, with its reference to the suffering of the Christ as such (using παθεῖν), should be excised from Acts 3 on two grounds. First, the idea of the suffering of Jesus 'plays no part in any other formulation of the primitive preaching'; and secondly, the thesis that the Christ (as distinct from the Son of man) should suffer, is a Lucan theologoumenon.[53] This proposal is used to support Robinson's doubtful argument, mentioned earlier, that Acts 2 and 3 contain two incompatible christologies, the second more primitive than the first.[54]

The first reason for discounting the authenticity of Acts 3: 18, that the suffering of Jesus does not belong to the early Christian kerygma, is difficult to sustain. Suffering belongs without question to the betrayal, denial, crucifixion, death and burial of Jesus; and these elements of the passion clearly feature in Peter's speech of Acts 2. Similarly, Paul's summary of the apostolic preaching in 1 Cor. 15: 3f. refers to the death of Jesus, which (*pace* Robinson) presumably implies and includes suffering.[55]

[50] E.g. Rom. 8: 34, *al.* Cf. also, however, Heb. 2: 9f. (the suffering of Jesus).

[51] See below, pp. 91f.

[52] The clear parallel between the suffering of Christ and the suffering of the Christian in 1 Peter (at 2: 21; 4: 1, 13, *al.*) is understandable if it is connected at all closely with Peter himself; for his sufferings as a Christian are all too apparent from the history of Acts (cf. Acts 4, 12, *al.*). On the general point, and against the view presented here, see U. Wilckens, *op. cit.*, pp. 117f., 157–63. See also K. Berger, 'Zum traditionsgeschichtlichen Hintergrund christologischer Hoheitstitel', *NTS* xvii (1970–1), pp. 391–425, esp. 391–411.

[53] J. A. T. Robinson, *Jesus and His Coming*, pp. 145f.; cf. K. Lake and H. J. Cadbury (ed.), *The Beginnings of Christianity*, i. 4 (London, 1933), *in loc.*, p. 37.

[54] Dr Robinson also uses it to establish his doubtful claim that the early church was unable to think of Jesus as the Christ before his exaltation. The primitive preaching instead asserts, he argues, even in Acts 2, that Jesus is the Christ by virtue of his resurrection (*Jesus and His Coming*, p. 146). On the other side, see S. S. Smalley, 'The Christology of Acts', *loc. cit.*, pp. 359f., 362; R. Longenecker, *op. cit.*, pp. 77–9.

[55] Cf. J. A. T. Robinson, *Jesus and His Coming*, pp. 145f. It is equally difficult to believe with Robinson that the suffering of Christ in Luke 24: 26f., 45f. (cf. Acts 17: 2f.; 26: 22f.) can be thought of apart from the crucifixion. Notice

The other reason for rejecting this verse from Acts, that the concept of the suffering of the Christ owes its origin to Luke's theology, is more pertinent. It may well be that in Acts, as in 1 Peter, we find this tradition of the suffering Christ becoming a theologoumenon, taken over by Luke. But even if that should be the case, we are not compelled to deny the existence of an earlier and historical background to the tradition. Similarly, the impressive connection already noticed between Χριστός and πάθημα in Acts and 1 Peter could be explained on the view that both are indebted to a developed, apologetic tradition; a primitive substructure is not necessarily implied. We now turn, therefore, to consider the arguments which may be adduced against the claim that the 'suffering of Christ' formula in Acts or 1 Peter (or both) is simply a late theological creation.

(i) Although this is debated,[56] a connection between messiahship and suffering may have existed in pre-Christian Judaism, and may have been taken over by Jesus in reference to his own identity.[57] (ii) As W. C. van Unnik points out,[58] there are messianic implications behind the trial narratives of the Gospels. The suffering and death of Jesus are related to his implicit and even explicit claim to be the Christ. (iii) According to both Mark (from Peter?) and Luke, Jesus stands in the line of the (messianic) prophets of God, who were equally open to suffering for their words and deeds.[59] (iv) There is an interesting association in Luke–Acts between the 'anointing' of Jesus as the suffering Christ, and the Spirit.[60] In spite of Luke's theological interest in the Spirit,[61] this association can hardly be regarded as totally

also the deliberate association in Acts 2: 36 between Christ and the crucifixion. The interpretation of Old Testament 'suffering' passages with reference to (Jesus) Christ, as in Acts, may have been too early for some Jews in Jerusalem (so K. Lake and H. J. Cadbury (ed.), *The Beginnings of Christianity*, i. 4, p. 37); but it need not have been too early for Peter and the first Christian apostles, who had been with Jesus during his ministry.

[56] See, *inter alios*, O. Cullmann, *Die Christologie des Neuen Testaments* (Tübingen, ²1958), pp. 51–9 (111–37); E.T. *The Christology of the New Testament* (London, ²1963), pp. 52–60 (111–36). More positively, W. D. Davies, *Paul and Rabbinic Judaism* (London, ²1955), pp. 274–84.

[57] Cf. Mark 9: 41; 12: 35–7; (14: 61f.), *al.*

[58] W. C. van Unnik, *loc. cit.*, pp. 101–16, esp. 105–16.

[59] Mark 8: 28; cf. Matt. 17: 10–13; Luke 24: 19f.

[60] See Acts 4: 26f. = Ps. 2: 2, using Χριστός and ἔχρισας; 10: 38, ὡς ἔχρισεν αὐτὸν ὁ Θεὸς Πνεύματι Ἁγίῳ καὶ δυνάμει; cf. Luke 4: 18f. = Isa. 61: 1. Cf. W. C. van Unnik, *loc. cit.*, pp. 113–15.

[61] Cf. S. S. Smalley, 'Spirit, Kingdom and Prayer in Luke–Acts', *Nov. T.* xv (1973), pp. 59–71.

redacted, in the face of its Old Testament background.[62] In 1 Peter we may compare 3: 18 and 4: 13f. (v) The confession of Jesus as a suffering Messiah was a difficult one for a Jew to make, and purports therefore to rest on some kind of authentic, historical basis.[63] There is no reason why this should not have been the teaching of Jesus itself. If the association between Christ and suffering appears in the apologetic tradition later on, this need not preclude its primitive derivation.[64]

IV

On the basis of our investigations into the common ground between the Petrine christology of Acts and the christology of 1 Peter, three summary considerations may be offered by way of conclusion.

First, there appear to be seminal links between Acts and 1 Peter in their common use of Χριστός as a name, and in their treatment of the theme of suffering in association with Christ.[65]

Secondly, if these links exist, their connection is no doubt historical rather than literary.[66] That is to say, an apostolic christological tradition lies behind both Acts and 1 Peter, and 'Peter', actually or indirectly, is its spokesman.

Finally, such a conclusion has inevitable and important implications for the question of the historicity of Luke–Acts, and, since this has been our immediate concern, for the christological content of Acts itself.[67] I see no less reason now than I did earlier for regarding the christology of Acts as other than essentially primitive in character, yet richly embryonic in content. Its undeveloped but high christology, possibly

---

[62] But note K. Berger, *loc. cit.*, pp. 393–400.

[63] Cf. W. C. van Unnik, *loc. cit.*, pp. 109–11.

[64] Cf. R. N. Longenecker, *op. cit.*, pp. 79–81.

[65] It may be that there are connections also between Acts and Mark, in terms of Peter and the 'sufferings of Christ' theme; cf. Mark 8: 31–8; 10: 28–30, *al.*

[66] E. G. Selwyn, *op. cit.*, p. 36. Selwyn draws out also the other connections between Peter in Acts and 1 Peter (pp. 33–6). Note also R. B. Rackham, *The Acts of the Apostles* (London, [14]1951), p. 24, who mentions the link between Acts 2: 23 and 1 Pet. 1: 2 (cf. verse 20) in their use of the term πρόγνωσις (these are the only two New Testament passages where this word occurs). Professor F. F. Bruce has pointed out to me in addition the contact in the use of ξύλον for the cross between Acts (5: 30; 10: 39; 13: 29) and 1 Peter (2: 24).

[67] It also moves us away from the position of D. L. Jones, *loc. cit.*, and towards that of C. F. D. Moule, 'The Christology of Acts', *loc. cit.*

running back to Jesus himself,[68] eventually flowers luxuriantly in
1 Peter.

In many ways this essay was Professor Moule's before it was given to
him. Not in the sense that he is responsible for its conclusions, still less
for its shortcomings; but in the sense that it owes so much, as always,
to his teaching and inspiration. It is offered to him now as a modest
token of high esteem and warm affection.

[68] So e.g. G. E. Ladd, 'The Christology of Acts', *Foundations* xi (1968), pp. 27–41,
esp. 32–4.

7

The Punctuation of Rom. 9: 5

BRUCE M. METZGER

Among problematic passages in the Pauline Epistles one of the most disputed involves the punctuation of Rom. 9: 5 and the question whether in this verse Paul calls Christ θεός. In view of the great number of special studies and articles that have been written on the problem, as well as the lengthy discussions in commentaries on Romans, there appears to be no exaggeration in F. C. Burkitt's comment that 'the punctuation [of Rom. 9: 5] has probably been more discussed than that of any other sentence in literature'.[1] The commonly received wording of the Greek text of the passage is as follows: ὧν οἱ πατέρες καὶ ἐξ ὧν ὁ Χριστὸς τὸ κατὰ σάρκα ὁ ὢν ἐπὶ πάντων θεὸς εὐλογητὸς εἰς τοὺς αἰῶνας ἀμήν. So far as Greek grammar is concerned, the latter part of the verse can be punctuated in at least eight different ways.

(1) The Textus Receptus, followed by the editions of B. Weiss, von Soden, H. J. Vogels, A. Merk, J. M. Bover, and G. Nolli, punctuates with a comma after σάρκα.

(2) The text of Westcott–Hort punctuates with a comma after σάρκα and another after πάντων. Both this way of punctuating and that mentioned in (1) may be rendered, 'who is over all, God blessed for ever' (AV, RV, ASV), or 'supreme above all, God blessed for ever' (NEBmg[1]), or 'who is above all, God for ever blessed!' (Jerusalem Bible).

(3) Placing a comma after σάρκα and also after θεός, one may translate, 'who is God over all, blessed for ever' (RSVmg).

(4) With a comma placed after πάντων and also after θεός, the passage may be rendered, 'who is over all, God, blessed for ever' (W. F. Gess).[2]

(5a) With a comma placed after ὁ ὢν and also after θεός, the words have been taken to mean, 'He who Is, God over all, blessed for ever'.[3]

(5b) Independently adopting the same punctuation, F. C. Burkitt

---

[1] *JTS* iii (1904), p. 451.
[2] *Christi Person und Werk*, II, i (Basel, 1878), pp. 207f.
[3] This is essentially the interpretation proposed by Christopher Wordsworth, *The New Testament of Our Lord and Saviour Jesus Christ, in the Original Greek: with Introductions and Notes*, new ed., ii (London, 1864), pp. 247f.

interpreted the words ὁ ὤν κ.τ.λ. as a parenthetical benediction which refers back to Paul's asseveration in verse 1 (οὐ ψεύδομαι). Burkitt paraphrased the meaning as follows, 'I lie not..., The Eternal (Blessed is His Name!), I call Him to witness'.[4]

(6) With a colon placed after σάρκα (Joseph Scaliger's ed. of the Greek N.T. (1620), WHmg, Nestle–Kilpatrick, Nestle–Aland, and the United Bible Societies' ed.), or

(7) With a full stop placed after σάρκα (Lachmann and Tischendorf) θεός may be taken either as predicate, 'He who is over all is God, blessed for ever' (RVmg²), or as subject, and εὐλογητός as predicate with the ellipsis of εἴη or ἐστίν, making the last part of the verse a doxology; thus, 'He who is God over all be (is) blessed for ever' (RVmg¹); or 'flesh; he who is over all, God, *be* blessed for ever' (ASVmg); or 'God who is over all be blessed for ever' (RSV); or 'May God, supreme over all, be blessed for ever!' (NEB); or 'Blessed forever be God who is over all!' (New American Bible).

(8) With a comma placed after σάρκα and a full stop after πάντων, the clauses may be rendered, 'and of whom is the Christ as concerning the flesh, who is over all. God be (is) blessed for ever' (RVmg³), or 'sprang the Messiah, who is supreme over all. Blessed be God for ever!' (NEBmg²).

It is obvious that these various ways of punctuating involve the most important christological consequences. In nos. 1 through 5*a* inclusive the clause that begins ὁ ὤν, with all that follows, including the designation θεός, qualifies ὁ Χριστός. In nos. 5*b* through 7 the words ὁ ὤν introduce an independent clause or sentence, and θεός denotes God the Father. No. 8 refers the ὁ ὤν clause to ὁ Χριστός, and the last part of the verse to God.

In deciding which of the ways of punctuating the sentence expresses most nearly the apostle's meaning, scholars have appealed to a variety of kinds of considerations, the cogency of which has been variously estimated. These include the evidence, such as it is, bearing on the punctuation of the passage in Greek manuscripts, its translation in the early versions, its interpretation in the Fathers, and the grammar and structure of the passage, considered in itself as well as in its wider context. The following pages seek to make a comprehensive survey and a fresh analysis of the main points that have been urged on one side and the other in construing the apostle's statement in Rom. 9: 5.

---

[4] *JTS* v (1904), p. 454.

I. THE PUNCTUATION OF ROM. 9: 5 IN GREEK MANUSCRIPTS

As is well known, during the earlier centuries of the transmission of the New Testament, scribes used marks of punctuation rather sporadically, not to say haphazardly. It follows, therefore, that the data concerning the punctuation of Rom. 9: 5 in Greek manuscripts must be assessed in the light of such scribal habits. Let us begin with the evidence of the later Greek manuscripts. According to Abbot,[5] reporting the investigation of C. R. Gregory, at least twenty-six minuscule Greek manuscripts 'have a stop after σάρκα, the same in general which they have after αἰῶνας or ἀμήν'. Abbot continues, giving as his opinion that 'in all probability, the result of an examination would show that three-quarters or four-fifths of the cursive MSS containing Rom. ix. 5 have a stop after σάρκα'.

As regards the earlier Greek witnesses, the following information concerning the papyri and the uncial manuscripts which contain Rom. 9: 5 has been provided through the kindness of Professor Kurt Aland, Director of the Institut für neutestamentliche Textforschung at Münster, and Dr. Klaus Junack, Kustos of the Institut.

The Chester Beatty Papyrus II ($\mathfrak{P}^{46}$, *ca.* A.D. 200), which reads χρς ὁ κατὰ σάρ[κα, has no mark of punctuation in the verse, but the scribe left a space after ἀμήν. Likewise no mark of punctuation occurs in the verse in either the fourth-century codex Sinaiticus or in the sixth-century codex Claromontanus (D^p). The latter is arranged in stichoi, which in verse 5 end with . . . πατέρες| . . . θεός| and . . . ἀμήν. The evidence of the other uncial manuscripts is as follows. A point standing in a middle position with respect to the line of writing (a colon) is present after σάρκα in A, B (*sec. man.*), F^p, G^p, Ψ, 049, and 056. A high point follows σάρκα in L, 0142, and 0151 (the last also has a space following the point). The scribe of C left a space after σάρκα.

Inasmuch as the last mentioned manuscript, being a palimpsest, offers some amount of difficulty in deciphering, it will be appropriate here to mention what other scholars have reported concerning the punctuation at Rom. 9: 5 in that witness. In Tischendorf's edition of

---

[5] Ezra Abbot, 'On the Construction of Romans ix. 5', *JBL* [i] (1881 (1882)), pp. 107f. (= *The Authorship of the Fourth Gospel and Other Critical Essays* (Boston, 1888), pp. 431f.).

the manuscript (Leipzig, 1843) a high point (a colon) and a space occur after σάρκα. Apparently these are corroborated by Lyon, who made the most recent careful examination of the entire manuscript,[6] for he includes nothing for this verse in his list of corrections of Tischendorf's readings. Earlier in the century Cuthbert Lattey reported the following information supplied by Père Boudon, S.J., who at Lattey's request made a careful inspection of the manuscript: 'Between σάρκα and ὁ ὤν there is a space hardly greater than that between any two consecutive letters, but there is quite clearly a small cross there, without any other sign or symbol. This small cross is very often found at the end of a verse, nearly always preceded by a point on a level with the middle of the letters, which point the cross often touches (·+); so after Acts 1. 5, etc.; without a point at the end of Acts 1. 14. Within a verse it is sometimes over the point, as in Acts 1. 7, after αὐτούς, and in Matt. 26. 69, after λέγουσα ... Finally the cross is also found by itself, within a verse, as in Acts 1. 11 (after εἶπαν, and finishing a line), Matt. 26. 58 (after ἀρχιερέως), Matt. 26. 73 (after Πέτρῳ).'[7]

In addition to the punctuation standing after σάρκα reported above, several uncials have additional marks of punctuation elsewhere in verse 5. According to information supplied by the Münster Institut, F^P also has a point in the middle position after πατέρες, after the first ὁ, after ὤν, after εὐλογοῦντες, after εἰς, after τούς, and after αἰῶνας, as well as a high point after the second ὤν, a low point after the second ὁ, and a cluster of two points and a comma after ἀμήν. G^P, besides having a point in the middle position after σάρκα, has a similar point after πατέρες, after the first ὁ, after ὤν, after θεός, and after αἰῶνας. K has a low point after πατέρες, two points (:) after σάρκα, followed on the next line by commentary, and two points (:) after ἀμήν, followed by commentary. L, besides having a high point after σάρκα, has a point in the middle position after πατέρες, a comma after θεός, and a point in the middle position after ἀμήν, followed by τέλος in the next line. P has a lacuna from 8:8 to 9:11. 056 has a high point after πατέρες and another after ἀμήν, followed by a space and commentary. 0142 has a point in the middle position after πατέρες and a high point after ἀμήν, followed by commentary. 0151 has two dots (:) after ἀμήν, followed by commentary on the next line. (This concludes the Münster report

[6] Robert W. Lyon, 'A Re-Examination of Codex Ephraemi Rescriptus', *NTS* v (1958–9), pp. 260–72.
[7] Cuthbert Lattey, *Exp. T.* xxxv (1923–4), pp. 42f.

concerning all known papyri and uncial manuscripts that contain Rom. 9: 5.)

In estimating the significance of the preceding data one should also take into account the quite erratic punctuation contained in early manuscripts for other verses of chap. 9. Thus, codex Vaticanus has a colon at the end of 9: 3, after both occurrences of Ἰσραήλ in verse 6, after Ἀβραάμ in verse 7, Ῥεβέκκα in verse 10, and αὐτοῦ in verse 22! Codex Alexandrinus has a colon after μεγάλη in verse 2, one between Χριστοῦ and ὑπέρ and another after σάρκα in verse 3, and one after Ἰσραηλῖται in verse 4.

In the light of the preceding data perhaps the most that can be inferred from the presence of a point in the middle position after σάρκα in a majority of the uncial manuscripts is that scribes felt that some kind of pause was appropriate at this juncture in the sentence. From such palaeographical information, however, one cannot determine what kind of punctuation, if any, Paul in dictating the epistle, or Tertius in transcribing it, would have regarded as appropriate. In any case, editorial conventions of punctuating Greek today are more precise and far more rigorously applied than was true when scribes copied literary documents in antiquity.

ADDENDUM: A CONJECTURAL EMENDATION OF THE TEXT OF ROM. 9: 5

Three centuries ago the Socinian Jonas Schlichting (*Lat.* Slichtingius) proposed, but later rejected, the conjecture that instead of ὁ ὤν Paul dictated ὤν ὁ, and that Tertius or a subsequent copyist reversed the sequence of the letters. The conjecture was taken up by Samuel Crell (not to be confused with the eminent commentator Johann Crell) in the *Initium Evangelii Sancti Johannis restitutum* (Amsterdam, 1726), published under the pseudonym of L. M. Artemonius, and was subsequently adopted by Whiston, Whitby, John Taylor of Norwich, Goadby, Wakefield, Bp. Edmund Law, and, in more modern times, by K. Barth and G. Harder. The conjecture, it must be admitted, is superficially attractive[8] in that it produces a clause parallel to those that

---

[8] For several examples of the same kind of textual corruption in manuscripts of the classics, see W. L. Lorimer's note entitled 'Romans ix. 3–5', in *NTS* xiii (1966–7), pp. 385f. Lorimer offers yet another conjecture: ὤν ὁ ἐπὶ πάντων θεός, ⟨ὁ ὤν⟩ εὐλογητὸς εἰς τοὺς αἰῶνας, ἀμήν.

4-2

precede: 'Whose is the adoption . . . whose are the fathers . . . of whom is the Christ . . . whose is God over all.'

There are, however, several reasons why the conjecture should be rejected. (*a*) The presence of καί before ἐξ ὧν suggests that the author intended this item to be the final one of the series of clauses that are introduced by ὧν. (*b*) If ὧν ὁ were original, one would have expected that εὐλογητός would have had the definite article. (*c*) It is not likely that Paul would affirm that the Jews had an exclusive interest in the one true God when he had earlier in the same epistle asserted the contrary ('Or is God the God of the Jews only? Is he not the God of Gentiles also? Yes, of Gentiles also', 3: 29). (*d*) It is unwise to adopt a conjecture arising from a doctrinal difficulty, especially when the text of the manuscripts is not so difficult as to be impossible.

II. THE TRANSLATION OF ROM. 9: 5 IN THE EARLY VERSIONS

Inasmuch as every translation is also a commentary reflecting the translator's interpretation of the vocabulary and syntax of the original, it is appropriate to inquire how the early versions of the Epistle to the Romans have construed the sentence under examination.

Among witnesses to the Latin Bible, codex Amiatinus, generally regarded as the best manuscript of the Vulgate, lacks marks of punctuation but divides the text into stichoi. Rom. 9: 5 in that manuscript reads as follows:

> quorum patres et ex quibus Christus secundum carnem
> qui est super omnia Deus benedictus in saecula amen.[9]

Although from a grammatical point of view it is possible to take the second stichos as an independent sentence, the rhythm of the sentence certainly leads the reader to regard *qui* as qualifying *Christus*. Like the Greek text of codex Claromontanus, the Latin text of this bilingual manuscript is also arranged in stichoi, which, according to Tischendorf's edition, correspond in Rom. 9: 5 to the divisions of the Greek text (see section I above). The peculiarity of the Greek text of codex Augiensis (F^p), namely having a point after virtually every word, is not true of the Latin text; according to Scrivener's edition, the only

[9] The text and stichoi of codex Amiatinus are reproduced by Wordsworth and White in their edition of the Latin Vulgate.

marks of punctuation in Rom. 9: 5 are suspended points standing after *carnem* and *amen*.

The recently published Old Latin fragments of Paul in the tenth century Monsa manuscript contains a certain amount of punctuation. In the case of Rom. 9: 5, however, the scribe dispenses with all punctuation, except for setting off *amen* by using a suspended point before and after the word.[10]

The Peshitta Syriac version (Bible Society's edition) reads, '... from whom the Messiah appeared in the flesh, who is God over all; to whom be praises and benedictions for ever and ever, amen'.

The Harclean Syriac (White's edition) reads, '... from whom (is) the Messiah, as regards the flesh, he who is above all, God blessed for ever, amen'.

Of the two principal Coptic versions the Sahidic (Horner's edition as well as the Beatty MS edited by Thompson) reads, '... out of whom the Christ came according to flesh, God who (is) over all, who is blessed for ever, amen'. The Bohairic (Horner's edition) reads, '... from them came the Christ according to flesh, he who is set [or, put] over all, God who (is) blessed for ever, amen'.

The Gothic version (Streitberg's edition) reads, '... from whom is Christ according to flesh, who is above all, God blessed for ever, amen'.

The Armenian version (Zohrab's edition) reads, '... from whom is Christ according to the flesh, who is above all, God blessed for ever, amen'.

The Ethiopic version (in Walton's Polyglot) reads, '... from whom Christ was born according to the flesh of man, who is God blessed for ever, amen'. The Bible Society's edition agrees, but adds 'and ever' after 'for ever'.

By way of summary of the evidence of the early versions, one observes a certain amount of variation in the manner in which the several translators have handled ἐπὶ πάντων, some putting it before 'God' and some after, and the Ethiopic omitting the phrase entirely. But almost all of the versions (the Latin is ambiguous) agree in taking ὁ ὢν κ.τ.λ. as describing Christ.

[10] See H. J. Frede, *Altlateinische Paulus-Handschriften* (Freiburg, 1964), p. 245.

III. PATRISTIC INTERPRETATION OF ROM. 9: 5

During the eighteenth and nineteenth centuries commentators on the Epistle to the Romans collected a wide spectrum of patristic testimonies bearing on the interpretation of 9: 5. What is perhaps the fullest such enumeration of Christian writers who have referred ὁ ὢν κ.τ.λ. to Christ was that assembled by Dean J. W. Burgon. This doughty defender of the Authorized Version counted up '55 illustrious names', 40 of Greek writers from Irenaeus in the latter part of the second century to John of Damascus in the eighth, and 15 of Latin writers, from Tertullian at the beginning of the third century to Facundus of the sixth, who 'all see in Rom. ix. 5 a glorious assertion of the eternal Godhead of CHRIST'.[11] Burgon's list, however, required some sifting, for he had included in his list of 'illustrious names' several writers who are anonymous and others whose testimony is quite ambiguous.[12]

Still, after making all necessary deductions, there is a not inconsiderable number of early Fathers who took the words ὁ ὢν κ.τ.λ. as qualifying ὁ Χριστός. Thus, in the second century they were taken in this way by Irenaeus (*Contra haer.* III. xvii. 2, ed. Harvey) and in the third century by Tertullian (*Adv. Prax.* 13 and 15), Hippolytus (*Cont. Noët.* 6), Novatian (*Trin.* 13), Cyprian (*Test.* ii. 6), and six bishops in a letter addressed to Paul of Samosata (*Concilium Antioch. adv. Paul. Samos.*, in Routh, *Reliquiae sacrae*, 2nd ed., iii, 291–2). For writers in the fourth and following centuries, it will be enough to mention, without specifying their works, the names of Athanasius, Epiphanius, Basil, Gregory of Nyssa, Chrysostom, Theodoret, Augustine, Jerome, Cyril of Alexandria, and Oecumenius.[13] Some of these Fathers quote Rom. 9: 5 many times. According to information kindly supplied by P. Bonifatius Fischer, the files of Latin patristic citations, collected in the Vetus Latina Institute at Beuron, contain for Rom. 9: 5 about three hundred items. Most of them, as would be expected in view of the

---

11 'New Testament Revision', *Quarterly Review* cliii (1882), pp. 54ff. (= American ed. *London Quarterly Review* cliii (1882), pp. 29f.); reprinted, with minor additions, in Burgon's *The Revision Revised* (London, 1883), pp. 212f.

12 For corrigenda to the Dean's list, see Abbot, *JBL* [i] (1881 (1882)), pp. 134ff. (= *Critical Essays*, pp. 387ff.).

13 For an extended list of patristic passages in which Rom. 9: 5 is cited, see Alfred Durand, 'La divinité de Jésus-Christ dans S. Paul, Rom ix, 5', *RB* xii (1903), pp. 550–70.

anti-Arian controversy, interpret the concluding words as descriptive of Christ.

Relatively few patristic writers took the words ὁ ὢν κ.τ.λ. as referring to God the Father.[14] Among the orthodox Greek Fathers one can mention only Diodore of Tarsus[15] and Photius.[16]

In assessing the weight of the patristic evidence one must put it within its proper perspective. On the one hand, certainly the Greek Fathers must be supposed to have possessed a unique sensitivity to understand the nuances of a passage written in their own language. On the other hand, however, in the present case the possibility must be allowed that dogmatic interests may have swayed (and in many instances undoubtedly did sway) their interpretation. It is therefore prudent to refrain from assigning much weight to the overwhelming consensus of patristic interpretation of the meaning of the passage in question. In fact, the prevailing patristic interpretation of the passage is altogether counterbalanced by what we have seen came to be the prevailing scribal tradition of punctuation in the later manuscripts (see pp. 97–9 above), each tradition neutralizing, so to speak, the force of the other.

IV. THE GRAMMAR AND STRUCTURE OF ROM. 9: 5

A discussion of grammatical and contextual aspects of the meaning of the passage under question necessarily involves probabilities of interpretation. In evaluating the several arguments one must weigh one set of considerations against another, with the result that, in some cases, the balance will be differently estimated by different exegetes.

(A) The expression τὸ κατὰ σάρκα qualifies the apostle's statement concerning the Christ: Paul here states that the Christ was descended from the Israelites. If Christ did not have some other relation, or stand

---

[14] The numerous patristic comments collected by Wetstein, stating that the words ὁ ἐπὶ πάντων θεός cannot be used of the Son, are not to the point, for, as Sanday and Headlam point out, in these passages the Son 'is called not ὁ ἐπὶ πάντων θεός, but ἐπὶ πάντων θεός, and some of the writers that he quotes expressly interpret the passage of the Christ elsewhere' (*A Critical and Exegetical Commentary on the Epistle to the Romans*, p. 234).

[15] In Cramer's *Catenae in Sancti Pauli Epistolam ad Romanos* (Oxford, 1844), p. 162, lines 25–7.

[16] *Contra Manichaeos* iii, 14 (Migne, *P.G.* cii, 157 B).

in some other position besides this one connected with the Jews, and different from it, there would seem to be no occasion for mentioning any such limitation. In other words, Paul's language here, having called attention to the human ancestry of Christ as a Jew ('according to the flesh'), naturally implies that he was more than a Jew. An altogether parallel case occurs in the opening salutation of this Epistle (1: 3–4). There Paul describes the human descent of Jesus Christ from David, but expressly limits it κατὰ σάρκα and then in contrast affirms that the same Jesus was installed as Son of God with power κατὰ πνεῦμα ἁγιωσύνης when he was raised from the dead. In fact, one may go so far as to affirm that there is no instance in the New Testament where κατὰ σάρκα is used, in which some such contrast is not plainly intended.

So far there can be little controversy. The main question, however, as related to the phrase τὸ κατὰ σάρκα in the present verse is, not whether a contrast is intended, but whether it is expressed. Diametrically opposite answers have been given to this question.

On the one hand, it has been argued[17] that the phrase τὸ κατὰ σάρκα *requires* an antithetical reference to Christ's divine nature, and that in fact such a declaration is set forth in the following words ὁ ὢν ἐπὶ πάντων θεός. But the assertion that κατὰ σάρκα *demands* that a following antithesis be expressed, not only cannot be proved; it is, in fact, contradicted by the presence of several examples in the Pauline Epistles where the antithesis is implied but not expressed. For example, in verse 3 of the same chapter, Paul refers to the Israelites as 'my kinsmen κατὰ σάρκα', and yet says nothing about them in any other relationship.

On the other hand, it has been argued by some scholars[18] that in Greek the phrase τὸ κατὰ σάρκα differs in force from κατὰ σάρκα, and that the former contains in itself an expression of contrast, thus excluding any further antithesis. But such a doctrinaire objection rests upon too rigid a view of the possibilities of the Greek language in expressing the apostle's thoughts. Apart from examples in the Greek classics where a similar prepositional phrase, preceded by the accusative of the article, occurs with a correlative contrasting expression,[19] the argument is

---

[17] For example, in the nineteenth century by J. P. Lange, *Commentary, ad loc.*

[18] Notably by W. A. van Hengel, *Interpretatio Epistolae Pauli ad Romanos*, ii (Utrecht, 1859), pp. 347–53.

[19] E.g., Xenophon, *Cyr.* v, 4, 11; Plato, *Minos*, 320 c; see Raphael Kühner–Bernhard Gerth, *Ausführliche Grammatik der griechischen Sprache*, 3te Aufl., ii, 1 (Hannover, 1898), pp. 317f.

beside the point, for on the supposition that ὁ ὤν κ.τ.λ. refers to Christ, we have not a formal antithesis, such as would be excluded by van Hengel's rule, but simply an appositional, descriptive clause, setting forth the exalted dignity of him who as to the flesh sprang from the Jews.

From the foregoing it appears that no absolutely necessary argument pro or con can be based on the presence of the expression τὸ κατὰ σάρκα. The most that can be said rests upon degrees of probability, and this has been set forth with admirable succinctness in the following series: '(a) The expression τὸ κατὰ σάρκα naturally and necessarily suggests the idea of contrast; (b) this contrast, though indeed it may not always be expressed, will probably be expressed whenever the thought can be brought out more clearly or more impressively by this means; (c) in the present case it is evident that the greatest force is given to the words, if the antithesis is distinctly stated; (d) therefore, in this case the phrase τὸ κατὰ σάρκα throws the presumption in favour of the view which holds that we have a statement of the antithesis within the sentence; (e) inasmuch as the clause ὁ ὤν κ.τ.λ. may be interpreted in such a way as to answer the purpose of an antithesis (even expressing it in the manner best adapted to the carrying out of a design which the writer manifestly has in mind), and inasmuch as there is nothing else in the verses which can answer this purpose, the probability is that this verse does express what τὸ κατὰ σάρκα suggests or calls for'.[20]

(B) The next words which require attention are ὁ ὤν ἐπὶ πάντων θεός. Certainly it must be admitted that the most natural way to take the grammar of these words is to refer ὁ ὤν to the immediately preceding nominative (ὁ Χριστός). An almost exactly parallel instance occurs in 2 Cor. 11: 31, where the apostle writes ὁ θεὸς καὶ πατὴρ τοῦ κυρίου Ἰησοῦ οἶδεν, ὁ ὤν εὐλογητὸς εἰς τοὺς αἰῶνας, ὅτι οὐ ψεύδομαι. Here the expression ὁ ὤν is obviously relatival in character and equivalent to ὅς ἐστιν. Put another way, in Rom. 9: 5 it is grammatically unnatural that a participle which stands in juxtaposition to the phrase ὁ Χριστὸς τὸ κατὰ σάρκα 'should first be divorced from it and then given the force of a wish, receiving a different person as its subject'.[21]

If, on the other hand, despite its awkwardness, the clause ὁ ὤν κ.τ.λ. is taken as an asyndetic doxology to God the Father, another difficulty

---

[20] Timothy Dwight, 'On Romans ix. 5', *JBL* [i] (1881 (1882)), p. 29.
[21] Nigel Turner, *Grammatical Insights into the New Testament* (Edinburgh, 1965), p. 15.

(besides its awkwardness) arises. In this case the word ὤν becomes superfluous, for 'he who is God over all' is most simply represented in Greek by ὁ ἐπὶ πάντων θεός.[22] The presence of the participle suggests that the clause functions as a relative clause (not 'he who is ...' but 'who is ...'), and thus describes ὁ Χριστός as being 'God over all'.

So far, therefore, as Greek grammar and usage are concerned, it must be concluded that the words ὁ ὤν are more naturally connected with ὁ Χριστός as a descriptive clause than with the following words as the beginning of a new and independent sentence.

(c) Yet another difficulty which stands in the way of construing verse 5b as an asyndetic doxology is that such an interpretation runs contrary to Pauline doxologies elsewhere. In every other case in the epistles ascribed to Paul (as well as in other New Testament epistles) instead of being asyndetic, doxologies are always attached to some preceding word. In Rom. 1: 25 Paul, having mentioned the Creator (τὸν κτίσαντα), continues with the statement, ὅς ἐστιν εὐλογητὸς εἰς τοὺς αἰῶνας · ἀμήν. In 2 Cor. 11: 31, as was pointed out earlier, Paul uses ὁ ὤν in the asseveration, ὁ θεὸς καὶ πατὴρ τοῦ κυρίου Ἰησοῦ οἶδεν, ὁ ὤν εὐλογητὸς εἰς τοὺς αἰῶνας, ὅτι οὐ ψεύδομαι. In Gal. 1: 5, after mentioning God the Father, Paul continues, ᾧ ἡ δόξα εἰς τοὺς αἰῶνας τῶν αἰώνων, ἀμήν. In 2 Tim. 4: 18, Heb. 13: 21, and 1 Pet. 4: 11 the writers use the same syntactical expression (ᾧ) in ascribing glory to God or to Jesus Christ. In Rom. 11: 36, Eph. 3: 21, 1 Pet. 5: 11, and 2 Pet. 3: 18 αὐτῷ links the doxology with what precedes. Finally, in Phil. 4: 20 and 1 Tim. 1: 17 the doxology follows directly upon τῷ δὲ θεῷ. In none of these cases is the doxology asyndetic; Paul and the other New Testament writers always link it to what immediately precedes in the sentence.

From the foregoing examples it must be concluded that the most natural way of construing Rom. 9: 5 is to take ὁ ὤν κ.τ.λ. with the immediately preceding ὁ Χριστὸς τὸ κατὰ σάρκα.

(D) There is still another consideration which also argues in favour of taking the words ὁ ὤν κ.τ.λ. as a descriptive clause referring to Christ rather than as a doxology to God the Father.[23] This involves

---

[22] According to Sanday and Headlam 'no instance seems to occur, at least in the N.T., of the participle ὤν being used with a prepositional phrase and the noun which the prepositional phrase qualifies' (*op. cit.*, p. 236).

[23] The language here is deliberately chosen, for, despite loose statements to the contrary, the words ὁ ὤν κ.τ.λ. constitute a doxology only if they are taken asyndetically; otherwise they are a descriptive clause (to be sure, of doxological

the position in the sentence of the word εὐλογητός, which occurs just where we should expect to find it, provided the clause qualifies ὁ Χριστός, but it does not occupy the place in the order of the sentence which it regularly holds in doxologies. An examination of the *usus loquendi* of εὐλογητός in the Septuagint shows that it almost[24] invariably stands first before the name of God.[25] Likewise in Semitic inscriptions asyndetic doxologies are always constructed with the verbal adjective (Heb. בָּרוּךְ, Aram. בְּרִיךְ) preceding the name of God, never following it.[26]

That is to say, throughout the Hebrew Bible and reflected in every instance except one in the Septuagint (see footnote 24), as well as in Semitic inscriptions, the consistent pattern for expressing doxologies is 'blessed be God' or 'blessed be the Lord', and not 'God blessed' or 'Lord blessed'. This being the case, it appears to be altogether incredible that Paul, whose ear must have been perfectly familiar with this constantly recurring formula of praise, should in this solitary instance have departed from the established usage. The passage therefore ought not to be considered as a doxology, or an ascription of praise to God, and rendered 'God be blessed', but should be taken as a declaration referring to Christ, 'who is blessed'.

(E) We may now look at the wider context in seeking to determine which interpretation best suits the argument in the preceding verses. Chapter 9 opens with an expression of the apostle's 'great sorrow and unceasing anguish' (verse 2) arising from the reluctance of Jews to become believers in Christ. With tender affection for his kinsmen by

content) qualifying ὁ Χριστός. Hence it is not to the point to argue, as some have done, that only in the later writings of the New Testament do we find doxologies to Christ (2 Tim. 4: 18; Heb. 13: 21; 2 Pet. 3: 18), as though this circumstance tips the scales in favour of taking Rom. 9: 5 as a doxology to God the Father.

[24] The only instance which appears to be an exception is Ps. 68: 19 (= LXX 67: 19–20), where the Septuagint reads κύριος ὁ θεὸς εὐλογητός, εὐλογητὸς κύριος ἡμέραν καθ᾽ ἡμέραν. Here, however, since the first εὐλογητός has no corresponding word in Hebrew, it appears to be an erroneous double translation, the first part of which is probably not a doxology, but a simple affirmation, as in the Old Latin version, *Dominus Deus benedictus est*. In the Hebrew it is, as in all other cases, 'Blessed be the Lord'.

[25] Gen. 9: 26; 14: 20; 24: 27, 31; Exod. 18: 10; Ruth 4: 14; 1 Sam. 25: 32, 39; 2 Sam. 18: 28; 1 Kings 1: 48; 5: 7; 8: 15, 56; 2 Chron. 2: 12; 6: 4; Neh. 4: 40; Ezra 7: 27; Ps. 18: 46; 28: 6; 31: 21; 41: 13; 66: 20; 68: 35; 72: 18; 89: 52; 106: 48; 119: 12; 124: 6; 135: 1; 144: 1; Zech. 11: 5.

[26] Mark Lidzbarski, *Handbuch der Nordsemitischen Epigraphik*, 1. Theil, *Text* (Weimar, 1898), p. 153.

race Paul goes so far as to say, 'I could wish that I myself were cut off from Christ for the sake of my brethren' (verse 3). It is particularly in view of the prerogatives which God had given to Israel that Paul feels so poignantly the incongruity of their present unbelief. The enumeration of these privileges and promises rises to a climax when the apostle reminds his readers that it was from their own Jewish lineage that the Christ in his human nature had come. In such a context it certainly is supremely appropriate to take the clause ὁ ὢν ἐπὶ πάντων θεὸς εὐλογητὸς εἰς τοὺς αἰῶνας as the capstone of a series which measures, on the one hand, the greatness of the divine privileges offered in the Gospel and, on the other hand, the inanity of the Jews in rejecting that Gospel. Such an interpretation gives a clear and coherent account of the passage and of Paul's emotions lying behind the passage.

On the other hand, to take the concluding words of verse 5 as a doxology introduces a discordant note into the development of the writer's thought and mood. It was not the habit of the apostle to break out into irrelevant ascriptions of praise, and certainly there is nothing in the immediate context requiring one. Although, in accord with abbrinical usage, Paul occasionally introduces an exclamation of praise (e.g. Rom. 1: 25; Gal. 1: 5; 2 Cor. 11: 32), he never does so except when God is the immediate subject of discourse. But here in Rom. 9: 5 there is no previous mention of the name of God. Moreover, in view of the apostle's lamentation over the lapse of the Jews from appropriating to the full their divinely granted prerogatives, there appears to be no psychological explanation that would account for the introduction of a joyful doxology addressed to the Father. Both logically and emotionally such a doxology would interrupt the train of thought as well as be inconsistent with the mood of sadness that pervades the preceding verses.

By way of summarizing the points made in this section concerning the grammar and structure of Rom. 9: 5, it is suggested that the rhythm of the sentence is more easy and natural if it be allowed to flow continuously down to 'amen'. In this way the declaration that Christ came τὸ κατὰ σάρκα finds an appropriate antithesis in the following description ὁ ὢν ἐπὶ πάντων θεός, the presence of the participle suggesting that the clause functions as a relative clause. On the other hand, to take the clause as an asyndetic doxology is contrary both to the usage of Paul in introducing such ascriptions of praise as an integral part of the sentence, and to the manner in which doxologies are constructed, according to which εὐλογητός stands first, and θεός in the predicate. Finally, whereas a clause that makes a solemn assertion concerning the person of Christ is in place in a sombre context, a joyful doxology addressed to the Father is out of harmony with the apostle's sorrowful mood.

V. CONCLUDING COMMENTS

So far in the discussion of the punctuation of Rom. 9: 5 we have examined evidence from Greek manuscripts, the early versions, and the Fathers, as well as a variety of grammatical considerations that bear upon the construction of the verse. In some cases the evidence is of questionable authority. Such, for example, are the traditions – so curiously antithetical – embodied on the one hand in the punctuation of later Greek manuscripts and on the other hand expressed in what can be fairly designated as the *consensus patrum*. At the same time, the interpretation of the meaning of the Greek as reflected in the early versions, several of which antedate the formation of either the palaeographical or the patristic traditions, favours taking the clause ὁ ὢν κ.τ.λ. as qualifying Christ. Likewise in the discussion of the balance of presumptions relating to the grammar and structure of the verse we found that the cumulative weight of the several kinds of considerations decidedly supports taking the concluding words of the verse as a description of Christ.

In the light of the foregoing discussion it can scarcely be denied that if one confines one's attention to the verse itself, the balance of probabilities favours referring θεός to Christ. But of course no single statement in a document should be interpreted in isolation from what that author has written elsewhere. In this case, although nowhere else in his genuine epistles[27] that have come down to us does Paul designate Christ as θεός, the apostle frequently speaks of Christ in the most exalted language. He calls him the Lord of glory (1 Cor. 2: 8) and the

---

[27] Tit. 2: 13 is generally regarded as deutero-Pauline. At the same time, as a modern writer points out, 'it may be argued that, whether or not they were written by Paul, the Pastorals are a homogeneous development of Pauline usage; thus the usage in Tit. 2: 13 *may* be interpreted as a continuation of Paul's own way of speaking already instanced in Rom. 9: 5' (Raymond E. Brown, 'Does the New Testament Call Jesus God?', *Theological Studies*, xxvi (1965), p. 560 note 35 (= *Jesus: God and Man, Modern Biblical Reflections* (Milwaukee, 1967), p. 21 note 35)).

Lord of the living and the dead (Rom. 14: 9). He represents him as the one through whom all things hold together (Col. 1: 17), as having a name that is above every name (Phil. 2: 9), and as the one to whom all things in heaven and earth and under the earth are to bow (Phil. 2: 10). He speaks of him as the image of God (2 Cor. 4: 4; Col. 1: 15) and as the power and the wisdom of God (1 Cor. 1: 24). Still more significant, Paul thinks of Christ as pre-existent (Gal. 4: 4; 2 Cor. 8: 9), and can even designate him not only as being ἐν μορφῇ θεοῦ but also, in some fashion, as involving τὸ εἶναι ἴσα θεῷ (Phil. 2: 6).

These and other statements like them in the Pauline Epistles indicate how very, very greatly the monotheism of rabbi Saul of Tarsus had been modified after his encounter with the risen Lord Jesus (Gal. 1: 16). The ultimate question is, of course, whether it is conceivable that Paul, as we know his mind from statements such as those just mentioned, would also have expressed his sense of Christ's greatness by calling him 'God (θεός – not, be it noted, ὁ θεός) blessed for ever'. To this question different exegetes, equally learned and equally devout, have given different answers. Those who interpret Rom. 9: 5 as containing a doxology to God the Father do so principally on the ground that elsewhere Paul stops short of designating Jesus as θεός. Thus the decisive argument is one which is external to the passage under consideration. On the other hand, the grounds which are urged by those who interpret ὁ ὤν κ.τ.λ. as descriptive of Christ fall within the limits of the wording of the passage itself. Both kinds of argumentation are licit, and may be of value and strength. But the exegete is confronted with the question which kind of considerations (those internal to the passage under consideration or those external) should be allowed the greater weight.

It appears to the present writer that normally considerations which belong to the words themselves, as they stand in the passage itself, should be permitted to carry the greater weight, because a writer may turn aside from his ordinary usage, or even start a new one, in some particular sentence. To deny that an author may on occasion, if he wishes, vary his style would mean that there could be no *hapax legomena* in his writings. But if one allows that such a principle holds good in purely lexical matters, there seems to be no reason why it should not also be allowed to operate with reference to *hapax legomena* among doctrinal statements. Let it be supposed, for the sake of the argument, that Paul on one occasion wanted to state that 'Christ is over all, God blessed for ever'. If now the exegete rigidly adheres to the principle that Paul's christological statements elsewhere in his epistles must be regarded as the controlling factor in estimating the meaning of any one particular statement, it is obvious that such a principle of interpretation will prevent the exegete from learning the mind of the apostle in the sole passage that stands outside the general run of such statements. In this connection it must be admitted that there are, of course, limits beyond which it is not thinkable that Paul would permit himself to go. For example, if we found a statement in his epistles which seemed to imply that the Son was superior in glory and majesty to the Father, it would be entirely proper for the exegete to seek to interpret that passage in accord with what Paul says elsewhere concerning the subordination of the Son to the Father. In the instance which has been under consideration, however, it appears to the present writer to be no great step from the high christology, expressed in the Pauline statements mentioned earlier, to the statement in Rom. 9: 5, as interpreted according to the internal grammatical and structural requirements of that passage.

It is, of course, most precarious to invoke psychological considerations as to what was, or was not, possible for Paul to write. Exactly opposite arguments of this kind have been urged against taking Rom. 9: 5 as referring to Christ. On the one hand, it has been alleged that Jewish monotheism was so deeply ingrained in the mind of the apostle that he could not have identified Jesus with God. On the other hand, it has also been argued that, if Paul frankly referred to Christ as God in Rom. 9: 5, he would have done so in his other epistles too.

One wonders, however, whether, as a recent writer has put it, 'we are in a position to say with an air of finality what was psychologically impossible for Paul. We are certainly not in a position to say that he was incapable of inconsistencies. His surviving works are small in quantity. If one or two thoughts which they contain do not seem to harmonize with the rest, we ought not to imagine that we can resolve the apparent discord only by finding a different interpretation of the Greek.'[28] The reason why there are so few statements in Paul's epistles bearing on the essential nature of Christ (ὁ ὤν . . .) is doubtless connected with a feature often noticed by others, namely that the apostle, for purposes of instruction bearing on Christian nurture,

---

[28] Arthur W. Wainwright, *The Trinity in the New Testament* (London, 1962), p. 57.

usually prefers to speak of the functional rather than the ontological relationships of Christ.[29]

The implications of the foregoing considerations, as they bear on the several patterns of punctuation that have been proposed for Rom. 9: 5 (see pp. 95–6 above), is that nos. 5*b* through 8, all of which make a more or less sharp break between θεός and what precedes, fail to commend themselves on the grounds set forth above under sections II and IV. Furthermore, the proposal to take ὁ ὤν as a surrogate for God (as in 5*a* and 5*b*) seems to be, in the context of Rom. 9, entirely impossible stylistically.

Among the other ways of punctuating the sentence, all of which appear to be legitimate on the basis of the preceding discussion, the one that seems to be most in harmony with the thought of the apostle, as well as in accord with the conventions of modern editors of Greek texts, is no. 1, namely καὶ ἐξ ὧν ὁ Χριστὸς τὸ κατὰ σάρκα, ὁ ὢν ἐπὶ πάντων θεὸς εὐλογητὸς εἰς τοὺς αἰῶνας, ἀμήν.

[29] So, e.g., Oscar Cullmann, *The Christology of the New Testament*, rev. ed. (Philadelphia, 1963), pp. 3ff.

8

Jesus: Anathema or Kyrios (1 Cor. 12: 3)

W. C. VAN UNNIK

In 1951 the churches of Greece celebrated the 1,900th anniversary of St Paul's coming to Europe, and organized a pilgrimage to all the places in the country in which the apostle preached according to the New Testament. It was a large ecumenical event in which leaders and youth-groups of many countries participated, together with a number of representatives of theological schools, mainly New Testament scholars. Whether the date was correct from the chronological point of view or not, may be a matter of dispute. But to me that question was of little importance as compared with the lasting effects the experience of this celebration had for me. One of them, and not the least, was my meeting with the Rev. C. F. D. Moule, then Dean of Clare College, Cambridge: a tiny figure under an enormous white linen hat, much like a mushroom, with sparkling eyes. That meeting resulted in a friendship that has grown in breadth and depth ever since, and all those who share with me that privilege know what that means. So it was St Paul who brought us together; hence it is obvious that I should look for a topic, for a contribution to the *Festschrift* in honour of him who has now occupied for many years the Lady Margaret's chair with such great distinction, in one of the apostle's letters to Greece. The editors defined the areas of christology and pneumatology in the New Testament as the main themes. Taking up these leads of 'reminiscence' and 'duty', I see these lines all point in one direction, namely 1 Cor. 12: 3: διὸ γνωρίζω ὑμῖν ὅτι οὐδεὶς ἐν πνεύματι θεοῦ λαλῶν λέγει · ΑΝΑΘΕΜΑ ΙΗΣΟΥΣ, καὶ οὐδεὶς δύναται εἰπεῖν · ΚΥΡΙΟΣ ΙΗΣΟΥΣ, εἰ μὴ ἐν πνεύματι ἁγίῳ.

This verse is still a *crux interpretum*, and different solutions have been proposed in the course of the years, most recently in studies by E. de Broglie, K. Maly, J. P. Versteeg and T. Holtz,[1] and in contemporary

---

[1] E. de Broglie, 'Le texte fondamental de Saint Paul contre la foi naturelle (1 Cor. xii. 3)', *RSR* xxxix (1951), pp. 253–66; K. Maly, '1 Kor. 12: 1–3, eine Regel zur Unterscheidung der Geister?', *BZ* x (1966), pp. 82–95; J. P. Versteeg, *Christus*

commentaries such as those of C. K. Barrett, H. Conzelmann and F. F. Bruce.[2] These books and articles form the background of this paper, to which readers may be referred for further clarification. I wish to apologize for the fact that I could not enter into a full discussion of the views expressed there, and that I have not more frequently indicated the points of agreement or disagreement. But the limits set to this paper prevented me from doing so.

The main problems are these:

(*a*) What is meant by ἀνάθεμα Ἰησοῦς? And is it not a complete truism to maintain that this can never be said under the inspiration of God's Spirit?

(*b*) Why can the Christian confession κύριος Ἰησοῦς only be made under the inspiration of the Spirit?

Is not that all self-evident? If so, it is hard to see why St Paul introduces it with the solemn declaration of a very important dogmatic statement: γνωρίζω.[3] It has often been thought that the apostle is giving here a criterion 'to distinguish the spirits'. But can it be supposed that the Christians in Corinth were so stupid as to think that 'cursed be Jesus' could be said by the Spirit of God?

An explanation that is much favoured today sees this word as directed against Gnostics who made a distinction between the ἄνω Χριστός and the κάτω Ἰησοῦς, the 'heavenly Christ' and the 'earthly Jesus', the former being confessed, the latter being cursed. In that case St Paul rejected this distinction by saying 'Jesus is Lord'. This explanation presupposes that St Paul had to do with 'Gnostics' in Corinth. It would take us too far afield if we were to discuss this thesis within the compass of this paper; therefore I cannot but state somewhat dogmatically that this thesis in general is, in my opinion, highly improbable; particularly in this case, because the contrast between the heavenly Christ and the earthly Jesus is only attested in much later sources, among Christian Gnostics who were familiar with Paul's letters. Be that as it may, this solution is only admissible if others are impossible. And the main reason which has prompted the present

---

en de Geest (Kampen, 1971), pp. 214ff.; T. Holtz, 'Das Kennzeichen des Geistes (1 Kor. xii. 1–3)', *NTS* xviii (1971–2), pp. 365–76.

[2] C. K. Barrett, *A Commentary on the First Epistle to the Corinthians* (London, 1968); H. Conzelmann, *Der erste Brief an die Korinther* (Göttingen, 1969); F. F. Bruce, *1 and 2 Corinthians* (London, 1971).

[3] This point was rightly stressed by F. J. Pop, *De eerste Brief van Paulus aan de Corinthiërs* (Nijkerk, 1965), p. 266.

contribution is that it seems to me that there is another way, unexplored so far, which is open as a means of understanding this verse.

In our discussion we shall concentrate our attention on the concrete expressions used in this verse, viz. *anathema Jēsous* and *Kyrios Jēsous*, and try to find out why Paul speaks of the absence and presence respectively of a relation with the Holy Spirit. This rule, which may seem self-evident, is laid down here *expressis verbis*, because in discussions of this passage there is sometimes a tendency to replace the former expression by words like 'the denial of the Christian faith', and the latter by something like 'the confession of the Christian faith'. St Paul however does not use such abstracts, but very definite formulas.

I

The great and obvious stumbling-block in this verse is the phrase ΑΝΑΘΕΜΑ ΙΗΣΟΥΣ, which, so far as I can see, is always and without exception translated as 'cursed be Jesus' (or an equivalent). Immediately some questions arise and certain observations can be made:

(*a*) Is it possible that Christians would utter these words? This idea is immediately rejected, but why does St Paul say so? He does not do it hypothetically, as if there could be people who might have dared to do so.

(*b*) It is remarkable that this utterance is not followed by words like μὴ γένοιτο. The apostle writes these words without any excitement or rebuke, which is rather strange.

(*c*) What is meant by this cursing? I know that swear words are often used just as forceful expressions without much thought. It can hardly be believed that that is the case here. But how could this be said about Jesus? The speaker does not say 'I reject Jesus', or something similar, but – according to the usual exegesis – wishes Jesus to be cursed. The case is here different from other places where St Paul uses the word ἀνάθεμα, because in Rom. 9: 3, 1 Cor. 16: 22, Gal. 1: 8 living persons are taken as the object of his wish. But how could that be said of Jesus who either was dead or lived in glory? How could a curse apply to him?

(*d*) It is always tacitly assumed without any argument that the verb to be supplemented is ἔστω, by analogy with 1 Cor. 16: 22 and Gal. 1: 8; whereas in the other declaration about Jesus, ἐστίν is added.[4] But

---

4 Cf. W. Foerster, *Herr ist Jesus* (Gütersloh, 1924), p. 122 n. 1: 'Wie zu den parallelen ἀνάθεμα ᾿Ιησοῦς ein ἔστω zu ergänzen ist, so zu κύριος ᾿Ιησοῦς ein ἐστίν' without further proof. This is typical.

grammatically these two statements have the same construction, and it is strange to give to the former the form of a wish and to the latter that of a declaration.

(*e*) According to Holtz these words were formed by St Paul by analogy with the Christian confession *Kyrios Jēsous*.[5] This seems somewhat improbable to me, for if he formed the expression *ad hoc*, why did he start with it without any introduction? It would have been highly startling and baffling to the Corinthian Christians, especially if it had been followed by the confession with which they were familiar. In order to understand what ἀνάθεμα meant for St Paul, let us free ourselves from all connotations we connect with the word 'cursed', and from the meaning 'excommunication' which it acquired in later Christian usage. Since there is in 1 Cor. 12: 3 no direct 'context' which might illustrate the word – the apostle uses it here as a well-known term – we shall have to look elsewhere in his letters.

A good starting-point is found in Rom. 9: 3, because there we find such a context: ηὐχόμην γὰρ ἀνάθεμα εἶναι αὐτὸς ἐγὼ ἀπὸ τοῦ Χριστοῦ ὑπὲρ τῶν ἀδελφῶν μου τῶν συγγενῶν μου κατὰ σάρκα.[6] After this, Paul enumerates the privileges by which the Jewish people were distinguished. St Paul wishes to be an *anathema* on behalf of his brethren. His attitude is compared by commentators[7] with that of Moses (Exod. 32: 32).[8] He 'erklärt seine Bereitschaft, dem Vertilgungs-fluch zu verfallen, wenn er dadurch sein Volk retten kann' (O. Michel). In various Jewish sources we find the idea that the death of somebody could be an atonement for the sin of others,[9] though there the idea is expressed by the word k^epara = ἱλασμός, and not ἀνάθεμα. However, the words used by St Paul suggest that for him to be an *anathema* can be beneficial to his fellow-Jews. It is clear from this

[5] T. Holtz, *loc. cit.*, p. 375 where he also mentions some predecessors.
[6] To avoid ambiguity in the use of ἀδελφός, Paul makes the double addition which stresses the national aspect; for him the bonds with his people had not been severed in becoming a follower of Jesus Christ.
[7] So e.g. C. K. Barrett, *A Commentary on the Epistle to the Romans* (London, 1957), p. 176; O. Michel, *Der Brief an die Römer* (Göttingen, 1963), p. 225, and many others; also in the margin of Nestle's edition of the New Testament.
[8] Although the very word ἀδελφός is not found in Exod. 32: 32: καὶ νῦν εἰ μὲν ἀφεὶς αὐτοῖς τὴν ἁμαρτίαν, ἄφες. εἰ δὲ μή, ἐξάλειψόν με ἐκ τῆς βίβλου σου (for the 'book' = 'book of life', see L. Kolp, 'Buch, IV', *RAC* ii, Sp. 627).
[9] Texts in H. L. Strack–P. Billerbeck, *Kommentar zum N.T. aus Talmud und Midrasch* (München, 1926), iii, pp. 260f.

passage, and from the wider context of Rom. 9–11, that he means the unbelieving Jews, who on the one hand have a special place in God's plan of salvation, belonging to God's elect people with certain prerogatives (cf. also Rom. 3:1ff.), and who on the other hand are disobedient to God's will, having rejected Jesus Christ, so that they are objects of God's ὀργή; for in this there is no distinction between Jew and pagan, as he has set forth in Rom. 1:18–2:29. What does *anathema* mean in this connection, and how can it benefit others?

It is common knowledge that ἀνάθεμα is a typically Jewish-Christian word and that it is used in the LXX as a translation of the Hebrew word *ḥērem*.[10] Wikgren wrote that in the New Testament 'the term means "cursed", but is moving away from the ritualistic force of the O.T. usage'.[11] It is doubtful if this is a correct description of the situation, since it does not explain the words of Rom. 9:3. Space does not permit a thorough discussion of the word,[12] but in examining the usage in the Septuagint we notice that it has two meanings: a thing that is devoted to God and a thing that is to be destroyed. These two sides are combined in Lev. 27:28f., particularly these words: πᾶν ἀνάθεμα ἅγιον ἁγίων ἔσται τῷ κυρίῳ. καὶ πᾶν, ὃ ἐὰν ἀνατεθῇ ἀπὸ τῶν ἀνθρώπων... θανάτῳ θανατωθήσεται. Here we find the well-known conception of holiness: what is consecrated to God must be taken out of general use and therefore destroyed. An extremely illuminating passage is Deut. 13:13–18. When there are people who try to lead a certain town to apostasy from God and to idolatry, then that city with all its inhabitants and its goods must be completely destroyed by sword and fire: ἀναθέματι ἀναθεματιεῖτε αὐτὴν καὶ πάντα τὰ ἐν αὐτῇ. Nothing may be spared: οὐ προσκολληθήσεται ἐν τῇ χειρί σου οὐδὲν ἀπὸ τοῦ ἀναθέματος, with this remarkable motive: ἵνα ἀποστραφῇ κύριος ἀπὸ θυμοῦ τῆς ὀργῆς αὐτοῦ καὶ δώσει σοι ἔλεος κ.τ.λ.[13]

[10] J. Behm, 'ἀνάθεμα', in Kittel, *TWNT* i, pp. 356f.; A. Wikgren, 'Anathema', *IDB* i, p. 125; C. Brekelmans, 'Ḥerèm, "Bann"', in E. Jenni–C. Westermann (ed.), *Theologisches Handwörterbuch zum A.T.* (München, 1971), i, pp. 635–7. It is very probable that the inscription from Megara that is often mentioned in the discussions of this word, and to which A. Deissmann was the first to draw attention (see his *Licht vom Osten*, Tübingen, ⁴1923, p. 74), reflects Jewish influence.

[11] A. Wikgren, *loc. cit.*, p. 125.

[12] For our purposes it is unnecessary to trace the historical development, although it would be interesting to investigate the interpretation of the LXX.

[13] Cf. also Deut. 7:26 (the same punishment is prescribed for Gentiles); Deut. 20:16ff. Deut. 13:13ff. is, I think, also the source of inspiration in Gal. 1:8f.:

This point is well illustrated in the famous story of Josh. 6–7: Jericho will be captured καὶ ἔσται ἡ πόλις ἀνάθεμα ... κυρίῳ σαβαωθ, except for Rahab and her house; ἀλλὰ ὑμεῖς φυλάξασθε σφόδρα ἀπὸ τοῦ ἀναθέματος, μήποτε ἐνθυμηθέντες ὑμεῖς αὐτοὶ λάβητε ἀπὸ τοῦ ἀναθέματος καὶ ποιήσητε τὴν παρεμβολὴν τῶν υἱῶν Ἰσραηλ ἀνάθεμα καὶ ἐκτρίψητε ἡμᾶς (Josh. 6: 17–18). Achan, however, is disobedient and takes some beautiful things from the *anathema*. When in the next expedition against Ai Israel is severely beaten and Joshua prays to God to know the reason why, the answer is that the people have stolen from the *anathema* and therefore they are defeated: ὅτι ἐγενήθησαν ἀνάθεμα. The Lord adds these words: οὐ προσθήσω ἔτι εἶναι μεθ᾽ ὑμῶν, [14] ἐὰν μὴ ἐξάρητε τὸ ἀνάθεμα ἐξ ὑμῶν αὐτῶν (Josh. 7: 12); Israel must sanctify itself, for: τὸ ἀνάθεμα ἐν ὑμῖν ἐστιν, οὐ δυνήσεσθε ἀντιστῆναι ἀπέναντι τῶν ἐχθρῶν ὑμῶν ἕως ἂν ἐξάρητε τὸ ἀνάθεμα ἐξ ὑμῶν (verse 13). Then Achan is found out and stoned with his whole family; [15] καὶ ἐπαύσατο κύριος τοῦ θυμοῦ τῆς ὀργῆς (verse 26). Here the motivation is similar to that in Deut. 13: 18. Although we notice in these O.T. passages a transition with regard to the concrete objects that are called *anathema* (the town and all that is in it; part of the booty; a curse that affects the people; the man who possesses that part of the 'ban' and is the cause of the curse), a clear concept of what was meant by *anathema* emerges. Apostasy from God and paganism must be blotted out completely by a 'ban', because they run counter to the will of God and arouse his wrath; if something is spared, the *anathema* spreads its pernicious effects on the whole people[16] and 'the Lord is not with them', so they are defeated. Only if the possessor of the *anathema* is destroyed is the wrath of God averted and blessing given. It is a serious lack, I think, in the studies devoted to *anathema* so far, that these aspects (God's wrath against the people, the averting of it and the return of God's

---

ἀλλὰ καὶ ἐὰν ἡμεῖς ἢ ἄγγελος ἐξ οὐρανοῦ ὑμῖν εὐαγγελίσηται παρ᾽ ὃ εὐηγγελισάμεθα ὑμῖν, ἀνάθεμα ἔστω... εἴ τις ὑμᾶς εὐαγγελίζεται παρ᾽ ὃ παρελάβετε, ἀνάθεμα ἔστω. This is a clear case of seducing to apostasy (an aspect which, as far as I can see, is not particularly stressed in the commentaries on Galatians, although it seems vital to me).

[14] See on this expression, my article 'Dominus Vobiscum', *New Testament Essays: Studies in memory of Thomas Walter Manson, 1893–1958* (Manchester, 1959), pp. 270–305.

[15] See on this punishment, H. W. Obbink, 'Enkele opmerkingen over de straf der steniging in het Oude Testament', *Hervormde Theologiese Studies* viii (Pretoria, 1951), pp. 110–18.

[16] Cf. 1 Sam. 15; although the actual term ἀνάθεμα and the verb are missing there.

blessing) seem to have been overlooked;[17] and yet they are essential elements in the whole concept.

This conceptual world may be very strange to us, but to St Paul it must have been a living reality, for it offers a clear answer to the question why he could wish to be an *anathema* on behalf of his unbelieving fellow-Jews. The sentence by which Michel paraphrased the idea of Rom. 9: 3, quoted above, is not complete, because it leaves unanswered the question why the sacrifice of destruction could save the people. It is found in these words of Deut. 13: 18: ἵνα ἀποστραφῇ κύριος ἀπὸ θυμοῦ τῆς ὀργῆς αὐτοῦ καὶ δώσει σοι ἔλεος.[18] The unbelievers deserved destruction under the wrath of God, but in their place St Paul wishes to be completely blotted out (ἀπὸ τοῦ Χριστοῦ, says he who lives ἐν Χριστῷ!) by taking upon himself the wrath of God and opening the way of God's mercy towards his people.

Now, having discovered the connotations which went with the word *anathema* for St Paul, we may return to our main question. In what way could this word be connected with Jesus? It should now have become clear that the combination *anathema Jēsous* was for St Paul not a swear-word or abnegation of Jesus by certain people, but had a very positive meaning, the underlying conception being seen in Rom. 9: 3 and Paul's Bible. The idea expressed by these words was that Jesus gave himself over as an *anathema* to complete destruction under the wrath of God and to separation from God, in order to save the people from that wrath and to give free course to God's mercy and blessing.[19]

Nowhere in the remaining letters of the apostle is this thought mentioned *expressis verbis*. This is not a very serious objection to this exegesis, because his epistles have preserved only a small part of his teaching and the light from Rom. 9: 3 is sufficient. There is, however, another text written by St Paul which offers a striking parallel to the thoughts connected with *anathema Jēsous* as we have defined them, and can help us to further clarification, although the idea is expressed in different wording. In his exposition of justification by faith and not by fulfilling the works of the Law in Galatians, St Paul writes (Gal. 3: 10):

[17] The conception of J. Pedersen, *Israel: Its Life and Culture* (London and Copenhagen, 1940), iii–iv, p. 29, that the soul of the enemies is 'incompatible with that of the Israelites', is too psychological, and does not do justice to the motifs mentioned in the texts.

[18] Cf. the prominent place of ἔλεος etc. in Rom. 9–11.

[19] Is this also the idea underlying John 11: 50: οὐδὲ λογίζεσθε ὅτι συμφέρει ὑμῖν ἵνα εἷς ἄνθρωπος ἀποθάνῃ ὑπὲρ τοῦ λαοῦ καὶ μὴ ὅλον τὸ ἔθνος ἀπόληται?

ὅσοι γὰρ ἐξ ἔργων νόμου εἰσίν, ὑπὸ κατάραν εἰσίν. γέγραπται γὰρ ὅτι ἐπικατάρατος πᾶς ὃς οὐκ ἐμμένει πᾶσιν τοῖς γεγραμμένοις ἐν τῷ βιβλίῳ τοῦ νόμου τοῦ ποιῆσαι αὐτά (Deut. 27: 26). St Paul reads this verse from Scripture not as a threat, but as a fact, because – this is the underlying thought – nobody is able to fulfil these commandments. Then he continues by saying in verse 13: Χριστὸς ἡμᾶς ἐξηγόρασεν ἐκ τῆς κατάρας τοῦ νόμου γενόμενος ὑπὲρ ἡμῶν κατάρα, ὅτι γέγραπται, ἐπικατάρατος πᾶς ὁ κρεμάμενος ἐπὶ ξύλου (Deut. 21: 23).[20] Because Jesus was crucified, this text could be applied to him, ξύλον and σταυρός being taken as synonyms.[21] In an interesting article the Dutch scholar W. S. van Leeuwen has investigated the ideas connected with this 'hanging on a tree' in Israel, and concludes that 'this death-penalty was used in Israel to take away the curse that was on and in the people through the wrath of God, and to restore the wholesome situation'.[22] This idea lies behind St Paul's argument.[23] The vicarious sacrifice of Jesus on the cross consisted in offering himself up by taking upon himself the curse according to the Law; he had now become κατάρα, and for him to be hanged meant the removal of the curse and therefore liberation for the people.

The conception behind Gal. 3: 13 is identical with that of *anathema*. Because St Paul argues in this passage in Galatians with these two Old Testament words using ἐπικατάρατος to describe what is going on, he had to use κατάρα and could not work with *anathema*. Moreover, he could make a link with the factual death of Jesus, his crucifixion.[24] From these data we may conclude that just as Paul could speak

[20] H. Ridderbos, *Aan de Romeinen* (Kampen, 1959), p. 205 (*ad* Rom. 9: 3) refers to this text in Galatians in connection with Exod. 32: 32, but does not mention 1 Cor. 12: 3 (this last text he mentions on p. 206, where he defines the word ἀνάθεμα as 'het door God of van Godswege aan de ondergang gewijde, ge-vloekte').

[21] W. S. van Leeuwen, 'Een zin van den kruisdood in de Synoptische Evangeliën, Ξύλον en Σταυρός', *Nieuwe Theologische Studiën* xxiv (1941), pp. 68–81, and the articles on ξύλον and σταυρός in Kittel, *TWNT*. Cf. Josephus' paraphrase of Gen. 40: 19, LXX: κρεμάσει σε ἐπὶ ξύλου, in *Ant. Jud.* ii. 5. 3. 73: αὐτὸν ἀνασταυρωθέντα.

[22] W. S. van Leeuwen, *loc. cit.*, p. 73 (my translation).

[23] Cf. also 2 Cor. 5: 21: τὸν μὴ γνόντα ἁμαρτίαν ὑπὲρ ἡμῶν ἁμαρτίαν ἐποίησεν, ἵνα ἡμεῖς γενώμεθα δικαιοσύνη θεοῦ ἐν αὐτῷ. That the crucifixion of Jesus is a 'stumbling-block for the Jews', precisely because of the curse that went with it, appears in Justin Martyr, *Dialogus cum Tryphone* 32, 1; 89, 2ff.

[24] It is irrelevant for our purpose to make a distinction between Paul's own thinking and his eventual dependence on tradition.

about Jesus as a κατάρα, the word ἀνάθεμα could be applied to him.

But, the apostle says in 1 Cor. 12: 3, nobody who speaks in the Spirit of God does so. Let it be observed that there is a difference here in the employment of the words. In Gal. 3: 13 Paul freely applies the word κατάρα to Jesus in the course of an argument and for a certain stage of the work of salvation, viz, the crucifixion; it demonstrates, with words taken from the Law, how Jesus liberated the people from the curse pronounced over them by the same Law. But that was not the last word St Paul had to say about the story of Jesus; for he not only died, but was also raised from the dead (cf. the kerygma in 1 Cor. 15: 3f.). But in 1 Cor. 12: 3 there is no question of a theological exposition, but of a kind of confession about the status of Jesus, and that makes all the difference, because now we are dealing not with a certain phase in Jesus' work of salvation, but with a pronouncement of what Jesus really *is*.

The pronouncement that Jesus had been an *anathema* could be made by any Christian with a perfectly good sense. It could follow from St Paul's teaching, who declared: οὐ γὰρ ἔκρινά τι εἰδέναι ἐν ὑμῖν, εἰ μὴ Ἰησοῦν Χριστὸν καὶ τοῦτον ἐσταυρωμένον (1 Cor. 2: 2); or from his teaching: ὅτι Χριστὸς ἀπέθανεν ὑπὲρ τῶν ἁμαρτιῶν ἡμῶν κατὰ τὰς γραφάς, καὶ ὅτι ἐτάφη (1 Cor. 15: 3f.). Particularly for Jewish-Christians, who were so well versed in the Scriptures, it would be meaningful to say that Jesus had been a curse. And even for unbelieving Jews that statement would be true, *teste Tryphone* in his dialogue with Justin a century later. What then was the difference? For the unbelieving Jews Jesus had been destroyed under the curse of God by his death on the cross, and the application of Deut. 21: 23 was the final word; whereas for the Christians this death on the cross, explained according to Deut. 21: 23, was not the last word, because the kerygma in 1 Cor. 15: 4 continues by saying: καὶ ὅτι ἐγήγερται τῇ ἡμέρᾳ τῇ τρίτῃ κατὰ τὰς γραφάς. But even if the words ΑΝΑΘΕΜΑ ΙΗΣΟΥΣ are an expression of Jesus' vicarious death on behalf of his people, the question still remains unanswered, why a Christian speaking in the Spirit of God cannot say so. A solution of this problem can only be found after some reflections on the other half of the verse.

II

We may now proceed to the second part of our verse, which is in opposite and complementary parallelism to the preceding clause. This implies that ἀνάθεμα is balanced by κύριος. Since so many excellent contributions have been devoted to the word κύριος, there is no need at the moment within the small compass of this article to enter into a full discussion. But a few observations are pertinent.

There is no other passage in the Pauline letters that offers a direct parallel to 1 Cor. 12: 3b. The two other texts that have this specific combination κύριος 'Ιησοῦς, viz. Rom. 10: 9 and Phil. 2: 11, miss the relation with the Holy Spirit; and that point is essential here. So we have no direct guidelines given by the author himself, and are bound to rely on a hypothetical reconstruction of the way of thinking that led him to this statement.

It is important to see that both in Rom. 10 and Phil. 2 the verb (ἐξ)ομολογεῖν is connected with this combination κύριος 'Ιησοῦς. It is a 'confession';[25] not however a confession before a hostile world, so much as a recognition[26] that the Lord is Jesus. Why is it necessary to acknowledge this? The context of Rom. 10: 6ff. is very significant, because the final goal of this 'confession' is salvation (cf. verse 9 σωθήσῃ, verse 10 εἰς σωτηρίαν, and verse 13 σωθήσεται in the quotation from Joel 3: 5 which brings the whole passage to its close). It is curious that the role of ὁμολογεῖν in the end is taken over by ἐπικαλεῖσθαι τὸ ὄνομα κυρίου.[27] He, Jesus, is that κύριος who is spoken of in the prophetic promise; he is called upon in order to receive final salvation. Holtz was quite correct in observing that the two sentences in Rom. 10: 9 do not stand in opposition to each other, but are almost identical.[28] Jesus, whom God raised from the dead, is this Lord who grants salvation to all who call upon him, according to the prophecy of Joel.

Two other New Testament passages illustrate how this recognition of Jesus as Lord is the decisive factor.

(a) Matt. 7: 21: οὐ πᾶς ὁ λέγων μοι Κύριε Κύριε, εἰσελεύσεται εἰς τὴν βασιλείαν τῶν οὐρανῶν, the supposition being that addressing Jesus as

---

[25] Because of the indication of the verb, it is better to speak here of a 'homologia' than of an 'acclamation', as is done by H. Conzelmann, *loc. cit.*, p. 243.

[26] W. Bauer, *Wörterbuch zum N.T.* (Berlin, ⁵1958), Sp. 1125, *s.v.* 4.

[27] In a forthcoming study, entitled 'With all those who call on the name of the Lord', I shall deal more fully with this text.

[28] T. Holtz, *loc. cit.*, p. 374.

'Lord' opens the entrance to the Kingdom of God; cf. the reference in 2 Clem. 4: 1–2: μὴ μόνον οὖν αὐτὸν καλῶμεν κύριον. οὐ γὰρ τοῦτο σώσει ἡμᾶς. λέγει γὰρ · Οὐ πᾶς ὁ λέγων μοι Κύριε Κύριε, σωθήσεται κ.τ.λ.

(b) Acts 2: 14ff.: The speech of Peter at Pentecost starts by explaining the outpouring of the Spirit by means of an extensive quotation from Joel's prophecy, which is closed by the very same verse, Joel 3: 5, as was cited by St Paul, and then changes over into a christological discourse (verses 22ff.) with only a passing reference to the Spirit (verse 33). This second part of the speech is an explanation of the 'name of the Lord', mentioned in the quotation from Joel (verse 21). Who is this κύριος who is to be called upon? That name is not disclosed by the prophet, but is now revealed by Peter. It is that of Jesus, who was crucified by the Jews (and we remember what crucifixion meant),[29] but was raised from the dead by God[30] and is now the 'Lord' at the right hand of God (verses 32–6, with the important quotation from Ps. 110: 1). Luke says that the purpose of this speech and other words of Peter was the admonition: σώθητε ἀπὸ τῆς γενεᾶς τῆς σκολιᾶς ταύτης (Acts 2: 40). We find here the same cluster of themes, though in a somewhat different wording, as in the Pauline passage in Rom. 10.

In analysing and comparing the above passages, we discover that here the decisive condition for man's salvation (by Matthew described as 'entering the kingdom of heaven') is to call on the *Kyrios*, who is none other but Jesus. For this reason the 'confession' Κύριος Ἰησοῦς is all-important, and the mark of Christianity by which it is distinguished from all other religions.

If the setting of this confession has become clear, we can now see a link between the two declarations in their parallelism and opposition: *anathema Jēsous* and *Kyrios Jēsous*. For if the interpretation of *anathema*, as set forth in this paper, is correct, both have to do with man's ultimate destiny. *Anathema* meant, as we saw, a means to remove sin and to restore communion with God; *Kyrios* in this connection is he who grants salvation. Both words belong to the same sphere; they are, so to say, means to the same end for men. But here they are put in opposition. *Anathema* implies the total destruction of him on whom it rests and complete separation from God, whereas *Kyrios* in this connection means resurrection from the dead by the act of God himself

[29] See pp. 120f.
[30] See Acts 3: 15; 4: 10; 5: 30; 10: 40; 13:30, 37; also in Paul, Rom. 4: 24; 6: 4; 8: 11; 1 Cor. 6: 14, ch. 15 *passim*; 2 Cor. 4: 14; Eph. 1: 20; Col. 2: 12; 1 Thess. 1: 10.

and being seated at the right hand of God, that is, fully sharing in his glory.[31]

Anathema, says Paul, cannot be said of Jesus, because although he died on the cross, and for that reason could be called a curse, it would imply his annihilation and separation from God. It would be an implicit denial of his resurrection (cf. 1 Cor. 15 and particularly verse 12). But the Christians believed in and confessed Jesus as *Kyrios*: ὃς παρεδόθη διὰ τὰ παραπτώματα ἡμῶν καὶ ἠγέρθη διὰ τὴν δικαίωσιν ἡμῶν (Rom. 4: 25);[32] Jesus who is *Kyrios*, seated at the right hand of the Father (Rom. 8: 34; 1 Cor. 15: 25f.). Why can Jesus only be called *Kyrios* 'in the Holy Spirit'? There is no indication that the answer should be sought in a (later) gnostic distinction between a Jesus κατὰ σάρκα and a Christ κατὰ πνεῦμα. The answer is, I think, much simpler. On both sides of the antithesis we find the name 'Jesus' *tout court*; in one case he receives the predicate *anathema*, in the other that of *Kyrios*, the exalted Lord. Christian tradition from the very beginning has made us so accustomed to this designation of Jesus as Lord, that we are hardly aware of the tremendous step that lies behind these 'simple' words. But in the missionary situation of the first century it meant an enormous change. The fact that the man Jesus of Nazareth had been crucified was a hard, historic fact, which could have been seen by everybody present. But the resurrection and exaltation of this man Jesus did not belong to this category of historic facts; it was attested by Jesus' disciples. But was this witness not λῆρος (Luke 24: 11)? God's activity in the raising up and exaltation of Jesus, as testified by the apostles and accepted in faith by the Christians, could not possibly be verified by the 'natural' man. This activity lies outside the boundaries of human observation. Here too the words of Paul, written in connection with the eschatological gifts of God, are completely relevant: τὰ τοῦ θεοῦ οὐδεὶς ἔγνωκεν εἰ μὴ τὸ πνεῦμα τοῦ θεοῦ (1 Cor. 2: 11).[33] It is only by a special revelation that one can know what has been done to Jesus by God, namely that he has become Lord. But then

[31] This is of course only one aspect of the Lordship of Jesus, namely why he was the Lord notwithstanding his death on the cross; but it goes without saying that his status as *Kyrios* had many more sides to it than this.

[32] See also Rom. 14: 9: εἰς τοῦτο γὰρ Χριστὸς ἀπέθανεν καὶ ἔζησεν, ἵνα καὶ νεκρῶν καὶ ζώντων κυριεύσῃ.

[33] The same idea, although in a different context and wording, is expressed in Matt. 16: 17: σὰρξ καὶ αἷμα οὐκ ἀπεκάλυψέν σοι, ἀλλ' ὁ πατήρ μου ὁ ἐν τοῖς οὐρανοῖς.

it also follows that to acknowledge Jesus as Kyrios is a work of the Holy Spirit.

From this vantage-point we can now understand the underlying thoughts of 1 Cor. 12: 3. When one only took into account the earthly side of what had happened to Jesus in his crucifixion, that side which was accessible to the observation of all men, it was possible to say, *anathema Jēsous*, in the light of texts like Deut. 27: 26. But this declaration is absolutely impossible for one 'speaking in the Spirit of God', because then the eyes have been opened by the Spirit to God's activity in the raising up and exaltation of that same Jesus. If *anathema Jēsous* had to be the final word, it would be a denial of God's action, and that would be impossible for one inspired by the Spirit of God. But thanks to God, that was not to be the last word; he had raised up Jesus and made him *Kyrios*. To see this is the work of the Spirit, and to acknowledge him as such, is the work of the Spirit. This short text must be read in the light of 1 Cor. 2: 8–10: εἰ γὰρ ἔγνωσαν (*sc.* οἱ ἄρχοντες τοῦ αἰῶνος τούτου τὴν σοφίαν τοῦ θεοῦ), οὐκ ἂν τὸν κύριον τῆς δόξης ἐσταύρωσαν. ἀλλὰ καθὼς γέγραπται· ἃ ὀφθαλμὸς οὐκ εἶδεν καὶ οὖς οὐκ ἤκουσεν καὶ ἐπὶ καρδίαν ἀνθρώπου οὐκ ἀνέβη, ὅσα ἡτοίμασεν ὁ θεὸς τοῖς ἀγαπῶσιν αὐτόν. ἡμῖν γὰρ ἀπεκάλυψεν ὁ θεὸς διὰ τοῦ πνεύματος.

This Christian community, in clear distinction from its pagan past, was reconciled with God through the death of his Son and assured by the apostle: σωθησόμεθα ἐν τῇ ζωῇ αὐτοῦ (Rom. 5: 10). They confessed Jesus as their Kyrios in his glory. This confession inspired by the Holy Spirit was as such a sign of the presence of the Spirit, for πάντες ἐν πνεῦμα ἐποτίσθημεν (1 Cor. 12: 13). This is the basis for the following exposition on the φανέρωσις τοῦ πνεύματος.

I hope that this explanation of the riddle in 1 Cor. 12: 3 may recommend itself by its inner consistency and agreement with the framework of Paul's thought. But whatever may be the result of a critical testing of this exegesis, one element in this paper is beyond doubt, viz. that it is offered to our friend Dr C. F. D. Moule as an expression of true κοινωνία τοῦ πνεύματος.

Additional Note: Some readers of this paper may be wondering why a discussion of the third text where the confession Κύριος Ἰησοῦς is found, namely Phil. 2: 11, is missing. The answer is that in my view this passage, important though it is, does not help to elucidate the point at issue, because it does not mention the way in which the 'name above all names' – if this is *Kyrios*, as seems very probable – was conferred on Jesus. In referring readers to the very full discussion of all problems involved and of the proposed explanations by Dr Martin,[34] I only wish to make two brief remarks, which unfortunately cannot be fully argued at the moment.

My first observation is that in the construction of this passage there is a curious change of subject. In verses 6–8 Jesus is the subject who does everything, while in the second part (verse 9) God is the subject and Jesus the object. Although the resurrection is not mentioned here, that fact is presupposed, and then the scheme of this passage fits exactly what we have found in our previous discussion. First Jesus acts and goes to the limit of human existence, to the death of the cross; not simple death, but that of the cross! Then God himself brings about the complete change, by which he who was despised and accursed is raised to the highest honour and will be acclaimed as Lord by all creatures. So the structure of this 'hymn' is additional confirmation of the thesis set forth in this paper.

The second remark is concerned with verses 10–11. In the light of the use of πᾶν and πᾶσα, the question whether Jesus is acclaimed Lord by the church or by the whole world is futile, because the former alternative is out of the question. The whole scene may be compared with such descriptions as 1 Enoch 62f. In this eschatological picture all men, even the godless rulers, are bowing before the Lord; in the end the *real* state of affairs is revealed, and sinners have to acknowledge him whom they have ignored on earth. But though they implore God's mercy, their repentance is too late. Here in Phil. 2: 10–11 we find an eschatological scene in which Jesus is acclaimed Lord by *all*. But that will be so in the end; it does not mean that this is now the case. At present Jesus is known and confessed only by the church, but as everywhere in early Christian eschatology the *eschaton* starts and is realized already in the church which has the ἀπαρχὴ τοῦ πνεύματος.

[34] R. P. Martin, *Carmen Christi: Philippians ii: 5–11 in Recent Interpretation and in the Setting of Early Christian Worship* (Cambridge, 1967).

9

1 Corinthians 15: 45 – last Adam, life-giving spirit

JAMES D. G. DUNN

How did Paul relate his present experience of the exalted Lord to the historical person Jesus? This is one of the key problems in Pauline christology and soteriology. And probably no other verse in the Pauline corpus poses the question more abruptly and more sharply than 1 Cor. 15: 45:

> οὕτως καὶ γέγραπται,
> Ἐγένετο ὁ πρῶτος ἄνθρωπος Ἀδὰμ εἰς ψυχὴν ζῶσαν·
> ὁ ἔσχατος Ἀδὰμ εἰς πνεῦμα ζωοποιοῦν.

For in this verse Paul seems to say not only that the central, constitutive element of the corporate Christian life is the experience of God's Spirit; but also that Jesus can be fully and adequately understood in terms of this Spirit. Not only is the earthly Jesus lost in the shadows behind the exalted Lord, but the exalted Lord seems to be wholly identified with the Spirit, the source of the new life experienced by believers.

It is unfortunate that the theological implications of this passage have not been more fully investigated in recent years, and that commentators seem to have been concerned more with the origins of Paul's ideas than with their place in his overall theology. It is to this task – the elucidation of 1 Cor. 15: 45 in its context within Pauline theology – that we now turn. I offer it to Professor Moule, my *Doktorvater*, as a small token of appreciation with warmest greetings and regards.

I

We take up first the exegesis of 1 Cor. 15: 45 in its immediate context. As in most of the letter, Paul is here addressing his gnostic opponents at Corinth. As part of their superior knowledge and higher wisdom it appears that they have denied the resurrection of the dead (15: 12). That is, presumably, they denied that their spiritual state was incomplete; already they were mature, already full, already reigning (3: 1f.; 4: 8; cf. 10: 1–12); they were already experiencing resurrection life in their experience of the Spirit; they had no place for a still future resurrection.[1] Above all, they denied that full redemption came through resurrection of the *body*; on the contrary, for a gnostic salvation would be wholly independent of the body; if anything was awaited as still future it would be release *from* the body. In short, they denied both the somatic and the future eschatological character of the resurrection.[2]

In refutation Paul argues first for a resurrection that is still future: as Christ's resurrection followed his death, so believers can look forward to resurrection after death (15: 13–23) (or transformation of σῶμα at the parousia – 15: 51f.); he then goes on to argue for a resurrection of the body – not the same body, though one in some degree of continuity with the present body (15: 35–50).[3]

The contrast between first Adam and last Adam occurs in the course of this latter argument. Paul justifies his belief in the resurrection body by contrasting the scriptural description of man's creation (Gen. 2: 7) with the mode of existence now enjoyed by the risen Christ. Man was created ψυχὴν ζῶσαν; Christ has become πνεῦμα ζωοποιοῦν. Or in other words, man was created σῶμα ψυχικόν; Christ became σῶμα πνευματικόν. The order of events is clear – first psychical then spiritual – the one from dust, the other from heaven. As the man made of dust is the pattern of psychical men, so the man from heaven is the pattern of spiritual men; that is, as earthly existence is an embodiment of ψυχή, σῶμα ψυχικόν, so resurrection existence is an embodiment of πνεῦμα, σῶμα πνευματικόν.

What has not been sufficiently realized in many expositions is the central significance of verse 45 in Paul's argument. The fact that verse

[1] Cf. 2 Tim. 2: 18; 2 Clem. 9: 1; Polycarp, *Phil.* 7; Justin, *Apol.* i. 26. 4; *Dial.* 80; Irenaeus, *Adv. haer.* i. 23. 5, ii. 31. 2; *Acts of Paul and Thecla* 14; Tertullian, *De Resurrectione Carnis* 19.

[2] H. von Soden, *Sakrament und Ethik bei Paulus* (Marburg, 1931), p. 23 n. 1; H. D. Wendland, *Die Briefe an die Korinther*, *NTD* vii (Göttingen, 1932, [10]1964), p. 125; Kümmel in H. Lietzmann–W. G. Kümmel, *An die Korinther* I/II, *HNT* ix (Tübingen, [4]1949), pp. 192f.; W. Schmithals, *Die Gnosis in Korinth* (Göttingen, [2]1965), pp. 147ff.; C. K. Barrett, *The First Epistle to the Corinthians* (London, 1968), pp. 347f.; J. H. Wilson, 'The Corinthians who Say There is No Resurrection of the Dead', *ZNW* lix (1968), pp. 90–107.

[3] Kümmel pp. 194f.; M. E. Dahl, *The Resurrection of the Body* (London, 1962), p. 94.

45 can be treated as a parenthesis[4] and the recognition that Paul's main concern throughout this passage is anthropological rather than christological[5] obscures how basic is the assertion of verse 45 to Paul's whole case. The series of contrasts of verses 42–4 have in themselves proved nothing, but were designed to lead up to the key antithesis of verse 44 between σῶμα ψυχικόν and σῶμα πνευματικόν, and the key statement, εἰ ἔστιν σῶμα ψυχικόν, ἔστιν καὶ πνευματικόν.

This simple affirmation is a classic example of Paul's apologetic skill. He appears to have taken over the ψυχικός/πνευματικός antithesis from his gnostic opponents.[6] But he subtly transposes it into his own terms, σ ῶ μ α ψυχικόν and σ ῶ μ α πνευματικόν. Such a use of σῶμα would normally have been unacceptable to the gnostics and his argument would have fallen to the ground, for σῶμα in the general usage of the time in reference to man means physical body and is not distinguished from σάρξ – that is, in gnostic thought it stood together with σάρξ and ψυχή in denigratory contrast to πνεῦμα.[7] But Paul introduces a distinction between σάρξ and σῶμα which outflanks the gnostics' position and leaves them open to Paul's counter-attack. He accepts the gnostic antithesis ψυχικός/πνευματικός and stands side by side with them in affirming that 'σάρξ καὶ αἷμα *cannot* inherit the kingdom of God' (15: 50). But he affirms also that pneumatic existence is a form of existence neither physical/fleshly nor *in*corporeal. There are many kinds of σώματα, heavenly as well as earthly, non-fleshly as well as fleshly (15: 40). So there is a σῶμα ψυχικόν and there is a σῶμα πνευματικόν. In short, Paul is combating the gnostics on their ground, but in his terms.[8] Given Paul's distinction between σῶμα and σάρξ and their own distinction between ψυχικός and πνευματικός they are bound to accept the fuller Pauline distinction between σῶμα ψυχικόν (bodily

---

[4] A. E. J. Rawlinson, *The New Testament Doctrine of the Christ* (London, 1926), p. 129 n. 1.

[5] R. Scroggs, *The Last Adam* (Oxford, 1966), pp. 85, 87; Barrett, p. 376.

[6] R. Reitzenstein, *Die hellenistischen Mysterienreligionen* (Leipzig/Berlin, ³1927) p. 74; J. Weiss, *Der erste Korintherbrief* (Göttingen, ¹⁰1925), pp. 371ff.; R. Bultmann, *Theology of the New Testament*, vol. i (E.T. London, 1952), p. 174; E. Brandenburger, *Adam und Christus* (Neukirchen, 1962), pp. 74f.; R. Jewett, *Paul's Anthropological Terms* (Leiden, 1971), pp. 340–4, 353f.

[7] See E. Schweizer, 'σῶμα', *TDNT* vii, pp. 1025–57.

[8] Cf. H. Clavier, 'Brèves Remarques sur la Notion de Σῶμα Πνευματικόν *The*,' *Background of the New Testament and its Eschatology: Studies in Honour of C. H. Dodd* (ed. W. D. Davies and D. Daube, Cambridge, 1954); p. 360; Jewett, pp. 266f.

existence vivified and determined by ψυχή) and σῶμα πνευματικόν (bodily existence vivified and determined by πνεῦμα).

The crucial step in Paul's argument is the next one – for now he must clarify and establish the *relation* between these two σώματα. And this he does in verses 45–9, where verses 46–9 are his exposition of verse 45. Verse 45 in other words is *not* the proof of verse 44b, contrary to common opinion; verse 44b needs no proof as such, since it is common ground with Paul's opponents. As the καί, not γάρ, indicates, Paul here takes the argument one stage further: 'Moreover as Scripture says, "The first man Adam became a living soul; the last Adam a life-giving spirit"'. In other words *he identifies the two kinds of* σώματα *with Adam and Christ*. Once this position is gained he has the upper hand over the gnostics; and the rest of the argument flows irrefutably on. If Christ is the type of σῶμα πνευματικόν then it is an eschatological, heavenly mode of existence which can be achieved only as Jesus achieved it, after death, or at the parousia. Everything therefore hangs on verse 45. The question obviously arises, Can Paul's assertion in verse 45 bear the heavy weight Paul puts on it?

Verse 45 is introduced by Paul as a scriptural quotation, and the whole verse stands under the οὕτως γέγραπται – including verse 45b, as the absence of δέ indicates.[9] Of course Gen. 2:7 to which Paul refers reads only, καὶ ἐγένετο ὁ ἄνθρωπος εἰς ψυχὴν ζῶσαν. Verse 45 must therefore be understood as Paul's pesher or midrash on Gen. 2:7. But how does Paul achieve this exegesis? It is unlikely that the only justification is the rabbinic hermeneutical principle of inferred antithesis.[10] It is possible but unnecessary to assume that he is reworking a rabbinic midrash on Gen. 2:7.[11] And it is probable that he is consciously aware of the Adam or Primal Man speculation which was current in his day (see below). But as with all Paul's midrashim, the exegesis of Gen. 2:7 in verse 45 is drawn principally from Paul's own understanding of Christ and the gospel (cf. 1 Cor. 9:8–10; 2 Cor. 3:7–18; Gal. 3:8; 4:21–31).[12] This is clearly indicated by Paul's insertion of πρῶτος (and Ἀδάμ) into the Gen. 2:7 clause. The understanding of 'the man' in Gen. 2:7 as πρῶτος Ἀδάμ is determined by Paul's under-

[9] Cf. Weiss, pp. 373ff.; H. Conzelmann, *Der erste Brief an die Korinther* (Göttingen, 1969), pp. 337f.
[10] Best exemplified in Matt. 5:43.
[11] Scroggs, pp. 86f.; cf. C. F. Burney, *The Aramaic Origin of the Fourth Gospel* (Oxford, 1922), p. 46.
[12] See J. D. G. Dunn, *Baptism in the Holy Spirit* (London, 1970), p. 126.

standing of Jesus as ἔσχατος Ἀδάμ. In other words, the point and force of the citation of Gen. 2: 7 lies not in the actual Genesis passage itself, but in the contrast between that Adam and the last Adam – a contrast drawn from Paul's own understanding of Christ.

Paul must play his trump card, Christ, at this point – for the argument up to and including verse 44b has in fact proved nothing against the gnostics. Only in the case of Christ does the relation between σῶμα ψυχικόν and σῶμα πνευματικόν become evident – their disjunction and temporal sequence. Only by reference to Christ can Paul hope to prove that spiritual embodiment is not something already enjoyed by the believer in the here and now, but a mode of existence which lies the other side of death and resurrection.

This brings us to the crux of the debate and the heart of Paul's theology. For Paul's whole case at this critical point rests on two assumptions. The first is that the exalted Jesus is *known* to possess a spiritual body. The second is that the exalted Jesus has a *representative* capacity in this mode of existence. Without these two assumptions Paul's case fails. But how well grounded are they for Paul? We will examine them in turn.

II

As Adam became εἰς ψυχὴν ζῶσαν so Christ became εἰς πνεῦμα ζωοποιοῦν. Clearly πνεῦμα ζωοποιοῦν means also or at least includes the idea of σῶμα πνευματικόν – otherwise the citation would not really be relevant; as Adam's existence as ψυχὴ ζῶσα means a bodily existence vivified and determined by ψυχή, so the risen Christ's existence as πνεῦμα ζωοποιοῦν means a bodily existence vivified and determined by πνεῦμα. But the reason why Paul writes πνεῦμα ζωοποιοῦν is not simply to achieve an aesthetically pleasing parallel with ψυχὴ ζῶσα, for that could have been achieved as well by writing πνεῦμα ζῶν. The principal reason is that Paul wishes to ground his assertion about the spiritual embodiment of the risen Christ *in the experience of the believing community*. Hence he characterizes Jesus not simply as πνευματικός but as πνεῦμα, not simply as ζῶν but as ζωοποιοῦν.[13] In other words, *the believer's experience of the life-giving Spirit is for Paul proof that the risen Jesus is σῶμα πνευματικόν*.

πνεῦμα ζωοποιοῦν cannot be understood except as a reference to the

[13] 'Non solum vivit, sed etiam vivificat' (Bengel); cf. Schweizer, *TDNT* vi, p. 420.

spiritual experience of the early believers. It is one of the chief merits of the *religionsgeschichtliche Schule* that it demonstrated so clearly the experiential basis of early theologizing. πνεῦμα denotes neither a theological dogma nor an idealized *Zeitgeist* but a spiritual experience – an experience of being taken hold of by a mysterious power, of being overwhelmed or inspired or directed or moved by a supernatural force.[14] 'Geist ist die göttliche, überirdische Macht. ... Die Wurzel seiner [Paul's] πνεῦμα-Lehre liegt also in der Erfahrung des Apostels' (Gunkel, pp. 79, 82). In many cases in early Christianity this experience of πνεῦμα was marked by ecstatic phenomena (Acts 2: 4, 33; 8: 18; 10: 46; 19: 6; 1 Cor. 1: 5, 7; Gal. 3: 5; Heb. 2: 4); in others by a strong emotional content (Rom. 5: 5; 1 Thess. 1: 6; κράзειν – Rom. 8: 15f.; Gal. 4: 6); sometimes it was an experience of liberation (Rom. 8: 2; 2 Cor. 3: 17; Gal. 5: 18), sometimes of intellectual illumination (2 Cor. 3: 16ff.; Eph. 1: 17f.; Heb. 6: 4); and so on.

Notice particularly the attribution of зωοποίησις to πνεῦμα in John 6: 63 and 2 Cor. 3: 6. For John Christianity was essentially a matter of 'having life' (20: 31) – that is, the experience of sheer exuberant vitality, like a stream of running water (7: 38) or a well bubbling up within (4: 14). So new and fresh was this experience of life that it could be spoken of in terms of birth or creation (3: 3ff.; 20: 22 – ἐνεφύσησεν). And this experience John not merely attributes to the Spirit (3: 5f. – ἐκ πνεύματος) but actually *identifies* with the Spirit (4: 10 – τὴν δωρεὰν τοῦ Θεοῦ;[15] 7: 39; 20: 22 – λάβετε πνεῦμα ἅγιον). (*Holy*) *Spirit is the name John gives to the experience of new life* – τὸ πνεῦμά ἐστιν τὸ зωοποιοῦν (6: 63). Likewise for Paul, the experience of life which set him free from the law of sin and death and from the dispensation of condemnation and death was the Spirit (Rom. 8: 2, 10; 2 Cor. 3: 7–9); 2 Cor. 3: 6 –

> τὸ γὰρ γράμμα ἀποκτείνει
> τὸ δὲ πνεῦμα зωοποιεῖ.

Hence in 1 Cor. 15: 45 πνεῦμα зωοποιοῦν can only refer to the early believers' experience of new life.

The significant factor however is that Paul identifies the risen Jesus with this life-giving Spirit; Jesus himself is the source of these experi-

---

[14] See particularly H. Gunkel, *Die Wirkungen des heiligen Geistes* (Göttingen, 1888); H. Weinel, *Wirkungen des Geistes und der Geister im nachapostolischen Zeitalter* (Freiburg im Breisgau, 1899).

[15] J. D. G. Dunn, 'A Note on δωρεά', *Exp. T.* lxxxi (1969–70), pp. 349–51.

ences of Spirit, or to put it the other way, the experience of life-giving
Spirit is experience of the risen Jesus. Moreover, and this is the crucial
point, this experience constitutes for Paul proof that Jesus is risen from
the dead and exists as σῶμα πνευματικόν. How so? Because for Paul that
which distinguishes Christian experience of πνεῦμα from comparable
experiences in other religions is precisely its Christ-relatedness, its
Jesus-content. Paul was of course well aware that similar pneumatic
phenomena were present in other sects, when worshippers 'would be
seized by some irresistible power' (NEB), 'irresistibly drawn...
towards dumb idols' (Jer. Bible – 1 Cor. 12: 2).[16] It is precisely for
this reason that at the beginning of his discussion of the spirituals or
spiritual gifts (12–14) he stresses the distinctive feature of the spiritual
experience of those 'in Christ' – not more exalted experiences, or
experiences of a totally different order, but experiences which are
centred on Christ. The test case he gives here is an inspiration which
recognizes the exalted status of Jesus as κύριος – only that power is
God's Spirit which inspires a man to confess 'Jesus is Lord' (1 Cor.
12: 3).

This Jesus-content of early Christian experience is even more marked
in the believer's assurance of sonship, when the Spirit cries within and
through him 'ἀββά' (Rom. 8: 15f.; Gal. 4: 6). For this experience
reproduces what had hitherto been the unprecedented and unique
spiritual experience of Jesus himself.[17] The intimate ἀββά-relationship
with God which until then only the historical man Jesus had enjoyed
was now experienced by those 'in Christ', so that they could think of
themselves not only as adopted sons of the Father and heirs of God,
but also as *fellow*-heirs with Christ (Rom. 8: 17). In consequence of
such experiences they believed that not only their relationship with
God was patterned on Jesus', but also, as we shall see below, that their
whole character was being transformed into the image of Christ.[18]

---

[16] See particularly E. R. Dodds, *The Greeks and the Irrational* (Berkeley, Cal.,
1951), pp. 64–101; W. F. Otto, *Dionysius Myth and Cult* (Bloomington, Ind.,
E.T. 1965).

[17] J. Jeremias, *The Prayers of Jesus* (E.T. London, 1967), pp. 54–65; *New Testament Theology*, vol. i: *The Proclamation of Jesus* (E.T. London, 1971), pp. 63–8.

[18] Professor Moule expressed this point well when he wrote: 'The diffused and
little defined and fitfully manifested Spiritual presence of God (viz. as we meet it
in the Old Testament) becomes sharply contracted to a "bottle-neck" so as to be
defined and localized in Jesus of Nazareth; God who formerly spoke at various
times and in many different fragments has now spoken to us in one who is a
Son. But the pattern, thus contracted to a single individual, widens again,

Such experiences they could only attribute to the risen Jesus acting upon them through the Spirit; there was a spiritual power moving in them which they could describe equally well as 'Christ in me' or 'the Spirit in me',[19] or, most striking of all, as 'the Spirit of Christ' (Rom. 8: 9), 'the Spirit of his Son' (Gal. 4: 6), 'the Spirit of Jesus Christ' (Phil. 1: 19). The 'intensive feeling of personal belonging and of spiritual relationship with the exalted Lord', which Bousset rightly calls the 'dominant' note in Paul's piety,[20] Paul on several occasions likens to the intimacy of a marriage relationship; most striking is 1 Cor. 6: 17 – as physical union means oneness of flesh, so union with the Lord means a oneness of Spirit.[21]

It was this Jesus-relatedness, this Jesus-content in their spiritual experience which constituted proof for the early believers that it was the exalted Jesus who was acting upon them – Jesus had become πνεῦμα ζωοποιοῦν. That is, he was the source of the power of new life which moved in and through them. The fact that Paul does not have to argue the point indicates that this type of experience was fairly general among believers, and perhaps particularly among the gnostics. Thus the affirmation of verse 45b is one which would be both understood and accepted by the gnostics at Corinth. It is in the implied, but in the context of Paul's argument, inevitable corollary that the punch comes – for existence as πνεῦμα ζωοποιοῦν means also existence as σῶμα πνευματικόν. In short, the nature of the believing community's experience of Spirit enables Paul to affirm that Jesus has become πνεῦμα ζωοποιοῦν, and therefore also σῶμα πνευματικόν.

> through his death and resurrection, to an indefinite scope, though never again to an undefined quality. However widely diffused, however much more than individual, it bears henceforth the stamp of the very character of Christ' (*The Holy Spirit in the Church* – an unpublished lecture (1963) quoted by E. M. B. Green, *The Meaning of Salvation* (London, 1965), pp. 175f.).
>
> [19] Rom. 8: 10; Gal. 2: 20; Eph. 3: 17. Rom. 8: 9, 11; 1 Cor. 3: 16; 6: 19; etc. Cf. 1 Cor. 12: 6; Phil. 2: 13; Col. 1: 29; Eph. 3: 20.
>
> [20] W. Bousset, *Kyrios Christos* (Göttingen, ⁶1967), p. 104; (E.T. New York, 1970), p. 153.
>
> [21] Note also Gunkel's comment on Paul's conversion: 'The first pneumatic experience of Paul was an experience of Christ' (p. 99) – a suggestion which may help to explain the ἐν ἐμοί of Gal. 1: 16.

III

The second assumption which underlies verse 45b is that Jesus has a representative capacity in his existence as πνεῦμα ζωοποιοῦν. The idea of Jesus as representative man comes to expression in several places in Paul's writings (notably Rom. 5: 12–21; 1 Cor. 15: 20ff.; Phil. 2: 7f.;[22] cf. Heb. 2: 5–18). Paul probably introduces the idea into 1 Cor. 15 partly at least because his gnostic opponents were influenced by the speculation concerning the Primal Man current at that time – as is shown particularly by Philo[23] and the Hermetic writings,[24] not to mention the apocalyptic concept of the heavenly (son of) Man.[25] This external evidence taken in conjunction with verse 46[26] certainly indicates that Paul was aware of some sort of gnostically influenced speculation about Jesus as Man, although the more elaborate divine *Urmensch* theses of Käsemann and Brandenburger both lack adequate foundation and are unnecessary to explain Paul's theology or argument at this point.[27]

However, what is all too often lost sight of in these debates is the fact that Paul's assertion here is again based on the believer's *experience*. *The community's experience of the exalted Jesus as* πνεῦμα ζωοποιοῦν *is what enables Paul to affirm the representative significance of Jesus' resurrection and resurrection body*. Paul's affirmation of the representa-

[22] R. P. Martin, *Carmen Christi: Philippians 2: 5–11* (Cambridge, 1967), pp. 207–11.

[23] *De Opificio Mundi* 134; *Legum Allegoriae* i. 31f.; W. D. Davies, *Paul and Rabbinic Judaism* (London, ²1955), pp. 44–52. Though see also Scroggs, pp. 115–22.

[24] *Poimandres* 12–17; R. Reitzenstein, *Poimandres* (Leipzig, 1904), pp. 81–116; though see also C. H. Dodd, *The Bible and the Greeks* (London, 1935), pp. 145–62. Cf. J. M. Creed, 'The Heavenly Man', *JTS* xxvi (1925), pp. 113–36.

[25] Dan. 7: 13f.; Enoch 48: 2f.; 69: 26–9; 71: 14–17; 2 Esdras 13; J. Weiss, *Earliest Christianity* (E.T. New York, 1937, reprinted 1959), pp. 485f.; Rawlinson, pp. 122–7; J. Jeremias, *TDNT* i, pp. 142f.; O. Cullmann, *The Christology of the New Testament* (E.T. London, 1959), pp. 166–70; W. G. Kümmel, *Die Theologie des neuen Testaments* (Göttingen, 1969), p. 139. Though see also Brandenburger, pp. 131–5; R. H. Fuller, *The Foundations of New Testament Christology* (London, 1965), pp. 233f.

[26] J. Moffatt, *The First Epistle of Paul to the Corinthians* (London, 1938), p. 263; J. Héring, *The First Epistle of Saint Paul to the Corinthians* (E.T. London, 1962), p. 178; Cullmann, pp. 167ff.; J. Jervell, *Imago Dei* (Göttingen, 1960), pp. 258ff.; Brandenburger, pp. 74ff., 155ff.; Barrett, pp. 374f.; Jewett, p. 353.

[27] The discussion is conveniently summarized and well assessed by Jewett, pp. 230–6.

tive significance of Jesus' risen state is not based merely on the belief
that post-mortem existence must be somatic – for then he could have
said merely, the last Adam became εἰς πνεῦμα ζῶν. It is the Christian's
experience of life as coming from the exalted Jesus which is determinative. Nor is he building on the foundation of a (gnostic) identity
between Jesus and the Primal Man, for it is precisely that equation
which Paul severs in verse 46: Jesus is ἔσχατος Ἀδάμ, not πρῶτος
Ἀδάμ; it is the *risen* Jesus who is the image of God, not any *Urmensch*,
let alone the first Adam.[28] Nor is he simply drawing out corollaries
from the sense of corporate oneness 'in Christ' which the worshipping
assembly experiences, although that is undoubtedly important for Paul
and probably contributes to his thinking here. The primary focus of
his thought at this point however is the believer's experience of the
life-giving Spirit. How so? Because in this experience the believer finds
himself being steadily transformed to become like Christ. *Paul's own
experience of the life of the Spirit bearing the imprint of Jesus' character
and conforming him to that image is the ground on which Paul asserts the
representative significance of Jesus' risen humanity.*

We enter here the deepest waters of Paul's Christ-mysticism. Paul's
experience as a believer is not merely of new life; it is also of decay and
death. Although the Spirit is life διὰ δικαιοσύνην, the body is dead διὰ
ἁμαρτίαν (Rom. 8: 10). The believer knows the life of the Spirit, but
he has to express it through the body of death (Rom. 7: 24f.; 8: 13;
2 Cor. 4: 11f.). Day by day he is being 'inwardly renewed', but at the
same time his 'outward humanity is in decay' (2 Cor. 4: 16). The
suffering this involves is a necessary preliminary to glory – suffering to
death is the way to glory (Rom. 8: 17). The significant feature of this
death–life experience is that for Paul *both the death and the life are
Christ's* – it is the outworking of Christ's death and risen life. Hence
the perfect tenses in Rom. 6: 5; Gal. 2: 19; 6: 14: the believer's experience is that of having been knit together with the ὁμοίωμα of Christ's
death; not only does he experience the life of Christ within but there
is also a dimension to his experience which can be described as a state
of having been crucified with Christ – still hanging there! So too the
significance for Paul of his suffering is that it is a suffering *with Christ*
(Rom. 8: 17), a sharing in Christ's own suffering (2 Cor. 1: 5). Paul

[28] Adam in Paul is always fallen man; only 'the resurrected and exalted Christ is
the perfect realization of God's intent for men' (Scroggs, pp. 91, 100; cf.
Jervell, pp. 263–8).

can even think of his suffering as a continuation and completion of Christ's (Col. 1: 24). Most striking of all is Phil. 3: 1of., where Paul expresses his longing to know Christ more fully, that is, to experience not just the power of his resurrection, but to share his sufferings, and so be more and more conformed to his *death*; only in this way will he attain the resurrection of the dead.

Integral to this whole train of thought of course is Paul's experience of Christ as Spirit. For the Spirit is the ἀρραβών of full redemption (2 Cor. 1: 21; Eph. 1: 14); that is to say, the experience of the Spirit is the first instalment, the beginning of the process of life and death which leads up and into the 'heavenly habitation' of the resurrection body (2 Cor. 5: 5).[29] Or in equivalent terms, the Spirit is the ἀπαρχή, the beginning of the full harvest of the resurrection body, so that the groaning and frustration of life in the present body of death is an expression of hope rather than of despair (Rom. 8: 23f.).[30] It is this death–life motif which lies behind Paul's talk of the continuing Christian experience as one of more and more being transformed into the image of Christ through the Spirit (2 Cor. 3: 18; Col. 3: 10; cf. Rom. 8: 29; 12: 2; 13: 14; 2 Cor. 4: 4; Col. 1: 18) – the process of the full personality of Christ coming as it were to birth in the believer with all the birth-pangs which that involves (Gal. 4: 19), a process which only ends when 'the body belonging to our humble state' is transfigured to become like Christ's glorious resurrection body by the power of the Spirit (Phil. 3: 21; Rom. 8: 11). That this whole train of thought is in Paul's mind in 1 Cor. 15: 45 is clearly indicated by verse 49, with its talk of believers coming to 'bear the image of the man of heaven' as something still future (φορέσομεν).[31] What verse 45 affirms is that this transformation into the image of the last Adam is the outworking of the life-giving power of the last Adam, a power which believers already experience.

It is to be noted that at no stage does Paul give way to the gnostic

---

[29] Cf. C. F. D. Moule, 'St Paul and Dualism: the Pauline Conception of Resurrection', *NTS* xiii (1966–7), pp. 106–23.

[30] Cf. E. Käsemann, 'The Cry for Liberty in the Worship of the Church', *Perspectives on Paul* (E.T. London, 1971), pp. 122–37. Notice also the use of παθεῖν in Gal. 3: 4: believers ἔπαθον the Spirit and his δυνάμεις.

[31] As most commentators agree, φορέσομεν is undoubtedly to be read rather than φορέσωμεν (*contra* Héring, p. 179; Scroggs, p. 110); otherwise we have a gnostic exhortation, not an anti-gnostic affirmation. The believer lives his present life ἐν ἀσθενείᾳ, ἐν φθορᾷ (verses 42f.).

views: that a fully matured Christian experience and state can be achieved here and now, and that the body is wholly evil. He recognizes that the full flowering of the life of Christ in him involves the experience of death as well as of life; he shares Christ's risen life through the Spirit, but not fully; there is still a future-ness in Christian experience, a not yet; he is in process of being transformed into the image of Christ, but he does not yet fully bear that image; the Spirit is only the ἀρραβών and ἀπαρχή of a life fully vivified and determined by the Spirit, that is, of the σῶμα πνευματικόν; otherwise 'hope' would be a meaningless concept (Rom. 8: 24f.).[32] At the same time Paul's talk of decay and death does *not* express a dualistic pessimism with regard to the body. For the full outworking of the Spirit's life-giving power is precisely the σῶμα πνευματικόν. The experience of decay and death of the body is a sign of hope not of pessimism, for it is the converse side of the coming to be of the spiritual body (2 Cor. 4: 7 – 5: 5). The point is that it is the experience of Christ as πνεῦμα ζωοποιοῦν which assures Paul that the present experience is only a foretaste, a process of coming to be of the full life of the Spirit, the full character of Christ – which assures Paul that Christ's glorified state is not an isolated or individual occurrence, but the beginning of a new kind of humanity. As (Christ) the life-giving Spirit is the ἀπαρχή of the resurrection body, so Christ (the life-giving Spirit) is the ἀπαρχή of the harvest of resurrected men.

To sum up, the nature of Paul's spiritual experience, with its distinctive Jesus content and Jesus character, enables, even requires, Paul to understand it not only in terms of the risen Christ, but also in terms of a Christ whose risen state is archetypal for believers' future state. Hence if Adam is the type of psychic existence, the Christ, the risen Christ, is the type of pneumatic existence. This experience of πνεῦμα ζωοποιοῦν now implies σῶμα πνευματικόν because that is the inevitable end result of a process already under way, the process of being transformed into the image of Christ by his Spirit. In short, verse 45b

---

[32] Reitzenstein, *Mysterienreligionen*, pp. 333ff. and Bousset, though not without justification, nevertheless seriously misinterpret Paul and leave him with no reply to the gnostics at this point (so too A. Schweitzer, *The Mysticism of Paul the Apostle* (E.T. London, 1931), pp. 167, 220). Paul does *not* regard the 'present Christian standing' as one of 'perfection' (*Vollkommenheit*); on the contrary, Phil. 3: 8–14. Nor does he believe that 'the natural being has completely died in him [the pneumatic Christian]' (Bousset pp. 118, 122; E.T. pp. 170, 174). On the contrary, Rom. 8: 13; Col. 3: 5; Eph. 4: 22.

constitutes proof because Paul's experience of the πνεῦμα ζωοποιοῦν convinces him that the exalted Jesus has a spiritual, somatic existence and that in that mode of existence he is the pattern and forerunner of a new humanity.

As we have already noted, the argument of verses 46–9 flows on directly from the assertion of verse 45. If the gnostics have appreciated the full force of that one pregnant phrase they cannot deny the rest, for verses 46–9 merely spell out the principal implications in verse 45b. Verse 46: the life-giving Spirit they all experience is the *risen* Jesus, the *last* Adam; the πνεῦμα ζωοποιοῦν, the σῶμα πνευματικόν, does not precede the ψυχή ζῶσα, the σῶμα ψυχικόν, it succeeds it – only after the decay and death of the latter does the former come into existence. Verses 47f.: the last Adam has *pneumatic* existence – it is in his risen existence, as the heavenly man,[33] σῶμα πνευματικόν, that he represents a new humanity; 'as we have borne the image of the man of dust (and still do), so we shall bear (φορέσομεν) the image of the man of heaven' – 'such is the influence of the Lord who is Spirit' (2 Cor. 3: 18).

IV

It remains simply to underline some of the christological corollaries which follow from Paul's experience-based christology.

(*a*) Paul identifies the exalted Jesus with the Spirit – not with a spiritual being (πνεῦμα ζῶν) or a spiritual dimension or sphere (πνευματικόν), but with the Spirit, the Holy Spirit (πνεῦμα ζωοποιοῦν). Immanent christology is for Paul pneumatology; in the believer's experience there is *no* distinction between Christ and Spirit.[34] This does not mean of course that Paul makes no distinction between Christ and Spirit. But it does mean that later Trinitarian dogma cannot readily look to Paul for support at this point. A theology which reckons seriously with the ἐγένετο of John 1: 14 must reckon just as seriously with the ἐγένετο implied in 1 Cor. 15: 45b.

Moreover, if christology is the key to Christianity, then the teeth of

---

[33] There may well be an allusion to the parousia here (Barrett, pp. 375f.; D. M. Stanley, *Christ's Resurrection in Pauline Soteriology* (Rome, 1961), p. 126), making a smoother movement in thought from Christ's resurrection to that of believers.

[34] 2 Cor. 3: 17 should not be cited as a parallel; see J. D. G. Dunn, '2 Corinthians 3: 17 – "The Lord is the Spirit"', *JTS*, n.s. xxi (1970), pp. 309–20; *contra* particularly I. Hermann, *Kyrios und Pneuma* (München, 1961).

that key are not only the historical Jesus and the kerygmatic Christ but also the life-giving Spirit. The new 'Quest' and interest in the 'titles of majesty' must not detract attention from the further dimension of christology – 'Christ in me, the hope of glory'.[35] In the debate between those who seek to ground an understanding of faith in the historical Jesus and those who start from 'the kerygma', the *experiential* basis of early Christianity must not be ignored. Men believed in Jesus as Christ and Lord because they experienced a to them supernatural vitalizing power – a power whose character, if Paul is to be our guide, directed them to the conclusion that Jesus was its living source. Paul's understanding of the exalted Christ emerged out of his experience of the Spirit, not *vice versa*.[36]

(*b*) The antithesis in verse 45 and the context of verse 45 make it clear that Jesus *became* Last Adam at his resurrection. As the first Adam came into existence (ἐγένετο) at creation, so the last Adam (as such) came into existence (ἐγένετο) at resurrection (1 Cor. 15: 20–2; Rom. 8: 29; Col. 1: 18). For Paul 'the resurrection marks the *beginning* of the humanity of the Last Adam'.[37] Christ's role as 'second man' does not begin either in some pre-existent state,[38] or at incarnation.[39] The 'man' of Phil. 2: 7f., 'that one man' of Rom. 5: 15ff., strictly speaking is not identical with the 'last Adam' of 1 Cor. 15: 45. It was not by incarnation that Christ became the image of God or sanctified humanity. On the contrary, in incarnation he took on the flesh of the first Adam, *sinful* flesh, *fallen* humanity, and by his death he destroyed it – dust to dust (Rom. 8: 3; 2 Cor. 5: 14).[40] For Paul the last Adam is precisely

---

[35] 'This certainty of the nearness of Christ occurs far more frequently in Paul's writings than the thought of the distant Christ "highly exalted" in Heaven' (A. Deissmann, *Paul* (E.T. London, ²1927, reprinted 1957), p. 140.

[36] Cf. Gunkel, p. 100. The same is true to a significant degree of his understanding of the earthly Jesus; see J. D. G. Dunn, 'Jesus – Flesh and Spirit: An Exposition of Romans 1: 3–4', *JTS.*, n.s. xxiv (1973), pp. 40–68.

[37] Scroggs, p. 92 (my emphasis); see also F. Büchsel, *Der Geist Gottes im Neuen Testament* (Gütersloh, 1926), pp. 406f.; Kümmel, p. 195; Jervell, pp. 258ff.; Hermann, pp. 61f.; Conzelmann, pp. 341f.

[38] *Contra* Weiss, *Korintherbrief*, p. 376; W. L. Knox, *St Paul and the Church of Jerusalem* (Cambridge, 1925), p. 134; Moffatt, p. 263; W. Manson, *Jesus the Messiah* (London, 1943), pp. 186, 189.

[39] *Contra* Cullmann, pp. 166ff.; Wendland, p. 136; Héring, p. 179; F. W. Grosheide, *The First Epistle to the Corinthians* (London, 1953), p. 388.

[40] Irenaeus's 'recapitulation' theory completely misinterprets Paul at this point (Bousset, pp. 348–60, E.T. pp. 437–50); as do most incarnation-based soteriologies (see e.g. A. R. Vidler's study of F. D. Maurice, *Witness to the Light*

the 'man' who *died*, who brought to an end the 'old man', destroyed sin in the flesh, in order that the 'new man' might come to be. The contrast in verse 45 is between death and life, not between two stages of evolution (1 Cor. 15: 22). In short, the new humanity stems from the resurrection; only those participate in the last Adam who participate in the life-giving Spirit; their hope of fulness of life, σῶμα πνευματικόν, is real only because Jesus has become πνεῦμα ζωοποιοῦν.

(*c*) In terms of the modern debate and of our opening question the significant feature to emerge from our study is that although Paul thinks almost exclusively in terms of the present Jesus experienced now as Spirit, he does not thereby ignore or deny the relevance of the historical man Jesus. For it is precisely the Jesus-, that is, the historical Jesus-, content and Jesus-character of the present experience of Spirit which is the distinctive and most important feature of the experience. Christ has become Spirit, *Christ is now experienced as Spirit* – that is true. But it is only because *the Spirit is now experienced as Christ* that the experience of the Spirit is valid and essential for Paul. The centrality given to the experience of the exalted Lord does not deny the relevance and importance of the historical Jesus for Paul; on the contrary it reinforces it, by binding the historical Jesus and the exalted Lord together in the single all-important experience of the life-giving Spirit. It is the *continuity* between earthly Jesus and exalted Lord, denoted by the clause ὁ ἔσχατος Ἀδὰμ εἰς πνεῦμα ζωοποιοῦν, which is the key to Paul's thought here and to much of his christology and soteriology as a whole.

(New York, 1948), pp. 29–57; R. C. Moberly, *Atonement and Personality* (1901), pp. 86–92). 'It is only in virtue of resurrection that He became the archetype and head of a new race (H. R. Mackintosh, *The Doctrine of the Person of Jesus Christ* (Edinburgh, 1912), p. 69). See also p. 136 n. 28.

10

Christ crucified
or second Adam? A christological debate
between Paul and the Corinthians

MARGARET E. THRALL

The Corinthians very clearly held views about Christian existence which Paul thought to be mistaken. It is often supposed that these beliefs were partly due to the influence of incipient gnosticism and partly to the work of rival missionaries. These influences may certainly have affected the situation. But were they the primary cause of the Corinthians' outlook? This essay will suggest that it was Paul's own presentation of Christ which had originally created the viewpoint which he was later compelled to contest. It will be argued that one aspect of his message had received exaggerated emphasis, and that the Corinthians had drawn from it a number of seemingly logical conclusions which Paul was unable to accept. His efforts to correct their misunderstanding – as it appeared to him – led to further deviation on their part, but also to a significant development in his own christological thinking.

1. PAUL'S ORIGINAL MESSAGE AT CORINTH

There are one or two hints in the Corinthian correspondence that Paul's basic gospel had become a matter of contention between himself and the congregation. There were complaints of its obscurity. In 2 Cor. 4: 3 he allows for the possibility that to some it may be 'veiled' and is probably alluding to a charge made by his critics.[1] Furthermore, in 2 Cor. 1: 18–19 he affirms in most emphatic language its fundamental consistency:

πιστὸς δὲ ὁ θεὸς ὅτι ὁ λόγος ἡμῶν ὁ πρὸς ὑμᾶς οὐκ ἔστιν Ναὶ καὶ Οὔ. ὁ τοῦ θεοῦ γὰρ υἱὸς Ἰησοῦς Χριστὸς ὁ ἐν ὑμῖν δι' ἡμῶν κηρυχθείς,...οὐκ ἐγένετο Ναὶ καὶ Οὔ, ἀλλὰ Ναὶ ἐν αὐτῷ γέγονεν.

---

[1] See F. F. Bruce, *1 and 2 Corinthians* (*NCB*, London, 1971), Floyd V. Filson, *The Interpreter's Bible*, vol. x (New York, 1953), Jean Héring, *La Seconde Épître de Saint Paul aux Corinthiens* (*CNT*, Neuchâtel, 1958), and R. H. Strachan, *The Second Epistle of Paul to the Corinthians* (*MNTC*, London, 1935), *in loc.*

These verses are usually thought simply to substantiate Paul's denial of vacillation in respect of his promised visits to Corinth, the subject of the preceding verses. But in that case one would expect verse 18 to be introduced by γάρ rather than by δέ. It would make equally good sense to take this short passage as a digression concerned with the consistency of Paul's gospel, though evoked by his denial of vacillation in his travel plans. If so, it would appear that some of the Corinthians were claiming that his presentation of Christ was unreliable or self-contradictory. Were they saying, perhaps, that he had first preached a Christ who appeared to be the positive answer to the problems of human existence but that his presentation had later changed, so that this positive answer appeared to be negated?

This brings us to the question of what Paul had originally preached to the Corinthians. Commentators do not seem to have paid much attention to the fact that within the Corinthian correspondence we have two rather different definitions of the content of his gospel. Several times he refers to the proclamation of the crucified Christ (1 Cor. 1: 17–18, 23; 2: 2). But in 2 Cor. 4: 4 he speaks of the gospel of the glory of Christ, who is the image of God.[2] And each of these two definitions has a parallel in some other letter where he is speaking of his original message to the congregation he is addressing. In Gal. 3: 1 his concern is with the crucified Christ, but in 1 Thess. 1: 10 he speaks of the risen Jesus, God's son who will come from heaven. Now it is obvious that the full Pauline kerygma included both elements (see 1 Cor. 15: 1–4). But the passages previously quoted do suggest that at times Paul may have appeared to emphasize the one aspect to the virtual exclusion of the other. His converts might then exaggerate this one-sided emphasis to an even higher degree, so that Paul himself would find it necessary to redress the balance. To do this he would have to shift his own emphasis, and this process could give rise to the charge of inconsistency in his preaching which may be reflected in 2 Cor. 1: 18–19.

If Paul's original preaching in Corinth had appeared to stress one aspect of the kerygma more than the other, which aspect was it? The evidence of our first extant letter seems quite clearly to show that he

[2] The contrast with 1 Corinthians is noted by Hans Windisch, *Der zweite Korintherbrief* (Göttingen, 1924), *in loc.*, but he provides no discussion of it. See also Alfred Plummer, *A Critical and Exegetical Commentary on the Second Epistle of St Paul to the Corinthians* (*ICC*, Edinburgh, 1915), *in loc.* Plummer denies any ultimate inconsistency in Paul's thought. This may be true, but he may have appeared inconsistent to the Corinthians.

emphasized the crucified Christ. But we have to remember that this letter is an attempt to correct erroneous behaviour and ideas, some of which may perhaps be derived from a mistaken understanding of Paul's own teaching.[3] His insistence, therefore, on the crucified Christ may similarly represent a correction of Corinthian misunderstanding. This would imply that it was the glorified Christ upon whom their whole interest was centred. It is therefore possible that Paul's own original presentation, while obviously including the claim that Christ 'died for our sins', had tended rather to stress his resurrection and glorification. In that case, it may be that the substance of his initial preaching in Corinth is better represented by the definition of the gospel in 2 Cor. 4: 4.

What, then, does he mean here when he speaks of 'the glory of Christ, who is the image of God'? According to some commentators,[4] it is Christ as the revelation of God that he primarily has in mind. This is certainly one element in his thought, but it is not, perhaps, the major element. Other scholars[5] would see an allusion to the belief in Christ as the Last Adam, the heavenly man and the pattern of eschatological humanity. Christ, here, is man re-endowed with the divine glory which, in Jewish thought, had originally belonged to the first Adam. This exegesis receives support from 2 Cor. 4: 6, where we have a similar reference to Christ's reflection of the divine glory, and where there is an obvious allusion to the book of Genesis (ὁ θεὸς ὁ εἰπών, Ἐκ σκότους φῶς λάμψει, cf. Gen. 1: 3). Robin Scroggs would see a further reminiscence of the creation story, as interpreted in rabbinic thought, when Paul specifically states that God's glory is seen ἐν προσώπῳ Χριστοῦ: he has transferred to Christ the rabbinic idea that the original countenance of Adam was so brilliant that it outshone the sun. If this is the background to verse 6, it is highly likely that in verse 4 the description of Christ as εἰκὼν τοῦ θεοῦ is also to be related to Genesis, where we read of the creation of man in the divine image (Gen. 1: 26–7). Thus, Paul is here describing Christ as the embodiment

---

[3] See 1 Cor. 5: 9–11. The slogan πάντα μοι ἔξεστιν (1 Cor. 6: 12) may derive from Paul's teaching on idol meats, and may have been mistakenly applied by the Corinthians to sexual relationships.

[4] See A. Plummer, *op. cit.*, *in loc.*, and R. V. G. Tasker, *The Second Epistle of Paul to the Corinthians* (*TNTC*, London, 1958), *in loc.*

[5] See F. F. Bruce, J. Héring, *op. cit.*, *in loc.*, Hans Lietzmann (revised by W. G. Kümmel), *An die Korinther I–II* (*HNT*, Tübingen, 1949), *in loc.*, Robin Scroggs, *The Last Adam* (Philadelphia, 1966), pp. 96–9, H. D. Wendland, *Die Briefe an die Korinther* (*NTD*, Göttingen, 1948), and H. Windisch, *op. cit.*, *in loc.*

of true humanity. In terms of current Jewish thought, he reproduces the original glory of the first man, and is therefore the progenitor and archetype of eschatological man.

We may conclude that, when Paul first preached to the Corinthians, he may have seemed chiefly to lay emphasis upon the risen Christ as a being of divine glory who was the first example of what all men might become. No doubt he himself supposed that he had also given due weight to the fact of Christ's death. But to the Corinthians this may have been only the negative, if essential, preliminary to the positive gospel of the glorified Christ.

2. CORINTHIAN CONCLUSIONS

In 1 Corinthians Paul is faced with a number of practical problems, both ethical and ecclesiastical. In addition, however, he has to deal with the Corinthians' general attitude. They are convinced that they are plentifully endowed with wisdom, and that they already enjoy the blessings of eschatological existence. Both convictions could well be the result of Paul's preaching of Christ as the glorious Last Adam.

Why did the Corinthians think themselves wise? It would not be unreasonable to suppose that they had some vague acquaintance with the thought-forms of Hellenistic Judaism. Some were themselves Jews (Acts 18: 8; 1 Cor. 7: 18; 1: 12, ’Εγὼ δὲ Κηφᾶ). And the fact that the Alexandrian Apollos had gained a substantial following (1 Cor. 1: 12; 3: 4) may suggest that his hearers were already to some extent familiar with the ways of thinking current in the Diaspora. Now it would appear that Paul's preaching of Christ as the image of God has its parallels in the Sophia-speculation of Judaism, where the designation 'image of God' is attributed to Sophia as a heavenly being.[6] Whether or not Paul himself explicitly equated Christ with the Divine Wisdom, it would have been easy enough for the Corinthians to make the identification. Furthermore, Christ as the one being in whom is seen the glory which once belonged to the first man could readily be understood as being himself the primal man, and this also would facilitate an identification with Wisdom, since Hellenistic Judaism had fused together these two figures.[7] If, then, Paul's presentation of Christ had encouraged the Corinthians to identify this heavenly being with the

[6] See F. W. Eltester, *Eikon im Neuen Testament* (Berlin, 1958), p. 133.
[7] *Ibid.*, p. 140.

figure of Sophia it is easy to see how they came to assert their own possession of wisdom. For had not Paul himself taught them that they were so closely united with Christ as to be one with him in spirit (1 Cor. 6: 17)? Might they not reasonably conclude that they shared Christ's character, and so were endowed with heavenly wisdom themselves?

It is likewise obvious that their belief in their present enjoyment of eschatological existence could have been the result of Paul's proclamation of Christ as the Last Adam and as the being with whom they were already united. Hence their denial of the resurrection from the dead. Through union with Christ they were already living the life of the resurrection.

3. PAUL'S REACTION AND ITS IMMEDIATE CONSEQUENCES

The conclusions which, we have suggested, the Corinthians drew from Paul's original message were logical enough, but their behaviour must have compelled him to recognize that their logic was mistaken. Their all-too-human conduct showed that, if they were possessors of wisdom, it was of an earthly rather than a heavenly character. Paul will thus have been led to stress the fact that the Christ he preached was also the Christ who had been crucified. For the crucifixion of the Redeemer means that all earthly wisdom has been totally devalued and negated, since in the world's eyes it would be incredibly foolish to regard this event as the means of salvation. Perhaps in retrospect Paul attributes to this element of the kerygma a greater significance than he explicitly gave it at the time of his first visit to Corinth. In any case, his experience with the Corinthians has now taught him that this is the christological assertion to which he must give the preponderant weight: the Redeemer is a crucified Redeemer.

What of his reply to their belief in their present enjoyment of eschatological blessings and spiritual glory? One aspect of his answer is not explicitly christological, but we shall see that the Corinthians may have drawn from it some negative christological conclusions, and that Paul himself was later forced to develop its christological implications. The argument is set out in 1 Cor. 4: 8–13. It is simply that apostolic existence is lacking in glory. The apostles are ἄτιμοι, by contrast with the Corinthians' assumption that they themselves are ἔνδοξοι (1 Cor. 4: 10). Now apostolic existence is the pattern for Christian existence in general. It follows that the Christian community has not yet attained the life of the eschaton, which is characterized by δόξα (1 Cor. 15: 42; Phil. 3: 21). This conclusion is further confirmed in 1 Cor. 15: 44–8. Paul does not here deny his original proclamation of Christ as the glorious Last Adam, but he rejects the Corinthians' understanding of it. Conformity to the likeness of the heavenly man is not a matter of present realization but a hope for the future.

How did the Corinthians, in their turn, respond to Paul's attempt to correct what he believed to be their errors?

Is it not highly likely that they would have accused him of preaching an inconsistent gospel?[8] He had originally presented them with a glorious heavenly Redeemer in whom such vague, mythical figures as Sophia had become reality. But now they were expected to look for salvation to the Redeemer's inglorious human death. Taught originally that they were united with this splendid eschatological figure, they might legitimately have hoped to enjoy here on earth his heavenly form of existence, but now all such enjoyment was apparently denied them.

Some may have gone further than this. On the basis of Paul's first argument against present enjoyment of eschatological existence they may have questioned the validity of his gospel itself, and may have become inclined to turn from Christ to Moses. Paul had shown that the life of the apostle was inglorious, and the Corinthians might well agree that this was a true picture of himself. But according to the presuppositions of Hellenistic religion this lack of glory in Paul could readily be held to invalidate the gospel he preached. This gospel was based upon his own vision of the risen Christ (Gal. 1: 11–12, 15–16; 2 Cor. 4: 4–6),[9] a vision of the glory of God in the face of Christ who is God's image. But was it not a well-established religious truth that a divine vision produced a transformation in the visionary? Did not the visionary become deified himself?[10] If Paul had really beheld the being of God reflected in the glorified Christ, ought he not to show some signs of transformation into a deified condition? And if he did *not* show any such sign, might one not conclude that his vision was illusory?

---

[8] See above, pp. 143–4.

[9] The following commentators see an allusion to Paul's Damascus experience in 2 Cor. 4: 6: P. Bachmann, *Der zweite Brief des Paulus an die Korinther* (*ZK*, Leipzig, 1909), *in loc.*, F. F. Bruce, F. V. Filson, A. Plummer, R. H. Strachan, R. V. G. Tasker, *op. cit.*, *in loc.*

[10] See W. Bousset, *Kyrios Christos* (3rd edit., Göttingen, 1926), pp. 164ff.

Whatever he had seen, it was not to be accounted a source of divine revelation or a means of contact between God and man. And so, if his gospel depended upon his own experience, his whole message would seem to be invalidated.

If some of the Corinthians were inclined to argue in this way, they may then have looked for some other source of divine revelation originating in an encounter between man and God, and they may have found their answer in Moses. For Moses, as interpreted in Hellenistic Judaism, had the credentials which Paul quite clearly lacked. Moses' encounter with God on Sinai had had visible results:

Then after the said forty days had passed, he descended with a counenance far more beautiful than when he ascended, so that those who saw him were filled with awe and amazement; nor even could their eyes continue to stand the dazzling brightness that flashed from him like the rays of the sun. (Philo, *Vit. Mos.* ii. 70 (Loeb translation))

Furthermore, this splendid transformation was not exclusive to Moses alone. Another passage in Philo shows that the Mosaic religion offers its adherents also the hope of transformation into a god-like condition:

Thus he [Moses] beheld what is hidden from the sight of mortal nature, and, in himself and in his life displayed for all to see, he has set before us, like some well-wrought picture, a piece of work beautiful and godlike, a model for those who are willing to copy it. (*Vit. Mos.* i. 158)[11]

Thus, Moses might seem genuinely to give the Corinthians what Paul had only appeared to provide.

If, therefore, a tendency had arisen in the Corinthian church to prefer Moses' vision of God to Paul's vision of Christ, the Corinthians may have been ready of their own accord to welcome the teaching of the visiting missionaries whose work in Corinth is reflected in 2 Corinthians. It has been suggested that they stressed the splendour of Moses, and fitted Jesus into the Mosaic tradition.[12] If, despite their doubts about Paul's version of Christianity, the Corinthians were disinclined

---

[11] See Dieter Georgi, *Die Gegner des Paulus im 2. Korintherbrief* (Neukirchen–Vluyn, 1964), pp. 145–61, 258–65, for the presentation of Moses as the θεῖος ἀνήρ *par excellence*, and the θεῖος ἀνήρ as the model for the rest of mankind.

[12] See Georgi, *op. cit.*, pp. 282–92, and Gerhard Friedrich, 'Die Gegner des Paulus im 2. Korintherbrief', *Abraham Unser Vater* (edit. O. Betz etc., Leiden, 1963), pp. 181–215.

to abandon Christ entirely, the form of the Christian faith preached by the newcomers may well have seemed to them a satisfactory compromise or synthesis.

4. FURTHER DEVELOPMENTS IN PAUL'S CHRISTOLOGICAL THINKING

The Corinthians' claim that he was inconsistent in his preaching Paul solemnly denies (2 Cor. 1: 18–19). But the tendency to prefer a Mosaic version of Christianity has to be dealt with at greater length. Paul proves the greater glory of the Christian ministry. He shows that this glory, which consists in assimilation to the character of Christ, is manifested in conditions of earthly weakness. It is the result of conformity to the earthly life and death of Jesus. Present unity with Christ means union with the crucified Christ, and the repudiation of a 'triumphalist' view of christocentric existence.

In 2 Cor. 3: 6–13 Paul demonstrates in general terms the superiority of the Christian apostle, and the new covenant which he serves, to Moses and the Mosaic covenant. In verses 14–17 he digresses on the theme of the present obstinate attitude of the Jews. But the conclusion of verse 17, with its allusion to the freedom produced by the Spirit, brings him back to the theme of verse 12, the confidence of the Christian apostle, and in verse 18 he brings to a climax his earlier argument for the superiority of the Christian ministry in words which directly relate this superiority to the apostolic reflection of the glory of Christ himself:

ἡμεῖς δὲ πάντες ἀνακεκαλυμμένῳ προσώπῳ τὴν δόξαν κυρίου κατοπτριζόμενοι τὴν αὐτὴν εἰκόνα μεταμορφούμεθα ἀπὸ δόξης εἰς δόξαν, καθάπερ ἀπὸ κυρίου πνεύματος.

This verse is usually taken to refer to Christians in general, rather than to the apostles alone. But in the phrase ἀνακεκαλυμμένῳ προσώπῳ we have a contrast with Moses (see verse 13) rather than with the Jews of the immediately preceding verses. It is the hearts of the Jews which are said to be veiled: the veiling of the face is attributed to Moses. The logical subjects of the contrast, therefore, are the Christian apostles, as in verses 12–13. The addition of πάντες after ἡμεῖς raises no substantial objection to this interpretation. Paul may wish obliquely to remind the Corinthians that his own experience, which is closely related to his gospel, is not isolated but is shared by the other apostles (cf. 1 Cor. 15: 3–11). It might seem that he would hardly restrict to the apostles the process of transformation into Christ's likeness. But he is not ultimately doing this, since he sees apostolic existence as the model for the life of all Christians (1 Cor. 4: 16).

The apostles, then, reflect the divine glory,[13] just as Moses did. Their glory excels his, however. Their faces are unveiled, and this means that their glory is permanent, whereas his was transitory (2 Cor. 3: 13). Their splendour increases, for they progress from one state of glory to a further state of glory.[14] The transformation of Moses was superficial, but the apostles are subject to a genuine inward change of character.[15] All this Paul intends to be applied primarily to himself, if the argument so far is correct. He has to claim some element of glory for his present apostolic existence, if his converts are not to forsake the religion of Christ for the religion of Moses.

Nevertheless, the fact remains that in the eyes of the Corinthians this assimilation to the glory of the Lord would still by no means be apparent. It was not visible in Paul's outward state. How were they to be expected to believe that he was gradually becoming like his Lord? The next step in his argument must be the demonstration that assimilation to the character of Christ necessarily demands an apparently inglorious form of apostolic existence. In 2 Cor. 4: 4–6 Paul reasserts the glory and lordship of Christ as the content of his gospel, and reaffirms his own vision of Christ's glory as the result of divine revelation.[16] To the Corinthians, all this would demand visible splendour as its authentication. Paul, however, continues (2 Cor. 4: 7):

Ἔχομεν δὲ τὸν θησαυρὸν τοῦτον ἐν ὀστρακίνοις σκεύεσιν, ἵνα ἡ ὑπερβολὴ τῆς δυνάμεως ᾖ τοῦ θεοῦ καὶ μὴ ἐξ ἡμῶν.

This is really a preliminary point: lack of human glory is a necessary condition for the recognition that it is God's power which is at work in the ministry of the apostles. It is in verses 10–11 that we arrive at the

---

13 The translation of κατοπτριζόμενοι as 'reflecting' is supported by E. B. Allo, *Saint Paul: Seconde Épître aux Corinthiens* (*Ét. Bibl.*, Paris, 1956), *in loc.*, and by P. Bachmann, J. Héring, A. Plummer, *op. cit.*, *in loc.* The linguistic arguments for the choice between 'reflecting' and 'beholding' seem evenly balanced. The implied contrast with Moses supports 'reflecting'.

14 See E. B. Allo, P. Bachmann, F. V. Filson, A. Plummer, R. H. Strachan, *op. cit.*, *in loc.*

15 See P. Bachmann, *op. cit.*, *in loc.*   16 See above, p. 148.

organic connection between the form of Paul's outward existence and his transformation into the likeness of Christ:

πάντοτε τὴν νέκρωσιν τοῦ Ἰησοῦ ἐν τῷ σώματι περιφέροντες, ἵνα καὶ ἡ ζωὴ τοῦ Ἰησοῦ ἐν τῷ σώματι ἡμῶν φανερωθῇ. ἀεὶ γὰρ ἡμεῖς οἱ ζῶντες εἰς θάνατον παραδιδόμεθα διὰ Ἰησοῦν...

The suffering and humiliation of the apostles is in some sense a repetition of the suffering of Jesus, the Christ who was incarnate and crucified. At the same time, they undergo a process of inward spiritual renewal, as Paul shows in verse 16:

ἀλλ' εἰ καὶ ὁ ἔξω ἡμῶν ἄνθρωπος διαφθείρεται, ἀλλ' ὁ ἔσω ἡμῶν ἀνακαινοῦται ἡμέρᾳ καὶ ἡμέρᾳ.

Thus, unity with Christ and transformation into his likeness take two forms within the framework of the apostle's present earthly life: conformity to Christ's suffering and inward change in character. Acceptance of this kind of existence, moreover, is the condition of final and complete conformity to Christ's eternal glory (2 Cor. 4: 17).

In this way, Paul has finally provided an answer to those of the Corinthians who may have been inclined to challenge the truth of his gospel on the grounds that his own life discredited the validity of his vision of the risen Christ and so cast doubts on his gospel itself, based, as it seemed to be, upon his own experience. Despite external appearances, his encounter with Christ had initiated a genuine process of transformation into the likeness of the Redeemer. His vision was therefore authenticated, and his gospel was also valid. Furthermore, he has solved a problem which must in the Corinthians' minds have remained outstanding after they had read 1 Corinthians. They must have asked what was the meaning of present unity with Christ, if it did not mean what they had originally supposed. Paul has now shown them that it means participation in the sufferings which characterize the earthly existence of the Redeemer, and so must characterize the lives of those who belong to him so long as they remain in the earthly sphere. Certainly he has been referring chiefly to himself and to his fellow-apostles. But he expects Christians in general to conform to the apostolic model, as we have seen.

The main argument has reached its conclusion. But it is possible that in 2 Cor. 5: 16 we may have another echo of the implicit christological debate which Paul has been conducting with his correspondents. Here we seem to have a further repudiation of the belief that christocentric existence conforms to the natural human desire for a life of power and splendour, together with a hint that even Paul himself might at times have shared this desire, and might have once supposed that it could be satisfied through adherence to Christ. The verse runs:

Ὥστε ἡμεῖς ἀπὸ τοῦ νῦν οὐδένα οἴδαμεν κατὰ σάρκα· εἰ καὶ ἐγνώκαμεν κατὰ σάρκα Χριστόν, ἀλλὰ νῦν οὐκέτι γινώσκομεν.

The exegesis of this verse is, of course, much disputed, and any interpretation which may be proposed requires detailed substantiation. We shall take two preliminary points for granted. The phrase κατὰ σάρκα is used adverbially, qualifying the verbs of knowing,[17] and the protasis in the second half of the verse is not to be understood as introducing an unreal condition.[18]

The crucial point for discussion is the meaning of knowing κατὰ σάρκα. What we need is some explanation which will make plausible Paul's admission that he may himself have known Christ in this way.[19]

It is widely accepted that the phrase means the passing of judgement upon a person on the basis of purely worldly standards and according to his external circumstances.[20] But how well does this fit the context? The immediately preceding verse is not directly concerned with emphasis on externals, but with ceasing to live for oneself. This is not a major objection, perhaps. But there is a further consideration of more weight. If knowledge κατὰ σάρκα is taken in this sense, the most plausible explanation of Paul's words about his own knowledge of Christ is that they refer to his estimate of Jesus before his conversion. He had judged Jesus, in the words of R. V. G. Tasker, 'in the light of the prejudices of his upbringing, and had concluded that it was impossible that one born in such obscurity, living in such restricted

---

[17] See E. B. Allo, P. Bachmann, F. F. Bruce, R. V. G. Tasker, H. D. Wendland, *op. cit., in loc.*

[18] See E. B. Allo, H. Lietzmann, H. Windisch, *op. cit., in loc.*

[19] According to R. Bultmann, *Exegetische Probleme des zweiten Korintherbriefes* (Uppsala, 1947), p. 17, Paul is merely quoting an extreme instance, to make clear the meaning of the first half of the verse: the phrase is essentially hypothetical. But it is surely preferable, if possible, to produce an interpretation which allows to the real condition some positive and non-hypothetical content.

[20] See E. B. Allo, F. F. Bruce, H. Lietzmann, R. V. G. Tasker, *op. cit., in loc.,* and R. Bultmann, *op. cit.,* p. 17.

circumstances and dying such a humiliating death, could be the Christ that the Jews were expecting'.[21] But this interpretation is not entirely convincing. H. Windisch says it is difficult to understand why Paul should speak here with such emphasis of his earlier misunderstanding of Christ, and notes that ἐγνώκαμεν κατὰ σάρκα is an odd expression for a judgement resulting in rejection.[22] E. B. Allo agrees that the apostle's Jewish past is not a matter of interest in this epistle.[23] And should we not have expected Ἰησοῦν rather than Χριστόν?

Another possibility may be worth considering. Does knowledge κατὰ σάρκα stand for an egocentric attitude towards other people? Does it mean the concern to know one's neighbour for the sake of promoting one's own interests and satisfying one's own desires?[24] This would certainly fit the immediate context, which speaks of living for oneself no longer. And it is congruous with one aspect of Paul's use of σάρξ. Bultmann claims that, according to Paul, life κατὰ σάρκα is life in pursuit of one's own ends,[25] and that in Gal. 5: 13–15 the term σάρξ is used to mean 'natural human self-seeking'.[26] We may also note that two other phrases in Galatians (5: 24; 2: 19–20), when set side by side, imply that 'the flesh' is a synonym for egocentric existence.

If, then, the general meaning of knowledge κατὰ σάρκα is self-seeking knowledge, what does it more precisely mean when Christ is its object? And what does Paul mean when he admits that he may himself have been guilty of it? The line of thought we have followed so far in this essay suggests a possible answer to these questions.

Self-seeking knowledge of Christ was certainly, in Paul's eyes, the attitude of the Corinthians. They had been convinced that adherence to Christ brought them present glory, present wisdom, and present power. They boasted of their exalted condition, taking an egocentric pride in what they believed to be the results of their union with Christ. They valued Christ because they believed him to satisfy their own desire for the possession of god-like power and for an obviously splendid form of existence. Insofar as Paul's words in 2 Cor. 5: 16 are an oblique attempt to correct the attitude of the Corinthians, the interpretation we have proposed of a 'fleshly' knowing of Christ seems to fit reasonably well.

---

[21] *Op. cit., in loc.*   [22] *Op. cit., in loc.*   [23] *Op. cit., in loc.*
[24] See A. Schlatter, *Paulus der Bote Jesu* (Stuttgart, 1934), p. 560.
[25] R. Bultmann, *Theology of the New Testament*, vol. i (E.T., London, 1952), p. 241.
[26] *Ibid.*, p. 239.

But what of Paul himself? Is it really conceivable that he had ever thought of Christ as the Redeemer figure who would satisfy the natural human desire for a life of power and glory? Perhaps he admits the possibility, simply because he has come to realize that such an attitude could logically have been derived from his own emphasis upon Christ as the glorious Last Adam with whom believers were united. But it is not entirely impossible that he did himself once see Christ as the source of some divine power which would enhance his own personal abilities and energies in an obvious fashion. There may be a hint in 2 Cor. 12: 7–10 that he had at one time expected something of the kind. It was only after intensive prayer for the abolition of his physical weakness that he came to believe that it was precisely within a condition of human weakness that Christ would display his power. This implies a prior state of mind in which he had supposed that a visible access of power was the result of adherence to Christ. Such a conclusion was not illogical.[27] It is possible that it was in part Paul's experience of its results within the Corinthian community which led him finally to abandon it, and to work out a different understanding of christocentric existence, based on conformity to the crucified Christ.

5. THE RESULTS OF THE CORINTHIAN DEBATE

We have suggested that Paul's attempts to deal with developments and attitudes in Corinth led to the modification and development of his own christological ideas. An original emphasis on Christ as the glorious Last Adam gave way to an insistence on the significance of the crucified Christ. It is to the crucified Christ that believers are now being assimilated. Conformity to Christ's glory, though an inward reality in the present, must await the Parousia for open and complete manifestation. Paul works this out primarily in relation to his own apostolic existence and the authentication of his gospel. But he also sees his own life as the model for that of his converts (1 Cor. 4: 16–17; 11: 1), so that he wishes it to apply to the Corinthians as well, and to all Christians in general.

So far Paul's christological thought may have progressed during the course of his correspondence with Corinth. But the evidence of Romans suggests that he was not content to leave the matter there. In Romans

[27] In Jewish thought, the glory lost by Adam at the Fall contained an element of physical splendour. Was it not reasonable to suppose that a similar splendour would be restored to man through unity with the Last Adam?

we seem to have a further synthesis, whereby the concept of Christ crucified, which has become predominant in Paul's thinking, is integrated with his original theme of Christ as Last Adam. D. M. Stanley notes that according to 1 Corinthians Christ assumes the role of Second Adam at his resurrection, but that in Romans he already acts as such in his voluntary acceptance of death (Rom. 5: 12–21).[28] His obedient submission to death is seen as the reversal of the first Adam's disobedience, and so as a genuine work of the Last Adam. Was this the result of Paul's controversy with the Corinthians? It is, at any rate, a final satisfactory synthesis of the Corinthians' perfectly valid claim that Christians were united with the one who was already the Last Adam and Paul's own perception that union with Christ meant present conformity to his sufferings and death.

[28] D. M. Stanley, *Christ's Resurrection in Pauline Soteriology* (Rome, 1961), pp. 275–6.

11

'Individualgeschichte' und 'Weltgeschichte' in Gal. 2:15–21

WERNER GEORG KÜMMEL

Die Frage, ob Paulus die Vorstellung der 'Heilsgeschichte' teilt und seiner Heilsbotschaft zugrunde legt, ist in den letzten Jahren heftig umstritten gewesen.[1] Vor allem G. Klein hat diese Annahme leidenschaftlich abgelehnt und seinem Generalangriff auf die 'Idee' der Heilsgeschichte in der Bibel[2] die Untersuchung einer Reihe paulinischer Texte vorausgehen lassen,[3] von denen seine Auslegung von Gal. 2: 15 – 4: 31,[4] soweit ich sehe, noch nicht die ihr gebührende Beachtung gefunden hat. Das ist umso merkwürdiger, als die anhand dieses Textes aufgestellten Thesen, daß es nach Paulus 'mit einer Verheißungsstruktur des Judentums nichts ist' und daß 'die Sicht der Weltgeschichte an konkret erfahrener Individualgeschichte hängt',[5] doch provozierend genug sind, um eine sorgfältige Nachprüfung ihrer exegetischen Grundlagen notwenig erscheinen zu lassen. Wenn diese Aufgabe hier in Angriff genommen werden soll, so verbietet es der zur Verfügung stehende Raum, den ganzen von Klein behandelten Abschnitt des Galaterbriefs ins Auge zu fassen, ich möchte mich vielmehr auf den einleitenden Abschnitt Gal. 2: 15–21 beschränken,[6]

---

[1] Vgl. zur Übersicht etwa Chr. Dietzfelbinger, 'Heilsgeschichte bei Paulus?', *Th. E.* (N.F.) cxxvi, 1965 (Lit. S. 5 Anm. 1) und L. Goppelt–G. Klein, 'Paulus und die Heilsgeschichte: Schlußfolgerungen aus Röm. iv und 1. Kor. x. 1–13', *NTS* xiii, 1966/7, 31ff.

[2] G. Klein, 'Bibel und Heilsgeschichte. Die Fragwürdigkeit einer Idee', *ZNW* lxii, 1971, 1ff.

[3] Diese Aufsätze sind, z. T. mit Ergänzungen, abgedruckt bei G. Klein, *Rekonstruktion und Interpretation. Gesammelte Aufsätze zum Neuen Testament, B. ev. Th.* l, 1969, 145–224.

[4] G. Klein, 'Individualgeschichte und Weltgeschichte bei Paulus. Eine Interpretation ihres Verhältnisses im Galaterbrief', zuerst *Ev. Th.* xxiv, 1964, 126ff., mit einem Nachtrag wieder abgedruckt a. Anm. 3 a. O., 180ff. (danach wird im Folgenden mit 'Klein' zitiert).

[5] Klein, 194, 218.

[6] Die Kommentare zum Galaterbrief und die Spezialarbeiten zu Gal. 2: 15–21 werden hier alphabetisch aufgeführt und im weiteren nur mit dem Autorennamen zitiert (die Abkürzungen entsprechen denenin der *RGG*[3] bzw. in meiner

zumal nach Kleins eigener Feststellung 'in dem Übergangsstück [d. h.
2: 15–21] die Basis zutage tritt, auf welcher die in Kap. 3 und 4
vorgelegte Stellungnahme zum Problem der Heilsgeschichte allererst
möglich wird'.[7]

I

Ehe wir uns Kleins Interpretation der einleitenden Verse des Abschnitts (2: 15, 16) zuwenden können, sind zunächst drei Vorfragen zu
klären. (*a*) Zur Bestimmung des syntaktischen Zusammenhangs der
Verse 15 und 16 geht Klein von der ohne weitere Begründung vorge-
tragenen Behauptung R. Bultmanns aus, 'daß V. 15 ein geschlossener
Satz ist, dem V. 16 als Gegen-Satz folgt',[8] und sucht auf dem Boden
dieser syntaktischen Feststellung das dialektische Verhältnis der beiden
Verse zu bestimmen. Doch trifft diese Behauptung schwerlich den
syntaktischen Charakter der beiden Verse. Denn bei dieser Annahme
muß nicht nur V. 15 als ein prädikatsloser Nominalsatz angesehen
werden, sondern der Leser oder Hörer kann auch schwerlich bemerken,
daß mit dem Partizip εἰδότες ein neuer Satz begonnen werden soll,
dessen Subjekt erst nach einiger Zeit nachfolgt. Vielmehr sind die
beiden Verse 15 und 16 offensichtlich als *ein* Satz angelegt: das in V. 15
genannte Subjekt ἡμεῖς wird zunächst durch die doppelte Apposition
φύσει – ἁμαρτωλοί und εἰδότες δὲ – Χριστοῦ Ἰησοῦ näher bestimmt;
nach dieser Unterbrechung wird das Subjekt durch καὶ ἡμεῖς wieder
aufgenommen und der Satz zu Ende geführt. Somit ist der ganze Passus
ἡμεῖς – Χριστοῦ Ἰησοῦ das grammatische Subjekt des Hauptsatzes εἰς

Einleitung in das Neue Testament, [17]1973): H. W. Beyer–P. Althaus, *NTD*,
[9]1962; O. Bauernfeind, 'Der Schluß der antiochenischen Paulusrede', in:
Theologie als Glaubenswagnis, Festschr. K. Heim, 1954, 64ff.; C. Bonnard, *CNT*,
1953; R. Bring, *Der Brief des Paulus an die Galater*, 1968; R. Bultmann, 'Zur
Auslegung von Gal. 2: 15–18', in: R. Bultmann, *Exegetica*, 1967, 394ff.; E. D.
Burton, *ICC*, 1921; G. S. Duncan, *Moffatt*, 1934; D. Guthrie, *CB*, 1969; V.
Hasler, 'Glaube und Existenz, Hermeneutische Erwägungen zu Gal. 2: 15–21',
Th. Z. xxv, 1969, 241ff.; K. Kertelge, 'Zur Deutung des Rechtfertigungsbe-
griffs im Galaterbrief', *BZ* (N.F.) xii, 1968, 211ff.; M.-J. Lagrange, *Ét. Bibl.*,
[2]1925; H. Lietzmann, *HNT*, [3]1932; W. Mundle, 'Zur Auslegung von Gal.
2.17: 18', *ZNW* xxiii, 1924, 152f.; A. Oepke, *Th. H.K.*, 1937; H. N. Ridderbos,
NIC, 1953; H. Schlier, *Meyer*, [12]1962; R. T. Stamm, *Int. B.*, 1953; U. Wilckens,
'Was heißt bei Paulus: "Aus Werken des Gesetzes wird kein Mensch gerecht?"',
EKK, Vorarbeiten i, 1969, 57ff.; Th. Zahn, *Zahn*, [3]1922.
7 Klein, 180.
8 Bultmann, 394; Klein, 181 Anm. 7, 184. So z. B. auch Bonnard, Lagrange,
Schlier.

Χριστὸν ᾽Ιησοῦν ἐπιστεύσαμεν;[9] innerhalb der doppelten Apposition zu dem ersten ἡμεῖς dient das δέ der Anknüpfung der zweiten, partizipialen Bestimmung des Subjekts, hat also kopulative Bedeutung,[10] während das die Wiederholung des ἡμεῖς einleitende καί steigernden Sinn hat ('sogar').[11] Dieses Verständnis des Satzes entspricht genau seinem Aufbau und hat zur Folge, daß die beiden Hälften der das Subjekt definierenden Apposition V. 15, 16a für den Hauptsatz 'wir kamen zum Glauben an Jesus Christus' wesentlich sein müssen.

(*b*) Die Kennzeichnung der zum Glauben gekommenen Judenchristen also 'von Natur Juden und nicht Sünder aus den Heiden' 'scheint [nach Kleins Meinung] ohne direkte Analogie im zeitgenössischen Judentum zu sein', da 'die gelegentlichen Charakterisierungen feindlicher Heiden als Sünder in den Psalmen Salomos Heiden und Juden nicht prinzipiell konfrontieren'.[12] Diese Behauptung entspricht aber nicht dem Befund, die in der Literatur[13] gesammelten Belege beweisen vielmehr das Gegenteil. Schon in den Septuaginta wird gelegentlich das auf die 'Völker' bezogene *reša'im* des hebräischen Textes durch ἁμαρτωλοί wiedergegeben (z. B. Ps. 9: 18; Jes. 14: 5), und in der nachalttestamentlichen Literatur begegnet die Parallelisierung von ἔθνη und ἁμαρτωλοί mehrfach.[14] Es ist aber nicht möglich, die Bezeichnung ἁμαρτωλοί in diesen Texten auf bestimmte feindliche Heiden einzuschränken,[15] und wenn die Bezeichnung der

[9] So auch Wilckens, 60 Anm. 23 und die Übersetzungen in den Kommentaren von Beyer–Althaus, Burton, Guthrie.
[10] Vgl. R. Kühner–B. Gerth, *Ausführliche Grammatik der griechischen Sprache* ii, 2, ³1904, 274 und zur Verwendung von δέ bei einer doppelten Apposition ebd. S. 243 Anm. 1; J. D. Denniston, *The Greek Particles*, ²1954, 163.
[11] So W. Bauer, *Griechisch-deutsches Wörterbuch zu den Schriften des Neuen Testaments*, ⁵1958, 777 (ii, 2); vgl. E. Schwyzer–A. Debrunner, *Griechische Grammatik* ii, 1950, 633.
[12] Klein, 182.
[13] Vgl. dazu außer (H. L. Strack)–P. Billerbeck, *Kommentar zum Neuen Testament aus Talmud und Midrasch* iii, 1926, 537 und K. H. Rengstorf, *TWNT* i, 1933, 237ff.: P. Volz, *Die Eschatologie der jüdischen Gemeinde im neutestamentlichen Zeitalter*, ²1934, 84; E. Sjöberg, *Gott und die Sünder im palästinischen Judentum*, 1939, 77, 211; Kertelge, 213 Anm. 7.
[14] Ps. Sal. 2: 1 ἔθνη ἀλλότρια = τὸν ἁμαρτωλόν (ähnlich 1: 1, 8; 8: 13; 17: 25); 1. Makk. 1: 34 ἔθνος ἁμαρτωλόν = ἄνδρας παρανόμους (vgl. 2: 48); Tob. 13: 8 ἔθνει ἁμαρτωλῶν = ἁμαρτωλοί; Jub. 23: 23f. die Sünder der Heiden = sündige Völker; 2 Esdras 4: 23 *gentes* = *tribus impiae*; Sib. v: 255 κακοί = die Heiden.
[15] So Klein, 182, ähnlich Kertelge, 213.

heidnischen Völker als 'Sünder' auch nicht häufig begegnet,[16] so ist sie doch in den verschiedensten Zusammenhängen und auch gerade im Judengriechisch sicher bezeugt und erklärt sich aus der jüdischen Überzeugung, daß die Heiden als Menschen, die das jüdische Gesetz nicht kennen, deswegen ἄνομοι und somit ἁμαρτωλοί sind.[17] Paulus kennzeichnet hier also die Juden, die zum christlichen Glauben gekommen sind, in traditioneller jüdischer Sprache als 'von Herkunft' Juden und nicht 'Sünder', wie es die Heiden ebenso 'von Herkunft' sind. φύσει bezeichnet dabei deutlich die durch die geschichtliche Befindlichkeit gegebene Besonderheit der Juden bzw. Heiden (ähnlich Röm. 2: 27 ἡ ἐκ φύσεως ἀκροβυστία, aber nicht wesentlich anders auch Röm. 2: 14).[18] D. h. diese Beschreibung der zum christlichen Glauben gekommenen Juden geschieht nicht vom christlichen, sondern vom jüdischen Standpunkt aus.

(*c*) Als die Einsicht, die die so beschriebenen Juden gewonnen haben, nennt Paulus: 'daß ein Mensch nicht aus Gesetzeswerken, sondern durch Glauben an Jesus Christus gerecht gesprochen wird'. Es leidet keinen Zweifel, daß mit diesem Satz die Juden und die 'Sünder aus den Heiden' in gleicher Weise gemeint sind, daß ἄνθρωπος also beide Gruppen von Menschen zusammenfaßt. Nach Klein sind damit 'die des δικαιοῦσθαι bedürftigen Subjekte nicht mehr geschichtlich spezifiziert, sondern in kategorialer Nivellierung aller geschichtlichen Unterschiede unter der Rubrik ἄνθρωπος zusammengefaßt... Juden und Heiden fallen gemeinsam unter die abstrakte Kategorie des "Menschen" überhaupt'; und Klein fügt ausdrücklich hinzu, daß damit nicht 'etwa ein begriffslos einfach für τις stehendes ἄνθρωπος unzulässig ausgebeutet' sei, zumal in Röm. 3: 28 ebenfalls der Begriff ἄνθρωπος 'zur Nivellierung des Unterschiedes zwischen Juden und Heiden eingesetzt' werde.[19] Dagegen ist zunächst einmal zu sagen, daß Paulus ἄνθρωπος mehrfach völlig unbetont im Sinne von τις oder 'man' gebraucht (1 Kor. 4: 1; 11: 28; Gal. 6: 1, 7) und daß der Leser

---

16 Immerhin kommt sie auch im Neuen Testament gelegentlich vor (nach der wahrscheinlicheren Auslegung): Mk. 14: 41 par. Mt. 26: 45; Lk. 24: 7; vielleicht Lk. 6: 32–4, wo die Matthäusparallele 5: 47 wenigstens einmal ἐθνικοί hat. So etwa K. H. Rengstorf, *TWNT* i, 332, dagegen Zahn, 122 Anm. 59.

17 Lk. 24: 7 εἰς χεῖρας ἀνθρώπων ἁμαρτωλῶν kann mit Apg. 2: 23 διὰ χειρὸς ἀνόμων wechseln wie ähnlich Ps. Sal. 17: 18 neben 17: 25.

18 Vgl. Zahn, 121; H. Köster, *TWNT* ix, 265.

19 Klein, 183f.; zu Röm. 3: 28 G. Klein, *Rekonstruktion und Interpretation*, 149 Anm. 17 (hier der Hinweis auf U. Mauser, 'Gal. iii. 20: Die Universalität des Heils', *NTS* xiii, 1966/7, 268, der dieselbe Deutung von ἄνθρωπος vertritt).

oder Hörer in Gal. 2: 16 durch nichts darauf aufmerksam gemacht wird, daß der Begriff ἄνθρωπος hier betont gebraucht sei (und das gilt für Röm. 3: 28 ebenso). Weiter zeigt eine Nachprüfung der Verwendung des Begriffs ἄνθρωπος bei Paulus überhaupt, daß Paulus ἄνθρωπος häufig im Gegenüber zu Gott gebraucht,[20] daß dieser Begriff nirgends aber, wenn wir Röm. 3: 28; Gal. 2: 16 noch beiseite lassen, als übergreifender Begriff gegenüber irgend einer Aufteilung der Menschheit in Gruppen begegnet.[21] Vor allem aber ist zu beachten, daß nach dem syntaktischen Aufbau des Satzes ἄνθρωπος in der zweiten Hälfte der Apposition zu dem ersten ἡμεῖς zwar die beiden Gruppen der ersten Hälfte der Apposition zusammenfaßt, daß der Ton dieser partizipialen Apposition aber auf der Aussage 'nicht aus Gesetzeswerken, sondern aus Glauben an Jesus Christus' liegt, daß das Subjekt des ὅτι-Satzes also ganz unbetont ist.[22] Der Begriff ἄνθρωπος in Gal. 2: 16 ist also keineswegs 'ein Ereignis von eschatologischem Charakter',[23] sondern hat den unbetonten Sinn von 'jedermann'.[24]

Aufgrund der Klärung dieser Vorfragen können wir uns nun der Interpretation des Zusammenhangs von V. 15 und 16 zuwenden. Hier ist von jeher umstritten, ob 2: 15ff. von Paulus noch als Fortsetzung der Anrede des Kephas durch Paulus in der antiochenischen Situation (2, 14b) gemeint ist oder nicht. Nun wird sich freilich das in V. 15 unvermittelt auftretende ἡμεῖς nur verstehen lassen, wenn Paulus den eben angeredeten Petrus und sich selbst zusammenfaßt und in dieser Form eine Aussage macht, die für alle Juden gilt, die Christen wurden. Aber andererseits weist nichts darauf hin, daß Petrus in V. 15 noch als angeredetes Gegenüber gedacht ist (es fehlt ja auch jede Anrede!), und es wird sich zeigen, daß V. 17, 18 nur verständlich sind, wenn hier

---

[20] S. W. G. Kümmel, *Das Bild des Menschen im Neuen Testament*, 1948, 21 Anm. 45 (E.T., 1963, 40 n. 45).

[21] Auch Röm. 2: 9 ist keine Ausnahme, weil hier zwar πᾶσα ψυχὴ ἀνθρώπου neben der Aufteilung der Menschen in Juden und Griechen begegnet, in 2: 10 aber parallel dazu neben der gleichen Aufteilung bloßes πᾶς steht.

[22] Auch in Röm. 3: 28 verhält es sich nicht anders; 'die Abfolge von V. 28 nach V. 29f.' wird keineswegs 'zum Rätsel' (so Klein, s. Anm. 19), wenn ἄνθρωπος in 3: 28 'man' oder 'jedermann' bezeichnet; vielmehr verlangt die Feststellung, daß der Weg der Gesetzeswerke zur Rechtfertigung ausgeschlossen ist, nach Paulus offenbar den Hinweis darauf, daß auf diese Weise nicht mehr nur die Juden die Möglichkeit zum Tun der Gesetzeswerke hatten, sondern daß Juden *und* Heiden, wie es Gott entspricht, gerechtfertigt werden können.

[23] Klein, 185; ebenso E. Güttgemanns, 'Heilsgeschichte bei Paulus oder Dynamik des Evangeliums?', *Studia Linguistica Neotestamentica*, B. ev. Th. lx, 1971, 54.

[24] So auch Burton, Schlier, Zahn; W. Bauer, s. Anm. 11, 137, 3 a γ.

nicht mehr das Verhalten des Petrus in Antiochien im Blick ist. Da
überdies an keiner Stelle innerhalb von 2: 15–18 der Übergang von
der Anrede an Petrus zur situationslosen Argumentation gegenüber
den Galatern erkennbar ist, wird man annehmen müssen, daß Paulus
zwar durch den Anschluß an 2: 14 dazu veranlaßt wird, seine
überleitenden Ausführungen über die Unmöglichkeit der Unterstellung
des Christen unter die Botmäßigkeit des Gesetzes in 2: 15–21 mit
ἡμεῖς zu beginnen, zugleich aber festzustellen haben, daß in dem
ganzen Abschnitt grundsätzlich von der Glaubensentscheidung aller
Judenchristen und von deren Folge für die Freiheit vom Gesetz im
Hinblick auf die galatische Situation gesprochen wird.[25] Nach Klein
hat nun Paulus in dieser Absicht zunächst die natürlich aufweisbare
Grenze zwischen Juden und Heiden durch die Bezeichnung der Heiden
als Sünder 'zu einer eschatologischen Grenze aufgeladen', diesen
'eschatologischen Unterschied' aber durch die gemeinsame Unterstellung von Juden und Heiden unter den Begriff des ἄνθρωπος
'sogleich wieder zum Verschwinden gebracht'. Indem so 'die eschatologische Grenze' von V. 15 in V. 16a 'glatterdings aufgehoben wird',
bleibt sie trotzdem als Wahrheit bestehen und wird 'von neuer
Wahrheit ... überholt'. In der Glaubensentscheidung, daß der
Mensch nur aus Christusglauben gerecht gesprochen werden kann,
stehen darum die Judenchristen mit den Heidenchristen gleich, aber sie
sehen, anders als die Heidenchristen, 'in ihrem vorgläubigen Seinsstand
nicht sowohl die Notwendigkeit für ihren jetzigen Glaubensstand als
vielmehr dessen zu überwindendes Hindernis'.[26] Es ist leicht zu sehen,
daß sich diese Interpretation Kleins angesichts der oben gegebenen
Antworten auf die Vorfragen nicht halten läßt.

Zunächst ist einmal klar, daß im Sinn des Paulus in V. 15 nicht von
einer eschatologisch aufgeladenen Grenze zwischen Juden und Heiden
die Rede sein kann, die bei der Christwerdung bestehen bleibt, aber
von neuer Wahrheit überholt wird. Vielmehr 'argumentiert [Paulus]
vom Standpunkt des normalen Juden aus',[27] den er geteilt *hat*,
erklärt aber in dem parallelen Partizipialsatz V. 16a, daß die inzwischen
gewonnene Einsicht, daß kein Mensch aus Gesetzeswerken gerecht

---

[25] So auch Klein, 181 mit Bring, 80, 86; Ridderbos, 98; Stamm, 482; Wilckens,
59; Zahn, 119f. Daß Paulus im Geist noch Petrus anrede, nehmen an Bauernfeind, 75; Beyer–Althaus, 20; Burton, 125; Duncan, 64; Guthrie, 89; Lagrange,
46; J. Munck, *Paulus und die Heilsgeschichte*, 1954, 119; W. Schmithals, *Paulus
und Jakobus*, 1963, 60.
[26] Klein, 182ff.   [27] Lietzmann, 15; ähnlich Duncan, 64.

gesprochen werden kann, zur Folge hatte, daß auch die Judenchristen, obwohl sie 'von Herkunft Juden' blieben, den Christusglauben angenommen haben, um auf diese Weise auch gerechtfertigt werden zu können. D. h. der von Paulus übernommene Gegensatz von Juden und Heiden = 'Sündern' wird nicht aufgehoben, weil die Judenchristen 'von Herkunft Juden' geblieben sind, er wird aber auch nicht 'von neuer Wahrheit ... überholt' (diese Dialektik ist unpaulinisch), sondern er wird in der Tat, trotz des Protestes von Klein, 'relativiert': die Judenchristen haben sich, ohne ihr Judesein aufgeben zu wollen oder zu können, im Wissen auf die alleinige Rechtfertigung aus Glauben den Heiden gleichgestellt und sind dadurch auch zu (gerechtfertigten) Sündern geworden, wie es V. 17 voraussetzt. Damit ist aber gegeben, daß die Judenchristen nach der Meinung des Paulus nicht im Unterschied zu den Heidenchristen, sondern *ganz genau wie* die Heidenchristen ihr vorchristliches Sündersein als das 'zu überwindende Hindernis' und damit natürlich zugleich als 'die Notwendigkeit für ihren jetzigen Glaubensstand'[28] anzusehen gelernt haben. Was die Rechtfertigung aus Glauben an Christus betrifft und damit die Hoffnung auf eschatologische Rettung, so stehen aufgrund ihrer Einsicht (εἰδότες) die Judenchristen mit den Heidenchristen jetzt völlig gleich (so auch Röm. 3: 28–30); das ändert aber nichts daran, daß sie 'von Herkunft Juden' bleiben und ihr Judesein sie nicht weniger, aber auch nicht mehr an der Möglichkeit gehindert hatte, gerechtfertigt zu werden, und daß dieser Zustand sich für beide nur durch den Glauben an Christus geändert hat. Garnichts aber sagt unser Text über den Hinfall einer 'Verheißungsstruktur des Judentums' aus, zumal im Galaterbrief, anders als im Römerbrief, das Verhältnis von Judenchristen und Heidenchristen zueinander überhaupt nicht im Blickfeld erscheint, weil im Galaterbrief ausschließlich Heidenchristen angesprochen sind (4: 8; 6: 12). Die Behauptung, daß es nach Paulus 'mit einer Verheißungsstruktur des Judentums nichts ist', kann darum an Gal. 2: 15f. nicht verifiziert werden, weil hier von keiner 'eschatologischen Grenze' die Rede ist, die dann 'glatterdings aufgehoben' werden könnte, und da andererseits von der 'Verheißungsstruktur des Judentums' in Gal. 2: 15f. darum nicht die Rede sein kann, weil Paulus hier von Gottes Verhalten gegenüber Israel oder dem jüdischen Volk überhaupt nicht redet. Die Verse tragen darum, richtig interpretiert, zu einer Antwort auf die Frage nach heilsgeschichtlichem Denken bei Paulus überhaupt nichts aus.

[28] Klein, 185.

II

Freilich kann diese Interpretation von Gal. 2: 15f. erst als sicher in Anspruch genommen werden, wenn sich zeigen läßt, daß die folgenden Verse mit ihr in Einklang stehen, und überdies muß die Frage noch beantwortet werden, ob der ganze Abschnitt Gal. 2: 15–21 die These stützt, daß bei Paulus 'die Sicht der Weltgeschichte an konkret erfahrener Individualgeschichte hängt'.[29]

Für das Verständnis des schwierigen Verses 17 muß davon ausgegangen werden, daß Paulus sich in 2: 15ff. nicht mehr mit dem Verhalten des Petrus in Antiochien auseinandersetzt.[30] Infolgedessen kann Paulus in V. 17 nicht sagen wollen, das Verhalten des Petrus könne zu der abzulehnenden falschen Folgerung führen, der Versuch, in Christus gerecht zu werden, sei selber Sünde.[31] Ferner hat Klein nachgewiesen, daß 'Logik und paulinischer Sprachgebrauch gebieten, daß in V. 17 nur der ἄρα-Satz verneint wird'.[32] Demnach *stellt* Paulus in V. 17a *fest*, daß die Judenchristen bei ihrem Bestreben, in Christus gerechtfertigt zu werden, auch selbst als Sünder befunden *wurden*, und lehnt nur die daraus gezogene Folgerung als unmöglich ab, durch diesen Vorgang sei Christus zum 'Diener der Sünde' geworden. Aber in wiefern gilt für die Judenchristen: 'Wenn wir in dem Bestreben, in Christus gerechtfertigt zu werden, auch unsererseits als Sünder befunden wurden', und in welchem Sinn kann daraus fälschlich geschlossen werden, Christus sei ein 'Diener der Sünde'? ζητοῦντες δικαιωθῆναι ἐν Χριστῷ V. 17 greift offensichtlich auf ἐπιστεύσαμεν ἵνα δικαιωθῶμεν ἐκ πίστεως Χριστοῦ zurück, sodaß nach Paulus der Anschluß der Judenchristen an den Glauben an die alleinige Rechtfertigung durch Christus bewirkt hat, daß auch die Judenchristen (doch wohl: wie die Heidenchristen) 'als Sünder befunden wurden'. Da nun καὶ αὐτοὶ ἁμαρτωλοί in V. 17a offensichtlich feststellen will, daß die Judenchristen *ebenso* wie irgend jemand sonst als ἁμαρτωλοί befunden wurden, läßt sich schwerlich bezweifeln, daß Paulus im Rückblick auf V. 15 in V. 17 sagen will: die Judenchristen erwiesen

---

[29] S. Anm. 5.   [30] S. o. S. 161f.

[31] Gegen W. G. Kümmel, *Römer 7 und die Bekehrung des Paulus*, 1929, 123; Ph. Vielhauer, *Oikodome*, Diss. Heidelberg 1939, 89; W. Schmithals, s. Anm. 25, 62.

[32] Klein, 189; so auch Burton, 126f.; Ridderbos, 101; M. Barth, 'Rechtfertigung', in: *Foi et salut selon S. Paul, An. Bibl.* xlii, 1970, 161 Anm. 57. Der mit εἰ eingeleitete Bedingungssatz ist daher kein Irrealis (gegen Bultmann, 396; W. G. Kümmel, s. Anm. 31).

sich ebenso wie die Heiden als Sünder, als sie erkannten, daß sie nur in Christus gerechtfertigt werden konnten. Klein hat also recht, wenn er aufgrund des Sprachgebrauchs des Paulus für εὑρίσκειν und aufgrund des Zusammenhangs feststellt: 'Im Akt des πιστεύειν der Judenchristen wird es manifest, daß auch die Juden der Gerechtigkeit ermangeln..., daß auch sie Sünder sind'.[33]

Nun zieht Paulus aus der Erkenntnis, die die Judenchristen bei ihrem Gläubigwerden gewannen, daß nämlich auch sie Sünder seien wie die Heiden (und darum nur durch die Rechtfertigung des Sünders gerettet werden konnten, Röm. 3: 23f.), die mögliche (oder auch gegen ihn vorgebrachte) Folgerung: 'Ist also Christus ein Diener der Sünde?', und das kann doch nur heißen: fördert nicht Christus die Sünde, indem er die Zahl der Sünder vermehrt? Paulus kann diese folgernde Frage aber darum radikal verneinen (und diese Verneinung dann in V. 18 begründen), weil nach seiner Meinung die Judenchristen durch ihre Christwerdung nicht erst zu Sündern *geworden* sind, vielmehr nur zum Vorschein kam, daß sie (wie die Heiden) Sünder *waren*. Das aber bestreitet Klein energisch: 'Im Glauben an Christus werden auch die Juden zu solchen, von denen sie sich bisher gerade *als* Juden, φύσει (V. 15), unterschieden: zu ἁμαρτωλοί', und daraus ergibt sich für Klein einerseits, daß die Frage, 'ob in dem εὑρεθῆναι ἁμαρτωλοί nur die Entbergung eines bisher schon vorhandenen Tatbestandes für die Erkenntnis oder die Konstituierung eines bisher nicht existenten Tatbestandes geschehe', 'unsachgemäß' sei, und andererseits, daß 'die Aufhebung des Vorrangs [der Juden] in Gal. 2: 15ff.... als Ereignis einer unvergleichlichen Disqualifikation' erfahren wird, 'die jegliche vorgegebene Ausgrenzung einer heiligen Gemeinschaft aus der umgebenden Welt der Sünde vernichtet und die Geschichte sui generis, die sich innerhalb der Ausgrenzung begab, ebenso als Bestandteil der sündigen Profangeschichte *erweist*, wie sie jene dazu allererst nun macht'. Und das bedeutet nach Klein, daß es mit einer Verheißungsstruktur des Judentums nichts ist, sofern damit '... eine theologisch weiterhin gültige Differenz zwischen Juden und Heiden substituiert wird'.[34] Dazu ist zunächst einmal zu sagen, daß der Leser verblüfft ist, wenn Klein der eindeutigen Feststellung, daß in V. 17a vom Manifestwerden der Sündigkeit der Juden die Rede ist, dann plötzlich die weitere Feststellung folgen läßt, daß die Juden im

[33] Klein, 187, 190, aber auch Lagrange, 49f.; Oepke, 47; Schlier, 95; Zahn, 126.
[34] Klein, 192, 194.

Glauben an Christus nach V. 17a zu Sündern *werden.* Und dieser Wechsel in der Interpretation von V. 17a wird in der Tat von Klein auch nicht durch die Exegese dieses Satzes begründet, sondern durch den Rückweis auf 'die durch das Nebeneinander von V. 15 und V. 16 bereits deutlich gewordene Dialektik'.[35] Wenn aber diese Dialektik in der von Klein angenommenen Form nicht haltbar ist (s. o. S. 162f.), dann fällt die einzige Begründung für die Behauptung dahin, daß Paulus in V. 17a von einem 'Sündigwerden' der sich zu Christus wendenden Juden rede. Und das trifft nun in der Tat nicht zu. Paulus stellt vielmehr in V. 17 eindeutig fest, daß die Judenchristen durch ihren Anschluß an Christus zugestanden haben, daß auch sie Sünder wie die Heiden *waren* und darum wie die Heiden nur 'in Christus gerechtfertigt werden' konnten.[36] Natürlich bedeutet das von dem in V. 15 aufgenommenen Standpunkt der Juden aus eine 'unvergleichliche Disqualifikation' und auch vom Standpunkt der Judenchristen aus eine völlige Gleichstellung der ehemaligen Juden und der ehemaligen Heiden vor dem Urteil Gottes. Aber absolut garnichts besagt diese Gleichstellung für die 'Verheißungsstruktur des Judentums', da diejenigen Christen, die 'von Herkunft Juden' waren, ja 'von Herkunft Juden' geblieben sind, und da sich die Frage, ob die den Juden geltenden Verheißungen Gottes durch das Christwerden der Juden für diese Juden hinfällig geworden sind, von Gal. 2: 15–17 aus überhaupt nicht beantworten läßt. Und ebensowenig läßt sich von diesen Versen aus die Behauptung verifizieren, daß sich durch die Gleichstellung der ehemaligen Juden mit den ehemaligen Heiden ἐν Χριστῷ 'die Geschichte sui generis [der Juden] ... als Bestandteil der sündigen Profangeschichte' *erweise*, weil die Frage nach Gottes Handeln gegenüber dem Volk der Verheißung hier völlig außerhalb des Gesichtskreises liegt. Denn nicht von 'Weltgeschichte' ist hier die Rede, sondern von dem Nebeneinander von 'Synagoge' und 'Kirche'. Aber stützt dieses Verständnis von Gal. 2: 15–17 dann nicht Kleins Behauptung, daß in diesen Versen 'die Sicht der Weltgeschichte an konkret erfahrener Individualgeschichte hängt'?

III

Diese Frage liegt umso näher, als Paulus zur Begründung der Ablehnung der Frage von V. 17a nun in V. 18 in die 1. Person Singular übergeht. Daß trotz dieses unvermittelten Wechsels in der Person des

---

[35] Klein, 191f.   [36] So auch Wilckens, 61 Anm. 26.

Verbums Paulus nicht in seinem individuellen Namen reden kann, ergibt sich aus der Unmöglichkeit, dann der Aussage 'Wenn ich wieder aufbaue, was ich aufgelöst habe, stelle ich mich als Übertreter hin' einen erträglichen Sinn abzugewinnen.[37] Aber ebenso spricht garnichts dafür, daß Paulus hier noch einmal an das Verhalten des Petrus in Antiochien denkt, der sich erneut den gesetzlichen Forderungen unterwarf (2: 12f.);[38] denn da V. 18 die Ablehnung der aus V. 17a abgeleiteten falschen Folgerung begründen will, muß sich diese Begründung auf das Verhalten der Judenchristen ganz allgemein bei ihrem Christwerden zurückbeziehen und kann nicht ein bestimmtes Verhalten des Petrus im Auge haben, und überdies konnten die Galater ja nach der allgemeinen Argumentation in V. 15–17 schwerlich bemerken, daß in V. 18 das in V. 12–14 erwähnte Verhalten des Petrus assoziiert werden solle. Wenn sich aber V. 18 auf das Christwerden der Judenchristen bzw. auf eine abzulehnende falsche Schlußfolgerung aus diesem Christwerden zurückbezieht, kann der Wechsel von 'wir' zu 'ich' in V. 18 nur stilistische Bedeutung haben, sodaß die 1. Person Singular das μὴ γένοιτο in verlebendigender Form mit einem möglichen gegensätzlichen, aber nicht verwirklichten Handeln der Judenchristen begründet. Ist die 1. Person Singular aber Stilform und damit 'überindividuell'[39] = jeder beliebige (Judenchrist), so ist damit zweierlei gegeben: (*a*) Paulus argumentiert im ganzen Zusammenhang anhand des faktischen (V. 17a), des möglichen (V. 18) und erneut des faktischen (V. 19f.) Verhaltens der Judenchristen; dabei stehen sich aber der Bericht über das Christwerden der Judenchristen V. 15–17a einerseits und die anschließende Argumentation V. 17b–21 andererseits nicht so gegenüber, daß in V. 15–17a kollektiv vom 'Akt des Gläubigwerdens' die Rede ist, in V. 18–21 aber vom 'neuen Stand des Glaubenden', was zur Folge hätte, daß in V. 18–21 aus sachlicher Notwendigkeit die 1. Person Singular auftritt, weil der mit Christus Gekreuzigte 'nur als dem vorgegebenen Kollektiv gegenüber Vereinzelter noch in den Blick geraten kann'.[40] Das trifft schon darum nicht zu, weil V. 19 in anderer Sprache erneut vom Christ*werden* der Juden-

---

[37] S. Klein, 196.

[38] So Klein, 196 mit Beyer–Althaus, Bonnard, Burton, Oepke, Schlier; W. Schmithals, s. Anm. 25, 62; Ph. Vielhauer, s. Anm. 31, 89.

[39] So Bonnard, 55; Burton, 132; Oepke, 47; Ridderbos, 102; Schlier, 96 Anm. 4; W. G. Kümmel, s. Anm. 31; J. Munck, s. Anm. 25, 121; Blaß–Debrunner, s. Anm. 10, §281.

[40] Klein, 195f. 201f.; ähnlich Kertelge, 219.

christen wie in V. 16f. die Rede ist; das trifft vor allem aber deshalb nicht zu, weil der in V. 15–17 anklingende Gegensatz von Juden und Heiden in V. 19–21 gar nicht mehr im Blickfeld ist, sondern ausschließlich das faktische oder mögliche Verhalten *der* Judenchristen. So sehr natürlich der *einzelne* Judenchrist 'an Christus glaubt' und 'mit Christus gekreuzigt' wird (V. 16, 19), so sehr ist für Paulus doch selbstverständlich, daß alle Getauften 'einer in Christus' sind (Gal. 3: 28), und der Gegensatz von 'Kollektiv' und 'Vereinzelter'[41] ist daher in diesem Zusammenhang völlig unsachgemäß.

(*b*) V. 18 begründet die Ablehnung der Folgerung, die Christwerdung der Judenchristen mache Christus zu einem Sündendiener, mit der Feststellung: 'Wenn ich nämlich wieder aufbaue, was ich abgerissen habe, erweise ich mich als Übertreter'. Schon dieser logische Zusammenhang zwischen V. 17 und 18 legt die Annahme keineswegs nahe, Paulus sehe in dem 'Abreißen', d. h. in der Aufgabe der Gesetzestreue und dem Gläubigwerden, die Übertretung, die zum Vorschein kommt, wenn die Judenchristen sich wieder unter das Gesetz begeben.[42] Und überdies verlangt V. 18 selber, daß das 'Wiederaufbauen' die Ursache für den Erweis als Übertreter ist und nicht das 'Abreißen'. Infolgedessen kann V. 18 als Begründung des μὴ γένοιτο in V. 17b nur bedeuten: Wenn auch die Judenchristen durch ihre Absicht, in Christus gerechtfertigt zu werden, als Sünder in Erscheinung traten wie die Heidenchristen, dann ist trotzdem Christus kein Förderer der Sünde, weil der Judenchrist vielmehr dann als Übertreter des Gesetzes sich erweist, wenn er das von ihm zurückgewiesene Gesetz wieder für sich in Kraft setzt.[43] Die Judenchristen (und *per analogiam* auch die galatischen Heidenchristen), die sich wieder unter die Botmäßigkeit des Gesetzes begeben und damit anerkennen, daß sie aus Gesetzeswerken gerechtfertigt werden wollen, erzeigen sich gerade dadurch als Gesetzesübertreter;[44] denn 'jeder beschnittene Mensch ist verpflichtet, das ganze Gesetz zu erfüllen' (Gal. 5: 3). Nur falls Judenchristen

---

[41] Klein, 202.

[42] So Bring, 98; Oepke, 47; Wilckens, 64 (als *mögliche* Auslegung); Zahn, 130, 132; O. Michel, *TWNT* v, 145; W. Schmithals, s. Anm. 25, 62.

[43] S. Klein, 198f. mit Bonnard, 55; Bultmann, 398f.; Burton, 130f.; Guthrie, 92; Lietzmann, 16; Mundle, 153; Ridderbos, 103; Schlier, 97; J. Schneider, *TWNT* v, 737f.

[44] Die Frage, warum Paulus hier den Begriff παραβάτης einführe (s. etwa Burton, 131; Klein, 199), ist unbeantwortbar; richtig Bultmann, 399: 'So hätte Paulus in V. 18 statt παραβάτην ἐμαυτὸν συνιστάνω auch sagen können: ἁμαρτωλὸς εὑρεθήσομαι.'

sich wieder unter das Gesetz begeben und dadurch die Zahl der
Gesetzesübertreter vermehren, kann Christus als 'Diener der Sünde'
bezeichnet werden; doch zeigt V. 19f., daß diese negative Möglichkeit
in Wirklichkeit nicht zutrifft, weil ja die Judenchristen für das Gesetz
tot *sind*. Versteht man V. 18 in dieser Weise, so ist der Vers als
Begründung des μὴ γένοιτο völlig verständlich und muß weder als
'Parenthese'[45] noch gar als Interpolation[46] angesehen werden.

IV

Vielmehr stellt Paulus neben die (hypothetische) negative Begründung
des μὴ γένοιτο in V. 18 nun in V. 19f. die (faktische) positive Begründung dieses μὴ γένοιτο:[47] 'Denn *ich* bin durch das Gesetz für das
Gesetz gestorben, um für Gott zu leben. Ich bin mit Christus gekreuzigt; *ich* lebe aber nicht mehr, Christus aber lebt in mir.' Da V. 19f.
also durch den Hinweis auf das faktische Geschehen die Unmöglichkeit
der Behauptung widerlegen will, das Christwerden der Judenchristen
habe Christus zum Diener der Sünde gemacht, muß V. 19f. auf die
Ausführung über das Christwerden der Judenchristen in V. 16, 17a
zurückgreifen und diese Wendung zu Christus mit neuen Begriffen
beschreiben. Der Rückgriff auf V. 16, 17a und der sachliche Parallelismus von V. 18 und 19f. fordern darum, daß auch die mit ἐγώ
eingeleitete Aussage in der 1. Person Singular in V. 19f. nicht als
persönliche Aussage des Paulus über sich selbst,[48] sondern wie V. 18
als stilistischer Gebrauch der 1. Person Singular verstanden werden
muß:[49] während es für die Judenchristen nicht zutrifft, daß sie sich
durch erneute Stellung unter das Gesetz als Übertreter hinstellen, gilt
es für sie, daß sie dem Gesetz gegenüber gestorben sind und nun *für
Gott* (nicht als Übertreter) *leben*, weil Christus in ihnen lebt und ihr
Leben im Fleisch ein Leben im Glauben an diesen Christus ist, der sich
für sie aus Liebe hingegeben hat. Warum Paulus in diesem Zusammen-

---

[45] Lietzmann, 17; Schlier, 96.   [46] Hasler, 246 Anm. 8.
[47] So richtig Klein, 199. Es trifft darum vermutlich zu, daß das γάρ in V. 19 wie
das γάρ in V. 18 an V. 17 anknüpfen soll (s. Anm. 45); aber γάρ *kann* hier auch
fortführenden Sinn haben (so Oepke, 48; vgl. die Beispiele für diesen Gebrauch
von γάρ bei W. Bauer, s. Anm. 11, 302, 4).
[48] So fälschlich Burton, 132; Duncan, 70; Hasler, 247; Oepke, 48; W. G. Kümmel,
s. Anm. 31.
[49] So Bonnard, 55; Ridderbos, 103; Schlier, 96 Anm. 4; W. Mundle, *Der Glau-
bensbegriff des Paulus*, 1932, 90 Anm. 1; P. Stuhlmacher, *Gerechtigkeit bei
Paulus*, 1965, 224.

hang den stilistischen Gebrauch der 1. Person Singular noch durch das hinzugefügte ἐγώ verstärkt (V. 19, 20a), ist naturgemäß nicht mit Sicherheit zu sagen; aber man kann vermuten, daß er dem nicht zutreffenden hypothetischen Argument in V. 18 gegenüber durch das vorangestellte ἐγώ die Realität der Aussage V. 19 über die Veränderung der Situation der Judenchristen dem Gesetz gegenüber betonen möchte; und möglicherweise ist auch der viel diskutierte Subjektwechsel zwischen V. 20a und 20b bei der Aufnahme des ἐγώ in V. 19 schon im Blick.[50] Auf keinen Fall aber läßt sich der Wechsel von der 1. Person Plural zur 1. Person Singular zwischen 2: 15–17 und 2: 18–21 damit begründen, daß die 1. Person Plural angewandt werden mußte, 'solange die aufweisbare Grenze zwischen Juden und Heiden auch die soteriologische zwischen Heil und Unheil ist' und sich 'die soteriologische Qualifikation des Menschen aus seiner Zugehörigkeit zu dem...empirischen Kollektiv' bestimmt, während die 1. Person Singular gebraucht werden mußte, sobald die Angehörigen der Kollektive 'theologisch unter die Kategorie des Menschen überhaupt fallen' und der Mensch nur noch als 'Vereinzelter' in den Blick geraten kann, sodaß der Gebrauch der 1. Person Singular in V. 18–21 'Widerschein des eschatologischen Geschehens selbst – in der Sprache' ist.[51] Diese Behauptung ist schon darum falsch, weil die ehemaligen Juden, die den Christusglauben annahmen, schon in V. 16b, 17 als 'Vereinzelte' in den Blick gefaßt sind, die sich aus der natürlichen Gegebenheit ihrer jüdischen Herkunft aussonderten, trotzdem aber im Plural von ihnen geredet wird, und weil, wie wir sahen, trotz des Übergangs zur 1. Person Singular in V. 18 weiter von den Judenchristen allgemein die Rede sein muß. Die Behauptung ist aber vor allem darum falsch, weil nach der Meinung des Paulus der Tod für das Gesetz dadurch zustande kommt, daß der Glaubende durch die Taufe in den Christus eingefügt wird (Gal. 3: 26–8; 1. Kor. 12: 12f.), sodaß trotz der individuellen Glaubensentscheidung gerade keine 'Vereinzelung' der Glaubenden stattfindet. Und es ist falsch, von einem durch den Übergang in die 1. Person Singular sichtbar werdenden 'anthropologischen' Stil zu reden,[52] weil das Nebeneinander von Gal. 2: 19f. und

---

50 Daß Paulus nicht nur die Stilform der 1. Person Singular kennt (vgl. W. G. Kümmel, s. Anm. 31, 121ff.), sondern auch das betonte ἐγώ rein rhetorisch gebrauchen kann, zeigen 1. Kor. 6: 12 und vielleicht 10: 30.

51 Klein, 201f.

52 So H. Conzelmann, 'Die Rechtfertigungslehre des Paulus: Theologie oder Anthropologie?', *Ev. Th.* xxviii, 1968, 398f., worauf Klein verweist.

3: 26–8 ebenso wie von 6: 14 und 6: 16 zeigen, daß Paulus von dem mit Christus gestorbenen Glaubenden immer sofort sagt: 'ihr seid alle einer in Christus', ihr gehört, ob vorher Beschnittene oder Unbeschnittene, zum 'Israel Gottes'.

Darum kann der Abschnitt Gal. 2: 15–21 nicht als Zeugnis für die 'paulinische Sicht von Individualgeschichte'[53] in Anspruch genommen werden. Auch wenn hier der theologische Sinn der Aussage Gal. 2: 16, 17a, 19f. und damit die Frage nicht erörtert werden kann, ob das paulinische Verständnis der Rechtfertigung sich nicht durch seinen eschatologischen Rahmen einer individualistischen und anthropologischen Deutung überhaupt entzieht,[54] kann es keinen Zweifel leiden, daß weder die Nebeneinanderstellung von φύσει Ἰουδαῖοι und ἐξ ἐθνῶν ἁμαρτωλοί in 2: 15 noch der Gebrauch von ἄνθρωπος in 2: 16 noch der Übergang in die 1. Person Singular in 2: 18 oder auch das ἐγώ in 2: 19 zu dem Urteil berechtigen, daß Paulus in diesem 'Übergangsstück' von 'Individualgeschichte' rede, der er dann in 3: 1ff. seine Sicht der 'Weltgeschichte' folgen lasse. Natürlich trifft es zu, daß niemand die paulinische 'Sicht der Geschichte zu verifizieren vermag', 'wer sich nicht mit Christus hat kreuzigen lassen', oder anders gesagt: die paulinische Sicht von Gottes Handeln in der Geschichte kann nur der Glaubende akzeptieren. Und *insofern* hängt natürlich bei Paulus, um die Sprache Kleins aufzunehmen, 'die Sicht der Weltgeschichte an konkret erfahrener Individualgeschichte'.[55] Aber die Entgegenstellung dieser beiden Begriffe ist überhaupt falsch, weil Paulus keine 'Individualgeschichte' kennt, die nicht immer auch durch die Zugehörigkeit des Individuums zu dem 'gegenwärtigen bösen Äon' oder durch das Herausgenommensein aus dem 'gegenwärtigen bösen Äon' und die Versetzung in die 'Herrschaft seines geliebten Sohnes' charakterisiert ist.[56] Denn eine 'säkulare' Existenz, die sich der bewußten oder unbewußten Entscheidung zwischen diesen beiden Äonen entzieht, kennt ja Paulus nicht. Aber wie man auch zu der uneingeschränkten

---

[53] Klein, 202.

[54] Vgl. dazu nur E. Käsemann, 'Rechtfertigung und Heilsgeschichte im Römerbrief', *Paulinische Perspektiven*, 1969, 108ff. und W. G. Kümmel, 'Die Theologie des Neuen Testaments nach seinen Hauptzeugen', *Jesus–Paulus–Johannes*, ²1972, 173ff.   [55] Klein, 218.

[56] Gal. 1: 4; Kol. 1: 13. Ich muß vermuten, daß G. Klein die paulinische Herkunft des Kolosserbriefs nicht zugestehen wird, treffe mich aber in dieser Annahme (meine Begründung bei W. G. Kümmel, *Einleitung in das Neue Testament*, ¹⁷1973, 294ff.) mit dem verehrten Forscher, den dieses *natalicium* grüßen soll.

Bestreitung heilsgeschichtlichen Denkens bei Klein[57] stehen mag, so dürften doch die vorstehenden Ausführungen gezeigt haben, daß Gal. 2: 15–21 Kleins These, daß 'die Sicht der Weltgeschichte an konkret erfahrener Individualgeschichte hängt', exegetisch nicht zu stützen vermag. Denn auch in diesem Text ist von 'Weltgeschichte' die Rede, wenn man sich der Terminologie Kleins bedienen will; oder besser gesagt: auch in diesem Text ist, um die Sprache des Paulus zu gebrauchen, von der eschatologischen Heilsgegenwart die Rede, weil 'jetzt der Tag des Heils' ist, der uns 'warten läßt auf die Offenbarung unseres Herren Jesus Christus' (2. Kor. 6: 2; 1. Kor. 1: 7).

'Individualgeschichte' und 'Weltgeschichte' in Gal. 2: 15–21

W. G. KÜMMEL

There has been much controversy in recent scholarship whether Paul shares the concept of Salvation History and makes it the basis of his message. In particular, G. Klein has argued that Paul's exposition of justification in Gal. 2: 15 – 4: 31 is contrary to any promises made to the Jews. It is rather an exposition of universal history, starting from his own concrete personal experience. The crucial passage for this interpretation is the opening section, 2: 15–21. The issue can only be decided on the basis of detailed exegesis of these verses.

Klein's argument presupposes that verses 15 and 16 are to be treated as separate sentences, referring to two different situations: the old dispensation, which is now past, and the eschatological time, which has now been reached. In this new age the distinction between Jew and Gentile no longer exists. Both alike are sinners, and so can only be justified through faith in Christ. This argument cannot be accepted, because the two verses must be taken as one sentence, in which the first verse is part of the subject of the whole sentence. The distinction between the two ages is neither implied nor expressed. Jews who are justified remain Jews, even though they recognise that the Law was powerless to make them righteous, so that from that point of view they were sinners like the Gentiles. It would be a complete misunderstanding to say that they actually had to *become* sinners in order to be justified (verse 17). On the contrary, the special position of the Jews requires that they should die to the Law in order to live in Christ, which in Paul's view happens in baptism (Gal. 3: 26–8; 1 Cor. 12: 12f.), so that it is in the new life in Christ that the distinction between Jew and Gentile is done away (verses 18–21).

[57] S. Anm. 2. Ich hoffe, mich dazu in anderm Zusammenhang äußern zu können.

In these last verses (18–21) Paul uses the 1st person singular, but the reason for the change seems to be purely stylistic. The idea that he is here speaking of his personal experience, before passing on to the universal exposition of 3: 1ff., cannot be maintained. What Paul says here has both individual and universal relevance, but it is addressed to the particular situation of the Jews. Klein's interpretation introduces a false antithesis. The truth is that this passage shows a consciousness of Salvation History, inasmuch as it illustrates Paul's conviction that 'now is the day of salvation' (2 Cor. 6: 2).

The basis of obligation in Paul's christology and ethics

G. M. STYLER

The relation of theology and ethics has long been and still remains a subject of debate among scholars. It is also one that is frequently included in examination papers for students. It was once set in the form, 'How close is the link between theology and ethics in the epistles of Paul?'; and one over-pedantic answer came back saying that it was *not* very close, since the theology was often presented in the first half of an epistle and the ethics in the second half. Perhaps this adequately represents the situation in Ephesians; but elsewhere, and particularly in Romans, the link is far closer and is established in principle inside the 'theological' half of the epistle, even if no detailed instructions on points of conduct are given until the later chapters.

Professor Moule has himself taken a prominent part in this debate,[1] arguing that the Christian experience of salvation through Christ does not weaken the obligation of moral conduct for Paul but strengthens it, and that what he rejects is legalism rather than the authentic content of law. The present paper is offered as a small contribution to the debate, under a title which no doubt promises too much in the space available. The word 'christology' will be used widely, to include the work of Christ as well as his person and nature; but towards the end something more precise will be said. One other disclaimer must be made. Although the relation of justification to ethical righteousness is central to the debate and will come into our discussion, little will be offered on the exact meaning of δικαιοσύνη in either sense.[2]

In the first section, I shall try to lay bare the logical substructure of Paul's soteriology, and to show that although words and images are used with varying reference and meaning there really is a strong structure, which holds the sense of Christian obligation in a firm grasp.

[1] C. F. D. Moule, 'Obligation in the Ethic of Paul', in W. R. Farmer, C. F. D. Moule, and R. R. Niebuhr (ed.), *Christian History and Interpretation* (Cambridge, 1967), pp. 389–406.
[2] A full treatment has recently been made by J. A. Ziesler, *The Meaning of Righteousness in Paul* (Cambridge, 1972).

In the second section I shall try to identify some of the main connecting links between christology and ethics and to prove their strength.

I

Four main points or stages can in principle be roughly distinguished in Paul's Christian assurance:

(A) the act of God in Christ;

(B) the initial response or conversion of the believer, marked by baptism;

(C) the continuing Christian life, with its duties and the expectation of growth in holiness, love and knowledge;

(D)[3] the final judgement and salvation.

These four letters will be employed as labels throughout this article, partly for brevity and partly to reduce the necessity of using Pauline words with a more restricted reference than Paul himself gave them. Short of using long phrases, one cannot quickly refer to these distinct stages except by labels. Established usage, it is true, uses 'justification' for (B) and 'sanctification' for (C). But it is obvious that Paul himself does not restrict δικαιοσύνη (and its cognates) to (B); it can mean 'ethical goodness', as well as justification;[4] and it is only a little less obvious that the cognates that make up 'sanctification', though often referring to (C), or (C) leading into (D), do not uniformly do so. Often enough the reference is to (B), as in 1 Cor. 6: 11, where the verb is a so-called baptismal aorist: 'you were sanctified'; or in the frequent use of ἅγιοι to denote Christians as such. Cases like these require a translation such as 'dedicated', or 'God's own people'. But there are others where 'holiness'[5] gives the meaning.

It would take too long to demonstrate the way in which word after word[6] can be used by Paul with varying reference, now to one and now to another of the stages. But a few must be mentioned because they are closely relevant to our theme. The verb ἐνδύεσθαι is used of putting on Christ at conversion and baptism, (B), as in Gal. 3: 27, or of putting

---

[3] English readers may be amused to see how convenient at least the first three of the letters are: (A) denotes the accomplished act of Christ; (B) the beginning of belief, and baptism; (C) the continuing Christian life. D is at any rate the initial letter of Last *Day*.

[4] And it can be used to refer to (A), as in the phrase 'the δικαιοσύνη of God'.

[5] In the 1946 edition of the New Testament, the RSV avoided the words 'sanctification' and 'holiness' in 1 Thess. 4: 3–7; but at the revision of 1952 these traditional words were restored.   [6] E.g. καταλλάσσειν.

him on in daily living, (C), with clear reference to moral conduct as in Rom. 13: 14.[7] The occurrences of the verb in 1 Cor. 15 are (D).

Similarly the Spirit is mentioned in connection with more than one stage. Examples of (A) are not numerous but can be found; e.g. it is closely associated with the resurrection of Christ, (A), in Rom. 1: 4.[8] Passages are of course numerous which connect the Spirit with the conversion and baptism of Christians (B), with the guidance and strengthening of them in their moral life (C), and, as guarantee or first instalment, with the life to come (D).

The examples we have mentioned all serve to underline the connection between (B) and (C). Some of them rely, it appears, on the use of the same word or phrase with a significant shift of reference and even of meaning. The δικαιοσύνη that is given us through faith on becoming a Christian is 'justification', 'acquittal', and 'acceptance'. It may be something real, not purely fictitious, but at least it is carefully shown to be independent of any moral conduct to which we may or may not be able to point. On the other hand the δικαιοσύνη which is now expected of us is actual moral conduct in daily living. The one word binds together two things which, however closely related, are not identical.

It is of the very essence of Paul's theology that the four stages adhere closely; and his habit of using a particular word or group of words to refer now to one stage and now to another has itself a cohesive effect. It may be objected that his inconsistent use of words only serves to conceal gaps in the thought which analysis or careful definition must expose, and that to bridge a gap by a junction that changes its nature halfway across is perilous. Nevertheless the connection of the four stages for Paul is vital; and his use of words makes this abundantly clear, even if, in some cases, it fails to shed much light on the nature of the connection. Beneath a liberty of language lies a firm substructure of belief.

Without such a firm substructure, and if the connecting links were not sound, Paul's theology of salvation would collapse. Any attempt to make each of the four divisions self-supporting is doomed to failure. God's act in Christ is decisive and complete, (A), and is described in aorist or perfect tenses of the indication. But it would not be efficacious for *us* apart from our acceptance of it in the act of faith, (B). It would

[7] Cf. also Col. 3: 12 (C); verse 10 is usually taken as (B), but (C) is not impossible.
[8] Cf. Rom. 8: 2 and 11.

be a foolish enterprise to make two separate lists of words describing God's gift of salvation, and claim that the words in one list describe what Christ has achieved, quite apart from the response of faith, and that the words in the second list represent what faith achieves, quite apart from the act of God in Christ.[9] Similarly we cannot isolate something which we suppose to have been achieved once for all, and as it were 'banked', in faith or baptism, (B), and claim for it an abiding validity apart from the discharge of obligations and growth in holiness which are expected to follow, (C). As has already been said, established convention uses 'justification' to denote (B), and 'sanctification' to denote (C). But this convention obscures both Paul's use of words and the tight link which he is striving to illuminate.

The speed with which Paul can move between (A), (B), and (C), without apparently any fear that his readers will not be nimble enough to follow his steps, reflects his confidence in the soundness of the logical substructure. There is an excellent example in 1 Cor. 5: 7–8:

(i) Cleanse out the old leaven that you may be fresh dough, (C),

(ii) as you really are unleavened, (B).

(iii) For Christ, our paschal lamb, has been sacrificed, (A).

(iv) Let us, therefore, celebrate the festival, not with the old leaven ..., but with the unleavened bread of sincerity and truth, (C).

The progress of thought is from (C) back to (B), and thence to (A), from which Paul leaps forward again to pick up (C), the ethical injunction. But we should take note of the fact that Paul *begins* this complex of thought and argument with the ethical injunction (C), and expresses it in language which is already determined by the picture of passover and unleavened bread. Now in the first instance that language can be used naturally only to express (A); its application to (B) and (C) is surely derivative, even forced. This particular image can scarcely be thought of as helping to *create* the links from (A) to (B) and (B) to (C); Paul can only have extended it in the way that he did because for him the links are already strongly established, a part of his basic Christian assurance.

Our concern is with the link that binds (C) to (B), or rather to (A)

9 Such an attempt to escape from the awkward tensions, sc. that Christ's work is complete but still has to be appropriated, that our appropriation of it is once-for-all and yet has still to be worked out in practice, and that the riches of the Christian life here are only a foretaste of the full treasure, has been compared by Professor Moule himself to the folly of taking down in a wind ropes which pull against one another to hold up a tent.

and (B) taken as a whole. The continuation of the Christian life can be thought of as growth into maturity, and the bearing of fruit. Equally it can be presented as moral obligation. The link is most aptly expressed in the tag 'become what you are'; Christians are to live the unleavened life because they really *are* unleavened.[10] Exactly the same logic underlies Paul's most famous expression of the link from (B) to (C), viz. in Gal. 5: 25: 'If the Spirit is the source of our life, let the Spirit also direct our steps.' But here at least the picture and the language can express the connection without any unnatural forcing; here, then, in the experience of the Spirit as both source of life and (in some sense) of moral conduct, we are presumably very near to the actual basis of Paul's thought.

There is no room to set out in detail the way in which the complex of bondage, ransom, deliverance, and freedom spreads over the whole area of soteriology. Only three things need to be said here. First, Paul's treatment bears witness to the strength of his grasp on moral obligation. His emphasis on deliverance, especially from law, would only too easily open the floodgates to antinomianism. But Paul refuses to open them. Instead, he argues that our freedom is the freedom that Christ has made possible; that is, it is a special kind of freedom, not to be confused with licence. In Gal. 5 he shows that the new life in the Spirit is not the way of licence, but it is not the way of law either; it has been well described as 'a highway above them both'. The harvest of the Spirit in the Christian life goes far beyond the most comprehensive list of works and duties that any law could prescribe: 'there is no law dealing with such things as these'.[11]

The second thing to notice is the way in which Paul gets into some confusion when handling these ideas in Rom. 6. We are free now from law, and sin, and death. But once again the result is not a freedom which acknowledges no sovereign or obligation. On the contrary, he alters his metaphor and asserts that we now have a new master, and are slaves

---

[10] ἵνα ἦτε νέον φύραμα, καθώς ἐστε ἄζυμοι. The RSV adds the word 'really' to underline this point. The point was slightly obscured in the first edition of the NEB: 'and then you will be bread of a new baking, *as it were* unleavened Passover bread'. This was corrected in the second edition to '*as Christians you are* unleavened Passover bread'.

[11] Gal. 5: 23 NEB, a translation which surely does justice to the meaning of the words and to Paul's argument. The usual translation is 'against such there is no law'. This is at best a massive understatement; as a piece of irony it is unconvincing. κατά can, of course, mean 'in opposition to'; but does it ever mean 'prohibiting' (of a law)?

of obedience, or righteousness, or indeed of God.[12] Elsewhere Paul uses the metaphor of purchase, which, like ransom, can involve the payment of a price. It is simplest to think of this as a slightly different metaphor, rather than as an extension of the same one. According to the metaphor of purchase, the Christian now belongs to God (or to Christ);[13] and this of course has ethical implications. It must be admitted that one could defend the unity of the whole image by saying that Paul draws on various aspects of sacral manumission: an effective freedom from human ownership is at the same time in legal theory slavery to the god. But if any explanation is needed beyond the tension actually encountered in the Christian experience, Old Testament usage will probably suffice: God 'redeems' a people *for himself*.[14] Paul apologizes in verse 19 for his awkward language, and apparently blames it on the limitations of his readers; with more justice he might have complained of the natural complexity of the subject, and the limitations of all metaphors.

The third point to notice briefly is that the purchase-image comes very close in meaning[15] to sanctification; the former pictures the believer as brought into God's ownership, the latter as brought within the sphere of God's own being and holiness.

The last, and for us the most important, complex to be examined is the believer's entry into the life of Christ. Our scheme is again helpful:

(A) Jesus himself died and rose again.

(B) On becoming a Christian the believer is included in that death and resurrection.

(C) But he must hope to display both the death and the power of the risen life effectively in his own conduct.

(D) Death awaits him in the future, and resurrection at the end.

It is not of course easy, or even sometimes possible, to classify Paul's statements rigidly in accordance with this scheme. So kaleidoscopic are the quick darts of Paul's thought that the reference can pass from one to another before a sentence comes to a point of rest. And even when there is no doubt of the division in our scheme into which a passage falls, yet

---

12 Rom. 6: 16, 18, and 22.

13 I Cor. 6: 19–20, and 7: 22–3.

14 Cf. 2 Sam. 7: 23 (= I Chron. 17: 21).

15 At I Cor. 6: 19–20 the statement 'You are not your own; you were bought with a price' follows immediately in support of the statement that the body is a temple of the Holy Spirit – which is another way of expressing the fact of sanctification, (B).

there can be a shift of theological application. For example, the death of Christ, (A), and the spiritual dying of believers, (B) or (C), can be thought of in a way that is essentially retrospective and negative, as a break with and escape from the old enemies, or in a wholly positive way, as an act of righteousness and obedience.[16]

Our division is convenient. But how much use does Paul in fact make of it? In particular, does he give much emphasis to the idea that the believer has already been included in Christ's resurrection, (B), and, living in the life of Christ now, must expect to display the power of the resurrection effectively, (C)? It is sometimes said that at this point, especially in affirming that the believer as such is risen with Christ, (B), Colossians and Ephesians go beyond the affirmations of the generally accepted epistles; and that the usual viewpoint of the latter is that although we are already included in Christ's death, (B), our inclusion in his resurrection lies in the future.[17] Certainly this seems so, if we judge by Rom. 6: 5–8: 'If we have been united with him in a death like his, we shall certainly be united with him in a resurrection like his. We know that our old self was crucified with him ... But if we have died with Christ, we believe that we shall also live with him.'

It is unnecessary to set out at length the passages from Colossians and Ephesians which supply what we are wanting.[18] Of the two epistles, Colossians is the one which associates the theological utterances more closely with particular ethical injunctions; Ephesians testifies to the connection in general, but postpones specific ethical exhortations until the second half of the epistle.

But I wish to challenge the view that Paul himself, to judge by the accepted epistles, did not hold the union of the believer with the resurrection of Christ, both in becoming a Christian, (B), and in the successes of the Christian life, (C). Point (B) is, in my opinion, effectively made in Rom. 6, as well as in Gal. 2: 19; and point (C) in this same extract from Galatians, and also elsewhere.[19]

In Rom. 6 Paul is asserting our effective union with Christ, and arguing that no place is now left in us for sin. We have (spiritually)

[16] Contrast e.g. Rom. 6: 10 with 5: 18–19, and Rom. 7: 6 with 2 Cor. 4: 10.
[17] (D), of course; but is (C) entirely excluded, at least as an occasional hope?
[18] The fullest is Eph. 2: 1–6, in which our ascension with Christ is included along with the resurrection as an accomplished fact. See also Col. 2: 12–13, where spiritual resurrection as well as death is included in baptism, and Col. 3: 1–3.
[19] 2 Cor. 4: 10–12 and 13: 4; Phil. 3: 10 and possibly also verse 11. Some of these are discussed below.

shared his death in baptism, (B), and we have a firm faith that we shall share his risen life, (D). But in verse 11 he says: 'So you also must consider yourselves dead to sin and alive to God in Christ Jesus.' This is followed, two verses later, by: 'Yield yourselves to God as men who have been brought from death to life.'

It is true that the affirmation is slightly muted: '*consider* yourselves alive' (λογίζεσθε), and '*as* (ὡσεί) dead men raised to life'. Such phrases betray the fact that our resurrection is not literal; but then neither is our inclusion in Christ's death. In Paul's spiritual experience both have their place. The verb λογίζεσθαι no doubt points us to a mode of reckoning which is not immediately obvious; but any suggestion that it means '*falsely* reckon' must be opposed. If there *is* some muting of the affirmation that the new life is ours already, then that is quite in line with Paul's custom of quickly checking any inclination to claim full and final achievement.[20]

For (C), the best example is 2 Cor. 4: 10–11: '... always carrying in the body the death of Jesus, so that the life of Jesus may also be manifested in our bodies. For while we live we are always being given up to death for Jesus' sake, so that the life of Jesus may be manifested in our mortal flesh.' It is just conceivable that in the former of the two verses the hope is of the bodily resurrection, (D); it seems to me quite inconceivable in the case of the latter verse, because the word used there is 'flesh'. That being so, the reference in *both* verses is surely to the experience of the resurrection in this present earthly life, (C); Paul first expresses his hope in somewhat formal terms, and then makes the point again in a slightly more concrete way. 2 Cor. 13: 4 contains the same hope of an effective demonstration of the resurrection through the apostle, this time with a note of menace: 'He was crucified in weakness, but lives by the power of God. For we are weak in him, but in dealing with you[21] we shall live with him by the power of God.' Clearly the reference is (C), not (D).

The most striking and important passage of all is, of course, Gal. 2: 19–20: 'I ... died to the law, that I might live to God. I have been

---

[20] Cf. Phil. 3: 12ff., and his rebuke to the Corinthians in 1 Cor. 4: 8ff. On the other hand the paradox in 2 Cor. 4: 12 ('death is at work in us, and life in you') reflects an authentic tension. The tension of 'become what you are', which is obvious in relation to δικαιοσύνη, holds in just the same way for 'alive to God in Christ'. In one sense we 'reckon' that we are already 'alive'; in practical achievement we still hope and pray to become so.

[21] εἰς ὑμᾶς; NEB 'in your service', which sounds more optimistic.

crucified with Christ; it is no longer I who live but Christ who lives in me; and the life I now live in the flesh I live by faith in the Son of God ...' This is not the final sharing of the risen life of Christ. But it is a real sharing, a spiritual sharing, or a sharing by faith. And the word 'faith' must not be reduced to the meaning of fictitious imagination, or anticipation of something wholly future; it is a life lived now 'in the flesh'. This is not the logical construction of a tidy scheme; it is something thrown up red-hot out of Paul's experience. And it is that experience which supplies the basis of Paul's thought, and therefore its logical substructure. I trust that it will not imply any loss of wonder and respect for this impressive testimony if we venture to label it as both (B) and (C).

I have already referred briefly to the role of the Spirit in both the beginning and the continuation of the Christian life. Along with the passages we have just been considering, it makes a striking picture. The Christian in a very real sense is included in the death and resurrection of Christ, and now lives – by faith, not sight, and not yet fully – by the power of his Spirit, who is the Spirit of God.[22] If Paul's words are taken seriously, he means far more than that the life of Christ supplies a model for our own; for him at least it supplies his whole being.

II

Our inquiry has shown how tightly Paul holds together the work fo Christ, our inclusion in it, our continuing life, and our future hope. In this complex, moral obligation has an important place, as an implication of the Christian's status in Christ. In this second section I shall make some suggestions which, if correct, may throw some light on the basis on which general moral obligation rests, and on the way in which Christian experience strengthens and enlarges it.

Let us consider three propositions, which can be logically distinguished:

(i) Through Christ, the *content* of obligation is developed and enriched.

(ii) Through Christ, the *motive* for grateful and obedient response is strengthened.

[22] The *full* picture should include, of course, the church as the body of Christ, and the individual as a member of the body. The omission of this part of the picture is not meant to imply that it is unimportant.

(iii) In Christ, we are brought close to the actual *basis* of obligation as such.

Of these three propositions, the first two are easy to understand and to accept; they could be true even if the third were rejected as either meaningless or false. In fact, it is clear that they are true for Christians. For them, as for Paul himself, the *content* of moral activity is enriched, indeed is transformed by the character and teaching of Jesus, by his life and death, and by the living guidance of the Spirit. Similarly, there is no doubt that the *motive-power* for moral conduct is strengthened almost out of recognition for those who respond in gratitude and obedience to God's love and pardon, effected in Christ and effective in the Spirit. These two propositions are straightforward, and need not be developed any further. It is the third which we must examine and try to understand.

But, before we do so, it is worthwhile to point out that in respect of all three propositions the control that is exercised by Christ over the Christian life and its obligations arises not only from the *past* fact of Christ, or even the past and present, but also, at least in some degree, from the fact of Christ as ultimate hope and ideal. The *goal* which he has revealed helps to set the direction in which travellers on the way must walk. Obviously the warnings of judgement provide a sanction for moral conduct, and the promises of reward an incentive. But the future life has a deeper relevance than as supplying sanction or incentive: it is revealed as the life which we are called to live here and now. To live a life now that is out of keeping with the final resurrection-life is not merely foolish; for Paul it is unthinkable. This is made clear in Romans 6: 5–12, which may be summarized as follows: 'As surely as we have been incorporated in Christ's death, we shall one day share his resurrection. We have shared in his death, and the break that he made with sin. Since we are also to share in his life, spiritually now and literally hereafter, we must make that break a reality in moral conduct.' In short, sin is unthinkable, because *inter alia* it is incompatible with the resurrection-life.

We must now turn to our third proposition, which is daring, hard to express, and harder still to prove: that in our incorporation into Christ we are brought close to the very basis on which obligation rests. It is important to distinguish it from the other propositions, and especially from the awareness of an enriched *content* to our obligations. But the distinction is as dangerous as it is convenient. In practice it is hard to separate the basic *idea* of obligation from our actual *obligations*. Has any man ever had *duty* but no *duties*? Further, the word 'basis' will prove misleading, if it is taken to mean that moral obligation in the abstract is temporally prior to our concrete duties. The moral demand is surely implicit in each circumstance or situation as it arises.

For the theist, the basis of all moral obligation must surely be in God himself, and in his will for men. For the Jew, the fullest revelation is in the Torah; for the Christian, in Christ. Even outside the biblical revelation, some knowledge of God's will has always been given and expressed in the moral standards and insights of mankind in general; and this knowledge of his will has often been independent of any knowledge on man's part of God himself. Paul concedes a positive value to these insights, in passages[23] which are too well known to need quoting. Although there is much to be condemned in pagan codes, and still more in pagan conduct, nevertheless there is an authentic element in the ordinary conscience and conduct of man as such; and, in some passages at least, Paul rates this at its full value. Yet how can this be conceded without devaluing conscious faith in God and the biblical revelation?

The answer lies in the doctrine of creation. Man is created in God's image, a moral being, capable of responding morally to the claims of his Creator and his neighbour. Moral conduct is a possibility and a duty for us in the context of a fellowship; ideally, a fellowship with other men under God; in practice, at least for many, a fellowship with other men without any consciousness of God. But, whether God is recognized or not, our moral response would never begin at all were it not for the moral nature and its potentialities with which the Creator has endowed us. It is he who has created the ideal of fellowship and its complex of possibilities and obligations; and this ideal stems from his own eternal being.

If this rough sketch of man's ideal life may be accepted, then the revelations of Moses and of Christ make a contribution which fits easily into place. Neither of them caused moral obligation to come into existence out of nothing; and neither of them caused it to be recognized for the first time. But each of them caused a spectacular advance in the moral insight and condition of those who received them. As their followers gained a clearer perception of God's presence and action, and a richer appreciation of fellowship inside a family, so they were struck

[23] E.g. Rom. 2: 15; I Cor. 10: 32; 2 Cor. 8: 21; Phil. 4: 8; I Thess. 4: 12.

and challenged by clearer and stronger moral insights. With every advance in insight and in fellowship, new possibilities give rise to new obligations. And with the appreciation of the depth of God's love in Christ, we are constrained by the most far-reaching obligations of all.[24]

At last we are in a position to see an important relationship between christology and ethics; and to see the way in which it will make a big difference *how* we state or define our christology. If Christ is teacher and revealer, but no more, then we can still claim a validity for the first two of our propositions on pp. 183–4. To acknowledge that he displays and teaches the ideal of love and fellowship on a new level is to acknowledge that he raises our moral sights to a new level and so opens up new possibilities and new obligations. Perhaps we could go further, and claim that his ideal and teaching are so comprehensive as to include and transform all the insights, and therefore all the obligations, that have gone before. But even *that* falls short of the Christian affirmation, as set out by Paul. The life we are to live is not just the life to which Christ points; it is the life of Christ himself.

The difference is an important one, and it is put in strong relief by the fine saying[25] of Rabbi Zusya of Hanipol: 'In the coming world they will not ask me, "Why were you not Moses?" They will ask me, "Why were you not Zusya?"'. Even with some adaptation, the Christian would not say this with reference to Christ. For Christ does not simply bid me be myself, he calls me to live in him. His Spirit is to be the source of our life, as well as the director of our path.[26]

We can take our final step, and claim that the life in Christ is not merely direction and motive-power, but the embodiment of the whole human ideal and the resultant obligation, if to the material already assembled in our first section we add the simple point that in Christ

---

[24] Rom. 13: 8; cf. Gal. 5: 13, 'through love be servants of one another'.

[25] Quoted by V. Gollancz, *A Year of Grace* (London, 1950), p. 402.

[26] Ethical systems are distinguished as heteronomous (with an external source of authority) or autonomous (with the source of moral authority internal to the agent). Neither kind of system in its pure form seems adequate: why should I respect an authority external to myself? Yet if the authority is wholly inside myself, what is there to prevent me from acting arbitrarily? My duty, if it is to be both *my* duty and my *duty*, must be something that I wholly accept as mine, and yet something that I have not invented. It is worth pointing out that the Pauline assurance of the indwelling Spirit as moral authority and guide does justice to both sides of this complex. The Spirit is the Holy Spirit, and yet is very closely united to man's own spirit; and so the source of moral authority is both internal to the agent and at the same time transcendent.

Paul sees the new Adam, the focus of the new creation. If we were right in connecting human obligation as such with creation in the image of God, then it is in keeping to connect the Christian's transformed world of obligation with the new creation.[27] The old obligations remain for those who are still living in the old creation; and the Christian will continue to respect them and to reverence their divine origin. His own obligations, however, are taken up and transformed in the new world which is opened up for him.

In some way, then, which it still remains hard to express, Christ in his very person is the point at which human ideals and obligations are renovated and transformed. What went before is now seen as a fore-shadowing of Christ; and Christ himself marks the goal of life as well as its origin. He confronts us with human obligation in its ultimate form; and does so not just by the legacy or teaching or insights that he has bequeathed, not just because of the life that he lived and its consequences; but because of the life that he lives, which is ours to live also.

---

[27] A comparison of Gal. 6: 15 with two similar verses may confirm the suggestion that for Paul the idea of 'new creation' has strong ethical implications. What really matters, he says, is not circumcision nor its absence, but 'new creation' (so, in Gal. 6: 15), or 'faith working through love' (so, in Gal. 5: 6), or 'keeping God's commandments' (so, in 1 Cor. 7: 19).

13

The Maranatha invocation and
Jude 14, 15 (1 Enoch 1: 9)

MATTHEW BLACK

The Maranatha formula at 1 Cor. 16: 22 (its only scriptural occurrence) constitutes a centuries-old *crux interpretum*; the literature on it alone is *unübersehbar*.[1] It is not, however, in the category of completely unsolved (or insoluble) New Testament problems. Modern study has gone so far in its elucidation of the formula to reduce the alternative meanings of the Aramaic words to three: (1) 'Our Lord has come!', (2) 'Our Lord is coming!', and (3) 'Our Lord, come!' The problem, as posed by most modern discussion, is (*a*) which alternative is to be preferred? For (1) is a confession, while (2) and (3) are invocations. (*b*) In what contexts and connections was the formula used, eucharistic (*Did.* 10: 6) or, especially in conjunction with *Anathema* (1 Cor. 16: 22), as part of an imprecation? (*c*) Finally, what, if anything, can be said about the origins of the formula in the Aramaic-speaking milieu of the primitive Church?

As in so many other areas of New Testament study here too Professor C. F. D. Moule has placed Biblical scholarship in his debt by a comprehensive and balanced discussion of the context of the formula.[2] He begins with a critical assessment of the widely popular view that the *maranatha* of 1 Cor. 16: 22 is to be understood as an invocation of Christ to be present in the eucharist.[3] The main grounds for this are

---

[1] The following selected list includes work on ἀνάθεμα: *TWNT*, *s.v.* ἀνάθεμα, μαραναθα; W. F. Albright, C. S. Mann, 'Two Texts in I Corinthians', *NTS* xvi (1970), pp. 271ff.; B. Botte, *Noël-Épiphanie, retour du Christ* (Paris, 1967), pp. 25–42; C. Spicq, 'Comment comprendre φιλεῖν dans 1 Cor. xvi. 22?', *Nov. T.* i (1956), p. 201; G. Bornkamm, 'Das Anathema in der urchristlichen Abendmahlsliturgie', *TLZ* lxv (1950), 227–30; R. Bultmann, *Theology of the New Testament* (London, 1965), vol. i, p. 52; S. Schultz, 'Maranatha und Kyrios Jesus', *ZNTW* liii (1962), pp. 125–44. J. Betz, 'Die Eucharistie in der Didache', *Archiv für Liturgiewissenschaft* xi (1969), esp. pp. 26ff. and 34ff.; W. Dunphy, 'Maranatha: Development in Early Christianity', *Irish Theol. Quarterly* xxxvii (1970), pp. 294ff.

[2] 'A Reconsideration of the Context of *Maranatha*', in *NTS* vi (1959–60), pp. 307–10.

[3] See R. Seeberg in *Religion und Geschichte* i (1906), pp. 118ff. (*Kuss und Kanon*); H. Lietzmann, *Messe und Herrenmahl* (1926), p. 229; J. A. T. Robinson, 'Traces

that other words and phrases in the same context can be interpreted eucharistically: 'the kiss' (v. 20), the 'anathema' upon anyone who does not love the Lord (v. 22), and the grace (v. 23) can all be supposed to be among the preliminaries to the Eucharist.[4] *Maranatha* also occurs in the *Didache* 10: 6 in a section connected at least in some way with the Eucharist.

But how much of this is really cogent? If I Corinthians was really intended to be (as it were) the homily, leading on into the eucharist, why is there so little trace of this in other New Testament epistles? Why does the *maranatha* in I Cor. xvi. 22 come at this particular point, *before* the grace (and the apostle's love)? Why does it occur where it does in the Didache? In spite of all that is said, is there sufficient evidence to suggest that it was meant to lead straight into the eucharist proper? And is there anything obviously eucharistic in the context of Rev. xxii?[5]

Professor Moule sought to revive and reconsider a quite different interpretation of the formula which was suggested in substance, at least, by E. Peterson's ΕΙΣ ΘΕΟΣ,[6] but going back ultimately to W. Bousset.[7] The suggestion was that *maranatha* was, in effect, part of the *anathema* at I Cor. 16: 22, i.e. it was a part of the ban-formula, an imprecation or curse. 'This is a less agreeable interpretation, but it is not to be lightly rejected. What if not only the *maranatha* of I Cor. xvi: 22 and *Did.* x: 6, but also the ἔρχου κύριε 'Ιησοῦ of Rev. xxii: 20 are not (at least primarily) eucharistic invocations but invocations (primarily at least) to reinforce or sanction the curse or ban?'[8]

Dr Moule supports his case for this interpretation by re-examining the contexts of I Cor. 16: 22, *Did.* 10: 6 and Rev. 22: 20: in the latter so far from appearing in a 'eucharistic context' the formula follows a tremendous curse (vv. 18f.). The contexts of I Cor. 16 and *Did.* 10 similarly support this interpretation. The argument is further strengthened by parallels with pagan 'sanction' and ancient cursing formulae.[9]

of a Liturgical Sequence in I Cor. xvi. 20–4', *JTS*, n.s. iv (1953), pp. 38ff.; O. Cullmann, *Christology of the New Testament* (1959), p. 210 etc.

[4] P. 307.   [5] *Ibid.*   [6] 1926.

[7] Moule, *op. cit.*, p. 307 n. 6. Moule notes that Bousset's *Herr ist Jesus* (1926), p. 22, is cited by Peterson, *op. cit.*, pp. 130ff., as having been retracted by Bousset later in his *Kyrios Christos*, p. 84.

[8] Moule, *op. cit.*, p. 308.

[9] E.g. R. Wünsch, *Antike Fluchtafeln, Kleine Texte* xx, 1907, pp. 13, 25, etc.; K. Preisendanz, *Papyri Graecae magicae* i (1928), lines 89–90; A. Deissmann, *Light from the Ancient East*, 1927, pp. 413ff.

A particularly significant example to which Dr Moule draws attention is a sepulchral inscription from Salamis (4–5 c. A.D.)[10] calling down a curse on anyone who interferes with the remains, in the form ἀνάθεμα ἤτω μαραν αθαν. 'The comment on this in Moulton and Milligan (*s.v.*, ἀνάθεμα) is: "the meaning of the Aramaic σύμβολον [i.e. μαραναθαν] being wholly unknown, it could be used as a curse – like unknown words in later days!" But is it not more natural to suppose that the μαραναθαν was here not a σύμβολον but a genuine invocation, that its meaning was understood (the slight misspelling is hardly an argument for complete misunderstanding), and that it was deliberately used to sanction the anathema?'[11]

In an article in the *Irish Theological Quarterly*,[12] Father Walter Dunphy points out that one line of patristic tradition uses *maranatha* in direct connection with *anathema*; e.g. 'Amandus declares excommunicated those who would tamper with his resting place and adds: *et sit anathema maranatha, quod est perditio in adventu Domini nostri Jesu Christi*'.[13] Fr Dunphy comments: 'This seems to give clear parousial reference to Maranatha, though many would say that the word is being used here without any real understanding of its meaning.' Such is clearly the case in other examples found in this line of interpretation (e.g. Tertullian, *de Pudicitia*, 14. 13; Canon 75 of the Fourth Council of Toledo (A.D. 633) *qui contra hanc definitionem praesumpserit, anathema maranatha, hoc est, perditio in adventu domini sit* (*TWNT* v, p. 470).

It seems fairly evident that the association with *anathema*, in these instances, fully bears out the Peterson hypothesis. It by no means follows, however, that *maranatha* must therefore necessarily have this same force in all or other contexts, e.g. at *Did.* 10 : 6 where it seems more likely that the reference is to the Parousia with no imprecatory force. This appears to be the position of K. G. Kuhn[14] and G. Bornkamm[15] who both allow that *maranatha* does *reinforce* the ban, but that it is going beyond the evidence to regard it as simply an apotropaic or exorcistic formula and nothing else. They interpret it as a eucharistic invocation or affirmation (the verb as indicative, not imperative): but the conception of the Lord's presence or coming also serves as a

---

[10] *CIG* iv, 9303. [11] Moule, *op. cit.*, p. 308.
[12] Vol. xxxviii, 4 (October 1970), pp. 294ff. (see above, p. 189). For the patristic tradition and further references, see B. Botte, *op. cit.*, pp. 25ff.
[13] Migne, *PL* lxxxvii, 1274. [14] *TWNT* iv, pp. 470ff.
[15] See above, p. 189 n. 1.

reinforcement of the ban. Certainly if, as seems likely, the formula was used as an apotropaic formula, it could have been invested with such a force in the Eucharist ('fencing the Table'). Its position at the conclusion of the eucharistic prayer at *Did.* 10: 6, however, after the celebration, does not seem, in that case, the most appropriate place for it: it may mean nothing more in this context than 'until He come' at 1 Cor. 11: 26, a looking forward to the Lord's Coming; the Parousia expectation was an integral element in the Eucharist. Within a eucharistic context it seems more likely to have been an invocation, therefore, or petition for the Lord's coming, i.e. it looks forward to the Parousia. The idea that it was an invocation for or affirmation of the Real Presence at the eucharist seems more a sixteenth than a first century idea, but this also may be wrong: 'Where two or three are gathered together in my name there I am in the midst of them'[16] (Matt. 18: 20).

Professor Moule traces the imprecatory use of the formula to its reference to the parousia. The parallel pagan formulae to which he drew attention seem to imply that the god would forthwith come and smite the delinquent. 'In view . . . of the Biblical expectation of a future general day of judgement, it seems more likely that the Christian formulae were directed – primarily at any rate – towards this expectation, and that *maranatha* meant "may the Lord *soon* come in judgement to redress wrong and establish right". This fits the appeal to repent (μετανοείτω) in *Did.* 10: 6 which would be reinforced by the expectation of the coming of the Lord in the near future (though perhaps to

---

[16] Cf. A. M. Hunter, *Exploring the New Testament*, p. 98, who argues that it is probably the earliest Christian prayer: 'What kind of prayer? We know that the early Christians expected Christ's "royal coming", or *Parousia*. We naturally therefore take it as a petition for Christ to come at the End. But in the *Didache* it closes the liturgy for the Lord's Supper. "Where two or three are gathered together in my name", Jesus had said (Matt. 18. 20) "there am I in the midst of them." Must it not also have been a prayer used by the early Christians at their eucharists when they invoked their living Lord to grace their meal with his presence, as he had done on the first Easter Day (Luke 24. 35; Acts 10. 41):

> Come, Lord Jesus, and be our Guest,
> And bless what Thou bestowèd hast.

Thus this little piece of Aramaic had a three-fold reference: (1) it looked back to the first Easter Day; (2) it invoked the presence of the risen Lord, through the Spirit, when the early Christians met to "break bread"; and (3) it called on the Lord to come in glory.

So far from being a piece of imprecatory mumbo-jumbo, *marana-tha* is probably the earliest Christian prayer.'

We can agree with (1), (2) and (3) but not with Dr Hunter's closing remark.

construe *maranatha* as an indicative, "the Lord is here", would be even more appropriate here).'[17]

So far as I know, Jude v. 14, 15 (citing 1 En. 1: 9) has never been adduced in consideration of the *maranatha* problem. Moreover, 1 En. 1: 9 is now extant in the 4Q Enoch fragments discovered at Qumran.[18] The following gives the Jude text and the text of the Greek Enoch, with the Ethiopic version and a translation of the extant Aramaic fragments of 4Q En. 1: 4–9.

EPISTLE OF JUDE 14, 15

Ἐπροφήτευσεν δὲ καὶ τούτοις ἕβδομος ἀπὸ Ἀδὰμ Ἐνὼχ λέγων·
ἰδοὺ ἦλθεν κύριος ἐν ἁγίαις μυριάσιν αὐτοῦ, ποιῆσαι κρίσιν κατὰ
πάντων καὶ ἐλέγξαι πάντας τοὺς ἀσεβεῖς αὐτῶν περὶ πάντων
τῶν ἔργων ἀσεβείας αὐτῶν ὧν ἠσέβησαν καὶ περὶ πάντων
τῶν σκληρῶν ὧν ἐλάλησαν κατ' αὐτοῦ ἁμαρτωλοὶ ἀσεβεῖς.

1 ENOCH 1: 9

ὅτι ἔρχεται σὺν ταῖς μυριάσιν αὐτοῦ καὶ τοῖς ἁγίοις αὐτοῦ,
ποιῆσαι κρίσιν κατὰ πάντων, καὶ ἀπολέσει πάντας τοὺς ἀσεβεῖς,
καὶ ἐλέγξει πᾶσαν σάρκα περὶ πάντων ἔργων τῆς ἀσεβείας αὐτῶν
ὧν ἠσέβησαν καὶ σκληρῶν ὧν ἐλάλησαν λόγων, ⟨καὶ περὶ
πάντων ὧν κατελάλησαν⟩ κατ' αὐτοῦ ἁμαρτωλοὶ ἀσεβεῖς.

𝔓⁷² αγιων αγγελων μυριασιν. Pseudo-Cyprian: *ecce venit cum multis millibus nuntiorum suorum.* ℵ, 8, 25, 56, sah. harc. εν μυριασιν αγιων. Al. ἐν μυριασιν αγιαις αγγελων (teste Tisch.)

ETH.

[3]The holy and great One will come forth from His dwelling... [5]and all shall be smitten with fear... [6]and the high mountains shall be shaken... [8]and He will make peace with them. [9]And behold! He cometh with ten thousands of His holy ones to execute judgement upon all, and to destroy all the ungodly, and to convict all flesh of all the works of their ungodliness which they have ungodly committed, and of all the hard things which ungodly sinners have spoken against Him...

[17] *Op. cit.*, pp. 309ff.
[18] See my article 'Christological Use of the Old Testament in the New Testament', in *NTS* xviii (1971/2), p. 10.

4Q ARAM.

The great Holy One will come forth from His dwelling [superscript 5][*and all will be afraid*] [superscript 6]*and all ends of the earth will shake* [superscript 8][*with the righteous He will make peace.*] [superscript 9][*When (Behold) He comes*] *with the myriads of His holy ones* [. . . כדי יאתה עם רבו[את קדישו[הי.] [*to execute judgement upon all; and he will destroy all the wicked and convict*] *all flesh, with regard to* [*all*] *their works* [*of ungodliness which they have committed in deed and in word, and with regard to all*] *the proud and hard* [*words which wicked sinners have spoken against Him*].

That Jude is referring to the Parousia seems fairly obvious, since it was for Christians this letter was written: in that case κύριος is the Lord Jesus. It does not seem to me that there is any ambiguity in the author's meaning though, of course, the Enoch reference is to the Lord God's coming in judgement.[19] The expectation of the 'Son of Man' coming attended by his holy myriads (and for judgement) appears at Matt. 25: 31. The tense ἦλθεν raises a difficulty. The context obliges us to give the verb a futuristic reference since it is to the Last Judgement, presumably at the Parousia, the author is referring, and is best explained as 'the form of prophetic utterance',[20] i.e. a prophetic perfect or a *perfectum futuri*.

What is now new and of some importance is that 1 En. 1: 9 has been found in Aramaic and circulated in Aramaic. And in Aramaic, '[Behold] the (our) Lord cometh!' (*Mara' 'atha'* or *'athe'* [perf. proph. or ptc.]) and *Mara(n) 'atha'* are verbally identical. Unfortunately the opening words of verse 9 are lost in the Aramaic: if we reconstruct them from the Greek, then 'when He (God, cf. v. 4 above) comes' was original.[21] The ἦλθεν of Jude could be a rendering of an Aramaic *perfectum propheticum* and so preserve a very old Greek text of 1 Enoch 1: 9. The

---

[19] The history of the tradition of the Enoch theophany goes back to a line beginning with the Sinai theophany in the Blessing of Moses (Deut. 33: 1ff.) and traceable in Judges 5: 4–5 (which may be the earlier of the two) to the Day of the Lord prophecies in Hab. 3: 3–6 and Mic. 1: 2–5a; the latter, in particular, has had an important influence on 1 En. 1. One of the main developments is that, whereas at Judges 5: 4–5 and Deut. 33: 1ff., the context points to a theophany of Yahweh in Israel's past, the Micah prophecy looks forward to a future Day of the Lord's coming in judgement. It is within this theophanic tradition that the New Testament Parousia expectation belongs; and most notably Jude 14–15 from 1 En. 1: 9.

[20] So R. Knopf, *Meyer Komm.*, *ad loc.*, K. H. Schelkle, *Herder Komm.*, *ad loc.*

[21] The Greek palimpsest reads οτει: modern editions read ὅτι but ὅτε is also possible.

'Behold' of the Ethiopic presumably is due to the influence of Jude, but, in that case, it is surprising that it has not also introduced the κύριος reading.[22]

It is a definite possibility that ἰδού should be restored in the Aramaic text. It seems unlikely, however, that the κύριος represents the original, although this term is found *simpliciter* for God both in the Greek and Aramaic fragments (e.g. 9: 6 (Gk.); 89: 31, 33, 36 (Aramaic)). The subject in the present context, however, looks back to verse 4, ὁ θεός. 'Behold the Lord cometh' (i.e. 'will surely come') is probably best explained as a Christian interpretation or accommodation of the original, interpreted, of course, of the Lord Jesus' coming. If it circulated in Aramaic it would read [*Hā'*]*Mara(n)* '*atha*'.

It is, of course, arguable that the coincidence of the formula with the opening words of 1 En. 1: 9 is entirely fortuitous; the Christian invocation could have circulated with a Parousia reference, as an independent liturgical formula. On the other hand, the coincidence seems too great to be purely accidental, and a liturgical phrase with a scriptural context (and authority) seems on the whole more likely; ὡσαννα has a similar basis in scripture.[23]

If the possibility is conceded, then the original setting of the *maranatha* formula at 1 En. 1: 9, where it refers to a divine judgement on the wicked, not only supports the Parousia reference in the New Testament but can also account for its use as a reinforcement of the ἀνάθεμα: no formula would lend itself more to the purpose of an imprecation or a ban. At the same time, it would be equally appropriate within a eucharistic setting, since the eucharist contains, as an integral element in its structure, the proclamation of the Lord's death 'until He come'.

There remains the philological problem. Is the verb ἀθα (*'atha'*) to be rendered as a present (present-future), future or imperative, (μαρανα) θα (as at Rev. 22: 20), or could it conceivably have originally been a participle (*'athē'*)? K. G. Kuhn lists the alternatives (with interpretations): (*a*) imperative, 'Lord come' (understood as a *petitionary prayer* for the Parousia); (*b*) 'Our Lord has come' (a *confession*, referring to the Lord's first coming in lowliness and humility); and (*c*) 'Our Lord

---

[22] The agreement of the Aramaic with 𝔓72 and (among other patristic sources) with Pseudo-Cyprian is noteworthy. See *Vetus Latina* xxvi 1 *Epistulae Catholicae* (1967), p. 426.

[23] Cf. Dalman, *Words of Jesus*, pp. 220ff.

is now here, is present' (namely, at divine service, above all in the celebration of the eucharist). Kuhn's final choice is for (*c*) and (*a*) in this order of priority.[24]

It will be noted that a futuristic meaning is not mentioned. This can only be defended if '*atha*' is regarded as a *prophetic perfect*: 'Our Lord will (soon) come (in the Parousia; cf. Phil. 4: 5, ὁ κύριος ἐγγύς). Kuhn argues that, while this construction is known to Biblical Hebrew, no single example is known over the whole range of Aramaic (*ibid.*, p. 472). This is a remarkable statement: the *perfectum futuri* is as well established in Syriac as in Biblical Hebrew (Nöldeke, *Syr. Gramm.*, § 258). The construction is rare in Palestinian Aramaic, but it is attested,[25] so that Dalman's ruling (*TWNT*, *loc. cit.*, note 29) that 'a future meaning for the Perfect is excluded' has to be set aside.

This is the alternative which is, in my judgement, the one to prefer: the reference is to the future expressed by a *perfectum futuri*, here virtually equivalent to a prophetic perfect, 'The Lord *will* (soon, surely) come' (i.e. at the *Parousia*). So far as the Greek letters of ἀθα are concerned, the form could be construed as an imperative (Kittel, p. 471 foot) or as a perfect, referring to the past. Just as Phil. 4: 5 (ὁ κύριος ἐγγύς) seems to reflect a future, Rev. 22: 20 ἔρχου κύριε Ἰησοῦ represents an imperatival interpretation. Perhaps the popularity of the formula was its ambiguity and hence flexibility: it could be fitted into different contexts, in the eucharist, as an imprecation, or as a confession ('The Lord has come').[26]

---

[24] *TWNT* iv, 473, 475.

[25] See M. Black, *op. cit.*, p. 11 note 4. Cf. H. L. Strack, *Abriss des biblischen Aramäisch* (Leipzig, 1896), citing Dan. 7: 27.

[26] The *Constitutiones Apostolorum* (vi. 26. 5) relates *maranatha* explicitly to the historical coming (ed. F. X. Funk, p. 414).

PART TWO

THE SPIRIT IN THE NEW TESTAMENT

14

Jesus und der Paraklet in Johannes 16

ERNST BAMMEL

I

In seinem berühmten Traktat über Rankes *Geschichte der Päpste* erklärt Macaulay in aller Deutlichkeit: auf dem Gebiet der natürlichen und geoffenbarten Theologie gibt es keinen Fortschritt.[1] Es denkt dabei sowohl an die Erkenntnismöglichkeit der Gegenstände, mit denen es die Theologie zu tun hat wie an die seelische Stimmung der Menschen, die sich dieselben aneignen. Da bleibt der Mensch, wie Macaulay, Goethes Mephisto nachredend sagt: 'wunderlich als wie am ersten Tag'.[2] Und die Gottesgelehrsamkeit verharrt – so verstand den Briten ein deutsches Gegenüber[3] – 'ewig auf demselben Fleck'.

Nicht jeder mochte mit der Meinung des englischen Geschichtschreibers übereinstimmen. Sein Landsmann W. R. Inge sah den Gedanken einer fortschreitenden Offenbarung im Christentum angelegt[4] und Hegel hatte schon zuvor die Rechtfertigung für die Ingeltungsetzung dieses Prinzips angegeben: es war die Überzeugung Jesu, daß es des 'Untergangs seines Individuums' bedürfe, um die 'Abhängigkeit der Jünger' zu beseitigen und den 'göttlichen Geist in ihnen selbst' zu erwecken.[5] Der Dekan der Paulskirche verwies dafür auf Joh. 16: 12, während der schwäbische Philosoph den vollen Wechsel und entscheidenden Fortschritt der Weltgeschichte in dem Wort Jesu von Joh. 16: 7c angedeutet sah. Beiden sagte das Wort der Schrift selbst, daß es einen Fortschritt gebe. Ihre Autorität war

---

[1] *The Complete Works of Lord Macaulay* ix (London, 1898), S. 291.

[2] Ebenda, S. 294.

[3] Es war Konst. Rößler (*Das deutsche Reich und die kirchliche Frage*, Leipzig, 1876, S. 440), dessen geistreiche Auseinandersetzung mit Macaulay auch heute noch des Reizes nicht entbehrt.

[4] *The Hibbert Journal*, 1927/8, S. 641. Ähnlich H. L. Jackson, *The Problem of the Fourth Gospel* (Cambridge, 1918), S. 139.

[5] *Hegels theologische Jugendschriften*, hsg. v. H. Nohl (Tübingen, 1907), S. 317: 'Erst nach der Entfernung seines Individuums konnte ihre Abhängigkeit davon aufhören und eigener Geist oder der göttliche Geist in ihnen selbst bestehen... Jesus hatte das Bewußtsein der Notwendigkeit des Untergangs seines Individuums.'

unbestritten; aber sie war dergestalt, daß sie über sich selbst hinauswies auf eine Bewegung, die über die in ihr selbst festgehaltenen Anfänge sich weiterentwickelt und deren Gewalt – das ist für beide anders als für Macaulay selbstverständlich – den Menschen verändert, ihn 'zum Bewußtsein bringt'.[6]

Es ist nicht unbezeichnend, daß dieses Stück des Neuen Testamentes es ist, das beiden sprechender als jede andere Stelle zu sein schien. Dies ist Grund genug, um die Verse selbst in Augenschein zu nehmen.

II

Mancherlei Thesen sind seit Wellhausens epochemachenden Forschungen über den ursprünglichen Bestand und die Zusätze der Abschiedsreden des Johannesevangeliums aufgestellt worden. Eine Richtung scheint sich in dieser Arbeit abzuzeichnen: von einem Gesamtschema abzusehen und die Lösung in der Einteilung in selbständige Einheiten zu erblicken. Übereinstimmung über die Abgrenzung derselben hat sich noch nicht herausgestellt. So wird es angezeigt sein, von kleineren Zusammenhängen auszugehen. Als ein solcher stellt sich zunächst einmal 16: 4b–30 dar. Während 16: 1–4a, 31–3 von der Verfolgung handeln, fehlt dies Thema ganz in den dazwischenliegenden Versen.[7] Diese werden abgeschlossen durch die chorartige Zustimmung der Jünger in V. 29f., eingeleitet aber durch eine Erklärung Jesu (V. 5a), der die Feststellung des Ausbleibens der Nachfrage nach dem Sinn der Aussage auf dem Fuße folgt. Dem sind parallel gebildet die Verse 16–18: der Zusage Jesu folgt nun wirklich die Frage, die Jesus selbst zu längeren Ausführungen über das Thema veranlaßt. Inhaltlich aber steht es so, daß nur der zweite Teil vom Weggang Jesu und der Folge desselben für die Seinen handelt. Im ersten Teil klingt dies Thema nur auf, um schon in V. 7b durch ein anderes ersetzt zu werden. Heben sich somit zwei Einheiten heraus, so ist auch damit zu rechnen, daß der Anfang der ersten hinzugekommen ist, um das Nachfolgende mit dem beherrschenden Thema des zweiten Teils des Kapitels zu verschweißen. Als tragend schält sich somit der Zusammenhang V. 7ff. heraus. Dabei ist freilich zu berücksichtigen, daß V. 14f. eine Erklärung von V. 13 sind: V. 14 verbindet die Aussage der vorangehenden Verse mit der

---

[6] Ebenda.

[7] Statt dessen ist viel (V. 6, 20–2) von der persönlichen Trübsal wegen des Scheidens Jesu die Rede.

vorherrschenden Christologie des Evangeliums, während V. 15 – auch textgeschichtlich nicht sicher bezeugt – als 'Anmerkung', sei es des Evangelisten,[8] sei es einer späteren Hand anzusehen ist.

Aber auch die Verse selbst sind kein einfach gewebtes Muster. V. 7f. und 13 enthalten Sprüche vom Parakleten.[9] Hans Windisch hat in seiner bahnbrechenden Untersuchung[10] sie mit drei vorangehenden Sprüchen zusammengestellt und zugleich vom umgebenden Kontext abgehoben. Sie gehören, recht gesehen, zusammen, wie die Bezugnahme auf den Parakleten durch ein bloßes ἐκεῖνος in V. 13 anzeigt.[11] Dazu: der Paraklet ist – der Bogen von V. 7f. zu V. 13 macht das deutlich – mit dem Geiste gleichgesetzt, eine Verbindung, die durchaus nicht üblich ist[12] und auch in den anderen Sprüchen vom Tröster nur durch eine nachhinkende Erläuterung (14: 17, 26; 15: 26) erzielt wird. Zwischen den Sätzen über den Parakleten aber stehen Verse, die erläutern (9–11) bzw. auf Jesus selbst zurückführen (12). Dies zeigt, daß selbst der kleinere Zusammenhang nicht aus einem Guß ist und darum Stück für Stück seinem Gehalt nach zu bestimmen ist.

Der letzte Spruch unterscheidet sich von den vorangehenden durch eine genaue Angabe über die von dem Parakleten erwartete Funktion. Das besondere daran ist, daß die Angabe sich in zwei Stufen entfaltet, einer ersten, die nur die Themen angibt und einer zweiten, die dieselben genauer ins Visier nimmt und eine nähere Erläuterung der Gegenstände

---

[8] So Bultmann, *Das Evangelium des Johannes* (Göttingen, 1941), S. 444 (E.T. p. 576).

[9] In 𝔓66 steht im oberen Rand εαν δε πορευθω πεμψω υμας. Der Text selbst fehlt für V. 6b bis 11a. Die Form der Angabe mag auf Nachlässigkeit des Korrektors beruhen (so V. Martin auf S. 52 der Erstveröffentlichung) oder aber ein Anzeichen für einen anderen Text sein. Falls das letztere der Fall, müßte es eine stark abweichende Fassung gewesen sein. Das ist nicht unmöglich, zumal auch im folgenden der Text ein eigener ist. Zwar wird in 15: 26 der Paraklet genannt und in 16: 13 eine (oder dieselbe) den Jüngern gegenüberstehende Größe, aber V. 15 ist ausgelassen, um V. 16 als eine Zusicherung eben dieser Größe erscheinen zu lassen. Der Vulgärtext von Tarragona, den E. S. Buchanan herausgegeben hat (*Evangelium sec. Johannem e codice rescripto Tarragonesi*, London, 1919) läßt die Verse 9–11 aus und gibt in den verbleibenden Versen eine Umformulierung, die mit den Begriffen *salvator* (= *paracletus* (*-itus*)), *spiritus hominum* und *spiritus filiorum dei* spielt.

[10] 'Die fünf johanneischen Parakletsprüche' in: *Festgabe Ad. Jülicher* (Tübingen, 1927), S. 110ff. (E.T. *The Spirit-Paraclete in the Fourth Gospel*, Philadelphia, 1968). Gegen Windisch wendet sich Fr. Büchsel, *Johannes und der hellenistische Synkretismus* (Gütersloh, 1928).

[11] Streng genommen handelt es sich also um vier (nicht fünf; so Windisch) Parakletsprüche in den Abschiedsreden.

[12] S. C. K. Barrett, *JTS* n.s. i, 1950, S. 11f.

gibt. Ist der Paraklet ansonsten und auch um Anfang (V. 7) wie am Ende (V. 13) als sich an die Jünger wendend angesehen, so ist das hier anders: schon in V. 8 ist der κόσμος angesprochen und dasselbe ist, eingeschlossen wie ausdrücklich (V. 11), in den drei folgenden Versen der Fall. Man wird in diesem Bezug das Gemeinsame zwischen der Themenangabe und der näheren Umschreibung zu sehen haben. Dennoch wird es angezeigt sein, beides von einander getrennt zu halten.

III

Die Tätigkeit des Parakleten[13] soll ein ἐλέγχειν gegenüber dem κόσμος sein. Zum Anklagen gibt es reiches Vergleichsmaterial.[14] Freilich ist es unsicher, wieweit es den Satz erhellen kann: handelt es sich hier doch ausgerechnet um den Tröster, dem die Rolle des Anklagens zugeschrieben wird. Dazu: paßt das Motiv in den Zusammenhang der Parakletsprüche? Sie wenden sich durchweg an die Jünger. Sogar in die Ausführungen zum vierten Spruch, in V. 10b ist dieser Bezug eingeflossen. Auch der größere Zusammenhang der Abschiedsreden ist, wie es 13: 33 deutlich markiert wird, ausschließlich an die kleine Schar gerichtet. Somit dürfte das ἐλέγχειν-Motiv weder mit den Parakletsprüchen selbst noch mit den Abschiedsreden in enger Verbindung stehen. Wohl aber gehört es mit den interpretierenden Versen 9–11 zusammen. Dort ist der Ausblick auf die Welt und die Ankündigung des Endes ihres Wesens der alles beherrschende Gedanke.[15] Das Wort ἐλέγχειν ist somit als Bindemittel anzusehen, das den Spruch vom Parakleten mit der nachfolgenden Erklärung zusammenfügt.

Das Wort ist an Stelle eines anderen eingesetzt worden. Fragt man nach dem Ausdruck, den es ersetzt hat, so kann man nur versuchen, ihn aus den Begriffen, auf die das Zeitwort hingeführt hat, zu erschließen und sieht dann, daß ἁμαρτία κ.τ.λ. viel weniger Gegenstände der Anklage[16] als der Unterweisung sind. Die Lehrtätigkeit

---

[13] Zum Begriff s. neuerdings H. Riesenfeld, *NTS*, 1971/2, S. 450.

[14] S. O. Betz, *Der Paraklet* (Leiden, 1963), S. 194ff.

[15] Etwas anders steht es lediglich im Codex Rehdigeranus, wo in V. 9 die drei ersten Worte fehlen und somit die Lehrtätigkeit des Parakleten mit dem Nichtglauben der Welt begründet wird. Die Fragen des gotischen Textes werden gesondert behandelt werden.

[16] Betz, S. 196, führt 1QH i. 25 als Parallele an. Indessen erscheinen die Begriffe – neben anderen – in ganz anderem Zusammenhang. Die Stelle steht Joh. 16: 8 fern.

des Parakleten ist auch im zweiten Spruch betont (14: 26) und im Schlußsatz der Kette (16: 13) wird die Formulierung von V. 8 durch ὁδηγήσει ὑμᾶς weitergeführt und überhöht. Somit darf angenommen werden, daß ein Begriff wie διδάξει ὑμᾶς ursprünglich in dem Spruch gestanden hat.

Es sind drei Gegenstände, bezüglich deren der Paraklet eine Wirksamkeit ausüben soll. Die Dreiheit wird keine zufällige sein. Sowohl für die Grundbegriffe des Gesetzes[17] wie das Zehntrecht[18] wie auch für die Beschreibung der βαρύτερα τοῦ νόμου[19] wird die Dreizahl verwendet. Gleichermaßen findet sie bei der Festlegung des praktischen Verhaltens dem Glaubensgenossen[20] wie dem Fremden[21] gegenüber Verwendung.

Überblickt man diese Triaden im jüdisch-christlichen Schrifttum,[22] so wird sich am ehesten der Gegenstand der βαρύτερα zum Vergleich anbieten.[23] Dem Wirken des Parakleten geht das Jesu voraus, wie die βαρύτερα auf den Normalvorschriften beruhen. Die Gegenstände, die mit dem Wirken des Parakleten verbunden werden, ἁμαρτία, δικαιοσύνη und κρίσις sind in der Tat solche, die in den Offenbarungsreden des Erlösers, wie sie sich im Johannesevangelium finden, kaum eine Rolle spielen.[24] Eine Ergänzung durch das Wirken eines anderen

---

[17] Apg. 15: 20 und die zahlreichen bei G. Strothotte, *Das Apostelkonzil im Lichte der jüdischen Rechtsgeschichte* (Diss. Erlangen, 1955), beigebrachten jüdischen Parallelen.

[18] Mt. 23: 23.

[19] Mt. 23: 23. Handelt es sich bei ἔλεος um die Liebeswerke, bei πίστις um den Glaubensweg, so ist die Bedeutung von κρίσις nicht recht klar. Vielleicht bezeichnet das Wort, was sonst bei Mt. durch δικαιοσύνη ausgedrückt wird. Lk., der was das Geringwertige anbelangt, die dreigliedrige Anordnung beibehalten hat (obzwar mit πᾶν λάχανον ein generalisierender Begriff hereinkommt) hat dies bei der Beschreibung des Wichtigen aufgegeben: κρίσις und ἀγάπη bezeichnen den einen Gerichtsvorgang nach seinen beiden Seiten. Vgl. auch Gal. 5: 14, insbesondere die frühen Auslegungen des Verses, die den Versuch machen, zwischen mehr oder weniger Wichtigem im Gesetz zu unterscheiden.

[20] S. *TWNT* vi, 914, bes. Anm. 279 (E.T. vi, 914 n. 279).

[21] Josephus, *contra Apionem* 2 §211; vgl. *TWNT* vi, 900 Anm. 139 (E.T. vi, 901 n. 139).

[22] Aseneth empfängt πνεῦμα ζωῆς, σοφία und ἀλήθεια (*Joseph und Aseneth* 19: 11). Vgl. Kants Trias: Gott, Freiheit, Unsterblichkeit und Bismarcks Äußerung über die geoffenbarte Religion: 'Gott, der das Gute will, ein höherer Richter und ein zukünftiges Leben.'

[23] Kaum ist mit Fr. Spitta (*Das Johannesevangelium als Quelle der Geschichte Jesu*, Göttingen, 1910, S. 319) und Windisch an die Bußpredigt zu denken; s. dazu B. Lindars, *Mélanges bibliques. Festschrift B. Rigaux* (Gembloux, 1970), S.275ff.

[24] Anders B. Lindars (s. Anm. 98).

wäre somit durchaus möglich, ja sachgemäß. D. h., die Themenangabe
steht mit derjenigen, die Ankündiger wie Angekündigten durch das
Wort ἄλλος parallelisiert und verbindet,[25] vor allem aber dem V. 13,
der dem Parakleten die Hinführung in alle Wahrheit, somit vielleicht
sogar eine größere Aufgabe und höhere Weihe zuschreibt, in
Verbindung.[26]

Des weiteren ist zu vergleichen mit den mancherlei Hoffnungen des
Spätjudentums, die sich auf einen bevollmächtigten Gesetzesdeuter
richteten.[27] Dort freilich handelt es sich um die Aufhellung von
Dunkelheiten der Thora, wie sie gegeben ist und um die Einordnung
von als zweifelhaft Erscheinendem in die Vorschriften des Gesetzes.
Nicht aber handelt es sich um die Verkündigung eines ergänzenden
oder gar neuen, alte Ordnungen aufhebenden Gesetzes.[28] Das ἀναγγέλλειν der kommenden Dinge kann sich dem unschwer verbinden,
wie das Beispiel des Habakukkommentars des Lehrers der Gerechtigkeit zeigt.[29] Wenn aber die volle Wahrheit für das Judentum im Gesetz
gegeben ist, so versteht sich ihreSichtbarmachung als ἐραστεύειν.[30] Das
Nämliche könnte auch durch ὁδηγεῖν ausgedrückt werden. Andere
Begriffe liegen jedoch erheblich näher. Wenn überdies bestimmte
Gegenstände des Interesses genannt werden, so fehlen dazu fast ganz
die Beispiele und rücken den Abschnitt an die Grenze des im
Spätjudentum Möglichen.

Die neue Lehre zu einem besonderen Zeitpunkt – das ist auch ein
Thema der synoptischen Evangelien. Ist schon die christologische

---

25 Joh. 14: 16. Anders H. Schlier (*Festschrift Jos. Schmid*, Regenburg, 1963,
S. 234f.), der zwar zugibt, daß nach Joh. 14: 26 Jesus der eine Helfer ist, aber
es als Mißverständnis bezeichnet, daraus zu folgern, daß der Geist ein zweiter
Jesus sei: 'Das gerade nicht.' Der personale Charakter des Parakleten wird
hier außeracht gelassen.

26 Auf anderer, in etwa paralleler Ebene stellte sich die Frage, ob das Evangelium
selbst im Hinblick auf ein zweites Werk entworfen sei. Sie hat, aus anderer
Richtung argumentierend, H. Preisker bejaht und geglaubt, daß das Vierte
Evangelium auf ein Seitenstück apokalyptischen Inhalts hin angelegt war
(*Theol. Blätter*, 1936, Sp. 185ff.). Die Frage braucht hier nicht entschieden zu
werden.

27 S. *TLZ*, 1954, Sp. 351ff. G. Jeremias, *Der Lehrer der Gerechtigkeit* (Göttingen,
1963), S. 285ff.

28 S. *TU* lxxxviii (1964), S. 120ff.

29 Vgl. auch das Bild Daniels im Spätjudentum, des Mannes, dem nachgerühmt
wird, nicht nur prophezeit zu haben sondern auch, daß er καὶ καιρὸν ὥριζεν
εἰς ὅν ταῦτα ἀποβήσεται (Jos., *Ant.* 10 §267).

30 S. Philo, *De spec. Leg.* i. 59: Μωυσῆς... ἀληθείας ἐραστὴς ὤν, und vgl. CD vii:
דורש התורה.

Belehrung nach der Darstellung des Markus auf den zweiten, der Passion zugewandten Teil der Wirksamkeit Jesu beschränkt, so ist die eigentliche eschatologische Verkündigung in die Leidensgeschichte selbst eingeschoben. Der Inhalt derselben ist das Äußerste dessen, was Menschen fassen können – darum dem kleinsten Kreise[31] innerhalb der Jüngerschaft anvertraut.[32] Diejenigen, die damit bekannt gemacht sind, werden zu Lehrern derjenigen, die durch Auferstehung und Wirken des Erhöhten zu weiterem Verständnis die Fähigkeit erlangen. Nicht weit verschieden von dieser Auffassung ist die andere, die dem erhöhten Herrn selbst eine Anweisung und neue Belehrung zuschreibt. Sie findet sich schon in Luk. 24: 25–7, 45f. und dann in großer Mannigfaltigkeit im apokalyptischen,[33] apokryphen[34] und gnostischen[35] Schrifttum. Ist die eine Form aus der Testamentsliteratur entwickelt,[36] so die andere aus den Visionsberichten. Beiden tritt der Gedanke der johanneischen Abschiedsreden an die Seite: der Erlöser selbst läßt die Seinen für eine Weile alleine,[37] während ein anderer Belehrung und Wegweisung übernimmt.

Ganz ähnlich steht es mit V. 13. Der Satz, der verschiedenen Bearbeitungen ausgesetzt war, dürfte so gelautet haben: . . . ὁδηγήσει ὑμᾶς εἰς τὴν ἀλήθειαν πᾶσαν.[38] Die Lesart ἐν κ.τ.λ. ist eine Erklärung von

---

[31] Mk. 13: 3 εἰς ἰδίαν. Die Namen (Andreas!) dürften aus alter Überlieferung stammen.

[32] Lk. ist dabei, daraus eine Szene zu machen.

[33] Ap. Joh., Past. Herm., Freer Logion, usw.

[34] *Gespräche Jesu mit seinen Jüngern nach seiner Auferstehung*, hsg. v. C. Schmidt (Leipzig, 1919); der Zusatz zum Markusevangelium im Briefe des Clemens, über den M. Smith (*Am. Soc. of Bibl. Lit.*, Dec. 1960) berichtet hat.

[35] *Sophia Jesu Christi*; *Pistis Sophia*; vgl. W. Bauer, *Das Leben Jesu im Zeitalter der ntl. Apokryphen* (Tübingen, 1909), S. 268, 373.

[36] S. *Verborum Veritas. Festschrift G. Stählin* (Wuppertal, 1970) S. 464.

[37] Es ist nicht unbezeichnend, daß der lukanische Gedanke der Lenkung durch den erhöhten Herrn den Abschiedsreden fremd ist.

[38] Die Wendung ist nicht eigentlich alttestamentlich. Sie begegnet nur in Dan. 9: 13 LXX, jedoch mit abweichender Wortstellung: ἐν πάσῃ ἀληθείᾳ. Ansonsten kommt bloßes ἐν ἀληθείᾳ häufiger vor, wie es auch in die Textüberlieferung von Joh. 16: 13 Eingang gefunden hat (א*; sehr interessant ist die Mischlesart des Breslauer Kodex 1: in veritate omnia). Der Ausdruck bezeichnet die Zuverlässigkeit der göttlichen Leitung (Dan. 3: 28; Sir. 27: 15: ἐν ἀληθείᾳ ὁδόν). Dem gegenüber ist schon Dan. 9: 13 LXX (im Text der Mas., einem Teil der LXX-Handschriften und Θ: δικαιοσύνῃ σου) etwas Unübliches. Dies gilt erst recht für die Wendung mit dem nachgeordneten Adjektive, die so auch kein gutes Griechisch ist. In verstärktem Maße stimmt dasselbe für εἰς ἀ. π., eine weder durch die LXX abgesicherte noch durch den griechischen Sprachgebrauch geforderte Wendung. Diese letztere mußte immer

εἰς, wie sie häufiger vorkommt,[39] hier aber den Sinn auf die Weise der Einwirkung beschränkt und damit gegenüber der Beifügung πνεῦμα τῆς ἀληθείας kaum etwas Neues gibt. Διηγήσει, obzwar eine sehr alte Lesart, entspricht nicht dem johanneischen Stil[40] und schreibt dem Parakleten eine Tätigkeit zu, die etwa derjenigen des Lehrers der Gerechtigkeit entspricht, nämlich die Erklärung einer bereits vorhandenen Wahrheit in Vollmacht.[41] Beide Lesarten, die sich ergänzen,[42] schränken die Wirksamkeit des Geistes auf in üblichen Begriffen Enthaltenes ein,[43] und weisen darin – *e contrario* – auf das Besondere und Befremdende der Aussage selbst hin.[44] Eine Eingrenzung anderer Art ist im Nachsatz gegeben. Die Übereinstimmung mit der Stimme Gottes[45] schließt die Mitteilung von Neuem nicht aus.[46] Es geht in dem Zwischengedanken von V. 13b um die Sicherheit der vom Geist gemachten Aussage; das ist ein in den Abschiedsreden nicht ungewöhnlicher Ton und könnte – jedenfalls in der Formulierung – eine

in Gefahr stehen, auf das theologisch Übliche und sprachlich weniger Fremde zurückgeführt zu werden. In ihr ist das Ursprüngliche zu sehen. Anders W. Michaelis, *TWNT* v, 104f. (E.T. v, 100f.) und E. Hirsch, *Studien zum vierten Evangelium* (Tübingen, 1936), S. 33; *Das Vierte Evangelium in seiner ursprünglichen Gestalt* (Tübingen, 1936), S. 45 (in seiner Auslegung nähert sich Hirsch – s. *Evangelium*, S. 360ff. – freilich der hier vorgeschlagenen Deutung an).

[39] S. Blass–Debrunner, *Grammatik* § 218.

[40] S. Joh. 1: 18.

[41] Vgl. Mk. 1: 27 und die Erklärung, die D. Daube (*N.T. and Rabbinic Judaism*, London, 1956, S. 205ff.) der Stelle angedeihen läßt.

[42] Merkwürdigerweise finden sie sich nur selten (in 1 got, vg^{pt}) in ein und denselben Handschriften.

[43] *Mutatis mutandis* geschah dasselbe mit dem Geistbegriff. In 3: 6 wie in 20: 19–23 werden im Unterschied zu den Abschiedsreden jeweils verbreitete Vorstellungen aufgenommen. Ein anderer Weg ist in der Pariser Johanneshandschrift beschritten worden: durch die Einführung von ὅταν δεχθῆτε τὸ πνεῦμα τῆς ἀληθείας ὅπερ ἐστὶ τὸ πνεῦμά μου (J. C. Thilo, *Codex Apocryphus*, Leipzig, 1832, S. 879) wird der Geist entpersonalisiert. Auf Joh. 17: 26 folgt in derselben Handschrift ein längerer Nachtrag. Neben solchen Worten, die aus Joh. 20 herübergenommen sind, finden sich auch herausragende Sätze. Darunter der folgende: ὁ παράκλητός ἐστιν ἐν ὑμῖν, διδάξετε ἐν τῷ παρακλήτῳ (Thilo, S. 880). Das Verständnis des Parakleten, wie es hier vorliegt, ist ganz der Geistesvorstellung angeglichen. Diese Zeile geht schwerlich auf alte Überlieferung zurück.

[44] Vielleicht ist auch die Auslassung von ἄρτι in V. 12 (das Material bei Hoskier, ii, 298) schon als Einschränkung zu verstehen (H. selbst hält die Lesart für möglicherweise ursprünglich).

[45] Im Zusammenhang ist daraus eine Betraunng durch den Erhöhten – verstärkt noch in der Lesart' ἀκούσει – geworden.

[46] Erst die Übersetzung von ἀναγγέλλειν durch 'expound' (so R. E. Brown z. St.) tut dies. Luther übersetzt ἀναγγέλλειν in Sap. 8: 8 durch 'erraten'.

bearbeitende Hand verraten. V. 13c schließt sich dem an und fügt doch etwas Bestimmtes hinzu: die Ankündigung der Abfolge der ἐρχόμενα und – so darf man schließen[47] – des Zeitpunkts des Eintritts derselben. In der Tat, dies ist auch gegenüber V. 8 etwas Neues und dürfte somit zum ältesten Bestand des Verses gehören.[48] Die christologische Erklärung, die ἀναγγελεῖ dann in V. 14 gefunden hat,[49] stellt sicher, daß die literarische Schichtung sich so wie in den vorangehenden Versen 8ff. vollzogen hat.

Wegführung[50] wird die dem Parakleten zugeschriebene Einfluß-nahme gennant – Aufschließen, 'Erraten' der Zukunft die von ihm erwartete Weisung. Der erstere Begriff kommt in den Psalmen[51] wie besonders in Weisheitsschrifttum vor. Geht es dort um die volle Potenz der Wahrheit – Gott ist ὁδηγός der σοφία (Sap. 7: 15) und Salomo bittet darum, daß die Weisheit ihn in seinem Tun leiten möge (Sap. 9: 11) –, so ist hier an die Enthüllung aller Wahrheit gedacht. Gibt es ein ὀρθοποδεῖν πρὸς τὴν ἀλήθειαν, also die Wahrheit als Zielbegriff auch andernorts im N.T.,[52] so ist doch hier an anderes, an die Kundmachung neuer Wahrheitselemente gedacht. Der Gebrauch von πᾶς und der Zusammenhang mit V. 8 stellen das sicher.

Es ist der Paraklet, dem diese Tätigkeit zugeschrieben wird. Das Spätjudentum erwog – bejahte oder auch verneinte[53] – die Frage, ob Gott beim Schöpfungswerk einen Teilhaber gehabt habe. Einer der Namen für diese Größe ist παράκλητος. Im Unterschied dazu spricht Joh. 16 vom Erlösungswerk, das als in Stufen sich vollziehend gedacht wird. Gewiß, der Paraklet wird hier mit Jesus verbunden: er wird vom Vater und Sohne ausgesandt[54] und seine Verkündigung ist ein Erinnern an die Botschaft Jesu. Aber ein Unterschied ist noch erkennbar. Jesus hat alles, was er gehört hat, weitergegeben (15: 15), und doch gibt es Gegenstände, die noch der Enthüllung harren: πολλὰ ἔχω ὑμῖν λέγειν

---

[47] Vgl. Sap. 8: 8, wo die Weisheit 'Zeiten und Stunden' erhellt.

[48] Anders Windisch, S. 122.

[49] Und zwar in rückschauender Darbietung: V. 15 ist Voraussetzung für V. 14.

[50] Nicht bloß 'Anleitung, Unterweisung'; so Michaelis, a. a. O.

[51] S. Betz, S. 187.

[52] Gal. 2: 14; G. D. Kilpatrick, *Bultmann-Festschrift* (Berlin, 1954), S. 265ff. Es handelt sich um die Entfaltung einer durch εὐαγγέλιον klar umgrenzten, als solcher bereits bekannten Wahrheit (s. Gal. 2: 5).

[53] Philo, *De opific. mundi* §23: οὐδενὶ δὲ παρακλήτῳ – τίς γὰρ ἦν ἕτερος; – μόνῳ δὲ ἑαυτῷ χρησάμενος ὁ θεός.

[54] Dies Element wird im Text der Pariser Handschrift von 16: 7 ausgelassen.

(16: 12).[55] Macht Jesus selbst eine καινὴ ἐντολή kund (13: 34), um Weiteres περὶ τοῦ πατρός (16: 15) anzukündigen, so wird in 16: 8 dem Parakleten eine διδαχή zugeschrieben. Ist Jesu eigene Verkündigung nach 14: 6 eine solche von dreifacher und somit letzter Vollkommenheit, so wird in 16: 8 das Nämliche vom Parakleten ausgesagt. Ohne Frage sind die eine eigenständige Tätigkeit des Parakleten anzeigenden Aussagen[56] die älteren.[57] Man hat sogar gemeint, daß sich als Folgerung daraus die Notwendigkeit ergebe, ἄλλος in 14: 16 als Einsatz anzusehen und demgemäß zu streichen.[58]

Dies freilich ist schwerlich aufrecht zu erhalten. Religionsgeschichtliche Forschung hat gezeigt, daß der Gedanke einer Abfolge von Rettergestalten verbreitet[59] und sogar in der Umgebung des Johannesevangeliums beheimatet ist.[60] Die Bezeichnung Paraklet kommt vor, während allerdings die Wirksamkeit dem, was aus dem Spätjudentum über den Fürsprecher bekannt ist,[61] nicht gerade entspricht.[62] Sogar die Abhebung der Tröstergestalten von einander durch die nähere Bezeichnung 'groß' oder 'hoch'[63] ist belegt. Weder die Beschränkung auf ein Vorläufer-Vollender-[64] noch auf ein Dreierschema: Vorläufer-Jesus-Paraklet[65] ist angezeigt. Hier nämlich sind es zwei und zwar, wie die Verhältnisbezeichnung ἄλλος anzeigt,[66] im Wesenlichen

---

[55] S. dazu die Erklärung W. Wredes, *Das Messiasgeheimnis in den Evangelien* (Göttingen, 1901), S. 193.

[56] Verständlicherweise hat der islamische Polemiker Ibn-Taimija den Schluß gezogen, der Paraklet müsse eine irdische Person sein, da er als anderer Paraklet bezeichnet und von ihm Reden, Hören und Gehörtwerden ausgesagt werde (E. Fritsch, *Islam u. Christentum im Mittelalter*, Breslau, 1930, S. 91).

[57] S. J. Wellhausen, *Das Evangelium Johannis* (Berlin, 1908), S. 77ff. Auf anderer Ebene zeigt sich eine Parallele in der Erörterung der Frage, ob das Vierte Evangelium in seiner Geistigkeit eine die Christusauffassung der Synoptiker weiterführende oder diese gar abstoßende Schrift sei; s. dazu H. Windisch, *Johannes und die Synoptiker* (Leipzig, 1926).

[58] Wellhausen, S. 65.

[59] S. W. Bauer, *Das Johannesevangelium* (Tübingen, 1933), S. 183f.

[60] Ebda S. 3f., 7f.

[61] S. S. Mowinckel, *ZNW*, 1933, S. 97f.; N. Johannsson, *Parakletoi* (Lund, 1940).

[62] Zur Kritik s. Merx, S. 374; C. K. Barrett, *JTS*, 1950, S. 11f.

[63] Vgl. Luthers: 'du höchster Fröster' (in: Nun bitten wir den Reiligen Geist). Die Formulierung ist in aller Wahrscheinlichkeit durch älteres Gut bestimmt worden.

[64] So G. Bornkamm, *Festschrift R. Bultmann* (Stuttgart, 1949), S. 12ff.; dazu Bultmann, *Beiheft*, S. 42f. (incorporated into E.T. pp. 567f.).

[65] So Windisch, a. a. O.

[66] G. Johnston, dessen Buch freilich viel zu wünschen übrig läßt (s. B. Lindars, *Theology*, 1971, S. 37f.), möchte ἄλλος adjektivisch zu πνεῦμα ziehen (*The Spirit-Paraclete in the Gospel of John*, Cambridge, 1970, S. 84).

gleichrangige Gestalten, mit denen wir es zu tun haben. So ist es angemessen, das Denkgerüst von den zwei Söhnen Gottes, die sich in der Sendung ablösen,[67] als nächsten Vergleichspunkt in betracht zu ziehen. Im Spätjudentum[68] wie im frühen Christentum[69] begegnet es.

Der Blick auf das Vergleichsmaterial zeigt aber auch, wie wandelbar die Anschauungen sind: daß das Verhältnis der einzelnen Gestalten zu einander Verlagerungen ausgesetzt ist.[70] Umbildungen, auch Namenswechsel konnten stattfinden. Eignet der philonischen Ausprägung eine deutliche Höherbewertung des υἱὸς πρεσβύτερος, des ὀρθὸς λόγος καὶ πρωτόγονος υἱός,[71] so ist dies für die johanneischen Formeln nicht ganz so ausgeprägt der Fall. Die Gänze der Wahrheit kann auch der Rest, der noch aussteht, sein.[72] Ἁμαρτία κ.τ.λ. mögen – müssen aber nicht unbedingt – Gegenstände vertiefter Geheimbelehrung sein.

Ihren besonderen Charakter gewinnt die Aussage durch die Angabe: συμφέρει ὑμῖν.[73] Ein Prinzip allgemeinerer Art, vergleichbar demjenigen von Joh. 11: 50, erheischt den Wechsel von Jesus zum Parakleten.[74] Die Abfolge von Erlösergestalten ist nicht mehr bloß eine im göttlichen Geheimnis beschlossene und fraglos hingenommene Tatsache sondern ein dem Weitergehen der Heilsereignisse dienliches Ereignis. Drückt sich in der Anschauung vom Ende der Gesandtschaften der Weisheit das Wissen um die negative Kehre und das andrängende Unheil aus,[75] so ist dieser Spruch von der frohen Erwartung – συμφέρει – eines weiterführenden Gnadenwegs erfüllt. Es ist dieselbe Zeit, in der auf jüdischer Seite die Anschauung vom sterbenden ersten

---

[67] Vielleicht kann die Erklärung von Lk. 15: 11ff. von daher eine Förderung erhalten.

[68] Philo, *De agricultura* §51.

[69] *Pistis Sophia*, S. 78 (S. 78 Schmidt); vgl. H. Leisegang, *Angelos* i, S. 24ff.; A. Marmorstein, *Angelos* ii, S. 155f.

[70] Im Kölner Mani-Kodex (Teilausgabe in *Ztschr. f. Pap. u. Epigraphik* v, 1970, S. 97ff.) wird Mani betont als Apostel Jesu beschrieben, während er sich im Schapurakan als 'Boten des wahren Gottes' bezeichnet (s. A. Adam, *Texte zum Manichäismus*, Berlin, ²1969, S. 6).

[71] S. Anm. 64.

[72] Anders Windisch, S. 120.

[73] Vielleicht hat ursprünglich etwas Ähnliches in 14: 28, wo dem εἰ ἠγαπᾶτέ με, ἐχάρητε ἂν nach Meinung Wellhausens (S. 68) die Ankündigung des Parakleten gefolgt ist, gestanden.

[74] Ed. Meyer, *Ursprung und Anfänge des Christentums* iii (Stuttgart–Berlin, 1923), S. 646, sieht in der parsischen Lehre, die dem Zoroaster die Unsterblichkeit verweigert, weil dann die Erlösung unmöglich wäre, eine Analogie zu Joh. 16: 7.

[75] S. *NTS* xviii, 1971–2, S. 124.

Gesalbten, dem Messias ben Joseph ensteht.[76] Wie dort diesem Tod als solchem kein Heilswert zukommt,[77] so steht es auch hier. Darin zeigt sich erst eigentlich, daß die Formel noch nicht voll verchristlicht dasteht.

Jedenfalls handelt es sich um eine Fortsetzung des Offenbarungsgeschehens. Das aber ist nicht im Sinne desjenigen, der die Abschiedsreden zusammengefaßt hat: er sieht in Erscheinung und Botschaft Jesu etwas Endgültiges. So ist es weniger wahrscheinlich, daß die Formeln durch den Endgestalter der Reden eingebracht worden sind,[78] als daß sie der ihm vorliegenden Überlieferung zugeflossen waren.

Die Vorstellung selbst, die die Variante einer allgemeineren ist, enthält kein im eigentlichen Sinne christliches Element. In der engeren wie der weiteren Gestalt ist sie im außerchristlichen Bereiche bekannt. So wird sie, mit christlichem Vorzeichen versehen, in früher Zeit als eine Weise, das Christusereignis in einen Rahmen zu stellen, Eingang gefunden haben. Der Grund dafür ist noch ertastbar. War es die Verlassenheit der Jünger[79] und mit ihnen der Gemeinde, die als quälende Frage hinter einem guten Teil der Abschiedsreden steht, so gab es der Antworten mehrere: sie ranken sich an einander hoch, um in der Wiedergabe der Bitte, ja des Verlangens[80] von 17: 24 Genüge zu finden. Eine der Antworten, alsbald zurückgelassen, ist in 16: 7b, 8, 13 zu sehen.

IV

Anders steht es mit den Versen 9–12. Mindestens die beiden ersten Näherbestimmungen handeln von Jesus, zeigen also den Parakleten in der Rolle des Erklärers oder auch Anklägers,[81] während die dritte sich aufs engste mit einem Wort berührt, das nach 12: 31 von Jesus selbst gesprochen ist. Hier besteht kein Fortschritt sondern eine Bewegung um die Gestalt Jesu herum.

---

[76] S. J. Klausner, *Die messianischen Vorstellungen des jüd. Volkes im Zeitalter der Tannaiten* (Berlin, 1904), S. 86ff.; Strack–Billerbeck, ii, 292ff.

[77] So Klausner, a. a. O.

[78] So Windisch, S. 112–21f.

[79] S. Kl. Haacker, *Die Stiftung des Heils: Untersuchungen zur Struktur der johanneischen Theologie* (Stuttgart, 1972), S. 137ff.

[80] Das Kapitel ist bestimmt von der Steigerung von ἐρωτάω (V. 9 u. ö.) zu θέλω. In dem eine unverlierbare Tatsache anzeigenden γνωρίζω (V. 26) ist es begründet, daß die Seinen zu Jesus dazugehören und nicht von ihm getrennt werden können. So mündet die Bitte in die Kundgebung eines Willens aus, ähnlich dem der testamentarischen Bestimmung, die am Ende von Q steht.

[81] Zum Problem S. W. Hatch, *Harvard Theological Review* 1921, S. 103ff.

Dabei kann kaum ein Zweifel bestehen, daß die Zuordnung der drei Kardinalbegriffe zu den ὅτι-Sätzen keine selbstverständliche ist.[82] Schon der Syrer hat dies empfunden und durch die Mehrzahlbildung ἁμαρτιῶν eine engere Verbindung zu der Vielzahl der Ungläubigen geschaffen.[83] Ganz besonders schwierig ist die Verbindung zum zweiten Begriff,[84] dem wiederum schon die syrische Übersetzung ihr erklärendes Bemühen zugewandt hat.[85] Klammert man diese Vordersätze ein, dann ist die Lage eine andere. Der Paraklet klagt an, daß die Welt Jesus bzw. seinem Zeugnis nicht geglaubt hat, er erklärt, daß er zum Vater geht[86] und macht gewiß, daß der Ankläger dem Gericht verfallen ist. Das ergibt einen durchlaufenden Sinn, wenn man es mit dem Prozeß Jesu in Verbindung setzt: es geht um die Nichtannahme des Zeugnisses Jesu durch die Welt, Jesu Rechtfertigung durch den Vater und die Entmächtigung des Fürsten dieser Welt.[87] Ist es bei Paulus und den Synoptikern die eigentliche Aufgabe des Geistes, die Christen in der Verfolgung stark zu machen, so fällt dem Parakleten hier etwas Ähnliches zu: durch die Deutung des Prozesses Jesu und die Zusicherung der Entmächtigung des Feindes wird der Christ dem Ausgeliefertsein an die Widerfahrnisse[88] enthoben. Konzentrieren die Synoptiker die Beschreibung des Wirkens des Geistes in der Verteidigung, die er durchführt, läßt Paulus den Triumph des Märtyrers im Gnadengeschenk des auf seine Lippen gelegten Vaterrufs

---

[82] Die von C. F. D. Moule (*An Idiom Book of N.T. Greek*, Cambridge, 1953, S. 147) heraus gearbeitete Schwierigkeit der ὅτι-Konstruktion würde dadurch gemildert.

[83] Zum Zusammenhang zwischen ἁμαρτίαι und Unglauben siehe Joh. 8: 21–4. Davon scheint auch die Afra beeinflußt zu sein, die in V. 8 (nicht in V. 9!) die Mehrzahl setzt. Sehr interessant ist die Erklärung, die der Stelle in Manis *Kephalaia* 14: 8ff. zuteil wird: der Paraklet wird die Welt überführen über die Sünde und mit den Jüngern reden über δικαιοσύνη, (Sünde) und Gericht. So ist eine doppelte Adressierung erreicht und das überführende Wirken der Welt gegenüber auf einen Punkt zurückgeschraubt, während die Hauptwirksamkeit das Reden (14: 9) bzw. das Predigen (14: 15) ist.

[84] Windisch, S. 120 Anm. 2, vermutet Textverderbnis. Spitta bezeichnet die Verse als 'eines der charakteristischen Mißverständnisse des Bearbeiters' (S. 320). Wellhausen erklärt freimütig: 'Den Sinn von 16: 11 begreife ich so wenig wie den von 16: 10' (S. 73).

[85] S. Merx, S. 402.

[86] Über V. 10b β s. S. 212f.

[87] Nahe kommt dieser Auslegung für einen Augenblick I. de la Potterie, der jedoch alsbald hinzufügt, das Zeugnis sei vom Evangelisten spiritualisiert worden (I. de la Potterie–S. Lyonnet, 'La vie selon l'Esprit (= *Unam Sanctam* 55), 1965, S. 99).

[88] Am Anfang (V. 1–4) wie Ende des Kapitels klar angezeigt.

bestehen,[89] so ist hier an die Anfechtung, die im folgelosen Unglauben der Vielen, im Tode Jesu und der Existenz einer widergöttlichen Macht besteht, gedacht. Alles drei ist mit der Theologie des Evangeliums eng verbunden.

Der Unglaube der vielen ist, wie Joh. 8: 45 zeigt, als Argument gegen Jesus verwendet worden. Sein gewaltsamer Tod hat als Zeugnis gegen die Wahrheit seiner Botschaft gedient (7: 20; 8: 48; 10: 20).[90] Jesus selbst ist mit dem Teufel in Zusammenhang gebracht worden.[91] Die einzelnen Punkte von Kap. 16: 9ff. finden sich als christliche Kontroversaussagen: (a) in 8: 40,[92] (b) in 7: 33f., (c) in 12: 30b (δι' ὑμᾶς), 31. Sie sind Ausschnitte von Auseinandersetzungen, stichwortartig und verkürzt wiedergegeben. Dieselben Aussagen werden Jesus zugeschrieben. Aber die Gewißheit, daß dem so ist, wird hier durch den Zuspruch einer anderen Person vermittelt, während sie in 12: 28 unmittelbar durch eine Himmelsstimme erzielt wird.

Dabei ist die Ausdrucksweise nicht ganz dieselbe wie sonst im Evangelium.[93] Vor allem aber entspricht dies nicht der Vorstellung vom Heiligen Geiste, wie sie anderswo in dieser Schrift entwickelt wird. So breit auch der Fächer der ins Johannesevangelium aufgenommenen Vorstellungen ist,[94] die hier angezeigte findet sich nicht. Auch der Paraklet der Abschiedsreden hat eine andere Aufgabe. Statt dessen ist das in 16: 9–11 angedeutete Amt dem des Geistes im synoptisch-paulinischen Schrifttum verwandt. Die Vorstellung darf darum als eigenständig, als Einsprengsel im Ganzen des Johannesevangeliums angesehen werden.

Die Verwandtschaft mit der synoptischen Vorstellung vom Eintreten des Geistes macht es wahrscheinlich, daß der Beistand in

---

[89] S. *Tutzinger Texte* (München, 1968), S. 83.

[90] 8: 32. Die Aussage, daß es zur Ausführung der ὥρα αὐτοῦ bedurfte (7: 30; 8: 20) ist die christliche Antwort darauf.

[91] Wurde etwa der ankündigte Paraklet von den Juden als der Teufel selbst bezeichnet?

[92] 8: 40, insbesondre V. 40b (ἄνθρωπον ὃς κ.τ.λ.) ist so zu verstehen.

[93] ὑπάγω ist hier (wie in der Einleitung V. 5) gebraucht, wo sonst in den Reden wie in der rahmenden Endgestaltung bevorzugt πορεύομαι und ἀναβαίνω stehen. Statt κέκριται findet sich in 12: 31, einem szenisch verankerten, somit nicht zur jüngsten Schicht gehörenden Wort, ἐκβληθήσεται.

[94] Neben derjenigen der Abschiedsreden sind mindestens zwei andere zu nennen. In 3: 8, 34; 4: 23f.; 6: 63 ist der zeitlose Widerstreit zwischen σάρξ und πνεῦμα ausgedrückt, während in 10: 22; vgl. 7: 39; 1: 32f. der Geist eine Kraft ist, die zu einem bestimmten Zeitpunkt empfangen wird. Die letztere Vorstellung steht der lukanischen nahe.

diesem Summarium ursprünglich als Geist bezeichnet worden war. Somit ist es mit der Kette von Parakletsprüchen erst dann zusammengewachsen, als diese selbst durch die Ergänzungen über den Geist[95] erläutert worden waren. Es wird dies geschehen sein, noch bevor die Parakletsprüche mit dem Haupttenor der Abschiedsreden zum Ausgleich gebracht wurden.

Das Summarium vom Zeugnis des Geistes über den Tod Jesu wird der Gemeinde ein besonders wertes Überlieferungsstück gewesen sein, dessen Wortlaut und Verbindlichkeit sichergestellt wurde und das, weil es als geistgewirkt galt, sich der Eingliederung in andere Worte über den Geist anbot. Luk. 12: 12 (διδάξει) zeigt anderseits das Bestreben an, dem Zeugnis des Geistes ein lehrkraftes Element beizugeben. Diese Umstände werden für die Aufnahme des Summariums in die Parakletkette maßgebend gewesen sein.

Dies ist die einzige konkrete Weisung des Geistes, die sich in dem Evangelium findet. Auch die Verheißung des Parakleten als einer zweiten Erlösergestalt findet sich nirgendwo außerhalb der Abschiedsreden. Ist das letztere eine religionsgeschichtlich erklärbare Vorstellung, so handelt es sich bei dem ersteren um eine echt christliche Verheißung und Erfahrung.[96] Diese ist in die weitere Vorstellung eingebettet worden, der damit das Schicksal widerfuhr, christianisiert zu werden.

Die Verschweißstelle zeigt an, worum es den Christen dabei ging. Die Verse 9–11 drücken die Erwartung, die Zuversicht und auch die Erfahrung aus, daß Angriff des Gegners und Anfechtung des eigenen Herzens nicht das Letzte seien, daß Gott 'zurecht' weisen werde. Die Form, in der dies ausgedrückt wird, ist von der Anleihe an ein vorgegebenes Schema nicht frei.[97] Aber den Christen geht es nicht um den Fortschritt zur Erlösung. Vielmehr ist es der Wille, die im Christusereignis wie der eigenen Erfahrung gegebene Wirklichkeit sicherzustellen, der sie veranlaßt, dieselbe so auszudrücken. Dem

---

[95] Daß diese Bestimmungen zusätzlich sind, hat Windisch, S. 122f. nachgewiesen. Vgl. auch Windisch in *Amicitiae Corolla. Festschrift J. R. Harris* (London, 1933) S. 312.

[96] Ebenso wie in der Apokalypse von Mk. 13 das den Beistand in der Verfolgung behandelnde Stück das eigentlich christliche Element darstellt.

[97] Es geschieht dies in dem Dreitakt, der auch Mk. 14: 62 und j. Taan. 2: 1 vorliegt und der für die Deutung des Todes charakteristisch zu sein scheint. Dem ἐγώ εἰμι von Mk. 14: 62 entspricht die negative Formulierung von V. 9, das ὄψεσθε... καθήμενον findet sich in V. 10 und die mit ἐρχόμενον κ.τ.λ. angedeutete Gerichtsszene ist in der Feststellung von V. 11 vorweggenommen.

entspricht es, daß in einer dogmatisierenden Sprache betont und überbetont wird, daß der Paraklet, was seine Beauftragung und seine Botschaft anbelangt, mit Jesus im Zusammenhang steht. Wenn das dahin ausgeführt wird, daß er 'nichts von sich selber sagt', so ist das mit 16: 8 and 13a schwer in Übereinstimmung zu bringen, ist Ausdruck der Spannung zwischen Stücken verschiedener Herkunft.[98]

V

Von dem leidenschaftlichen Willen beseelt, der eigenen Erfahrung höchste Dignität zu geben und doch die Glaubensgüter der Vergangenheit nicht aufzugeben, haben Montanus[99] und Mani[100] sich den Mantel des Parakleten umgeworfen – bei Mohammed taten es seine Anhänger.[101] [102] Lessing und Hegel streckten sich dem Zeitalter des

[98] Die Eingliederung des Stücks einmal in den Zusammenhang der Paraklet-Kette, zum anderen in den Gesamtzusammenhang der Abschiedsreden hat eine Verschiebung des Sinns zur Folge gehabt. So ist δικαιοσύνη im Sinne des Bearbeiters nicht seine (Jesu) Gerechtigkeit (so Windisch, S. 120) sondern Gottes Gerechtigkeit, die Jesus zum Vater gehen läßt. Eine ganz eigenartige, auf der Spannungsweite von ἐλέγχειν aufgebaute Erklärung gibt B. Lindars a. a. O.

[99] Eine eigentliche Gleichsetzung wird freilich erst von den vergröbernden Ketzerbestreitern der späteren Zeit behauptet. Hieronymus gibt genauer an: 'Paracletum in Montanum venisse contendunt' (contr. Vigil. 9. II). Auch machten die Montanisten einen Unterschied zwischen dem Parakleten und dem Geist (s. A. Schwegler, Der Montanismus, Tübingen, 1841, S. 39).

[100] Vgl. F. C. Burkitt, The Religion of the Manichees (Cambridge, 1925), S. 94; O. Klima, Mani (Prag, 1962), S. 234ff. Auch dort handelt es sich nicht um Gleichsetzung. Nach Keph. 14: 32 kam der lebendige Paraklet herab und sprach mit Mani. So drückt es auch der Kölner Kodex aus: ἄφιξις τοῦ παρακλήτου τῆς ἀληθείας (64: 1f.). Daraus hat sich in der volkstümlichen, sich nicht an die Eingeweihten wendenden Lebensgeschichte Manis die Gleichsetzung von Paraklet und Religionsstifter ergeben (so in 17: 4f. und 70: 20f. nach der Angabe von Henrichs-Könen, S. 163), ein Gebrauch, der in der alten Kirche polemisch aufgenommen wurde (so z. B. Adam, Texte, S. 96f.: ἐτόλμησεν ἑαυτὸν παράκλητον καὶ ἀπόστολον Ἰησοῦ Χριστοῦ ὀνομάζειν). Damit erweist sich die Auslegung, die F. Flügel, Mani (Leipzig, 1862), S. 163, gibt ('nur...ein menschlicher Lehrer'), als einseitig.

[101] Material bei M. Steinschneider, Polemische Literatur (Leipzig, 1877), S. 328, und Fritsch, S. 76, 90–2. Dem entspricht es, daß Mohammed Jesus als seinen Bruder bezeichnete (Asin., Nr. 45, 184). Diese Auslegung war dem Verfasser des Traktats De tribus Impostoribus (hsg. von G. Bartsch, Berlin, 1960, S. 60) bekannt.

[102] Auch die Ananiten haben von dem Parakleten gewußt und, wie es scheint, in Anan die Erfüllung der Verheißung gesehen (Schahrastani–Cureton, S. 167f.; Haarbrücker, i, 254).

Geistes entgegen.[103] War in der ersteren Vorstellung die Möglichkeit der Ergänzung oder Ablöse des Gegebenen, auch der Bestätigung der eigenen Person gegeben, so rückt die letztere das mit der Ankündigung Gemeinte in die Zukunft, gibt ihr einen unpersönlichen, dafür aber weltgeschichtlichen und insofern 'alle Wahrheit' einschließenden Ausdruck. Beiden Ausprägungen gemeinsam ist nächst dem Bezug auf die Abschiedsreden der Gedanke eines wie auch immer gearteten Fortschritts.[104]

Dem Gedanken kann auch eine kirchengeschichtliche Wendung gegeben werden. So hat A. Loisy der Stelle eine Erklärung angedeihen lassen, die Wellhausen zu der Charakterisierung veranlaßte: 'Der Pater Loisy nimmt sozusagen für den Parakleten gegen Jesus Partei, im Interesse für die Autonomie der lebendigen katholischen Tradition'[105] Und Fr. Mußner hat jüngst die apostolische Tradition und das kirchliche Lehramt als in den Parakletsprüchen angelegt aufweisen wollen.[106] Den katholischen Exegeten ist kein geringerer als Ed. Meyer an die Seite getreten; er sieht in Joh. 16: 13 'die ganze Entwicklung der katholischen Kirche bis zum Vatikanum herab' 'vorgebildet'.[107]

Der johanneische Kreis, dem das Leitbild von Fortschritt und Vollendung, was den Christen und die Gemeinde anbelangt, durchaus nicht fremd ist,[108] ja der demselben durch das Wort προάγειν einen Namen gegeben hat, der in seiner theologischen Darbietung die Begriffe aufnahm, wo er sie fand, hat doch, wo es um den Gegenstand des Glaubens ging, keine anhaltende Neigung gehabt, nach Neuem zu greifen. Eine erste Weise, das sichtbar zu machen, war das Aussprechen

---

[103] Das Erbe der idealistischen Auslegung ist noch bei Hirsch (*Das Vierte Evangelium*, S. 360ff.) erkennbar.

[104] Vielleicht so am wenigsten bei Montanus; dies insbesondere, wenn die Harnack–Bonwetsch'sche These über den konservativen Charakter der durch seinen Namen bezeichneten Bewegung zurecht besteht. Darum hat Wellhausen recht, wenn er meint, Montanus habe den Parakleten völlig mißverstanden, wenn er ihn zum Verkünder der nahen Parusie gemacht habe (*Johannes*, S. 124).

[105] *Johannesevangelium*, S. 118.

[106] *Bibl. Zeitschr.* 1961, S. 56ff. Vgl. dazu Haacker, S. 157ff.

[107] *Ursprung und Anfänge* iii, 647.

[108] S. Joh. 20: 31 (πιστεύητε) und vgl. 1 Joh. 2: 12ff., wo bestimmte Grade des Christseins gemeint sind. Auch das χρῖσμα gehört in den Zusammenhang. Mit ihm ist die Belehrung περὶ πάντων (1 Joh. 2: 27; vgl. V. 20, *var. lect.* πάντα) verbunden. Nach dem Philippusevgl. 112 besitzt der Gesalbte 'alles': Auferstehung, Licht, Kreuz, heiligen Geist. Hier liegt die christliche Form der jüdischen Anschauung von den zwei Stufen der Aneignung des Gesetzes vor.

der Überzeugung, daß der Paraklet von Vater und Sohn gesandt werden würde. Eine andere – in einer schon zugespitzen Lage – war das beschwörende Hinweisen auf die Gefahr, durch eigenes Dichten und Trachten 'Jesus zunichte zu machen'[109] und die Aufforderung, bei ihm zu 'bleiben'.[110] Eine dritte mündet in die Parole aus, nicht voranzuschreiten, ohne in der Lehre Christi zu bleiben.[111]

Ed. Schwartz formulierte einst, das Vorhandensein des vierten Evangeliums mache deutlich, daß das Christentum bis ins zweite Drittel des zweiten Jahrhunderts hinein eine Bewegung der 'unbegrenzten Möglichkeiten' gewesen sei.[112] Was immer daran richtig sein mag, dies ist sicher, daß das Evangelium selbst Reichweiten anzeigt und Verknotungen aufweist, die den Verfassern der anderen Evangelien verborgen geblieben sind. Eine der Möglichkeiten ist in Joh. 16: 6ff. schlaglichtartig an die Wand geworfen. Es grenzt an Träumereien sich vorstellen, was hätte entstanden sein können, wenn der Evangelist selbst den Weg weitergegangen wäre, auf den ihn Mani und der Islam gewaltsam umzulenken suchten. So ist es eine Möglichkeit geblieben, die für einen Augenblick nur aufgenommen, dann entschlossen eingegrenzt und beiseite gelassen wurde, weil sie dem, worum es den Männern der Urkirche eigentlichst ging, zuwiderzulaufen schien.

Jesus und der Paraklet in Johannes 16

ERNST BAMMEL

There is an ongoing debate whether the Bible allows the possibility of fresh revelation of divine truth after the definitive revelation in Christ. John 16: 7–13 is a crucial passage in this debate, and appeal is made to it by both sides.

The relevance of this passage to this issue can only be assessed on the basis of a critical evaluation of its sources and their place in the religious ideas of the time. Verses 7f., 13 depict the Paraclete in the manner of a second teacher, who comes when the Redeemer is withdrawn in order to complete the teaching which has been given. The triad ἁμαρτία, δικαιοσύνη and κρίσις can be compared with triads which sum up the essence of the Law or of the secret knowledge in Jewish and Gnostic writings. The idea of a

---

[109] 1 Joh. 4: 3. Zur Ursprünglichkeit der Lesart λύειν s. Harnack, *Studien zur Geschichte des N.T. und der alten Kirche* i (Berlin, 1931), S. 132ff.

[110] Dasselbe wird in Kap. 15 des Evangeliums im Bilde vom Weinstock gesagt und eingeschärft.

[111] 2 Joh. 9.   [112] *Nachr. d. Göttinger Gel. Gesellschaft* (1908), S. 558.

second teacher also appears in Jewish apocalyptic and Gnostic literature. It is thus probable that these verses reproduce ideas current in John's world.

By contrast verses 9–11 explain the triad of verse 8 in phrases which place all the emphasis on response to Jesus himself. All three have close links with recurring themes of the Fourth Gospel. But whereas these ideas are spoken elsewhere by Jesus himself, here they are mediated by the Paraclete. This is reminiscent of the function of the Spirit in Paul and the Synoptic Gospels. It thus seems likely that these verses too are a Spirit-passage, which has been incorporated into the Paraclete-passage in the course of construction of the discourse. But the author has taken care to avoid the suggestion that the work of the Spirit-Paraclete is a new act of redemption by his insistence that the Spirit's work is not his own but is derived directly from Jesus.

John 16: 7–13 only envisages the possibility of new teaching by the Spirit or a further redeemer-figure, a tendency which is later openly embraced by Montanus and Mani, and appears also in some modern Catholic exegetes in relation to the development of doctrine. But in fact the Johannine circle was opposed to the idea. In this passage we see one aspect of the 'limitless possibilities' (Ed. Schwartz) of Christianity in the first hundred years of its existence momentarily entertained and then resolutely set aside.

15

Ascension du Christ et don de l'Esprit d'après Actes 2: 33

J. DUPONT

Le thème général de ce recueil d'études offertes en hommage au Professeur C. F. D. Moule trouve, pour ce qui concerne les Actes des Apôtres, une expression heureuse dans la manière dont le jubilaire résume le contenu christologique de cet ouvrage: 'Jesus is shown in Acts as raised from death, exalted to heaven, destined ultimately to return, and meanwhile represented in the church's activities and expansion by the Holy Spirit, whose advent is the result of Christ's "withdrawal".'[1] Parmi les thèmes que ce résumé évoque, ceux de l'exaltation céleste et de l'envoi de l'Esprit sont étroitement liés en Act. 2: 33: 'Exalté par la droite de Dieu et ayant reçu du Père la promesse de l'Esprit Saint, il a répandu ce que vous-mêmes voyez et entendez.' Le Professeur Moule s'est intéressé à ce verset et à l'éclairage qu'il reçoit du Ps. 68: 19;[2] c'est lui aussi qui a orienté dans ce sens les recherches d'un de ses élèves, B. Lindars, auquel on doit sur ce sujet quelques pages qui méritent de retenir l'attention.[3] S'il n'y a plus quelque chose de très nouveau à dire en la matière, une mise au point sur ce qui a été dit pourra cependant rendre service. Notre exposé n'a pas d'autre ambition.

Pour expliquer Act. 2: 33 les exégètes recourent ou ne recourent pas au Ps. 68: 19. Ceux qui n'y recourent pas constituent la très grande majorité. Parmi eux nous choisirons trois exégètes récents, pour caractériser les orientations que peut prendre l'interprétation du verset des Actes quand on fait abstraction de son arrière-plan scripturaire. Nous parlerons ensuite des exégètes qui font appel au psaume, et nous préciserons la manière dont ils présentent leur argumentation.

[1] C. F. D. Moule, 'The Christology of Acts', dans L. E. Keck et J. L. Martyn, *Studies in Luke–Acts. Essays presented in honor of Paul Schubert* (Nashville–New York, 1966), pp. 159–85 (165).

[2] C. F. D. Moule, 'The Ascension – Acts i. 9', *Exp. T.* lxviii (1956–7), pp. 205–9 (p. 206 n. 3).

[3] B. Lindars, *New Testament Apologetic: The Doctrinal Significance of the Old Testament Quotations* (Londres, 1961). Voir p. 44 n. 1: 'I am indebted to Professor C. F. D. Moule for drawing my attention to this reference.'

J. Dupont

L'INTERPRÉTATION RÉDACTIONNELLE

1. *O. Bauernfeind*, dans son commentaire publié en 1939,[4] fournit un bon point de départ à notre enquête. Cet auteur souligne l'art avec lequel Luc a composé le discours de la Pentecôte en le conduisant progressivement jusqu'au v. 33, où le discours atteint son but et où, en même temps, la conclusion se trouve habilement préparée. L'importance du travail attribuable au rédacteur ne saurait cependant faire méconnaître l'influence que des formulations antérieures ont exercée sur le texte. On en trouve particulièrement la trace dans l'expression τήν τε ἐπαγγε-λίαν ... λαβὼν παρὰ τοῦ πατρός. Prise en son sens naturel, cette affirmation implique que Jésus ne possédait pas l'Esprit durant son ministère terrestre: il ne l'aurait reçu qu'au moment de son exaltation céleste. Cette manière de voir se retrouve dans les formules traditionnelles qui nous ont été conservées en 1 Tim. 3: 16 et Rom. 1: 4. Mais elle ne correspond pas à la pensée de Luc: pour lui, Jésus a reçu l'Esprit lors de son baptême. Le désaccord de ce verset avec les vues de Luc montre qu'il reprend ici une formule antérieure.

2. *E. Haenchen*[5] a repris l'explication proposée par Bauernfeind, mais en lui apportant un sérieux correctif. Haenchen croit aussi que Act. 2: 33 s'inspire d'une formule traditionnelle dans le genre de celles de Rom. 1: 4 ou 1 Tim. 3: 16, où il était dit que Jésus a reçu l'Esprit lors de sa glorification. Mais Luc ne se contente pas de répéter la formule. Il l'adapte à ses propres vues en précisant qu'à Pâques Jésus a reçu l'Esprit, non pour lui-même, mais pour le communiquer à ses disciples. Il n'y a donc plus de désaccord entre ce verset et la conception d'après laquelle Jésus a reçu l'Esprit (pour lui-même) lors du baptême.[6]

3. *U. Wilckens*, dans son ouvrage sur les discours missionnaires des Actes,[7] rejette l'explication de Haenchen. Il estime que le v. 33 doit

---

[4] O. Bauernfeind, *Die Apostelgeschichte* (Leipzig, 1939), pp. 48s.

[5] E. Haenchen, *Die Apostelgeschichte* (Gœttingue, [10]1956), p. 150 = 15e éd., 1968, p. 146.

[6] Signalons aussi l'explication proposée par E. Grässer, *Das Problem der Parusie-verzögerung in den synoptischen Evangelien und in der Apostelgeschichte* (Berlin, 1957), p. 210. D'après cet auteur, les formules traditionnelles qui parlent de l'élévation pascale de Jésus la mettent en rapport avec son prochain avènement. En Act. 2: 33, l'idée de la parousie est remplacée par celle de l'envoi de l'Esprit; ailleurs, il est question du pardon des péchés (5: 31; cf. 13: 27s.; 26: 18) ou de la tâche d'annoncer le salut (26: 23).

[7] U. Wilckens, *Die Missionsreden der Apostelgeschichte. Form- und traditions-geschichtliche Untersuchungen* (Neukirchen–Vluyn, 1961 = 2e éd., 1963), pp. 59s., 94s. et 150s.

être considéré comme une création de Luc. Inutile d'y chercher l'écho d'une formule traditionnelle. Luc s'intéresse ici à l'effusion de l'Esprit, point de départ du temps de l'Église. Il tient en même temps à assurer la continuité entre les deux grandes périodes de l'histoire du salut: entre le temps de Jésus qui s'achève avec l'Ascension et l'histoire de l'Église qui commence avec la venue de l'Esprit. Jésus avait reçu l'Esprit au début de son ministère, et c'est lui-même qui, après l'avoir promis avec insistance, le donne à ses disciples pour qu'ils rendent témoignage de lui. L'Esprit joue ainsi le rôle de trait d'union entre les deux étapes de l'histoire du salut. Cela correspond trop bien aux vues de Luc pour qu'on puisse songer à l'existence d'une formulation antérieure.[8]

Nous ne nous attarderons pas à discuter ces explications. Elles négligent manifestement un aspect de la question, celui que soulignent précisément les auteurs dont nous allons parler. Pour éclairer Act. 2: 33, il ne suffit pas d'opposer ce verset à Rom. 1: 4 ou à 1 Tim. 3: 16; il semble bien plus important d'observer sa ressemblance avec Éph. 4: 8.

ACTES 2: 33 ET PSAUME 68: 19

1. *H. J. Cadbury* a publié en 1933 une étude sur les discours des Actes, où il s'occupe de la manière dont on y présente l'argument scripturaire.[9] À propos d'un oracle prophétique, on montre qu'il ne s'applique pas à son auteur (David, quand il s'agit d'un psaume), mais que, trouvant son accomplissement en Jésus, c'est lui qu'il visait. En Act. 2: 34, le début du verset, 'Car David n'est pas monté aux cieux', suppose qu'il a été question d'un psaume parlant d'une montée aux cieux: commençant par un γάρ, l'explication précise que le trait ne concerne pas l'auteur présumé du psaume. Le γάρ remplit le même rôle en 13: 26,

---

[8] U. Wilckens développe et précise les indications que H. Conzelmann avait proposées sommairement dans *Die Mitte der Zeit. Studien zur Theologie des Lukas* (Tubingue, ³1960), p. 162. Cet auteur ne revient pas sur la question dans son commentaire: *Die Apostelgeschichte* (Tubingue, 1963), p. 30. Notons encore l'opinion de G. Stählin, *Die Apostelgeschichte* (Gœttingue, 1962), pp. 49s.: établi 'Fils de Dieu en puissance' (Rom. 1: 4) en vertu de son exaltation céleste, Jésus se trouve en mesure de réaliser la promesse eschatologique concernant l'Esprit, don du Père en même temps que du Fils, par qui il parvient aux hommes. On se demande si ces considérations théologiques ne veulent pas éviter les problèmes relatifs à l'histoire de la tradition.

[9] H. J. Cadbury, 'The Speeches in Acts', dans F. J. Foakes Jackson et K. Lake, *The Beginnings of Christianity*, i. 5 (Londres, 1933), pp. 402–27 (voir 408s.).

tandis que 2: 30 emploie οὖν dans le même sens. Mais 2: 33 ne rend pas compte des termes utilisés dans l'explication du verset suivant. Ce qu'on y dit d'une exaltation par la droite de Dieu, ou à sa droite, ne correspond qu'assez vaguement à l'idée d'une montée aux cieux. Cette expression se comprendrait mieux si, à la suite de F. H. Chase,[10] on suppose que le v. 33 contenait primitivement une citation du Ps. 68 (gr. 67): 19, qui serait devenue peu reconnaissable dans la rédaction actuelle. En faveur de cette hypothèse, il est possible de faire valoir quelques traces significatives: les mots du psaume ἀναβὰς εἰς ὕψος trouveraient leur écho dans le participe ὑψωθείς, et l'expression ἔλαβες δόματα dans le participe λαβὼν (τὴν ἐπαγγελίαν).

2. *W. L. Knox*, dans son petit livre sur les Actes des Apôtres paru en 1948,[11] explique que la marche des idées serait bien meilleure dans le passage qui nous occupe si l'on pouvait supposer que la source utilisée par Luc faisait allusion au Ps. 68: 19. Ce psaume était assigné à la Pentecôte, où l'on commémorait la promulgation de la Loi, et l'exégèse rabbinique interprétait le verset en l'appliquant à Moïse: Moïse serait monté au ciel pour y recevoir la Loi et la rapporter aux hommes. Act. 2: 33 reporterait sur le Christ et l'Esprit ce que les rabbins disaient de Moïse et de la Loi. L'intérêt que présentent les explications de Knox ne saurait faire oublier leur fragilité. Elles paraissent peu convaincantes en ce qu'elles font appel à des traditions juives assez tardives, et en ce que, prêtant à la source de Luc une allusion au Ps. 68, elles ne cherchent pas à en trouver au moins quelque vestige dans le texte actuel.[12] La tentative de Knox a cependant le mérite de pressentir une orientation dans laquelle l'exégèse ne tardera pas à s'engager, mais sur des bases plus solides.[13]

3. *G. Kretschmar* fournit l'apport décisif en ce sens dans un important

[10] F. H. Chase, *The Credibility of the Acts of the Apostles* (Londres, 1902), p. 151.

[11] W. L. Knox, *The Acts of the Apostles* (Cambridge, 1948), pp. 85s.

[12] Voir nos observations critiques dans *Les Problèmes du Livre des Actes d'après les travaux récents* (Louvain, 1950), p. 97; repr. dans *Études sur les Actes des Apôtres* (Paris, 1967), p. 100. Également dans notre étude sur 'L'utilisation apologétique de l'Ancien Testament dans les discours des Actes', *Ephemerides Theologicae Lovanienses* xxix (1953), pp. 289–327 (p. 299 n. 15) = *Analecta Lovaniensia Biblica et Orientalia* II, xl (Louvain, 1953), p. 13 n. 15 = *Études sur les Actes des Apôtres*, p. 255 n. 15.

[13] F. F. Bruce, *The Acts of the Apostles* (Londres, 1951 = 2e éd., 1952, p. 95) signale prudemment Ps. 68: 19 comme simple parallèle pour Act. 2: 33, sans aller jusqu'à en faire une source d'inspiration. Il n'en fait plus mention dans son *Commentary on the Book of the Acts* (Édimbourg, ²1956).

article publié en 1955.[14] L'attention de cet auteur se porte sur l'accord dont témoignent Éph. 4: 7–12; Act. 2: 33 et la tradition johannique[15] dans leur manière d'associer l'exaltation céleste du Christ et l'effusion de l'Esprit. Cet accord suppose une tradition ancienne. À en juger par la forme de la citation du Ps. 68: 19 en Éph. 4: 8, on peut lui attribuer une origine palestinienne. Il est possible que Act. 2: 33 ait été influencé par le même verset psalmique; ce serait un indice supplémentaire de l'antiquité de cette tradition.

Pour déterminer la signification de l'association entre exaltation du Christ et don de l'Esprit, Kretschmar souligne l'importance du fait que le judaïsme avait déjà fait de la Pentecôte une fête commémorative de la promulgation de la Loi, ou de la conclusion de l'Alliance sinaïtique. Le premier témoignage de cette interprétation se trouve peut-être en 2 Chron. 15: 8–15. La chose est claire en tout cas avec le Livre des Jubilés et les textes de Qumrân. Il n'y a donc aucune difficulté à supposer que les premiers chrétiens ont compris les événements de la venue de l'Esprit au jour de la Pentecôte en fonction des traditions relatives au Sinaï. C'est précisément l'arrière-plan qui donne toute sa portée au récit de Act. 2: 1–13.[16] Cet arrière-plan permet de se rendre compte que l'appel au Ps. 68: 19 implique une typologie qui reporte sur le Christ et le don de l'Esprit ce que l'exégèse juive disait de la montée de Moïse vers Dieu, et de la Loi qu'il en avait rapportée.

Ces explications de Kretschmar ont immédiatement reçu l'assentiment de *C. F. D. Moule*.[17] Cité en sa forme rabbinique en Éph. 4: 8, le verset du psaume fait peut-être l'objet d'une allusion, dans sa forme biblique, en Act. 2: 33. Ce que les interprètes juifs disaient de Moïse, monté sur la montagne pour y recevoir de Dieu la Loi et la rapporter aux hommes, est appliqué par les chrétiens au Christ, nouveau Moïse. *R. Le Déaut* reprend la même thèse à son compte, admettant, lui aussi, que Act. 2: 33 a peut-être été influencé par la tradition qui a inspiré

---

[14] G. Kretschmar, 'Himmelfahrt und Pfingsten', *ZKG* lxvi (1954–5), pp. 209–53.

[15] Jean 15: 26; 16: 17; cf. 14: 16; 7: 39, ainsi que la 'Pentecôte johannique', Jean 20: 22s.; cf. 20: 17 pour l'Ascension (Kretschmar, p. 214).

[16] Sur ce point, la thèse de Kretschmar a été reprise par M. Sabbe, 'Het Pinksterverhaal', *Collationes Brugenses et Gandavenses*, iii (1957), pp. 161–78. Nous avons repris la question sous la même perspective dans notre article 'La première Pentecôte chrétienne (Ac. 2, 1–11)', dans *Fête de la Pentecôte* (Bruges, 1963), pp. 39–62; repr. dans *Études sur les Actes des Apôtres*, pp. 481–502.

[17] C. F. D. Moule, dans *Exp. T.* lxviii (1956–7), p. 206 n. 3.

Éph. 4: 8.[18] Le prudent 'peut-être' des auteurs précédents disparaît dans une étude de *C. Ghidelli*,[19] qui ne tient pas seulement compte des arguments de Kretschmar, mais aussi de ceux de Cadbury. Nous avons adopté plusiers fois nous-même une position analogue.[20]

4. *B. Lindars*, dans son ouvrage de 1961,[21] a repris la question sous un angle un peu différent: celui de la critique littéraire, et aussi celui de l'histoire des idées théologiques. Nous n'avons pas à le suivre sur ce dernier terrain; mais ses observations littéraires, qui fournissent des précisions nouvelles, concernent directement notre sujet. Elles tendent d'abord à reconnaître la part rédactionnelle attribuable à Luc en Act. 2: 33. Il faut mettre au compte de son intervention les expressions τήν τε ἐπαγγελίαν et τοῦτο ὅ; il en va de même pour τοῦ πνεύματος τοῦ ἁγίου et pour ἐξέχεεν, qui font écho au texte de Joël cité au v. 17. L'emploi de l'expression τῇ δεξιᾷ τοῦ θεοῦ veut préparer la citation du Ps. 110: 1 au verset suivant (v. 34); mais elle pourrait aussi avoir été amenée par le dernier stique du Ps. 16 (v. 11c), qui a été omis au v. 28: τερπνότητες ἐν τῇ δεξιᾷ σου εἰς τέλος.[22] Il reste les mots ὑψωθεὶς ... λαβὼν παρὰ τοῦ πατρός; si l'on tient compte en même temps de l'affirmation du v. 34: οὐ γὰρ Δαυὶδ ἀνέβη εἰς τοὺς οὐρανούς, leur rattachement au Ps. 68: 19 ne paraît pas pouvoir être mis en doute. Mais sous quelle forme le verset du psaume a-t-il été utilisé? C'est sur ce point que les explications de Lindars méritent l'attention.

On sait que le verset est cité explicitement en Éph. 4: 8, sous une forme qui diffère sensiblement de celle dont témoigne la LXX. Le fait que la construction passe de la deuxième à la troisième personne reste

---

[18] R. Le Déaut, 'Pentecôte et tradition juive', *Spiritus* vii (1961), pp. 127–44 (139); repr. dans *Fête de la Pentecôte* (Bruges, 1963), pp. 22–38 (32s.).

[19] C. Ghidelli, 'Le citazioni dell'Antico Testamento nel cap. 2 degli Atti', *Il Messianismo. Atti della XVIII Settimana Biblica* (Brescia, 1966), pp. 285–305 (305).

[20] Signification de la Pentecôte: *Les Béatitudes* i (Bruges–Louvain, ²1958), p. 327 n. 1. Appel à Éph. 4: 8–11 pour éclairer Act. 2: 33, dans *Les Actes des Apôtres* (Paris, ²1958), p. 47. Fait précis d'une allusion au Ps. 68: 19 en Act. 2: 33: 'L'interprétation des psaumes dans les Actes des Apôtres', dans *Le Psautier, Ses origines, ses problèmes littéraires, son influence. Études présentées aux XIIes Journées Bibliques de Louvain (29–31 août 1960)* (Louvain, 1962), pp. 357–88 (368s. et 379) = *Études sur les Actes des Apôtres*, pp. 283–307 (292 et 300); ''Ανελήμφθη (Actes 1, 2)', *NTS* viii (1961–2), pp. 154–7 (p. 156 n. 3) = *Études sur les Actes des Apôtres*, pp. 477–80 (p. 479 n. 8); *La première Pentecôte chrétienne*, p. 39 (481); *Les Actes des Apôtres* (Paris, ³1964), p. 47.

[21] *New Testament Apologetic*, pp. 39, 42–4 et 51–9. Cet auteur est malheureusement très peu averti du travail de ses devanciers.

[22] Il n'y a pas lieu d'exclure une influence du Ps. 118: 16 (p. 44).

accessoire: l'adaptation au contexte peut justifier ce changement. Il n'en est pas de même pour le complément τοῖς ἀνθρώποις, ni surtout pour la substitution de ἔδωκεν à ἔλαβες. Les mêmes traits se retrouvent dans le targum. Cela ne prouve pas encore une influence de l'araméen. À cette hypothèse Lindars en préfère une autre, celle qui fait appel à deux explications indépendantes l'une de l'autre: Éph. 4: 8 citerait le verset d'après un *midrash pesher*,[23] dont l'interprétation serait parallèle à celle qui nous parvient dans le targum.

Pour en savoir davantage sur la nature de ce *midrash pesher*, il faut se tourner vers les Actes. En Act. 2: 33, l'allusion au Ps. 68: 19 intervient dans un commentaire du Ps. 110: 1: il s'agit de montrer que la session à la droite de Dieu est liée à une fonction médiatrice, celle qui consiste à communiquer l'Esprit. Le thème général est celui que Éph. 4 développe à partir des idées exposées dans 1 Cor. 12; mais l'allusion au Ps. 68 conserve le verbe λαμβάνω. Lindars se demande en outre si le verbe ἐξέχεεν n'a pas été substitué à ἔδωκεν. Cette hypothèse permettrait de découvrir en Act. 2: 33 le chaînon intermédiaire entre la formulation de la LXX et la citation d'Éph. 4: 8. Disons tout de suite qu'il nous paraît difficile de suivre notre auteur dans une conjecture aussi dangereuse.

Mais Lindars croit découvrir en Act. 5: 31–2 un troisième témoin de son *midrash pesher*. Dans ce passage, en effet, l'expression ὕψωσεν τῇ δεξιᾷ αὐτοῦ est immédiatement suivie par la précision [τοῦ] δοῦναι. Il est ensuite question de μετάνοια et de 'témoignage'; ces traits relèvent manifestement d'amplifications rédactionnelles. Il s'agit après cela de retrouver le texte qui sert de base à l'argumentation; pour y arriver, Luc est obligé de répéter maladroitement le verbe dans une proposition relative: τὸ πνεῦμα τὸ ἅγιον ὃ ἔδωκεν ὁ θεός. Il serait donc possible de reconnaître dans ce passage le présence du thème attesté en 2: 33 et en Éph. 4: 8. L'élévation céleste du Christ y est liée au don de l'Esprit, en des termes qui s'inspirent du Ps. 68: 19.

Les reconstitutions de Lindars ne manquent pas de hardiesse; mais elles sont au service d'un argument de convergence, qui n'est pas négligeable. Nous nous demandons s'il ne serait pas possible de prolonger cet argument dans une direction où l'auteur fait soudain preuve d'une prudence qui nous paraît excessive. Il admet que le Ps. 68 faisait partie du répertoire de la liturgie juive de la Pentecôte. Il n'ignore pas l'exégèse juive qui découvrait dans le v. 19 du psaume une allusion à

---

[23] Voir E. E. Ellis, *Paul's Use of the Old Testament* (Édimbourg–Londres, 1957), pp. 45 et 139–47.

Moïse donnant la Loi au peuple, et il reconnaît que cette interprétation pouvait conduire les chrétiens à calquer sur ce modèle l'image du Christ communiquant l'Esprit à son Église. Mais il se méfie d'une typologie qui ne lui paraît pas pouvoir se concilier avec la date ancienne à laquelle il place son *midrash pesher*. Cette méfiance n'est pas fondée. Il n'est pas difficile de se rendre compte que la typologie est inscrite dans les termes mêmes dont use Act. 5 : 31 : τοῦτον ὁ θεὸς ἀρχηγὸν καὶ σωτῆρα ὕψωσεν. La comparaison avec 7 : 35 est éclairante : τοῦτον (τὸν Μωϋσῆν) ὁ θεὸς ἄρχοντα καὶ λυτρωτὴν ἀπέσταλκεν; voir aussi 7 : 25 : ὅτι ὁ θεὸς διὰ χειρὸς αὐτοῦ δίδωσιν σωτηρίαν αὐτοῖς.[24] La manière dont Act. 5 : 31 parle du Christ correspond à celle dont le chapitre 7 parle de Moïse, en termes qui d'ailleurs dépassent Moïse et s'appliquent au Christ, dont Moïse n'est que la figure. La typologie de Moïse est donc présente dans les discours des Actes, et rien n'empêche de la supposer à la base de l'interprétation qui applique le Ps. 68 : 19 à l'ascension du Christ et à l'envoi de l'Esprit. On pourrait même se demander si ce n'est pas là qu'il faut chercher le point de départ des développements théologiques dans lesquels Paul met en valeur le contraste entre la Loi et l'Esprit.

CONCLUSION

1. Des considérations diverses ont conduit les exégètes à penser que Act. 2 : 33–4 contient un rappel du Ps. 68 : 19. L'attention de H. J. Cadbury se porte avant tout sur l'argumentation développée dans ce passage : elle ne prend son sens qu'à partir d'un texte scripturaire qui n'est pas cité au v. 33, mais dont les termes correspondraient à ceux du Ps. 68 : 19. G. Kretschmar s'intéresse au fait que les premiers chrétiens ont interprété l'ascension du Christ en fonction des traditions juives sur la promulgation de la Loi au Sinaï, et en relation avec la signification qui s'attachait alors à la fête de la Pentecôte. Ce cadre assure toute sa portée à la citation du Ps. 68 : 19 en Éph. 4 : 8, il favorise aussi l'hypothèse d'une allusion au même verset psalmique en Act. 2 : 33. B. Lindars s'attache à faire le discernement entre les éléments qui relèvent du travail rédactionnel de Luc et ceux qui remontent à une tradition

---

[24] Le rapprochement doit se faire aussi avec Act. 3 : 15, ou le titre d' ἀρχηγὸς τῆς ζωῆς attribué au Christ paraît devoir s'entendre en fonction du rôle joué par Moïse. Il faudrait également tenir compte de l'oracle sur le Prophète semblable à Moïse : Act. 3 : 22; 7 : 37 (Deut. 18 : 15,18). Sur le parallèle latent entre Moïse et le Christ, voir notre article 'L'utilisation apologétique de l'Ancien Testament', p. 294 = *Études sur les Actes des Apôtres*, p. 250.

antérieure. Il croit pouvoir dégager ainsi de Act. 2: 33–4 et 5: 31–2 un *midrash pesher* qui utilise le Ps. 68: 19 dans un sens analogue à celui qu'Éph. 4: 8 lui prête. Est-il besoin de souligner que ces différentes voies d'approche ne s'excluent nullement? Elles sont manifestement complémentaires, et les résultats de l'une devraient corroborer ceux de l'autre.

2. Parmi les questions soulevées par le discours de la Pentecôte et les autres discours missionnaires du Livre des Actes, une des plus intéressantes est celle du parti qu'on peut tirer de ces textes pour la connaissance des origines de la christologie. Le fait que le rédacteur final y a mis son empreinte personnelle ne résout évidemment pas le problème. Il faut s'interroger sur la documentation dont il disposait. À ce point de vue, les allusions scripturaires méritent une attention toute particulière, surtout dans le cas où elles semblent relever d'un stade antérieur à celui de la rédaction actuelle. L'allusion au Ps. 68: 19 en Act. 2: 33–4 nous en fournit un bon exemple. Il faut donc élever les plus sérieuses réserves à l'égard de la méthode suivie par les exégètes qui négligent cet aspect du problème et qui, sans tenir compte du parallèle fourni par Éph. 4: 8, se contentent d'opposer Act. 2: 33 à Rom. 1: 4 ou à 1 Tim. 3: 16.

3. Un mot encore sur la portée christologique de Act. 2: 33, compte tenu de sa référence implicite au Ps. 68: 19. L'interprétation christologique qu'on donne au verset du psaume se rattache à un ensemble plus large: celui d'une interprétation de l'événement de la Pentecôte chrétienne à partir de la signification que la tradition juive attribuait à la fête en la mettant en relation avec la théophanie du Sinaï. Pour faire une place au Christ dans ce cadre, il était normal qu'on s'inspire du rôle de Moïse lors de la promulgation de la Loi. L'exégèse rabbinique du Ps. 68: 19 permettait d'établir un parallèle entre la montée de Moïse et l'ascension de Jésus, entre le don de la Loi et le don de l'Esprit. La perspective n'est pas celle d'une question de théologie systématique sur le moment où Jésus aurait reçu l'Esprit, pour lui-même ou pour d'autres. La pensée se meut sur un terrain beaucoup plus concret: on se trouve en face d'événements dont il s'agit de dégager la signification profonde. C'est l'originalité même du christianisme qui se trouve mise en valeur dans le parallèle antithétique qui oppose au don de la Loi le don de l'Esprit, au rôle joué par Moïse celui qu'on attribue au Christ, monté au ciel et assis à la droite de Dieu.

J. Dupont

Ascension du Christ et don de l'Esprit d'après Actes 2: 33

J. DUPONT

In the course of his speech at Pentecost, Peter refers to the gift of the Spirit by the exalted Christ to the church (Acts 2: 33), using language which seems to recall Ps. 68: 19. It is disputed, however, whether there is an actual allusion to this text. The majority of critics do not seriously entertain the possibility at all, regarding Acts 2: 33 either as a Lukan adaptation of a formula comparable to Rom. 1: 4; 1 Tim. 3: 16 (Bauernfeind, Haenchen), or as a creation of Luke himself (Wilckens). Other scholars have shown, on the other hand, that the whole context is illuminated if the verse is seen against the background of a Jewish midrashic tradition, in which Ps. 68 is interpreted of the promulgation of the Law at Sinai. The application of this tradition to the Christian idea of the gift of the Spirit is confirmed by Eph. 4: 8. Moreover the citation of Ps. 68: 19 in the latter passage has important agreements with the Targum against the Hebrew and the Septuagint. That Luke was capable of using this tradition in this way is suggested by his use of a typology of Moses elsewhere (compare Acts 5: 31 with 7: 35).

The presence of an intentional allusion to Ps. 68: 19 in Acts 2: 33 has been argued by Cadbury, Kretschmar and Lindars along different lines of approach. But these are complementary, not mutually exclusive, and tend to support the contention. The speeches in Acts are Lukan compositions, but the scriptural quotations in them are pointers to the underlying traditions, which give valuable information about the origins of christology. In the case of Acts 2: 33, recognition of an allusion to Ps. 68: 19 has important consequences. It means that Christianity can take over the Jewish ideas connected with the feast of Pentecost, and interpret them afresh in the light of the Christ event. The gift of the Law through Moses on Sinai, which this psalm celebrates according to rabbinic exegesis, is now replaced by the gift of the Spirit through the exalted Jesus, the second Moses.

16

Τὸ πνεῦμα Ἰησοῦ
(Apostelgeschichte 16: 7)*

G. STÄHLIN

I

'The word πνεῦμα is a problem to translators', sagt der verehrte
Jubilar zu der einen Stelle, an der das Wort πνεῦμα in dem von ihm

* H. von Baer, *Der Heilige Geist in den Lukasschriften.* Stuttgart, 1926 – C. K.
Barrett, *The Holy Spirit and the Gospel Tradition.* London, 1954 (= [1]1947) –
F. Baumgärtel, Art. πνεῦμα B.C 11; in: *TWNT* vi (1959), 357–66 – W. Bieder,
Art. πνεῦμα C13-112; ebd. 367–73 – ders., 'Gebetswirklichkeit und Gebets-
möglichkeit bei Paulus'; in: *TZ* iv (1948), 22–40 – F. Büchsel, *Der Geist Gottes
im Neuen Testament.* Gütersloh, 1926 – R. Bultmann, *Theologie des Neuen
Testaments.* Tübingen, 1953, 151–62 – Yves M.-J. Congar, 'Le St. Esprit et
le Corps apostolique réalisateurs de l'œuvre du Christ'; in: *RSPT* xxxvi
(1952), 613–25; xxxvii (1953), 24–48 – H. Conzelmann, *Die Apostelgeschichte.*
Tübingen, 1963 ([2]1972) – ders., *Die Mitte der Zeit: Studien zur Theologie des
Lukas.* Tübingen, [5]1964 – H. E. Dana, *The Holy Spirit in Acts.* Kansas City,
1943 – A. Dietzel, 'Beten im Geist'; in: *TZ* xiii (1957), 12–32, bes. 28–32 –
P. Feine, *Theologie des Neuen Testaments.* Berlin, [8]1951, 137–9, 408f. – H.
Flender, *Heil und Geschichte in der Theologie des Lukas.* München, 1965 – H.
Gunkel, *Die Wirkungen des Heiligen Geistes nach der populären Anschauung der
apostolischen Zeit und der Lehre des Apostels Paulus.* Göttingen, [3]1909 (= [2]1899) –
E. Haenchen, *Die Apostelgeschichte.* Göttingen, [6]1968 – A. Harnack,
Beiträge zur Einleitung in das Neue Testament, iii: *Die Apostelgeschichte.* Leipzig,
1908 – I. Hermann, *Kyrios und Pneuma: Studien zur Christologie der paulinischen
Hauptbriefe.* München, 1961 – E. Kamlah, Art. 'Geist'; in: *TBL* i, 479–89 – H.
Kleinknecht, Art. πνεῦμα A; in: *TWNT* vi, 330–57 – K. Lake, 'The Holy
Spirit'; in: *The Beginnings of Christianity* i: *The Acts of the Apostles* v. London,
1933, 96–111 – G. W. H. Lampe, 'The Holy Spirit in the Writings of St
Luke'; in: D. E. Nineham (ed.), *Studies in the Gospels: Essays in Memory of
R. H. Lightfoot.* Oxford, 1955, 159–200 – S. K. Meurer, *Die Anwaltschaft des
Geistes Gottes im biblischen Zeugnis.* Diss. Basel. Wuppertal–Elberfeld, 1969 –
C. F. D. Moule, '2 Cor. 3: 18b'; in: Heinrich Baltensweiler–Bo Reicke (Hgg.),
*Neues Testament und Geschichte: Historisches Geschehen und Deutung im Neuen
Testament, Oscar Cullmann zum 70. Geburtstag.* Zürich–Tübingen, 1972, 231–7 –
K. L. Schmidt, 'Das Pneuma Hagion als Person und als Charisma'; in: *Eranos-
Jahrbuch* xiii (1945): *Der Geist.* Zürich, 1946, 187–235 – E. Schweizer, Art.
πνεῦμα, πνευματικός D–F; in: *TWNT* vi, 387–450, 330–3: Literatur – ders.,
'The Spirit of Power: The Uniformity and Diversity of the Concept of the Holy
Spirit in the New Testament'; in: *Interpretation* vi (Richmond, Virg., 1952),
259–78 – E. Sjöberg, Art. πνεῦμα C III; in: *TWNT* vi, 373–87 – G. Stählin,

229

kommentierten Kolosserbrief vorkommt.[1] In der Tat, man sagt wohl nicht zuviel, wenn man noch einen Schritt weitergeht und feststellt: das Wort πνεῦμα gehört zu den problemreichsten neutestamentlichen Vokabeln und Begriffen.[2] Es ist oft ungemein schwierig, die genaue Vorstellung und den Gedankengehalt zu erfassen, die in dem häufig formelhaft gewordenen Gebrauch von πνεῦμα[3] und in bestimmten Wortverbindungen, in denen es steht,[4] verborgen sind. Zu den schwierigsten und zugleich wichtigsten Problemen gehört das Verhältnis von Pneumatologie und Christologie, d. h. die Frage: wie stellt sich den neutestamentlichen Autoren das Nebeneinander und Miteinander von Christus dem Herrn und dem Heiligen Geist dar? Dieses Problem ist in nuce enthalten in der Wendung τὸ πνεῦμα ᾿Ιησοῦ (die im Neuen Testament nur einmal vorkommt, Apg. 16:7), wie auch in den nahe verwandten Wendungen τὸ πνεῦμα Χριστοῦ und τὸ πνεῦμα τοῦ κυρίου (vgl. S. 232f).

II

Der uns beschäftigende Vers Apg. 16: 7 steht in dem bedeutsamen Abschnitt (15: 40 – 16: 10), in dem Lukas den Anmarschweg des Paulus und seiner Begleiter, Silas (von 15: 40 ab) und Timotheus (von 16: 3 ab), zu ihrer Missionswirksamkeit in Europa darstellt. Diese Reise ist gekennzeichnet durch ein eigentümliches Nebeneinander – teils Mit- teils Gegeneinander – von Planung des Apostels und

Die Apostelgeschichte. Göttingen, [3]1968 – E. Stauffer, *Die Theologie des Neuen Testaments.* Stuttgart, [3]1947, 144–7 – F. C. Synge, 'The Holy Spirit in the Gospels and Acts'; in: *CQR* cxx (1935), 205–17 – F. Terry, 'Jesus and the Era of the Spirit'; in: *Hib.J.* li (1952/3), 10–15 – H. Weinel, *Biblische Theologie des Neuen Testaments.* Tübingen, [4]1928, 381–5 – H. Windisch, 'Jesus und der Geist nach synoptischer Überlieferung'; in: S. J. Case (ed.), *Studies in Early Christianity presented to Frank Chamberlin Porter and Benjamin Wisner Bacon.* New York–London, 1928, 209–36 – J. E. Yates, 'Luke's Pneumatology and Lk. 11, 20'; in: F. L. Cross (ed.), *Studia Evangelica* ii (*TU* lxxxvii). Berlin, 1964, 295–9 – Th. Zahn, *Die Apostelgeschichte des Lucas* i. Leipzig, 1919, ii. Leipzig–Erlangen, 1921.

[1] C. F. D. Moule, *The Epistles of Paul the Apostle to the Colossians and to Philemon* (Cambridge Greek Testament Commentary). Cambridge, 1957, 52 zu Kol. 1: 8.

[2] Vgl. vor allem die Darstellungen von Kamlah, Lampe, K. L. Schmidt und Schweizer.

[3] Z. B. in den Präpositionalwendungen διὰ πνεύματος, ἐν πνεύματι, κατὰ πνεῦμα oder in dem mit den verschiedensten Verben verbundenen Dativ τῷ πνεύματι.

[4] Z. B. πνεῦμα καὶ δύναμις, πίμπλημι πνεύματος, γεννάομαι ἐκ τοῦ πνεύματος, τὸ πνεῦμα τῆς ἀληθείας, τὸ φρόνημα τοῦ πνεύματος, ἡ κοινωνία τοῦ πνεύματος.

höherer Führung; vgl. Apg. 15: 36, 40f.; 16: 3, 7 mit 16: 6f., 9. Man muß diesen Abschnitt jedoch in einem weiteren Rahmen sehen: Lukas kennzeichnet manche Pläne des Apostels als konform mit dem göttlichen Willen oder direkt von ihm eingegeben, so besonders die den letzten Hauptteil der Apostelgeschichte (19: 21 – 28: 31)[5] bestimmenden Pläne; vgl. 19: 21; 20: 22 mit 23: 11 sowie Röm. 1: 15; 15: 23f., 28f. Am eindeutigsten und präzisesten ist hier die Einheit eines Entschlusses des Apostels und der Führung des Geistes schon in Apg. 19: 21 ausgedrückt. Aber die Apostelgeschichte (16: 6f.; 22: 18–21), insbesondere Zeugen des sog. 'westlichen' Textes (Apg. 17: 15; 19: 1; 20: 3)[6] berichten auch von Plänen des Paulus, die durch ein Eingreifen von oben vereitelt oder wenigstens modifiziert wurden.[7] In solchen Fällen steht dann auf der einen Seite ein θέλειν (16: 7 vl; 19: 1 vl; 20: 3 vl), πειράζειν (16: 7), die ἰδία βουλή (19: 1 vl) oder sogar ein Einspruch (22: 19f.) des Apostels, auf der anderen ein κωλύειν (16: 6; 17: 15 vl; Röm. 1: 13), ἐγκόπτειν (Röm. 15: 22), μὴ ἐᾶν (Apg. 16: 7) oder ein entsprechender Spruch des Kyrios (22: 21) oder des Geistes (19: 1 vl; 20: 3 vl).

Diese Vorgänge gehören zu einer umfänglichen Gruppe von Eingriffen in das irdische Geschehen, die Lukas in mannigfaltiger Weise beschreibt oder auch nur andeutet: als Herrenvisionen (9: 3 parr; 9: 10 par; 22: 17f.), als Engelerscheinungen (8: 26, 39 vl; 10: 3, wohl auch 16: 9),[8] als Geistesweisungen (8: 29; 10: 19 = 11: 12; 13: 2; 19: 1 vl; 20: 3 vl, wohl auch 15: 28).[9] Die Vielfalt dieser Vorgänge, die sicher tiefer begründet ist als nur in schriftstellerischer Freude an der

---

[5] Vgl. F. V. Filson, 'The Journey Motif in Luke–Acts'; in: W. W. Gasque– R. P. Martin (edd.), *Apostolic History and the Gospel. Biblical and Historical Essays presented to F. F. Bruce on his 60th Birthday.* Exeter, 1970, 68–77, bes. 72f.

[6] Die Frage liegt nahe, ob in diesen Angaben des 'westlichen' Textes nicht doch alte Überlieferung enthalten ist, die – vermeintlich zur Ehre des Paulus? – unterdrückt wurde. Darum werden im folgenden solche 'westlichen' Textformen in den Kreis der Untersuchung mit einbezogen. Vgl. P. Feine–J. Behm–W. G. Kümmel, *Einleitung in das NT*, Heidelberg, [17]1973, 154f.

[7] Diese Berichterstattung steht aber in Einklang mit Angaben, die Paulus selbst in seinen Briefen macht; vgl. Röm. 1: 13; 15: 22; 1. Kor. 16: 12. Auffällig ist vor allem Röm. 15: 22; denn hier werden Pauli Pläne immer wieder (τὰ πολλά) durchkreuzt, obwohl er nach einem göttlichen Missionsprinzip (V. 20f.; Jes. 52: 15; vgl. O. Michel, *Der Brief an die Römer.* Göttingen, [11]1957, 330) zu wirken sucht.

[8] Vgl. Stählin 214 z. St.

[9] Wie in diesen Fällen der Führung dienen Vorgänge gleicher Art der Bestätigung und Stärkung der Boten, so die Herrenvisionen in 18: 9f.; 23: 11, die Engelerscheinung in 27: 23 und die Sprüche des Geistes in 20: 23; man kann also auch hier das gleichsam 'triadische Führungsgremium' beobachten.

Abwechslung,[10] hat einen gemeinsamen Ursprung: es sind lauter Mittel einer einheitlichen höheren Führung von teleologischer Zielstrebigkeit.[11] Aus dieser Einheit wird man auch die beiden Bezeichnungen des Geistes in Apg. 16: 6 und 7, vor allem die singuläre Wendung πνεῦμα ᾽Ιησοῦ, zu verstehen haben. Lukas meint in V. 6 und 7 sicher einen und denselben Geist.[12] Aber wieder ist es kaum nur stilgemäße Abwechslung wie in dem vergleichbaren Fall von Apg. 5: 3 und 9; vielmehr ist in V. 7 doch wohl ein bewußter und wohlbedachter Gebrauch einer besonderen Bezeichnung anzunehmen.

III

Was aber will Lukas mit der singulären Wendung τὸ πνεῦμα ᾽Ιησοῦ[13] sagen? Welches Verhältnis des πνεῦμα zu Jesus will der Genitiv aussagen? Ist diese lukanische Wendung als völlig synonym anzusehen mit den paulinischen Wendungen (τὸ) πνεῦμα Χριστοῦ (Röm. 8: 9c, auch 1 Petr. 1: 11) bzw. τὸ πνεῦμα ᾽Ιησοῦ Χριστοῦ (Phil. 1: 19) und (τὸ) πνεῦμα κυρίου (2 Kor. 3: 17b)?

---

[10] Zweifellos liebt Lukas die Abwechslung, auch über die Erfordernisse eines guten Stils (vgl. z. B. 16: 6 κωλύω mit V. 7 οὐκ ἐάω) hinaus (vgl. die Berichte von Ananias und Sapphira, von Theudas und Judas sowie die Bekehrungsberichte von Paulus und Cornelius). Aber jenes vielfältige Erzählen von höheren Eingriffen beruht wohl in einigen Fällen auf verschiedenen Berichten, die Lukas als Tradition zugekommen waren, öfter jedoch auf seinem theologischen Interesse an dem Zusammenwirken von Mächten wie Geist und Engel (8: 26ff.), Kyrios und Geist (2: 33), Kyrios, Geist und Engel (10: 3ff., wohl auch 16: 6ff.) oder auch von zwei Herrenerscheinungen (9: 3ff., 10ff.) bzw. zweierlei Geistesweisungen (20: 22f.; 21: 4, 11). Dieses Motiv des Zusammenspiels von mehreren Weisungen von oben ist zusammen mit den Motiven der Wiederholung und der Ausführlichkeit bei manchen dieser Berichte als Indiz für die Bedeutung zu werten, die Lukas diesen Ereignissen beimaß.

[11] Es ist darum nicht vorstellbar, daß z. B. Weisungen des Kyrios und solche des Geistes in Gegensatz zueinander stehen. Apg. 21: 4, verglichen mit 19: 21; 20: 22f.; 21: 11, scheint allerdings einen solchen Fall anzuzeigen. Aber wahrscheinlich ist hier eine Leidensweissagung seitens des Geistes und eine Warnung seitens der Geistträger in eins zusammengezogen; vgl. einerseits Mk. 8: 31f., andererseits Apg. 21: 11f. sowie Stählin, 273 zu 21: 4.

[12] Mit dieser Feststellung begnügen sich vielfach die Exegeten, z. B. T. Zahn, 561, E. Haenchen, 424; andere, z. B. H. W. Beyer, H. Conzelmann, setzen die Gleichheit einfach voraus.

[13] Die Überlieferung ist freilich nicht einheitlich. Aber die geringe Bezeugung der Lesart τὸ πνεῦμα κυρίου und die späte Bezeugung des einfachen τὸ πνεῦμα durch die Handschriften des byzantinischen Reichstextes lassen τὸ πνεῦμα ᾽Ιησοῦ eindeutig als die ursprüngliche Lesart erschließen.

Τὸ πνεῦμα Ἰησοῦ (*Apg. 16: 7*)

Gerade die Wendung τὸ πνεῦμα τοῦ κυρίου, die sich auch in der Apostelgeschichte findet (5: 9; 8: 39, sowie als vl zu 16: 7, vgl. Anm. 13), ist für unsere Fragestellung von großer Bedeutung. Ursprünglich bezeichnet sie den Geist Jahwes (vgl. LXX Jdc. 3: 10; 6: 34 B; 11: 29; 13: 25; 1. Sam. 10: 6; 11: 6; 2. Sam. 23: 2; 1. Rg. 18: 12) genau wie ὁ ἄγγελος τοῦ κυρίου den Engel Jahwes (vgl. LXX Gen. 16: 7ff.; 22: 11, 15; Ex. 3: 2; 4: 24). Aber auf Grund der Übertragung des Herren-Titels auf Jesus (vgl. Apg. 2: 36) konnte τὸ πνεῦμα τοῦ κυρίου als der Geist des Herrn Jesus Christus und ὁ ἄγγελος τοῦ κυρίου als der Engel des Herrn Jesus Christus verstanden werden. Wahrscheinlich haben wir an der Mehrzahl der einschlägigen Stellen dieses Verständnis vorauszusetzen. Unter dieser Voraussetzung erscheint es wahrscheinlich, daß Christus für Lukas der κύριος πνεύματος (vgl. 2. Kor. 3: 18) ist, d. h. der Herr, der über den Heiligen Geist als Herr verfügt.[14] Dann aber verfügt der Erhöhte im Unterschied vom irdischen Jesus doch auch über die Engel.[15] Er ist der Kyrios, dem der ἄγγελος τοῦ κυρίου wie das πνεῦμα τοῦ κυρίου zu Gebote steht. Diese Annahme wird sich uns im folgenden bestätigen.[16]

Wenn Lukas in Apg. 16: 7 bewußt τὸ πνεῦμα Ἰησοῦ schrieb, so kann das in seinem Sinn eigentlich nur bedeuten: hier in dieser Geistesweisung, die den Missionaren nur noch *eine* Richtung für die Fortsetzung ihrer Reise offen ließ, die nach Westen, zu der am weitesten auf Europa zu vorgeschobenen Hafenstadt Kleinasiens Troas, war derselbe Jesus[17] am Werk, der von Gott zum Herrn und Messias erhöht wurde (2: 36) und dem zugleich mit seiner Erhöhung der Heilige

---

[14] Vgl. Schweizer, *TWNT* vi, 402.

[15] Anders H. Conzelmann, *Die Mitte der Zeit*, 122 (zu Lk. 21: 27), 161 Anm. 3.

[16] Vgl. unten S. 238ff.

[17] Vgl. Apg. 2: 32 und 36, wo die Identität des irdischen, gekreuzigten Jesus mit dem auferweckten und zum Kyrios erhöhten durch οὗτος ὁ Ἰησοῦς unterstrichen wird (vgl. 1: 11; 10: 42, wo dasselbe οὗτος die Identität des Gekreuzigten und Erhöhten mit dem als Richter Wiederkommenden unterstreicht). Dagegen ist es weniger wahrscheinlich, daß Lukas auch 16: 7 den speziellen Gedanken ausdrücken will: der Heilige Geist, der hier an den Aposteln wirkte, war – nicht nur der Geist des erhöhten Herrn, sondern – schon der Geist des auf Erden wandelnden Jesus; so H. von Baer, 42, und ähnlich G. W. H. Lampe passim: Es ist derselbe Geist, in dem der irdische Jesus und dann die Apostel wirkten. Diese Deutung geht von dem irrigen Gedanken aus, daß mit dem bloßen Namen 'Jesus' notwendig auf den irdischen Jesus Bezug genommen werde. Aber an mehreren Stellen der Apostelgeschichte ist mit 'Jesus' deutlich nur der Erhöhte (6: 14; 7: 55; 9: 5 parr, 17) oder *auch* der Erhöhte (z. B. 4: 2, 18; 5: 40; 8: 35; 17: 18; 28: 23) gemeint.

Geist übertragen worden war (V. 33). Der Gedanke des Lukas, der sich für ihn aus Apg. 2: 33–6 ergibt, ist der: Jesus erhält die verheißene Geistesgabe, nicht nur um sie an Pfingsten den an ihn glaubenden Jüngern mitzuteilen, sondern auch dazu, daß er, der Herr des Geistes, durch diesen Geist und durch die von ihm bewegten Menschen zum Herrn schlechthin, zum Herrn über die ganze Welt werde. Diesem Ziel aber dient vor allem die Mission, und für sie und in ihr entfaltet der Geist Jesu darum sein entscheidendes Wirken.[18] Man kann deshalb das Thema für das zweite Buch des Lukas so formulieren: 'Die Zeit der Herrschaft Jesu Christi durch das Pneuma.'[19]

Der Einsatzpunkt der neuen Periode ist die Erhöhung Jesu, von

[18] G. W. H. Lampe 196 schreibt mit Recht: 'Above all, the Spirit operates in the Church's mission...of which it is both the driving force...and the guide that ...directs their course (sc. of the missionaries).' Man könnte aus dem Zusammenhang der Verse Apg. 2: 33ff. und speziell aus dem Zitat in V. 34f. den Gedanken herauslesen, daß die Geistesgabe der Erreichung des in diesem Zitat bezeichneten Zieles der Erhöhung dienen solle: die Feinde des neuen Kyrios zu überwinden (vgl. Anm. 22 zu 1. Kor. 15: 25). Doch der Kampf gegen die Feinde Gottes bzw. Christi tritt in der Apostelgeschichte auffallend zurück. Exorzismen spielen eine relativ geringe Rolle; sie werden außer in 16: 16–18 (und 19: 13ff.) nur in summarischen Berichten kurz erwähnt 5: 16; 8: 7; 19: 12. Den menschlichen Feinden gegenüber aber befindet sich das junge Christentum nie in der Offensive (auch nicht Stephanus 7: 51–3, vgl. 6: 9ff.) außer mit der freilich oft als Angriff und Verurteilung erfahrenen Verkündigung des Evangeliums. Den Ausgangspunkt von Konflikten bilden meistens feindselige Anschläge und Pläne der Gegner, die in der Regel auf mannigfaltige Weise vereitelt werden, und manche Gegner werden für Christus gewonnen. Eben dies – der siegreiche Fortgang der Mission –, wird man sagen dürfen, ist die Art und Weise, in der die Gottesverheißung von Apg. 2: 35 erfüllt wird. Eine Ausnahme könnte man höchstens 12: 23 finden; aber dieser durch den 'Engel des Herrn' vollzogene Strafakt paßt nicht zu dem sonstigen Wirken des Erhöhten. Ähnliches gilt von dem durch den Geistträger Petrus vollzogenen doppelten Strafakt in 5: 1–11. Beide Stücke wirken im Rahmen der Apostelgeschichte wie Fremdkörper; sie repräsentieren eine Geisteshaltung, der Lukas mit seiner Grundanschauung fern steht. Vgl. Stählin, 85, 171f.

[19] Diese Kennzeichnung trifft die Intention des Lukas m. E. besser als der Titel 'die Zeit des Geistes'; vgl. K. Lake 108: 'The whole background of the book (sc. of Acts) is the guidance of the Holy Spirit'; H. E. Dana hält geradezu 'The Activity of the Holy Spirit' für den angemessenen Titel des Buches. Noch weniger zutreffend ist aber m. E. der Titel 'Die Zeit der Kirche'; vgl. H. Conzelmann, *Die Mitte der Zeit*, 9, 158. Jedenfalls ist der Beginn der Christusherrschaft als Merkmal der neuen Periode für Lukas mindestens ebenso wichtig wie die Gründung der Kirche, zumal sich das Wort ἐκκλησία im ökumenischen Sinn nur einmal in der Apostelgeschichte findet, und das in einem Summarium 9: 31. Die im Sinn des Lukas entscheidenden Korrelatbegriffe sind Geist und Herrschaft Christi. Vgl. auch W. Michaelis, *Reich Gottes und Geist Gottes nach dem Neuen Testament*. Basel, 1931.

Τὸ πνεῦμα Ἰησοῦ (*Apg. 16: 7*)

Lukas allein unter allen neutestamentlichen Autoren anschaulich gemacht in der Himmelfahrt Jesu, und die 'Ausgießung' des Geistes als der erste Herrscherakt des zur Rechten Gottes Erhöhten (2: 33). Der Ehrenplatz zur Rechten Gottes (vgl. noch 2: 34; 5: 31; 7: 55f.) kann nur bedeuten: Jesus handelt fortan über der Welt als gleichberechtigter Stellvertreter Gottes, und der Heilige Geist, durch den er vorzüglich wirkt, erscheint an einigen Stellen als der Stellvertreter Christi.[20] Es ist jedoch schlechterdings unmöglich, die hier gemeinte Stellvertretung so mißzuverstehen, als wäre nun derjenige, der sich vertreten läßt, ausgeschaltet oder untätig.[21] Gott bleibt der primus agens, und Jesus wird nicht etwa erhöht, um in majestätischer Ruhe auf seinem Ehrenplatz zur Rechten Gottes zu thronen,[22] sondern um als sein Stellvertreter zu wirken. Diese Stellvertretung aber findet im Rahmen eines allerseits aktiven, 'trinitarischen' Zusammenwirkens statt.

[20] Schon Tertullian (*Adv. Marc.* 3: 6; *Adv. Prax.* 24) hat Christus den vicarius patris genannt und (*Praescr.* 28; *Adv. Valent.* 16; *De Virg. Vel.* 1) den Heiligen Geist Christi vicarius bzw. vicarius Domini; vgl. Y. M.-J. Congar 622 Anm. 32. Bei Tertullian sind diese Begriffe jedoch subordinatianisch verstanden; vgl. A. v. Harnack, *Lehrbuch der Dogmengeschichte*. Tübingen, [5]1931, 580f. mit 581 Anm. 4; F. Loofs, *Leitfaden zum Studium der Dogmengeschichte*. Halle, [4]1906, 157f.

[21] Vgl. D. Sölle, *Stellvertretung*. Stuttgart, 1965, bes. 86–93, und dazu H. Gollwitzer, *Von der Stellvertretung Gottes*. München, 1967.

[22] Einige Stellen der Apostelgeschichte wie 1: 11; 2: 35; 3: 21 könnten so mißverstanden werden, als sei Jesus in den Himmel aufgenommen, um hier die Vollendung seiner Herrschaft, seine Parusie, das Jüngste Gericht und die Vollendung des Alls zu erwarten. Diese Vorstellung verbindet der Hebräerbrief mit der sessio ad dexteram (vgl. bes. 10: 13): 'Christus wartet auf die Unterwerfung seiner Gegner...Wie Gott nach der Schöpfung Ruhe von seinen Werken empfangen hat (Gen. 2: 2), ebenso der Christus. Die Ruhe ist das Zeichen der Vollendung' (O. Michel, *Der Brief an die Hebräer*. Göttingen, [6]1966, 340f.). Für Lukas wie für Paulus dagegen ist es nicht 'Wartezeit' und 'Ruhezeit', sondern Zeit höchster Aktivität: Herrschen heißt unablässig handeln. Paulus versteht (anders als Lukas, vgl. Anm. 18) das βασιλεύειν Christi als steten Kampf mit dem Ziel der endgültigen Unterwerfung aller Feinde 1. Kor. 15: 25: Subjekt des τιθέναι ist hier Christus, in dem zitierten Psalm (110: 1) und überall, wo dieser Psalm sonst im Neuen Testament zitiert wird (auch Apg. 2: 35; vgl. Anm. 18), dagegen Gott (auch in dem passivum divinum in Hebr. 1: 13 !). Die zweite, nicht minder wichtige Form des Handelns des erhöhten Christus ist die Fürsprache vor Gott, so bei Paulus (Röm. 8: 34), Johannes (1. Joh. 2: 1) und auch im Hebräerbrief (7: 25, wohl auch 9: 24), der auf einen Ausgleich der Vorstellungen verzichtet. Bei Lukas aber herrscht der Erhöhte, indem er das Werk seiner Boten auf Erden lenkt und den Segen seines Heilswerks an den Menschen wirksam werden läßt (z. B. Apg. 5: 31); vgl. S. 237.

IV

Hinter und über allem, genau wie schon über dem Wirken des irdischen Jesus, steht der Plan *Gottes*[23] (βουλή Apg. 2: 23; 4: 28; 20: 27; πρόγνωσις 2: 23; θέλημα 22: 14, auch 21: 14; τὸ ὡρισμένον Lk. 22: 22; προορίζω Apg. 4: 28 und bes. δεῖ 3: 21; 4: 12; 14: 22; 27: 24; vgl. πάντα τέτακται 22: 10 u. a.).[24] Gott ist es aber auch, der vor allem selber wirkt, nicht nur seine größte Tat, die Auferweckung Jesu (vgl. Anm. 41) samt seinen Erscheinungen 10: 40, und seine Erhöhung 5: 31. Gott wirkt auch das Entscheidende in der Mission: die Verkündigung (17: 30; vgl. 4: 29) und die Wunder der Boten (15: 12; vgl. 4: 30[25]), überhaupt alles, was diese vollbringen (14: 27; 15: 4; 21: 19), sodann die Berufung (2: 39) und die Wahl (15: 14) des neuen Gottesvolkes sowie den Glauben der Hörer (14: 27; 26: 29, wohl auch 16: 14). Dazu darf man auch einige der Geschehnisse zählen, die Lukas in der Form des Passivs berichtet, insbesondere den Bau (9: 31) und das Wachstum (5: 14 u. o.) der Gemeinde. Aber man wird damit zu rechnen haben, daß oft, wo ein solches passivum divinum steht, als Subjekt des Aktivs im Sinn des Lukas ebenso der erhöhte Christus wie Gott selbst gedacht werden kann; das ist ebenso oft eine offene Frage wie an anderen Stellen die, wer mit dem κύριος gemeint ist: so wie Christus z. B. in Apg. 2: 47b (neben ὁ θεός in 2: 47a!) der κύριος sein kann, der die Gemeinde der Geretteten vermehrt, so kann er auch das Subjekt des Aktivs zu den Passiva in 2: 41; 5: 14; 6: 7; 11: 24 sein. Dieselbe Frage stellt sich z. B. auch einerseits zu 11: 21 (vgl. V. 20), 23; 13: 47 (vgl. 26: 17f.); 15: 36; 19: 20; 20: 32, andererseits zu 10: 45 (ἐκκέχυται, vgl. 2: 17f. neben 2: 33); 2: 4; 4: 31 (vgl. 5: 32; 11: 17; 15: 8 neben 2: 33; 9: 17). Gerade bei dem πλησθῆναι τοῦ ἁγίου πνεύματος wird man mit beiden Möglichkeiten rechnen müssen, gleichzeitig aber festzustellen haben, daß Lukas beides sich vorstellen kann, ohne einen grundsätzlichen Unterschied zu machen, genau wie Paulus in vergleichbaren Fällen (vgl. z. B. 2. Kor. 5: 10 mit Röm. 14: 10). So erklärt sich die

---

[23] Vgl. H. Conzelmann, *Die Mitte der Zeit*, 141–4, 199f.

[24] Den später so wichtigen terminus technicus für den Heilsplan Gottes οἰκονομία (vgl. O. Michel, Art. οἰκονομία in: *TWNT* v, 154f.) verwendet Lukas noch nicht.

[25] Die Hand Gottes ist Bild für seine Macht in der Lenkung des Geschehens (4: 28; 11: 21), und bei den Wundern (4: 30; 13: 11), nicht aber für die Macht seines Geistes wie mehrfach im Alten Testament, wo die Hand Gottes und sein Geist parallel gebraucht werden können; vgl. z. B. 1. Rg. 18: 46; 2. Rg. 2: 16; Ez. 1: 3; 8: 3.

zweifellos auffällige 'Vermischung von Aussagen über das Walten Gottes und Christi'.[26]

Darum ist es aber auch abwegig, Jesus als 'Werkzeug' in Gottes Heilsplan zu bezeichnen;[27] der Ehrentitel Kyrios und das Sitzen zur Rechten Gottes besagen vielmehr: das Wirken Christi und das Wirken Gottes ist eine unauflösbare Einheit. Jesus hat als der Erhöhte dieselbe Herrschermacht wie Gott; in dieser Hinsicht besteht kein Unterschied zwischen Lukas und Paulus.[28] Man kann auch schwerlich die 'Funktion' Gottes und die Jesu in der Apostelgeschichte so unterscheiden, daß die eine in der Durchführung des Heilsplanes bestehe, die andere in Wirkungen im Leben der Kirche. Denn einerseits stehen im Wirken an der Kirche Gott und Christus so nahe beisammen, daß die Aussagen über den Anteil des einen und des anderen nicht scharf unterschieden werden, andererseits geschieht die Durchführung des göttlichen Heilsplans in der dritten Periode der Geschichte nach lukanischer Sicht gerade vornehmlich durch Christus und den Geist. Darum könnte man sagen: Lukas behandelt in seinem zweiten Buch das Thema: 'Wie der Erhöhte die Geschichte seiner Sache führt und damit den Plan Gottes verwirklicht.'[29]

V

Im Rahmen dieses Plans betreibt der Kyrios Jesus sein 'Werk', das zugleich Gottes Werk ist (vgl. 14: 26; 15: 18 vl; 13: 41; 5: 38). Für dieses Werk bestimmt *er* die Werkzeuge: 1: 2 (in Bestätigung der Wahl von Lk. 6: 13–16); 1: 24f.; 9: 3–16 parr,[30] gibt ihnen seine

---

[26] H. Conzelmann, *Die Mitte der Zeit*, 162 Anm. 2; vgl. auch ebd. 165.

[27] Diese Kennzeichnung (H. Conzelmann ebd. 161) ist bestimmt durch einen etwas einseitigen Subordinatianismus, den Conzelmann dem Lukas zuschreibt. Das Schema 'Subordination und Auszeichnung' beschreibt den Sachverhalt wohl kaum ganz zutreffend (ebd. 167). Zwar ist Jesus Gott als sein Stellvertreter 'untergeordnet'; aber er ist sein *vollmächtiger* Stellvertreter (vgl. auch S. 235, 241f.). Darum die 'Promiskuität zwischen Gott und dem Kyrios' (ebd. 206).

[28] Anders Conzelmann ebd. 164.

[29] Vgl. I. Hermann 99. – Natürlich kann man das Thema auch anders formulieren, je nach dem man das Hauptinteresse der lukanischen Geschichtsschreibung bestimmt; vgl. S. 234.

[30] Es ist für die Beweglichkeit und Sorglosigkeit gegenüber Spannungen und Widersprüchen in der Berichterstattung des Lukas bezeichnend, daß in einem der drei Berichte von der Bekehrung des Paulus, einer Rede vor Juden (22: 14f.), Gott, in den beiden anderen (9: 15; 26: 16f.) Christus als der Wählende genannt wird. Für Lukas ist dies kein Widerspruch; vgl. S. 236f., 240.

Aufträge: 1: 2; 26: 18; 22: 21; 13: 47 – indem er sie als seine Zeugen beruft: 1: 8, 22, 24; 22: 15; 26: 16 und ihnen so das Botenamt überträgt: 20: 24, vgl. 1: 17, 25; 6: 4; 21: 19 – und rüstet sie aus für dieses Amt: 1: 5, 8; 2: 4; 9: 17.[31]

Der Kyrios Jesus bestimmt auch die großen Linien und die Ziele für das Wirken seiner Boten: 1: 8; 9: 15; 22: 15, 21 (vgl. 26: 20); 23: 11 (vgl. 19: 21); 27: 24 und gibt in diesem weiten Rahmen Einzelanweisungen für Orte und Wege des Wirkens, auch für das Bleiben an einem Ort 18: 9f. (vgl. 1: 4). Als der Herr des Tempels (Lk. 19: 45f.; vgl. 2: 49) erteilt er[32] den Auftrag zum Wirken im Tempel zu Jerusalem 5: 19f. Er bringt die Mission weit über Jerusalem hinaus in Gang: ins Küstengebiet von Palästina 8: 39f. (ob es hier das πνεῦμα κυρίου oder der ἄγγελος κυρίου ist, der Philippus nach Asdod entrückt, auf jeden Fall geschieht es nach dem Willen des κύριος). Durch ein Zusammenwirken von Engel und Geist wie auch durch eigenes Eingreifen (10: 11ff.) bestimmt der Kyrios den – nach Lukas – entscheidenden Schritt zur Heidenmission 10: 3ff. Aber auch in dem vielleicht gleichzeitigen Wirken[33] der 'Hellenisten' unter den Heiden 11: 20f. ist der Herr selbst am Werk V. 21.[34] Eine ähnliche Bedeutung muß Lukas auch der Bekehrung des Äthiopiers, wie bei Cornelius durch ein Zusammenwirken von Engel und Geist bewirkt 8: 26–39, beigemessen haben, wenn er auch nichts von einer späteren Missionstätigkeit des Mannes berichtet. Vor allem aber bestimmt der Herr auf eine besonders mannigfaltige Weise – durch ein doppeltes eigenes Eingreifen (22: 6–11 parr und V. 17–21) sowie durch einen menschlichen Boten (22: 12–16), den er nach 9: 10–16 in einer Vision gleichfalls selber beauftragt – den Paulus zum apostolischen Wirken und später durch Geistesworte 20: 23; 21: 11

---

[31] Wenn daher das Wirken von Männern wie Stephanus und Barnabas gekennzeichnet wird durch die Wendung 'erfüllt mit dem Heiligen Geist' (6: 5; 11: 24), so besagt das: sie sind vom Herrn gewählt, berufen und ausgerüstet; die Beauftragung durch die Gemeinde folgt nur der Vorwahl des Herrn (vgl. 1: 24).

[32] Vgl. das S. 233 zum ἄγγελος κυρίου Gesagte.

[33] Zu den konkurrierenden Berichten über den Beginn der Heidenmission vgl. Stählin 116.

[34] Vgl. Anm. 25. Man kann hier eine nachträgliche Bestätigung der selbständigen Entscheidung jener Boten durch den Herrn der Mission sehen. Dasselbe gilt auch für andere Abschnitte, etwa das Wirken des Philippus in Samarien – die Fortsetzung (8: 14ff., 26ff.) kann als Bestätigung angesehen werden – und das Wirken des Paulus in Philippi; hier wäre die Bestätigung etwa in 16: 14, 18, 26 zu finden; doch sieht Lukas den Weg des Paulus nach Philippi vermutlich noch unter der Weisung von 16: 9f.

(aber vgl. schon 9: 16) zum apostolischen Leiden. Der Herr ist es auch, der seinen Werkzeugen von Fall zu Fall neue Aufgaben stellt: Philippus durch seinen Engel (8: 26), Petrus, den der Herr (12: 11, 17) durch seinen Engel aus dem Gefängnis befreit (12: 7ff.), wohl nicht zuletzt, weil er ihn zum Wirken in einem neuen Bereich (ἕτερος τόπος V. 17) brauchen will, vor allem aber wieder Paulus und seinem Mitarbeiter (von 11: 25f. an) Barnabas 13: 2. Hier spricht zwar τò πνεῦμα τò ἅγιον zu den Leitern der Gemeinde; aber dieser Geistes-spruch ist die Antwort auf einen Gebetsgottesdienst, der dem Kyrios gilt, dem erhöhten Herrn der Gemeinde;[35] demnach ist er es, der in dem μοι (V. 2) spricht, derselbe, der die jetzt Auszusondernden und Auszusendenden schon vorher berufen hatte.[36] Der Geist ist – wohl durch den Mund von Propheten – Träger der Antwort auf das Gebet, so wie anderswo (10: 3f., 30f.; Lukas 1: 13; 22: 43) ein Engel oder wie Apg. 22: 17–21 der Herr selbst.[37] In der Fortsetzung gibt

[35] Mit Gebeten zu Jesus, dem Erhöhten, rechnet Lukas ganz allgemein für die von ihm dargestellte Periode. Jesus, der nun der Kyrios ist, wird als solcher auch angerufen. Dies eben ist das entscheidende Merkmal der Christusgemeinde im Unterschied von der sie umgebenden jüdischen und heidnischen Welt; darum nennen sich die Christen οἱ ἐπικαλούμενοι τò ὄνομα κυρίου, vgl. 9: 14, 21; 22: 16; 2: 21; Röm. 10: 13 und bes. 1. Kor. 1: 2. Deshalb ist der Anruf Jesu als des Kyrios der erste Akt, der entscheidende Bekenntnisakt des Getauften (Apg. 22: 16). Es mag auffallen, daß in der Apostelgeschichte Gebete zu dem erhöhten Herrn relativ selten erwähnt werden: außer 13: 2 noch 1: 24; 7: 59f.; 22: 17, vgl. Anm. 37. Sie sind jedoch als Beispiele für einen allgemeinen Brauch anzusehen. Verwandt mit den genannten Beispielen sind auch die Berichte in 9: 10–16; 22: 10, 17–21; allerdings steht hier der Anruf κύριε im Rahmen von Herrenerscheinungen im Unterschied von 7: 59f., wo die Erscheinung (V. 55f.) und die Gebete nach Zeit und Ort geschieden sind.

[36] Der Vorgang der Weisung vollzieht sich hier und an anderen Stellen (vgl. S. 250f. zu 16: 6f.) auf dem Weg einer doppelten Vermittlung: das Wort Christi wird der Gemeinde bzw. den Boten durch den Geist zugesprochen, der seiner-seits durch den Mund von Propheten redet. Es ist derselbe Vorgang, der Apk. 19: 10d in knapper, verschlüsselter Form umschrieben wird; vgl. E. Lohse z. St. (*NTD* ³1971, 100).

[37] Der Erhöhte antwortet hier auf ein an *ihn* gerichtetes Gebet; denn mit προσευ-χόμενος V. 17 wird ἐπικαλεσάμενος τò ὄνομα αὐτοῦ V. 16 aufgenommen, und dieses αὐτοῦ ist auf Christus zu beziehen, der vorher zu Paulus gesprochen hatte V. 14f. Der besonderen Bedeutung des Gebetes entsprechend, die Lukas schon im Leben Jesu immer wieder sichtbar macht, zeigt er auch besonders oft, wie Offenbarungen, höhere Weisungen und Weissagungen als Antworten auf Gebete erfolgen. Lukas 3: 21f.: Geisterscheinung und Himmelsstimme sind Antwort auf Jesu Gebet bei der Taufe; 6: 12f.: die Wahl der Zwölf beruht für Lukas zweifellos auf einer als Gebetsantwort empfangenen göttlichen Weisung; 9: 18–23: Jesu Verhalten und seine Antwort an die Jünger setzen voraus, daß er im Gebet eine Ankündigung seines Leidens erhalten hatte;

der Herr auf dem gleichen Wege auch die Richtung für den neuen Arbeitsauftrag an 13: 4 und setzt später – im Zusammenhang einer entscheidenden Wende der Mission – solche Weisungen fort 16: 6f., 9. So jedenfalls, daß wie in der Erscheinung von Troas doch wohl auch schon in den Geistesweisungen von 16: 6f. der Herr[38] selber spricht, verstehen die Boten das Geschehen V. 10. Endlich wird auch die Schlußphase des paulinischen Wirkens, in der er ein letztes Mal nach Jerusalem und dann nach Rom geführt wird, vom Herrn bestimmt in der triadischen Form (vgl. Anm. 9) des Zuspruchs durch den Geist 19: 21; 20: 22, durch Christus selbst 23: 11 und durch einen Engel[39] 27: 23f. Alle diese Einzelschritte aber stehen unter der Maxime τοῦ θεοῦ θέλοντος 18: 21, bei der Lukas nicht nur an den Plan, sondern auch an die Einzelentscheidungen Gottes als letzte Instanz denkt. Wie für das Wirken der Boten gilt die conditio Jacobaea aber auch für ihr Leiden 21: 14 (vgl. das δεῖ in 9: 16, auch in 14: 23).

Über die Führung des Missionsablaufs im großen wie im einzelnen hinaus wirkt der erhöhte Herr auch unmittelbar im Wirken seiner Apostel: wenn immer sein *Wort* verkündigt wird, spricht er selbst; das ist der Sinn der Wendung ὁ λόγος τοῦ κυρίου, die sich besonders oft in Nebenüberlieferungen des Acta-Textes findet: 6: 7 vl; 8: 25; 12: 24 vl; 13: 5 vl, 44 vl, 48f.; 14: 25 vl; 15: 35f.; 16: 32 vl; 19: 10, 20 vl. Das entspricht wieder genau der Gewißheit, daß im λόγος τοῦ θεοῦ Gott selber redet; vgl. z. B. 10: 36; 13: 46; 16: 6 vl. Der Kyrios ist es auch, der in den das Wort begleitenden und bestätigenden *Wundertaten* am Werke ist 14: 3 (vgl. Mk. 16: 20), auch wieder analog den Aussagen, durch die dasselbe von Gott bekannt wird 19: 11 (vgl. Hebr. 2: 4). Insbesondere wirkt Jesus der Erhöhte auch dort selber, wo etwas in seinem *Namen* geschieht; vgl. 3: 6, 16; 4: 10, 12; 10: 43; 16: 18. Denn

9: 28–31: wiederum erhält Jesus als Antwort auf ein Gebet, zusammen mit der Verklärungsvision, eine Leidensweissagung durch den Mund der Propheten Mose und Elia; darauf beruht dann wieder (wie V. 22) seine eigene Leidensankündigung (V. 44). Aus der Apostelgeschichte ist noch zu erwähnen: 4: 24–31 und 8: 15, 17 ist die Geistesgabe, 12: 6ff. und 16: 25f. das Befreiungswunder Antwort und Erfüllung der Gebetsbitten; 9: 12 und 10: 9ff. erfahren die Beter durch Gesichte, daß ihre Gebete Gehör finden.

38 Die Lesart κύριος V. 10 ist stark bezeugt. Wenn dagegen θεός die ursprüngliche Lesart ist, wollte Lukas sagen, daß der Ruf nach Makedonien gemäß dem göttlichen Plan für den Weg der Mission erging.

39 Lukas nennt hier einen 'Engel Gottes'; aber er tut das mit Rücksicht auf das vorausgesetzte Verständnis der heidnischen Hörer, zu denen Paulus hier spricht; ähnlich ist es auch 10: 3, vgl. V. 30; 11: 13.

in seinem Namen ist der Kyrios Christus selbst mit seiner Macht gegenwärtig genau wie der Kyrios Jahwe in seinem Namen.

In dem allen ist aber das eigentliche Handeln des Erhöhten ein *Wirken zum Heil*, zunächst zum Heil der von den Boten angesprochenen Juden 5: 31; 3: 26; 13: 38f.: hier weisen die durch ihre Stellung stark betonten Wendungen διὰ τούτου und ἐν τούτῳ deutlich hin auf den, der nicht nur in der Botschaft spricht, sondern auch in dem Geschehen der Vergebung und Rechtfertigung als der Wirkungen dieser Botschaft gegenwärtig am Werke ist, gemäß dem biblischen Glauben, daß das Wort wirkt, was es sagt. Eben dies wird auch den heidnischen Hörern und den heidenchristlichen Gemeinden des Paulus zugesprochen 13: 47; 26: 18; 20: 32. Auch dies kann wieder auf Gott selbst zurückgeführt werden 11: 18; vgl. insbesondere 14: 27 mit 16: 14, ferner 15: 4, 12; 21: 19.

Trotz der erwähnten zahlreichen Analogien und Parallelen im Handeln Gottes und Christi im Geschehen von Mission und Kirche wird man doch als übergreifende Sicht des Lukas feststellen können: ähnlich wie in der alttestamentlichen Geschichte Gott die alleinige Führungsmacht ist – vgl. die großen Überblicke in Apg. 7: 2–50 und 13: 16–41 – so ist in der neutestamentlichen Geschichte seit Ostern Christus das am stärksten hervortretende Subjekt des gesamten Geschehens.[40]

Hier stellt sich zwangsläufig die Frage, ob bei Lukas von einer Subordination Christi unter Gott die Rede sein kann. Die Antwort muß lauten: wenn überhaupt, dann nur in einem begrenzten Sinn (vgl. Anm. 27). Natürlich kann man von einer Art ʻ Unterordnung' Christi sprechen, wenn Gott ihn ʻerstehen läßt', d. h. sendet Apg. 3: 26; 13: 23; vgl. V. 26; 10: 36, von den Toten auferweckt 2: 24, 32; 3: 15 u. o.,[41] zu seiner Rechten bzw. durch seine Rechte erhöht 2: 33; 5: 31 und so zum Kyrios macht 2: 36 und wenn Christus damit zugleich als Vermittler der verheißenen Gabe Gottes (Lk. 24: 49) von Gott den Heiligen Geist empfängt. Aber die Erhöhung zum Kyrios bedeutet nichts

---

[40] Vgl. G. Delling, ʻIsraels Geschichte und Jesusgeschehen nach Acta'; in H. Baltensweiler und B. Reicke (Hgg.), *Neues Testament und Geschichte. Festschrift O. Cullmann*. Zürich–Tübingen, 1972, 187–97, bes. S. 190f.; I. Hermann 99.

[41] Auffälligerweise spricht Lukas nur zweimal vom Auferstehen (ἀνίσταμαι) Jesu 10: 41; 17: 3; ἐγείρομαι gebraucht er statt dessen im Unterschied von Paulus nur selten (Lk. 9: 22; 24: 6, 34) und auch hier wahrscheinlich in passivischem Sinn. Darum wird man ἀνάστασις bei Lukas durchweg besser mit ʻAuferweckung' als mit ʻAuferstehung' wiedergeben.

anderes, als daß die 'Unterordnung' zu Ende ist und daß Jesus nun als Throngenosse des Vaters neben diesem und mit diesem in Machtvollkommenheit herrscht und wirkt; freilich vollzieht sich dieses Wirken in einem Zusammenhang, den man, wie schon oben gesagt (S. 235, vgl. Anm. 9), als 'trinitarisch' bezeichnen kann.[42]

VI

So wie das Wirken des Erhöhten in der Apostelgeschichte umschlossen ist vom Plan Gottes und sich weithin mit Gottes eigenem Wirken deckt, so überschneidet sich das *Wirken des Heiligen Geistes* im großen und im einzelnen mit dem Wirken des Kyrios. Dabei kann nie von 'Konkurrenz' die Rede sein, sondern nur von engstem Zusammenspiel. In nuce ist das schon in Apg. 1:8 zu beobachten. Dieses letzte Wort Jesu zwischen Auferstehung und Erhöhung hat eine programmatische Bedeutung für das ganze Buch, die schlechterdings nicht überschätzt werden kann. Diese Tatsache ist längst erkannt; nur ist der Sinn dieser Bedeutung oft einseitig bestimmt worden; denn sie ist nicht so sehr in Bezug auf den Weg des Evangeliums von Jerusalem 'bis ans Ende der Erde' zu sehen – das ist die übliche Einschätzung des Verses – als vielmehr in Bezug auf das Wirken des Kyrios und des Pneuma in dieser Geschichte.

Was den Kyrios anbelangt, so sind hier bereits drei Hauptelemente seines Wirkens anvisiert: Er beauftragt die von ihm gewählten Jünger mit dem Zeugendienst,[43] er bestimmt ihren Weg durch die Welt, er rüstet sie aus[44] mit der Macht des Heiligen Geistes (vgl. oben S. 237ff.).

Ebenso werden hier bereits grundlegend wichtige Elemente für das Wirken des Pneuma berührt: es ist einerseits charismatische Gabe und dynamische Kraft, die Triebkraft des Zeugnisses in den Zeugen (vgl. 18:5 vl), andererseits eine personhafte Macht, die 'kommt', durch den Mund der Zeugen spricht (vgl. 5:32) und ihren Weg dirigiert (vgl. 16: 6f. und dazu Anm. 36, 54).

[42] Unter den neutestamentlichen Vorstufen des späteren Trinitätsdogmas hat die lukanische Konzeption des trinitarisch bestimmten Geschehens zweifellos eine hervorragende Bedeutung.

[43] Aus dem Futur ἔσεσθε muß man (wie aus ἔση 22: 15) trotz des unmittelbar daneben stehenden rein futurischen λήμψεσθε einen imperativischen Klang heraushören.

[44] λαμβάνω ist Korrelat zu δίδωμι (vgl. z. B. 8: 17–19), dessen Subjekt auch bei λαμβάνω mit bedacht werden muß.

Das Neben- und Miteinander von personalen und impersonalen Aussagen über den Geist[45] ist für die biblische Vorstellungs- und Gedankenwelt entscheidend wichtig. Frühe Vorstufen der heidnischen Religionen, die in die Bibel hineinwirken, sind bestimmt von animistischen Vorstellungen vom Geist, die ein personales Element einschließen, und von dynamistischen, die ein impersonales Bild vom Geist voraussetzen. Zahlreiche Nachwirkungen dieser beiden Vorstellungsformen finden sich in der neutestamentlichen Redeweise,[46] ohne daß man die damit ausgedrückten Vorstellungen noch als animistisch oder dynamistisch bezeichnen dürfte. Auf den höheren Stufen insbesondere der griechischen Religion aber ist und bleibt das πνεῦμα ein Neutrum; es wird nie Person.[47] Dagegen erscheint im Alten Testament *rûach* als personhaftes Wesen,[48] und in der rabbinischen Literatur wird vom Geist oft in persönlichen Kategorien geredet.[49] Aber 'seine Gegenwart kann auch mit unpersönlichen Ausdrücken beschrieben werden ..., ohne daß damit eine andere Geistvorstellung vorausgesetzt wäre als die hinter den persönlichen Ausdrücken liegende'.[50] Dasselbe gilt auch von der neutestamentlichen, auch speziell von der lukanischen Geistvorstellung. Die personhaften Ausdrucksweisen sind außerordentlich mannigfaltig, vor allem solche der Bewegung: ἔρχομαι 19: 6,[51] ἐπέρχομαι 1: 8 (vgl. Lk. 1: 35; auch καταβαίνω 3: 22), ἐπιπίπτω Apg. 10: 44 (11: 15); 8: 16.[52] Der Geist sendet Boten 13: 4; 10: 20,[53] setzt Bischöfe ein 10: 28, faßt Beschlüsse 15: 28, hindert die Ausführung menschlicher Pläne 16: 6,[54] und macht

---

[45] Zu dem Thema 'Der Geist als Person und als Charisma' vgl. vor allem die wichtige Untersuchung von K. L. Schmidt.

[46] Vgl. bes. H. Gunkel, passim; R. Bultmann 153f.

[47] Vgl. H. Kleinknecht 357.   [48] Vgl. F. Baumgärtel 362.

[49] Vgl. E. Sjöberg 385.   [50] Ebd. 386.

[51] Vgl. Lukas 11: 3 D; E. Schweizer, *TWNT* vi, 407 mit Anm. 504.

[52] Es ist allerdings die Frage, ob ἐπιπίπτω hier personal zu verstehen ist (wie Mk. 3: 10; Lukas 15: 20; Joh. 13: 25 vl; Apg. 20: 10, 37) und nicht vielmehr in Analogie zum 'Überfall' unpersönlicher 'Mächte' wie φόβος (Lk. 1: 12; Apg. 19: 17; Apk. 11: 11), σκότος (Apg. 3: 11) oder ἔκστασις (Apg. 10: 10 vl); vgl. zu allen drei Begriffen Gen. 15: 12 LXX. Freilich ist auch gerade in diesem Vorstellungsbereich, wenn es um übermenschliche Mächte geht, mit einem personhaften Moment zu rechnen; vgl. vor allem Mk. 3: 11: τὰ πνεύματα τὰ ἀκάθαρτα...προσέπιπτον αὐτῷ.

[53] Das Ich des Geistes identifiziert sich hier mit dem Engel (vgl. V. 3, 5) und kann es deshalb tun, weil in beiden der Kyrios spricht; vgl. Flender 128.

[54] Das Bild eines personalen Handelns des Geistes entsteht hier durch ὑπό (nicht διά) τοῦ ἁγίου πνεύματος, ganz entsprechend V. 7. Vgl. das ὑπό in Mk. 4: 1 gegenüber Lk. 4: 1, 14.

den Apostel zum Gefangenen[55] 20: 22.[56] Vor allem aber: der Heilige Geist *spricht* wie schon im Alten Testament 1: 16; 4: 25; 28: 25 so auch jetzt 8: 29; 10: 19 (11: 12); 13: 2; 21: 11 (wie übrigens auch der böse Geist 19: 15); er bezeugt 22: 23, lehrt Lk. 12: 12, weissagt Lk. 2: 26. Ferner setzen – auf Seite des Menschen – die Haltungen des ἀντιπίπτειν 7: 51, ἀνθίστασθαι 6: 10,[57] ψεύδεσθαι 5: 3, πειράζειν 5: 9 wie des βλασφημεῖν Lk. 12: 10 gegen den Geist (vgl. auch λυπεῖν Eph. 4: 30) für diesen eine personale Vorstellung voraus.[58] Überhaupt gehört zu dieser Vorstellung des Geistes, daß er in mehrfacher Weise dem Menschen gegenübersteht, in seinem Reden, Senden, Hindern usw., obwohl in allen diesen Fällen damit zu rechnen ist, daß der Geist in der praktischen Erfahrung in Menschen und durch Menschen wirkt. Von dem Geist und Jesus wird dagegen nie ein solches Gegenüber ausgesagt (außer Lk. 3: 22); vgl. Lk. 4: 1, 14; 10: 21. Weiter entsteht ein solches personales Bild des Geistes vor allem auch dort, wo ihm Funktionen zugeschrieben werden, die sonst Gott oder Christus zukommen: wie Gott betraut der Geist Männer mit Ämtern, vgl. Apg. 20: 28 mit 1. Kor. 12: 28, auch 1. Tim. 2: 7; 2. Tim. 1: 11, und setzt so geistliches Recht.[59] Wie Christus vertritt er die Christen vor Gott; vgl. Röm. 8: 26f. mit 8: 34; Hebr. 7: 25; 9: 24[60] und wird ihnen zum Beistand vor Menschen; vgl. Lk. 12: 12 mit 21: 15 (sowie Joh. 14: 16 mit 1. Joh. 2: 1). Wie Christus ist er auch Quelle der παράκλησις für die

---

[55] 20: 22 ergibt zusammen mit 19: 21 dasselbe Bild der willig bejahten Gebundenheit des apostolischen Dienstes, wie es Paulus selbst in 1. Kor. 9: 16–18 entwirft.

[56] Gegenstück ist Lk. 13: 16. Auch sonst kennzeichnen die gleichen Bilder und Wendungen eine auffallende Analogie im Wirken des Heiligen Geistes und der widergöttlichen Macht; vgl. Mt. 12: 28 mit V. 24, 27; Apg. 16: 6 mit 1. Thess. 2: 18; Apg. 10: 44 (11: 15) mit Mk. 3: 11. Vgl. auch Anm. 77 sowie G. Stählin, 'Die Feindschaft gegen Gott und ihre Stelle in seinem Heilsplan für die Welt'; in: Otto Michel–Ulrich Mann (Hgg.), *Die Leibhaftigkeit des Wortes. Festgabe für Adolf Köberle zum 60. Geburtstage*. Hamburg, 1958 (47–62), 55f.

[57] Man wird darum fragen können, ob die Stelle bei Pr.–Bauer *s.v.* ἀνθίστημι nicht ebenso unter 1. (τινί persönlich) wie unter 2. (τινί unpersönlich) angeführt werden müßte.

[58] Anders Synge 207, der überhaupt die Personhaftigkeit des πνεῦμα leugnet (214f.), u. a. mit der Begründung, daß von Paulus und Lukas χάρις oft im selben Sinne wie πνεῦμα gebraucht werde. Damit wird Synge jedoch der Mannigfaltigkeit der lukanischen Geistesaussagen nicht gerecht; vgl. dagegen E. Schweizer, *The Spirit of Power*.

[59] Vgl. H. D. Wendland, 'Geist, Recht und Amt in der Urkirche'; in: *Archiv für Evangelisches Kirchenrecht* ii (1938), 289–300.

[60] Vgl. E. Fuchs, *Die Freiheit des Glaubens*. München, 1949, 115–21; K. L. Schmidt 206; E. Sjöberg 387.

Gemeinden; vgl. Apg. 9: 31; 1. Kor. 14: 3 mit Phil. 2: 1; 2. Thess. 2: 16. Personal wirkt auch das Zusammenspiel von Engel und Geist, wie es in Apg. 8: 36ff. und 10: 3ff. geschildert wird im Unterschied etwa von der Vorstellung von Apk. 17: 1ff. und 21: 9ff., wo beide Male auf die Stimme eines Engels eine Entrückung durch den Engel ἐν πνεύματι (vgl. Apg. 8: 39) und eine Vision folgen.

VII

Bei dem vielfältigen Zusammenwirken des erhöhten Herrn und des Heiligen Geistes ist beides zu beobachten: zunächst ist das πνεῦμα die charismatische Gabe des Kyrios 2: 33, 38, und so scheinen ihm auch einige festgeformte, aus einer bildhaften Tradition aufgenommene Wendungen wie 'geben', 'ausgießen',[61] 'erfüllen mit' fast den Charakter einer unpersönlichen 'Substanz' zu verleihen.[62] Aber bei Lukas ist πνεῦμα nie mehr eine unpersönliche, vitale Naturkraft. Es kann zwar das Erscheinungsbild eines enthusiastisch-ekstatischen Phänomens besitzen, aber es steht immer und überall in direktem Bezug zu dem Gott der Bibel und damit (in der Apostelgeschichte) zugleich zu dem erhöhten Kyrios. Der Mensch erfährt das πνεῦμα zugleich als Gottesgegenwart in seinem Inneren und sich gegenüber.[63]

[61] Die Vorstellung, die für die frühe Christenheit hinter der aus Joel 3: 1f. (vgl. H. W. Wolff, *Biblischer Kommentar AT* xiv 5. Neukirchen–Vluyn 1973, 78) und Sach. 12: 10 stammenden Wendung ἐκχέω τὸ πνεῦμα steht, ist verschieden bestimmt und abgeleitet worden: (1) von dem Übergießen mit Öl bei der Salbung (vgl. Apg. 10: 38, auch 1. Joh. 2: 27), so H. E. Dana 44, (2) von dem Bild der Joel 3: 1 benachbarten Stelle 2: 23: 'wie einen befruchtenden Regen', so J. Behm, Art. ἐκχέω; in: *TWNT* ii, 460; Pr.–Bauer *s.v.* ἐκχέω 2, (3) von der eschatologischen Wasser- und Geistgabe Jes. 44: 3; Ez. 36: 25–7, so u. a. O. Böcher, 'Wasser und Geist'; in: *Verborum Veritas (Festschrift G. Stählin)*. Wuppertal 1970 (197–209), 198f., 206. Dies ist wohl am wahrscheinlichsten, zumal Joel 3: 1f. und Sach. 12: 10 in den Kreis der gleichen eschatologischen Erwartung gehören. Eine Verbindung mit der andersartigen Bildvorstellung der Taufe (vgl. βάπτω, λουτρόν) ist erst sekundär hergestellt worden; vgl. Tit. 3: 5f.

[62] Synonym mit diesen Wendungen ist indes die nichtlukanische Wendung 'den Geist senden', die mehrfach eindeutig eine persönliche Vorstellung des Geistes voraussetzt, vor allem als Parallele zur Sendung Jesu; vgl. Gal. 4: 6; Joh. 14: 26; 15: 26; 16: 7, aber auch 1. Petr. 1: 12 (vgl. V. 11). Doch könnte auch Lk. 24: 49 diese personale Vorstellung in Verbindung mit der impersonalen (ἐπαγγελία = die verheißene Gabe des Geistes) vorliegen; denn ἐξαποστέλλω hat wie ἀποστέλλω im Neuen Testament fast durchweg personale Objekte.

[63] An dieser Stelle wird ein wesentlicher Unterschied der Christologie des Lukas gegenüber der des Paulus, speziell im Verhältnis zu ihrer Pneumatologie,

Dem entspricht es, daß man in vielen Aussagen der Apostelgeschichte über das πνεῦμα einen eigentümlichen Schwebezustand zwischen Personhaftigkeit und Unpersönlichkeit beobachten kann. Schon 1: 8 wird derselbe Vorgang mit dem impersonalen 'geben' bzw. 'empfangen' und mit dem personalen 'kommen auf' bezeichnet, und das Pfingstgeschehen beschreibt Lukas 2: 4 einerseits mit dem impersonalen πλησθῆναι, andererseits mit der personalen Wendung τὸ πνεῦμα ἐδίδου ἀποφθέγγεσθαι. Im Sinn dieser Wendung ist wohl auch sonst die Verbindung von πλησθείς bzw. πλήρης πνεύματος mit der Rede des Geistträgers zu verstehen, wie bereits Lk. 1: 41, 67 so vor allem Apg. 4: 8, 31; 7: 55; 13: 9, und auch die ähnlichen Aussagen 6: 10; 18: 5 vl; 18: 25. Auch Apg. 5: 32 ist in diesem Zusammenhang zu erwähnen, weil der Heilige Geist hier einerseits Gabe Gottes, andererseits Zeuge des Evangeliums von Christus ist, gemeinsam mit den menschlichen Zeugen, in denen er redet.[64]

M. E. geht man nicht fehl, wenn man gerade diesen schwebenden Doppelcharakter als charakteristisches Merkmal der lukanischen Geistesvorstellung bezeichnet. Es hat darin seinen entscheidenden Grund, daß der Geist Gottes sich selber den Menschen als Gabe gibt.[65]

Auch im Verhältnis von Kyrios und Pneuma stellt sich wieder die Frage einer Subordination (und zwar nach beiden Richtungen!), und wieder erscheint es bei genauerer Betrachtung zweifelhaft, ob die Frage legitim ist. Man kann zwar bei Markus und Matthäus feststellen, daß der irdische Jesus als dem Geiste untergeordnet erscheint (vgl. Mk. 1: 12 par); aber Lukas hat das in seinem Evangelium konsequent vermieden; vgl. Lk. 4: 1, 14 mit Mk. 1: 12; Mt. 4: 1.[66] Doch auch das umgekehrte Verhältnis einer Subordination kann nicht eindeutig behauptet werden. Eine gewisse Unterordnung des Pneuma liegt insofern vor, als Christus den Geist gibt, ihn auf Menschen ausgießt,

---

sichtbar: für Paulus kann Christus wie der Geist das Subjekt der Einwohnung in Christen sein; vgl. Röm. 8: 10 mit V. 9 und 11. Dagegen kennt Lukas keinen Χριστὸς ἐν ἐμοί. Im Handeln am Menschen können Christus und der Geist bei ihm auswechselbar sein, nicht aber in der Einwohnung. Weil die Christologie des Paulus ungleich reicher ist als die des Lukas, ist die Vertauschbarkeit von Christus und Geist im Denken des Paulus umfassender als in dem des Lukas. Etwas Ähnliches wie für Paulus gilt auch für Johannes; vgl. 1. Joh. 3: 24; Joh. 14: 23 mit V. 17.

64 Ein bezeichnendes Beispiel ist wohl auch in dem Nacheinander einer geistgewirkten ἔκστασις, die für eine Vision und eine Audition qualifiziert (Apg. 10: 10ff. = 11: 5; vgl. 22: 17f.), und eines Geistesspruches 10: 19 (11: 12) zu sehen.

65 Vgl. K. L. Schmidt 191.   66 Vgl. H. Conzelmann 168 mit Anm. 2.

Menschen damit erfüllt. Auch die Wendungen πνεῦμα κυρίου, πνεῦμα Χριστοῦ und πνεῦμα Ἰησοῦ besagen, daß der Kyrios den Geist als Möglichkeit seines Wirkens zur Verfügung hat; d. h. der Geist steht zu dem erhöhten Christus im selben Verhältnis wie im Judentum zu Gott.[67] Das liefe darauf hinaus, wie schon einmal gesagt, daß Jesus der Herr des Pneuma ist.[68] Aber das ist gleichsam nur die eine Seite; die andere, mindestens ebenso wichtige, ist die, daß der Geist auch dann im höchsten Maße – und in gewisser Weise selbständig – aktiv ist. Sein Wesen ist δύναμις, vgl. Apg. 1: 8; 10: 38; Lk. 4: 14; 24: 49, sein Sein ist ἐνεργεῖν, vgl. 1. Kor. 12: 11: wie hier Paulus dem Pneuma dasselbe ἐνεργεῖν πάντα zuschreibt wie Gott selbst (V. 6), so wirken in der Apostelgeschichte der erhöhte Christus und der Geist Gottes in so enger Gemeinschaft des Wirkens, daß man von einem und demselben Werk und Wirken sprechen kann.[69]

Diese Einheit des Wirkens ist in der konzentriertesten Form in der singulären Bezeichnung τὸ πνεῦμα Ἰησοῦ ausgesprochen. Es ist derselbe Geist wie in V. 6 das Subjekt des κωλύειν und zugleich derselbe Herr wie der, der durch das Traumgesicht von Troas die Missionare nach Europa weist. Mit der Wendung τὸ πνεῦμα Ἰησοῦ ist dieselbe spannungsvolle, logisch nicht aufzulösende Einheit umschlossen wie in 2. Kor. 3: 17f.: in dem πνεῦμα κυρίου ist der Kyrios am Werk, dem der Geist zu Gebote steht, der also der κύριος πνεύματος ist, und zugleich der Geist, dessen machtvolles Wirken identisch ist mit dem des Herrn, ja der selbst identisch ist mit diesem Herrn: ὁ κύριος τὸ πνεῦμά ἐστιν.[70]

VIII

Zum Schluß sei die Frage erwogen: *Wie* ist das μὴ ἐᾶν des πνεῦμα Ἰησοῦ zu denken? Lukas zeichnet nur bei der dritten Wegweisung in Apg. 16 (V. 9) das knappe, anschauliche Bild einer Vision mit einer Audition. Man wird darin eine Steigerung gegenüber den ersten beiden Weisungen mit ihren äußerst mageren Angaben sehen dürfen. Viel-

---

[67] Vgl. E. Sjöberg 385f.; I. Hermann 56, 75, 140.

[68] Vgl. E. Schweizer, *TWNT* vi, 402, sowie oben S. 233f.

[69] Vgl. A. Wikenhauser, *Die Apostelgeschichte und ihr Geschichtswert*. Münster 1920, 25; H. von Baer 39, ähnlich die wertvolle Untersuchung von I. Hermann über die Identität von Kyrios und Pneuma bei Paulus. Die Behauptung von Flender 122, 125, daß die Bereiche des Wirkens von Pneuma und Kyrios klar voneinander geschieden werden, läßt sich m. E. nicht erhärten.

[70] Etwas anders deutet diese schwierige Stelle C. F. D. Moule in seiner neuen bedeutsamen Untersuchung.

leicht ist aber auch schon die zweite Weisung eine Steigerung gegenüber der ersten, insofern hier der Kyrios Jesus selbst die Weisung durch seinen Geist gibt. Aber wie? Ob es richtig ist, Lukas mangelndes Interesse an dem Wie solcher Weisungen von oben zuzuschreiben,[71] möchte ich bezweifeln; in anderen Fällen zeigt er sich doch sehr daran interessiert. Es ist wohl das Anliegen, die Zielstrebigkeit dieser Kette von höheren Weisungen eindrücklich zu machen, wenn er sie in solcher äußerster Knappheit, gleichsam Schlag auf Schlag, nur eben erwähnt.

Man wird es trotzdem nicht als illegitim bezeichnen dürfen, wenn der heutige Ausleger sich die Frage stellt und dem Leser zu beantworten sucht, was damals geschehen ist und wie Lukas das Geschehen geschildert hätte, hätte er Anlaß genommen, es eingehender darzustellen.

Es sind fünf Arten von Vorgängen, die man hinter der knappen Wendung οὐκ εἴασεν vermutet hat:

1. Zur ersten Art ist eine Reihe von verschiedenen innerweltlichen Vorgängen zu rechnen, die den Versuch des Paulus, nach Bithynien weiterzureisen, vereitelt haben könnten:

(*a*) Die Krankheit, die Paulus während seines Aufenthaltes in Galatien befiel (Gal. 4: 13f.; vgl. Apg. 16: 6).[72]

(*b*) Eine Verfolgungssituation ähnlich der im Pisidischen Antiochien (13: 45f., 50f.), in Ikonium (14: 5f.), Lystra (14: 19), Philippi (16: 19ff.) usw., die jedesmal Störungen und Änderungen im Wirken der Missionare verursachten.

(*c*) Feindseligkeit der Bevölkerung in den Landstrichen, durch welche Paulus weiterziehen wollte.[73]

(*d*) Zerstörung von Straßen und Wegen durch Wolkenbrüche,[74] Flutkatastrophen oder Erdbeben.[75]

Derartige Vorgänge können jedoch zwar gewiß als gottverhängte,[76] aber kaum gerade als geistgewirkte Behinderungen angesehen werden.

---

[71] Vgl. Kleinknecht 356, der behauptet, das Neue Testament zeige generell weniger Interesse am Wie des Pneuma-Wirkens als das Griechentum.

[72] So M. Dibelius, *Aufsätze zur Apostelgeschichte*. Göttingen 1951, 169 Anm. 2.

[73] Haenchen 427 meint, daß aus dem Verhältnis der Galater zu ihren nördlichen Nachbarn ein Hemmnis für die Weiterreise durch Bithynien entstanden sein könnte.

[74] Ich habe selbst im Jahr 1959 erlebt, daß der Versuch, Antiochien in Pisidien zu besuchen, daran scheiterte, daß die dorthin führenden Straßen durchs Gebirge durch starke Regenfälle schlechthin unpassierbar geworden waren.

[75] Mit der Möglichkeit der Behinderung (außer durch Krankheit, s. unter *a*) durch Vorgänge von den unter *b* und *d* genannten Arten rechnet M. Dibelius a. a. O 170.

[76] Gunkel 5. Als Ausnahme nennt er 2. Rg. 2: 14f. Aber die Teilung des Jordanwassers wird hier nicht direkt auf den Geist, sondern auf Gott zurückgeführt;

2. Aus eben diesem Grunde – daß Einwirkungen Gottes auf die Natur nie als Geisteswirkung hingestellt wurden[77]– deutet H. Gunkel die Vorgänge von Apg. 16: 6f. wie 20: 22 auf Impulse, welche mit unbeschränkter Gewalt die Menschen überkommen, so daß sie das ausführen müssen, was eine geheimnisvolle Kraft ihnen eingibt. Man wird eine solche Deutung, angesichts vieler entsprechender, antiker wie moderner, psychischer Phänomene nicht ausschließen dürfen. Aber sie ist doch ein Beispiel von vielen für die etwas einseitige dynamistische Deutung der pneumatischen Phänomene, die Gunkel in seiner religionsgeschichtlichen Entdeckerfreude bevorzugte.[78]

3. Ganz ähnlich, aber der Geistesvorstellung des Lukas mehr adäquat als der Gedanke an einen irrationalen, geheimnisvollen Kraftimpuls ist der an eine innere Weisung, die Paulus (oder einer seiner Begleiter) empfing. Denn das ist wohl eine auch sonst als lukanisch bezeugte Vorstellung, so in Lk. 2: 27 und 12: 12; auch in anderen Fällen, in denen die Empfänger einer Geistesweisung allein sind, wird man diese Vorstellung annehmen dürfen, so Apg. 8: 29; 10: 19 (11: 12), auch wohl 20: 22. Wenn man hiermit auch in den Fällen von Apg. 16: 6f. rechnet, könnte man daran denken, daß die warnenden Weisungen als geistgewirkte Antworten des Kyrios auf geistgewirkte Gebete ergingen, in denen Paulus um Klarheit über den weiteren von ihm einzuschlagenden Weg bat.[79] Dann läge hier eine Erfahrung ähnlich der von Apg. 13: 2 vor (s. oben S. 239, aber auch S. 250).

4. Als Antwort auf Gebete könnte man sich auch Visionen vor-

---

denn die Propheenjüngert folgern zwar aus dem Wunder: der Geist Elias ruht auf Elisa; aber dieser selbst ruft Gott an: 'Wo ist denn nun der Herr, der Gott des Elia?' – und darauf teilt sich das Wasser.

[77] Oder auch als vom Teufel bewirkte Hindernisse; vgl. 1. Thess. 2: 18, wo es aber näher liegt an ein Eingreifen der Juden oder der Behörden zu denken als an Krankheit oder stürmisches Wetter; vgl. G. Stählin, Art. ἐγκόπτω in *TWNT* iii, 856; E. von Dobschütz, *Die Thessalonicherbriefe*. Göttingen 1909, 124; nur stimmt es nicht, daß Paulus 'in jeder Hemmung ein Werk des Teufels erblickt'. Wohl aber werden Hindernisse für das Missionswerk zunächst als ambivalent empfunden; vgl. die passiva Röm. 1: 13; 15: 22, auch Apg. 17: 15 vl, die im Sinn des Paulus jedoch als passiva divina zu verstehen sind.

[78] Gunkel 21, vgl. den ganzen Abschnitt S. 20–3. Seine Deutung der Geisteswirkungen erweist sich schon darin als einseitig, daß sich, wie er selbst sah (S. 25), einige der paulinischen Geistesgaben nur mit einer etwas gepreßten Deutung seiner Theorie einfügen lassen.

[79] W. Bieder, *Gebetswirklichkeit* usw. 35 mit Anm. 25; zum Wirken des Geistes im Gebet vgl. Dietzel 28 ff.

stellen, wie Apg. 22: 17ff.; Lk. 3: 21f.; 9: 28ff., und tatsächlich hat man auch schon bei den beiden ersten Weisungen in Apg. 16 (V. 6f.), wie bei der dritten (V. 9) an Visionen gedacht,[80] im Blick darauf, daß durch die Prophetie des Joel (2: 28) ὁράσεις καὶ ἐνύπνια als Wirkungen des Geistes angekündigt wurden (Apg. 2: 17).[81] Die Frage ist nur, ob Lukas, wenn er an Visionen, etwa gar an Christusvisionen, dachte, es so ausgedrückt hätte, wie er es in 16: 6f. tut.

5. Die beste Deutung scheint mir die auf prophetische Worte zu sein, weil dies dem wichtigsten Merkmal des Geisteswirkens bei Lukas am meisten entspricht (vgl. oben S. 244): πνεῦμα und λόγος sind Korrelatbegriffe.[82] Das erweist sich im Phänomen der alttestamentlichen Prophetie.[83] Das machen auch frühe griechische Vorstellungen vom πνεῦμα deutlich.[84] Die enge Verbindung von Geist und Wort bezeugen die Evangelien, z. B. Mk. 13: 11 parr; Lk. 2: 26; 10: 21, und in mannigfaltiger Weise auch die Apostelgeschichte,[85] vor allem gleich im Pfingstbericht und in der Verbindung, die sie schon 1: 8; vgl. 5: 32, zwischen πνεῦμα und μαρτυρία herstellt.[86] Das Alte Testament wird im Neuen als Rede des Geistes verstanden; vgl. Mk. 12: 36 par; Apg. 1: 16; 4: 25; 28: 25. So spielen denn auch Worte neutestamentlicher Propheten in der Apostelgeschichte eine große Rolle; vgl. 11: 28; 21: 4, 11, wohl auch 13: 2, 4; 20: 23, 28. Man wird die Bedeutung der Prophetie[87] für die frühe Christenheit schon deshalb kaum über-

---

[80] So u. a. A. Harnack 115, 121. Er rechnet zu den Wir-Stücken der Apostelgeschichte nicht nur 16: 9 (was im Blick auf V. 10 vertretbar ist), sondern auch – etwas willkürlich (doch vgl. oben S. 240) – V. 6f., weil der zweite Teil der Apostelgeschichte keine pneumatischen Stücke enthalte, außer 19: 2ff. und den Wir-Stücken, dem 'eigensten Werk' des 'pneumatischen Wunderarztes' Lukas.

[81] Vgl. H. von Baer 16 Anm. 9; er rechnet (ebd. 42) in V. 7 mit einer 'typischen pneumatischen Christophanie'.

[82] Vielleicht besteht schon ein ursprünglicher Vorstellungszusammenhang, wie es der parallelismus membrorum zwischen dem Wort des Herrn und dem Hauch seines Mundes, z. B. in Psalm 33: 6, nahelegt.

[83] Vgl. Sigmund Mowinckel, '"The Spirit" and the "Word" in the Pre-exilic Reforming Prophets'; in: *JBL* lxxx (1934), 199–227.

[84] Vgl. dazu Kleinknecht 343.

[85] Vgl. Synge 209, der darauf hinweist, daß der Heilige Geist in Verbindung mit Reden 5 mal im Lukasevangelium und 23 mal in der Apostelgeschichte vorkommt; ferner vgl. z. B. Meurer 75.

[86] Vgl. E. Schweizer, *TWNT* vi, 406 f. mit Anm. 492.

[87] Die Bedeutung der Prophetie für Lukas bezeugt z. B. die Einfügung von προφητεύσουσιν in den Text der Pfingstpredigt (2: 18). Vgl. zu diesem Thema bes. E. E. Ellis, 'The Role of the Christian Prophet in Acts'; in: W. Gasque– R. P. Martin (Hgg.), *Apostolic History and the Gospel. Festschrift F. F. Bruce.* Exeter 1970, 55–67.

schätzen können, weil sie ein wesentliches Unterscheidungsmerkmal vom zeitgenössischen Judentum darstellte, in dem immer wieder die Klage laut wurde, daß es keine Propheten mehr gebe.[88]

Wenn in Apg. 16: 6f. an prophetische Sprüche zu denken ist, so könnte sie Paulus selbst gesprochen haben[89] – denn er wird 13: 1 den Propheten zugerechnet und bekennt sich 1. Kor. 14 selbst als Träger solcher Geistesgaben – oder auch Silas,[90] der nach Apg. 5: 32 gleichfalls ein Prophet war.[91] Solche Sprüche können wie die der alttestamentlichen Propheten eingeleitet worden sein mit dem Wort 'So spricht der Herr' (z. B. 2. Sam. 12: 7 u. o.) oder auch, vielleicht wahrscheinlicher, mit dem Wort 'So spricht der Heilige Geist' (wie Apg. 21: 11). Solche prophetischen Worte, die eine vom Geist geschenkte Eingebung (vgl. oben Nr. 3) als Grundlage haben, bezeugen eine gottgeschenkte Einsicht in Gottes sonst verborgenen Willen, eine Einsicht, die zugleich unmittelbare Weisungen zu konkretem Handeln gibt, denen gegenüber kein Widerspruch möglich ist.[92] Denn in diesen Weisungen spricht der Kyrios Jesus selbst (vgl. Anm. 36), der im Strom der zufällig scheinenden Ereignisse der Weltgeschichte bestimmte Dinge vollmächtig bestimmt, die nach dem Heilsplan Gottes notwendig sind.

Wenn wir abschließend nochmals die Eingangsfrage stellen, welches Verhältnis des πνεῦμα zu Jesus der Genetiv Ἰησοῦ aussagen will, so ist nach dem oben Ausgeführten eine doppelte Antwort zu geben, d. h. man wird in der Wendung τὸ πνεῦμα Ἰησοῦ zwei in einer spannungsvollen Einheit zusammengehörige Gedanken vereinigt finden: 1. Jesus ist der Herr des Geistes, über den er als Kyrios verfügt. 2. 'Der Geist Jesu' ist die Geistesmacht, in der der Kyrios Jesus selbst gegenwärtig ist und wirkt.

---

[88] Vgl. K. L. Schmidt 202f.; Rudolf Meyer, Art. προφήτης κ.τ.λ., in *TWNT* vi, 817f.

[89] So Synge 210.   [90] Vgl. Th. Zahn 561.

[91] An andere Propheten ist kaum zu denken. Die Apostelgeschichte kennt nur judäische Propheten, setzt sie aber auch im Missionsgebiet voraus 20: 23. Im Unterschied von dieser Stelle, wo κατὰ (πᾶσαν) πόλιν sich auf Städte mit bereits bestehenden Missionsgemeinden beziehen wird, sind dort, wo die Geisteswirkungen von Apg. 16: 6f. sich ereignen, noch keine christlichen Gemeinden vorhanden, in denen Propheten aufstehen könnten; E. Schweizer 402 Anm. 462.

[92] Vgl. E. Schweizer, ebd. 406 mit Anm. 491; 404f.

Τὸ πνεῦμα ᾽Ιησοῦ (Apostelgeschichte 16: 7)

G. STÄHLIN

Πνεῦμα in the New Testament is always a difficult word to interpret, but nowhere does one find greater difficulties than when trying to determine the relation between the Spirit and the exalted Lord. This is the problem behind the seemingly simple expression τὸ πνεῦμα ᾽Ιησοῦ (Acts 16: 7).

It occurs in one of a series of divine directions concerning missionary projects. The giving of these directions is expressed in a number of different ways. But the guidance at work in all these different ways is one and the same, the guidance of the κύριος ᾽Ιησοῦς, who, at the same time as his exaltation as Lord, was entrusted with the gift of the Spirit (Acts 2: 33). He is the principal actor in the story as told by Luke in his Book of Acts. Therefore he should not be thought of as a tool of God, but rather as God's representative, κύριος of equal power with God himself; and the Spirit of the Lord is his Spirit – therefore rightly called 'the Spirit of Jesus' – just as, according to the understanding of Luke, the angel of the Lord is his angel, and 'the word of the Lord' is his word, equal in power to the 'word of God'.

The work of the Lord Jesus and God's work are an indissoluble unity. The same is true with regard to the work of the Spirit and Christ's work. Within this frame there is no room for conceptions of a consequent subordination, either with regard to the Spirit or with regard to Christ. Rather there is a close cooperation of Kyrios and Spirit which is, in the most concentrated form, expressed by the unique phrase τὸ πνεῦμα ᾽Ιησοῦ.

Luke follows the biblical and Jewish tendency to think of the Spirit in a personal way. But often he speaks of the Spirit also as of something that is given. One observes a certain ambiguity; but this ambiguity of personal and impersonal conceptions and representations seems to be characteristic of Luke's pneumatology.

As to the manner by which the Spirit of Jesus made the missionaries understand that he would not allow them to enter Bithynia, it is unlikely that guidance through natural events is meant, or psychic impulses of irresistible power, or even a vision as in verse 9. One might think of an inner certainty brought about by the Spirit. But it is more likely to be the word of Christ spoken under inspiration by a prophet (probably Paul, or perhaps Silas).

'The Spirit of Jesus' is the Spirit who belongs to Jesus as to 'the Lord of the Spirit' (cf. 2 Cor. 3: 18), and at the same time he is the personal spiritual power whereby the Lord Jesus is present and active in the church.

17

'Grievous wolves' (Acts 20: 29)

G. W. H. LAMPE

Paul's address to the elders of Ephesus is the only speech in Acts, comparable in scope with the missionary sermons and apologiae, which is addressed to an exclusively Christian audience; and Luke's placing of it at the conclusion of Paul's missionary enterprise indicates that he intends by means of this speech to offer important comments for his readers on the nature of Paul's achievement and the relation of his pioneer mission to the continuing pastoral ministry of the elders in the Pauline churches. Several important themes are thus brought together in the Miletus speech. There is a retrospective summary of Paul's missionary work: his proclamation to Jews and Greeks; we are reminded that the content of the apostolic gospel, or preaching of the kingdom, was repentance and faith towards God and the Lord Jesus; Paul is portrayed as the ideal archetype of the missionary-pastor, and this picture is linked, through the quotation of a dominical saying, with the figure of Jesus himself; and Paul's approaching 'passion' at Jerusalem is set in parallel with the Gospel story itself through the first of three predictions of his coming sufferings.

Into this biographical and theological comment on Paul, Luke introduces a prophecy of the future: the elders must take heed to themselves and to their flock to exercise pastoral care and oversight of the church, God's purchased possession, in which they have been appointed overseers by the Holy Spirit – which may mean, either that their possession of charismatic gifts marked them out for this ministry, or that they had been designated for it by the testimony of prophets in the Ephesian congregation. This duty is especially urgent because, 'after my departure grievous wolves will come in among you, not sparing the flock, and from your own ranks men will arise speaking distortions of the truth to draw away the disciples to follow them'.[1] Their orders, therefore, are 'Be watchful'.

This part of the speech belongs, as has often been observed, to a class of Christian literature common in the New Testament and other early

---

[1] Acts 20: 29–30.

Christian writings. This consists of pessimistic forecasts, not only of persecution and other external pressures to be inflicted on the Church by its enemies, but also of some kind of 'counter-evangelism' by anti-Christian prophets and teachers in which, as in the Church's own mission, the spoken word will be reinforced by works of supernatural power ('signs and wonders'), bringing about widespread apostasy and disruption of the Christian community. This will be in addition to perplexity and dissension caused by heretical deviationists among those who still profess to be believers. Prophecies on these lines are frequent in the New Testament from the apocalyptic discourses in the Gospels to the Revelation of John, and a very typical example occurs in the apocalypse in the *Didache*: 'In the last days false prophets and corrupters shall be multiplied and the sheep shall be turned into wolves and love shall be turned into hate.'[2] When such 'woes' are attributed to Jesus or an apostle they are cast in the form of actual predictions of the future; in the later New Testament writings which do not explicitly claim apostolic authorship future prophecy tends to be replaced by present warnings and admonitions; sometimes, as in the Pastorals, the expected troubles are supposed to have already begun within the lifetime of the apostolic writer himself.

Predictions of this kind are part of an ancient tradition in eschatology. Jewish and Christian apocalyptic envisages the future in terms of a crescendo of tribulation that leads to God's final intervention to vindicate the righteous and overthrow the forces of evil. There must be an increase of violence, unrighteousness and apostasy before the judgement, the destruction of the heathen and the vindication of God's people:[3] a pattern which reflects the actual sequence of events, and the hopes of the faithful loyalists, in the Maccabaean crisis.[4] The woes in Christian apocalyptic[5] are part of this tradition which, in its general insistence that things must get worse before God makes them better, has certain presuppositions in common with Greco-Roman interpretations of history as a decline from an heroic age into decadence, to begin again from a renewed golden era when the cycle of the ages comes round. Yet the conventional generalizations of eschatological prophecy usually tend to turn into more specific and detailed predictions when the writers are alluding to contemporary history; and this is the case with the New Testament prophecies of apostasy and dissension in the

---

[2] *Did.* 16. 3.
[3] 1 En. 91: 5–10.
[4] Cf. Dan. 11: 31; 12: 1.
[5] E.g. Mark 13: 6ff. and parallels.

Christian society. Nowhere, it is true, do they disclose precise information about the nature of the troubles or their cause; but there are enough indications in the New Testament and the Apostolic Fathers to suggest that in the late first and early second centuries the Church was faced with a powerful counter-attack from the side of Judaism which, though it probably included teaching of a Gnostic or Essene type, on the lines of the false teaching at Colossae, concentrated its onslaught on the Church's claim to be the authentic Israel, the true heirs and descendants of the patriarchs and the prophets. This claim was contested with the aid of prophecy, particularly the interpretation by prophets of the scriptural prophecies, and the backing of signs and wonders. If, as is so often supposed, the Epistle to the Hebrews was addressed to Christians confronted by both the pressure and the attraction of Judaism, the kind of literature to which the Miletus prophecy of 'grievous wolves' belongs can help us to envisage, if only in very general terms, the situation which evoked that letter.

According to the speech to the elders, the 'heroic age' of Paul's ministry is to be succeeded by a time of danger and trouble. The admonition 'Take heed (προσέχετε) to yourselves' recalls the Gospel warnings: 'Beware (προσέχετε) of false prophets who come to you in sheeps' clothing, but inwardly are rapacious wolves';[6] 'Beware' of men who will persecute Christ's missionaries;[7] 'Beware' of the leaven of the Pharisees and Sadducees;[8] 'Take heed (προσέχετε) to yourselves' lest 'that day' come upon you unawares.[9] 'Grievous wolves' will 'come in' (from outside) to attack the flock, and men will arise (from within) who will not merely teach a deviationist form of Christianity but actually 'pull away' (ἀποσπᾶν) Christian believers (from the faith). This suggests that preachers or teachers from outside the Church, non-Christian missionaries, are persuading members to apostatize and to subvert the faith of other Christian disciples in their turn; to 'draw away' disciples must presumably mean to persuade them to deny that Jesus is the Christ. In such a crisis the word for the overseers, 'Be watchful' (γρηγορεῖτε) recalls the warning of Mk. 13: 35, 37, addressed, not wholly unlike this admonition, to servants appointed to guard the master's house until his return.

The general picture indicated here is reproduced in the Pastoral Epistles, which strikingly echo the main themes of the whole Miletus

---

[6] Matt. 7: 15.   [7] Matt. 10: 17.
[8] Matt. 16: 6/Luke 12: 1.   [9] Luke 21: 34.

speech, the Johannine Epistles, Jude and 2 Peter, and, in a vaguer way and to a more limited extent, the Synoptic Gospels. It recurs in 1 Clement and Ignatius, and it receives some further illumination in retrospect from Justin's *Dialogue*.

A dramatic aspect of the picture is presented in the phrase 'grievous wolves'. The Old Testament prophets describe as 'wolves' the false princes of Israel, with whom are closely associated false prophets.[10] In the Gospels they are enemies of the Christian mission, and of Christ's flock generally.[11] More specifically, they are, for Matthew, false prophets,[12] as they are for the *Didache*;[13] they may be false teachers, as Ignatius implies,[14] or, as in *2 Clement*,[15] the metaphor can be applied to persecutors; and the idea of 'wolves in sheeps' clothing' can be transferred from Matthew's false prophets to heretics in the Church or, more generally, to Christians whose conduct contradicts their profession.[16] False prophecy presented as grave a problem for the early Church as for Israel in the days of Jeremiah. This was inevitable, since prophecy played a dominant role in the Church's life, though we have inadequate evidence about how the gift was exercised and by whom.

Christians believed that with the advent of the Messiah, announced by John, the greatest of the prophets, the hope of a re-kindling of prophecy in Israel had been fulfilled. Luke, in his Infancy stories, lays great emphasis on prophetic inspiration and utterance as part of the attendant circumstances of the Messiah's birth, and the argument of Peter's speech in Acts 2: 1–36 turns, first, upon the identification of the Pentecostal gift with prophecy,[17] and, secondly, on the conviction that this is now bestowed, in fulfilment of the expectation of Joel 3: 1–5, upon all those who acknowledge Jesus as Lord and Messiah. It becomes a standard argument in later Christian apologetic that with the coming of Christ the gift of prophecy has been transferred from the old Israel to the Church.[18] It seems, nevertheless, that although the gift was possessed by many in the Church, and although Paul, who reckoned it to be of the highest value for evangelism and edification, envisaged it as

---

[10] Ezek. 22: 27–8; cf. Zeph. 3: 3–4. [11] Matt. 10: 16/Luke 10: 3; John 10: 12.
[12] Matt. 7: 15. [13] *Did.* 16. 3.
[14] *Philad.* 2. 2. [15] 5. 2–4.
[16] Just. *dial.* 35. 3; *1 apol.* 16. 13.
[17] Acts 2: 4, 11, 17–18, where note in v. 18 Luke's addition, 'and they shall prophesy' to his citation from Joel.
[18] Just. *dial* 87. 3; Or. *hom. 5 in Lc.* (*GCS*, p. 30. 24; *PG* 13. 1812B); id. *fr. 50 in Lc.* 11: 11 (*GCS*, p. 257. 33); Cyr. H. *catech.* 13. 29).

a normal and frequent activity in congregational worship and thought that ideally it might be given to the entire community,[19] it was not in fact exercised by all Christians without distinction. It was but one of many charismata, apportioned by the Spirit among different individuals,[20] and by the time of the *Didache* prophets take a leading part in the life and worship of the churches, perform similar functions to those of the *episcopi* and *diaconi*, and receive first-fruits like high priests.[21] Within the New Testament period there seems to have been a definite, though to us obscure, distinction between occasional prophesying by 'ordinary' Church members, on the one hand, and the exercise of a ministry by 'specialist' prophets, on the other. Thus, despite his belief in a general 'outpouring' of the prophetic gift at Pentecost and the implications of the manifestations of the Spirit at Samaria and Ephesus,[22] Luke demonstrates the importance of the ministry of 'specialist' prophets.[23] Such men predict the future, sometimes using symbolical actions in the manner of the Hebrew prophets;[24] they exhort;[25] their functions seem to be parallel to, and overlap with, those of 'teachers',[26] particularly in the exposition of scripture;[27] and, according to Paul, the prophetic charisma brings understanding of God's revelations.[28] Prophets designate men for specific tasks or offices in the Church.[29] Above all, prophecy witnesses to Jesus. It is the mode in which the Spirit in the Church attests to the Church its central and fundamental faith in Jesus as Lord. Through the ministry of prophets the witness of Jesus himself, the 'faithful and true witness' is re-presented in the Church by the continuing inspiration of the Spirit: 'the testimony of Jesus is the Spirit of prophecy'.[30]

Prophecy combines free spontaneity with the incontrovertible authority of divine revelation. It is not easily fitted into the framework of ecclesiastical organization. Difficulties had already arisen in Corinth, where Paul was so anxious to exalt rationally controlled prophecy above

[19] 1 Thess. 5: 19–21; 1 Cor. 14: 1, 4–5, 22–30, 39.
[20] 1 Cor. 12: 28; cf. Rom. 12: 6. [21] *Did.* 11, 13, 15.
[22] Acts 8: 18; 19: 6. [23] Acts 11: 27; 13: 1; 15: 32; 21: 10.
[24] Acts 11: 28; 21: 10. [25] Acts 15: 32.
[26] Acts 13: 1; 15: 32, 35; cf. 1 Cor. 12: 28, etc.
[27] The remarkable reapplication of scriptural prophecies to Christian eschatology in the Revelation of John may be an example of their work.
[28] 1 Cor. 13: 2.
[29] Acts 13: 1–3; 1 Tim. 1: 18; 4: 14; possible also Acts 20: 28.
[30] Rev. 3: 14; 1: 5; 19: 10.

the less orderly charisma of 'tongues'.[31] That women should exercise the prophetic gift caused him embarrassment,[32] and he was driven flatly to refuse to admit the possibility that a prophet might be right and he himself be wrong.[33] Where the Church's most fundamental faith in Jesus Christ was attested by prophecy, and where the manifest working of the prophetic Spirit was a sign and guarantee both that the Church was the authentic Israel and that Israel's eschatological hope was being fulfilled for the Church, false prophecy presented a peculiarly dangerous threat: a menace which might subvert the core of the Christian community's faith and life. Where the prophetic gift was believed to have been universally 'outpoured' and potentially available to every believer, and where little distinction was drawn between prophets and any other teachers, it was especially hard to tell true teaching from false; for both could claim the authority of inspiration, either directly or through what they would claim to be Spirit-dictated interpretations of scripture, and both might support their teaching with signs and wonders. Furthermore, to criticize or try to test a genuine prophet could be the unforgiveable sin.[34]

The difficulty was already acute in Paul's time. The ability to distinguish true spirits from false was very important at Corinth,[35] where it proved actually necessary to remind Christians that no one could rightly claim to be an inspired prophet when formally pronouncing a curse on Jesus.[36] For, as this rather enigmatic passage reminds us, the problem was often not merely that of distinguishing true prophets from charlatans.[37] False prophets or teachers could be formidable anti-Christian missionaries. They might, indeed, claim some sort of authority from Christ even while they subverted the gospel and were 'workers of lawlessness',[38] and thus appear as 'wolves in sheeps' clothing'; they might claim to be acting in Christ's name, just as in Jeremiah's day prophets prophesied 'falsely in my (i.e. God's) name',[39] even while they advanced messianic claims for themselves.[40] A characteristic mark of their activity, according to the Synoptic Gospels, is deception: the misleading, if this were possible, of God's very elect,

[31] I Cor. 14: 32–3.
[32] I Cor. 11: 5; 14: 34–5.
[33] I Cor. 14: 37–8.
[34] *Did.* 11. 7.
[35] I Cor. 12: 10.
[36] I Cor. 12: 3.
[37] As in *Did.* 11, 12.
[38] Matt. 7: 22–3.
[39] Jer. 27: 15; 29: 9.
[40] Mark 13: 6/Matt. 24: 5; Luke (21: 8) interprets the false teaching as the announcement of an imminent eschatological fulfilment.

and the performing of great signs and wonders.[41] Luke omits the mention of these, but in the story of bar-Jesus the rather vague allusions in the Gospels, which are repeated and applied to the antichrist by the *Didache*,[42] are concretely realized in the person of a false prophet who is also a *magus*, a Jew who tries to prevent the conversion of a highly important Gentile to Christianity. Luke's narrative[43] may be stylized in the form of a conventional miracle-story from the mission field, but bar-Jesus is quite a credible figure, reminiscent of another Cypriot-Jewish magician, Simon, who induced Drusilla to transgress the Law by marrying Felix after leaving her husband Aziz.[44] Bar-Jesus, unlike Simon, is a propagandist for Judaism, a counter-missionary against the Church, and his activity is described in terms which recall the warnings of 2 Timothy[45] against men who, in the coming times of trouble, 'withstand'[46] (for the writer lapses from the prophetic future tense into the present tense of contemporary description) the truth, as Jannes and Jambres withstood Moses. The furious denunciations of these deceivers are too vague to allow us to identify them. They are γόητες whose activities seem to be accompanied by persecution of the Church,[47] and they win popularity by substituting 'myths' for Christian truth.[48]

Whether or not the 'heresy' of the Pastorals includes gnostic elements, it is very possible that it is primarily a Judaizing movement. The false teachers profess to be 'teachers of the Law',[49] a term which denotes scribes or rabbis.[50] This legalism is associated with 'myths' or 'Jewish myths'.[51] Ignatius[52] connects such 'myths' with 'living according to Judaism'; they may therefore be haggadic teaching and Jewish exegesis of scripture. With them are linked 'genealogies' which may reflect controversies between Christians and Jews about descent from Abraham and hence the claim to be Israel, and the ancestry of the Messiah.[53] Apostasy is prevalent; it has been foretold by 'the Spirit,[54] by which is probably meant 'in scripture'. This seems to have been brought about by the teaching of false prophets, 'deceitful spirits and teachings of demons', and this includes encratite doctrine denying the implications of belief in Creation,[55] a heresy which is not incon-

---

[41] Mark 13: 22/Matt. 24: 24.　　　[42] 16. 4.

[43] Acts 13: 6–12.　　　[44] Jos. *Ant.* 20. 7. 2.

[45] 3: 8.　　　[46] Cf. Acts 13: 8, ἀνθίστατο; 2 Tim. 3: 8, ἀνθίστανται.

[47] 2 Tim. 3: 12.　　　[48] *Ibid.* 4: 4.　　　[49] 1 Tim. 1: 7.

[50] Luke 5: 17; Acts 5: 34.　　　[51] 1 Tim. 1: 4; 2 Tim. 4: 4; Titus 1: 14.

[52] *Magn.* 8. 1.　　　[53] Cf. Theodoret's comments *ad loc.*

[54] 1 Tim. 4: 1.　　　[55] 1 Tim. 4: 1–5.

sistent with gnosticizing or Essenizing Judaism. Other passages in
1 Timothy suggest that these counter-missionary activities have produced strife and dissension in the community and hasty attempts to
depose presbyters: a situation closely parallel to that which evoked
Clement's letter to Corinth.[56]

The impression that the troubles of the Church in the Epistles to
Timothy are part of the post-apostolic crisis envisaged in the Miletus
speech, 1 Clement, and much other literature, and that they are due, at
least in part, to a Jewish counter-mission using the weapon of prophecy,
is strengthened by the injunctions given in the Epistle to Titus: to
appoint presbyter-bishops to maintain true teaching; to beware of the
many false teachers, especially those 'of the circumcision', who subvert
entire households; not to attend to Jewish 'myths' and commandments of men (relating, apparently, to food taboos); and to avoid
questionings (perhaps disputes about the interpretation of scripture),
genealogies, and strife and quarrels about the Law.[57]

A similar situation may lie behind the obscure denunciations in Jude
and 2 Peter. There is the same insistence here on a golden 'apostolic'
age of true belief, contrasted with the apostasy and degeneracy of the
present time, brought about by false teachers. 'The faith once for all
delivered to the saints' is imperilled by opponents who deny 'Jesus
Christ, our only Master and Lord'.[58] Although Jude does not expressly
call these teachers false prophets, this seems to be implicit in his description of them as 'dreamers', probably meaning that they are false
seers, claiming to see visions, and as sharers in Balaam's error who at the
same time stir up fratricidal strife, like Cain, and rebellion against Church
authority, like Korah.[59] It is probably against their claims to prophetic
inspiration that Jude insists that these creators of division are totally
unspiritual ('psychic'), altogether lacking the Spirit that inspires the
prayers of those who 'fortify' themselves in their most sacred faith.[60]

Like Jude and the Miletus speech, 2 Peter tries to follow the convention of putting the situation it describes in the future; the apostle, soon
to die, looks ahead to the time when false teachers will arise. He
contrasts their artificial 'myths' with the message of the Old Testament
prophets, confirmed by his own eye-witness testimony to the power of
the Lord Jesus Christ and his *parousia*,[61] probably meaning by this

---

[56] 1 Tim. 6: 3ff.; 5: 19. [57] Titus 1: 5ff., 10f., 14f.; 3: 9.
[58] Jude 3–4. [59] *Ibid.* 8, 11.
[60] *Ibid.* 19–20, NEB. [61] 2 Pet. 2: 1ff.; 1: 13–16.

term the coming of Christ in the Incarnation,[62] and not, as at 3 : 4, his future coming. It would thus seem that the false teachers in 2 Peter, as in Jude, deny Jesus Christ, in the sense that they deny that the Messiah has come in the person of Jesus. The fact that they introduce their 'heresies' from outside,[63] and that these are therefore not simply deviations arising from within the Church, confirms the probability that these teachers are out to subvert the gospel itself. Part of their argument rests on the delay in the promised parousia,[64] an apparently weak point in the Christian position which Clement also had to try to defend.[65] It is possible that they were also selecting certain utterances of Paul as another target for attack – a favourite opportunity, since the apostle's own day,[66] for Judaizing misrepresentations – for 'Peter', while calling to his aid Paul's God-given wisdom, apparently concedes that some Pauline 'obscurities' offered a dangerous handle to his opponents.[67]

However this may be, it seems that the false teachers were claiming prophetic gifts, for they are said to correspond in the Church to the false prophets in Israel, and they follow in the path of Balaam.[68] The orthodox defence against this prophesying is to lay stress on the authoritative tradition of the 'holy prophets' of the Old Testament and 'your apostles', as transmitters of the 'commandment of the Lord and Saviour'.[69] Indeed, since the Old Testament prophecies were uttered under inspiration from the Holy Spirit, and not by the human will of the prophet, no individual is entitled to interpret them, even, as we may infer, if he himself claims the gift of prophecy, since the same Holy Spirit now speaks only through, and in accordance with, this authoritative prophetic-apostolic tradition.[70]

The menace of false prophets appears more explicitly in the Johannine Epistles. They are equated with 'antichrist', expected in the last times. They have left the Christian community, but by doing so have shown that they never truly belonged to it.[71] The essence of their falsehood is the denial that Jesus is the Messiah, which also involves denial even of God as Father.[72] These teachers, again, are not mere deviationists within Christianity; to counter their preaching John has

---

[62] As in Ign. *Philad.* 9. 2.
[63] 2 Pet. 2: 1.
[64] *Ibid.* 3: 4.
[65] *1 Clem.* 23. 3.
[66] Cf. Rom. 3: 8.
[67] 2 Pet. 3: 15–16.
[68] *Ibid.* 2: 1, 15.
[69] *Ibid.* 3: 2; cf. Eph. 2: 20; Ign. *Philad.* 5. 1, 9. 1; Polyc. *ep.* 6. 3.
[70] 2 Pet. 1: 20–1. [71] 1 John 2: 18ff. [72] *Ibid.* 2: 22.

to reassert the basic Christian credal affirmations: 'Jesus is the Messiah', 'Jesus is the Son of God.'[73] Yet it is as prophets that they deny these truths; and so, since many false prophets have come into the world, inspiration has to be tested: 'Do not believe every spirit, but test the spirits, whether they are from God.'[74] There is the Spirit of truth, and the really existing, but false, spirit of error;[75] and the criterion is the content of the teaching, for the Spirit of God is recognizable wherever the prophetic spirit acknowledges that Jesus is Messiah come in flesh, that is to say, that in the concrete person of the historical Jesus the Messiah has truly come,[76] whereas no spirit is from God that does not acknowledge Jesus. It seems most probable that in 2 Jn. 7, as in this passage, the message of the 'deceivers' or false prophets, who are an embodiment of *the* deceiver, the antichrist, is that Jesus is not Messiah come in flesh, and that J. C. O'Neill is right in believing that their teaching is not the docetic heresy combated by Ignatius, but an attack on the essential Christian faith. This view finds confirmation in the assertion that no one who does not adhere to the teaching of the Christ, that is, the doctrine concerning the Christ, 'has God', whereas he who does adhere to it has both the Father and the Son, and, in the same context, in the proposal of a total boycott, in the spirit of Deut. 13: 12ff., of any visitor to the congregation who does not accept the true doctrine.[77]

It is true that in the Revelation of John the situation is different from this; there the role of false prophecy is to lead Christians into the idolatrous worship of the beast through delusive propaganda and the working of miracles.[78] But for the most part the New Testament writings suggest that in the post-apostolic period the Church had good reason to fear a successful campaign by Judaizing propagandists, accompanied by persecution, which may have already begun to make itself felt in Paul's time at Corinth and in which teachers who claimed to be inspired prophets preached against the messiahship of Jesus. It is true that there is little direct evidence of organized counter-missionary activity from the side of Judaism; we hear chiefly of defensive measures against the Church, such as physical persecution,[79] the exclusion of Christians from the synagogues, and the introduction of the twelfth of

---

[73] *Ibid.* 5: 1, 5.   [74] *Ibid.* 4: 1.   [75] *Ibid.* 4: 6.
[76] *Ibid.* 4: 2–3; see J. C. O'Neill, *The Puzzle of 1 John* (London, 1966), pp. 46–8.
[77] 2 John 9–11.   [78] Rev. 16: 13; 19: 20; 20: 10.
[79] As in Acts 9: 1–2; 1 Thess. 1: 14–16; cf. Just. *dial.* 16. 4.

the *Eighteen Benedictions* in which Nazarenes and Minim are formally cursed.[80] There may, however, be an authentic echo of some more aggressive counter-action in Justin's repeated assertion that the Jewish authorities organized a mission to contradict Christian preaching,[81] and Eusebius, even though he pictures it anachronistically, may preserve a vestige of independent tradition when he says, 'We find in the writings of the ancients that the priests and elders of the Jewish people living at Jerusalem sent letters . . .to all the Jews everywhere, slandering the teaching of Christ as a new heresy, alien to God, and warned them by letters not to receive it. Jewish envoys (identified by Eusebius with the 'apostles' sent out by the Jewish patriarch of his own time to the Diaspora synagogues) went all over the world to calumniate the message (λόγος) concerning our Saviour.'[82]

The hints and suggestions of the New Testament, however, that a campaign of this kind was mounted, including the strong possibility that the background of the Epistle to the Hebrews is to be found in the situation which I have indicated, is supported by the evidence of Clement and Ignatius. From these writings, too, we gain the impression that the era of 'grievous wolves', besides introducing Christian heresies of a generally gnostic type, also brought a more serious attack at what the Judaistic Christian author of the *Clementine Recognitions* calls the one point of difference between Christian and non-Christian Jews: the decisive question whether or not Jesus is in fact the Messiah.[83]

The dissensions at Corinth which evoked *1 Clement* involved much more than merely personal quarrels on the lines of the divisions which occurred there in Paul's time: so Clement himself tells us.[84] He describes the trouble as a 'detestable and unholy *stasis*',[85] using the strong term which Luke applied to the dispute between 'some from Judaea' and Paul and Barnabas over the necessity of circumcision, to the strife which Paul was accused of fomenting in Diaspora Judaism, and to the furious quarrel in the Sanhedrin between Pharisees and Sadducees in which Paul was almost torn in pieces.[86] Clement contrasts this sedition with the former virtues of the Corinthian church, which he enumerates[87] in terms of faith and piety (εὐσέβεια), sobriety, hospi-

80 Cf. Just. *dial.* 16. 4.
81 *dial.* 17. 1; 108. 2.
82 Eus. *Isa.* 18: 1–2 (*PG* 24. 213D).
83 *Recog. Clem.* 1. 43.
84 *1 Clem.* 47.
85 *Ibid.* 1. 1.
86 Acts 15: 2; 24: 5; 23: 7, 10.
87 *1 Clem.* 1. 2.

tality, knowledge (all of which are especially closely paralleled in Luke–Acts, the Pastorals and 2 Peter). There had been a 'golden age' at Corinth, and Clement's panegyric on this is reminiscent of the account of Paul's ministry in the Miletus speech which in fact has a direct parallel in Clement's citation of the dominical saying about giving and receiving.[88] There had been an 'outpouring' of the Spirit,[89] resulting in peace and good works.[90]

This ideal state of affairs has been shattered by envy (3ῆλος).[91] This attitude is characteristic not only of factious people within the Church,[92] but also of opponents of Christianity. According to Luke it is the motive of the unbelieving leaders of Judaism who obstruct the conversion of Israel to faith in Christ, both in Jerusalem and in the Diaspora.[93] Clement's examples of *zelos* and its deadly effects – it leads, literally, to death[94] – are consistent with the possibility that for him, too, it denotes the attitude of Jewish opponents of Christianity and Judaizing traitors to the faith, and it is significant that after his long warning against *zelos* he goes on to develop the argument of his letter in terms of anti-Jewish apologetic.

Clement's series of examples of *zelos* and, on the other hand, of heroic victims of it and resisters to it, strongly resembles the 'succession lists' of the false and true traditions in Israel, contained in the speech of Stephen. The tradition of apostasy, and of envy and hatred of the righteous, began with the patriarchs' jealousy (3ηλώσαντες) of Joseph[95] and culminated in the murder by the leaders of Judaism of the Righteous One.[96] It has always confronted the true line of descent from Abraham, the authentic Israel of Joseph, Moses, the prophets, Jesus, and, by implication, the Church. Clement begins[97] with Cain's fratricidal jealousy of the righteous Abel, a type of Christ,[98] and proceeds by way of Esau, the persecuting brothers of Joseph, Moses' countryman who forced him to flee from Egypt, Aaron and Miriam, Dathan and Abiram, to David's enemies, the Philistines and Saul. Of these, Joseph's brothers, the Israelite opponent of Moses, and Aaron appear in Stephen's 'false succession', and David in his corresponding catalogue of the true Israel. The probability that Clement's selection of

---

[88] *Ibid.* 2. 1.

[89] Cf. Acts 2: 18, 33; 10: 45; Titus 3: 6.

[90] *1 Clem.* 2. 2.

[91] *Ibid.* 3. 1.

[92] Rom. 13: 13; 1 Cor. 3: 3; 2 Cor. 12: 20; Jas. 3: 14–16.

[93] Acts 5: 17; 13: 45.

[94] *1 Clem.* 9. 1.

[95] Acts 7: 9.

[96] Acts 7: 52.

[97] *1 Clem.* 4.

[98] Cf. Heb. 12: 24 and also Matt. 23: 35/Luke. 11: 51.

'anti-heroes' indicates that the source of ζελos at Corinth was Jewish counter-missionary activity is strengthened by his choice of heroes. Besides Abel, Jacob, Joseph, Moses and David,[99] it includes Enoch and Noah,[100] Abraham,[101] Lot,[102] Rahab,[103] and those who went about in sheepskins and goatskins, that is, Elijah, Elisha and Ezekiel, the prophets, and Job who was righteous and true.[104] The list is, of course, closely parallel to, and probably influenced by, the roll of heroes of faith in Hebrews 11. Clement lays the emphasis on the loyal steadfastness of their faith and righteousness. Enoch was righteous in obedience. Noah proclaimed regeneration (παλιγγενεσία) and through him God saved the creatures who entered the ark in concord (ὁμόνοια); he thus represents the Church's saving mission and its baptism. Abraham is the hero of faithful obedience and hospitality, but the application of his story is different from that in Acts 7: 2–8. Here, too, it is used as anti-Jewish apologetic, but Clement's point is not that Abraham left a settled abode to follow God's call as a homeless wanderer, but that he went out from 'a scanty land, a feeble kindred, and a mean house' to inherit the richness of God's promise. The implication is that the true (Christian) descendant of Abraham has left the poverty of Judaism to gain the riches promised to the true Israel of faith – and, it is to be inferred, must not let himself be tempted to return. Lot is included as a type of steadfast loyalty to the Master,[105] in contrast with his wife, the representative of apostates (ἑτεροκλινεῖς, ἑτερογνώμων, οὐκ ἐν ὁμονοίᾳ, δίψυχοι, διστάζοντες). Rahab, besides exemplifying hospitality, stands for those who do not betray (true) Israelites to persecutors, and, as a prophetess, she recognizes that salvation for her people lies in joining (the true) Israel.[106]

Clement adds to his Old Testament examples 'the athletes who lived nearest our time' (ἔγγιστα γενομένους ἀθλητάς), in particular, Peter and Paul. He does not mean that they died very recently: only that they belong to the Christian era, as opposed to the Old Testament characters (ἀρχαῖοι).[107] He does not tell us specifically how ζελos brought about their 'labours' and 'endurance', and if he is referring to the circumstances of their deaths at Rome we cannot know whether Jews or Gentiles were the source of this 'envy'. But, apart from mentioning that the two apostles died, and implying that their deaths were glorious,

---

99 *1 Clem.* 4.
100 *Ibid.* 9.
101 *Ibid.* 10.
102 *Ibid.* 11.
103 *Ibid.* 12.
104 *Ibid.* 17.
105 *Ibid.* 11.
106 *Ibid.* 12.
107 *Ibid.* 5. 1.

Clement probably adds nothing to the information about their 'labours and endurance' which he could not have derived, like ourselves, from the traditions recorded in Acts. Both Peter and Paul 'bore witness' (μαρτυρέω).[108] This verb, as used in the New Testament, never necessarily connotes 'martyrdom' and probably never actually does so; the noun, μάρτυς, probably does so only at Rev. 2: 13; 17: 6, and just possibly at Acts 22: 20. Here, too, the verb may well refer to the apostles' entire career of missionary witness, and not to the manner of their deaths. Within the period recorded in Acts Peter underwent 'not one or two but many labours'[109] and the unusual expression, 'went to his due place of glory' (ἐπορεύθη εἰς τὸν ὀφειλόμενον τόπον τῆς δόξης;[110] cf. '(Paul) went to the holy place'[111]), may possibly contain a verbal reminiscence of the enigmatic statement in Acts 12: 17 that Peter 'went to another place' (ἐπορεύθη εἰς ἕτερον τόπον). Clement's information about Paul could also be read out of Acts: 'seven (i.e. 'countless') times in bondage','exiled' (from Jerusalem), 'stoned' (at Lystra), 'preached in the east and west','taught righteousness' (cf. Acts 13: 10; 24: 15), 'reached the goal of the west' (Rome), 'witnessed before the rulers (or governors, ἡγούμενοι)' (cf. Acts 9: 15, Paul's speeches before Felix and Festus, perhaps the implications of the appeal to Caesar, and possibly cf. also the prophecy of Lk. 21: 12). If this is so, then Clement is saying that Peter and Paul are shining examples of those who suffer, for the Christian gospel, from *Jewish* envy. Clement goes on to say that *zelos* also caused Christian women to suffer persecution. If we ignore the very probably corrupt allusion to 'Danaids and Dircae',[112] which, if it were correct, would indicate pagan persecution, we may again refer Clement's statement, either partly or wholly, to persecution of Christian women by Jews in the apostolic age, as recorded in Acts 8: 3 ; 9: 2 and 22: 4.

The pressure of the same *zelos* has caused women to desert their Christian husbands,[113] a situation envisaged by Luke, alone of the Synoptists, in his prophecy of the effects of hatred and persecution on the lives of disciples.[114] The fact that Clement expects the same 'contest' at Rome[115] indicates that *zelos* and *stasis* are much more than a merely local difficulty at Corinth; *stasis* is provoked by an external agency, the source of *zelos*, and the 'repentance' for which Clement

---

[108] *Ibid.* 5. 4, 6.
[111] *Ibid.* 5. 7.
[114] Luke 14: 26; 18: 29.

[109] *Ibid.* 5. 4.
[112] *Ibid.* 6. 2.
[115] *1 Clem.* 7. 1.

[110] *Ibid.*
[113] *Ibid.* 6. 3, cf. 1 Tim. 3: 6.

calls probably includes the return of apostates as well as the ending of schism. This is suggested, too, by his description of the dissident leaders at Corinth as *archegoi* of 'abominable *zelos*'[116] who rush into strife and *stasis* and thus 'estrange us from what is right', that is, cause apostasy. The language of *1 Clement* 15, and its selection of Old Testament texts, suggest that these leaders may be dissembling Judaizers. Accordingly, Clement appeals to the Corinthians not to become 'deserters' (λιποτακτέω, αὐτομολέω).[117] There is the usual vague denunciation of 'evil works of abominable desire',[118] but we are not told precisely what the false teaching was nor why it proved alluring. From the apocryphal citation at 23: 3, however, and the accompanying scriptural texts, 'He shall come quickly and not tarry' and 'The Lord shall suddenly come . . .',[119] it seems that, as 2 Peter also indicates, loss of hope of an early parousia made Christians become receptive towards it, and this may be borne out by the fact that Clement thinks it necessary to digress at some length on the evidences for resurrection.[120] The main thrust of the attack, however, may be inferred from Clement's insistence that Christians are truly 'the people Jacob, the Lord's portion',[121] the real 'Judah' whose 'praise' is with God;[122] that the patriarchs are *our* fathers;[123] that priests, levites, kings in the line of Judah, and Jesus according to the flesh, are all descendants of Jacob;[124] and that all from the beginning, like Christians, have been justified by faith. What Clement has to defend is the Christian claim, set out by Paul in Romans, that the authentic Israel are those who share Abraham's true righteousness of faith.

If it is this very claim which was under attack, the situation implied in Clement's letter illuminates and confirms the evidence of the New Testament that Judaizing missionary activity, accompanied by persecution, exerted severe pressure on the sub-apostolic Church. It is worth notice that Clement speaks of loyalists at Corinth having been subjected to actual persecution, like Daniel and Ananias, Azarias and Misael,[125] and that it is in this context that he insists so strongly that Church order is based on the ancient cultic ordinances of *Israel*.[126]

Ignatius, too, writes to churches in peril from dissension and schism, and, like Clement, he seeks to fortify their resistance by laying stress on

---

[116] *Ibid.* 14. 1.
[117] *Ibid.* 21. 4; 28. 2, cf. 28. 4 ἀποδιδράσκω.
[118] *Ibid.* 28. 1.
[119] Isa. 13: 22; Mal. 3: 1.
[120] *1 Clem.* 23–5.
[121] *Ibid.* 29. 2–3, cf. 31. 2–4.
[122] *Ibid.* 30. 6, cf. Rom. 2: 29.
[123] *Ibid.* 30. 7.
[124] *Ibid.* 32. 2.
[125] *Ibid.* 45. 1–7.
[126] *Ibid.* 40ff.

ministerial order. The threat comes largely from docetic heresy, but it is clear from *Magnesians* and *Philadelihdans* that Judaizing propaganda is also exerting a dangerous influence. Christianity has therefore to be defended in two directions: as a new doctrine and way of life against any reversion to antiquated Jewish teaching and practice, and at the same time as the religion of Israel, proclaimed by the prophets and continuous with the faith of the patriachs. 'Do not', he writes, 'be led astray by heterodoxies or old fables ... For if to this present time we live according to Judaism, we acknowledge that we have not received grace. For the most divine prophets lived according to Christ Jesus. Therefore also they were persecuted, being inspired by his grace, so that the disobedient might be persuaded that there is one God, who manifested himself through Jesus Christ his son ...'.[127] Similarly he asks, 'If those who followed a way of life in ancient practices (i.e. the prophets) came to newness of hope, no longer keeping sabbath, but living according to Sunday (κυριακήν), on which also our life rose through him and his death ... how shall we be able to live apart from him?'.[128] Ignatius appeals for loyalty: 'Having become his disciples, let us learn to live according to Christianity. For he who is called by another name than this is not of God. So then, lay aside the evil leaven that has grown old and sour, and change over to the new leaven, who is Jesus Christ ... It is absurd to speak of Jesus Christ and Judaize. For Christianity did not come to faith in Judaism, but Judaism in Christianity.'[129] Hence he writes, in another letter, 'If anyone interpret (i.e. in exegesis of scripture) Judaism to you, do not listen to him. For it is better to hear Christianity from a circumcised man than Judaism from an uncircumcised. If both do not speak about Jesus Christ, these men are to me gravestones and tombs of the dead!'[130]

The lines which Judaizing attacks and the Christian response to them followed in this period appear again in much clearer form in Justin's dialogue with Trypho. It would be beyond the scope of this essay to consider that evidence, which reinforces the conclusion to which the New Testament and early extra-canonical writings point, that much of the false teaching and false prophecy to which the Church was subjected in the late first and early second centuries was a Judaizing counter-mission, sufficiently formidable to give Christian leaders good reason to fear the onslaught of 'grievous wolves'.

[127] *Magn.* 8. 1–2.
[128] *Ibid.* 9. 1–3.
[129] *Ibid.* 10. 1–3.
[130] *Philad.* 6. 1.

18

Christ and Spirit in 1 Corinthians

E. EARLE ELLIS

The meaning of πνεῦμα in Pauline thought and the relationship of πνεῦμα to Christ have stimulated much discussion and raised a number of issues that cannot be pursued here.[1] It may be helpful, however, to indicate the perspective from which the present essay is written. With W. D. Davies, I. Hermann and others this writer regards the decisive influence on Paul's understanding of Spirit, apart from his personal experiences, to be his heritage from the Old Testament and Judaism.[2] The Spirit apparently is identified with the Old Testament spirit of Yahweh, at least in so far as the latter is understood as the spirit of prophecy (1 Cor. 7: 40; cf. Eph. 1: 13f.). Within this context it is probably to be understood primarily as power rather than substance though for Paul the distinction may not have been meaningful. Although its manifestations may not always appear to be so, the Spirit is personal: it 'bears witness', 'intercedes', 'comprehends', 'teaches' 'dwells', 'wills', 'gives life', and 'speaks'.[3] Also, in Paul's usage, no discernible difference appears between the (divine) Spirit, Spirit of God = Spirit of Christ (Rom. 8: 9), Spirit of the Lord and the holy Spirit.

I

The meaning of πνεῦμα, particularly within 1 Corinthians, may be seen more clearly by observing (1) its connection with the closely related concept δύναμις, (2) its function within the charisms, and (3) the infrequent

[1] Most of the significant literature is given in E. Schweizer, 'πνεῦμα', *TDNT* vi (1968), 334, 415–37; I. Hermann, *Kyrios und Pneuma* (München, 1961); and A. Wikenhauser, *Pauline Mysticism* (Edinburgh, 1960). Some representative works are: H. Gunkel, *Die Wirkungen des heiligen Geistes* (Göttingen, 1888); A. Deissmann, *Paul* (New York, 1957 (1912)), pp. 138–44; W. Bousset, *Kurios Christos* (Nashville, 1970 (1913)); R. B. Hoyle, *The Holy Spirit in St Paul* (London, 1927); J. Weiss, *Earliest Christianity* (New York, 1959 (1937)), ii, 463–71; W. D. Davies, *St Paul and Rabbinic Judaism* (London, 1948).
[2] Davies, *op. cit.*, pp. 177–226; Hermann, *op. cit.*, pp. 123–31.
[3] Rom. 8: 16, 26; 1 Cor. 2: 11, 13; 3: 19; 12: 11; 2 Cor. 3: 6; cf. Rom. 8:11; 1 Tim. 4: 1.

but significant plural use of the term. Πνεῦμα and δύναμις sometimes appear together as parallel terms:

> It is sown in dishonor, it is raised in glory:
> It is sown in weakness, it is raised in *power*:
> It is sown a natural body, it is raised a spiritual body.
> . . . The first man Adam became a living being.
> The eschatological Adam became a life-giving *spirit*.
>
> (1 Cor. 15: 43–5)

The combined use of the terms in Rom. 1: 3f. reflects the same meaning, the miraculous power of God manifested in the resurrection of Christ:[4]

> . . . (God's) Son: who was from the seed of David
>   according to the flesh,
> Designated Son of God in *power* from the resurrection of the dead
>   according to the *spirit* of holiness.

As an eschatological reality present in the Christian community, 'the concept of power is linked indissolubly with that of Spirit'.[5] In some passages, however, Paul draws a distinction between 'spirit' and 'power' in which πνεῦμα appears to be connected especially with 'inspired speech' and δύναμις with (other) miraculous acts. This is most clearly expressed by the chiastic pattern in Rom. 15: 18f.:[6]

> . . . Christ wrought through me. . . by word and work,
> By the *power of signs and wonders*, by the *power of the Spirit*.

That is, the δύναμις of God, which is here the more inclusive concept, may be expressed as the Spirit-carried 'word' or as a miraculous 'work'. In a somewhat different verse-pattern the same distinction is present in 1 Cor. 2: 4:

> (My kerygma was) not in persuasive words of (human) wisdom,
> But in demonstration of *Spirit and power*:
> That your faith might not rest in the wisdom of men,
> But in the *power of God*.

[4] Cf. Eph. 1: 17–20; compare 1 Cor. 6: 14 ('through his power') with Rom. 8: 11 ('through his Spirit').
[5] W. Grundmann, 'δύναμις', *TDNT* ii (1964/1935), 312.
[6] *Ibid.*, p. 311.

In this passage Origen apparently was the first to identify 'spirit' with (Old Testament) prophecy and 'power' with miracles.[7] His interpretation is supported by the literary pattern, by Paul's comment in 2 Cor. 12: 12 that his ministry to the Corinthians did include miraculous 'powers',[8] and by the similar contrast of 'spirit' and 'power' elsewhere.

Two other Pauline passages may be mentioned.[9] In 1 Thess. 1: 5 Paul and his co-workers write, 'our gospel did not come to you in word only but also in *power* and in *holy Spirit* and much assurance' (πληροφορία). 'Assurance', a word that is closely coupled to 'spirit', can mean the conviction that accompanies prophetic understanding and proclamation.[10] It appears to be used similarly here[11] and, if so, serves to qualify 'spirit' in that way. Although it is not clearly defined, the same distinction probably is present in Gal. 3: 5: 'the one who supplies the *Spirit* to you and works miracles (δυνάμεις) among you'.

In these texts God's δύναμις, manifested in the resurrection of Christ, is operative through the exalted Christ in two distinct ways: in the Spirit (inspired perception and speech) and in power (miracles). This interpretation is strengthened by a few traditions in the Gospels and in Acts. In Acts 6: 8, 10, Stephen is represented thus: ... 'full of grace and *power* he did great wonders and signs ... And they were not able to withstand the *spirit* and wisdom with which he spoke.' 'Spirit and wisdom' are probably a hendiadys. In such a combination 'spirit' is usually the more inclusive term with wisdom as a gift of the Spirit or one expression of the Spirit's work, i.e. in prophetic perception (1 Cor. 12: 8; cf. Col. 1: 9) or teaching.[12] Thus, Sirach (24: 1, 23ff.) identifies

---

[7] Origen, *Contra Celsum* 1. 2.
[8] Cf. W. Bousset, 'Der erste Brief an die Korinther', *Die Schriften des Neuen Testaments* ii (Göttingen, 1917), p. 83.
[9] But cf. also Eph. 3: 5–7, 16; Heb. 6: 5.
[10] Cf. C. F. D. Moule, *Colossians and...Philemon* (Cambridge, 1958), p. 86 (on Col. 2: 2): 'the conviction is the result of insight, of understanding'. According to *1 Clem.* 42. 3 the apostles, having been 'assured' by the resurrection, were then confirmed 'in the word of God with full assurance of the Holy Spirit' (πληροφορίας πνεύματος ἁγίου).
[11] Cf. L. Morris, *Epistles to the Thessalonians* (Grand Rapids, 1959), p. 57: '...the primary meaning is the assurance the Spirit gave to the preachers'.
[12] The 'wise' (*maskilim*) at Qumran are those prophetic persons who by God's Spirit are given understanding in the Scriptures. Cf. 1QS 9:17–19; 1QH 12:11f.; E. Lohse, *Colossians and Philemon* (Philadelphia, 1971), pp. 25, 27 (on Col. 1: 9); E. E. Ellis, 'The Role of the Christian Prophet in Acts', *Apostolic History and the Gospel*, ed. W. Gasque and R. P. Martin (Grand Rapids and Exeter, 1970), p. 59.

wisdom as Torah, i.e. as the prophetic teaching that flows from the (divine) 'spirit of understanding' (cf. 39: 6). Not essentially different, Wis. 7: 22–7; 9: 17 virtually equates 'wisdom' with 'your holy spirit', whose coming makes men 'prophets'.[13] Mark 6: 2 may be understood in the light of this background: 'what is the *wisdom* given to this one, and what sort of *miracles* (δυνάμεις) are being done by his hands?'

With these passages in mind we may return to 1 Corinthians. In 1 Cor. 1: 18–31 the 'word of the cross' effecting salvation is identified as δύναμις θεοῦ (1: 18), and is then specified in terms of Christ (crucified), 'the power of God and the wisdom of God' (1: 24). The idea is very similar to 1 Cor. 2: 4, in which Paul's kerygma 'in the power of God' is specified in terms of 'spirit and power'. 1 Cor. 2: 1–5 is a bridge passage between the two expository pieces, 1 Cor. 1: 18–31 and 1 Cor. 2: 6–16.[14] The latter is concerned with the role of the pneumatics, those endowed with the 'spiritual' gifts of inspired perception and speech. In the former, *viz.* 1 Cor. 1: 24, Christ is identified with the power of God in the community, both as miraculous act (δύναμις) and as prophetic word (σοφία). Via the 'bridge' in 1 Cor. 2: 4 (δύναμις/πνεῦμα) we may infer that he is identified also with τὸ πνεῦμα τὸ ἐκ τοῦ θεοῦ in 1 Cor. 2: 12. In both cases the nature of that identification remains unstated, and it may be clarified by an examination of the role of Christ and the Spirit in Paul's discussion of charisms in 1 Cor. 12–14.

II

The Spirit appears in 1 Cor. 12: 4–6, in parallel with the Lord (Christ) and God, as the source of the charisms 'those gifts of the eschatological age that create and empower the Christian community. In the following verses (12: 7–13) the Spirit alone is the source: 'the one and the same Spirit' distributes all the charisms 'as it wills' (11). Clearly the Spirit is not just 'the spirit of prophecy'; it is the source of other gifts, including the miracle of the new life itself (13). The inclusive meaning of Spirit and its use in parallel with Christ are similar to 1 Cor. 15: 45 and

---

[13] Cf. W. Bieder, 'πνεῦμα', *TDNT* vi (1968), 371; U. Wilckens, 'σοφία', *TDNT* vii (1971), 501f.; J. Lindblom, *Prophecy in Ancient Israel* (Oxford, 1962), pp. 175–9. Cf. Sirach 24: 33; Luke 11: 49; Philo, *Quaes. Exod.* ii. 29; *de gig.* 47, 54ff.

[14] Note the 'homiletic midrash' pattern: theme and proem text (1 Cor. 1: 18f.) + exposition (1: 20–30: σοφία/μωρία) + concluding text (1: 31). Similarly in 1 Cor. 2: 6–9, 10–15 (ἄνθρωπος/πνεῦμα, εἶδον), 16.

1 Cor. 6: 17. All three passages identify the Spirit, in the words of E. Schweizer, 'with the exalted Lord, once this Lord is considered not in himself but in his work toward the community'.[15]

Elsewhere, however, Paul in a similar fashion identifies the Spirit with God. As Professor Moule's perceptive essay has shown,[16] he probably does so in 2 Cor. 3: 16f. ('the Lord is the Spirit') even if christological connotations also are involved. He clearly does so in 1 Cor. 3: 16f. by the equation of 'the temple of God' with the indwelling of the holy Spirit.[17] Also, the far-ranging parallelism between Christ and Spirit, noted by Deissmann,[18] is found on a more limited scale between God and the Spirit:

> You must consider yourselves to be dead indeed to sin
> but living τῷ θεῷ in Christ Jesus.   (Rom. 6: 11)

> You have died and your life is hid with Christ ἐν τῷ θεῷ.
>   (Col. 3: 3)

> Through the law I died to the law that I might live θεῷ . . .
> I have been crucified with Christ; but I live,
> no longer I, but *Christ lives in me*.   (Gal. 2: 19f.)

Such parallels suggest the essential equivalence of the varying expressions denoting the resurrection life: 'with reference to God' or 'in God', 'Christ in me' or 'in Christ', 'in the Spirit' or 'according to the Spirit' (Rom. 8: 5, 9). Similar instances are the phrases, the mind of Yahweh, the mind of Christ (1 Cor. 2: 16), the mind of the Spirit (Rom. 8: 6) and, returning to 1 Cor. 12: 4–6, the ascription of the charisms to the Spirit, to Christ (cf. Eph. 4: 7f.) and to God.

At the same time things are said of Christ (or God) that cannot be said of the Spirit.[19] The relationship, therefore, includes distinction as well as identity, and the oscillation in terminology is reminiscent of that

---

[15] Schweizer, *op. cit.*, p. 433. Cf. Eph. 4: 4–6 (Spirit, Lord, God), 7–11 (Christ alone is the source).

[16] C. F. D. Moule, '2 Cor. 3: 18b', *Neues Testament und Geschichte, Oscar Cullmann zum 70. Geburtstag* (Tübingen, 1972), pp. 235f. One should perhaps compare this passage with the exposition in Eph. 4: 8–11 in which ascriptions to God (Ps. 68) are given an eschatological application to Messiah.

[17] Hermann, *op. cit.*, pp. 133f.; what is said in 2 Cor. 3: 17 of the Lord (Christ) and his Spirit is said in 1 Cor. 3: 16 of God and the Spirit.

[18] Deissmann, *op. cit.*, pp. 138ff.

[19] Cf. A. Wikenhauser, *Pauline Mysticism* (Edinburgh, 1960), pp. 80–91.

between Yahweh and the Spirit of Yahweh in the Old Testament.²⁰ The distinction is perhaps best expressed in Gal. 4: 6: 'God sent the spirit of his Son into our hearts.' The spirit of God in its eschatological role is (solely) at the disposal of the Son, the resurrected Lord, who as the Spirit lives and works among his people.²¹

Πνεῦμα is used in 1 Cor. 12: 1–3 and 1 Cor. 14 in the more restricted sense of 'the spirit of prophecy'.²² This meaning was present in the Old Testament and Judaism,²³ and it continues in early Christianity.²⁴ It is given there a special christological orientation that is most explicit in Rev. 19: 10: 'The spirit of prophecy is the witness to Jesus.' 1 Cor. 12: 1–3 makes the 'witness to Jesus' the hall-mark of a (prophetic) utterance in 'holy Spirit' or in 'the Spirit (or a spirit) of God'. The passage serves to clarify the relation of Christ and Spirit in 1 Cor. 2: 'the spirit that is from God' (2: 12) not only manifests the 'mind of Christ' (2: 16) but also gives the 'witness of God' (2: 1, ℵᶜ BD), which is the witness to 'Jesus Christ . . . crucified' (2: 2; cf. 1: 18).

Πνευματικά is used similarly in these passages of 'prophetic' gifts of inspired speech and discernment – a hymn, a teaching, a revelation, a ongue, an interpretation (14: 24). The term is not equivalent to the more general χαρίσματα, although it may be identified with the 'greater charisms'.²⁵ Likewise, the pneumatics (πνευματικοί), those who manifest the gifts of inspired speech, are closely associated with the 'prophet' (14: 37). As Professor Schweizer has observed, πνευματικός is probably the broader concept of which προφήτης is a special type.²⁶ Apparently πνευματικός/πνευματικά, used both in the general meaning of resurrection life (1 Cor. 15: 44) and in the more restricted meaning of 'prophetic' persons or powers, are of Christian coinage. In both meanings they represent a development of the same twofold use of πνεῦμα. Like πνεῦμα they are inseparable from the exalted Christ, who is the 'life-giving Spirit' and the 'wisdom of God'.

---

²⁰ Cf. A. R. Johnson, *The One and the Many in the Israelite Conception of God* (Cardiff, 1961), pp. 15f. But see also Hermann, *op. cit.*, pp. 82f.

²¹ Hermann, *op. cit.*, pp. 65f., 105. Cf. C. F. D. Moule, 'The Holy Spirit in the Scriptures', *The Church Quarterly* iii (1970–1), 285f.

²² See above, pp. 270ff.

²³ Hos. 9: 7; cf. 1QS 8: 16. Cf. the Targum on Judg. 3: 10; 1 Sam. 10: 6; Isa. 63: 10; Philo, *de fuga* 186; *vita Mosis* ii. 40.

²⁴ E.g. 1 Thess. 5: 19; 1 Pet. 1: 10f.; Acts 13: 2; 21: 11; Rev. 2: 7; cf. 11: 8; *Did.* 11: 7ff.

²⁵ Cf. Rom. 1: 11; 1 Cor. 14: 1 with 1 Cor. 12: 31.

²⁶ Schweizer, *op. cit.*, p. 423; cf. 1 Cor. 14: 1.

III

One further question may be raised: what was there in the Corinthian situation that caused Paul to underscore the unity of the Spirit with the exalted Christ specifically with reference to the prophetic gifts of inspired speech and discernment? Two answers may be suggested. First, as 1 Cor. 1–4 reveals, some of the 'philosophic' Corinthians have displayed an attitude of factious rivalry and have viewed it (proudly) as a manifestation of wisdom (cf. 3: 18). They have displayed it not only in an intellectual dialectic of 'persuasive words of wisdom' but also in ethical attitudes, 'jealousy and strife', a boasting 'in men', and arrogance (3: 3; 4: 6–8, 18f.).[27] In short they have reflected a 'fleshly wisdom', a 'wisdom of this age' (1: 20; 3: 18f.; cf. 2 Cor. 1: 12). In contrast to it Paul, in the context of an 'eschatological' exposition of scripture, sets forth a wisdom that consists in and is imparted by the crucified and exalted Christ (1: 23f., 30) speaking through the pneumatics (2: 13). He and Apollos have conformed their life-style to that wisdom (2: 5–9; 4: 1), and he urges the Corinthians also to forgo boastful 'dialectics' and to live 'according to scripture' (3: 20; 4: 6 RSV).

The plural use of 'spirits' in 1 Cor. 14 may supply a second answer to our question: the Corinthians are described as 'zealots for spirits' (πνεύματα, 14: 12), and must be reminded that 'the spirits of the prophets subject themselves to the prophets' (14: 32). The πνεύματα here are not to be equated with the πνευματικά, nor do they represent simply the variety of spiritual charisms. They are probably to be understood rather as the angelic beings that, under Christ, mediate the πνευματικά and minister with and through the pneumatics.[28]

The evidence for this interpretation cannot be detailed here. In brief, one may say that in the Old Testament the angelic mediation of Yahweh's word was a recognized form of prophetic experience[29] and that the prophets were included in heavenly (angelic) councils,[30] were conducted by interpreting angels and guarded by angelic armies.[31]

---

[27] Cf. H. Conzelmann, *Der erste Brief an die Korinther* (Göttingen, 1969), pp. 57, 74.
[28] Rightly, O. Everling, *Die paulinische Angelogie und Dämonologie* (Göttingen, 1888), pp. 11–48, 43f. Otherwise: M. Dibelius, *Die Geisterwelt im Glauben des Paulus* (Göttingen, 1909), p. 74. Cf. E. E. Ellis, '"Spiritual" Gifts in the Pauline Community', *NTS* xx (1973–74), 1–17.
[29] E.g. 1 Kings 13: 18.
[30] Cf. 1 Kings 22: 19; Isa. 6: 1–8; Jer. 23: 18; R. N. Whybray, *The Heavenly Counsellor in Isaiah xl. 13–14* (Cambridge, 1971), p. 52.
[31] Ezek. 40: 3; Zech. 1: 9, *passim*; 2 Kings 6: 16f. ('with us').

In apocalyptic Judaism the role of angels, often designated 'spirits',[32] is given elaborate expression. At Qumran 'the spirit of truth' appears to be identified with both God's holy Spirit and with the angel of truth or light;[33] conversely, angels can themselves be called 'holy spirits' or spirits 'of truth' or 'of knowledge'.[34] The holy Spirit or holy spirits have a special relationship to 'the wise' (משכילים), i.e. the teachers,[35] who are represented as recipients and transmitters of mysteries, possessors of wisdom, discerners of spirits and interpreters (מליצים).[36] As such, they bear a striking resemblance to the pneumatics in the Pauline community.[37] These similarities lend weight to the parallel between the angelic spirits given to the wise at Qumran and the 'spirits' sought by the Corinthian pneumatics.

Paul himself,[38] as well as other New Testament writers,[39] also associates angelic (and demonic) spirits with prophets and/or 'spiritual' gifts. His usage, together with the parallels in Judaism and early Christianity, strongly supports the interpretation of the 'spirits of the prophets' given above. The apostle identifies the power at work in the pneumatics both as the holy Spirit (1 Cor. 12: 3, 11) and as angelic spirits (1 Cor. 14: 12, 32). The oscillation, like that between Christ and the Spirit, probably reflects the Old Testament conception of 'the one and the many' in which God may be present 'in person' in his angelic messengers.[40]

If Paul recognizes the role of angels in the pneumatic gifts, why does he mention it only in the passing references in 1 Cor. 12–14? First, he may regard the 'pneumatic' Corinthians' zeal 'for spirits' (14: 12) as an erroneous tendency, clearly evident in other churches, towards a veneration of angels.[41] Second, this tendency may have facilitated their

[32] Cf. Jub. 2: 2; Enoch 15: 6ff.
[33] Cf. 1QS 4: 21f. with 1QH 12: 11f.; 1QS 3: 18–25.
[34] 1QH 8: 11f.; 1QM 13: 10; 1QH 3: 21ff.; cf. 11: 9–13.
[35] Cf. A. R. C. Leaney, *The Rule of Qumran* (London, 1966), pp. 72f., 230; F. F. Bruce, in *Neotestamentica et Semitica*, ed. E. E. Ellis and M. Wilcox (Edinburgh, 1969), pp. 228f.
[36] See above, note 35. Further, 1QH 12: 12f.; 2: 13f.; 1QS 3: 13f.; 9: 14, 17.
[37] Cf. 1 Cor. 2: 7, 13f.; 12: 10; 14: 29; Eph. 3. Cf. Eph. 4: 12f.; Col. 1: 26–8; 2: 2 with 1QS 4: 21f.
[38] 1 Cor. 13: 1; 11: 4, 10.
[39] Rev. 12: 10; 19: 10; 22: 6; Heb. 1: 14 (διακονία); 1 John 4: 1–3.
[40] Johnson, *op. cit.*, pp. 28–32. See above, pp. 273f.
[41] Cf. Col. 2: 18; Rev. 19: 10; G. Johnston, *The Spirit-Paraclete in the Gospel of John* (Cambridge, 1970), pp. 119–26: the Spirit-Paraclete doctrine is part of a polemic against an incipient angel cult with affinities to Qumran.

indiscriminate acceptance of ecstatic phenomena even of demonic origin (12: 3). Paul reckons with such activity of (evil) angels in the preaching of his opponents, pneumatics who impart 'a different spirit', serve a pretended 'angel of light', and boast of visions and revelations.[42] These factors also give Paul adequate reason to avoid any emphasis on angelic spirits, and to stress instead the Spirit's unity with Christ, its witness to him and its role in edifying his body (12: 4–6, 3, 25–8). By this emphasis the Apostle calls his readers back to the centrality of Jesus Christ, the indelible mark of the Pauline gospel.

[42] 2 Cor. 11: 4, 13–15; 12: 1, 11; Gal. 1: 8; Col. 2: 18; 2 Thess. 2: 2.

19

Christus, Geist und Gemeinde
(Eph. 4: 1–16)

R. SCHNACKENBURG

Die Anschauungen über den Geist im Epheserbrief sind bisher wenig untersucht worden.[1] Das ist aus mehreren Gründen leicht begreiflich. Das zentrale Thema dieses theologischen Lehr- und Mahnschreibens[2] ist die Kirche, näherhin das ihr anvertraute und in ihr sich verwirklichende 'Christusgeheimnis', ihre Einheit aus ehemaligen Juden und Heiden (2:11–18; 3:4–6, 9f.). Dabei wird auch die enge Beziehung der Kirche zu Christus, ihrem himmlischen Herrn, profiliert herausgearbeitet, besonders unter dem Gedanken, daß sie als der 'Leib Christi' zu Christus als ihrem 'Haupt' gehört (1:23; 4:12, 16; 5:23, 30); doch kann sie auch als auf Christus gegründeter Gottesbau (2:20–2) und als seine Ehefrau (5:22–33) betrachtet werden. Der Geist ist zwar aus dieser ekklesiologischen Sicht nicht weg zu denken (vgl. den Gottesbau ἐν πνεύματι 2:22); aber er nimmt darin doch nicht eine so dominierende Stellung ein wie Christus selbst, der faszinierend den Blick auf sich lenkt. 'In Christus Jesus'[3] hat Gott seinen großen Heilsplan durchgeführt, und dieses Christusgeschehen ist unmittelbar konstitutiv für

---

[1] Die Kommentare begnügen sich mit Erklärungen zu den einzelnen πνεῦμα-Stellen. E. Schweizer widmet dem Eph. in seinem Artikel zu πνεῦμα im *TWNT* vi (Stuttgart, 1959) etwas mehr als eine halbe Seite (443). Längere Ausführungen finden sich bei E. Percy, *Die Probleme der Kolosser- und Epheserbriefe* (Lund, 1946), 299–309 und 317–24. Die Literatur zum σῶμα τοῦ Χριστοῦ wird manches Einschlägige enthalten, was ich nicht berücksichtigt habe.

[2] Die briefliche Form stellt nur einen ziemlich äußerlichen Rahmen dar; vgl. C. L. Mitton, *The Epistle to the Ephesians: Its Authorship, Origin and Purpose* (Oxford, 1951), p. 4. Auch ein kultischer Sitz im Leben erscheint mir fraglich; der Verfasser hat sich nur einen gehobenen, liturgisch geprägten Stil angeeignet. H. Schlier, *Der Brief an die Epheser* (Düsseldorf, ⁶1968), S. 21, betrachtet den Eph. (den er für einen echten Paulusbrief hält) als 'Weisheitsrede'. J. Gnilka, *Der Epheserbrief* (Herders Theolog. Kommentar x/2, Freiburg–Basel–Wien, 1971), S. 33, möchte ihn als 'liturgische Homilie' kennzeichnen, die in die Form eines Briefes gekleidet wurde.

[3] Zu der ausgeweiteten und ziemlich vagen Verwendung dieser Formel vgl. J. A. Allan, 'The "In Christ" Formula in Ephesians', in: *NTS* v (1958–9), pp. 54–62; zu ihrer theologischen Zielsetzung ('*Gott* handelt *in* Christus im Hinblick auf *uns*') vgl. J. Gnilka, *op. cit.*, 66–9.

die Kirche (vgl. 1: 20–3; 2: 14–18; 5: 23, 25f.), die in der Sicht des Verfassers schon mit dem Kreuzestod Christi existent wird (2: 15; 5: 25). Nur unter einem Aspekt tritt der Geist innerhalb dieser ekklesiologischen Konzeption stärker hervor: dort, wo von der Einheit des Leibes gesprochen und zur Einheit der Kirche gemahnt wird (2: 18; 4: 3, 4). So verdient der Abschnitt, der am Beginn des paränetischen Teils steht (4: 1–16) und darum bemüht ist, der Gemeinde die 'Einheit des Geistes' ans Herz zu legen (4: 3) und sie zur 'Einheit des Glaubens und der Erkenntnis des Sohnes Gottes' zu führen (4: 13), besondere Beachtung. Wenn irgendwo, dann muß sich in dieser tiefschürfenden theologischen Motivation zeigen, wie der Verfasser das Verhältnis von Christus, Geist und Gemeinde sieht.

Der Geist kommt auch noch in anderen Zusammenhängen vor. Er hat eine offenbarende, das Christusgeheimnis erschließende Funktion, wie sich besonders an den 'heiligen Aposteln und Propheten' zeigt (3: 5), aber auch für alle Christen in dem Gebetswunsch deutlich wird, daß Gott ihnen 'den Geist der Weisheit und Offenbarung' schenken möge (1: 17). Die Christen sind mit dem heiligen Geist 'versiegelt' worden, er ist die 'Anzahlung' auf das volle Erbe (1: 13f.), durch ihn sollen sie erstarken am inneren Menschen, um immer mehr mit den Heilskräften erfüllt zu werden (vgl. 3: 16–19); ihn, mit dem sie versiegelt wurden, sollen sie nicht betrüben (4: 30). Die letztgenannten Texte nehmen Taufgedanken auf, die auch sonst das Schreiben durchziehen und in 4: 4f. in nächster Nachbarschaft mit dem Geist als Einheitsprinzip des Leibes Christi auftauchen. Schließlich erkennt man noch einen anderen Sitz im Leben für den Geist: den Gottesdienst der Gemeinde. Die Mahnung, sich nicht mit Wein zu berauschen, sondern sich 'mit Geist zu erfüllen', wird dann nämlich präzisiert: 'Sprecht einander in Psalmen, Hymnen und geisterfüllten Liedern zu!' (5: 18f.), und das weist auf die gottesdienstlichen Versammlungen, wie immer sie näherhin zu denken sind.[4] Diese vielfältigen Zusammenhänge, in denen der Geist im Epheserbrief genannt wird, und die Art und Weise, wie Prophetie, Taufe und Kult zur Sprache kommen, zeigen das eine, daß der Verfasser schon in einer Tradition theologischer Reflexion und in einem vorgeschrittenen Stadium urchristlichen Gemeindelebens steht.

---

[4] Die Art des Gottesdienstes (Eucharistiefeier, Agape, oder beides noch verbunden? mit mehr Liturgie angereichert?) ist wegen der Anspielung auf den Weingenuß umstritten, vgl. die Kommentare. F. Hahn, *Der urchristliche Gottesdienst* (Stuttgart, 1970), S. 68f., reiht diesen Gottesdienst in die nachapostolische Zeit ein.

Seine besondere Nähe zum Kolosserbrief, die kaum ohne Kenntnis dieses Schreibens zu erklären ist (vgl. 5:19f. mit Kol. 3:16f.), bestätigt das, braucht uns hier aber nicht näher zu beschäftigen.[5] Die unterschiedlichen Zusammenhänge und Verwendungsweisen von 'Geist' im Epheserbrief haben sicher dazu beigetragen, daß man den Geist-Aussagen dieses Schreibens keine besondere Aufmerksamkeit widmete, und in der Tat wird man auch nicht von einer ausgeprägten oder einheitlichen Geistlehre sprechen können. Aber für die zentrale Ekklesiologie ist es nicht unwichtig, wie das Pneuma mit ihr verbunden und in sie integriert wird. Welche Funktion und Bedeutung hat der Geist in dem und für das Verhältnis von Christus und Kirche? Wie sieht der Verfasser die Beziehung zwischen dem Geist und dem zur Höhe aufgestiegenen, zur Rechten Gottes inthronisierten Christus, und wie wird er für die mit Christus aufs engste verbundene Kirche wirksam? Dafür lassen sich aus dem Abschnitt 4:1–16, mit dem wir uns befassen wollen, einige Erkenntnisse gewinnen, die auch gewisse Rückschlüsse auf den geschichtlichen Ort des Schreibens gestatten.

Ehe wir uns jedoch der Exegese zuwenden, muß eine im anglikanischen Raum entwickelte These genannt werden, die den Hintergrund der Geist-Aussagen in der Feier eines christlichen Pfingstfestes erblicken will. Das Zitat in 4:8 und den anschließenden christlichen 'Midrasch' hatte schon G. B. Caird mit Pfingsten in Verbindung gebracht.[6] J. C. Kirby weitete dann die These in Anbetracht des durchgängigen liturgisch-hymnischen Stils auf das ganze Schreiben aus und suchte sie breiter zu begründen.[7] Die Funktion des Zitats in 4:8 ist bei der Exegese zu prüfen; die Nachprüfung der ganzen These überschreitet den Rahmen dieser Arbeit. Sie scheint mir, aufs ganze gesehen, nicht genügend fundiert zu sein; aber sie hat das Verdienst, die Frage nach dem Geist und seiner Beziehung zu Christus und der Kirche für den Epheserbrief dringlicher zu stellen.

---

[5] Vgl. unter den zahlreichen Untersuchungen besonders C. L. Mitton, *op. cit.*, 55–97; J. Gnilka, *op. cit.*, 7–13; ferner W. G. Kümmel, *Einleitung in das Neue Testament* (Heidelberg, 13. Auflage des von P. Feine und J. Behm begründeten Werkes, 1964), S. 259f. Die Priorität und Benutzung des Kol. durch den Eph.-Autor dürften feststehen; eine längere Zwischenzeit ist dann nicht erforderlich, wenn der Eph.-Autor eigene theologische Ziele verfolgte und sich nicht eng an seine Vorlage band.

[6] G. B. Caird, 'The Descent of Christ in Ephesians 4:7–11', in: *Studia Evangelica* ii, ed. by F. L. Cross (Berlin, 1964), pp. 535–45.

[7] J. C. Kirby, *Ephesians, Baptism and Pentecost* (London, 1968), besonders S. 125–49.

EIN LEIB UND EIN GEIST

Unter den sieben Ausdrücken, die der Gemeinde ihre Einheit in wohlüberlegter Anordnung und Aufeinanderfolge zum Bewußtsein bringen sollen (4: 4–6), stehen an erster Stelle 'ein Leib und ein Geist'. Die unverbunden einsetzende Aufzählung hat schwerlich den Sinn, die Mahnung fortzusetzen; vielmehr soll sie die Aufforderung von V. 3 ('bemüht euch, die Einheit des Geistes durch das Band des Friedens zu bewahren') motivieren.[8] Die Einheit des Geistes ist der christlichen Gemeinde vorgegeben, besteht für sie als von Gott geschenkte Realität und soll als solche im Verhalten der Gemeinde manifestiert und im praktischen Bemühen aktiviert werden. Für diese Einheit aber ist der Geist der maßgebliche Faktor und das bleibende Prinzip. Auch in V. 3 ist mit dem πνεῦμα schon der göttliche Geist gemeint, also das gleiche πνεῦμα, das dann in V. 4 nochmals in Verbindung mit dem 'einen Leib' genannt wird. Darum heißt es auch, daß die Adressaten die Einheit des Geistes *bewahren* sollen. Das 'Band des Friedens' ist durch eine Reminiszenz aus Kol. 3: 14 eingedrungen, wo anschließend (V. 15) ebenfalls von der Berufung 'in einem einzigen Leib' die Rede ist. Der Autor des Epheserbriefes hat die Kolosser-Paränese selbständig aufgenommen und vertieft, auch hinsichtlich des Geist-Gedankens, der in jenem anderen Schreiben fehlt.

Der Verfasser hat die eindrucksvoll gesteigerte, durch die πάντα-Formeln bei dem einen Gott und Vater voll ausklingende Aufzählung der Einheitsmomente, wie mir scheint, nicht schon (etwa in der Liturgie) vorgefunden, sondern selbst geschaffen, allerdings unter Verwendung festgeprägter Wendungen. Am ehesten hat er sich dabei der Taufkatechese angeschlossen. Die 'Berufung', die sich für die Christen bei der Taufe konkret erfüllt und die Hoffnung auf das volle Erbe aus sich heraussetzt (vgl. 1: 14, 18; ferner 1 Petr. 1: 3), dient als unmittelbare Begründung (καθώς) für die Aussage, daß die Gemeinde 'ein Leib und ein Geist' ist. Der anschließend genannte 'eine Herr',

---

[8] Imperativisch möchte die Darstellung in V. 4–6 verstehen M. Dibelius, *An die Kolosser, Epheser, an Philemon* (Handbuch zum NT 12, dritte Auflage, neubearbeitet von H. Greeven, Tübingen, 1953), S. 79. E. Gaugler, *Der Epheserbrief* (Zürich, 1966), S. 165, versteht die Aufzählung als Explikation des Begriffes ἑνότης 'im Sinn der Schilderung des normalen Zustandes'. E. F. Scott, *The Epistles of Paul to the Colossians, to Philemon and to the Ephesians* (The Moffatt N.T. Commentary, London, 1930, [9]1958), p. 203, spricht von 'the conditions of unity in the Church'. Besser noch versteht man die Aufzählung als Motivation, vgl. H. Schlier, *op. cit.*, 187; J. Gnilka, *op. cit.*, 200.

der Inhalt des 'einen Glaubens' ist, wird in der *einen* (allen gemein-samen) Taufe bekannt (vgl. Röm. 10: 9a). Erst danach richtet sich der Blick auf den einen Gott und Vater, der 'über allen und durch alle und in allen' ist. So ist es nicht schwer, die theologische Tradition zu erkennen, in der der Verfasser steht: Tauferfahrung und Taufbekennt-nis der Gemeinde, wie sie Paulus interpretiert. Man kann besonders an das Wort des Apostels in 1. Kor. 12: 13 erinnern: 'In einem einzigen Geist wurden wir alle für einen einzigen Leib[9] getauft, ob Juden oder Griechen, Sklaven oder Freie . . .' Der *eine* Geist korrespondiert dem *einen* Leib; er ist das den Leib aufbauende und zusammenfügende Prinzip. Weil alle den gleichen Geist empfangen, werden sie alle in den einen Leib einbezogen; sie werden Glieder am Leib Christi (vgl. 1. Kor. 12: 27; Eph. 5: 30).

Diese paulinischen Gedanken sind im Epheserbrief aufgenommen und durch die Fortführung des σῶμα-Modells weiter entfaltet. Hier ist Christus in betonter Weise das Haupt des Leibes (1: 22; 4: 15; 5: 23), das nicht nur die beherrschende und leitende Stellung hat, sondern auch den Leib aufbaut, zusammenhält und sein Wachstum betreibt (4: 16). Berücksichtigt man den paulinischen Grundgedanken und bedenkt man gleichzeitig die theologische Weiterführung des Epheser-Autors, so kann man der Folgerung nicht entgehen, daß Christus als das Haupt *durch den Geist* wirksam ist, im ganzen Umfang der dem Haupt zugeschriebenen Funktionen. Das wird zwar nirgends aus-drücklich ausgesprochen, steht aber hinter der gesamten Konzeption unseres Abschnitts. Eine gewisse Bestätigung liegt auch in dem ἐν πνεύματι von 2: 22. Weil in 4: 3–6 der Nachdruck auf den Geist als Einheitsprinzip fällt, muß er für die Ausführung in 4: 7–16 als maßgeb-licher Faktor, als stillschweigend vorausgesetzte Realität zwischen dem himmlischen Christus und der irdischen Gemeinde, als Mittel und Modus des Einwirkens Christi auf seine Kirche angesehen werden.

Um die Gedanken des Autors bei der Formel 'ein Leib und ein Geist' noch schärfer zu erfassen, muß man auf 2: 14–18 zurück-greifen.[10] In unverkennbarer Korrespondenz folgen hier ἐν ἑνὶ σώματι

---

[9] Zu der verschieden gedeuteten Wendung εἰς ἓν σῶμα in 1. Kor. 12: 13 vgl. R. Schnackenburg, *Baptism in the Thought of St Paul* (Oxford, 1964), S. 26f.
[10] Für diese Texteinheit nehmen manche Exegeten an, daß der Autor einen Hymnus verarbeitet hat, u. a. G. Schille, *Frühchristliche Hymnen* (Berlin, 1965), S. 24–31; J. Sanders, 'Hymnic Elements in Ephesians 1–3', in: *ZNW* lvi (1965), pp. 214–32, näherhin 216–18; J. Gnilka, 'Christus unser Friede – ein Friedens-Erlöserlied in Eph. 2, 14–17', in: *Die Zeit Jesu* (Festschrift für H. Schlier,

(V. 16) und ἐν ἑνὶ πνεύματι (V. 18) aufeinander. Zunächst ist durch das Thema dieses Abschnittes klar, daß der Autor die Einheit auf die Vereinigung von ehemaligen Heiden und Juden in der Kirche bezieht (vgl. V. 11–13). Sodann wird diese Einheit auf das Kreuzesgeschehen zurückgeführt, wo Christus, 'unser Friede', die beiden Gruppen zur Einheit zusammenschließt (V. 14) und 'die zwei in sich (in seiner Person)[11] zu einem einzigen neuen Menschen schafft' (V. 15). Schließlich – und das ist die bemerkenswerteste Wende – besteht für den Autor diese neue Einheit, die eine Kirche aus Juden und Heiden, seit jenem Geschehen am Kreuz. Denn im Blute Christi sind die einst 'Fernen' (Heiden) zu 'Nahen' geworden (V. 13), in seinem Fleisch hat er die trennende Scheidewand, die Feindschaft, niedergerissen (V. 19) beziehungsweise das 'in Satzungen bestehende Gesetz der Gebote' (das an jener Trennung und Feindschaft schuld war), vernichtet (V. 15).[12] Der Kreuzestod Jesu, bei Paulus streng soteriologisch interpretiert (ὑπὲρ ἡμῶν), erlangt für den Autor des Epheserbriefes sogleich einen ekklesiologischen Wert, ja er kann das traditionelle ὑπέρ (vgl.

Freiburg–Basel–Wien, 1970), S. 190–207; Id., *Der Epheserbrief*, S. 147–52. In der Rekonstruktion des Liedes stimmen diese Forscher nicht überein. Kritisch dazu: R. Deichgräber, *Gotteshymnus und Christushymnus in der frühen Christenheit* (Göttingen, 1967), S. 165–7; H. Merklein, 'Zur Tradition und Komposition von Eph. 2, 14–18', in: *BZ* xvii (1973), S. 79–102. Auf jeden Fall dürfte die Korrespondenz von ἐν ἑνὶ σώματι und ἐν ἑνὶ πνεύματι vom Eph.-Autor geschaffen sein.

11 Durch dieses ἐν αὐτῷ (viele Handschriften lesen ἐν ἑαυτῷ) wird die Kirche aufs engste mit Christus verbunden, ihre Erschaffung nicht nur als Frucht seines Sterbens verstanden, sondern unmittelbar in seine Hingabe am Kreuz verlagert (5: 25). Christus in seiner Person wird zu dem *einen* Leib aus den bisher getrennten beiden Gruppen. Man kann kaum bezweifeln, daß dahinter bestimmte Adam-Anthropos-Spekulationen stehen. Für das viel erörterte religionsgeschichtliche Problem scheint mir die vom hellenistischen Judentum herkommende Linie beachtlich zu sein, vgl. C. Colpe, 'Zur Leib-Christi-Vorstellung im Epheserbrief', in: *Judentum, Urchristentum, Kirche* (Festschrift für J. Jeremias, Berlin, 1960), S. 172–87; H. Hegermann, *Die Vorstellung vom Schöpfungsmittler im hellenistischen Judentum und Urchristentum* (Berlin, 1961); E. Schweizer, 'Die Kirche als Leib Christi in den paulinischen Antilegomena', in: *TLZ* lxxxvi (1961), Sp. 241–56 (abgedruckt in: *Neotestamentica*, Zürich–Stuttgart, 1963, S. 293–316); E. Brandenburger, *Adam und Christus* (Neukirchen, 1962), besonders S. 151–3; J. Gnilka, *Epheserbrief*, S. 101ff.

12 Die Wendung ἐν τῇ σαρκὶ αὐτοῦ kann entweder mit dem Vorangehenden (V. 14) oder mit dem Folgenden (V. 15) verbunden werden. Die Meinungen darüber sind geteilt. Entsprechend ἐν τῷ αἵματι V. 13 scheint mir die Anknüpfung an den zuvorstehenden Satz den Vorzug zu verdienen (mit Schlier, *Eph.* S. 125). Doch ändert auch die von der Mehrzahl angenommene andere Meinung, die sich auf den Satzrhythmus berufen kann (vgl. die Stellung von λύσας), nicht viel am Hauptsinn.

5: 2) unmittelbar mit der ἐκκλησία verbinden (5: 25), so daß der irritierende Eindruck entsteht, die Kirche existiere schon beim Kreuzestod. Doch will der Verfasser kaum mehr sagen, als daß die Kirche der liebenden Hingabe Christi alles verdankt.[13] Wenn die Kirche schon im gekreuzigten Christus präsent wurde, dann ist auf jeden Fall mit ἐν ἐνὶ σώματι in V. 16 der Leib der Kirche mitgemeint, wenn nicht vorzugsweise und ausschließlich gemeint.[14] Durch das Kreuz, an dem Christus mit seinem Fleisch verblutet, bewirkt er die Versöhnung der beiden bisher getrennten Gruppen mit Gott 'in einem einzigen Leib', den sie eben dadurch und seither bilden. Durch ihn haben die beiden jetzt 'in einem einzigen Geist' den Zugang zum Vater (V. 18). Das dazwischen in V. 17 stehende Schriftzitat, das sich an Jes. 57: 19 anlehnt, will sicher nicht auf die Wortverkündigung Jesu zurückgreifen, sondern lokalisiert gemäß dem Kontext diese 'Friedensverkündigung' im Kreuzesgeschehen. Von da an besteht der ekklesiale Leib Christi, der von dem einen Geist durchwaltet wird. So erlangt auch der Geist von vornherein eine ekklesiale Valenz; er ist stärker als bei Paulus in diese Funktion eingewiesen und auf diese Sicht eingegrenzt. Die Einheit ist durch Christus vorgegeben; aber Christus wirkt durch den Geist und bewirkt durch den einen Geist, daß die beiden bisherigen feindlichen Menschheitsgruppen als mit Gott und untereinander Versöhnte den gleichen Zugang zu Gott dem Vater haben.

DER ZUR HÖHE AUFGESTIEGENE

Mit V. 7 setzt eine neue Betrachtung ein, die das Thema von der Einheit der Gemeinde festhält und weiter verfolgt, und zwar in paränetischer Absicht, 'damit wir alle zur Einheit des Glaubens und der Erkenntnis des Sohnes Gottes gelangen' (V. 13). Aber der Verfasser ist überzeugt, daß Christus selbst den Aufbau und die Einheit seines

---

[13] Über die zu 5: 25 entwickelten Ansichten referiert J. Gnilka, *Epheserbrief*, S. 279f.; er weist mit Recht auf den Wechsel des Bildes (Bräutigam und Braut oder Ehemann und Ehefrau) hin, der zu jener Formulierung zwang. Gemeint sei die Entstehung der Kirche im Tod Christi.

[14] Auch über die Deutung von ἐν ἐνὶ σώματι sind die Meinungen geteilt: Kreuzesleib, ekklesialer Leib oder beides? Vgl. die Diskussion bei E. Gaugler, *Der Epheserbrief*, 115–17; der '*eine* Leib' dürfte für den Eph.-Autor aber doch sogleich die eine Kirche aus Juden und Heiden sein, die sich dem Versöhnungsgeschehen am Kreuz verdankt. Der Autor bewegt sich, wie 4: 4 zeigt, in festen Assoziationen; vgl. auch 5: 23 αὐτὸς σωτὴρ τοῦ σώματος. An keiner Stelle des Eph. wird sonst σῶμα auf den individuellen Leib Christi bezogen.

Leibes betreibt und alles dafür Erforderliche tut. Dabei hat er speziell die der Kirche verliehenen, zur 'Zurüstung der Heiligen' bestimmten, ein 'Werk des Dienstes' erfüllenden, für den 'Aufbau des Leibes' sorgenden (V. 12) Amtsträger im Sinn, die in V. 11 aufgezählt werden. Dieses dem Autor dringliche Anliegen, die Stellung und Funktion der in der Gemeinde und für die Gemeinde tätigen Amtsträger aufzuzeigen, begründet er theologisch aus dem Wirken des 'zur Höhe' aufgestiegenen Christus. Wieder – wie im ganzen Schreiben – argumentiert er für seine ekklesiologische Konzeption aus dem Verhältnis Christus–Kirche; aber es ist das einzige Mal, daß er im Blick auf die irdische Kirche, die noch dem Irrtum, der Verführung und Gefährdung ausgesetzt ist (vgl. V. 14), so 'konkret' wird und uns einen Durchblick auf die Struktur der empirischen Gemeinde zu seiner Zeit gestattet. Die Sorge um die Einheit und das innere Wachstum der Gemeinde hat ihn dazu bewogen. Das Amtsverständnis, das in dieser Sicht hervortritt, ist für uns von besonderem Interesse; aber es läßt sich nicht erhellen, wenn wir dem Autor nicht in seinem Gedankengang genau folgen.

Der Epheser-Autor ist sich trotz aller engen Bindung der Kirche an Christus doch bewußt, daß der Kyrios von seiner irdischen Gemeinde geschichtlich-räumlich entfernt ist. Das kommt in dem Schriftzitat von V. 8 zum Ausdruck: Christus ist 'in die Höhe aufgestiegen'. Die eigentümliche Verwendung der Psalmstelle (68: 19), die ursprünglich vom Siegeszug Jahwes handelt, der zum Sion hinaufsteigt, Gefangene macht und Huldigungsgeschenke unter den Menschen empfängt, ist oft genug beachtet und reflektiert worden.[15] Die gegenüber dem masoretischen Text und der Septuaginta entscheidende Änderung von 'Gaben-Empfangen' zu einem 'Geben von Gaben' findet sich auch im Targum zu den Psalmen, das zwar in seiner überlieferten Gestalt spät ist, aber auch ältere Auslegungstraditionen übernommen haben kann; denn die Deutung auf Mose, der zur Höhe aufsteigt, um die Tora in Empfang zu nehmen, ist auch noch in anderen rabbinischen Schriften bezeugt.[16] Darf man darum einen Einfluß jüdischer Interpretation annehmen, vielleicht im Zusammenhang mit dem Pfingstfest?

---

[15] Vgl. außer den Kommentaren B. Lindars, *New Testament Apologetic: The Doctrinal Significance of the Old Testament Quotations* (London, 1961), pp. 52–4; G. B. Caird, *art. cit.*; M. McNamara, *The New Testament and the Palestinian Targum to the Pentateuch* (Rom, 1966), pp. 78–81.

[16] Siehe bei P. Billerbeck, *Kommentar zum Neuen Testament aus Talmud und Midrasch* iii (München, 1926), S. 596–9; vgl. M. McNamara, *op. cit.*, 80.

B. Lindars meint, daß wahrscheinlich nur 'a real case of coincidence' vorliegt.[17] Aber es ist auffällig, daß der anschließende christliche Midrasch (V. 9f.) nicht das 'Geben' begründet, obwohl dieses der Angelpunkt des Gedankenganges ist, sondern den Text als solchen wie selbstverständlich voraussetzt. Was den Autor zu seinem Kommentar in V. 9f. veranlaßt, ist die Deutung des 'Aufgestiegenen' auf Christus. So hat er das ἔδωκεν sicher schon vorgefunden, und zwar, wie das oben Gesagte nahelegt, in einer jüdischen Auslegungstradition. Ihr gegenüber kam es dem christlichen Autor darauf an, den Text auf Christus zu beziehen. Da das Zitat im Neuen Testament einmalig ist, also in der älteren Gemeinde sicherlich noch keine Rolle spielte, dürfte es sich schon um eine spätere Stufe christlicher Schriftauswertung handeln, wie sie zum Teil (wieder mit anderen Schriftstellen, doch auch nicht unbeeinflußt vom jüdisch-haggadischen Schriftgebrauch) im Johannesevangelium begegnet.[18] Das Charakteristische für diese urchristliche Schriftinterpretation ist immer der christologische Bezug.

Spielt unsere Stelle auf das christliche Pfingsten an? Das wäre der Fall, wenn man der Auslegung G. B. Cairds folgen dürfte, der erklärt: 'It is a Christian Pentecostal psalm, celebrating the ascension of Christ and his subsequent descent at Pentecost to bestow spiritual gifts upon the church.'[19] Aber V. 9–10 lassen sich nicht auf ein *nachfolgendes* Herabsteigen Christi beziehen. Wenn diese Exegese für V. 9 noch möglich ist, so wird sie durch V. 10 zunichte gemacht. Denn die Aussage dieses Verses tendiert auf den Aufstieg Christi, 'um das All zu erfüllen'. Außerdem wäre es einmalig, wenn die pfingstliche Ausgießung des Geistes direkt als Herabkunft Christi bezeichnet würde (vgl. αὐτός); Christus würde dann völlig mit dem Geist identifiziert werden, und das ist weder bei Paulus (auch nicht in 2. Kor. 3: 17) noch bei Johannes (vgl. 14: 16f. mit 18–20; 20: 22) der Fall. Diese Exegese hat auch nicht viel Zustimmung erfahren.[20]

---

[17] *Op. cit.*, 52f.

[18] Für Jo. 7: 38 ist das durch sorgfältige Forschungen nachgewiesen, vgl. R. Schnackenburg, *Das Johannesevangelium* ii (Herders Theol. Komm. zum NT iv/2, Freiburg–Basel–Wien, 1971), S. 215–17. Ein weiteres Beispiel ist Jo. 19: 37; vgl. dazu meinen Beitrag 'Das Schriftzitat in Joh. 19: 37' für die Festschrift für J. Ziegler (Würzburg, 1972).

[19] *Art. cit.*, 541.

[20] Doch wurde diese Auffassung schon im vorigen Jahrhundert vertreten; dagegen wandte sich E. Haupt, *Die Gefangenschaftsbriefe* (Meyers Kommentarwerk 8, Göttingen, ⁸1902), *ad loc.*; in der Gegenwart auch J. J. Meuzelaar, *Der Leib des Messias* (Assen, 1961), S. 136f.

Für V. 9 stehen sich noch immer hauptsächlich zwei Erklärungen gegenüber: die seit dem Altertum weit verbreitete und bis heute einflußreiche[21] Deutung auf den Abstieg Christi in die Unterwelt, das Totenreich, und die Auffassung, daß der christliche Midrasch in V. 9f. den im Zitat genannten ἀναβάς auf Christus deuten will, der in die Niederung der Erde herabgekommen und dann 'über alle Himmel' aufgestiegen ist. Die letztgennante Auffassung scheint mir aus folgenden Gründen den Vorzug zu verdienen: (*a*) Der Kommentar von V. 9f. will das Wort ἀναβάς interpretieren und auf Christus hin auslegen. Es ist eine auf den Text bezogene Exegese nach jüdischer Methode. Das wird durch den Anfang von V. 11 bestätigt: Nachdem der ἀναβάς bestimmt ist, wendet sich die Erklärung dem ἔδωκεν zu. (*b*) Das Anliegen des Verfassers wird verständlicher, wenn er sich einer jüdischen Exegese gegenübersieht, die den Vers auf Mose bezog. (*c*) Aber warum sagt der Autor dann nicht einfach: Dieser Hinaufgestiegene ist Christus, ähnlich wie Paulus den mitwandernden Fels in 1. Kor. 10: 4 auf Christus deutet, oder wie der Epheser-Autor selbst in 5: 31f. Gen. 2: 24 auf Christus und die Kirche bezieht? Wahrscheinlich deshalb, weil er mit der Erklärung in V. 9f. noch eine tiefere Absicht verfolgt. Der in den Himmel aufgefahrene Christus soll zugleich in seiner überragenden Stellung (auch in seiner Mose übertreffenden Bedeutung?) aufgezeigt werden. Es ist das gleiche Anliegen, das er schon in 1: 20–3 verriet: Christus ist der herrscherlich zur Rechten Gottes Inthronisierte und damit zugleich das Haupt der Kirche, die sein Leib ist. (*d*) Der merkwürdige Ausdruck τὰ κατώτερα μέρη τῆς γῆς erklärt sich wahrscheinlich aus dem gleichen christologischen Denken, das auch den Christushymnus von Phil. 2: 6–11 leitet: Das Kommen auf die Erde ist für den, der vorher bei Gott in gottgleicher Würde weilte, eine tiefe Erniedrigung, die dann allerdings zu einer überhohen Erhebung geführt hat. Das Hinabsteigen in die 'tieferen Teile, nämlich auf die Erde' (gen. apposit.) ist der stärkste Kontrast zu dem Aufstieg 'über alle Himmel empor'. (*e*) Das bedeutet aber keineswegs einen Abstieg in ein unter der Erde befindliches Gebiet (das Totenreich). Wenn es der Sinn des Ab- und Aufstiegs ist, 'das All zu erfüllen', könnte nur an eine Bezwingung unterirdischer

---

[21] Siehe u. a. E. F. Scott, *ad loc.*; J. Huby, *S. Paul, Les Épîtres de la Captivité* (Verbum Salutis viii, Paris, [19]1947), p. 210; F. Büchsel im *TWNT* iii (Stuttgart, 1938), S. 641–3; Ch. Masson, *L'Épître de S. Paul aux Éphésiens* (Comm. du N.T. ix, Neuchâtel–Paris, 1953), p. 190; M. McNamara, *op. cit.*, 81.

Mächte gedacht sein. Für das Weltbild des Epheser-Autors muß das ausgeschlossen werden, weil er die widergöttlichen geistigen Mächte in den unteren Himmeln, der Luftregion, lokalisiert (vgl. 2: 2; 6: 12). In Phil. 2: 9 empfängt der im Himmel inthronisierte Christus zwar die Huldigung der 'Himmlischen, der Irdischen und der Unterirdischen'; aber die letzte Gruppe wird im Eph. nicht genannt. Vielmehr sind die in 1: 21 genannten Mächte, die Christus zu Füßen gelegt sind, die gleichen, denen in 3: 10 ihr Aufenthalts- und Wirkbereich ausdrücklich 'in den Himmeln' zugewiesen wird.[22]

Bei dieser Auslegung läßt sich eine unmittelbare Anspielung auf das christliche Pfingsten nicht erkennen. In seinem Kommentar zu dem Schriftzitat in V. 9f. zeigt der Verfasser ein ausgesprochen christologisches Interesse; eine liturgische Reminiszenz wird nicht erkennbar. Möglich bleibt noch, daß das Schriftzitat zur Deutung des Pfingstereignisses beigezogen wurde; aber auch das ist wenig wahrscheinlich, weil gerade der Geist nicht genannt wird.

Bei den 'Gefangenen', die der in die Höhe Aufsteigende nach dem Schriftzitat macht, denkt der Autor natürlich an die widergöttlichen Gewalten, und dieser Gedanke wird auch bei dem 'Erfüllen des Alls' von V. 10 nachklingen. Aber er übergeht diesen Gedanken hier rasch (anders als in 1: 21–2a), weil es ihm im Zusammenhang auf die andere Funktion des siegreich aufgestiegenen Christus ankommt: das Gaben-Austeilen an seine Kirche. Auch in 1: 22b–23, am Ende jener ersten Ausführung über die Erhöhung Christi, konzentrierte sich der Blick auf die Kirche, den Segensbereich des herrscherlichen Christus (seine von ihm durchwaltete 'Fülle'). Auf das Heilswerk, das Christus in und mit seiner Kirche durchführen will, und nicht auf die Niederwerfung der gottfeindlichen Gewalten (die nur die Voraussetzung und Kehrseite seiner Heilsherrschaft ist), legt der Verfasser den Nachdruck. Doch in 4: 7–16 beherrscht der ekklesiale Aspekt ganz und gar die Gedankenführung, und dazu bietet ihm das 'Gaben-Geben' des Schriftzitats den Ansatzpunkt. Man erkennt dieses Interesse schon

---

[22] Zu ἐν τοῖς ἐπουρανίοις siehe den Exkurs bei H. Schlier, *Der Epheserbrief*, S. 45–8. – F. Büchsel, *art. cit.* 642, argumentiert von Eph. 1: 20 her, daß das Eingehen Christi ins Totenreich, nicht die sieghafte Unterweltsfahrt eines Himmelswesens gemeint sei. Aber im Zusammenhang mit dem Zitat und dem Hinblick auf den ἵνα-Satz V. 10 wäre diese Emphase schwer verständlich. Wenn der ἀναβάς auf Christus gedeutet werden soll, ist seine Herabkunft auf die Erde viel näherliegend, weil dieser Gedanke eine breitere Basis in der urkirchlichen Christologie hat, vgl. besonders das Johannesevangelium.

äußerlich an der gehäuften Wortfolge: ἐδόθη – τῆς δωρεᾶς τοῦ Χριστοῦ (V. 7) – ἔδωκεν δόματα (V. 8) – αὐτὸς ἔδωκεν (V. 11). Da das Schriftzitat begründend eingeführt wird (διὸ λέγει), kann kein Zweifel sein, daß es dem Verfasser nur um dieses Schenken Christi geht, im Schriftzitat also aller Nachdruck auf dem ἔδωκεν δόματα liegt.

DIE GABEN CHRISTI FÜR SEINE KIRCHE

Die Gaben Christi, die er nach seiner 'Himmelfahrt', das heißt nach seiner Auferstehung und (der damit eng verbundenen) Einsetzung im Himmel (vgl. 1: 20),[23] seiner Kirche gibt, werden in V. 11 konkret auf die dort genannten Amtsträger gedeutet. Es heißt nicht, daß Christus ihnen Geschenke gab, sondern daß er sie selbst als seine Gaben für den Aufbau seines Leibes gab. In dem ganzen Abschnitt kommt es dem Verfasser auf diese Männer an, die einen besonderen Dienst in der Kirche ausüben, obwohl er letztlich den ganzen Leib, der sich von Christus, dem Haupt, her in Liebe aufbaut, im Blick hat (V. 16). Aber die in dem eigentümlichen Leib-Bild von V. 16 genannten 'Unter-stützungsbänder' (διὰ πάσης ἁφῆς τῆς ἐπιχορηγίας), die den ganzen Leib zusammenfügen und zusammenhalten, können wieder nur jene Dienst-Ausübenden sein.

Darum dürften schon in V. 7 diese Amtsträger angesprochen werden – entgegen einer verbreiteten Auffassung, die 'jeden einzelnen von uns' auf alle Gläubigen beziehen möchte.[24] Diese exegetische Streitfrage hat für die besondere, von Paulus in gewisser Weise abweichende Sicht des Epheser-Autors ein erhebliches Gewicht, da sie sein Amtsverständnis betrifft. Folgende Gründe scheinen mir für die engere Deutung auf die Amtsträger zu sprechen: (*a*) Mit V. 7 beginnt nach dem fast doxologi-schen Abschluß in V. 6 ein neuer, weiterführender Gedankengang. Das wird auch durch δέ angezeigt. Diese Konjunktion soll schwerlich

---

[23] Die sichtbare Himmelfahrt im lukanischen Sinn ist nicht vorausgesetzt. Das 'Hinaufsteigen' Christi ereignet sich für den Verfasser in der Auferstehung, die sogleich – ohne ein erkennbares zeitliches Intervall – zur himmlischen Inthronisation wird. Die lukanische Himmelfahrt mit Darstellungsmitteln einer sichtbaren Entrückung ist eine spezielle, von Lukas entwickelte An-schauung. Vgl. G. Lohfink, *Die Himmelfahrt Jesu: Untersuchungen zu den Himmelfahrts- und Erhöhungstexten bei Lukas* (München, 1971), besonders S. 87.

[24] So die meisten neueren Ausleger außer H. Schlier, *Der Epheserbrief*, S. 191, der mir das Richtige zu sehen scheint, auch wenn er Eph. 4: 7, 11 undiffe-renziert neben Röm. 12: 5f. und 1. Kor. 12: 28 stellt.

die vorher genannten πάντες unter dem Aspekt 'jeder einzelne' neu in den Blick bringen, sondern sie hebt den ganzen Abschnitt V. 1–6 vom folgenden ab. (*b*) Das wird durch den Wechsel der Personalpronomina bestätigt. In V. 1–6 waren durchweg die Adressaten in der zweiten Person angesprochen; jetzt redet der Verfasser in der ersten Person (ἡμῶν). Erst nach der Ausführung über die Amtsträger stoßen wir in V. 13 auf einen Wir-Stil, bei dem die Adressaten mitgemeint sind; aber da ist bezeichnenderweise hinzugesetzt οἱ πάντες. (*c*) Die in V. 7 genannte χάρις ist nicht die allen Christen verliehene Erlösungsgnade (vgl. 1:7; 2:5, 8), sondern die spezielle Gnadengabe, die zur Ausübung eines Dienstes verliehen wird. Die nächste Parallele ist 3:8, wo 'Paulus' über sein Verkündigungsamt spricht (ἐμοὶ ... ἐδόθη ἡ χάρις αὕτη). Auch die δωρεά Christi, nach deren Maß jene Gnade jedem einzelnen verliehen wurde, findet in 3:7 eine Parallele, nur daß hier von der δωρεά Gottes die Rede ist. (*d*) Der Satz von V. 7 soll durch das Schriftzitat in V. 8 begründet werden (διὸ λέγει). Das darin genannte 'Gaben-Geben' aber wird dann in V. 11 klar und eindeutig auf die Amtsträger gedeutet. Dadurch ist die Aussage von V. 7 an das Folgende gebunden und muß von daher interpretiert werden. (*e*) Unsere Deutung wird nochmals durch V. 16 bestätigt; denn hier stoßen wir bei 'jedem Band der Unterstützung', das auf die Amtsträger zu beziehen ist, auf eine sehr ähnliche Formulierung: ἐν μέτρῳ ἑνὸς ἑκάστου μέρους. Diese Beifügung ist eine unverkennbare Wiederaufnahme von V. 7, eine nochmalige Erinnerung, daß 'jeder einzelne', der in der Gemeinde und für die Gemeinde einen Dienst erfüllt, dies doch nur gemäß der ihm verliehenen Gnade, aus der Kraft und Bestimmung, die ihm von Christus verliehen wurde, tun kann.

Paulus freilich gebraucht ähnliche Formulierungen wie in Eph. 4:7 für die ganze Gemeinde beziehungsweise alle Charismatiker in ihr; für Korinth gewinnt man den Eindruck, daß jedes Gemeindemitglied mit irgendeinem Charisma begabt ist (vgl. 1. Kor. 1:7; 7:7; 12:4–6, 13, 27). Für alle Charismatiker sagt der Apostel: 'All das wirkt ein und derselbe Geist, der jedem für sich zuteilt, wie er will' (12:11); oder in Röm. 12:6: 'Wir haben aber verschiedene Charismen *gemäß der Gnade, die uns verliehen ist* ...'. Außer der besonderen Gnade des Apostelamtes, die Paulus für sich selbst öfters hervorhebt (Gal. 2:9; Röm. 1:5; 12:3; 15:15; 1. Kor. 3:10; Phil. 1:7), betrachtet er also auch die Befähigungen anderer Christen als gleicherweise von Gott verliehene 'Gnaden' oder Charismen. Die Charismenliste in 1. Kor. 12:

10-2

28 enthält außer der ersten Gruppe 'Apostel, Propheten und Lehrer' noch eine ganze Reihe von anderen charismatischen Fähigkeiten, die sämtlich dem gemeinsamen Nutzen (vgl. 12: 7), dem Aufbau der Gemeinde (vgl. 14: 4f., 12) dienen sollen. Auch in der Charismenliste Röm. 12: 6–8 werden neben Prophetie und Lehre noch mannigfache andere Charismen (vor allem diakonische) genannt. In Eph. 4: 11 dagegen haben wir eine kategorische Aufzählung von fünf Gruppen vor uns, die der himmlische Herr seiner Gemeinde als seine Gaben für ihren Aufbau gegeben hat. Außerdem ist folgendes beachtlich: Keine Andeutung, daß es sich nur um eine exemplarische Auswahl handelt; fünf offenbar festgeprägte Bezeichnungen; schließlich Ausdrücke, die sämtlich und ausschließlich auf Verkündigung und Lehre beziehungsweise Leitung der Gemeinde ('Hirten') hinweisen. Umstritten ist es, ob die 'Hirten und Lehrer', die gemeinsam unter einem Artikel genannt werden, zwei verschiedene Gruppen oder den gleichen Personenkreis betreffen; doch hat diese Frage für unsere Betrachtung kein großes Gewicht.[25]

Man muß darum bezweifeln, daß Eph. 4: 11 einfach eine Charismenliste ist wie die in 1. Kor. 12: 28 und Röm. 12:6–8. Sie ist auf bestimmte Dienste reduziert, die der Verfasser für besonders dringlich, ja (als 'Gaben' Christi) für unentbehrlich hält, um den Aufbau des Leibes Christi zu ermöglichen. Die an erster Stelle genannten 'Apostel und Propheten' haben für ihn sogar eine 'fundamentale' Bedeutung, da auf ihnen der ganze 'Gottesbau im Geiste' aufgerichtet ist; sie sind und bleiben das Fundament, während Christus selbst der Eck- oder Schlußstein ist, der dem ganzen Gebäude den Zusammenhalt gibt und seinen weiteren Aufbau ermöglicht (2: 20–2).[26] Schaut man nun die

[25] Man wird mit Dibelius–Greeven, Schlier und J. Gnilka (alle *ad loc.*) eher dafür plädieren müssen, daß Hirten und Lehrer zwei verschiedene Personengruppen sind. Die Lehraufgabe wird erst in den Pastoralbriefen den Presbytern, die (kollegial) die Gemeinden leiten, zugesprochen. Die Bezeichnung 'Presbyter' fehlt im Eph. wie in allen Paulusbriefen. Dann ist es um so bedeutsamer, daß die 'Hirten' den Lehrern vorangestellt werden.

[26] Zu dem Bild vgl. außer den Kommentaren besonders J. Pfammatter, *Die Kirche als Bau* (Rom, 1960), S. 78–107 und 140–51; F. Mußner, in: *Neutestamentliche Aufsätze* (Festschrift für J. Schmid, Regensburg, 1963), S. 191–4; B. Gärtner, *The Temple and the Community in Qumran and the New Testament* (Cambridge, 1965), S. 60–6; G. Klinzing, *Die Umdeutung des Kultus in der Qumrangemeinde und im Neuen Testament* (Göttingen, 1971), S. 184–91. – Die Deutung des ἀκρογωνιαῖος (Eckstein oder Schlußstein?) ist immer noch kontrovers. Der auf J. Jeremias zurückgehenden Deutung auf den krönenden Schlußstein (*TWNT* i, 792f.; iv, 278f.) haben sich viele Ausleger angeschlossen,

drei weiteren Bezeichnungen an, kann man kaum der Folgerung entgehen, daß die 'Evangelisten, Hirten und Lehrer' die maßgeblichen Amtsträger zur Zeit und im Blickkreis des Verfassers sind. Wahrscheinlich will er die entscheidenden Dienste für das Leben und Wirken der Kirche vollständig aufführen, da keinerlei Fortsetzung angedeutet ist und für die anschließende Darstellung ihre Funktionen vollkommen ausreichen. Man darf aufgrund von 2: 20–2 sogar vermuten, daß die Apostel und Propheten (vgl. auch 3: 5) zu seiner Zeit schon Größen der Vergangenheit oder doch im Aussterben begriffen waren. Sie werden in 4: 11 aber an der Spitze mitaufgeführt, weil sie die ersten und 'grundlegenden' Gaben des Herrn an seine Kirche waren. Ihnen schließen sich die 'Evangelisten, Hirten und Lehrer' an, ohne daß ein Unterschied markiert wird. Gewiß haben sie nicht die gleiche Bedeutung wie die Apostel und Propheten, deren Rang durch die Reihenfolge gewahrt bleibt; aber auch sie werden gleicherweise als Gaben des Herrn für seine Kirche betrachtet, sie stehen in der gleichen Linie, mehr noch: sie übernehmen die wesentlichen Funktionen der Apostel und Propheten, nämlich Verkündigung und Lehre und, damit eng verbunden, die Leitung der Gemeinden. Die Evangelisten, in der neutestamentlichen Literatur nur noch in Apg. 21: 8 (Philippus) und 2. Tim. 4: 5 (der Briefempfänger) genannt, sind offenbar Verkündiger, die nicht den Rang eines Apostels haben, aber die apostolische Verkündigung fortsetzen. Sie sind sicher in einem größeren Gebiet, jedenfalls über einzelne Gemeinden hinaus tätig. Dagegen sind die 'Hirten und Lehrer' die ortsgebundenen Amtsträger in den Gemeinden.

Diese Beobachtungen lassen sich im Vergleich mit 1. Kor. 12: 28 noch präzisieren. In der Liste von 1. Kor. 12: 28 stehen am Anfang drei Bezeichnungen, die durch diese Stellung und durch eine nummerierte Aufzählung hervorgehoben sind: 'Gott bestimmte in der Kirche erstens Apostel, zweitens Propheten, drittens Lehrer.' Diese Trias dürfte Paulus schon vorgegeben sein; wahrscheinlich war sie auch sonst bekannt und spielte überhaupt für die Anfangszeit eine große Rolle. Die Apostel waren die bevollmächtigten Verkündiger und Missionare, die Propheten die in nicht wenigen Gemeinden und im Gesamtraum der Kirche tätigen Geistträger, die mancherlei 'Offen-

---

zuletzt J. Gnilka *ad loc.*; dagegen verteidigen die Deutung auf den Eckstein u. a. J. Pfammatter, *op. cit.*; F. Mußner, *art. cit.*; K. Th. Schäfer, 'Zur Deutung von ἀκρογωνιαῖος in Eph. 2: 20', in: *Neutestamentliche Aufsätze* (Festschrift für J. Schmid, Regensburg, 1963), S. 218–24; R. J. McKelvey, 'Christ the Cornerstone', in: *NTS* viii (1961–2), S. 352–9.

barung' und Weisung, Deutung und Ermutigung gaben, die Lehrer schließlich die in allen Gemeinden notwendigen Interpreten und Befestiger des Evangeliums, Tradenten der apostolischen Verkündigung und Lehre.[27] Wahrscheinlich liegt der Liste in Eph. 4: 11 immer noch diese alte Trias zugrunde, doch jetzt charakteristisch erweitert. Die Apostel und Propheten sind das Fundament geblieben; aber da sie größtenteils schon der Vergangenheit angehören, setzen Evangelisten, Hirten und Lehrer die weiterhin notwendigen Aufgaben fort. Dabei tritt als besondere und wichtige Funktion die Leitung der Gemeinden hervor; sie wird auch in anderen neutestamentlichen Dokumenten unter dem Hirtenbild hervorgehoben.[28] In den paulinischen Missionsgemeinden hatten in der Gründungszeit die 'Sich-Abmühenden' und 'Vorstehenden' nur eine geringere Bedeutung (vgl. 1. Thess. 5: 12f.; 1. Kor. 16: 15f.). Das wurde mit dem Tod des Apostels anders; die Gemeinden mußten zu einer strafferen Verfassung auf örtlicher Ebene übergehen. In diese Zeit gehört auch der Epheserbrief. Das Leitungsamt ist auf dem Weg zur Verselbständigung und erlangt größere Bedeutung, vor allem für die innere Einheit der Gemeinde und die Festigung im Glauben (vgl. Eph. 4: 14). So müssen die Hirten auch Lehrer sein oder Männer neben sich haben, die die apostolische Tradition und Lehre zuverlässig weitergeben.[29]

Aus dem Gesagten ergibt sich eine bestimmte Sicht des Verfassers auf das Verhältnis von Christus und Kirche, Geist und Amt. Die Einheit der Gemeinde, die ihm so sehr am Herzen liegt, ist für ihn kein menschliches Werk, sondern im Ursprung der Kirche aus Christus und in ihrer engen Verbindung mit Christus, ihrem Haupt, begründet. Die in der *einen* Taufe und in dem *einen* Glauben an den *einen* Herrn manifestierte, durch den *einen* Geist bewirkte Einheit muß aber auch im Leben der Gemeinde festgehalten (4: 3) und in ihrer Existenz inmitten der Welt verwirklicht werden. Denn trotz aller hohen

---

[27] Vgl. H. Greeven, 'Propheten, Lehrer, Vorsteher bei Paulus', in: *ZNW* xliv (1952/3), S. 1–43.

[28] Vgl. Apg. 20: 28; 1. Petr. 5: 2f.; Jo. 21: 15–17; auch die ἡγούμενοι von Hebr. 13: 7, 17, 24; vgl. Lk. 22: 26 sind hier zu nennen. Zur Bezeichnung der Führer der Gemeinden als Hirten vgl. J. Jeremias im *TWNT* vi (1959), S. 497.

[29] Die in Eph. 4: 11 genannten Ämter werden näher besprochen und in die urkirchliche Entwicklung eingeordnet bei H. Merklein, *Das kirchliche Amt nach dem Epheserbrief* (ungedr. Dissertation Würzburg, 1971). Manche Anregungen für den obigen Beitrag verdanke ich dieser Untersuchung.

theologischen Gedanken über die Kirche sieht der Verfasser die irdische Gemeinde wie ein Schiff auf schwankenden Wogen bedroht, durch das 'Würfelspiel' der Menschen heimtückisch dem Irrtum ausgesetzt (V. 14).

In dieser Situation liegt ihm daran, die in den Gemeinden wirkenden Amtsträger, die Evangelisten, Hirten und Lehrer, zu stärken. Der Geist übt durch diese Männer eine zweifache Funktion aus: Er sorgt für die Weitergabe, Bewahrung und Vertiefung der apostolischen Tradition, und er wirkt auf die Einheit der Gemeinde hin. Das erste ergibt sich aus dem Zusammenhang von 4: 12–16, aber auch aus der ganzen Anlage des Schreibens und dem darin zutage tretenden Selbstverständnis des Verfassers. Denn es dürfte sich um das pseudonyme Schreiben eines Mannes handeln, der in paulinischer Lehrtradition stehend, selbst tiefe Einsichten in das Christusgeheimnis gewonnen hat (vgl. 3: 3) und sich unter die Autorität des großen Heidenapostels stellt (vgl. 3: 8). Auf die Einheit der Gemeinde wirken diese Hirten und Lehrer gerade durch ihre Bewahrung der apostolischen Lehre und Tradition hin.

Damit öffnet sich auch ein wenig der Hintergrund des Schreibens: Es stammt aus einer Zeit des Übergangs von der apostolischen zur nachapostolischen Epoche und spricht in eine Situation hinein, in der die aus ehemaligen Juden und Heiden zusammengesetzte Gemeinde in mancherlei Anfechtung steht, die ihre Einheit bedroht. Um die inneren Spannungen und äußeren Gefahren zu überwinden, entwickelt der Autor eine tiefe Theologie der Kirche und, verbunden damit, auch eine Theologie des Amtes. Auf paulinischen Gedanken aufbauend, setzt er doch neue Akzente, die in den fortgeschrittenen Verhältnissen seiner Zeit nötig wurden. Er nimmt seine Leser in eine Sicht auf Christus und Kirche, Geist und Amt hinein, die auch heute noch ihre Bedeutung hat, nicht zuletzt für das ökumenische Anliegen.

Christus, Geist und Gemeinde (Eph. 4: 1–16)

R. SCHNACKENBURG

The importance of the Spirit in Ephesians tends to be overlooked because of the dominating interest in Christ and the church. But in fact the author uses the idea of the Spirit in a wide range of applications, which suggests that he stands at the end of a process of theological reflection. He is dependent on Colossians for much of his thought, but not bound by it. The most important passage for his teaching on the Spirit in relation to the exalted Christ and the life of the church is 4: 1–16.

The author's chief aim is to promote the unity of the church (4: 3), for which the Spirit is the operative factor and the abiding principle. This idea is derived from Paul's teaching on baptism (1 Cor. 12: 13). There is one Spirit, just as there is one Body. Christ is the Head, at work in the Body through the Spirit (cf. 2: 22). This idea is already apparent in 2: 14–18, where the diverse elements which go to make the church are brought into unity through the death of Christ. They are reconciled to God and to one another through his cross, so that by his work through the Spirit they may have equal access to the Father.

Christ is no longer with the church in person, for he has ascended on high (4: 8 = Ps. 68: 19). The author takes advantage of Jewish traditions of this citation, which he exposes in the Jewish manner, first by interpretation of ἀναβάς and then by interpretation of ἔδωκεν. It is a mistake to see here an allusion to the event of Pentecost. It is rather a christological assertion, the risen Christ being conceived of as enthroned. But the central interest is Christ's gifts to the church.

These gifts are not spiritual qualities or abilities, but the men themselves who hold office in the church. Unlike the charismata-lists of Rom. 12: 6–8 and 1 Cor. 12: 4–11, the gifts enumerated here are definite functionaries, who are indispensable for the structure and well-being of the church. Apostles and prophets are mentioned first, but they belong to the early days. The other three ministries, evangelists, pastors and teachers, no doubt reflect the conditions of the writer's own day, after the death of Paul, when the functionaries who replace the original apostles assume increasing ecclesiastical importance.

Ephesians belongs to the time of transition from the apostolic to the sub-apostolic age, when the church, composed of both Jews and Gentiles, is threatened by divisive forces. To cope with this situation the author develops the theology of the church, and with it a theology of the ministry as Christ's gift to the church, building on and extending the teaching of Paul himself.

20

Christus und Geist im Kolosserbrief

E. SCHWEIZER

C. F. D. Moule hat in seinem Kommentar zu Kol. 1:8 schon angemerkt, daß in diesem Brief 'praktisch nichts über den heiligen Geist gesagt ist'.[1] Vielleicht macht es ihm daher ein wenig Freude, wenn ich seine Anregung aufnehme und dem damit gestellten Problem etwas nachgehe. Meine eigentliche Absicht dabei ist nicht, die Verfasserfrage neu aufzurollen. Fiele es mir sowieso schon schwer, dem ganzen Charme des Jubilars, seiner tiefen Güte und Bescheidenheit zu widerstehen und etwas anderes zu behaupten als er,[2] wäre das ausgerechnet in einem Geburtstagsartikel doppelt schwierig. Mein Anliegen ist das theologische Problem, wie es dazu kommt, daß Paulus oder sein Schüler die Aussagen vom Geist derart zurücktreten lassen kann. Das schließt die Frage ein, in welcher Weise er diese durch andere Aussagen ersetzt. Um der Einfachheit willen verwende ich im Folgenden 'Paulus' und 'paulinisch' nur für die allgemein anerkannten Briefe (Röm., 1., 2. Kor., Gal., Phil., 1. Thess., Phlm.), ohne damit den Entscheid über die Echtheit oder Unechtheit des Kolosserbriefs schon vorwegzunehmen.

1. DIE KRAFT DES NEUEN LEBENS

Das Zurücktreten der Geistaussagen wird schon im ersten Abschnitt, in der Danksagung für den Stand des Gemeindelebens und der Fürbitte sichtbar. Den Ausdruck 'Frucht bringen' (Kol. 1:6) kann auch Paulus verwenden (Röm. 7:4f.). Freilich ist für Paulus Frucht nicht an sich schon positiv zu werten. Man kann ebenso 'Gott' wie 'dem Tode' Frucht bringen. Wenn es sich daher um das erste handelt, dann ist es Wundergeschehen, Leben 'in der Neuheit des Geistes'

---

[1] The Cambridge Greek Testament Commentary, Cambridge, 1958, S. 52 (meine Übersetzung).

[2] Während C. F. D. Moule, *op. cit.*, 13f. vorsichtig für paulinische Autorschaft eintritt, bestätigen mir die in diesem Aufsatz gezeigten Tatsachen meine Sicht, daß zwar nichts eindeutig dagegen spricht, daß aber die Annahme eines Schreibens eines Paulusschülers wesentlich wahrscheinlicher ist.

(Röm. 7: 6). So spricht denn auch Gal. 5: 22 von der 'Frucht des Geistes'. Noch eindrücklicher ist der Vergleich mit der Danksagung und Fürbitte am Anfang des 1. Thessalonicherbriefes, wo gleich zu Beginn nicht nur auf die 'Fülle' des Gemeindelebens, sondern vor allem auch auf den 'heiligen Geist' hingewiesen ist (1: 5). Man wird den Unterschied nicht überbewerten; denn das Subjekt des Frucht-bringens ist ja im Kolosserbrief das 'Evangelium' mit seinem 'Wort der Wahrheit' und erst von da aus dann auch die Gemeinde (1: 10). Daß dabei nur in positivem Sinn von Frucht gesprochen werden kann, ist ja selbstverständlich. Vor allem aber zeigt die Wendung, daß der Verfasser durchaus noch um die tiefere Verwurzelung des ganzen Gemeindelebens im Handeln Gottes weiß. Es bleibt bei ihm festge-halten, daß es sich dabei nicht um ein selbständig gewordenes, von Gottes Handeln losgelöstes moralisches Verhalten handelt. Aber es ist an die Kraft des Wortes erinnert, nicht an die des Geistes. Natürlich sind auch für Paulus 'Jesus', 'Geist' und 'Evangelium' so etwas wie Synonymbegriffe (2. Kor. 11: 4). Immerhin merken wir an, daß hier nur der letzte Ausdruck aufgenommen ist, während der Hinweis auf den Geist ganz fallen gelassen ist – vielleicht darum, weil 'Wort' oder 'Evangelium' leichter festlegbar, bestimmbar, gegen Verfälschung abschirmbar ist als 'Geist'.

In Kol. 1: 12 wird auf den 'Vater' verwiesen, der die Gemeinde 'befähigt' hat für das 'Los der Heiligen im Licht'. Abgesehen von der stark mit den Qumranschriften und der Bekehrungsterminologie von Apg. 26: 18[3] verwandten Sprache dieser Verse, die wahrscheinlich auf liturgische Vorlagen zurückgeht, ist wiederum darauf aufmerksam zu machen, daß 2. Kor. 3: 6 dasselbe Verbum steht, daß es dort aber 'der Dienst des Geistes, nicht des Buchstabens' ist, zu dem der Apostel durch Gott befähigt wird. Das Ziel der 'Befähigung' wird also bei Paulus als dynamisches Geschehen unter der Herrschaft des Geistes, in Gegensatz zum festlegbaren, fixierten 'Buchstaben' beschrieben, im Kolosserbrief als ein Raum, in den hinein man definitiv versetzt ist. Wieder ist die Differenz nicht zu überziehen. Einmal ist im zweiten Korintherbrief vom Apostel, im Kolosserbrief von der Gemeinde die Rede. Vor allem aber ist hier liturgische Sprache verwendet, die gerne in der Kategorie der von einander geschiedenen 'Räume' des Heiligen und Unheiligen, des Lichtes und der Finsternis denkt. So ist die Neigung zu verspüren, die Christologie stärker vom bleibenden Sein,

---

[3] F. F. Bruce, *Commentary on the Book of the Acts* (London, 1965), zur Stelle.

vom Statischen her anzugehen als vom Ereignis.[4] Doch mag auch dies auf liturgische Formulierungen zurückgehen.

In Kol. 1:11 wird das neue Leben der Gemeinde als ein solches in 'Kraft' (neben δύναμις steht auch das bei Paulus fehlende Wort κράτος) beschrieben, ähnlich in 1:29 das Wirken des Apostels (ἐνέργεια ... ἐνεργουμένη ... ἐν δυνάμει), überall ohne Hinweis auf den Geist. In einem vergleichbaren Kontext spricht Röm. 15:13, 19 von der 'Kraft des heiligen Geistes' in der Gemeinde und der 'Kraft des Geistes', die im Apostel wirkt. Auch nach 1. Thess. 1:5 wirkt das Wort des Apostels in 'Kraft und heiligem Geist und Fülle', nach 1. Kor. 2:4 'in Erweis des Geistes und der Kraft'. Erst recht ist beim Verbum der Rückweis auf den Geist Gottes üblich. Hat nach Röm. 7:5f. einst unter dem Gesetz die Sünde 'gewirkt', indem sie dem Tode Frucht brachte, so lebt die Gemeinde jetzt 'in der Neuheit des Geistes', nicht mehr unter dem 'Buchstaben'. Auch nach 1. Kor. 12:11 ist es 'der eine Geist', der alles 'wirkt' und jedem seine Gnadengabe zuteilt (vgl. noch Gal. 2:8f.). Wenn 2. Kor. 4:12 vom 'Wirken' des 'Lebens' im Gegensatz zu dem des 'Todes' die Rede ist, dann ist seit 3:6 klar, daß 'der Geist lebendigmacht, der Buchstabe aber tötet', und 4:13 weist denn auch nochmals auf 'den Geist des Glaubens' zurück. Auch in Gal. 3:5 ist Gottes 'Wirken von Krafttaten' unter den Galatern identisch mit der 'Darreichung des Geistes' durch ihn. Wiederum ist der Unterschied nicht radikal. Natürlich muß auch Paulus nicht jedesmal, wenn er von der Kraft des neuen Lebens oder des apostolischen Wirkens spricht, ausdrücklich auf den Geist hinweisen. Umgekehrt weiß auch der Kolosserbrief eindeutig, daß solche Kraft nie einfach menschliche Leistung, sondern eben die 'Macht der Herrlichkeit Gottes' ist. Dennoch ist, wenn man alle bisher genannten Stellen zusammennimmt, das Zurücktreten des Rückweises auf den Geist auffällig. Überall ist zwar festgehalten, daß Frucht, Fähigkeit und Vermögen der Gemeinde

---

[4] Bei Paulus erscheint Christus als Subjekt der Errettung: Gal. 1:4 und 1. Thess. 1:10; in Röm. 7:24f. (vgl. 2. Kor. 1:10) ist es Gott 'durch Christus', während hier Christus der 'König' des neuen Reiches ist und erst nachträglich noch als Urheber der 'Sündenvergebung' (so nicht bei Paulus) erscheint. Dazu kommt, daß der Hymnus Kol. 1:15–20 völlig auf den der Gemeinde gegenüberstehenden Erhöhten ausgerichtet ist und ihn anspricht, wobei nur zur Begründung seiner Würde auf seine Tätigkeit in Schöpfung und Erlösung zurückgegriffen wird. Wie es in der von ihm geschaffenen und umschlossenen Welt überhaupt zur Erlösungsbedürftigkeit kam, muß nicht gesagt werden, weil nicht heilsgeschichtlich erzählt, sondern der Erhöhte gepriesen wird (E. Schweizer in *E.K.K.*, Vorarbeiten, Neukirchen, 1969, 24f. = *Beiträge zur Theologie des NT*, 1970, 134ff.).

nie in ihr selbst begründet, von Gottes Handeln unabhängig, sind; aber es wird auch nicht ausdrücklich vom Geiste Gottes gesprochen, der in ihnen wirkt, sondern vom Wort der Wahrheit, das sie gehört haben, vom Los der Heiligen und dem Reich des Sohnes der Liebe, in das sie versetzt sind. Es scheint also eine gewisse Tendenz zu herrschen, eher von beschreibbaren, in der Verkündigung und Lehre einigermaßen begrenzbaren und gegen Irrlehre abzusichernden Gegebenheiten auszugehen als vom Wirken des unverfügbaren Geistes. Gegenüber Paulus scheint eine leise Verschiebung vom Dynamischen zum eher statisch Verstehbaren vorzuliegen, ohne daß dadurch die Aussagen geradezu unpaulinisch würden.

2. DIE NEUE ERKENNTNIS

Schon in Kol. 1:6 wird das neue Leben darauf begründet, daß die Kolosser 'die Gottesgnade in Wahrheit erkannt haben' (ἐπιγινώσκειν). Paulus verwendet das gleiche Verbum; doch ist volle Erkenntnis für ihn eigentlich erst im Eschaton möglich, nämlich so, daß Gott selbst uns erkennt (1. Kor. 13: 12). Darin gründet die Tatsache, daß unser Erkennen Gottes immer auf einer Bewegung Gottes auf uns hin beruht (schon vor dem Eschaton Gal. 4:9; vgl. 1. Kor. 8: 3). Wo also Erkenntnis schon hier möglich wird, da ist es der Geistträger (πνευματικός), der 'erkennt' (1. Kor. 14: 37). Nur der Geist schenkt Geistbegabten Erkenntnis Gottes 1. Kor. 2: 11 ff.; Röm. 8: 16. Im gleichen Kontext der Danksagung am Briefeingang wie Kol. 1: 6 weist 1. Thess. 1: 6 auf die Annahme des Wortes 'mit Freude des heiligen Geistes' hin. Immerhin fehlt dieser Hinweis auf den Geist auch in der Danksagung und Fürbitte von Phil. 1: 3–11, und wenn dort die Erkenntnis (ἐπίγνωσις 1: 9) als Funktion der Liebe zum Zweck des rechten Entscheidens (δοκιμάζειν) für das Handeln beschrieben ist, dann wird auch Kol. 1: 9f. diese praktische Ausrichtung der Erkenntnis deutlich sichtbar. Ähnliches gilt für den Vergleich von Kol. 1: 28 mit Röm. 15: 14. Nach beiden Stellen wirkt sich die Weisheit oder Erkenntnis vor allem in der Zurechtweisung der Brüder aus. Nun ist gewiß auch im Kolosserbrief nicht vergessen, daß solche Erkenntnis nur von Gott selbst geschenkt werden kann. Kol. 1: 27 sagt dies auch ausdrücklich, steht also in der Nähe von Stellen wie 1. Kor. 2: 1, 7, auch 13: 2 und 2. Kor. 4: 1ff. Freilich stehen alle diese paulinischen Stellen deutlich im Zusammenhang mit Ausführungen über das Wirken des Geistes, während es nach dem Kolosserbrief einfach Gott ist, der der Gemeinde 'das Geheimnis (nämlich Christus) kundtut'.[5] Auch hier ist also die Begründung aller Erkenntnis im Handeln Gottes nicht vergessen; wiederum fehlt aber jeglicher Hinweis auf den Geist. Dafür findet sich der Rückverweis auf die apostolische Verkündigung (1: 28) und vor allem die christologische Aussage, daß Christus selbst das 'Geheimnis Gottes' ist (1: 27; 2: 2) und darum alle 'Schätze der Weisheit und Erkenntnis' in sich birgt (2: 3).

Noch deutlicher wird dieser Sachverhalt, wo von 'Weisheit und Einsicht' (σοφία, σύνεσις) gesprochen wird (1: 9; 2: 2f.). Die Zusammenstellung erscheint auch 1. Kor. 1: 19, freilich als alttestamentliche Formel. Wiederum ist aber der Ton bei Paulus etwas verschieden. Zunächst steht nämlich für ihn die 'Weisheit' im Gegensatz zu 'Geist und Kraft' (1. Kor. 2: 4); doch präzisiert der Apostel im Folgenden, daß es die 'Weisheit der Menschen' ist, der die 'Kraft Gottes', die 'menschliche Weisheit', der die Lehre des 'Geistes', die 'fleischliche Weisheit', der die 'Gnade Gottes' entgegensteht (1. Kor. 2: 5, 13; 2. Kor. 1: 12). So gibt es denn auch für ihn eine 'Weisheit Gottes' (1. Kor. 1: 21, 24; 2: 7), die auch er mit Christus ineinssetzen kann (1. Kor. 1: 30: σοφία ... ἀπὸ θεοῦ).[6] Daß allerdings solche Weisheit immer vom Geist gegeben ist, sagt 1. Kor. 12: 8. Einerseits zeigt also der Kolosserbrief nichts mehr von der, freilich durch die korinthische Situation mitbedingten, Reserve des Paulus gegen alle Weisheit und Erkenntnis; andererseits spricht Paulus nicht von 'geistlicher Weisheit' wie Kol. 1: 9. Was das bedeutet, darüber werden wir im Abschnitt 5 nachzudenken haben; doch wird schon hier deutlich, daß der Kolosserbrief undialektischer von der in der Christologie ein für allemal gegebenen Erkenntnis und Weisheit reden kann, ohne auf das stets unverfügbare Geschehen des Geistes reflektieren zu müssen.

Auch der Kolosserbrief nennt Glaube und Hoffnung neben der Erkenntnis. In 1: 23, einer Mahnung, die an 1. Kor. 15: 58 erinnert, erscheinen beide Begriffe, in 2: 7 der Glaube. An beiden Stellen ist damit das *Bleiben* beim Evangelium, beim ihnen gelehrten Glauben

---

[5] Nicht direkt verwandt sind die Hinweise auf (eschatologische) Einzeloffenbarungen 1. Kor. 14: 2; 15: 51; Röm. 11: 25.

[6] Es ist aber wohl zu beachten, daß Paulus Christus nicht direkt mit der Weisheit Gottes identifiziert, als wäre sie gewissermaßen in ihm verfügbar vorhanden. Christus ist nach ihm 'für uns' 'von Gott her' zur Weisheit 'geworden'. Das heißt: nur im Ereignis des Handelns Gottes, das unseren Glauben schafft, wird die Gleichsetzung Wirklichkeit.

betont. Bei Paulus hingegen wird etwa Röm. 15: 13 das *Wachsen* in
der Hoffnung 'in der Kraft des heiligen Geistes', Gal. 5: 5 das *Warten*
auf die 'Hoffnung der Gerechtigkeit' aus Glauben 'kraft des Geistes'
betont,[7] und wenn der Apostel Gal. 3: 1ff. zum Bleiben im Glauben, ja
zur Rückkehr dazu aufruft, dann erinnert er ausführlich an den Empfang des Geistes, der es doch unmöglich macht, jetzt 'im Fleisch' zu
enden. Es zeigt sich also auch hier, daß Glaube und Hoffnung weniger
als etwas verstanden werden, auf das man eindeutig verweisen kann,
denn als etwas, das immer neu unter der Wirkung des Geistes wachsen
und gestaltet werden muß.

All dies ist nicht unpaulinisch. Paulus kann ebenfalls von Erkenntnis
und Weisheit reden, nicht nur von Glaube und Hoffnung. Es wird aber
deutlich, daß im Kolosserbrief die Aussagen über die rechte Erkenntnis
überwiegen, und daß dabei wohl einmal von 'geistlicher Weisheit und
Einsicht' die Rede ist, daß aber nie der Geist als die allen Glauben, alle
Hoffnung und alle Erkenntnis stets neu bewirkende Kraft erscheint.
An seine Stelle tritt die Christologie mit dem Hinweis darauf, daß in
ihr ein für allemal alle Geheimnisse gegeben sind. So wird denn auch
dort, wo von Glaube und Hoffnung gesprochen wird, eher von einem
Besitzstand ausgegangen, der durch das Evangelium und seine Lehre
gegeben ist, eher zum Bleiben als zum Wachsen aufgerufen. Wieder
darf der Tatbestand nicht karikiert werden; auch Kol. 1: 6, 10 spricht
vom Wachsen des Evangeliums in Kolossä und daher vom Wachsen
der Gemeinde in der Erkenntnis. Dennoch ist ein neuer Ton und das
Abrücken von der Pneumatologie zur Christologie hin nicht zu
überhören.

3. DER GRUND DES NEUEN LEBENS

Vielleicht zeigt sich dieser Tonunterschied gerade an der Stelle, die
deutlicher als irgendwo sonst die typisch paulinische Verbindung von
Indikativ und Imperativ enthält. Gal. 5: 25 lesen wir: 'Leben wir im
Geist, so laßt im Geist uns wandern (στοιχεῖν)', Kol. 2: 6: 'Wie ihr
Christus Jesus übernommen habt, so wandelt in ihm (περιπατεῖν).'
Beides ist nicht einfach dasselbe. Die Fortsetzung Kol. 2: 7 zeigt, daß
an den richtig gelehrten Glauben gedacht ist, den man ein für allemal

---

[7] Vgl. auch den Aufruf zum 'Werden' in 1. Kor. 15: 58, nicht zum 'Bleiben' (Kol.
1: 23); und den weithin uneschatologischen Charakter der Hoffnung im Kolosserbrief (G. Bornkamm, *Geschichte und Glaube* ii, München, 1971, pp. 206–13).

'übernommen' hat, und in dem man nun wandeln soll, während bei
Paulus vom nicht so einfach verfügbaren und festlegbaren Geist die
Rede ist, in dem sie schon immer 'leben' und nun 'wandern' sollen.
Ebenso steht die verwandte Stelle Phil. 3: 16 'Wohin wir gelangt sind,
darin laßt uns wandern' im Kontext der Aussage, daß auch Paulus
das Ziel nicht erreicht hat, sondern ihm nachjagt (V. 12–14). Wie in
Gal. 5: 25 ('leben'), ist also auch hier das Unterwegssein schon die
Voraussetzung der Mahnung und geht es nicht einfach darum, pauli-
nische Christologie zu 'übernehmen'. Ähnlich ist auch das 'Wandeln in
Weisheit' (Kol. 4: 5) zu beurteilen, nur daß hier die Verantwortung
gegenüber den Nichtchristen betont ist.[8] Nun wird bei Paulus überhaupt gerade beim Aufruf zum neuen Wandel (περιπατεῖν) der
Gegensatz des Wandels 'im Geist' zu dem 'im Fleisch' offen oder
latent thematisch. Am deutlichsten geschieht dies Röm. 8: 4; aber
auch Gal. 5: 16 redet vom 'Wandeln im Geist', 2. Kor. 12: 18 vom
'Wandeln im gleichen Geist'. Ohne daß der Gegenbegriff 'Geist'
ausdrücklich genannt wird, beschreibt 2. Kor. 10: 2f. das Leben des
Glaubens als ein 'Wandeln im', aber 'nicht nach dem Fleisch', und
der ordentliche Wandel von Röm. 13: 13 wird als 'Anziehen des
Herrn Jesus und nicht mehr nach dem Fleisch Leben' näher bestimmt,
während 14: 15 und 6: 4 vom Wandel in der Liebe und in der Neuheit
des Lebens reden. 1. Kor. 3: 3 bedeutet 'nach Menschenweise wandeln'
dasselbe wie 'nicht geistlich' (πνευματικός) sein.

Die Formulierung 'in ihm (Christus)' taucht auch Kol. 2: 10 in
Verbindung mit dem Verbum 'erfüllt sein' als Feststellung des
Standes der Kolosser auf. Wo Paulus vom 'Erfüllen' spricht, da denkt
er eher an ein noch zu Geschehendes als an etwas schon Erreichtes.
Gott (nicht Christus) 'erfüllt' mit Freude und Friede, damit die
Gemeinde wachse in der Hoffnung durch die Kraft des heiligen
Geistes (!)[9] (Röm. 15: 13).

Ähnliches läßt sich beim Aufruf, alles 'im Namen des Herrn Jesus'

---

[8] Gerade weil hier wie 2. Kor. 1: 12 an die Situation der Verkündigung gedacht ist,
ist bemerkenswert, daß Paulus dort erklärt, er sei 'nicht in fleischlicher' Weisheit'
gekommen. Da Paulus auch eine göttliche Weisheit kennt, die in seiner Verkündigung wirksam wird, ist dies kein absoluter Gegensatz; doch setzt der
Kolosserbrief die rechte Christologie und die rechte Weisheit weit fragloser
als der Paulus der Korintherbriefe einfach voraus.

[9] Vielleicht ist zu vergleichen, wie Kol. 3: 13f. vom 'Begnaden' (χαρίζεσθαι) und
vom Frieden (εἰρήνη) Christi reden, während Paulus von Gott oder dem
Menschen als Subjekt des Begnadens und vom 'Gott des Friedens' oder dem
'Frieden Gottes' spricht.

zu tun (Kol. 3: 17), erheben. Die nah verwandte Stelle 1. Kor. 10: 31 spricht vom Tun 'zur Ehre *Gottes*'. Doch läßt sich auch Röm. 14: 4ff. vergleichen, wonach wir in allem 'dem Herrn' stehen oder fallen, ihm essen oder nicht essen, ihm leben oder sterben. Genau das kann auch Kol. 3: 17 gemeint sein; doch ist jedenfalls die Formulierung des Römerbriefs weit besser geschützt vor einem formelhaften Mißverständnis. Dort ist es der Herr, der in jedem Augenblick über uns steht und bestimmt, ob wir stehen oder fallen, essen oder nicht essen, leben oder sterben. Auch wenn sich nach 1. Kor. 5: 4 die Gemeinde 'im Namen unseres Herrn' versammelt, dann ist die Präsenz dieses Namens so ernst genommen, daß Paulus vom dort gefällten Gerichtsspruch wahrscheinlich den leiblichen Tod des Sünders erwartet.[10] Schließlich ist an den Christushymnus Phil. 2: 10 zu erinnern, wo sich 'im Namen Jesu' alle Knie im Himmel, auf Erden und in der Unterwelt beugen. Hier ist das Ereignis der Machtausübung des 'Herrn' erst recht deutlich. So ist es denn nicht zufällig, daß in 1. Kor. 6: 11 der 'Name des Herrn Jesus Christus' synonym mit dem 'Geiste unseres Gottes' zusammensteht. Daß bei der Formel vom 'Namen Jesu' der Geist erwähnt wird, ist nicht zu erwarten. Daß dies bei Paulus doch einmal geschieht, zeigt, was auch im Kontext aller anderen Stellen deutlich wird: daß nämlich durchwegs an das gedacht ist, was Paulus sonst mit dem Wirken des Geistes bezeichnet, an das Ereigniswerden der Macht Gottes.

Noch typischer ist die Rede von der 'nicht mit Händen gemachten Beschneidung' oder der 'Beschneidung Christi' Kol. 2: 11. Zunächst erinnert das sehr an Paulus. 2. Kor. 5: 1 erscheint der 'nicht mit Händen gemachte', ewige Bau, der schon im Himmel bereit liegt. Vor allem aber setzt Röm. 2: 29 die Beschneidung 'am Sichtbaren, am Fleisch' derjenigen 'im Verborgenen' gegenüber. Aber wieder taucht dabei die Rede vom Geist auf, wenn diese Beschneidung als die 'des Herzens' bezeichnet wird, die 'im Geist, nicht im Buchstaben' erfolgt und Lob bei Gott, nicht bei den Menschen bringt. Wieder ist also der scharfe Gegensatz eines Lebens, das sich auf das Sichtbare verläßt, von dem lebt, was der Mensch beurteilen und messen kann, zu einem Leben, das sich allein auf Gott, auf das Verborgene, nicht Vorweisbare, nicht Meßbare verläßt, also zu einem Leben 'im Geist' deutlich. So sind

---

[10] Entgegen J. Cambier, *NTS* 15 (1968/9), S. 221ff. halte ich die Stelle nicht bloß für eine Exkommunikationsformel, sondern verstehe sie als Gerichtsspruch, der den Tod des Sünders herbeiführen soll.

denn auch nach Phil. 3: 3 diejenigen, die 'kraft des Geistes Gottes dienen', '*die* Beschneidung'. Schließlich ist bei Paulus auch die Taufe, von der ja Kol. 2: 11 redet, durchaus als Geschehen des Geistes verstanden (1. Kor. 12: 13).

Das Ergebnis ist dem der andern Abschnitte ähnlich. Nirgends findet sich etwas, was bei Paulus unmöglich wäre. Ja, die typische Verbindung von Indikativ und Imperativ findet sich kaum je außerhalb des Corpus Paulinum und zeigt jedenfalls, wie gut der Verfasser paulinische Theologie mit ihrer Gründung aller Ethik im Heilshandeln Gottes verstanden hat. Dennoch ist der Ton ein anderer geworden. An die Stelle des Geistes tritt ausschließlich der Herr Christus. Wo bei Paulus eindeutig von einem Geschehen, einem Unterwegssein des Menschen auf Gott hin und einem Unterwegssein Gottes auf den Menschen hin gesprochen ist, da bleibt im Kolosserbrief offen, ob nicht an den im Evangelium durch die Lehre des Apostels richtig überlieferten und von der Gemeinde so übernommenen Christus gedacht ist.

4. DAS LEBEN 'DROBEN'

Eben bei dem erwähnten Verständnis der Taufe findet sich der wohl bekannteste, oft besprochene Unterschied zwischen dem Kolosserbrief und den (übrigen?) Paulusbriefen. Sie ist nicht nur ein Mitbegraben-, sondern auch ein Mitauferstandensein mit Christus (2: 12). Diese Auffassung führt dann zum Satz von der Gemeinde, die nicht mehr 'in der Welt' lebt (2: 20). Freilich darf wiederum nicht mehr behauptet werden, als der Text hergibt. Einerseits kommt nämlich Röm. 6: 11 schon nahe an eine solche Aussage heran; andererseits betont Kol. 3: 1–5, daß das 'Droben' noch gesucht werden, im ganzen Existenzvollzug stets neu verwirklicht werden muß, weil das neue Leben immer noch 'mit Christus in Gott verborgen' ist bis zur Parusie. Es kommt dazu, daß Paulus in Korinth, wo er wohl den Römerbrief geschrieben hat, eine enthusiastische Frömmigkeit vorgefunden hat, die sich schon im Himmel lebend wähnte und die Welt mit ihren Forderungen und Aufgaben hinter sich gelassen hat. Umgekehrt sind die Kolosser von einer jüdisch-neupythagoreischen Weltschau geprägt, die zwar nicht daran zweifelt, daß Christus, wie die Kolosser es in ihrem Hymnus (1: 15–20) ja regelmäßig sangen, Haupt des ganzen Alls ist, die aber ängstlich darauf bedacht ist, die Seele durch asketische Praxis von allem Irdisch-Materiellen zu lösen, damit diese bei ihrer Himmelreise nach dem Tode ungehindert durch die 'Elemente' aufsteigen kann, von der Erde durch Wasser, Luft und Feuer bis zum Äther, und so Christus als das oberste Haupt auch wirklich erreicht.[11] Solcher asketischer Skrupulosität gegenüber muß dann freilich betont werden, daß mit der Taufe alles schon geschenkt ist, daß der Getaufte grundsätzlich schon 'droben' mit Christus lebt, also das Irdisch-Materielle nicht mehr fürchten muß, als könnte es ihn vom Aufstieg zu Christus abhalten. Wiederum wäre also solche Verlagerung des Gewichtes bei Paulus selbst möglich. Und doch ist nicht zu übersehen, daß er anders spricht. Das 'obere (ebenfalls ἄνω) Jerusalem' steht Gal. 4: 26 nicht etwa allem Irdischen, Weltlichen entgegen, sondern dem 'jetzigen Jerusalem', das dem 'nach dem Fleisch gezeugten', sklavenmäßig lebenden Sohn entspricht. 'Oberes' Jerusalem ist die Gemeinde also, weil sie nicht von ihrem Werk lebt, sondern 'durch die Verheißung (Gottes) gezeugt' ist.[12] Auch die 'obere Berufung' in Phil. 3: 14 meint wohl die von oben, nicht vom Menschen her, sondern von Gott her wirksame Berufung. Paulus denkt also viel dialektischer. Die Verbindung zwischen dem Leben des Glaubens 'im Fleisch', das doch schon in der Taufe nicht nur mit dem gekreuzigten, sondern auch mit dem auferstandenen Herrn zusammengeschlossen ist, und dem Leben der Auferstehung kann nur durch das Wirken des Geistes hergestellt werden. Er ist die Erstlingsgabe, die das Kommende schon zuspricht (Röm. 8: 23), er das Unterpfand, in dem die künftige Auferstehung schon in die Gegenwart hineinwirkt (2. Kor. 1: 22; 5: 5). Es ist daher 'der Geist dessen, der Jesus auferweckt hat', der auch die zu ihm Gehörenden einst auferwecken wird (Röm. 8: 11.)[13] Darum bleibt das 'Mitleben' mit Christus für Paulus ein zukünftiges Geschehen (Röm. 6: 8), das sich im ganzen Wandel des Glaubens schon hier durchsetzen und bewähren muß (Röm. 6: 4). Gewiß kann auch Paulus so etwas wie räumliche Terminologie benützen. Wir leben 'im

---

[11] Zum religionsgeschichtlichen Hintergrund vgl. den bei E. Schweizer, 'Die "Elemente der Welt" Gal. 4: 3, 9; Kol. 2: 8, 20', in *Verborum Veritas* (Wuppertal, 1970), S. 257 = E. Schweizer, *Beiträge zur Theologie des Neuen Testamentes* (Zürich–Stuttgart, 1970), 160 zitierten neupythagoreischen Text aus dem 1. Jahrhundert v. Chr., der ungefähr alle in Kol. 2 erscheinenden typischen *termini* enthält.

[12] Man beachte den Wechsel zwischen der Formulierung von dem durch den Menschen '*nach* dem Fleisch' Erzeugten und der vom '*durch* die Verheißung (Gottes)' Erzeugten (*TWNT* vii, S. 131, 20ff.).

[13] Falls hier der Genetiv, nicht der Akkusativ zu lesen ist.

Geist' oder 'im Fleisch' (Röm. 8: 9); aber beide 'Räume' liegen auf Erden, ineinander verschoben, sodaß Paulus auch vom Glaubenden sagen kann, daß er natürlich noch 'im Fleisch', aber gerade so nicht 'nach dem Fleisch' lebe (2. Kor. 10: 3). So steht der Kolosserbrief hier dem Sprachgebrauch von Jak. 3: 15, 17, wonach die 'von oben kommende Weisheit' der 'irdischen, psychischen, dämonischen', die Streit hervorruft, entgegengesetzt ist, doch etwas näher als Paulus dies tut.

Es ist von hier aus auch konsequent, daß ungeschützter als bei Paulus vom 'neuen' oder 'vollkommenen' Menschen die Rede sein kann (Kol. 1: 28; 3: 10). Nun spricht zwar auch Paulus vom 'alten Menschen' (Röm. 6: 6 wie Kol. 3: 9), den wir abgelegt haben, und vom 'neuen Sauerteig' der Gemeinde (1. Kor. 5: 7). Sprachlich wäre die Formulierung also zweifellos möglich. Doch ist dieser 'alte Mensch' bei Paulus schwerlich rein individualistisch gedacht, wie wahrscheinlich doch im Kolosserbrief; Röm. 6: 6 meint wohl das Hinter-sich-lassen 'Adams', also eines ganzen Herrschaftsbezirkes. Daher zieht der Glaubende in der Taufe auch nicht den 'neuen Menschen' an, sondern Christus (Gal. 3: 27; Röm. 13: 14). Das heißt aber, daß die Neuheit für Paulus nicht eigentlich im Getauften lokalisiert ist, sondern in dem, auf den er, in den hinein er getauft wird. Er allein lebt wirklich 'droben' als der Auferstandene und umgibt und bestimmt den Täufling so als Macht. Darum ist es auch bei Paulus immer die Gemeinde als ganze, die als 'neuer Sauerteig' oder als 'heilige Braut' (2. Kor. 11: 2) erscheint. Auch gehört die Terminologie vom 'alten Menschen' deutlich in die Gegenüberstellung von Adam und Christus (1. Kor. 15: 45, 47). In der Situation von Kolossä hingegen geht es ja um eine neue Gesetzlichkeit asketischer Prägung, also, paulinisch gesprochen, um Mose und Christus. Dort aber kann nicht mehr nur von der Verborgenheit des Neuen gesprochen werden, sondern muß der scharfe Gegensatz des Geistes zum Fleisch hervortreten. Paulus könnte daher solche Gesetzlichkeit auch kaum als bloßen 'Schatten' gegenüber der 'Sache' (σῶμα) selbst beschreiben wie Kol. 2: 17.[14] Wo Paulus von den 'Vollkommenen' spricht, da sind es die mit dem Geist Begabten, die πνευματικοί (1. Kor. 2: 6, 13f., vgl. 14: 20), die, die 'durch die Kraft des Geistes Gott(es) dienen', sich Christi rühmen und nicht mehr auf das Fleisch vertrauen (Phil. 3: 3, 15).

---

[14] Röm. 8: 10, 13 zeigt, daß gerade σῶμα eher auf der Seite des Abzulehnenden im Gegensatz zum Geist steht.

Läßt sich also die Wahl des Gegensatzes zwischen 'Welt' und 'droben' von der kolossischen Situation her verstehen, so fehlt doch die Dialektik der paulinischen Lehre vom Geiste, der gerade im 'Fleisch' oder in der 'Welt' den Glaubenden nicht mehr 'nach dem Fleisch', nach den Maßstäben der Welt leben, sondern ihn umgekehrt von der 'Verheißung' oder vom 'Droben' sich bestimmen läßt. Weiß auch der Kolosserbrief, daß das neue Leben nicht einfach undialektisch verstanden werden, daß das 'Droben' nur 'gesucht' werden kann, so könnte doch erst der Verweis auf den Geist eindeutig sichern, daß solches 'Suchen' schon ganz und gar Gottes Werk an uns, also gerade die Präsenz des Zukünftigen oder Oberen ist, die sich mitten im 'Fleisch' oder der 'irdischen Welt' vollzieht.

5. DIE AUSSAGEN ÜBER DEN GEIST

Am auffälligsten sind die Aussagen über den Geist selbst. Es sind nur vier Stellen. In Kol. 2: 5 ist 'Geist' wahrscheinlich rein anthropologisch zu fassen. An der ganz parallelen Stelle 1. Kor. 5: 3 (wie auch 7: 34) steht als Gegenbegriff bezeichnenderweise 'Leib', nicht 'Fleisch' wie Kol. 2: 5. Dabei ist die Gegenwart des Apostels 'im Geist' so ernst genommen, daß sie die Vollmacht des Urteils, das den Sünder dem Tod überliefert, garantiert (1. Kor. 5: 4f.). Wo 'Fleisch' als Gegensatz erscheint (V. 5), ist es der dem Todesgericht überantwortete Mensch, sodaß 'Geist' sein von Gott begnadetes, im jüngsten Gericht einst gerettet werdendes Ich meint. Dieser Sprachgebrauch liegt also der harmlosen Verwendung von 'Fleisch' und 'Geist' in Kol. 2: 5 ganz fern. So ist eigentlich nur 2. Kor. 7: 1 wirklich parallel, eine Stelle, die zu einer unpaulinischen Interpolation gehört.[15]

Sonst findet sich das Substantiv 'Geist' im Kolosserbrief nur noch in der Wendung 'eure Liebe im Geist' (1: 8). Das erinnert sachlich an Röm. 15: 30 ('die Liebe des Geistes'), formal an Röm. 14: 17 ('Freude im heiligen Geist'.) Doch ist an der ersten Stelle klar festgehalten, daß der Geist selbst Subjekt solcher Liebe ist,[16] und an der zweiten Stelle sichert die Fortsetzung ('wer nämlich in ihm [dem Geist] Christus Gehorsam leistet...') das rechte Verständnis: der Geist ist die eigentliche Kraft der Freude. Dieses Wissen wird auch noch hinter

[15] *TWNT* vii, S. 125 Anm. 219; viii, S. 370 Anm. 245; S. 392, 22–4.
[16] Vgl. Röm. 5: 5: der Geist gibt Gottes Liebe (Gott ist Subjekt, V. 8) in unsere Herzen.

Kol. 1: 8 stehen; aber es fragt sich, wie weit es noch wirkungskräftig ist. Jedenfalls besteht die Vermutung, daß der Ausdruck nur noch eine 'geistliche' Liebe von einer rein weltlichen unterscheiden will, also weniger den Grund und die Kraft solcher Liebe beschreiben will als ihre Art und Weise, sie also eher als zum Bereich des Religiösen gehörend klassifizieren als sie auf Gottes eigenes Tun zurückführen will.

Mindestens ist dies an den beiden Stellen wahrscheinlich, wo nur noch das Adjektiv steht. Die 'geistlichen Lieder' von Kol. 3: 16 bedeuten kaum etwas anderes als der entsprechende deutsche Ausdruck: Lieder mit einem religiösen, nicht mit einem weltlichen Inhalt. Wo Paulus davon spricht, daß er 'im Geiste singt' (1. Kor. 14: 15), empfindet er diese Aussage von dem ihm übergeordneten, göttlichen Subjekt seines Singens so stark, daß er gleich zufügen muß, daß er, im Unterschied vom Glossolalen, dabei doch auch seinen 'Verstand' beteiligt weiß. Daher wählt er auch nicht zufällig das Substantiv 'Geist', nicht bloß das Adjektiv, das eine Eigenschaft ausdrückt. Endlich ist auch die 'geistliche Weisheit und Einsicht' von Kol. 1: 9 schwerlich mehr als eine auf geistliche, d. h. religiöse Inhalte bezogene Weisheit. Jedenfalls ist der scharfe Gegensatz von 1. Kor. 1: 18 – 3: 3, wo Paulus alles daran liegt, festzuhalten, daß Gott selbst und sein Geist Subjekt aller Erkenntnis und alles Lehrens bleibt, nirgends mehr expliziert.

Wiederum läßt sich nicht sagen, daß der Tatbestand eindeutig gegen Paulus spricht. Auch Paulus braucht das Adjektiv 'geistlich' mehr als einmal. Nur ist bei ihm an allen Stellen vom Kontext her deutlich, daß er ernsthaft daran denkt, daß der Geist der eigentliche Wirker, der Geber, das Subjekt alles Handelns ist.[17] Im Kolosserbrief hingegen stellt sich die Frage, ob man das alles mithören muß, weil es vorausgesetzt ist und daher nicht mehr ausdrücklich wiederholt wird, oder ob das theologische Interesse an der Aussage vom Geist abgeklungen ist, der Verfasser sie also jedenfalls nicht mehr als im Zentrum stehend ansieht. Die Antwort wird nicht nur, aber auch dadurch bestimmt, ob man voraussetzt, daß Paulus selbst hier schreibt, oder ob man mit einem Paulusschüler rechnet.

[17] Das gilt wohl auch für 1. Kor. 10: 3f., obwohl dort noch am ehesten der hellenistische Gegensatz von Profan-Weltlichem und Göttlichem, Gewöhnlichem und Außergewöhnlichem nachwirken könnte.

6. SCHLUSSBETRACHTUNG

Es besteht kein Zweifel daran, daß die Geistaussagen im Kolosserbrief außerordentlich stark zurücktreten, und daß umgekehrt die Christologie sich stark im Vormarsch befindet, jedenfalls die Pneumatologie, zum Teil aber auch die Theologie überdeckt. Das braucht noch nicht unpaulinische Autorschaft zu beweisen. Auch im Philipperbrief stehen zwar in 1:19, vor allem in 3:3, ziemlich sicher ebenfalls in 2:1 noch zentrale Sätze über den Geist Gottes; immerhin sind dies, wenn man 1:27 als möglicherweise und 4:23 als sicher anthropologisch zu verstehende Stellen ausklammert, auch die einzigen Verse, in denen der Geist vorkommt. Doch wird die Verschiebung des theologischen Gewichtes im Kolosserbrief deutlich.[18]

Nun hängt das natürlich auch mit der besonderen Situation in Kolossä zusammen. Es gibt ja für Paulus überhaupt keine ewig gültige Normaltheologie, sondern nur ein theologisches Eingehen auf die immer neuen Fragen von der immer gleichen Grundlage aus, die aber nie definitiv in festen Sätzen festgelegt werden kann. Dennoch erklärt dies nicht alles. Daß Paulus der judaistischen Werkgerechtigkeit in Galatien entgegen die Wirksamkeit des Geistes, die sich dialektisch mit dem Leben des Glaubens im Fleisch und dem noch nicht erlangten Ziel verbindet, betont, ist einsichtig. Er hat aber in Korinth eine Überbetonung des Geistes vorgefunden, die in eine Schwärmerei hineingeführt hat, in der die Welt versank und der Glaubende sich schon im Himmel lebend wähnte. Paulus hat darauf nicht etwa mit einer vorsichtigen Zurückstellung aller Geistaussagen geantwortet, sondern hat im Gegenteil erst recht vom Geist gesprochen, und zwar gerade so, daß er jede billige Verwechslung des heiligen Geistes Gottes mit dem menschlichen, religiösen Innersten scharf attackierte. Er hat auch in dem in Korinth verfaßten Brief nach Rom, wo ihm keine deutlich erkennbare Fehlentwicklung entgegentrat, sehr ausführlich und klar vom Geist gesprochen. Die asketische Skrupulosität der Kolosser, begründet in der Angst, die Seele nicht rein genug zu halten von allem Irdisch-Materiellen, ließ den Briefschreiber das 'Schon' betonen: schon sind sie mit Christus auferstanden, schon leben sie nicht

---

[18] Vgl. Anm. 2 und den Hinweis auf die nur in Kol., Eph. und den Pastoralbriefen fehlende Anrede '(meine) Brüder', die sonst für Paulus so charakteristisch ist, bei E. Schweizer, *Neotestamentica* (Zürich–Stuttgart, 1963), S. 429 (= *ZNW* 47, 1956, S. 287).

mehr in der Welt; also müssen sie keine Angst haben, einmal nicht zu Christus aufsteigen zu können, weil sie noch zu sehr den 'Elementen der Welt' verhaftet wären. Zugleich weiß der Verfasser des Kolosserbriefes, gut paulinisch, um die Notwendigkeit, den Indikativ immer neu auch als Imperativ zu hören, d. h. das 'Droben' zu suchen und die am Irdischen haftenden 'Glieder' zu töten (3: 1, 5); nur daß dies nicht durch asketische Lösung von allem Materiellen geschehen kann, sondern durch den Gehorsam, der Unzucht, Unreinheit, Leidenschaft usf. flieht. Daß gerade hier zur Klärung dieser Dialektik nicht auf den Geistbegriff zurückgegriffen wird, ist doch wohl nur so zu erklären, daß das rasche Reden vom Geist trotz aller Korrekturen in den großen Paulusbriefen, gefährlich geworden ist. Allzu viele berufen sich wohl schon auf die Geistlehre des Paulus. Muß nun in Kolossä nicht vor dem Unglauben, Kleinglauben oder dem Müdewerden im Glauben gewarnt werden, sondern vor der falschen Gläubigkeit, die durchaus einsatzbereit, ja 'begeistert' ist, freilich in falscher Richtung, dann ist der Rückgriff auf den Geist schwierig. Die lange Diskussion des Paulus mit den Korinthern demonstriert ja *ad oculos*, wie genau und ausführlich dann gesprochen werden muß, um nicht dauernd mißverstanden zu werden, um nicht Gottesgeist und Menschengeist hoffnungslos in einander verschwimmen zu lassen, sodaß alles in sein Gegenteil verkehrt würde.

Es läßt sich also verstehen, daß der Kolosserbrief den Kampf eher auf dem Feld der Christologie führt. Hier können leichter falsche Sätze von richtigen geschieden werden; hier kann eher auf die einmal übernommene 'Erkenntnis', die empfangene 'Lehre' verwiesen werden, auch wenn dann natürlich dazu aufgerufen werden muß, das Erkannte jetzt im ganzen Leben zu verwirklichen. Freilich müßte das Zurückstellen der Geistaussagen dann gefährlich werden, wenn das nicht mehr mitgehört wird, was der Schreiber des Briefes, ob es Paulus oder sein Schüler ist, noch selbstverständlich mithört: das in den großen Paulusbriefen vom Wirken Gottes durch seinen Geist zu Lesende.

Diese gewisse Einseitigkeit macht die Großartigkeit des Kolosserbriefes aus. Hier ist der Versuch gemacht, in einer Lage, in der die Einzigkeit Christi zwar theoretisch festgehalten, ja überschwänglich gepriesen wurde, in der diese aber faktisch nicht mehr recht zur Wirkung kam, alles auf die Christologie zu konzentrieren. Mit einer vor ihm kaum je erreichten imponierenden Radikalität reklamiert der Verfasser die ganze Welt für Christus und schließt alles in ihn ein, sodaß er, bis an die Grenze der 2. Tim. 2: 18 verworfenen Haeresie vorstoßend, sogar vom Schon-auferstanden-sein der Gemeinde Christi reden kann. Daß dies nicht zu einer reinen, undialektisch verstandenen *theologia gloriae* führt, daß der eschatologische Vorbehalt von 3: 1–4 zu einem bewußt ethischen Aufruf, ja zum ersten Mal zur Aufnahme einer Haustafel[19] führt, das verdankt der Briefschreiber der Erinnerung an die mächtigen Aussagen vom Geist, der im Fleisch doch gegen das Trauen auf das Fleisch ankämpft. Sollten sie allerdings vergessen werden, dann bestünde die Gefahr, daß man eine immer weiter ausgebaute, nach allen möglichen Seiten hin abgesicherte und weiterentwickelte christologische Lehre als Ersatz für ein Leben im Geist und aus dem Geiste verstände, daß man also Christologie als ein zu übernehmendes Gedankengebäude und nicht mehr als ein das ganze Leben bestimmendes und bewirkendes Fundament ansähe.

Wenn ein junger Mann einem Mädchen sagt 'Ich liebe dich', dann muß dieser Satz gewiß entfaltet werden. Der Mann wird ihn daher in immer neuen Situationen explizieren und wird klären müssen, was dies konkret heißt. Dennoch kann die vollkommenste Erläuterung dieses Satzes mit der genauesten Beschreibung des gemeinsamen Lebens und die größte intellektuelle Anstrengung vonseiten des Mädchens nicht zum wirklichen Verstehen führen, solange das Mädchen nicht davon bewegt und überwältigt wird. Daß das Bewegt- und Überwältigt-werden durch den Satz von Gottes Liebe nicht auf der religiösen Anstrengung des Menschen beruht, sondern noch einmal Gottes eigenes Handeln am Menschen ist, das ist der Sinn der paulinischen Geistlehre. Darum muß er sie den Galatern, die auf ihre Werkgerechtigkeit bauen, ebenso scharf entgegenrufen wie den Korinthern, die auf ihre religiösen Fähigkeiten und Erkenntnisse vertrauen. Im Kolosserbrief liegt der eindrückliche Versuch vor, einmal die Ganzheit des Glaubens, sein Gottes- und sein Weltverständnis von einem einzigen Punkt aus, nämlich von der Christologie her zu explizieren. Der Versuch ist gelungen, solange man die paulinischen Geistaussagen noch mithört. Er muß mißlingen in einer Zeit, die das nicht mehr tut. So teilt der Kolosserbrief Verheißung und Gefahr jeder Dogmatik, die entschlossen von einem Zentrum her das Ganze des Glaubens in eine

---

[19] Nicht zu übersehen ist, daß hier auch die Mahnung an die Übergeordneten, also die Männer, Väter und Herren direkt in die Haustafel mitaufgenommen ist (vgl. dazu E. Lohse, *Die Briefe an die Kolosser und an Philemon*, Göttingen, 1968, S. 220–32).

bestimmte Zeit und Situation hinein zu sagen versucht. Keine theologische Aussage, die überhaupt etwas vermitteln will, das aufhorchen läßt, wird diesem Wagnis entgehen können. Keine rechte theologische Aussage wird sich darum aber auch den kritischen Rückfragen nach den in ihr liegenden stillschweigenden Voraussetzungen entziehen können, sobald diese Voraussetzungen nicht mehr selbstverständlich mitgedacht werden. So hat der Kolosserbrief in besonders ausgeprägtem Maße teil an der Verheißung, die jeder entschlossenen Theologie gegeben, und zugleich an der Gefahr, die ebenso von allem Anfang an in ihr eingeschlossen ist.

Christus und Geist im Kolosserbrief

E. SCHWEIZER

Why does the author of Colossians (perhaps a pupil of Paul) so rarely mention the Spirit, and on occasions replace statements about the work of the Spirit by other expressions?

There is no doubt that the theological emphasis in this letter is on Christ rather than Spirit. The shrouding of the doctrine of the Spirit is evident from the writer's treatment of (1) the power of the new life in Christ; (2) the new, Christian, understanding of 'the grace of God in truth'; (3) the basis of the new life in Christ; (4) and the idea of the life 'above'. Moreover the four statements about the Spirit in Colossians (2: 5; 1: 8; 3: 16; 1: 9) point in the same direction. The result cannot be regarded as un-Pauline, although the evidence points rather towards a later period with a decline of interest in the person of the Spirit.

The investigation of these issues confirms the impression that there is a clear shift of emphasis in Colossians from pneumatology to christology. But this change arises from the Colossian situation, in which it seems that rash talking about the Spirit has led to certain dangers, so that a corrective to enthusiastic false faith has become necessary. Orthodoxy is more easily maintained with regard to a clearly defined doctrine about Christ, than with regard to the Spirit. It must be recognized, however, that the new weight given to christology in Colossians also has its dangers, for it can lead in the life of the Christian to a diminished dependence on the work of God through his Spirit. Certainly the grandeur of this letter is its christological concentration; the author reclaims the whole world for Christ. The letter thus shares to a special extent both the promise and the danger of every dogmatic work which tries in one situation to speak of the Christian faith in its totality.

21

Were there false teachers in Colossae?

MORNA D. HOOKER

It seems to be accepted by all commentators and writers on Colossians that the basic reason for the letter's composition was the existence of some kind of aberration in the Colossian community. Sometimes this is referred to as a 'heresy'; more cautiously it is described as 'false teaching' or 'error'. Its proponents are variously thought to be members of the Christian community spreading corruption from within, or outsiders attacking the Church's beliefs; the teaching has been interpreted as Jewish, as Gnostic, or as a mixture of the two. But that the Church was under some kind of serious attack, and that the letter was written to meet this attack, does not seem to be questioned.

The content and character of this 'false teaching' have to be deduced from what appears to be Paul's rejoinder, and this, as always, is an extremely difficult task, as prone to misinterpretation as the incidental overhearing of one end of a telephone conversation. In this particular case we think we recognize the voice as Paul's,[1] but we know very little indeed about those to whom he is speaking; and from the snippets of conversation which we overhear it is very easy to make false deductions. However, when Paul says 'don't', it is logical to suppose that he thinks such a warning is necessary; and when he elaborates a particular aspect of Christian teaching, it seems likely that he considers that this is being neglected. So, from the Christological 'hymn' in Colossians 1, and from the warnings about regulations in Col. 2, there has emerged a picture of a false teaching whose advocates do not recognize the uniqueness of Christ, but try to set him in some kind of hierarchy of powers, and who are attempting to subject the Colossian Christians to a strange mixture of Jewish and ascetic practices.

The attraction of this theory is that it offers an explanation of the epistle. It is an axiom of Pauline studies that every letter has a *Sitz im Leben*: the apostle always wrote to a particular situation, and for a

---

[1] If Colossians is non-Pauline (and its special relationship to Ephesians seems to us to make this very difficult to maintain), then the problem of understanding the letter becomes more complex, but our discussion here is not radically affected.

particular purpose, and the exegete's task is to recover that situation and purpose. If Paul did not write this letter because he felt that the church was in danger from false teaching, then we are left wondering why he sent it at all. What was the situation in Colossae, and what was the relevance of what he says in this letter to that situation? Is Colossians an exception to the general rule, written by Paul when he was perhaps occupying his time in prison in writing pastoral letters without any particular or pressing purpose in mind?

A further advantage of the traditional explanation is that it offers some kind of link between the christology of chapter 1 and the admonitions of chapter 2; in both sections, Paul is understood to be correcting beliefs integral to the Colossian error. It is because the false teachers believe that the world is governed by angelic powers that they think the way of salvation is through knowledge of these spiritual beings and observance of religious practices, such as fasting.

The strangest feature about this reconstruction of the situation behind the Colossian epistle is the extraordinary calm with which Paul confronts it. If there were within the Colossian Christian community any kind of false teaching which questioned the uniqueness of Christ, which suggested, for example, that he was a member of some kind of gnostic series of spiritual powers, then Paul would surely have attacked such teaching openly and explicitly. Even if such false teaching was as yet outside the church, but constituted a real danger to the faith of the Colossians, we should expect a much clearer refutation of these false ideas. The teaching in Col. 1 is entirely positive, and it is only the assumption of some kind of situation such as has been outlined that leads commentators to assume that what Paul affirms, others have been denying. If false teaching exists, then it cannot be serious, either in character or magnitude; one glance at Galatians reminds us of the way in which Paul reacts when he feels that faith in Christ is being undermined. There is therefore no real basis for assuming that the christology of chapter 1 is developed in opposition to false beliefs in the Colossian church which could in any sense be described as 'heretical' or 'dangerous'.

It is, of course, fashionable to attempt to reconstruct some kind of pre-Christian 'hymn' behind the christological section in chapter 1.[2] There is, however, no real evidence, in spite of the ingenuity of

---

[2] See, e.g., E. Käsemann, *Essays on New Testament Themes* (London, 1964) pp. 149ff.

exegetes, that such a hymn ever existed. And though the exclamations of recognition, surprise, and illumination uttered by the Colossians when they heard Paul's new version of something familiar to them may be that part of the conversation which is lost to us, such a reaction on their part is sheer speculation. Certainly Paul is here describing the supremacy of Christ, and the comprehensive character of his work in creation and redemption. This does not mean, however, that he is refuting teaching which has suggested that others have a role in this work. It is illuminating to compare Col. 1 with Heb. 1, a passage which it in many ways resembles. In Hebrews, the author leaves us in no doubt that he is arguing for the supremacy of Christ as compared with other, lesser, beings, such as angels; Heb. 1 offers us more evidence for the existence of a 'heresy' – in which angels could play a large role – than does Col. 1![3]

One must also be cautious about constructing too much on the basis of Paul's warnings in chapter 2. In verse 4 he explains that he is reminding the Colossians of certain facts in order that no one should delude them. The warning is a general one, and we should not assume too readily that Paul believes that the Colossians are in imminent danger from particular 'false teachers'. In verse 16, he urges the Colossians to allow no one to condemn them on the basis of certain regulations. Here the situation is more specific, but there is no hint that Paul supposes that his readers have already succumbed to the possible danger, which is contrasted to what they have received through Christ. Exhortation to avoid a certain course of action certainly does not necessarily indicate that those addressed have already fallen prey to the temptation, as every preacher and congregation must be aware. Only in verse 20 is there a possible indication that his readers have allowed themselves to be misled by 'false teaching' consisting of various negative rules listed in verse 21. Δογματίζεσθε is often taken to mean that the Colossian Christians have already submitted to these regulations. It is probable, however, that Paul is asking 'Why subject yourselves?', or 'Why submit?' – i.e. to any attempt which may be made to impose such regulations – rather than 'Why *do* you subject yourselves?'.[4] In view of the lack of

---

[3] Cf. T. W. Manson, 'The Problem of the Epistle to the Hebrews', *BJRL* xxxii (1949), pp. 160ff., who suggested that Hebrews was written by Apollos to Colossae.

[4] Cf. C. Masson, *L'Épître de Saint Paul aux Colossiens* (Neuchâtel and Paris, 1950), *in loc.* Note the present tense of the verb, which may be understood as middle or passive. For a possible parallel, see I Cor. 10: 30.

any other indication that the Colossians have submitted to such regulations, it seems more likely that Paul is issuing a warning than an accusation.

In chapter 2, then, we do have indications of pressure upon the church. But it is by no means certain that this ought to be described as 'false teaching'. Since commands such as 'do not touch, do not taste', are clearly taught, and since Paul undoubtedly regarded such teaching as false, our objection may seem pedantic. Yet it is unfortunate if labels are used which imply too much; and the phrase 'false teaching' does tend to imply a system of teaching, a particular school or religious sect. It is perhaps for this reason that commentators wish to link up the warnings of chapter 2 with the speculations supposedly attacked in chapter 1, although there is no necessary or obvious link. But were the pressures upon the Christian community in Colossae of this kind? In looking for particular 'heresies' and sects which we may categorize, it is easy to overlook the less obvious but possibly far greater pressures upon the young Christian community. Although we may not be able to reconstruct the situation of the Colossian Christian community, we may certainly conclude that one element in the contemporary scene was the general acceptance in pagan society of immorality; another was the – very different! – heritage of Judaism. To the newly-baptized Christian, called to be 'holy and blameless and irreproachable' (1: 22) and surrounded by the lax morality of the pagan life he had abandoned, the pressure to achieve purity by keeping the regulations of Judaism must have been enormous. The convert who accepted so much from Judaism would naturally tend to accept these also. There is no need to postulate the arrival in Colossae of 'false teachers' or 'Judaizers' to explain Paul's warnings.

We have noted the absence from Colossians of the distress which permeates Galatians. Nor is there any angry outburst, such as we find in Phil. 3: 2, or hint of a problem of rebellion, as in the Corinthian correspondence. Indeed, a closer examination of Paul's language in Colossians suggests a situation very different from the troubled state of some of his churches. He thanks God specifically for the faith and love of the Colossians (1: 4) who are described as πιστοί in the opening salutation (1: 2), and he mentions the fruitfulness of the gospel among them (1: 6) and their love in the Spirit (1: 8). Since we often find hints of the theme of a Pauline letter in its opening paragraph, it may be that Paul is deliberately reminding the Colossians of the reality of their faith; but he in no way suggests that it is weak.

A similar impression is given in chapter 2, where we find Paul rejoicing because of the good order and the firmness of the Colossians' faith (verse 5), urging them to live as those who are 'rooted and built up in him and established in the faith' (verse 7). Again, Paul may be reminding his readers of the basis of their faith, but his language does not suggest that he regards them as in danger of apostasy.

The evidence which has led commentators to speak of false teachers attacking the Christian community consists, on the one hand, of the warnings in 2: 4, 8 and 20, which we have suggested may be more general in their reference; and on the other hand, of the christological statements in chapter 1. Although, as we have seen, the idea of false teaching offers some kind of explanation of the existence of these two themes in one letter, it leads in turn to the difficulty of holding together in one system the different beliefs which Paul is said to be attacking. The regulations referred to in chapter 2 seem to be mainly Jewish in character; the christology of chapter 1 is said to oppose beliefs which seem to be more 'gnostic'. We might expect to find syncretism in Colossae, and it is therefore possible that the two sets of ideas cohere; but they do not necessarily or inevitably belong together.

In attempting to reconstruct the situation behind Paul's writings, the danger of circularity is inevitable; it is all too easy to use what hints there are in a letter to build a false picture of events, and then read this back into what is said. Our own attempt to answer the problem of Colossians can, of course, like any other, only use the evidence of the letter itself, and is open to the same danger of circularity. We suggest, however, that there may perhaps be a sufficient explanation of the letter in the facts which are outlined in it by Paul. Clearly he regards the Colossian Christian community as part of his pastoral responsibility, although he has not been to the city himself; the gospel was brought to them by Epaphras – but he acted as Paul's representative, 1: 7.[5] Paul's ministry includes the Colossians: his sufferings are 'for your sake', 1: 24; his commission was 'to you', 1: 25; he is striving 'for you ... and for all who have not seen my face', 2: 1; although absent in body, he is present in spirit, 2: 5. It is natural that Paul should write to the church in these circumstances if the opportunity arises. This opportunity is possibly afforded by the return of

[5] Reading ὑπὲρ ἡμῶν with 𝔓⁴⁶, ℵ* A B D* G, against ὑμῶν read by C K L P. See C. F. D. Moule, *The Epistles to the Colossians and to Philemon* (Cambridge, 1958), p. 27 n. 1.

Onesimus to his master, 4: 9; the letter to the Colossians is actually sent by the hand of Tychicus, 4: 7, but he was perhaps travelling to the Lycus valley to accompany and support Onesimus.

Even if the letter is written out of a general pastoral concern for the Christians in Colossae, rather than because of some dangerous error there, we may expect Paul's words to reflect knowledge of the state of the church. Aspects of the gospel which he includes in his thanksgivings, as well as points which he emphasizes in his exhortations, may well indicate tendencies within the community, news of which has obviously reached Paul. We must therefore briefly look at the main theme of the epistle.

Paul begins, as usual, after the opening salutation (1: 1–2), with the customary thanksgiving for his readers. He singles out their faith, which is ἐν Χριστῷ 'Ιησοῦ, and their love to all the 'saints', both faith and love being dependent upon ἐλπίς (verses 4–5): this, as Professor Moule has pointed out,[6] is remarkable – and significant; for at once the Colossians' faith (which they possess because they are in Christ) and their Christian love (which they are displaying) are linked with hope, the goal of Christian life, which is to be an important theme in the epistle. Paul reminds them that they have already heard[7] of this hope in the gospel, which is bearing fruit and increasing in them as in the rest of the world (verses 5–6).

Thanksgiving merges into prayer, and Paul prays that the Colossians may be filled (πληρόω) with the knowledge of God's will, in all wisdom and spiritual understanding (verse 9); here we have language which has suggested that Paul may be contrasting true knowledge and wisdom with some false system. However, ἐπίγνωσις, σοφία and σύνεσις (the latter two especially) are all terms with an Old Testament background,[8] and ἐπίγνωσις is used by Paul in Romans of response to God's revelation (1: 28 and 10: 2); σοφία can certainly mean a human wisdom which is opposed to God's – see especially 1 Cor. 1–3, although it should be

---

[6] C. F. D. Moule, *op. cit.*, *in loc.*

[7] Assuming, *contra* Lightfoot and Moule, that the hearing precedes the time of writing, and not the hypothetical false teaching. Since it is Epaphras, not Paul, who has preached the gospel to them, it is natural that Paul should refer to what they have already heard. Cf. E. Lohse, *Die Briefe an die Kolosser und an Philemon*, Göttingen, 1968, *in loc.*

[8] 'Επίγνωσις is not common in the LXX, though the verb ἐπιγινώσκειν is widely used; the verb γινώσκειν, similarly, is much more frequent than the noun γνῶσις. Both σοφία and σύνεσις occur frequently, especially in the wisdom books.

noted that no particular 'philosophy' or 'heresy' comes under attack there. These words do not necessarily refer to a particular rival philosophy, or represent the vocabulary of some gnostic system. Professor Moule cautions us: 'it is well to remember . . . that they can still be found in non-technical senses in the New Testament, and it is a mistake to assume that they must invariably carry some abstruse inner meaning'.[9]

True knowledge of God's will leads to action, and this brings us to the second petition in Paul's prayer – that his readers may live worthily of the Lord, bearing fruit and increasing in the same knowledge (ἐπίγνωσις) of God, being strengthened according to the might of his glory – that is, of his revelation in Christ.[10] The relation between knowledge of God and of his will (verse 9) and behaviour (verse 10) is clear: the strength with which the Colossians are strengthened (ἐν πάσῃ δυνάμει δυναμούμενοι) is dependent upon him – κατὰ τὸ κράτος τῆς δόξης αὐτοῦ. The passage also seems to be intended to emphasize the completeness of the goal; as well as the verb πληρόω in verse 9, and the use of synonyms, Paul uses πᾶς five times in three verses (ἐν πάσῃ σοφίᾳ . . . εἰς πᾶσαν ἀρεσκείαν, ἐν παντὶ ἔργῳ ἀγαθῷ . . . ἐν πάσῃ δυνάμει . . . εἰς πᾶσαν ὑπομονήν).

In verse 12 we return to thanksgiving, as Paul summarizes the facts of their redemption, the basis on which his prayer is built: the Colossians have been qualified by God for a share in the inheritance of the saints in light, having been rescued out of the power of darkness, and transferred to the kingdom of God's Son. In him we have redemption – the forgiveness of sins.

It is at this point that Paul launches into what is often described as a christological 'hymn'. Whether or not the passage had an independent existence before its use here, we should expect it – like other, similar christological sections in the Pauline literature – to be relevant to the context. If we leave this passage aside for a moment, we see that the argument in verse 21 takes up again the theme of verses 13–14: those who were at one time alienated (21) are those who have now been given a share in the inheritance of God's holy ones (12); those who were hostile in mind and evil deeds (21) are those who have been rescued from the power of darkness (13) and whose calling is the knowledge of God and every good deed (9–10); those who are reconciled through the death of Christ (22) are those who have been transferred into his kingdom (13);

[9] *Op. cit.*, p. 159.   [10] Cf. C. F. D. Moule, *in loc.*

those whom he now presents as holy, blameless and irreproachable (22) are those who in him have redemption, the forgiveness of sins (14). It is possible, of course, to argue that verses 15–20 are therefore an addition to the main theme; but if Paul placed this section here, it was because he thought it relevant to his argument. The theme of these verses is the position of Christ, first in relation to 'all things' in general, and secondly in relation to the church. Everything was created and continues to exist, ἐν αὐτῷ ... δι' αὐτοῦ καὶ εἰς αὐτόν. This is often interpreted as Paul's reaction to those who believe in a gnostic 'hierarchy' and see Christ as one of a series of spiritual beings. But the point which is made is as much their coherence in him as his supremacy over them;[10a] and at least half the 'hymn' is concerned with Christ's relationship with the church. We suggest that the themes which are found in these verses are intended to underline the points which Paul has made in verses 13–14, and which he will take up again in verses 21–3. The supremacy of Christ to all things in heaven and earth guarantees the reality of the Colossians' rescue from the power of darkness; they have been transferred to the kingdom of one who is stronger than any spiritual powers which may have enslaved them in the past. The statement that all things were created in, through and for Christ tells us something about the final scope of this kingdom: in Christ, God's purpose for the world is being fulfilled, and everything finds its existence and meaning in him. The fact that Christ is head of the body, and that he is first-born from the dead, means that he is in everything pre-eminent. Interestingly enough, it is only at this point in these verses that statements about Christ lead to the conclusion that he he is therefore pre-eminent, and it is in relation to the church, not the spiritual powers, that this deduction is now made. The final statement that through him all things are reconciled (ἀποκαταλλάξαι) to him, defined in terms of 'making peace by the blood of his cross', confirms the earlier statement in verse 14 that in him 'we have redemption, the forgiveness of sins', and is echoed in verse 22 – 'you ... he has now reconciled (ἀποκατήλλαξεν) in his body of flesh by his death'.

These verses, then, give us christological statements which back up the reality of what Paul has said about the Colossians' redemption in verses 12–14, a theme which he takes up again in verses 21–3. Their redemption is guaranteed by Christ's relationship to God, to the world, and to the church. It is worth noting that the introductory clause, ὅς

[10a] Note how language used of Christ in 1:15; 3:2; 1:13, 18 echoes terms in 1:16.

ἐστιν εἰκὼν τοῦ Θεοῦ τοῦ ἀοράτου, is probably a deliberate echo of Gen. 1:26;[11] Christ, not Adam, is the one who is the image of God, at once the revealer of God's will to the world, and himself obedient to that will. Since Christ replaces Adam as God's vicegerent on earth, we should expect him to be supreme over the whole of creation.[12] Similarly, as the first-born from the dead, and head of the new humanity, it is not surprising to find that other men are dependent upon him.

Why did Paul think it necessary to write these things to the Colossians? Was it because false teachers were insisting on the authority and role of other powers besides Christ? Or was it because, living in a world which took the existence of such spiritual powers for granted, and wrested from their pagan beliefs and superstitions by Christian preachers, the Colossians would naturally have qualms about these beings, and wonder whether they still had power to influence their destiny? To suppose that belief in such forces can only be the result of explicit 'false teaching' in the Colossian Christian community is to underestimate the pressures of the pagan environment, and to forget the background of these converts. Paul himself does not deny the existence of the supernatural forces; for the Colossians, living in a world seemingly inhabited by hostile men and hostile spiritual beings, the reminder that Christ was greater than all others, and the one who had all things in his control, must have been very necessary. The reassurance which Paul gives seems more suited to calm such fears than to correct veneration of angelic powers. A Christian pastor in twentieth century Britain might well feel it necessary to remind those in his care that Christ was greater than any astrological forces; if Christians succumb to the temptation to read their horoscopes in the newspaper, then they are yielding to the pressures of contemporary society and falling prey to superstition, not to false teachers who are deliberately invading the church. Astrological powers and predictions which today are treated only semi-seriously were, in first century Colossae, undoubtedly forces to be reckoned with – but forces which, according to Paul, had come under the control of Christ. Col. 1 is not the only place where Paul states this conviction; in Rom. 8: 31–9 Paul declares that since God is on our side (in Christ) no one can be against us; no disaster or spiritual power can separate us from the love of God in Christ Jesus our Lord. It is worth noting that these verses form the

[11] C. F. D. Moule, *in loc.*
[12] Cf. M. D. Hooker, *The Son of Man in Mark* (London, 1967), pp. 11–74.

climax to a section in Romans in which Paul has worked out the significance of what he said about Christ and Adam in 5: 12–21, in relation to both mankind and creation. We are sons of God, and therefore heirs with Christ (8: 14–17); we have received the Spirit, and wait for the completion of our adoption, the redemption of our body, for which we still hope (8: 23–5); we are destined to be conformed to the likeness of God's Son, who is therefore πρωτότοκος (8: 29–30). Here we have the idea of Christ as true Man, the prototype of the new humanity which becomes – in and through Christ – what Adam was intended to be from the beginning. Creation, too, is to be released from bondage and to be set free (8: 18–22). In view of this certain hope – in which you have been saved (verse 23) – it is not surprising that Paul declares that no force in heaven or earth, physical or supernatural, can separate Christians from God's love. It is this cosmic understanding of the role of Christ that lies behind the assurances of Col. 1 also.

The 'hymn' of Col. 1 does, of course, move beyond Romans 8 in that Christ is now seen as the agent of creation. Already, however, we have met the idea that Christ is the one in whom and through whom mankind and creation are restored (cf. also 1 Cor. 8: 6). Moreover, since this restoration fulfils the original intention of creation, it is perhaps a natural development to say that Christ is the one in whom and through whom all things were *created*. This step seems to have been made within the context of a developing 'Wisdom christology'.[13]

Paul, then, stresses the position and the power of Christ, in order to remind his readers of the importance of what has already happened and of what will happen; in verse 23 we have again a reference to the hope of the gospel. He urges them to remain faithful and firm – a general warning which is perhaps more relevant to the kind of situation which we have suggested, than in the more urgent situation assumed by most commentators, which would require a more pointed warning. The gospel in which they hope has been preached ἐν πάσῃ κτίσει – a further echo of the theme of its universal scope, already elaborated in verses 15–20.

At this point Paul somewhat abruptly introduces the theme of his

---

[13] The suggestion of C. F. Burney, in 'Christ as the ΑΡΧΗ of Creation', *JTS* xxvii (1926), pp. 160ff., that the background of the hymn is to be found in a combination of Gen. 1: 1 and Prov. 8: 22, and that Paul gives us here a rabbinic exposition of běrêshîth, is a very attractive one. If he is right, the very Jewish character of such an exposition would make any reference to 'gnostic' terminology even more unlikely.

own ministry. He is a servant of the gospel, and his ministry is 'to you' (verse 25). He refers first to his sufferings, which are 'for your sake', and which are in some mysterious way linked to the sufferings oj Christ. One is puzzled not only by the meaning of verse 24, a notoriously difficult passage, but also by its sudden introduction. Is Paul, in prison, trying to understand the meaning of his ministry in this situation, and seeing his sufferings as his share in the 'messianic woes', the necessary preliminary to the fulfilment of the hope of the gospel, and the final working out of the picture in verses 15–20?[14] He speaks also of another aspect of his ministry, however, namely the task of making fully known the word of God – the mystery of God, which is Christ in you, the hope of glory. Again we have the theme of the hope of the gospel, a hope which is dependent upon Christians' union with Christ. Paul's mission is to all men – the phrase πάντα ἄνθρωπον comes three times in verse 28 – and we note again how this aspect of his ministry, like suffering, is a sharing in the work of Christ; his aim is to present (παραστήσωμεν – cf. verse 22) all men mature (τέλειον) in Christ.

In 2: 1–5, Paul turns from his wider ministry to his concern for those in the Lycus valley in particular. He desires their encouragement, and their possession of the understanding which consists in knowledge of Christ. Once again, we meet this emphasis on Christian knowledge, which suggests that Paul is well aware of the temptation to which the Colossians might succumb, of pursuing other varieties of knowledge. This danger is specifically mentioned in verse 4, although with no indication that Paul has any particular false teacher in mind. Paul, who has never visited the Colossians, nevertheless regards himself as their apostle, and naturally feels anxiety for these converts; although physically absent, he is with them in spirit (2: 5), 'warning every man and teaching every man in wisdom, that we may present every man mature in Christ' (1: 28).

From their relationship to himself, Paul turns to the more fundamental relationship of the Colossians with Christ. As they received Christ Jesus the Lord (through the preaching of Epaphras) so they must live, 'rooted and built up by him and established in the faith, just

---

[14] In Rom. 8, too, Paul reminds us that we must share the sufferings of Christ if we are to share his glory. See Rom. 8: 17, and cf. 2 Cor. 1: 5 and 4: 7–18, where the comfort and glory which come through suffering are already a present experience.

as you were taught' (2: 6–7): Paul confirms the teaching which the Colossians have already been given. They are to beware lest anyone now kidnap them through philosophy and empty deceit. Paul's vivid metaphor of 'kidnapping' perhaps looks back to the imagery of 1: 13, where the Colossians' conversion was spoken of in terms of a rescue from the powers of darkness, and a transference to the kingdom of Christ. They must beware lest they are snatched out of this kingdom. But who is it that might 'kidnap' the Colossians? Paul uses the indefinite τις, and although Lightfoot points out that he sometimes uses this word to refer to exponents whose name he knows, this does not exclude the possibility that here it simply means 'anyone'. Lightfoot also notes that the form of the sentence – βλέπειν μή with the indicative – 'shows that the danger is real'.[15] We would not for a moment deny that Paul believes that the dangers surrounding the Colossian Christian community are real, or that he thinks it necessary to warn them against the temptation to turn to various theosophies. What we are questioning is the theory that they are under attack by a specific group of teachers who are advocating a particular doctrine which can properly be termed 'the Colossian error'. Paul's warnings here seem to us to be just as applicable to the situation which we have suggested existed in Colossae, in which all kinds of alternative philosophies and doctrines might assail the young convert. Here, Paul defines the 'philosophy and empty deceit' as being 'according to human tradition, according to the στοιχεῖα of the universe, and not according to Christ'. There has been much debate regarding the meaning of στοιχεῖα, and also concerning the precise nature of the opposing teaching, which from this description might be either 'gnostic' or Jewish. Perhaps the answer to this second question is that it is unnecessary to choose between 'gnostic' and Jewish, or to solve the problem by speaking of an amalgam; Paul has in mind *any* 'philosophy' which looks for salvation anywhere outside Christ. 'For in him the whole fullness of deity dwells bodily, and you have come to fullness of life in him' (verses 9–10). There is no need for the Colossians to look anywhere else for completion. He is the head of all ἀρχαί and ἐξουσίαι (10) – for he has disarmed them, triumphing over them in the cross (14–15). Once again, what Paul has to say about ἀρχαί and ἐξουσίαι seems to suggest that the Colossians are still worried about the power of these spiritual beings, and need encourage-

---

[15] J. B. Lightfoot, *St Paul's Epistles to the Colossians and to Philemon* (London, ²1876), *in loc.* The indicative is, however, a future one.

ment to be confident in Christ's power over them. Paul also refers, however, to the fact that the Colossians have been circumcised in Christ. Once dead in trespasses and the uncircumcision of their flesh, God has made them alive with Christ; their trespasses have been forgiven, and the bond with its legal demands has been cancelled. Here Paul's argument seems more appropriate to meet fears that salvation in Christ is not complete, that something more is needed to qualify the Colossians to be full members of the community of the saints (1: 12), and that some method of dealing with trespasses is still needed. This suggests that Paul has in mind pressures on pagan converts to 'complete' their conversion by accepting Judaism and all its demands. This seems confirmed by the following verses, 16–19, which urge the Colossians not to allow anyone to condemn them in matters of 'food and drink, or with regard to a festival or a new moon or a sabbath' – scruples which, on the whole, seem to be Jewish in character. Paul's reference to these as the 'shadow of what is to come' reminds us of the argument of the epistle to the Hebrews (cf. 10: 1); the shadow which is contrasted with the reality in Christ probably refers to Jewish regulations, recognized now by Paul to be futile and unnecessary.

The Colossians must therefore beware those who advocate these religious practices, for by pursuing them one can be disqualified (verse 18; cf. 1: 12). To rely on such things is to be puffed up by a mind of flesh, the very opposite of the attitude which should be seen in Christians, which is the holding fast (κρατῶν, verse 19; cf. κατὰ τὸ κράτος τῆς δόξης αὐτοῦ, 1: 11) to the Head, from whom the whole body takes its strength and in whom it grows. Failure to hold fast to him means a failure to grow to maturity.

The fact that Paul refers in this chapter both to the defeat of the ἀρχαί and ἐξουσίαι, and to the futility of religious practices, has been interpreted by some commentators as an indication that the 'error' comprised these two elements of belief in spiritual powers and the search for salvation through ritual observances. It is perhaps Paul himself, however, who has deliberately fused these two themes. If in Galatians he can describe the circumcision of Christians as a return to bondage to the στοιχεῖα, similar to their previous enslavement to beings which are not gods (Gal. 4: 8–9), it is not surprising if his warning to the Colossians is couched in similar language. They, too, had formerly been in bondage to these spiritual powers; the submission of all spiritual powers to Christ means not only that the Colossians can be free from fear of the forces which oppressed them in the past, but also that they need not submit to any others.[16]

If, then, they have died with Christ from under the power of these στοιχεῖα τοῦ κόσμου, why should they submit to δόγματα about what may be touched and what may be eaten? These same δόγματα have been abolished through Christ's death (2: 14). Such precepts are human in origin, and have only the appearance of wisdom, being unable to achieve what they claim to do. We have already suggested that the verb δογματίζεσθε does not necessarily indicate that the Colossians have already submitted to these regulations, though certainly the urgency of Paul's appeal suggests that he fears they may do so. The danger, however, seems to be one familiar in the Pauline literature – the temptation to succumb to pressure from Jews or Jewish Christians, and to seek Christian perfection by means of religious observance. There is no indication here of an 'error' which is unique to the Colossians.

In chapter 3, Paul states his case positively: if the Colossians have been *raised with Christ*, who is at the right hand of God, they must seek and set their mind on the things which are above, not things which belong to the earth. At this point Paul reminds his readers once again of the Christian hope – a hope which is not limited to life on the earth, but which looks for a final conformity to the glory of God (verses 1–3).

The logical outcome of this dying and rising with Christ is that they must put to death desires belonging to the earth, and put away the evil practices of their old lives. They have put off the old man, with all its practices, and put on the new man, which is being renewed according to the image of its creator (9f.). Paul here takes up the familiar theme of Christ as the Second Adam,[17] and also takes us back to the imagery of 1: 15–20. The renewal of Christians is conformity to Christ, who is *the* image of the creator, the invisible God: in him, Christians have become what he is.[18] Paul also picks up again the theme of knowledge in the enigmatic phrase εἰς ἐπίγνωσιν, indicating perhaps that it is in this conformity to God's purpose that men come to true knowledge of him. In this new humanity, created in Christ, there is neither Greek nor Jew, circumcision nor uncircumcision; a reminder not only of the unity

[16] Cf. E. Percy, *Die Probleme der Kolosser- und Epheserbriefe* (Lund, 1946), pp. 160–9. Percy interprets the θρησκεία τῶν ἀγγέλων of Col. 2: 18 in this light. Cf. Gal. 3: 19.

[17] C. F. D. Moule, *in loc.*

[18] Cf. M. D. Hooker, 'Interchange in Christ', *JTS*, n.s. xxii (1971), pp. 349–61.

found in Christ, but of the fact that circumcision is not necessary, and that Gentiles are no longer excluded from God's people. Those who (verse 12) are the chosen of God, holy and beloved (as Christ is, 1:13), must put on attitudes belonging to the Lord, into whom they have been called in one body (verses 13–15). It is perhaps worthy of note that the final ethical section in 3:18 – 4:6, often seen as entirely separate from the main argument of the epistle, continues this theme of unity in Christ, and order in creation.

Paul's teaching in Colossians, then, seems to us to be quite as appropriate to a situation in which young Christians are under pressure to conform to the beliefs and practices of their pagan and Jewish neighbours, as to a situation in which their faith is endangered by the deliberate attacks of false teachers; in view of the absence from Colossians of any clear reference to the supposed error, or hint of distress on Paul's part, this explanation seems to us far more probable. Paul's emphasis on Christian hope and on maturity in Christ is understandable if the Colossians were subject to the obvious temptation to look for perfection in the regulations of Judaism. Even after reading his pastoral letter, these converts from paganism may well have found themselves wondering *how* they were to obey his exhortations to put off the things belonging to the old man and put on those belonging to the new; a code of rules is much simpler to obey, and enables one to measure one's progress! The christological section in chapter 1 is equally relevant to this situation, since it confirms both the reality of the redemption which already belongs to the Colossians in Christ, and the scope of their Christian hope: if Christ is supreme over all powers, then the Colossians need neither fear them nor obey them, for they have been set free from those powers which dominated them in the past, and must not submit to others now.

If our interpretation is correct, then this has certain consequences for our understanding of the christological passage in Col. 1. If no Colossian 'error' existed, then Paul's christological statement here was not, as has been suggested, developed or formulated in any attempt to combat false teaching. It may, however, have been developed and formulated (whether composed specifically for its present position or not) in order to demonstrate that both creation and redemption are completed in Christ because he has replaced the Jewish Law. Paul's argument that Christians need neither fear nor obey other 'powers' depends upon the supreme authority of Christ, of whose kingdom the

Colossians are members; legal requirements have been done away with because they are only a shadow of the reality which exists in Christ. The logic of Paul's argument is clear, and the link between the christology of Col. 1 and the exhortation of Col. 2 is explained, if this section in 1: 15–20 is, as has been suggested, an exposition of Christ as the replacement of the Jewish Torah, in terms which have been taken from the wisdom literature.[19] It is Christ, in whom all treasures of knowledge and wisdom are hid (2: 3), who is the true Wisdom of God (1 Cor. 1: 24, 30), who was with God from the beginning and through whom and by whom the universe was created (1: 15–18; cf. Prov. 8. 22 and Gen. 1: 1). But for the Jew, the Wisdom of God is identical with the Torah.[20] In claiming for Christ what has been said of Wisdom, Paul is claiming that he has replaced the Jewish Torah; it is Christ, not the Torah, who is older than creation, the instrument of creation, the principle upon which creation itself depends and to which it coheres.[21] This kind of reinterpretation, although startling in the audacity of its claims regarding Jesus of Nazareth,[22] is nevertheless precisely the kind of development which we should expect to take place in a period in which Christian thinkers were grappling with the problem of the relationship between Judaism and the person of Jesus Christ. Although Jesus is for them the Messiah, the fulfilment of the promises made in

---

[19] See W. D. Davies, *Paul and Rabbinic Judaism* (London, ²1955), pp. 147–52, 172–5.

[20] Cf. W. D. Davies, *op. cit.*, p. 170: 'It is important to emphasize that in the Judaism of Palestine in Paul's day and elsewhere the identification of the Torah with Wisdom was a commonplace.' For examples, see Ecclus. 24: 23 and Baruch 4. 1.

[21] For the role of Wisdom in creation, see Job 28: 23–7; Prov. 8: 22–31; Ecclus. 24: 1–12. W. D. Davies, *op. cit.*, pp. 170–1, points out that various characteristics of Wisdom in relation to the creation are ascribed to the Torah in rabbinic writings. In particular, Prov. 8: 22f. is applied to the Law in Sifre Deut. 11: 10; the Law is described as the instrument by which the world was created in Pirkê Aboth 3: 23; and it is said that the world was created for the sake of the Torah in Gen. Rabbah 12: 2.

[22] As Professor Moule aptly points out, *op. cit.*, pp. 3–4. Paul has already taken a vital step towards this interpretation, however, in speaking of Christ as the counterpart to Adam, whose behaviour and destiny affect the universe as well as mankind. Cf. Rom. 5 and 8; 1 Cor. 15. In 2 Cor. 3–4 we find the idea of Christ as εἰκὼν Θεοῦ in whom God's glory is revealed, in a context which contrasts the lasting glory of Christ with the fading glory of Moses; it was natural that the theme of δόξα should form a bridge between Christ as Second Adam and as greater than the Law. See also the discussion of the theme of Christ in relation to creation in C. F. D. Moule, *Man and Nature in the New Testament* (London, 1964).

the Torah itself, he is nevertheless also greater than the Torah: what the Law could not do, God has achieved in his Son (Rom. 8: 3); the ministry of the new covenant is more glorious than that of Moses (2 Cor. 3: 4–18); it is Christ who is 'our wisdom, our righteousness and sanctification and redemption' (1 Cor. 1: 30) – these things belong to those who are in him, not to those who are obedient to the Law. The Colossians have been brought into the inheritance of God's people, not through obedience to the Law, but because they have been transferred into the kingdom of God's beloved Son, and have redemption in him (1: 12–13). In working out what these claims meant – a traumatic experience for those nurtured in the Jewish faith – it was perhaps inevitable that the role of Christ in relation to creation and redemption should in time be expressed in the kind of language which we find in Colossians 1: 15–20: Jesus Christ had indeed replaced the Torah as the revelation both of God's glory and of his purpose for the universe and for mankind. It is this fundamental truth which is expressed in Colossians, in terms which demonstrate its relevance for those who have been rescued from the grasp of alien powers, and who are subject to the constant temptation to look for perfection through religious rites and regulations, instead of simply relying upon the one in whom all the fullness of God dwells, and in whom they find fulfilment and the confident assurance of final glory.

22

The Spirit in the Apocalypse

F. F. BRUCE

The invitation to contribute to a volume in honour of a friend and colleague of many years' standing was one to be accepted with alacrity, not unmixed with misgivings about the possibility of producing something adequate to the occasion. Ever since I heard his lecture 'From Defendant to Judge – and Deliverer' and first read his *Idiom Book of New Testament Greek*, I have been impressed by the diversity and depth of Professor Moule's scholarship; but the quality of the man himself is more impressive still. In view of the prescribed subject-matter of the volume, it occurred to me that a study of the Spirit in the Apocalypse would both fall within its scope and help to set in perspective one aspect of a book to which I have paid considerable attention in recent years. The result is now offered as a tribute, *quantulumcumque*, to one who has given me more than he can ever receive.

I. THE SEVEN SPIRITS

The epistolary salutation 'Grace to you and peace', following the names of the writer and of the persons addressed, is familiar to readers of the New Testament letters; in most of the Pauline letters the salutation continues '. . . from God the Father and our Lord Jesus Christ'.[1] When, therefore, in Rev. 1: 4f. we find the address and salutation, 'John to the seven churches that are in Asia: Grace to you and peace from him who is and who was and who is to come . . . and from Jesus Christ the faithful witness', we recognize a familiar form, even if the details of the wording are peculiar. What does provoke surprise, however, is the phrase 'and from the seven spirits who are before his throne', which follows the mention of 'him who is and who was and who is to come' and precedes that of 'Jesus Christ the faithful witness'. Whatever the seven spirits may be, it is strange to find them placed between the eternal God and Jesus Christ in this way. Yet to conclude

[1] Cf., in addition to the Pauline letters, 1 Pet. 1: 2; 2 Pet. 1: 2.

'without hesitation', as R. H. Charles does,[2] that the reference to the seven spirits here is an early interpolation is a precarious course in default of textual support.

In the context of trinitarian orthodoxy the accepted interpretation has seen in the seven spirits a reference to the personal Spirit of God in his sevenfold plenitude of grace. Victorinus of Pettau, the earliest Latin commentator on the Apocalypse,[3] applies to this passage an earlier Christian interpretation of Isa. 11: 2, LXX (attested in Justin),[4] according to which the seven designations of the Spirit of the Lord to be bestowed on the Davidic prince denote seven gifts or 'powers' (δυνάμεις) of the one Spirit[5] – an interpretation well known from the words of the *Veni Creator*:

> Thou the anointing Spirit art
> Who dost thy sevenfold gifts impart.

But such dependence on the LXX text, not to say such an application of it, is unlikely in the Apocalypse.

It is necessary, however, to look at other references to the seven spirits in the Apocalypse. If in Rev. 1: 4b the seven spirits are described as being 'before the throne' of God – i.e. in the presence of God in his heavenly dwelling-place – the setting is portrayed with more detail in John's vision of heaven in chapter 4, where he sees burning 'before the throne . . . seven torches of fire, which are the seven spirits of God' (verse 5). Elsewhere the seven spirits appear as attributes or accessories of the risen Christ. In the second part of the vision of heaven, for example, the Lamb – i.e. the Davidic Messiah who has won his victory through suffering and death – is endowed 'with seven horns and with seven eyes, which are the seven spirits of God sent out into all the earth' (5: 6). Perhaps it is only the eyes and not the horns which symbolize the seven spirits;[6] even so, the fact that shortly before the seven spirits have been symbolized by the seven torches burning in front of the throne shows that in John's imagery there is no sense of incongruity in having two different symbols in a single vision denoting one and the same reality. The Old Testament background to Rev. 5: 6

---

[2] *The Revelation of St John*, ICC (Edinburgh, 1920), i, p. 11.

[3] *Comm. in Apocalypsin*, ed. J. Haussleiter, *CSEL* xlix (Vienna, 1916), pp. 16, 18.

[4] *Dial. c. Tryph.* 87. 2; cf. Irenaeus, *Haer.* iii. 18. 2.

[5] MT has only six; after 'the spirit of knowledge' LXX adds 'and of piety' (καὶ εὐσεβείας).

[6] The relative οἵ agrees with ὀφθαλμούς as the nearer antecedent, but that need not exclude κέρατα from the total antecedent.

is clearly to be discerned in Zech. 4: 2, 10b, where the seven lamps on the golden lampstand which Zechariah sees in his fifth night-vision are explained as 'the eyes of Yahweh, which range throughout the whole earth'. (That the function of Yahweh's eyes in Zech. 4: 10b is transferred to the eyes of the Lamb in Rev. 5: 6 is material for the christology of the Apocalypse.) In Zechariah's language there may be some allusion to the court emissaries of the Persian Empire popularly known as the King's Eyes.[7]

But if in Rev. 5: 6 the seven spirits are sent out into all the earth, the question arises of their relation to the seven chief angels. This question is also posed by the preamble to the church of Sardis: 'The words of him who has the seven spirits of God and the seven stars' (Rev. 3: 1). Not only are the seven spirits here accessories of the risen Christ, as in Rev. 5: 6, but the 'seven stars' hark back to the inaugural vision of the book, in which the risen Christ holds in his right hand seven stars which are identified with 'the angels of the seven churches' (Rev. 1: 16, 20). But the angels of the seven churches are not the seven chief angels, so the καί which links the seven spirits and the seven stars in Rev. 3: 1 is probably copulative, not epexegetic.

The seven chief angels are presented in Rev. 8: 2 as 'the seven angels who stand before God' and blow the seven trumpets of doom (they may be identical with the seven angels of Rev. 15: 1ff. who pour out the seven last plagues on the earth). The 'seven angels who stand before God' (cf. Luke 1: 19, where Gabriel introduces himself as one of them) are those described by Raphael (another of their number) in Tobit 12: 15 as 'the seven holy angels who present the prayers of the saints (cf. Rev. 5: 8; 8: 3f.) and stand before the presence of the Holy One'; their names are listed in 1 Enoch 20: 2–8 ('the archangels' names are seven'). Once more an analogy with Persian court practice suggests itself: we may think of the 'seven princes . . . who saw the king's face, and sat first in the kingdom' (Esther 1: 14).[8] If we think further of the Amesha Spentas of the Gathas, we should bear in mind that they sometimes number seven only when the supreme lord Ahura Mazdah is reckoned as one of them.[9]

---

[7] Cf. Herodotus, *Hist.* i. 114, v. 24; Aristophanes, *Acharn.* 92, 94, 124.
[8] Cf. Ezra 7: 14.
[9] Cf. J. H. Moulton, *Early Religious Poetry of Persia* (Cambridge, 1911), pp. 58ff.; in fact, there were considerable variations in the conception of Ahura Mazdah's relation to the (other) Amesha Spentas; if originally he was distinct from them, he may have been included with them by the time Zoroastrianism influenced

It may well be that 'from a religio-historical standpoint', as Eduard Schweizer says, the seven spirits 'are simply the seven archangels'.[10] But John is never in bondage to the religio-historical roots of his symbolism; with sovereign freedom he bends and re-shapes it to serve his special purpose. If in his initial salutation he invokes a blessing on the seven churches from the seven spirits, placing them between God and Christ, who in this book shares the attributes of God, something more than a reference to angels is implied. If an allusion to the sevenfold phraseology of Isa. 11: 2 LXX is improbable, it is also improbable that the number seven is due to the number of the churches of Asia;[11] the seven churches disappear from sight at the end of chapter 3, to reappear only in the epilogue (22: 6–21), but the seven spirits are prominent in chapters 4 and 5. The most probable account of the matter is that given by I. T. Beckwith:[12] by the 'seven spirits' we are to understand the one Spirit symbolized by the seven torches (Rev. 4: 5) and the seven eyes (Rev. 5: 6), two symbols from Zechariah's fifth vision, the reality symbolized being identified with the symbols;[13] and the order of Rev. 1: 4f. is dictated by the order of appearance in the vision in chapters 4 and 5, where God is seated on the heavenly throne (4: 2f.), before which 'burn seven torches of fire, which are the seven spirits of God' (4: 5), and to which, as the vision proceeds, the Lamb advances to take the sealed scroll from the hand of God (5: 6f.). If the number seven is not derived from Isa. 11: 2, nevertheless that text, in so far as it speaks of the Davidic Messiah as endowed with the Spirit of Yahweh, is one of the sources of our seer's depiction of the 'seven spirits' as accessories of the Lamb (cf. also Isa. 42: 1; 61: 1).

If we are to relate the 'seven spirits of God sent out into all the

Judaism. Cf. B. Geiger, *Die Amǝša Spǝntas: ihr Wesen und ihre ursprüngliche Bedeutung* (Vienna, 1916); G. Widengren, 'Stand und Aufgaben der Iranischen Religionsgeschichte', *Numen* i (1954), pp. 16ff.; R. C. Zaehner, *Dawn and Twilight of Zoroastrianism* (London, 1961), pp. 45ff. *et passim*; M. Boyce, 'Zoroaster the priest', *BSOAS* xxxiii (1970), pp. 22ff.

[10] *TDNT* vi (Grand Rapids, 1968), *s.v.* πνεῦμα, p. 450.

[11] So H. B. Swete, *The Holy Spirit in the New Testament* (London, 1909), p. 274 ('The spirits are seven because the churches are seven').

[12] I. T. Beckwith, *The Apocalypse of John* (London–New York, 1919), pp. 426f.

[13] Cf. also G. B. Caird, *The Revelation of St John the Divine* (London, 1966), p. 15. When account is taken of the seer's use of symbolism, it is unnecessary to suppose that Rev. 1: 4 'shews us how far were the New Testament times in general from reaching a fixed Trinitarian formula, such as is outlined in the baptismal commission' (H. W. Robinson, *The Christian Experience of the Holy Spirit* (London, 1928), pp. 233f.).

earth' to the one Holy Spirit, we may think of the Paraclete's ministry of convicting the world in John 16: 8, but for the most part the Spirit appears in the Apocalypse in a different perspective from that in which he is presented in other writings of the Johannine corpus. There is no word in the Apocalypse of his indwelling believers in general (cf. John 14: 17; 1 John 2: 20, 27; 3: 24) apart from his using the prophets as his mouthpiece – unless indeed all true believers are viewed here as prophets.[14] Whether that is so or not, this brings us to the central role of the Spirit in the Apocalypse.

II. THE SPIRIT OF PROPHECY

On this subject the key-passage is Rev. 19: 10, 'the testimony of Jesus is the Spirit of prophecy'. The expression 'the Spirit of prophecy' is current in post-biblical Judaism: it is used, for example, in a Targumic circumlocution for the Spirit of Yahweh which comes upon this or that prophet. Thus the Targum of Jonathan renders the opening words of Isa. 61: 1 as 'The Spirit of prophecy (*rûaḥ nᵉbû'āh*) from before the Lord God is upon me'. The thought expressed in Rev. 19: 10 is not dissimilar to that in 1 Pet. 1: 11 where 'the Spirit of the Messiah' (meaning perhaps the Spirit of messianic prophecy) is said to have spoken in the Old Testament prophets[15] who foretold 'the sufferings destined for the Messiah and the subsequent glories'. There too Jesus is the theme of the witness borne by the prophetic Spirit; the prophets did not know who the person or what the time would be, but at last the secret is out: the person is Jesus; the time is now.

In Rev. 19: 10, however, it is through *Christian* prophets that the Spirit of prophecy bears witness. What the prophets of pre-Christian days foretold is proclaimed as an accomplished fact by the prophets of the new age, among whom John occupies a leading place.

When the word 'prophets' is used generally in the Apocalypse, Old Testament prophets may be included, but New Testament prophets are in the forefront. 'Saints and apostles and prophets' are called upon to rejoice over the downfall of great Babylon because 'in her was found

[14] Cf. E. Schweizer, *TDNT* vi, p. 449 n. 816: 'It seems to me...that acc. to 19: 10 all members of the community (at least potentially, Loh. Apk. on 19: 10) are prophets.'

[15] Cf. *1 Clement* 22: 1, where a quotation from Ps. 34 (LXX 33): 11–17 is introduced by the words: 'All these things are confirmed by faith in Christ, for he himself through the Holy Spirit encourages us as follows.'

the blood of prophets and of saints, and of all who have been slain on earth' (Rev. 18: 20, 24). The comprehensive terms of the last clause may imply that from great Babylon, as from the generation of Jesus' day in Luke 11: 50f., reparation should be required for 'the blood of all the prophets shed from the foundation of the world'.[16] But first and foremost the saints and prophets directly killed by great Babylon are in view, for when John sees great Babylon in the guise of the scarlet woman, she is 'drunk with the blood of the saints and the blood of the witnesses of Jesus' (Rev. 17: 6).

The burden of the prophecy entrusted to John and his fellow-prophets, then, is 'the testimony of Jesus' (ἡ μαρτυρία 'Ιησοῦ). The genitive 'Ιησοῦ is most probably objective, as it is in the preceding clause of Rev. 19: 10 where the angel declines to accept John's homage on the ground, as he says, that 'I am a fellow-servant with you and your brethren who hold the testimony of Jesus', and also as it certainly is in the phrase τῶν μαρτύρων 'Ιησοῦ quoted above from Rev. 17: 6. True, Jesus himself is 'the faithful witness' (Rev. 1: 5; cf. 3: 14) and the whole Apocalypse is his testimony to his people (Rev. 22: 16, 20).[17] But they in their turn are his witnesses, like Antipas the Pergamene martyr,[18] whom he calls 'my faithful witness', or indeed like John himself, exiled to Patmos for 'the word of God and the testimony of Jesus' (Rev. 1: 9).[19] When the followers of Jesus are assaulted by the dragon and his agents, 'they have conquered him by the blood of the Lamb and by the word of their testimony, for they loved not their lives even unto death' (Rev. 12: 11). No doubt their Lord was bearing *his* testimony in theirs, and suffering in them, but it is through their own testimony that they conquer, and their own testimony is that which they bear to Jesus and his redeeming power. It is this testimony, John is assured, that is the very substance of the Spirit of prophecy.

We may recognize here an insight similar to that found in 1 Cor. 12: 3 and 1 John 4: 2f., where the test of the genuine Spirit of prophecy (in the church) is the testimony which it bears to Jesus. If that testimony is true – if it affirms the lordship of Jesus (according to Paul) and his

---

[16] In Matt. 23: 35 'the blood of all the prophets' is generalized to 'all the righteous blood shed on earth'.

[17] Cf. Rev. 1: 1.

[18] In Rev. 2: 13 (cf. 17: 6) μάρτυς has clearly begun its transition from 'witness' to 'martyr'.

[19] Cf. Rev. 1: 2, where John 'bore witness to the word of God and to the testimony of Jesus Christ'.

real incarnation (according to John) – it is to be accepted; if it denies these truths, it is to be banned.

Again, when Jesus in John 15: 26f. tells his disciples that, when the Paraclete comes, 'he will bear witness to me; and you also are witnesses', it is probably implied that the Paraclete's witness will be borne in them; and the same implication is probably present in Acts 5: 32 where Peter and his fellow-apostles, making their defence before the Sanhedrin, say 'we are witnesses to these things, and so is the Holy Spirit whom God has given to those who obey him'.

The same perspective pervades the Apocalypse, with the distinctive feature that here the Spirit who bears his testimony in the witnesses of Jesus is specifically the Spirit of prophecy. So the ministry of the two witnesses of Rev. 11: 3ff. is statedly a prophetic ministry; the Spirit of prophecy is not explicitly mentioned, but is certainly to be inferred, in the record of their testimony.[20] (When, in Rev. 11: 11, πνεῦμα ζωῆς from God enters them three and a half days after their martyrdom, this is the 'breath of life' as in Gen. 2: 7 and not the prophetic Spirit.) Features of their ministry are purposely included so as to place them in the succession of Moses and Elijah, and in verse 3 their function is further described in symbols taken from the same night-vision of Zechariah as has been drawn upon in Rev. 4: 5 and 5: 6.

In addition to 'the Spirit of prophecy', we have in Rev. 22: 6 a reference to 'the spirits of the prophets' ('the God of the spirits of the prophets', John is told, 'has sent his angel to show his servants what must soon take place'). The plural expression denotes not the one Spirit of prophecy but rather the spirits of the individual prophets, as in 1 Cor. 14: 32, where it appears in the anarthrous form: 'spirits of prophets are subject to prophets'. There may be an echo in Rev. 22: 6 of the Old Testament phrase, 'God of the spirits of all flesh' (Num. 16: 22; 27: 16); he who creates and controls all human spirits has a special concern for 'the spirits of the prophets' who are his spokesmen on earth.

When the Spirit of prophecy comes upon him, John speaks of himself as being, or becoming, 'in Spirit' (ἐν πνεύματι). So his inaugural vision

---

[20] The adverb πνευματικῶς in the vision of the two witnesses is used of the interpretation of Jerusalem, 'where their Lord was crucified', as 'the great city which is *spiritually* called Sodom and Egypt'. Whereas the adverb is commonly rendered 'allegorically' (RSV; cf. NEB 'in allegory'), E. Schweizer takes it to mean 'in prophetic rather than ordinary speech' (*TDNT* vi, p. 449 with n. 819).

is introduced with the words 'I became in Spirit on the Lord's day' (Rev. 1: 10); his second vision, in which he was rapt to heaven, is similarly introduced with 'immediately I became in Spirit' (Rev. 4: 2); and for two later visions – that of the scarlet woman and that of the bride of the Lamb – he is carried away 'in Spirit' by an angel to an appropriate vantage-point (Rev. 17: 3; 21: 10). In these last two passages especially, his language is strongly reminiscent of Ezekiel's, although Ezekiel uses other expressions than 'in Spirit'. Ezekiel's nearest approach to this phraseology is in Ezek. 37: 1: 'the hand of Yahweh was upon me and carried me out in the Spirit of Yahweh'. Elsewhere he says 'the Spirit lifted me up, and took me away' (Ezek. 3: 14; cf. 8: 3, etc.). The Spirit performs for Ezekiel the service that one of the seven angels performs for John, but the same type of ecstasy is described under the variant terminology.

III. WHAT THE SPIRIT SAYS TO THE CHURCHES

The exhortation at the end of each of the letters to the seven churches (preceding the promise to the overcomer in the first three, following it in the last four), 'He who has an ear, let him hear what the Spirit says to the churches',[21] should give the reader pause. For each of these letters is sent in the name of the exalted Christ, who is introduced by one designation or another, largely drawn from John's description of him in his inaugural vision. Thus the letter to the Ephesian church, for instance (Rev. 2: 1–7), begins with 'The words of him who holds the seven stars in his right hand (cf. 1: 16), who walks among the seven golden lampstands' (cf. 1: 13), but towards the end comes the exhortation to the attentive hearer to pay heed to what *the Spirit* says (2: 7a). The conclusion is plain: it is not that the Spirit is identical with the exalted Lord,[22] but that the exalted Lord speaks to the churches by the Spirit – and the Spirit can scarcely be other than the Spirit of prophecy. The words which John writes to the churches by the Lord's command he writes as a prophet.

Nor is it only in these letters that he speaks by the Spirit of prophecy in the name of the exalted Lord. One prophetic utterance thus made in his name is of special interest. When John sees the kings of the earth mustering for the battle of Har-Magedon 'on the great day of God the

[21] Rev. 2: 7a, 11a, 17a, 29; 3: 6, 13, 22.
[22] As E. Schweizer suggests (*TDNT* vi, p. 449).

Almighty', a voice declares: 'Lo, I am coming like a thief! Blessed is he who is awake, keeping his garments that he may not go naked and be seen exposed!' (Rev. 16: 15).[23] The voice is self-evidently that of the exalted Lord, but it echoes a logion ascribed in the Gospels to the earthly Jesus, in a life-setting which is perfectly appropriate. The thief simile, which has already been used by the exalted Lord in the letter to the church of Sardis as an incentive to stay awake (Rev. 3: 3), is used by Jesus in a Q logion (Matt. 24: 43 ‖ Luke 12: 39), where the day of visitation comes unexpectedly as a thief.[24] We may infer that a prophetic utterance in the name of Jesus was liable to take up an authentic *verbum Christi* and adapt or point it to the current situation, as here the logion is elaborated by the blessing pronounced on the man who is alert and ready dressed, so that when the alarm is sounded he has no need to take to flight naked, like the man 'who is stout of heart among the mighty' in Amos 2: 16.

This raises the question of the place of such prophecy in other parts of the New Testament. It is sometimes argued that the first-century churches were not much concerned to distinguish the words of the earthly Jesus, preserved by tradition, from the words of the risen Lord, conveyed through prophets – so much so that words of the latter category might be given a context in the historical ministry and so recorded in the Gospels. But the Apocalypse at least, because of its peculiar character, cannot be cited as a general precedent. It might indeed be adduced as an analogy to the Olivet discourse of Mark 13: 5ff., although this discourse is introduced by a conversation (Mark 13: 1f.) whose most natural life-setting is that which the evangelist gives it. It might be adduced also as an analogy to the revelation of 1 Thess. 4: 15ff., which Paul communicates 'by the word of the Lord', though this could equally well mean his application of a logion received by tradition. The prophetic genre has its own characteristics, which cannot be transferred without more ado to other literary genres. Paul, like John, sends letters to various churches, and occasionally claims as authority for what he writes the mind of the Spirit or the commandment of the Lord, but he sends his letters in his own name (quite emphatically so), not in the name of the Lord.

A closer parallel to the Apocalypse is presented by the Odes of

---

[23] R. H. Charles (*The Revelation of St John* ii, p. 49) maintains that Rev. 16: 15 is an intrusion here, either from the middle of Rev. 3: 3 (so also J. Moffatt) or from before 3: 18 (so Th. Beza).   [24] Cf. 1 Thess. 5: 2; 2 Pet. 3: 10.

Solomon which, while they are not apocalyptic, breathe the spirit of prophecy, especially where Christ himself is the speaker. He says, for example, 'I rose up and was with them, and speak by their mouths' (Ode 42: 6). But this apparently refers not to prophets in particular but to those who love him in general (Ode 42: 4), and especially in the context of persecution, so that it is to the same effect as the passage in the Lukan edition of the Olivet discourse where Jesus tells his disciples that when they are brought to trial for their faith, 'I will give you a mouth and wisdom' (Luke 21: 15).[25]

IV. THE RESPONSIVE SPIRIT

The Spirit in the prophets is immediately responsive to the will of heaven.[26] So, when John is directed by a heavenly voice to write, 'Blessed are the dead who die in the Lord henceforth' (Rev. 14: 13), the Spirit adds his Amen: 'Blessed indeed, . . . that they may rest from their labours, for their deeds accompany them!'[27] For apostates and confessors alike it is true that 'their deeds accompany them' beyond the grave, but whereas for the former this means tribulation, for the latter it means rest (cf. 2 Thess. 1: 6f.). The significance and construction of 'henceforth' (ἀπ' ἄρτι) are debatable: the 'saints, those who keep the commandments of God and the faith of Jesus' (Rev. 14: 12) may be given this beatitude as an incentive to endure from now on[28] – but their lot, if they suffered martyrdom, was never anything but blessed. Perhaps ἀπ' ἄρτι means 'after they have suffered martyrdom' or, as A. Debrunner has conjectured, it should be spelt ἀπαρτί, 'verily'.[29]

Again, when 'the Spirit and the Bride say, "Come"' (Rev. 22: 17a), this is their response to the Lord's announcement in verse 12, 'Behold,

---

[25] In Mark 13: 11, 'it is not you that speak, but the Holy Spirit' (cf. Matt. 10: 20).

[26] Similar responses are made by the angel of the waters (Rev. 16: 5) and by the altar (16: 7); cf. 18: 20, where heaven, together with the saints, apostles and prophets, is called upon to acquiesce with joy in the divine judgement on great Babylon.

[27] Cf. *Pirqe Aboth* 6: 9 ('in the hour of man's departure neither silver nor gold nor precious stones nor pearls accompany him, but only Torah and good works').

[28] The adverb ἀπ' ἄρτι is naturally construed with ἀποθνήσκοντες, not with μακάριοι. Cf. H. B. Swete, *The Apocalypse of St John* (London, 1906), p. 184; R. H. Charles, *The Revelation of St John* i, p. 370.

[29] *Coniectanea Neotestamentica* xi (1947), p. 48, quoted with approval by A. Oepke, *TDNT* v (Grand Rapids, 1967), p. 867 n. 50 (*s.v.* παρουσία).

I am coming soon'. The Spirit may be envisaged as indwelling the beloved community ('the Bride'), prompting this response, or (more probably) the Spirit is the Spirit of prophecy, who takes the initiative in making the response, and is seconded by the community as a whole, so that 'the Spirit and the Bride', in H. B. Swete's words, is an expression 'practically equivalent to "the Prophets and the Saints"'.[30]

The words immediately following, 'And let him who hears say, "Come"' (Rev. 22: 17b), constitute a call to those who are listening to the reading of the Apocalypse in the churches (cf. Rev. 1: 3) to interpose at this point with their own 'Come!' We cannot dissociate this passage from the use of the invocation *Maranatha* in the early church – a subject to which Professor Moule has made his own characteristically illuminating contribution.[31] In the eucharistic setting in which the invocation appears in the *Didache* (10: 6), it is preceded by the call:

> 'If anyone is holy, let him come;
> if anyone is not, let him repent.'

The invitation 'let him come' (ἐρχέσθω) presents a marked affinity to the words in the Apocalypse which follow the call to the hearer: 'And let him who is thirsty come (ἐρχέσθω), let him who desires take the water of life without price' (cf. Isa. 55: 1) – take it from the Alpha and Omega who, as Rev. 21: 6 declares, has the authority and the will to grant it.

The water of life is drawn from the river of Rev. 22: 1f., which flows through the New Jerusalem. The imagery is derived from the life-giving river of Ezek. 47: 1 ff., but when we consider that in the New Testament the figure of the water of life appears only in the fourth Gospel and the Apocalypse, we are bound to think of the 'rivers of living water' promised by Jesus in John 7: 37ff. The evangelist explains this living water as a figure of the Spirit, and similarly (although the seer does not himself make the identification explicitly) the water to be had without price in Rev. 21: 6b and 22: 17b may be identified with the Spirit – but if so, it is now the Spirit of life, not the Spirit of prophecy, that is in view.

To revert to the invitation, whereas the *Didache* holds out the hope of repentance to one who is not holy, the situation in the Apocalypse is

---

[30] *The Apocalypse of St John*, p. 306 (he compares Rev. 16: 6; 18: 24).
[31] C. F. D. Moule, 'A Reconsideration of the Context of *Maranatha*', *NTS* vi (1959–60), pp. 307ff.

more urgent, and room for repentance is practically excluded: 'Let the evildoer still do evil, . . . and the holy still be holy' (Rev. 22: 11).

Here Professor Moule's 'reconsideration of the context of *Maranatha*' is specially relevant. In 1 Cor. 16: 22, he reminds us, *Maranatha* is clearly associated with the anathema pronounced on 'any one' who 'has no love for the Lord', while in Rev. 22: 20 the invocation 'Amen: come, Lord Jesus!' is preceded by 'the tremendous curse' of verses 18f. on any one who tampers with 'the words of the book of this prophecy'. The curse is introduced with 'I testify' and followed by the words, 'He who testifies to these things says, "Surely I am coming soon"'.

Probably the invitation to the seeker and the ban on the reprobate are both associated with the invocation 'Come!' The nearness of the Lord, which is a comfort to believers, means judgement for the impenitent. In Rev. 21: 7f. the overcomer's heritage of divine sonship is proclaimed in the same breath as the sentence to the 'second death' on those who in speech or conduct have forsworn the faith.

When the Lord manifests his real presence in the holy supper, the humble are encouraged to draw near and partake; the self-centred and hard-hearted are warned off lest they eat and drink judgement to themselves: ἑκὰς ὢ ἑκὰς ἔστε βέβηλοι. The Lord's coming in the Apocalypse is more than his eucharistic presence, but it is anticipated in his eucharistic presence, as the separation of the righteous from the unrighteous at his coming is anticipated by the two-way fencing of the holy table. The most solemn act of the church's worship could thus have provided an appropriate occasion for the public reading of the Apocalypse, and such an occasion may have been in the seer's mind as he wrote the concluding sentences of his book.

23

The Spirit in gnostic literature

R. MCL. WILSON

In a volume relating to the New Testament, the inclusion of a paper devoted to gnostic literature may at first sight seem anomalous. At least it would appear to require some justification, especially if the term 'gnostic' is considered to refer only to the Christian heresy, which did not reach its full development until after the New Testament period. Adequate reasons for the inclusion of such a paper are, however, not far to seek. For one thing, it is now increasingly recognized that gnosticism may no longer be treated as merely a Christian heresy of the second century, if it is to be fully understood. Its full development, in terms of clear-cut systems, is admittedly later than the New Testament, but there are at least anticipations long before, and an influential body of scholars would maintain that in some sense the gnostic movement is even prior to Christianity, and may have influenced the New Testament itself. Again, our division of history into periods is in large measure arbitrary, purely a matter of convenience, to restrict the field of study within manageable limits. In point of fact we may often have to go back before the period with which we are concerned in order to find the explanation for developments within it; and we may also require to move down beyond the end of the period into a later age before we can detect the final outcome of trends and tendencies already present and recognizable in our period itself. Finally, it may not be inappropriate to observe that the scholar to whom these pages render homage has himself been known to stray on occasion beyond the narrow confines of the New Testament period proper.

Some of the problems are already evident, even at this early stage. What is the relation between the New Testament and gnosticism (or, in a somewhat wider sense, gnosis)? What trends and tendencies can be detected in the New Testament itself, or more broadly in the New Testament period, which were later to be developed in one way or another in gnostic literature? To what extent is the development due to the infiltration of alien ideas, and from what sources? How far is it a case, not of the introduction or substitution of alien ideas, but of the more subtle modification which results from convergence of ideas, when concepts that are similar but in fact distinct are simply conflated or identified?

This leads directly to problems of method. Some of these questions, it should be said at once, do not admit of a simple and straightforward answer. It is for example a fundamental error to assume that the relationship between Christianity and gnosticism (or gnosis) was a one-way process, so that any parallels must be considered evidence either of New Testament influence upon gnosticism or of the influence of gnosis upon the New Testament. There *are* clear cases, where a New Testament influence is guaranteed by an express quotation or at least a manifest allusion: the Excerpta ex Theodoto (3) refers to the spirit breathed into the apostles, Exc. 16 to the dove which descended upon the flesh of the Logos, and the Valentinian Marcus according to Irenaeus (1: 15. 3) to the Spirit of God which spoke in Jesus. Even here, however, it is sometimes a question whether the explicit reference is not due to the reporter, rather than to the actual system. Judgement is rather more difficult in cases like the Apocryphon of John,[1] where reference is frequently made to the coming of a 'helper' who is sometimes identified as a spirit.[2] Is this to be claimed as a development from the Johannine Paraclete? There is a similarity which makes the suggestion attractive, but the term Paraclete itself is not used, and there may be other possibilities to be considered. It is for example open to question whether in English the word 'spirit' in these passages should be left in lower case, or capitalized to suggest a divine hypostasis, if not the Holy Spirit of 'orthodox' theology. In any case, a more direct link connects with the βοηθός of Gen. 2: 18, LXX.

It may be granted that there are some instances of clear influence from the New Testament, but this does not justify us in concluding that the whole gnostic movement was merely a phenomenon within

[1] Text in W. C. Till, *Die gnostischen Schriften des koptischen Papyrus Berolinensis* 8502 (TU60, Berlin, 1955), pp. 78ff. (= *BG*); M. Krause and P. Labib, *Die drei Versionen des Apokryphon des Johannes* (Wiesbaden, 1962) (the Nag Hammadi Codices II, III and IV = *CG*); S. Giversen, *Apocryphon Johannis* (Copenhagen, 1963) (*CG* II). English translations in W. Foerster, *Gnosis* i (Oxford, 1972), pp. 105ff. (*BG*).

[2] *BG* 47. 2–4 (a spirit from the perfection is poured upon Sophia, and her consort descends to put right her deficiency); 53. 5–10 (the good spirit, identified as the Epinoia of light, is sent as a helper to Adam); 63. 16–19 (the spirit descends to awaken the nature that is like him. This spirit remains for a time, working on behalf of the 'seed' (64. 4–9), and appears to be the 'spirit of life' (66. 16, 67. 9). The latter term has clear links with the creation story in Genesis, for which see below).

Christianity. We have also to take account of the use of πνεῦμα and related concepts both in Greek and in Jewish thought prior to the New Testament period.[3] According to Kleinknecht,[4] πνεῦμα in Greek thought, despite the Stoics, has only a secondary significance, in contrast to the dominant role which it plays in the New Testament. For our present purpose, however, the interest lies not so much in the significance of concepts in their original context, but in the effects of convergence. What happened when a Gentile, nurtured on Greek conceptions of πνεῦμα, encountered the Old Testament conceptions of spirit in Greek dress in the Septuagint? Something of the answer can be seen from Hellenistic Judaism, particularly Philo;[5] but it has to be remembered that Philo was a Jew interpreting his own tradition in Greek terms, not a Gentile approaching that tradition from a different background. 'If in terms of terminology Philo is close on the one hand to pantheistic Stoicism and on the other to dualistic gnosticism, yet in terms of content he is neither a pantheist nor a dualist, but as a Jew in Greek clothing an ethical theist.'[6]

On the Palestinian side Sjöberg rightly remarks that Palestine was no isolated region at this period, but influenced by the surrounding Hellenistic culture.[7] The problem here is to determine just how strong that influence was at any given period, in any given area, or in any particular book. It may suffice to observe that section D of the Kittel article, on 'the development to the pneumatic Self of Gnosis', begins with a discussion of the Qumran Scrolls. The well-known doctrine of the two spirits, deriving ultimately from Persian dualism, may be reflected in references to the spirit of wickedness in the system of the Valentinian Ptolemy (Iren. 1: 5. 4; he is the 'world-ruler', not the Demiurge), the spirit of truth in the Hypostasis of the Archons (96: 24, 35; in the latter context there are however Johannine elements), or the spirit of knowledge (combined with that of love) in Exc. 7. Possibly the ἀντίμιμον πνεῦμα in the Apocryphon of John should be included here too.[8] Clear evidence of Jewish influence which need not

---

3 See E. Schweizer and others in Kittel, *TWNT* vi, pp. 330–450, partially translated by A. E. Harvey in *Spirit of God* (London, 1960); full translation in Kittel–Bromiley, *TDNT* vi, pp. 332–451; also Schweizer's article in W. D. Davies and D. Daube (ed.), *The Background of the New Testament and its Eschatology* (Cambridge, 1956), pp. 482–508.

4 *TWNT* vi, p. 355.   5 Cf. Bieder, *TWNT* vi, pp. 370–3.

6 *Ibid.*, p. 373 (my translation).   7 *Ibid.*, p. 379.

8 *BG* 63. 9; 67. 15 (the context refers to the spirit of life); 71. 4–5; 74–5. It is not certain whether this should be identified with the ἀντικείμενον πνεῦμα of 55. 7.

have been mediated through Christian channels (although of course it could have been) is provided by the use made of the Genesis creation narrative. In the book Baruch, for example, Eden and Elohim make man as a symbol of their unity and love, and set in him their powers, Eden the soul and Elohim the spirit. Abandoned by Elohim, Eden in revenge commands her angels to afflict the spirit of Elohim in man (Hippol. 5: 26. 8, 17 etc.). Even clearer are those systems akin to the Apocryphon of John (*BG* 51. 16), where the Demiurge breathes his spirit into the hitherto inert and lifeless torso.[9] Elsewhere we find the familiar motif of the spirit brooding over the waters of the primeval chaos.[10]

The search for possible influences and sources is however not the only line of approach. It is already evident from the references given above (which do not include explicit allusions to the Holy Spirit) that the word 'spirit' is used in the gnostic texts, as in the New Testament and elsewhere, in several different ways. There are good and evil spirits, spirits of truth and error, opposing and 'counterfeit' spirits. Here the gnostic texts are more or less at one with a wide range of literature, complete evaluation of which would involve an investigation of angelology and demonology beyond the scope of the present paper. One point of interest however shows the transmission of such ideas from one tradition to another: the Gospel of Philip ('saying' 61) says that among the unclean spirits there are male and female, who force themselves upon unattached members of the opposite sex; only if the image (the Gnostic) and the angel (his angelic counterpart) are united are their assaults in vain. The motif of male and female spirits recurs in a Manichean fragment from Chinese Turkestan.[11]

Secondly, there is the anthropological use, of the spirit in man. Here Dr Schweizer lays his finger upon a problem that perplexed generations.[12] God in the Genesis creation story (to confine the discussion to

9 The texts do not always expressly refer to 'spirit', but the dependence on Genesis is clear. According to L. Schottroff, *Der Glaubende und die feindliche Welt* (Neukirchen, 1970), p. 39, the Golem motif is not to be explained from Genesis. Yet as she herself remarks, the framework in the gnostic texts is almost without exception the Old Testament paradise story.

10 The Megale Apophasis (Hippol. 6: 14. 4, 6); Exc. 47; the Sethians (Hippol. 5: 19. 17); Poimandres 5(?). The Apocryphon of John (*BG* 45. 6–12) 'corrects' Moses on this point.

11 Ménard, *L'évangile selon Philippe* (Strasbourg, 1967), p. 179. A Gospel of Philip was in use among the Manichees, and there are grounds for assuming that it was the Nag Hammadi document (Puech in Hennecke–Schneemelcher, *New Testament Apocrypha* i (London, 1963), pp. 272, 277).

12 *TWNT* vi, p. 387, 27–41.

the biblical material) breathed into man the breath of life, 'and man became a living soul'. There is therefore some relation between the Spirit of God and the soul in man. But if the soul is a portion of the divine Spirit, must it not be automatically saved after death? Or must we distinguish from it another human ego which can receive or reject, keep pure or defile this part of the divine Spirit? Or should we understand this portion of the divine Spirit in terms of the possibility of free decision? This problem of the relation between the human soul and the divine Spirit – with the related problems of determinism and free-will, divine sovereignty and human responsibility – can be traced in the literature in various forms and in various stages of discussion; but this lies beyond the scope of this paper. It must suffice to illustrate from a few examples in the gnostic literature. According to Saturninus (Iren. 1 : 24. 1) the supreme power sent to man a 'spark of life' which raised him up and made him live. At death this spark 'hastens back to his own kind', which would seem to imply salvation for all such sparks, and therefore for all men. Yet in the next section we read that Saturninus distinguished two kinds of men, good and evil, and that the Saviour came for the destruction of the evil and the salvation of the good. The latter have just been identified as those who believe in Christ, who are 'those who have the spark of life in them'. Reference has already been made above to the book Baruch, where the spirit derives from Elohim, the soul from Eden. The good angel Baruch attempts to intervene on behalf of the spirit, attacked by the angels of Eden, but cannot move the spirit so strongly as Naas, his opponent, moves the vital soul – until at last he finds Jesus. The Valentinians took a somewhat different line, distinguishing three kinds of men, pneumatic, psychic and material; but the problem still remains. What is the essential difference between the pneumatic and the hylic, which marks the one for salvation and the other for damnation, and accords to the psychic between them a measure of choice and free will, and at best a partial salvation at the end of it all? Heracleon (fr. 13) distinguishes between the pneumatics and 'the mere "calling", apart from the Spirit': 'the temple forecourt is a symbol of the psychics who attain a salvation outside the Pleroma'.

Finally, there is the question of John in the Apocryphon (*BG* 64. 14–16):[13] 'Will the souls of all be saved into the pure light?' To this

---

[13] The text here seems to require correction in the light of the parallel in Codex III from Nag Hammadi. See the apparatus to Till's edition, *TU* lx (1955), pp. 168–9; also the Codex II version, p. 25. 17f. Krause, pl. 73. 17f. Giversen.

Christ replies, 'those on whom the spirit of life comes down and who have united with the power will be saved' (*BG* 65. 3–6). Here, it seems, we must pay close attention to the words employed: the vital point is not so much the reference to the spirit of life but the fact that it 'comes down', and that the saved 'have united with the power'. There is a difference between the spirit that is in man and the saving power: the former is breathed into man by the Demiurge at the instigation of Auto- genes and the four lights – who aim by this process to recover from Ialdabaoth the divine power that is in him (*BG* 51. 1–20). The 'saving power' (*BG* 53. 4ff.) is something different, although it must bear some sort of relationship to the spirit in man. In gnostic thought, after all, the 'essential man' is consubstantial with the divine, and the divine spirit which comes to redeem the soul (or the spirit in man) is only seeking to redeem its own.[14] A simpler scheme would have dis- tinguished the soul or 'breath of life' in man as the common property of all, and the saving power, be it gnosis or the Spirit of Life, as given only to the few; but the pattern has been complicated by the idea of consubstantiality, and by failure to recognize the wide semantic range of the term 'spirit'.

Thus far attention has been concentrated on texts which refer either to spirits of good or evil, or to the spirit in man, although it has been noted that there are cases where it is open to question whether the word 'spirit' should not be capitalized and considered an allusion to the Spirit of God. In a third group of passages the issue is placed beyond doubt by explicit references in the context to the Holy Spirit. Thus the Apocryphon of John (*BG* 71. 5–10) expressly identifies the Spirit and the Epinoia of light. Heracleon (fr. 17) says 'the water which the Saviour gives is from his spirit and his power', and later (fr. 27) that 'through the Spirit and by the Spirit the soul is drawn to the Saviour'. Reference has already been made to Exc. 16, concerning the dove – 'which some call the Holy Spirit, the followers of Basilides the servant, the Valentinians the spirit of the "thought" of the Father'. Such passages may serve by way of transition to those which refer explicitly to the Holy Spirit.

Here it may be useful, for comparison and contrast, to note the three

---

[14] The statement in the Berlin text (*BG* 53. 10–14; no parallel in Codex II) that the Epinoia of light 'works at the whole creation...setting it up in her own perfect temple' seems to contain echoes of the Wisdom tradition (cf. Prov. 8: 22ff., 9: 1); but this cannot be followed up here.

heads under which Dr Haenchen sums up Luke's teaching concerning the Spirit in Acts.[15] It is first of all 'the gift which every Christian receives at baptism'. This of course entails another solution to the problem noted by Dr Schweizer, parallel to the solution adopted in the Apocryphon of John: it is not the natural endowment of the *human* spirit which has saving power, but the Spirit bestowed in baptism. Secondly, Luke describes the Spirit as 'the equipment possessed by individual Christians for a given task at a particular moment' – a use which was already possible for Judaism; and thirdly, the Spirit 'gives specific directions for the Christian mission at important junctures', like the *bath qol* in Jewish tradition.

These three points already provide a standard to measure the extent to which the gnostic literature has moved away from the New Testament, so far as Luke is representative. It may indeed be significant that the index to a two-volume collection of gnostic texts contains only half-a-dozen references to Acts, none of them relating to the Holy Spirit.[16] For one thing, the Gnostics simply were not interested in the Christian mission as such. We know but little of their organization and ecclesiastical structure, if they had any, but it is clear that there was nothing comparable to the missionary labours of a Paul. Equally, there is little if any sign that they thought of the Spirit as 'equipment for a given task at a particular moment'.[17] Only the first of Dr Haenchen's three heads really comes into consideration, and here the Spirit (with the exception of such passages as that from the Apocryphon of John) tends to be not a gift received at baptism but a permanent element in the constitution of the πνευματικός.[18] Some indeed claimed that they were saved 'by nature'.

What then is the nature and function of the Holy Spirit in the gnostic

---

[15] E. Haenchen, *Die Apostelgeschichte* (Göttingen, 1965), p. 83 (E.T. Oxford, 1971, pp. 92f.). Cf. also G. W. H. Lampe in D. E. Nineham (ed.), *Studies in the Gospels* (Oxford, 1955), pp. 159ff.

[16] W. Foerster, *Die Gnosis* (Zürich and Stuttgart, 1969, 1971), ii, pp. 482f. C. H. Talbert, *Luke and the Gnostics* (Nashville, 1966), argues that Luke–Acts was written for the express purpose of serving as a defence against gnosticism.

[17] According to Exc. 24. 1, however, 'the Valentinians say that the spirit which each of the prophets received specially for his ministry is poured out on all in the church; therefore the signs of the Spirit – healings and prophesyings – are accomplished through the church'.

[18] The Gospel of Philip however ('sayings' 59, 67) makes a distinction between those who have received on loan, and must repay, and those who have received as a gift. In 'saying' 95 the Holy Spirit is among the things 'possessed' by the anointed.

literature? Here it should be remembered at the outset that the documents at our disposal belong in their present form to the second Christian century at the earliest. Reference has already been made above to some cases of fairly obvious New Testament influence, and there are other instances in which elements have clearly been taken over from Christianity. The most obvious is the use of the formula 'Father, Son and Holy Spirit' (e.g. Acts of Thomas 27; Gospel of Philip, 'sayings' 11 and 67); although it should at once be added that the use made of the formula requires investigation. The Ophites of Irenaeus (1. 30. 1), for example, have a primal triad of Father, Son and Holy Spirit; but the Spirit here is described as the First Woman, who cannot cope with all the light infused into her by the Father and the Son. The surplus of the light overflows into the underlying waters and assumes from them a body, and so the cosmic process is set in motion. The point here is that the word for Spirit is in Hebrew feminine, which leads to the conception of the Spirit as a female entity – a motif which recurs in several other systems. It also prompts the question whether we may not have here a vestige of an older pre-Christian speculation which has been only crudely Christianized. Confirmation for this suggestion is perhaps afforded by the fact that some of the allusions to the Spirit in other texts have all the appearance of secondary interpolations, as when in the Apocryphon of John (*BG* 71. 5–10) the Spirit is dentified with the Epinoia of light. Such allusions are not integral toi the system, but appear to have been added to give a veneer of Christianity. Our difficulty here is that while we may suspect the existence of non-Christian systems, or even documents, underlying the Christian gnostic texts, we have as yet no such document in its original non-Christian form, and our reconstructions therefore must remain conjectural; nor can it be assumed without more ado that what is non-Christian is also pre-Christian.

Similar identifications reflecting Christian influences occur in other passages. Heracleon (fr. 13) identifies the whip of John 2: 15, as well as 'the linen cloth, the winding-sheet and all such things', as 'an image of the power and energy of the Holy Spirit'. Commenting on 1 Cor. 15: 50, the Gospel of Philip ('saying' 23) identifies the blood of Jesus as the Holy Spirit. In Basilides (Hippol. 7: 26. 9) the light which descended from above on Jesus is identified with the Spirit of Luke 1: 35. The Gospel of Philip however ('saying' 17) rejects this interpretation, on the ground that the Spirit itself is female, and Hippolytus

(6:35. 3–7) notes that there was 'great dispute' among the Valentinians at this point; the 'Italians' affirmed that the body of Jesus was psychic, and that the Spirit came upon him at his baptism; the 'orientals' on the other hand held that the body was pneumatic, the Holy Spirit (Sophia) and the power of the Most High (the Demiurge) having come to Mary 'in order that that which was given to Mary by the Spirit might be formed'.

This 'great dispute' would appear to derive at least in part from divergent views (not to say confusion!) regarding the relation of the Holy Spirit and Sophia. To the Ophites (Iren. 1: 30. 1ff.), the Holy Spirit is one of the three primordial principles, Sophia the overflow of the light deposited in the Spirit. It is Sophia, the mother (of Ialdabaoth), who contrives to deprive Ialdabaoth of his trace of light, and empties Adam and Eve of their trace of light, 'so that the spirit which came from the Source should not suffer abuse or reproach'.

In Barbelognosis, according to Irenaeus (1: 29. 4), the Holy Spirit is on a lower level, and is identified with Sophia (cf. Hippol. 6: 35. 3). In the Apocryphon of John, however (*BG* 38. 6–14), Sophia and the Spirit are distinguished, and the latter is called 'Zoë, the mother of all'. Yet Sophia is also called 'the mother' (*BG* 37. 15f.; 42. 15–43. 2) and it is to Sophia that Gen. 1: 2 is made to refer (*BG* 44. 19–45. 5). Further complications are introduced with the appearance of Eve, who in Gen. 3: 20 is called 'the mother of all living'. The good spirit sent as a helper to Adam is identified as the Epinoia of light, 'who was called by him Zoë' (*BG* 53. 4–10). This Epinoia is hidden in Adam, and Ialdabaoth tries to bring her out by creating Eve from Adam's side (*BG* 59. 6–19; here again the Apocryphon 'corrects' Moses). But the tree of the knowledge of good and evil is also identified as the Epinoia of light (*BG* 57. 8–12), and later 'the maiden who stood beside Adam' appears to be no longer the Epinoia but a created woman (*BG* 62. 6–11). We have thus at least four different entities – the Spirit, Sophia, the Epinoia of light and created Eve – who have somehow to be discovered in the narrative of Genesis. The question is whether the whole speculation results from exegesis of Genesis, or whether it is not rather eisegesis of an existing system into the creation story – just as Philo read his Greek philosophy between the lines of the Old Testament.

In Valentinianism, the syzygy of Christ and the Holy Spirit is produced for the consolidation of the Pleroma, after the fall of Sophia (Iren. 1: 2. 5; cf. Hippol. 6: 31. 2–4). On their return to the Pleroma they leave with Sophia a certain 'fragrance' of immortality (Iren. 1: 4. 1; cf.

Basilides in Hippol. 7: 22. 14). Here the Spirit and Sophia are already distinct – but Sophia is also called Holy Spirit. Later on (Iren. 1: 5. 3) the 'mother' is named 'Ogdoad, and Sophia, Earth, Jerusalem, Holy Spirit and, with a masculine reference, Lord'. She occupies the 'place of the Middle', above the Demiurge but below or outside the Pleroma. One of the clues to understanding here lies in the recognition of the parallelism of the different realms; the lower regions are structured on the pattern of those above, so that the corresponding names from a higher level can be applied on the lower. The process would appear to have begun in Barbelognosis, and to have been further elaborated and developed in Valentinianism.

In the passages so far mentioned, the Spirit plays a subordinate role. If for the Ophites she is one of the three primal principles, she is none the less the third, and receptive rather than active, while in the other systems the Spirit appears to be a comparatively minor entity. We may add that in Basilides (Hippol. 7: 22. 10–15) the second Sonship makes use of the Spirit as a wing on its ascent to the heavens. The Spirit cannot itself enter into the highest realm, but is left with a fragrance of the Sonship. Later it is said that the place of the Sonship is above the exalted Spirit (*ibid.*, 25: 1) and that the Spirit is a boundary between the higher and lower regions (*ibid.*, 27: 1, 6f., 10; cf. the Valentinian Horos). In a fragment in Clement of Alexandria it is described as a ministering spirit (*Strom.* 2: 8. 36. 1). This makes the system of the Apocryphon of John all the more remarkable, for here the primal being from whom the aeons themselves take their origin is described as 'the Holy Spirit' (*BG* 22. 19–23): 'The true God, the Father of the All, the Holy Spirit, the invisible, who is above the All, who exists in his imperishability, is in the pure light into which no eye may look.' He is not to be thought of as God, but is more excellent than the gods, and the Apocryphon continues with a lengthy statement of negative theology. Now in the section concerning the emanation of the aeons this supreme being is consistently called 'the invisible spirit' (pp. 30–7), save that at *BG* 34. 16–18 we have the statement that 'all things were established through the will of the Holy Spirit, through the Autogenes'. At 37. 2–9 Sophia is said to have acted 'although the spirit had not consented or granted it, nor again had her partner consented, the male virgin spirit'. This must prompt the question whether on the following page the statement that Sophia hid her gruesome offspring 'that none might see it except the Holy Spirit – whom they call Zoë, the Mother of all' (38. 10ff.) does not contain some insertions. The reference to Zoë has all the appearance of an interpolation, and if the word 'Holy' be considered an accommodation to the Christian conception of the Spirit, then the original might have been 'that none might see it except the (invisible) spirit', who presumably already knew, and who in 46. 19 is described as 'the holy invisible spirit'. In this case we should have further evidence of the Christianizing of what was originally a non-Christian system. Since all the entities in the Pleroma are of course 'spirit', and could qualify for the epithet 'holy', the process of assimilation would not be difficult; but we must beware of assuming at the outset that Christian influence is present wherever the phrase 'Holy Spirit' occurs. There may indeed be a New Testament echo in the reference to the punishment of those who blaspheme against the Holy Spirit (*BG* 70. 18–71. 2; cf. the Gospel of Thomas, log. 44, and synoptic parallels), but – particularly if we take the version in Thomas into account – the Spirit here would seem to be not the third person of the Christian Trinity, but the supreme being of a gnostic system. In the Sophia Jesu Christi (*BG* 125. 4–5) we have a reference to 'the great invisible spirit' – which recurs in one of the titles of the Nag Hammadi Gospel of the Egyptians: 'The sacred book of the great invisible spirit.'[19]

This survey is by no means exhaustive, and much still remains to be done when the complete edition of the Nag Hammadi texts becomes available. Yet some things are already clear: the Gnostics share with the New Testament and other literature of the early Christian centuries the idea of good and evil spirits; like their contemporaries they grappled, not always or altogether successfully, with the problem presented by the conception of spirit in man. On occasion they borrowed from the New Testament, and there are indications at certain points of an attempt to assimilate gnostic and Christian conceptions, to give a Christian veneer to what was originally non-Christian. The material provides interesting examples of the interplay and interaction of Christian and non-Christian ideas in what was still a formation period for some aspects of Christian theology. This survey has been confined to material from gnosticism proper, but it may be worth noting that in Mandeism Ruha has become a female demon; yet the Mandean texts still preserve traces of the myth which underlies such documents as the Apocryphon of John.

[19] Text published by J. Doresse, *Journal Asiatique* ccliv (1966), pp. 317–435; German translation by H. M. Schenke in *NTS* xvi (1969–70), pp. 196ff.

PART THREE

CHRIST AND SPIRIT TODAY

24

Conversion and conformity:
the freedom of the
spirit and the institutional church

C. K. BARRETT

This subject,* as I understand it, presents one theme under two aspects, first as it concerns the individual, and then as it concerns the community. What is it, first, that makes a Christian? Is it an inward event, a conviction, a change of course, an act or disposition of penitence and trust, a being apprehended by Christ Jesus, followed by a lasting determination to apprehend that for which one was apprehended? In a word, Is it conversion? Or is it conformity to the social group which bears the name Christian? Such conformity might be in the realm of behaviour, of doctrine, of social alignment, or of all three; it means joining the Christian party, thinking as it thinks, or at least behaving, morally and liturgically, as it behaves. And, secondly, What is it that constitutes the Christian society? Is it the free movement of the Spirit, who, like the wind, breathes where he wills, animating a number of men and associating them with one another, perhaps only temporarily, in a loosely articulated common life, where a common inspiration, a shared conversion, make it natural for them to think, live, and pray together in free association? Or is the true Christian society constituted and marked out by a unique structure which prints a Christian character upon those who accept its discipline and excludes those who do not? That is to say, Is the Christian society distinguished by inspiration, or by a particular form of organization?

It will be observed that in this exposition of the title I have changed the wording by substituting for the conjunctive 'and' the disjunctive 'or'. This I have done simply in the interest of clarity; a proposition is often best stated by setting over against each other two extreme alternatives. It is not my intention to suggest that the question is as

---

* I was asked to speak on this theme at the Anglo-Scandinavian Theological Conference held in Durham in August 1971. The present paper is a revision of what I said on that occasion.

simple as the two crude extremes suggest; indeed it is not simple at all. Something of its complexity has been brought out by Jaroslav Pelikan's study of the theme in Luther.

The development of Luther's character was a quest for certainty. In the radicalism of 1520...he could claim to be announcing publicly 'the counsel I have learned under the Spirit's guidance'. But...by the later 1530s his quest for certainty had taken the form of asserting: 'This is the reason why our theology is certain: it snatches us away from ourselves and places us outside ourselves.' When 'structure' meant the objective authority of an ecclesiastical institution arbitrarily enforced from without, Luther opposed it in the name of the freedom of the Spirit – the old Luther no less than the young. When 'spirit' meant the free-floating subjectivity of an individual who had 'swallowed the Holy Spirit, feathers and all', Luther opposed it in the name of the gift of grace – the young Luther no less than the old. It was as a young man that Luther had learned, in the bitter experience of his guilt and penance, how unreliable a foundation for certainty his own subjective feelings could be. And he was no longer a young man when he still felt able to boast that he, too, 'had been in the Spirit and seen the Spirit, perhaps even more of it (if it comes to boasting of one's flesh) than those fellows with all their boasting will see in a year'.[1]

The question of Spirit versus Structure, Inspiration versus Institutionalism, is far from simple in regard to Luther, who did not simply reform himself out of one into the other, and then with advancing years fall back into a new version of that out of which he had emerged. It is perhaps even less simple in regard to the New Testament.

The question is a complex one, but it is open to various kinds of simplification, which inevitably end in misleading results.

It may for example be withdrawn from the field of theology and treated in psychological and sociological terms. These are hinted at in the passage I have quoted from Dr Pelikan. He is an exceptional individual who never questions his own subjectivism, and doubts whether his conversion is an illusion. How are my feelings related to truth? Which feelings am I to trust? How can I be convinced that I am right at the moments when I am certain of salvation, and wrong at the times (which may be more frequent) when I doubt this, and everything else? In other words, Can I depend on a conversion experience alone? Does not such an experience need to be coordinated with an

---

[1] J. Pelikan, *Spirit versus Structure: Luther and the Institutions of the Church* (London, 1968), pp. 134f.

institutional framework, so that I may find reinforcement for my faith in the fact that I am accepted by a society which not merely knows what it believes but is so organized as to be authentically recognizable as the church of Christ? This in turn shifts the question from the individual to the corporate level. What is the ground of the church's self-confidence? its confidence, that is, that it is in fact the church? Just as few individuals feel strong enough to stand on nothing but their own convictions, few societies have been able to exist for long simply in terms of their own charismatic self-consciousness. In both the Old Testament and the New the phenomena of inspiration are exposed to criticism, and the criticism is not only theologically directed but instinctive. Prophesying is a religious phenomenon, and the mere fact of ecstasy proves little in regard to the truth. And what happens in the normal intervals between the outbursts of spiritual activity? Does the charismatic body cease to exist when it is not functioning in this way? How, moreover, can it guarantee its own continuity, and, from day to day, year to year, century to century, demonstrate its identity? Under the influence of such questions as these it is natural to reach the practical solution (which, in practice, may in the end turn out to be not far wrong), We need a certain amount of conformity, but not too much. Not too much, or the spontaneity and inspiration of the Spirit, the supernaturalness of Christianity, will be lost; but enough to give solidity to individual faith, and to safeguard the church from doctrinal vagaries which might in the end turn it into something radically different from what it originally was. This is an attractive, common-sense answer to the question; but a little reflection will show that it is neither precise enough, nor profound enough. The question whether the church is an institution or not, and the question whether the individual becomes and is a Christian in virtue of his conformity to the church institution, or in virtue of his personal relation to God, are theological questions, and not to be answered in terms of a convenient practical compromise. The Christian life, whether of the individual or of the society, must be defined in terms of its origin. If an institution is given in and with that origin, the questions are answered, whether as a result the individual and the society are left to struggle indefinitely with the ambiguities of their own subjectivity, or are bound to an inescapable institutionalism.

From this observation it is tempting to go to the opposite extreme, and conclude that inspiration and institutionalism must both be maintained at full strength, and held in tension. The definition of the individual Christian and of the church would thus be a dialectical one. The individual's Christian existence would depend wholly upon his personal faith and possession of the Spirit: Without faith it is impossible to please God (Heb. 11: 6); If any man has not the Spirit of Christ he does not belong to Christ (Rom. 8: 9). Equally it would depend wholly upon his membership of the church: *extra ecclesiam nulla salus*. The society's Christian existence similarly would depend wholly on the dwelling of the Spirit within it; equally it would depend wholly upon the provision of a suitable framework for the Spirit's activities. The two balancing propositions would in each case have to be kept in tension.[2] It is not however clear that the New Testament speaks in these terms.

A more promising suggestion is that the convert is required to be a conforming member of a church which in addition to being the home of the Spirit also exhibits a special institutional structure which is prescribed for it by its own origin in the purpose of God. A certain structure is needed in order that the church by its very being may bear witness to the Gospel that generates it; but only one structure will achieve this result. Any other might be worse even than none, since it would reduce the church not to a formless collection of inspired individuals but to a signpost pointing in the wrong direction. The best example of an argument on these lines is A. M. Ramsey's *The Gospel and the Catholic Church*,[3] the only seriously theological and biblical defence of episcopacy in recent years. This is indeed an argument to be taken seriously, though its edge is blunted by the fact that similar claims have been made for independency and presbyterian church polity. The New Testament scholar is likely to view them all with some scepticism.

An even more radical problem is raised by the famous conflict of two generations ago between Sohm and Harnack. Sohm argued that any form of church law, that is, any sort of institutional structure, was simply incompatible with the church's origin. The adoption of a system of church law was the church's fall from the purely spiritual freedom in and for which it was brought into being. Harnack on the other hand argued that from the beginning the church possessed a legal framework,

---

[2] I draw attention to the important parallel discussions of christology and the church by J. L. Leuba in *L'Institution et L'Événement* (Neuchâtel and Paris, 1950).　　　　　[3] London, 1936.

a developing system of ordinances which did not contradict but were a function of its origin in the Gospel. The very utterances of the charismatics could become legally binding commands. According to R. Bultmann[4] the debate is not yet closed.

Um Recht und Unrecht der beiden einander widersprechenden Anschauungen beurteilen zu können, muß man sich den Unterschied deutlich machen zwischen der Ekklesia als einem historischen Phänomen und der Ekklesia als der eschatologischen, vom Walten des Geistes geleiteten Gemeinde, als welche sie sich selbst versteht. Harnack faßt die Ekklesia als historisches Phänomen ins Auge, Sohm versteht sie von ihrem eigenen Selbstverständnis aus.

To Dr Bultmann's profound discussion of these two views of the church, and of the relation between them, we shall return,[5] with a considerable measure of agreement. His comment on the Sohm–Harnack debate for the present provides us with the cue for embarking on the main part of this paper.

The theme we are to discuss is one that is often obscured by generalizations based rather on presupposition than on observation. This is to be avoided at any cost, and in order to keep clear of it I shall not at this stage discuss even Dr Bultmann's exegetically based conclusions. The right course will be first to examine, with our problem in mind, a number of specific New Testament situations, and to observe how the problem arises and how it is dealt with. We shall consider the situations connected with the names Jesus, Paul, and John. Jesus himself gathered a group of followers and provoked the opposition of many. He and his followers were confronted by the highly institutionalized religion of his adversaries. The position of Paul and John was different, not only in that they were themselves professed followers of Jesus and not initiators of new movements, but also in that their environment included Christian as well as Jewish institutions. In principle, however, the situations were not fundamentally different, and comparisons can be made. In order to facilitate, and to give objectivity to, these comparisons, it will be useful to have a common set of questions which can be addressed to each of the three situations in turn. Pursuit of the answers will lead us in different directions, but we shall have at least common starting-points. The following questions are suggested by our theme, and seem to be suitable to the material on which we have to

[4] *Theologie des Neuen Testaments* (Tübingen, 1948–53), pp. 441f.
[5] Pp. 377f.

work. (1) What response did the preacher in question expect from his converts? (2) What was his attitude to existing institutions? (3) What steps did he take to establish new institutions conformable to his own purpose and message?

A. Our inquiry into the work of *Jesus* will differ from that into Paul and John not only for self-evident theological reasons but also because his work lay in the first instance within the old framework of Judaism and not the new framework of Christianity. In this sense at least it is right to speak of his teaching as a presupposition of New Testament theology rather than as a part of it,[6] and of his work as a foundation of the Christian structure, rather than as a piece of it. At the same time, all we know of what he said and did is known only through the medium of the structures of thought and organization which arose after the resurrection. There is nothing new in this observation, but it is particularly important in the present inquiry; I shall return to this point later.[7]

(1) Jesus appears in all the synoptic gospels as a preacher and teacher: What did he require of those who accepted his message? A full answer to this question could be given only on the basis of a much more detailed analysis of the message itself than can be attempted here. It seems that he announced the near arrival of that for which Judaism as a whole was waiting and praying – the kingdom of God. The kingdom was not yet here, for men must still pray for its coming (Matt. 6: 10; Luke 11: 2); yet the present moment was uniquely related to its future coming, and Jesus' exorcisms were a sign of its presence (Matt. 12: 28; Luke 11: 20; cf. Mark 3: 27). It was precisely the relation between Jesus and the kingdom that determined the nature of the response that his hearers were invited to make. This was expressed in a personal attitude to Jesus, which involved faith and obedience. That the obscure, humble, unqualified, and unauthorized preacher should be the representative of the kingdom was too unlikely to be capable of demonstration, yet the connection is one of the major themes of the seed parables, which contrast, for example, the minute mustard seed with the huge mustard plant (Mark 4: 30ff.), yet presuppose the fact that the plant is impossible and unthinkable apart from the seed. This is the secret (μυστήριον) possessed precisely by those who are around Jesus (οἱ περὶ αὐτόν – that is, his party, his group; Mark 4: 10f.). To throw in one's lot with Jesus is to commit oneself to the view that what he says about the

---

[6] See Bultmann, *op. cit.*, p. 1.   [7] Especially p. 381.

kingdom is right, and that it is his men who will participate in it. This is a venture of faith – a gamble, a risk like that taken by the man who finds treasure in a field, or the merchant who stakes his fortune on one pearl (Matt. 13: 44ff.). It is not enough to be a good Jew. The man who has kept all the commandments is told to sell his property and follow Jesus (Mark 10: 17–22); conversely, to be ashamed of Jesus and his teaching is to lose everything (Mark 8: 38). 'Following Jesus' has an ethical content; those who are 'about him' are those who do the will of God (Mark 3: 31–5); and between their poverty, purity, meekness, steadfastness, their pursuit of righteousness, mercy, and peace, and the possession of the kingdom (Matt. 5: 3–12; Luke 6: 20–3) there is the same mysterious link as that which unites the seed and the crop.

Jesus, then, required personal loyalty to himself, and this loyalty found ethical expression, which is illustrated rather than codified in the Beatitudes, and summed up in principle rather than in detail in the two great commands of love to God and to the neighbour (Mark 12: 28–34). There is little to indicate that it also found dogmatic expression. The question whether Jesus applied to himself any title whatever is disputed. Messiahship in some sense seems to be inseparable from his ministry, or at least from its outcome in crucifixion, but he did not proclaim himself as Messiah,[8] and preferred to give no account of the authority with which he acted (Mark 11: 27–33). His disciples accepted the authority; they could hardly be expected to accept an account of it which he did not give. So far there is little enough of conformity to distinguish the life of a disciple; his relation to an institution will be considered below.

(2) The institutions Jesus found in existence were Jewish. They were detailed, comprehensive, and pervasive. In some respects Jesus conformed to them. He made regular use of the synagogue (e.g. Luke 4: 16). The synoptic gospels represent him as having spent only a short time in Jerusalem; but when there he not only visited the Temple but cleansed it, and forbade profane use of it, as the rabbis did.[9] He ordered a cleansed leper to make the prescribed offering (Mark 1: 44), and

---

[8] See my *Jesus and the Gospel Tradition* (London, 1967), pp. 19–24 – and many other modern discussions of the subject.

[9] Interpreting Mark 11: 16 in terms of Berakoth 9: 5. It is possible (see H. W. Bartsch, *NTS* xi (1965), p. 394) that the meaning is: He would not permit anyone to carry a cult vessel through the temple; that is, he put a (temporary) stop to the temple-worship. This interpretation would range this verse with the 'non-conformist' material, but would not radically change the total picture.

himself wore the *ṣiṣith* (Mark 6: 56). His conformity however was confined within relatively narrow limits. The so-called cleansing of the Temple (Mark 11: 15ff.) may in fact have been a warning sign that its end was near. His observance of the Sabbath left much to be desired (e.g. Mark 2: 23 – 3: 6); he openly attacked the oral tradition which gave to the written law its coherence and universal applicability (Mark 7: 6–13), and on divorce varied the written law itself (Mark 10: 2–12). Fasting was in any case (save on the Day of Atonement) a supererogatory work; he regarded it as inapplicable to himself and his followers, since it was no longer necessary to put pressure on God to do what he was already doing (Mark 2: 18ff.).

'Institution' in the Jewish field means Torah; and the attitude of Jesus to Torah is too large a subject to be discussed here. The few points already cited are sufficient to show that his attitude was not simple; certainly they are sufficient to show that he did not affirm the law without qualification and criticism, and it is clear that he came into mutual conflict with its authorized exponents. It is equally clear that he did not conduct a campaign for the abolition of the law. He was content to live within it, as its master not its slave. So far as it provided an adequate channel for God's claim upon man and man's obedience to God he affirmed it; where it was inadequate he himself replaced it, in the interests of a higher claim and a more complete obedience. His personal authority clashed most frequently with that of the scribes, as official representatives of Jewish institutions, but Mark 2: 28; 7: 19; 10: 5f. can hardly be reckoned less than supersession of the institution itself.

(3) Did Jesus establish new institutions? It has been rightly pointed out that unlike the Qumran sectaries, who drew up an elaborate institution for a limited group who adopted a distinctive interpretation of Judaism, Jesus addressed his mission to Israel as a whole.[10] Inevitably, however, the result of his work was to create a minority group of those whose acceptance of his message and loyalty to his person distinguished them from other Jews. They were not distinguished by dogmatic propositions to which they were expected to conform; were they expected to conform to an organization? Apparently not; on the contrary, concern for such conformity was discouraged. The exorcist 'who does not belong to our party' (ὃς οὐκ ἀκολουθεῖ ἡμῖν, Mark 9: 38) so far from being prevented from continuing his work is said

[10] See E. Schweizer, *Church Order in the New Testament* (Studies in Biblical Theology xxxii; London, 1961), §2a.

to be 'on our side'. There are signs of institutionalism in the synoptic gospels, but for the most part these either arise from the initiative of the disciples and are suppressed by Jesus, or are late parts of the tradition. It is, for example, disciples who introduce the characteristically institutional notion of a hierarchy in which one is greater than another; their interest in the matter is rebuked, and they are told, paradoxically, that humble service is greatness (Mark 9: 33ff.; 10: 42ff.).[11] Matt. 16: 19; 18: 18 show disciples assuming the authority of rabbis to permit and forbid by the issuing of *halakoth*; but it is unlikely that these verses, in their present form, go back to Jesus. A possible exception to Jesus' disinterest in institutions may lie in the provision made for the continuance of those common meals which he shared with his disciples; this however leads to a problem so difficult that though it must be mentioned it cannot be discussed. It is not simply that the command τοῦτο ποιεῖτε εἰς τὴν ἐμὴν ἀνάμνησιν is wanting in Matthew and Mark, and in the Western Text of Luke, being given only in 1 Cor. 11: 24f. and in the longer text of Luke 22: 19b, 20. The words where we do encounter them are not easy to combine with the apocalyptic outlook of the Last Supper, which seems to exclude the possibility of any continuing institution in this world. Did Jesus expect an extended period to intervene between his resurrection and the coming of the Son of man? If he did not, he will hardly have provided for his followers an institution they would never need.

One further point must be made explicitly here. Jesus did not, in the manner of our title, set inspiration over against institutionalism. There is in the synoptic gospels notoriously little about the Holy Spirit, and most of such material as there is belongs to the same post-resurrection context as the institutional material. In the time of Jesus himself it is not the freedom of the Spirit but obedience – though a freely chosen and individually given obedience – that fills the place of conformity to an institution.

B. To study *Paul* through Acts is a process similar to that of studying Jesus in the gospels: the image is refracted through the minds of others. With Jesus, this is unavoidable; the gospels may not be satisfactory historical sources, but they are the only sources we have. With Paul we are more fortunate; we have some of his letters, and at this point I

---

[11] Contrast Luke 22: 26, which seems to presuppose the existence in the church of ὁ μείζων and ὁ ἡγούμενος.

shall use only his own words. To say this is not to write off the historical value of Acts altogether, still less is it to deny Luke a voice in discussion of our subject; but his voice is not Paul's voice, and it is important to distinguish them.[12]

Restriction of our inquiry to the epistles gives rise to some difficulty in the answering of the first question, for the epistles were directed to those who already were Christians, and had made at least the initial response to Paul's Gospel. There are however a number of indications of what that response had been.

(1) Paul's preaching, like that of the exponents of Hellenistic Judaism, included an attack on idolatry and a proclamation of the one biblical God, set in the context of the primitive Christian eschatological hope. Thus the Thessalonians had turned from their idols to serve the living and true God, and to await his Son from heaven (1 Thess. 1: 9f.). The preaching, however, was more than an intellectual critique of current theological views; it reached its hearers not as the word of man only, but as the word of God (1 Thess. 2: 13; cf. 1: 5); it rested not upon human wisdom, but on the power of God and the work of the Spirit (1 Cor. 2: 4f.). Again, Jesus the Son of God was not an absent apocalyptic figure whose arrival might be hoped for at a more or less remote last day; he was a historical person, who had died and was proclaimed as Christ crucified (1 Cor. 2: 2; cf. 1: 18, 23). In addition to his crucifixion, the two fundamental propositions about him, which were proclaimed and accepted as a confession of faith by those who became Christians, were (*a*) Jesus is Lord, and (*b*) God raised him from the dead (Rom. 10: 9; cf. 1 Cor. 12: 3; also 15: 3f.). To accept Jesus as Lord acknowledged a claim for moral reform; the resurrection made this possible; and moral renewal was part of the process of becoming a Christian:

Fornicators, idolaters, adulterers, catamites, sodomites, thieves, rapacious men, drunkards, abusive men, and robbers – none of these shall inherit the kingdom of God. And that is what you were, some of you; but you were washed, you were sanctified, you were justified, in the name of the Lord Jesus Christ and in the Spirit of our God (1 Cor. 6: 9ff.).

This passage has been quoted in full because it brings out in the most vivid manner possible the essentially moral experience of conversion which Paul sees as the foundation of Christian life, and at the same time

[12] See p. 381.

points to a different though closely related set of ideas. Ἀπελούσασθε certainly refers to cleansing from moral evil by a renewal of the will (cf. Rom. 12: 2), but it also suggests baptism, though by avoiding the verb βαπτίζειν and using the middle voice Paul succeeds in laying the stress elsewhere; and ἡγιάσθητε could be rendered, You became ἅγιοι, that is, members of the holy people of God. Paul's attitude to baptism is not easy to assess. On the one hand, he seems to have assumed that all his readers had been baptized, and can argue from the fact (Rom. 6: 3); on the other, he took little note of whom he baptized, did not regard baptizing as part of his work, and firmly resisted the Corinthian tendency to regard baptism as effective *ex opere operato* (1 Cor. 1: 14–17; 10: 1–13). Membership of the holy people, however, was an essential part of the response to the Gospel. It was, for example, a crucial question whether this was achieved by faith only, or by circumcision, and a related question how the people of God were to be defined and where they were to be found – how, that is, they were related to the physical family of Abraham. Those who became Christians became members of a body, as closely and as necessarily related to one another as hand and foot. In this mutual relationship they shared a common life, one manifestation of which was that they ate and drank together at a common meal.

What then did it mean to become a Christian in Thessalonica or in Corinth? The convert recognized a personal obligation to Jesus as the κύριος – the person who was the κύριος in virtue of the eschatological act in which God raised him from the dead. In this loyalty and recognition there were the seeds of a dogmatic development, which recognized that the God of the Old Testament, who had sent his Son, was the only God, and that Jesus was the envoy and Son of this God, whose death meant deliverance (Rom. 3: 24); and more than the seeds of moral renewal. Both the moral renewal and the eschatological dogmatics were expressed in the death and resurrection of baptism, which opened the door to the society of the converted, all of whom were similarly related to Christ and were thus related to one another, and had received the same Spirit (1 Cor. 12: 13).

(2) What has just been said poses a problem, and did so already for Paul. As a Jew he had believed, and as a Christian he did not cease to believe, that God had in the past elected a particular people to be his own, to recognize him as the one true God, to serve him in a moral life directed by commandments which he himself had supplied, and to look

for the coming of the anointed one. How then was the new people, elected by God, believing in his unity and holiness, assembled in the name of the anointed one, and living a new moral life, related to the old? It is natural to answer such a question as this in terms of the institutions which give identifiable form to the bodies that adopt them.

It is clear that there is a sense in which Paul valued the institutions of Judaism.

What then does the Jew possess which others have not? What profit is there in circumcision? Much in every way. In the first place, they were entrusted with the oracles of God (Rom. 3: 1f.). They were made God's sons, they were shown his glory, with them he made the covenants, to them he gave the law and the temple-worship (λατρεία, *'abodah*) and the promises; to them belong the fathers of the race and from them (on the human side) springs the Christ himself (Rom. 9: 4f.).

The law included not only moral but also ceremonial, institutional, features, and Paul refers explicitly to the temple-worship. Both were the gift of God himself: it was impossible therefore to suppose that they could be other than good. Good things however can be abused: *corruptio optimi pessima*. Paul's affirmation (Rom. 10: 4) that Christ is the end (τέλος) of the law is by no means so negative as might at first sight appear; but even if τέλος means *goal* rather than *termination* it remains true that it was Christ, not the law, weakened as it was by the flesh (Rom. 8: 3), that achieved this goal; and Paul's own relation to the law is made clear elsewhere. He was dead to it (Gal. 2: 19), and dead to it in order that he might live to the God who gave it. Most important of all is the passage in 1 Cor. 9: 19–23, where Paul says that although he is ἔννομος Χριστοῦ he is not under the law; he is not even a Jew – a member of the institution Israel – though he can on occasion become a Jew; this and all else he is and does διὰ τὸ εὐαγγέλιον, for the sake of the Gospel.

The Jew who is called by God to become a Christian should not pretend that he is something he is not (1 Cor. 7: 18); apart from this, and the reminder that the Jew has the terrible advantage of living under a law that condemns him, Paul who values them highly in their origin has little good to say of what the institutions of Judaism had become. God's calling is not limited to a physical line of descent (Rom. 9: 6–13). Those who receive circumcision as a supplement to their faith have fallen from grace and finished with Christ (Gal. 5: 4); of those who try to force circumcision on Gentile Christians he can say, I wish they would castrate themselves (Gal. 5: 12). A strong Christian is not interested in the Jewish calendar or in food laws (Rom. 14: 2, 5; 1 Cor. 8: 4); Gentiles who adopt such Jewish customs are falling back into heathenism (Gal. 4: 9).

Paul was hardly less critical of the incipient Christian institutions that he found about him. We have seen that the new people of God was normally entered by baptism, and that its common life included a common meal. It appears that in Corinth, and no doubt elsewhere, there was a tendency to believe that the new life, thus entered and thus sustained, was guaranteed an absolute security against sin and death. Nothing, said Paul, could be further from the truth. Under the old covenant, baptism into Moses, and the use of spiritual food and drink, did not prevent the Israelites from falling into sin, or save them, when this happened, from appropriate punishment. Christian baptism and the Christian meal will have no greater prophylactic effect (1 Cor. 10: 1–13). It is not the *opera*, duly performed, but the faith that gives them their meaning, and the divine power to which faith looks, that save. Paul regarded himself as an apostle, and recognized the existence of other apostles – undoubtedly significant persons in the new Christian institution. That he was aware of pseudo-apostles (2 Cor. 11: 13) is not relevant to our inquiry, though it may have contributed to a generally sceptical outlook; more important is the fact that he attributed no great dignity to the undoubtedly genuine and pre-eminent apostles popularly known as pillars: 'Whatever they were makes no difference to me – God shows no favouritism' (Gal. 2: 6). The true apostle, no lord over his converts' faith (2 Cor. 1: 24), was in fact marked out by obloquy and suffering:

I think God has put on us the apostles as last in the show, as men under sentence of death, for we became a spectacle to the whole world, angels and men alike. . . We have become as it were the world's scapegoats, the scum of the earth, to this day (1 Cor. 4: 9–13).

Indeed, in Paul's view apostleship was not an institution; it was an error to turn it into one.

(3) What institutions did Paul provide for the Christians who came into being as a result of his preaching? We have seen that he retained baptism and the common meal; that he valued them appears from, for

example, Rom. 6 and 1 Cor. 10; that he was aware of the dangers as well as the benefits they conveyed we have already seen. It might be said that it was precisely the institutionalizing of them that turned benefit into peril. For the rest, when Paul used the language of institutional and conventional religion – priest, offering, incense, and the like – he used it not in a cultic but in an everyday setting.[13]

The Pauline churches were not without ministers of a sort. The reference in Phil. 1: 1 to ἐπίσκοποι and διάκονοι we cannot interpret, for Paul makes no other use of the words, and to explain them in terms of the usage of half a century later is methodologically false. They may well have been financial officers; if so, they point to a measure of institutionalization, though not of a religious or ecclesiastical kind. There were teachers who received some sort of reward for their services (Gal. 6: 6); there were those who presided (e.g. Rom. 12: 8), though we do not know what they presided over – there is nothing in 1 Cor. 11 to suggest the existence of liturgical presidents. In any society there are inevitably those who take the lead (1 Cor. 16: 15f.; 1 Thess. 5: 12f.), and Paul believed that such men should be loved and respected in return for the work they did for the church. There were house groups (e.g. Rom. 16: 5), and it may be supposed that those in whose houses the groups met took some responsibility for organizing the meeting. Paul himself took steps to regulate the conduct of church meetings, and a code of practice grew up in the churches. Paul could and did appeal to it (1 Cor. 11: 16). He urged his people to exercise discipline. He was unwilling to appeal to his own authority in this respect, but could suggest both punishment (1 Cor. 5: 3ff.) and the remission of punishment (2 Cor. 2: 5–8). The only 'institution' however that Paul seems to have proposed for this purpose was the church meeting.

Paul was profoundly conscious that his converts became, as Christians, members of a body; but he thought in terms of organism rather than of organization. He did not ask for conformity, beyond the acceptance of Jesus as Lord; variety was a good thing, which he defended (1 Cor. 12: 4–11), and in disputed matters he wished each Christian to be fully convinced in his own mind (Rom. 14: 5), even if this meant disagreement with him, Paul. Each man, and apparently

---

[13] Cf. E. Käsemann, 'Gottesdienst im Alltag der Welt', *Exegetische Versuche und Besinnungen* ii (Göttingen, 1964), pp. 198–204. Cf. pp. 248f. (in 'Paulus und der Frühkatholizismus'); also *E. V. u. B.* i (Göttingen, 1960), pp. 121ff. (in 'Amt und Gemeinde im Neuen Testament'). All these essays are of the greatest importance for our subject.

each woman (1 Cor. 11: 5), might take part in the church meeting, just as each arranged and made his own contribution to the collection (1 Cor. 16: 2). The church was not an institution to which one conformed, but a body of which one was a member. Each received his own gift of the Spirit, and it was in accordance with these various gifts that God was served and the body built up (1 Cor. 12: 7; Rom. 12: 6).

c. Jesus we know, and Paul we know; but who was *John*? The name is simply a convenient symbol for the kind of Christian life and thought[14] represented in five books of the New Testament. This means that we are released from the historical problems that beset our work on Jesus and Paul, and can ask directly the three questions we are applying to the various fields in the New Testament.

(1) According to some, the Fourth Gospel itself is preaching, an evangelistic message addressed to the Hellenistic world, it may be, or to the Diaspora Synagogue. I should prefer to say that it presupposes such mission preaching, but is itself addressed, like the Epistles and the Apocalypse, to Christians. The preaching presupposed, however, was intended to elicit a response, and this (though the verse is also applicable to the believer) is summed up in John 20: 31: 'These are written that you may believe that Jesus is the Christ, the Son of God, and that believing you may have life in his name.' A standard of belief, to which the Christian must conform, is here set up, but it does not go much further than Paul's 'Jesus is Lord', though it uses different language. The gospel contains other dogmatic formulations (e.g. 1: 49; 4: 42; 6: 69; 11: 27), which however are probably to be taken as partial statements of what is most comprehensively but also most enigmatically expressed at 8: 24: 'Unless you believe that I am, you shall die in your sins.' Jesus is the sole and sufficient revelation of the invisible Father (1: 18; etc.) and to receive him is the way to regeneration and life (1: 12; etc.). There are according to John two related marks of discipleship: one is to abide in the word of Jesus (8: 31); the other is love, expressed primarily within the Christian circle (13: 35). Was anything more than this expected of the convert? This turns mainly on the interpretation of 3: 5 and 13: 8, which may be taken to mean, Unless you are baptized you cannot be a Christian. That each passage contains an allusion to baptism is probable; that it should be no more

---

[14] There is a measure of unity, but there is also a good deal of diversity in the Johannine literature; see below, p. 376.

than an allusion is probably significant. John like Paul was aware of baptism as an all but universal rite of initiation, but did not (in the manner of Matt. 28: 19; Mark 16: 16) explicitly require it as a condition of membership of the church. Revelation too, which speaks explicitly of 'following Jesus', may make similar allusions (7: 14; 22: 14) in the language of washing. It is safe to say that the Johannine Christian had accepted Jesus as the way to God (10: 9; 14: 6), the revelation of God (1: 18; 14: 9), the Saviour of the world (4: 42), and had received some instruction in appropriate dogmatic expression of this conviction; he had probably been baptized, and had thus entered the community of the friends of Jesus (15: 14f.), whose distinguishing mark was love.

(2) For John, Judaism had practically ceased to be the serious alternative to Christianity that it still was for Paul. There is thus little direct polemic against the institutions of Judaism. Judaism is indeed an enemy that is vigorously attacked, and Jews have thrust Christians out from their institutions (ἀποσυνάγωγος, 9: 22; 16: 2), but this very fact means that Christians do not need to be told not to adopt Jewish practices. Circumcision can be mentioned and used in an argument (7: 22f.) without any polemical flavour. This is not because John thinks that Christians are free to use circumcision, but because he knows that there is no risk of their doing so. The same attitude is sharpened further in Revelation: those who claim to be Jews are not so (for Christians are the true people of God); they are a synagogue of Satan (2: 9). Since Judaism, having rejected its own Messiah, is wrong at the heart there is no point in attacking particular manifestations of it.

I return to the observation that though John notes that, during the ministry, the disciples (but not Jesus – 3: 22; 4: 2) baptized he does not explicitly refer to a Christian water baptism. It is an analogous fact that he omits all reference to those words and acts of Jesus at the Last Supper that are held to have instituted the eucharist. This means neither that John was unaware of Christian baptism and the holy meal, nor that he wished to suppress them. We have seen that baptism appears to be alluded to; and the discourse on the Bread of Life has eucharistic echoes (with which may be compared Rev. 3: 20). Why does John write in this way? Many answers have been given to this question; none is so convincing as the view that John wished to attach these two rites not to particular occasions and commands, however august, but to the life, death, and resurrection of Jesus as a whole. The probable motivation for this (in addition to John's natural theological insight) was that baptism and the eucharist were becoming institutionalized and conventionalized; John intended not to abolish but to revitalize them, and to do so by relating them personally to Jesus himself.

It is a consequence of this attitude of John's to existing Christian institutions that we may continue our discussion in terms of the third question; it is not easy to distinguish between the provision of an institution and the criticism and renewal of an existing one.

(3) It has often been held, probably rightly, that in Revelation the references to the angels of the churches (2: 1, 8, 12, 18; 3: 1, 7, 14), and the picture of elders and living creatures worshipping God in heaven (4: 1–8), reflect the ministry and the worship of the church on earth. There is little to help us here. It is also clear that the churches to which the book was addressed were hard pressed by pernicious doctrinal and moral influences, and that resistance to these called for strict discipline. We are not however informed in any detail how this discipline was applied. The same observation and limitation apply to the saying of John 20: 23: 'If you forgive the sins of any, they are forgiven them; if you retain the sins of any, they are retained.' We shall return to this passage.[15]

The clearest picture of the church as a community exercising discipline over its members is to be found in 2 and 3 John. The second epistle begins by reiterating the commandment of mutual love (5), but love is defined as walking in accordance with 'his commandments' (ἵνα περιπατῶμεν κατὰ τὰς ἐντολὰς αὐτοῦ, 6). The commandments are not defined, but are narrowed down to one (αὕτη ἡ ἐντολή ἐστιν) – presumably the commandment that we should love one another. The observance of the commandments is threatened, however, by those who embrace false doctrine; they do not confess that Jesus Christ came in the flesh. These are deceivers, and behind them stands the arch-deceiver, Anti-Christ. Advanced spirits (πᾶς ὁ προάγων, 9), who do not abide in the teaching, are without God (θεὸν οὐκ ἔχει). Treatment of such persons is specified in verses 10f. They are not to be received εἰς οἰκίαν – into the house church, perhaps, or given hospitality in a Christian's home; the true believer must cut them dead (χαίρειν αὐτῷ μὴ λέγετε). To give them a greeting is to share in their wicked works. No clearer statement of the general principle of excommunication could be given: the heretic is cut off from the body. The third epistle deals with specific cases. The recipient, Gaius, has welcomed missionaries approved by the writer (the Elder); these men take no pay from the

---

[15] See p. 376.

heathen, to whom they go, and need, and merit, the church's support (5–8). Not so Diotrephes, who receives neither the Elder, nor the missionaries (τοὺς ἀδελφούς), and forbids and expels from the church those who wish to receive them (9f.). Here is a disciplinary institution in action; and the Elder, it seems, intends to reply in the same vein (10). To analyse and define the relative positions of the Elder, Gaius, and Diotrephes (not to mention Demetrius, 3 John 12) is impossible within the limits of this essay.[16] It is enough to point out that each acts in the same way, repulsing those travelling Christians of whom he disapproves, and doing his best to see that the church as a whole follows his example. In the development of institution and institutionalism the church has now reached the end of the New Testament road.

At this point, the question with which this paper deals takes a particularly acute form, and it is important to consider the unity of the Johannine literature. If 2 and 3 John are read alone it is natural to draw the conclusion that we have already reached one of the shadier areas of ecclesiastical history, in which Christian love, though still professed, gives place to power politics. Force and something approaching violence are being used in order to uphold the authority of one particular teacher who is determined that the church shall contain only Christians who are prepared to conform to his views. One can well imagine both the Elder and Diotrephes quoting John 20: 23; the question is whether they also quoted John 20: 22, that is, whether they understood the exercise of Christian discipline as a *charisma*, capable of being discharged only by those who have received the Spirit and are engaged upon the continuation of Jesus' mission. To say this is indeed not to put an end to the problem, for 1 John makes it clear that the support of the Spirit could be claimed on both sides of a dispute; it was necessary to test the spirits to see whether they came from God, and it is clear that 1 John's (anti-gnostic) test was both doctrinal and moral – prophets who did not believe in the incarnation, prophets who did not love, could only be false prophets (2: 22; 4: 2f., 8f.). Others no doubt had other tests; what is important here is that the writer of the epistle is content to bear witness and to leave the matter to his readers. He writes to them not because they do not know the truth but because they do know it (2: 21). They all have a χρῖσμα from the Holy One in virtue of which they all have knowledge. This is their protection against false doctrine; it is spiritual, not institutional.

---

[16] See also E. Käsemann, 'Ketzer und Zeuge', in *E. V. u. B.* i, pp. 168–87.

The importance of the material we have just looked at is that it raises the whole problem of conversion and conformity, inspiration and institution. In virtue of their inward conversion all Christians are inspired; confident that they know the truth they expect all their fellow Christians to agree with them. When they find that their brothers do not agree but sometimes hold seriously divergent views on important matters they are apt to use the instruments of institutionalism to compel the wanderers to come in. The process, however, is put into operation on both sides, with results sometimes amusing, sometimes tragic, and seldom edifying. If space permitted we could trace further development of the position in 2 and 3 John in 2 Peter and Ignatius. In a full treatment of the subject it would be important to note the contrast that becomes apparent when one moves up to and over the edge of the New Testament; but we must be content with the ground already very lightly covered.

Before we attempt to reach any conclusions of our own, it will be rewarding to look at a few aspects of the matter as they have been raised and discussed by others.

For example, I referred above[17] to Dr Bultmann's comment on the old dispute between Harnack and Sohm. Rightly he sets the question in the light of the eschatological convictions of the primitive church, and rightly also criticizes Sohm on the ground that, though he proceeds on the basis of the church's understanding of itself as an eschatological community whose existence is determined by theological considerations (and that means, in practice, by the Spirit) rather than by the historical considerations which Harnack, as a matter-of-fact historian, could not miss, he fails to recognize that the church's understanding of itself had to be expressed in historical terms. One might indeed go further than Dr Bultmann, and say that the biblical type of eschatology is not a matter of the non-historical but rather of a special piece of history; the eschatological community is not a heavenly phenomenon which somehow finds itself unexpectedly transported to earth, but the earthly community of a particular period, namely the last, in which God's purpose is at length fulfilled. Looking at the church as a historical phenomenon, Dr Bultmann, following Holl,[18] perceives that the inspired utterances of the charismatics formed one of the bases of

---

[17] See p. 363.

[18] See also E. Käsemann, 'Sätze heiligen Rechtes im Neuen Testament', in *E. V. u. B.* ii, pp. 69–82.

church law; conversely, the first office-bearers in the ecclesiastical institution were the preachers of the word. In his description however of the church's eschatological understanding of itself he puts together material that is of more than one kind. The church understands itself 'als die eschatologische Gemeinde der κλητοί, der ἐκλεκτοί, der ἅγιοι, und der Glaubende führt seine Gliedschaft nicht auf seinen Entschluß zurück, sondern auf den Ruf Gottes und auf das Sakrament der Taufe, die ihn (paulinisch formuliert) in das σῶμα Χριστοῦ einfügt'.[19] There is a sense in which all these terms – election, calling, holiness, baptism – can be brought together and described as mythological; but they are only superficially related in this way, and each of them calls for strict analysis.[20] Election, calling, and holiness are in part at least historical terms, and since the work of Markus and Karl Barth[21] it must be seriously asked whether the earliest Christian understanding of baptism was in any strict sense of the term sacramental; the evolution of baptism into a sacrament is (it may be) part of the process and problem we are studying.

Another important contribution to our subject is that of W. Bauer in his *Rechtgläubigkeit und Ketzerei im ältesten Christentum.*[22] Bauer emphasizes what he calls 'die elastizität des paulinischen Geistes' (p. 236). Paul was a many-sided thinker. His christology, for example, on the one hand pointed to Docetism, on the other hand spoke also of a Christ who had come in the flesh, 'born of a woman'. He upheld the bodily resurrection, but this was not a matter of flesh and blood. 'Er war Pneumatiker wie keiner, und doch auch wieder der Mann der kirchlichen Ordnung' (p. 236). In consequence of this *Weiterzigkeit,* the Pauline epistles can hardly be said to know a heretic, 'im Sinne des Mitchristen, von dessen abweichender Glaubenshaltung man überzeugt ist, daß sie ihm den Heilsweg verschließt' (p. 236). This attitude was to undergo a change. Bauer contrasts Paul's patient attempt to persuade aberrant Corinthians of the truth of his view of the resurrection with that of Justin, for whom such men are only 'so-called Christians'; and I Cor. 5: 1–5, where a man is delivered to Satan only for a very grave ethical offence, with I Tim. 1: 20, where Hymenaeus and Alexander are given the same treatment because they have made shipwreck of the faith.

Bauer's observations, which bear especially on the question of heresy

[19] *Op. cit.,* p. 442.
[20] Elsewhere Bultmann makes large contributions to this analysis; it cannot be pursued here.
[21] M. Barth, *Die Taufe – ein Sakrament?* (Zürich, 1951); K. Barth, *Church Dogmatics* iv 4 (Edinburgh, 1969).   [22] Tübingen, 1934; E.T. 1972.

and orthodoxy, and the steps the church found it necessary to take in order to keep its doctrine as pure as it desired, are of great value, and he has described with great perceptiveness a development that did take place. Yet he has not perhaps fully taken into account (though he does recognize it) that along with Paul's *Weitherzigkeit* went a profound concern not for orthodoxy in the narrower sense of the term but for the purity of the Gospel. Bauer rightly says that in Galatians Paul's attack is directed primarily not against divergent brethren, but against false brethren, ψευδάδελφοι, who misuse the rulings established in Jerusalem. But Paul was theologian enough to detect the principle involved, and to attack it not only when it was expressed in a demand for circumcision, or, more generally, for works of the law, but also when it appeared in the form of human wisdom (1 Cor. 2: 4; 2 Cor. 1: 12). Paul had evolved no machinery to deal with the danger; it would be wrong to conclude that he would altogether have rejected the use of such machinery.

Perhaps the most important contribution to the discussion of this subject is that of H. von Campenhausen, in *Kirchliches Amt und geistliche Vollmacht in den ersten drei Jahrhunderten*,[23] which is as remarkable for its balance as for its learning. What is to be seen throughout the period he deals with is, according to von Campenhausen, the interplay of regular official ministry and free spiritual authority. There can be no simple solution of the problem of the origin of the church's ministry in terms of one or other of these two.

Die kirchliche Ordnung beginnt nicht mit der 'Stiftung' eines maßgebenden Amtes durch Jesus selbst, an das der Glaube dann ein für allemal gebunden wäre; am Anfang erscheint aber ebensowenig die chaotische Freiheit des 'Geistes' und der einzelnen vom Geist begabten Personen. Weder die autoritäre, 'katholische' noch die liberal-protestantische Auffassung der Kirche besteht vor den tatsächlichen Gegebenheiten des Urchristentums (p. 324).

Office and *charisma* alike were subordinate to the word or testimony which they served, and in which Christ himself was present as the living Word. The weakening of either tended towards *schwärmerisch* or authoritarian distortion of the concept of the church.

In Jesus only was there a perfect combination of official and charismatic authority. Between him and the later ministry the apostles occupy a unique place, since their authority rests upon their meeting with the risen Lord, and can therefore be neither repeated nor transmitted. All

[23] Tübingen, 1953.

later ministries derive their authority from the witness to Christ borne by the apostles, and it is thus only in the third generation that the tension of spiritual and official authority arises.

There is no place for an official ministry in Paul's conception of the church, though he knew that certain persons were endowed with special gifts and functions for the benefit of the community. Over against the Pauline churches others grew up which were based on the Jewish pres-byteral model. As early as Acts and 1 Peter the two systems began to run together, but the inevitable consequence of ecclesiastical development was the strengthening and emphasizing of the official element. This devel-opment was carried further by the general conditions of life in the second century, when it became more and more necessary to hold fast to tradi-tion. This is certainly understandable, but the result was unfortunate.

Der ursprüngliche Sinn der evangelischen Vollmacht beginnt sich zu verdunkeln. Die Kirche lebt nicht mehr im radikalen Sinn aus der Vergebung Christi und versteht ihre Heiligkeit wie eine menschliche Aufgabe, die von den Christen zu erfüllen und zu fordern ist. Darum wird auch die Autorität des Amtes einseitig verstanden und vorzüglich moralisch und pädagogisch, juristisch und politisch gefaßt (p. 329).

This seems to point us in the right direction, though there are some points on which von Campenhausen invites disagreement. He is for example right in speaking of the uniqueness of the apostles, but it was a uniqueness that expressed itself in ways that had clear parallels in other Christians. Thus it is not true that the apostles 'sind keine Charis-matiker; denn ihre Vollmacht entspringt keiner besonderen geistlichen "Gabe", sondern gründet sich auf ihre geschichtliche Begegnung mit dem auferstandenen Herrn' (p. 325). That they had seen the risen Lord is true, and it was an indispensable qualification; yet Paul can also speak (e.g. Rom. 12: 3) of ἡ χάρις ἡ δοθεῖσά μοι – the gift that gave him his unique apostolic authority. Equally, he recognizes that he is authorized by the message he bears; he does not authorize the message (Gal. 1: 8). This duality, which von Campenhausen demonstrates for the ministry, belongs properly to every department of its life and to every age of its history, including the apostolic.

Whether we speak of conversion or of conformity, of inspiration or of institutions, their value consists simply in the witness they bear – to the Gospel. They are to be judged and controlled not by being balanced against one another, but by this absolute standard, and it will follow from this that the optimum proportion of one to the rest will vary from

time to time and from place to place. When this is said, it can nevertheless be seen, in the light of the New Testament evidence, that they are
unlikely ever to be of equal importance, and that, conversely, some are
more likely to be dangerous than others.

In the New Testament two strands are intertwined. In the teaching of
Jesus, in the epistles of Paul, and to a great extent in the Johannine
literature, we find that men respond to God in simple terms of faith and
love. They are encouraged to think and act in a non-conformist rather
than a conformist way. Certain basic principles emerge for the intellectual expression of their faith, and certain guidelines are laid down for the
practical operation of love; these however are elementary and elastic.
But Jesus is known to us through the gospel tradition, and the life of
Paul is narrated in Acts; and in the gospels and Acts, and to some extent
in the framework of the Johannine literature, a different tendency can
be observed, in which emphasis is laid upon the importance and value
of rules of faith and practice, and on the organization of the Christian
brotherhood. It would be wrong to suggest that this process had gone
far. Not only the synoptics but Acts also sees the development of the
church as controlled from point to point by the gift and direction of the
Spirit, who remains sovereign, appointing, for example, those who are
to act as presbyter-bishops (Acts 20: 28). In substance if not in time we
are far from the uneasy contiguity in which institutionalism and
inspiration are found in Ignatius. The institutional tradition begins as
soon as it becomes apparent that the people of God have a life to live
in the conditions of space and time, and this has already happened in
the New Testament. It is not however the institution that creates the
people of God, but the immediacy of inspiration, which forms the
primary and indispensable witness to the creative act of God in his
Son,[24] and it is to him alone, to his life, death, and resurrection that
men must be conformed. It is for the institution to draw to itself as little
attention as possible, and, as far as may be, to act as a further witness to
Christ crucified and risen, and to the fact that it is none other than the
Spirit who guides the church into all the truth.

[24] Cf. E. Käsemann, *Der Ruf der Freiheit* (Tübingen, 1972), p. 72: 'Der Enthusias-
mus ist unentbehrlich, wo das allgemeine Priestertum wirklich erweckt und
die Gemeinde durch die Laien repräsentiert und beweglich gemacht werden
soll...Wer Freiheit will, muß dem heiligen Geist die Zügel etwas mehr
überlassen, als Kirchenleitungen und Pastoren im allgemeinen gewohnt sind
und für richtig halten. Es ist sehr problematisch, ob Ordnung sein letztes Wort
ist, obgleich Unordnung wenig erfreulich wirkt.'

25

Structure and energy in Christian communication

F. W. DILLISTONE

The New Testament is, at first sight, simply a collection of literary forms: gospels, letters, travel records, apocalypses. But literary forms provide one of the chief means by which a man communicates his knowledge, his concerns, his intentions, his expectations to others. A key problem in the interpretation of the New Testament, as indeed it is in the task of communicating the Christian faith today, is that of the relationship between form and content, between medium and message, between structure and meaning. From one point of view communication may be seen as a simple, direct process. From another it can be seen as a highly concentrated dialectic or interaction between two parties: a transmitter and a receiver, an individual who is eager to project or impart information and those who may or may not be immediately ready to engage in the activity of accepting it. It is when communication is regarded from the latter point of view that urgent questions begin to arise.

How, for example, can a form be devised which will adequately express the communicator's intention? How can he be sure that the form he uses will be familiar to his neighbour at the receiving end? Is the form a constant or must it be continually adapted to new circumstances? And perhaps most important of all, how does his desire or intention to communicate affect the form and how does the form itself affect what the initiator wishes to communicate and what the neighbour actually receives? These questions are of central importance both in the task of interpreting the New Testament and in the task of communicating the Gospel in any particular age.

I

The problem can be immediately illustrated by reference to a passage in a recent book by Professor E. L. Mascall. In discussing the formulation of Christian theology, he writes:

Here I can only state my own position which I believe to be that of the central Greek tradition in both East and West and which was plainly expressed by Pope John in his inaugural address to the Second Vatican Council that 'the substance of the ancient doctrine contained in the "deposit of faith" is one thing; its formulation is quite another'.

To pronounce such a formula as this is not to close discussion. It may be by no means easy in any particular case to decide whether two different formulas express the same substance of doctrine or not. . . The Church is no stranger to this kind of situation. It occurred, to give one instance, in the third century, when it had to be settled whether when Dionysius of Alexandria used the formula 'three *hypostases* and one *ousia*' to describe the Holy Trinity he was expressing the same basic doctrine as was Dionysius of Rome who used the formula 'three *personae* and one *substantia*'.[1]

The general picture which comes into view as we study these statements by Pope John and Dr Mascall is that of a 'substance', a 'deposit', a basic 'essence', which has to be described by means of some kind of verbal formula. The deposit is firm and unchanging: the descriptions vary from age to age, from culture to culture. The task of the theologian or indeed of any Christian communicator is to make sure that his own formulation adequately represents the original 'substance' and this he does by constantly testing his particular formulation against the Church's tradition stretching back to the earliest confession of the essential Christian verities.

This concern which I have illustrated from the more 'Catholic' wing of Christendom also operates in a slightly different way within 'Protestant' circles. Here it usually expresses itself by making a contrast between the Gospel and the forms in which it needs to be communicated. Such phrases are used as 'the essential core of the Gospel', 'the heart of the Gospel', the 'pure' or the 'true' or the 'unchanging' Gospel. If this is preserved, it is claimed, we can afford to be flexible and pragmatic in the choice of 'forms' to communicate it to those who have not yet embraced the Christian faith.

I take as an example a little book by Francis A. Schaeffer entitled *Escape from Reason*. His concern as defined in the Foreword is the problem of 'learning how to speak meaningfully' to any particular generation. The responsibility of the Christian church 'is not only to hold to the basic, scriptural principles of the Christian faith, but to communicate these unchanging truths into the generation in which it is

---

[1] *Theology and the Future*, 31.

living'. Where are these 'basic principles', 'unchanging truths', 'unchangeable facts' to be found? In the Bible which is 'God's communication of propositional truth, written in verbalized form'. But this truth must be constantly re-translated into changing historical situations and into the dialects and thought-forms of succeeding generations. Even when the 'unchanging truth' is not as closely identified as by Dr Schaeffer with Biblical propositions but rather with the essential Gospel at the heart of the Bible, the assumption is still made that it is possible to determine first what is this Gospel and then to proceed with the task of relating it to the shifting language- and thought-forms of any particular period.

II

Clearly these ways of solving the problems of communication are part and parcel of total views of the universe and of life in society. The first I shall call the 'homes and gardens' mentality: the second the 'community and crisis' mentality. One of the oldest and most elementary drives in the heart of man is to build himself a stable dwelling-place, a home in which he and his family can find shelter and safety. He dreams about his home: he imagines the *form* it might take. He gathers materials – wood or stone – and fashions them in such a way as to conform as nearly as possible to the pattern already formed in his own mind.

This apparently simple process has attained the distinction of being one of the normative ways by which the human imagination has envisaged the creation of the universe. In Greek and in mediaeval Christian speculation no image of God was more prominent than that of the supreme Architect. The universe, it was believed, had first been conceived in the mind of God. Then, with perfection of order and measurements he had taken formless matter and moulded it into his imagined design. The imperfection and intractability of matter meant that on earth the perfection of form could never be fully realized: the idea, the image in the mind of God, this alone was perfect in proportion and regularity. But it was still possible, even under material conditions, to construct approximate representations of what was only existent in its eternal and ideal form in the realm of the spirit.

This whole conception has made an extraordinary appeal to western man in particular. Even today it is in *building* that he finds one of his deepest satisfactions. But not only does he need shelter: he needs daily bread. So he wrestles with the soil and brings water to his plot of land, confident that he can reap far more than he sows though confident also that the essential nature of what he plants will be reproduced in the expanded harvest. Here the crucial element in his view of the universe is not the form created within his mind and then constructed out of formless matter but rather the form already residing in the seed, the plant, the genus, which, if given proper conditions, will be retained through the life-cycle of the growing organism and be revealed most clearly when it reaches maturity.

Here again is one of the determinative patterns of the human imagination. In nature, it appears, there are certain given forms. Their number is legion but each has a distinctive part to play in the movement of the whole towards its final perfection. The seed, the germ is there: it is capable of growth and development: but through all the many changes of environmental conditions the essential form remains unchanged. It is this which constitutes the criterion and meaning of the whole process.

It is not difficult to see how these two general outlooks could affect men's thinking about the transmission of divine truth. According to the first view the essential pattern of truth concerning God and man and the universe has existed from all eternity within the mind of God. In sundry ways and in divers manners this pattern has become visible through the works of creation. Above all it has been manifested openly in and through the new 'temple' of God constructed out of human flesh, the tabernacle in which God's glory has been perfectly revealed (John 1: 14). The pattern, having thus been expressed in human form, can now be reproduced in human life with varying degrees of fidelity. But the theologian must always strive to make his verbal forms approximate as closely as possible to the pure spiritual ideals which gained expression through the human career of Jesus the Christ.

According to the second view our primary datum is a world of forms each of which has the capacity of developing to its full potential. But as every gardener knows, many seeds never show themselves above ground and those that do often show defects of one kind or another. So it is with the form of humanity. Only once, in this view, was the perfection of the human form manifested in the world. He was truly man and through his incarnation, death and resurrection the form of humanity was taken up into the godhead. The task of the theologian now is to discover the essential form of words which belonged appropriately to the description of his humanity and to allow that form to exercise its influence upon all other forms of human language, drawing them towards that perfection which is part now of its own existence insofar as it remains faithful to its archetype, the One who assumed human form and brought it to its perfection through uniting it with the life of God himself.

III

I turn to what I have called the 'community and crisis' mentality. If one basic instinct causes man to seek the shelter and security of a settled home, another impels him to seek the means of attaining order and stability in his social life. A free-for-all cannot continue indefinitely. Some principle of order must be established between equals besides that which exists within a family unit on grounds of age or physical strength.

The obvious way of establishing such a stability is by some process of *exchange*. If I possess something of yours and you possess something of mine we are then held together by a common bond. Something of me has entered into you and vice versa. The bond may not be strong enough to hold when new conditions arise but for the time being the all-important matter is the *form of the covenant*. The exchange may be effected through food, clothes, blood, breath, jewels etc.: but the most significant exchange of all is through a solemn word, an oath, a promise, a covenant. My word is added to your total resources, your word to mine. The word normally denotes not simply a tangible gift but a promise of my presence, my strength, my assistance, my support in specified circumstances. Life is no longer entirely unpredictable. I can, because of the covenant, rely upon the behaviour and attitudes of my neighbour in a way which would otherwise have been impossible.

This simple pattern of covenant-making lies behind great systems of law which have ultimately been constructed to govern the relations between individuals and societies. And it has been entirely natural for man to picture his relations with his God in similar terms. Pre-eminently amongst the Hebrews the concept of covenant became determinative in their religious life. God, they were led to believe, had covenanted himself to a particular tribe. He had promised them his blessing and support and expected in return a promise of loyalty and service. God, conceived as the great Law-giver, became central in the religious and social life of ancient Israel. The form of words establishing the covenant attained a sanctity above all other verbal exchanges.

To live for ever in harmonious relationship with God and the neighbour within the order established by the covenant would appear to be the *summum bonum* of human existence. Yet, within recorded history, life has never for long worked out this way. Certainly so far as Israel was concerned history was punctuated by crises of greater or lesser dimensions, sometimes, it seemed, through the sheer malice of evil powers, sometimes through the sheer fecklessness and disloyalty of the chosen people themselves. How could disaster be interpreted? How could deliverance from disaster be interpreted? Not by reasoned argument but by gathering the critical events into *a story*. The story had a beginning, a middle and an end. The story could interpret the onset of the crisis, the interplay of the chief actors within the crisis, the proximate or the final outcome of the crisis. Through the *story* men gained some sense of order even in the midst of seeming catastrophe. Events were not entirely in the saddle. Through the story events were seen to be the manifestation of the majestic activity of God himself, judging and redeeming his people.

Again it is not difficult to see how these two general outlooks would affect men's thinking about the transmission of divine truth. According to the first view the essential truth concerning the relations between God and man has existed from all eternity in covenant-form. God's purpose for man: man's obedient response to God: both have been foreordained within the divine counsels. In other words there are certain basic laws which make life human. Unless man conforms to these laws which have been partially disclosed through the social experience of Israel and fully revealed in and through the teaching of Jesus the Christ, he goes against the whole purpose of human existence and breeds anarchy and disorder rather than the co-operation in goodness which is the will of God for all mankind. To hold to the form of the eternal covenant in the midst of all the changes and chances of this mortal life is the chief duty and responsibility of man.

According to the second view history records far greater crises than can be encompassed within a well-defined pattern of keeping or transgressing specified ethical injunctions. There are build-ups of corporate pride, there are aggressive movements of nations, there are wars and rumours of wars, there are cruelties of individual tyrants, there are follies of individual fanatics. The prophets of Israel cried out in warning, pleaded with compassion. All these events were to be viewed not as outside the control of God but as set within his purpose which was a purpose of *redemption*. Out of the clash of good and evil forces a new creation would come into being. The story of Israel's deliverance from Egypt constituted a paradigm, an essential form which would find its fulfilment when the Messiah came. And the early Christian witnesses became true successors of the prophets as they made the story-form their instrument for interpreting the crucial events in and through which, they believed, God's final purpose of redemption had been proleptically achieved.

IV

At the beginning of the seventeenth century Western Christendom embraced four theological traditions corresponding roughly to those which I have sketched in the earlier part of this essay. The Augustinian outlook expressed itself most characteristically through *architectonic* forms: the earthly building which is a copy of the heavenly: geometrical and musical forms which are reflections of divine proportion and harmony. The Thomistic emphasis was on *biological* forms: the combination of form and matter in every living thing: the subtle distinction between initial form, intermediate form and final form: the further distinction between potential form and immediately sensed positive form: the emphasis upon the 'organic pattern of all the final, formal causes of all things, which is the first and final cause of the determinate universe as a whole' and which 'may be termed the soul of the universe'.[2]

The Reformed outlook, brilliantly expressed in Calvin's *Institutes*, is essentially *governmental* and therefore concerned with forms of law and order. Covenant, law, order of nature in heaven and on earth, providence, justice and wisdom tempering and directing events in the best-conceived order to a right end – these are key concepts and terms in Calvin's exposition. He had been trained in the law. He was entirely familiar with the making of constitutions. His whole outlook on life and society was directed towards the establishment of 'the rule and law of good governing' on one side, 'obedience and discipline' on the other.[3] It was only natural that the written forms of Holy Scripture should be regarded by him as the indispensable instruments for the expression of the Divine Law and for the instruction in obedience of God's people.

The Lutheran can be best described as *redemptive* and therefore concerned with forms relating to critical situations in human experience.

---

[2] F. S. C. Northrop. *The Meeting of East and West*, 277.   [3] *Institutes* 14. 10. 28.

Deliverance and redemption, saviour and helper, victor and overcomer, are key words in Luther's teaching and preaching: they are set in the context of the great hostile forces which constantly seek to annihilate man – sin and death and hell and the devil. Luther had known in his own experience what it meant to be tempted, to be overcome, to be imprisoned, to be in despair. These were the types of human experience which he found vividly depicted in the Old Testament accounts of crises in the lives of patriarch and prophet and of Israel itself. These however were but shadows compared with the stupendous crisis of the ages to which the New Testament bears witness. Every form of speech used in this central witness Luther lays hold of to convey his own testimony to the saving work of Christ on our behalf. These are the forms which for him never grew stale or outworn. If anything in the world is permanent and unchanging it is the word which proclaims Jesus of Nazareth as Saviour *pro me*.[4]

Of these four types of form, the first and the third were obviously least open to development and change. The great challenge to the first was to come through the inventions of the telescope and the clock and the formulation of Newton's Laws of Motion. The new forms were mechanistic rather than geometrical, dynamic rather than static. Yet it was still possible for the general outlook which I have called Augustinian to be maintained by conceiving God as the supreme watchmaker rather than architect and by attributing unchangingness to laws of motion rather than to laws of measurement and weight.

The great challenge to the third was to come with the invention of new methods of travel and communication and the consequent possibility of setting up new social orders in virtual independence of previously existing structures. The new forms were democratic rather than authoritarian, related to a changing world rather than fixed within an unchanging divine order. Yet it was still possible for the Calvinistic framework to be maintained in general outline with God conceived as the supreme overlord who allowed his servants to devise new forms of government which did not actually contravene or contradict the essential moral laws which had once for all been revealed in his Word.

The second outlook which I have called the Thomistic was to receive its challenge later and at first in a less spectacular way. The nineteenth century witnessed the rise of a new interest in the biological sciences

---

4 See Ian D. K. Siggins, *Martin Luther's Doctrine of Christ*, Chapter 4.

and this interest gained its focus in the doctrine of evolution as enunciated by Darwin and his followers. The general idea of form being maintained through long periods of growth and development was in no way novel: what was startlingly new were the ideas that man had evolved from lower forms of animal life and that the forms of species had not been fixed at the time of creation but that novelties could emerge through processes of natural selection. The concept of a single creative life-force could perhaps be reconciled with the traditional doctrine of the one World-Soul: but could the idea of changing forms be reconciled with that of a comprehensive organic pattern within which all individual forms were determined by their relation to it?

The fourth outlook, the Lutheran, was also to receive its major challenge in the nineteenth century but from a quite different source. The advance of historical studies which gradually brought about a totally new understanding of the way civilizations had risen and fallen and of the movements of men and nations outside the range of the Biblical accounts, naturally caused men to question their accuracy in recording events, whatever might be said about their proclamation of saving truth. In particular were the *stories* of redemption as told in the Old Testament true accounts of what actually happened or were they the fabrications of pious imaginations? And how far could it still be affirmed that the death and resurrection of Jesus had been the determinative liberating act related to all men at all times? Was the gospel-story a *form* of universal and unchanging character?

V

The twentieth century has witnessed an unparalleled upheaval and transformation (whether or no it be regarded as 'progress') in all departments of thought and practice. Perhaps the greatest change of all has come about through the growing recognition that the age-long search for *uniformity* in the organization of human thought or behaviour is simply incapable of realization. The hope that advances in knowledge of the structure of the universe or of the history of mankind would enable us at length to establish a single uniform system of thought and an all-embracing uniform code of conduct, though still entertained in some quarters, is by most regarded as neither attainable nor even desirable. Such notions as relativity, discontinuity, randomness, complementarity, have come to be regarded not only as necessary for the understanding of reality but as creatively advantageous for the ordering of human affairs.

One consequence of this new attitude is that whereas up until the beginning of this century the proponents of each of the four approaches with which I have been concerned still looked and hoped for the ultimate victory of the system to which they were respectively committed, victory at least in the sense of the recognition of the superiority if not of the exclusive validity of their own formulation: increasingly in this century has come the recognition that a plurality of forms can be a strength rather than a weakness and that the method of interchange, interaction, inter-relationship is far to be preferred to that of the one-track mind, the exclusive pursuit of one definitive structure, the attempt to include all phenomena within a single determinative formula. This does not mean however that the *families* of forms or *types* of structure which I have already delineated lose their identity within some boundless plurality. Rather it implies that there are certain types of phenomena which call for certain types of formal representation and that through these *types* there is both a link with the past and the establishment of a principle of order in the present.

What I have called the *architectonic* or the Augustinian is represented today by the analogue model approach. This derives from the conviction that there is a *structure* or *web of relationship* (Max Black's terms) in an original, whether the original be the universe as a whole or some part of it. A working model can be constructed whose form corresponds in some striking way to what is known of the structure of the original. The construction is normally made through some new medium which is relatively familiar to the circle of those who use it. So reality takes approximate shape within a medium and through a form which in itself stimulates the imagination and which through its use begets a deepening understanding of the original phenomenon.

The *biological* or Thomistic family of forms has taken on a wholly new significance and character through the growing acceptance of the concept of evolution. There has indeed been the danger that evolution would come to be defined in a singular and simplistic way and made the rigid criterion of some new scientific orthodoxy. But so long as an openness of detailed interpretation is maintained there can be little doubt that forms suggestive of an evolving process are indispensable for the communication of the 'livingness' of which our whole experience makes us aware.

What is all-important in an evolving process is the occurrence of constant breaks and re-combinations. Any hardening into an unchangeable form implies death. But where there is re-form, re-adaptation, re-combination within new environments and circumstances, there is the continuance of *life*. A form from the past then is never completely evacuated. Rather it is taken up into a new situation: it is transformed within the totality of an ongoing, living process. Reality gains expression through a sequential form which is never final but which is a temporary (and adequate for the time being) stimulus both to the imagination and to the understanding.

Governmental forms have probably resisted change more effectively than any others. However much man valued and depended upon the laws of Newtonian mechanics, he valued and depended even more upon social law as it had come to be formulated within Western civilization. It gave a firm structure of order within which he could both feel reasonably secure and at the same time enjoy a reasonable freedom.

But a growing acquaintance with other types of society and other systems of law brought the theory of one absolute expression of divine law under severe challenge and now, as in the natural order so in the moral, the construction of models becomes more important than the definition of exact and unchanging codes of conduct. These models take the form of dramatic simulations. It is recognized that the moral order is structured and that man can set up symbolic dramas which direct the social conscience towards this structure. But there can be no finality about any humanly constructed code or rule of conduct. It can point towards the ordered structure which is constantly relating itself to changing social circumstances: it can never embody it in any absolute form.

Finally *redemptive* forms have taken on a new importance and a new range of relevance through the widely diffused appeal to the principle of the dialectic. The life of society, it is claimed, is never in steady equilibrium. Always possibilities of alienation are present and under conditions of special stress alienation issues in open conflict and a struggle for freedom. But history reveals that revolution never establishes a final liberation. It in turn becomes institutionalized. New alienations appear and sooner or later the task of redemption has to be performed afresh.

The inner dynamic of this historical process, however, creates forms which are never static but inter-related in a Yes–No polarity. By their very nature these forms cannot be final or absolute. They depend upon

one another, they spring out of one another, they relate now to subjection, now to dominance, now to alienation, now to reconciliation,
now to passivity, now to revolt in a dialectic which never ceases. There
may seem to be periods of history when inertia reigns but this impression is mistaken. Forces are gathering which are bound to erupt. Once
again the drama of redemption will be played out and a new form of
reconciliation will temporarily take shape.

VI

What are the implications of all this for the interpretation and communication of the New Testament witness to Jesus of Nazareth? If
my analysis is in any way correct it means that we have to work with
four groups or types or families of *forms* in seeking to do justice to its
total testimony.

In the first place Jesus is presented as the Son, the first-born of all
creation, the image of the invisible God, the logos and sophia of God.
Through this group of models we can focus our attention upon him
through whom all things were created and in whom all things cohere.

But not only is he seen within the context of the total pattern of the
universe: he is also seen as the fountainhead of its evolving life in and
through the Spirit. As breath, as water, the Spirit generates and
regenerates, creates and recreates, within the total process which has as
its goal 'the manifestation of the sons of God' (Rom. 8: 19). A variety
of New Testament forms explores the nature of this universal operation.
All bear witness to the central revelation through him whose total
life-cycle was dependent upon the Spirit, even Jesus of Nazareth.

Within the context of the social order Jesus is presented as the Lord,
the Head over all things, the Heir of all things. Each of these titles
belongs to and depends upon a wider contextual framework, a social
order imagined in terms of the universalization of some particular
expression of organic wholeness (a body, a family, a tribe). His own
parables which made present to his hearers the operation of the Reign
of God provide the pattern according to which forms bearing a
continuing witness to the Lordship of Jesus are to be constructed.

But again not only is he seen as Lord and Head over all things: he is
also seen as the agent through his Spirit of every critical break-through
to new freedom and new potency. 'If it is by the Spirit of God (the
finger of God) that I cast out demons, then the Kingdom of God has

come upon you' (Matt. 12: 28; Luke 11: 20). The paradigm-form of the Gospels through which witness is borne to the redemption wrought by Jesus through his Spirit in particular instances: the kerygma-form of the wider New Testament through which witness is borne to the once-for-all redemption wrought by Jesus through death and resurrection: these are the dominant forms of our earliest Christian writings just because the sense of having been delivered out of the power of darkness into the glorious liberty of the children of God was so vivid and so strong.

Architectonic, biological, governmental, redemptive forms – all are needed to bear witness adequately in our own time to 'the things concerning Jesus'. The only 'content' of the New Testament is Jesus himself, speaking and acting in the power of the Spirit. Some forms emphasize structure, some energy. All are needed to direct our gaze towards him in and through whom has been revealed the manifold, the pluriform wisdom of God.

ὁ σωτὴρ ἡμῶν as an African experience

JOHN MBITI

1. THE TITLE 'SAVIOUR' IN THE NEW TESTAMENT

It is surprising, and perhaps disturbing, that the title Saviour is so sparingly used of God and Jesus in the New Testament. In contrast, it had acquired common usage in the ancient Mediterranean world of the Egyptians, Hebrews, Greeks, and Romans, in reference to men, divinities (gods) and God as the case might be. But since New Testament times, *Saviour* has become, together with *Lord*, the most universal title of Jesus. Indeed it could be argued that the Christian Faith coheres in the one concept of the Saviourhood of Christ.

No satisfactory explanation has been put forward for the scarcity of the title Saviour with regard to Jesus. Foerster thinks that for the Jews it would have connoted a national liberator, while for other people the title was linked up with the Roman emperor. Hence the fear that it might have kindled false hopes and ideas 'which the Gospel could not fulfil'. For the same reasons the restraint continued in post-apostolic times.[1] Taylor blames the restraint to its use in Greek religion and Caesar worship.[2] These two explanations do not satisfy since the same situation pertained to the title *Lord* which gained such rapid currency in the early church. Indeed, Cullmann considers the centrality of the title Lord (*Kyrios*) to have eclipsed the *Sōtēr* title.[3] If this were the case, however, *Sōtēr* would have dislodged *Kyrios* from its centrality when the former came into full use later on, and this did not happen. Furthermore it is impossible to imagine that the early Christians would not have been able to find a compromise in the use of the two terms if ever the question of 'conflict' or 'eclipse' had arisen.

That God is Saviour is a Jewish concept which went back to pre-

[1] W. Foerster, article 'σωτήρ' in *TDNT* viii, E.T. 1971, pp. 1020f.
[2] V. Taylor, *The Names of Jesus* (London, 1953), pp. 108f.
[3] O. Cullmann, *The Christology of the New Testament* (E.T. London, 1963), p. 238; cf. pp. 243–5.

Christian times, and reference to it in the New Testament takes the notion for granted (Luke 1: 47; 1 Tim. 1: 1; 2: 3; 4: 10; Titus 1: 3; 2: 10; 3: 4). On the other hand, it has been pointed out, Saviour was not a current Messianic title in the New Testament period.[4] Note would need to be taken, however, of the view that linguistically the name Jesus (Jeshua) connoted Saviour (Moshiya, Jeshua); and as such it may have been pointless, in the Palestinian church at least, to attach a title to a personal name when both had virtually the same meaning.

The Saviourhood of Jesus derived from partly the transfer and/or extension of the concept from God (in Judaism) and partly the growing realization of the meaning of his death and resurrection, even if the linguistic nicety of the actual title *Sōtēr* only took shape in Hellenistic Christian communities at a later date.

Could the scarcity of the title Saviour in the early church be a purely statistical rather than theological, political or linguistic scarcity? Even when used of God among the Hebrews, the title of Saviour is strikingly rare compared to that of Lord. God is only occasionally referred to as Saviour in the Old Testament, and since this is not one of the Messianic titles, it would not have been natural or normal for the title Saviour to be appended to Jesus as commonly and readily as that of Lord, even if his very person and ministry implied the concept of salvation. Used of God, the Saviour title is rare both in the Old Testament and in the New Testament; this same rarity is maintained with regard to Jesus in the New Testament. In contrast, the concept of salvation and related ideas is more abundant in connection with God in the Old Testament, and both God and Jesus in the New Testament. The concept thus seems to have antedated the formal application of the title Saviour within the church for both God and Jesus. And when its use does begin there is a tendency, at least in the Pastorals, for both God and Jesus to be mentioned simultaneously in a manner which does not apply at all or only rarely to other titles.

By the second century, the title Saviour had gained currency and popularity, much more for Jesus than for God. It appears in the late New Testament epistles, in Ignatius, Polycarp and Gnostic writings of that period. Yet it is significant to note its absence from the *Didachē*, *Barnabas* and the *Shepherd of Hermas*.[5] Possibly in the same century

---

[4] W. Foerster, *op. cit.*, pp. 1013ff.
[5] Cf. W. Foerster, *op. cit.*, pp. 1018f.

it also made its integral appearance in the acrostic ΙΧΘΥΣ ('Ιησοῦς Χριστὸς Θεοῦ Υἱὸς Σωτήρ).[6]

From an early period of the church, Saviour has become the commonest and most important title for Jesus after that of Lord (and in some cases it is used more frequently than any other title). It is as such that it has come down to us through the centuries, and has been planted as part and parcel of the Christian message in African societies. It has been taken for granted in missionary work, so much so that the scripture translations into African languages are of 'The New Testament of our Lord and Saviour Jesus Christ', and the Gospel is preached as 'accepting Jesus Christ as my personal Saviour'. This essay will examine how African Christians seem to experience the meaning of 'Saviour' which has been made such an indispensable part of the Christian message, and which seems to be a much more personalizable title than 'Lord'. It seems that the missionary movement responsible for the modern spread of Christianity in Africa brought the title Saviour so fully established for Jesus (and much less so for God the Father), that for many Christians it is more or less a proper name like Jesus or Christ as much as it is a title.

2. 'SAVIOUR' IN AFRICAN BACKGROUND

In traditional African life the name or title Saviour is rarely used whether in connection with God or men, although God's acts of saving people from calamity, danger or death are commonly acknowledged. In this usage, God is the final resort, to whom people turn when all other means of help is exhausted. They solicit his intervention by calling on him through prayer and sacrifice. They also acknowledge his 'saving' response when the danger is over.

There is also a notion of salvation on a moral level, particularly in the dispensation of justice when man seems to flout justice and oppress the weak, or when the situation is such that man cannot pass a clear judgement. The case is then left to God as the final judge and dispenser of justice. This is often implied in covenant-making, taking oaths and in pronouncing formal curses.[7] The question of eschatological salvation

---

[6] F. L. Cross (ed.), *The Oxford Dictionary of the Christian Church* (London 1958), p. 506, points out that it is not known for certain whether the symbo gave rise to the acrostic or the acrostic to the symbol.

[7] For further information, see J. S. Mbiti, *Concepts of God in Africa* (London–New York, 1970), pp. 69f., *et passim*.

does not arise since African concepts of time lay emphasis on the present and the past, and do not accommodate any eschatological stretching of time.

In recent political history of Africa, some leaders have been called 'saviour' in admiration of what they did to rid their people of colonialism and exploitation. Only in one case, however, has an African leader adopted 'saviour' as a title for himself, and this was Kwame Nkrumah, former President of Ghana, who called himself *Osagyefo* (in Akan, literally 'One who saves the battle'). It is pointed out that the term was used as an honorific title for chiefs, and it has not been often used of Christ (except occasionally in lyrics and prayers, as honorific for God or Christ).[8]

On coming to African peoples, the Christian message found a well-established notion that God rescues people when all other help is exhausted, and that this rescue is primarily from material and physical dilemmas. God does not save because he is Saviour; rather, he becomes Saviour when he does save. The concept of saving is a dynamic one which is rooted in a particular moment of desperation.

It seems that this traditional African understanding of God's intervention to rescue people in desperation has continued to form much of the background to the way Christians understand and experience the notion of ὁ σωτὴρ ἡμῶν, an otherwise typically Christian term; and that, theologically, soteriological notions are either altogether eclipsed or only secondary in this African experience. The material for this investigation comes primarily from the so-called independent (or separatist) churches. It is within these churches that African Christians have more freely externalized their experience of the Christian faith than is otherwise the case in the mission-dominated or historical churches. In the latter, there is an obvious and often superficial endeavour to conform to orthodox missionary vocabulary and teaching, whether or not the people concerned actually understand the meaning of what they say. One leaves the possibility open that Christians in the historical churches have a more orthodox theological grounding; but they are under greater pressure to conform to 'the tradition of the (missionary) elders', and consequently it is not often clear what their true experience of the Christian faith might be.

[8] I am grateful to Professor Kwesi A. Dickson for a personal communication concerning the use of Osagyefo.

3. 'OUR SAVIOUR' IN AFRICAN CHRISTIANITY

The concept of ὁ σωτὴρ ἡμῶν is applied more or less indiscriminately to both Jesus and God, particularly as evidenced in the independent churches. This comes out in a number of ways, such as catechisms, prayers, hymns and the names by which these churches go. Their names imply the power of Jesus and God, which is the power to 'save' principally in a physical rather than spiritual dilemma.

Some examples of these names will illustrate the point. In Kenya alone there are Churches with the following names: 'Believed Power of Jesus Christ in Kenya', 'Children of God Regeneration Church', 'Christian Theocratic Holy Church of God', 'Church of the Almighty (Kenya)', 'Church of the Power of Jesus Christ', 'Power of Jesus Around the World Church', 'Church of Saviour's', 'Faith Miracle Church', 'Water of Life Church', 'Water and Holy Salvation Church', 'Wokofu (Salvation) African Church', and so on.[9] Elsewhere we have similar names, such as: 'Divine Healers Church' (Ghana), 'Église de la Foi en Messie Jésus-Christ' (Zaire, broken away from the Roman Catholic Church), 'Holy Flock of Christ' (Nigeria), 'Living Sheep Society' (Ghana, cf. the preceding name), 'Regeneration Church of Christ' (Nigeria, cf. a similar name in the Kenya listing above), 'Society for the Salvation of Souls' (Egypt, arising from the Coptic Orthodox Church in 1925, although it has never seceded as such), 'Society of the One Almighty God' (Uganda), 'Soldiers of God' (Rhodesia/Zimbabwe), 'Soldiers of Salvation' (Madagascar, but suppressed by French colonialists), 'Swazi Church God in Zion' (Swaziland), and many others.[10]

These names are significant, at least in an African setting where names often carry meanings. It is obvious that for the independent churches they summarize what the followers consider to be their most significant and central experiences of the Christian faith. The power of God is experienced in one's commitment to Christianity. This power of God causes no problem since in African religion it is one of the chief attributes of God. Therefore, to become a Christian is in effect to commit oneself to the almighty power of God and implicitly of Jesus; one does not lose by embracing the new faith. Indeed the power of God,

[9] D. B. Barrett (ed.), *Kenya Churches' Handbook* (Nairobi, 1972).
[10] D. B. Barrett, *Schism and Renewal in Africa* (Nairobi and Oxford, 1968), *passim*.

which is traditionally acknowledged, is, through faith in Christ, transformed or extended to be not only creative and governing power but also 'saving power'. God is then not only the almighty and powerful God, but also the saving God, since this is what he has demonstrated in and through Jesus, and since this is also the central message of Christianity as brought to us. God is 'our Saviour' because he is almighty, and not because of the act of Christ on the cross and his resurrection. Similarly, Jesus is 'our Saviour' as well, not so much because of the cross but because he is linked up with the God who, by virtue of his almightiness, can and does rescue or save the needy. It is as if the almightiness of God becomes personalized at the level of 'saving', 'rescuing' the individual.

Without this personalization of the power of God, 'Saviour' would otherwise be meaningless except as an attribute of admiration. It seems that Jesus is the one who facilitates or mediates this personalization of God's mighty power, and the personalization is experienced in terms of rescuing or saving individuals who subsequently constitute a particular (independent church) group.

The experience of God or Jesus as 'our Saviour' means not only being rescued but also being protected. This is evident from church names like 'Holy Flock of Christ', 'Christian Theocratic Holy Church of God', 'Believed Power of Jesus Christ in Kenya', 'Living Sheep Society', 'Soldiers of God' and so on. In effect this means that God's or/and Jesus' rescue is final and continuing. This idea parallels the African traditional notion that when all other help has failed, the needy is committed to God. The difference may only lie in the fact that, whereas in traditional life people turn to God as the final resort to rescue or save them, in the Christian experience the Saviour is both the first and final resort. Therefore in the Christian experience, one may enter through faith into a relationship with God or Jesus (or both) which guarantees an abiding and undiminishing state of rescue and protection. A Christian is, therefore, a member of those who have been 'rescued', and constitute a 'safe' flock which nothing can threaten since it is under the protection of personalized mightiness of God. They are the 'living sheep', the 'soldiers', the 'healed ones', the 'regenerated' ones, of God or Christ, ὁ σωτὴρ ἡμῶν.

Because of the Christian personalization of God's power, new symbols and metaphors have come into use which were either completely unknown or very rarely used in traditional African life. Such are the 'flock', 'living sheep', 'soldiers', 'society of God', 'God in Zion', 'divine healers', and so on, terms which describe the (new) relationship between people and God or Jesus. The relationship is possible only because both are 'our Saviour'. It is noteworthy in this connection that in one case the 'African Apostolic Church of Johane Maranke' (in Rhodesia) has substituted for the episcopal structure of church ranks, one which ranges from evangelist (the lowest office) rising through baptizer and prophet to healer.[11] This means that the highest ministerial office is one of healing, of keeping safe and secure. Consequently this is the peak of the Christian experience of God and Jesus as 'our Saviour'. Divine healing is an extension of the 'saving' benefits of God and Jesus.

Healing brings or increases life. For that reason, there are independent churches known as 'Water of Life Church', 'Water and Holy Salvation Church', 'Children of God Regeneration Church', 'Regeneration Church of Christ', 'Living Sheep Society', and so on. This is a major, if not central, outcome of coming into a faith relationship with 'our Saviour'. The question is not so much one of 'salvation from what', as it is 'salvation into what'. The answer is clearly that Christians are rescued or saved into a life, a life whose source and sustainer is God or Jesus 'our Saviour'.

Redeemed life is manifested corporately through the fellowship of members of each independent church. In that corporateness they 'feel at home'.[12] There are, therefore, many names of churches incorporating this idea of the shared life, the common life of those who have put their faith in 'our Saviour', such as: the 'Balokole' ('Saved Ones', found all over eastern Africa as a revival movement rather than a sect), 'God is our Light Church' (Sierra Leone), 'God's All Times Association' (Ethiopia), 'African Brotherhood Church' (Kenya), 'Holy Flock of Christ' (Nigeria), 'African God Covenant Brotherhood Church Society' (Kenya), 'Friends of the Holy Spirit' (Kenya), 'Negro Church of Christ' (Nigeria), 'Church of the Holy Apostles of the Lamb' (Kenya), 'Church of Holy Communion of God' (Kenya), 'Communion Church of Africa' (Kenya), and many others.

This fellowship or communion is derived from the common life rather than the celebration of the eucharist which is never or rarely

[11] D. B. Barrett, *op. cit.*, p. 177.
[12] This observation has been popularized by F. B. Welbourn, *East African Rebels* (London, 1961); F. B. Welbourn and B. A. Ogot, *A Place to Feel at Home* (London and Nairobi, 1966).

celebrated in many independent churches. To be a member of any of these churches is, *ipso facto*, to enter into a relationship of communion with other members and, jointly, to express the new life received through faith in 'our Saviour'. It is almost immaterial whether 'our Saviour' is God or Jesus, and in practice it is both, jointly and interchangeably. Indeed it is also to be noted that the Holy Spirit features prominently in the life and some names of the independent churches, and one may suspect that he too is regarded, when convenient, as 'our Saviour'.

But it is not only by the act of entry into membership of an independent church that people realize or experience the meaning of 'our Saviour'. The experience is ritualized and celebrated, giving it an ongoing continuity and renewal. A clear illustration may be cited from the Fang people of Gabon, where a Bwiti cult has been born out of Christian and African traditional ideas. Of this it is reported that 'the Bwiti view of the career and character of the Saviour accords with the qualities of leadership demanded in such a dynamic cult, where local cult leaders depend for their success on gathering and holding together nuclear cult membership'. They ritualize and hence re-enact the life of Jesus in an all night long ceremony and dance, because members of this cult 'find a certain inadequacy in quiet prayer, but feel, to the depths of their being, that he who knows the power of the dance dwells in God . . . For the first hours of the night they dance the birth of Christ (starting from 8 p.m.) and in the last hours they dance His death (ending at sunrise). It was Jesus, they say, as *emwan mot* – the Son of Man – who taught us how to be born and how to die, and we must forever celebrate these two intelligences that he brought us.' The dance forms are traditional African dances, but they have new content in their songs which recount the events of the birth and death of Christ. At Easter time, the passion of our Lord is dramatized in 'an exciting chase and capture of the Saviour before the "crucifixion". In this even Jesus is pictured as trembling at the knowledge of his death; and fearing about his compact with God he flees through the village cult chapel. He is chased by his "persecutors" in a big cry which lasts for about one hour.' To mark the birth of Jesus (the Saviour), they use a dance form traditionally used for women's fertility ceremony or annual village purification ceremonies. The re-enacting of his birth in the traditional setting no doubt dramatizes life's perpetuity, hence its safety, as wrought by the Saviour.

The account of ritualizing the Saviour continues by saying that 'in practically all the many dances of the all-night ceremony there is a central and leading dancer called *Nganga*. This is the Saviour. Sometimes he is lost to view as one of a swirling group of many dancers, at other times he leads the dance group, and at others he dances alone. Now he is being born, now he is leading a mock hunt for witches, now he is purifying the chapel or invoking the presence of the ancestors. Now he is being crucified. The *Nganga*, this central figure, is always Christ . . . But it is clear that he has a multiplicity of other meanings. For it is apparent that no man can be Saviour to the Banzie unless he also addresses himself to their preoccupations with the problems of fertility, witchcraft and purification. The figure of Christ in Bwiti ritual is a symbol that addresses itself to all these problems. The symbol is chiefly Christ, but it is a figure that also binds in itself all the many ancestral figures that have, like Christ, borne the burden of enabling the Fang, as men, to adjust to the new problems of their life and death.' For members of this cult, 'religious experience' is the feeling that comes upon them after an exhausting night of dancing.[13]

We cannot, obviously, draw generalizations from this one case. But studies of independent churches show that the ceremony and the ritual play a great role in the life of their members. This is a typical African religious trait of celebrating life. It is for this reason that, for example, they emphasize baptism, healing sessions, exorcisms and purification rituals, as well as the drumming, clapping, dancing, (spirit) possession and glossolalia, which go on in many of their religious services. This is acted rather than reflected theology, and it is through it that the concept of the Saviour seems most readily accessible to many African Christians. He has to be 'humanized' through being one of us, and this is most demonstrable in the ritualization of the events of Christ's life and his power to 'save' people in the context of their practical concerns.

4. ὁ σωτὴρ ἡμῶν – FROM WHAT?

It is impossible to treat an essay of this nature without asking ourselves 'from what' is the experience of 'salvation' most meaningful among African Christians. Earlier on we asserted that in fact the question is not uppermost in the minds of those who turn to the Christian faith.

[13] J. W. Fernandez, 'The idea and Symbol of the Saviour in a Gabon Syncretistic Cult', in *International Review of Missions* liii (1964), pp. 281–9.

The reason is that the issue is already faced in the traditional setting. People know the answers to such a question already, even before they hear and receive the Christian message – whether their answers are theologically adequate or not. For 'our Saviour' to be meaningful, he (whether God the Father or Jesus Christ) must be able to *deliver* from and keep away practical enemies to the life of the individual and the community. The people know these enemies; they have through their history tried to ward them off, to fight them off, to keep them at bay. Unless the Christian faith comes to assist them in this battle, it does not bring them the type of 'salvation' they want and appreciate. That which attacks, destroys, bridles, and protects against these enemies of life, is clearly salvatory. The enemies in traditional life are innumerable and include: sickness, witchcraft, sorcery, magic, barrenness, failure, troublesome spirits, danger, misfortune, calamity, and death, as far as the individual is concerned; and drought, war, oppression, foreign domination, slavery, locust invasion, epidemics, floods, and so on, as far as the wider community is concerned. These categories, obviously, overlap on both the personal and community levels.

African traditional religion is not a 'salvation' religion like Christianity and Islam. Therefore it has not evolved concepts of how one may ultimately be redeemed from these enemies of the individual and the community. This is left to 'random' acts of various kinds in which measures are taken as the need arises. For communal dilemmas, God (or some major divinity where the cosmology allows this) is invoked chiefly through sacrifices, offerings and prayers conducted by the ritual elders, priests and rain-makers. He is thus regarded, whether or not he is given the title, as 'redeemer' with reference to particular necessities.

For the individual, steps like anti-witchcraft measures, exorcisms, the use of traditional 'medicines' (where 'medicine' has to be understood in a broad sense to include physical, ritual and mystical measures), divination, offerings to the living dead (i.e. spirits of close relatives who have recently died up to four or five generations back, and are still remembered personally by living people who knew them), prevention and counter-measures, are taken, for which the local 'medicine' man features prominently as the agent of 'rescue' and 'prevention'. In a sense, therefore, the safety of the individual is not the immediate concern of God, since there are these other sources of help mediated through the 'medicine' man and the diviner. Only, or mainly, when the human-controlled or directed rescue seems to fail, is the 'hopeless' case brought before God either directly (through invoking him or sacrificing to him), or indirectly by taking it for granted that it is in his nature and concern to help 'if he wants'. An African proverb summarizes this concept: 'Katonda (God) redeems the afflicted according to his will.'[14]

In traditional life the situations are many which require the intervention of the rescuer, whether as a human-controlled agent or as God. Against such a background the Christian message was brought to African peoples, principally as a message of salvation. One response to it was that they would reject it if it did not penetrate to these areas, which, in their experience, required or called for 'salvation'. Another response was that they would accept it and force it to fit into that which needed 'redemptive' application. In the event, both responses are operative. The Christian message in Africa has been astonishingly welcome within the short period of less than one hundred years since modern missionary expansion into Africa, to such an extent that currently Christians in Africa are increasing at the rate of 6 per cent of the population per annum (of whom 2.5 per cent may be accounted for through the natural population growth, and 3.5 per cent through direct conversions). At this rate, Africa is destined to have an enormous Christian population of more than 350 million by the year A.D. 2000.[15]

African Christians are embracing the Christian message of redemption partly because of the ready-made traditional situations requiring salvation as they see it, and partly because they can apply their understanding of redemption to those needs and to new ones created by modern social, economic and political changes. The list of dangers has in fact increased since the introduction of Christianity to African societies, and hence the need for redemption has similarly grown stronger. A sociologist makes a relevant observation when, in writing on conversion, he says, 'it would appear, then, that the beliefs and practices of the so-called world religions are only accepted where they happen to coincide with responses of the traditional cosmology to other, non-missionary, factors of the modern situation'.[16]

[14] A. M. Lugira, 'Redemption in Ganda', in *Cahiers des Religions Africaines* iii, (1969), p. 18.
[15] For a fuller account of the prospects for Christianity in Africa, see D. B. Barrett and J. S. Mbiti, *The Future of Christianity in Africa* (New York, 1972).
[16] R. Horton, 'African Conversion', in *Africa* xli (1971), pp. 85–108; see p. 104.

There is ample evidence to indicate that the chief preoccupation of African Christians is 'redemption' from physical dilemmas. When the spiritual comes into the picture it is either secondary or only remotely subsequential. For this reason we have not touched the question of sin, since African experience of salvation is chiefly one of deliverance from physical evils or dilemmas. In a careful and thorough study of one of the independent churches, Aladura (in Nigeria and neighbouring countries), the investigator comes to the conclusion that the message of this church has not taken up 'the full seriousness of sin in men that could be dealt with only in this way' (of God's atonement through the Cross of Jesus).[17] The idea of deliverance is the commonest theme in the original hymnology of this church. It is deliverance from evil power, death, calamity, dangers, persecutions, witches, troubles (grief, fear, sorrow), sickness or pain, darkness, and so on; a category which is virtually the same as in pre-Christian life situations. It is also to be noted that some of the hymns address themselves to political deliverance of African peoples, a tendency found also elsewhere in African independent churches.

Even if the question of sin features a great deal in missionary or historical churches, it is highly doubtful that African Christians understand its centrality in the New Testament teaching about atonement and redemption. A great deal of what is said about being 'saved from sin' is simply a parrot-type indoctrination from the bringers of the Christian message. Converts appreciate more deliverance from the physical evils than anything else that would be in the nature of spiritual or moral depravity. Again this comes out clearly in the catechisms, hymns and prayers produced by independent churches, where Christians do not feel so much under pressure to conform to missionary expectations. Yet in no way should these statements be taken to mean that African Christians are conscious of redemption from sin; rather, they are more conscious of physical deliverance than of spiritual, even if the same Saviour saves them in both situations.

To show the efficacy of 'our Saviour', African Christians in both historical and independent churches sometimes swing to the extreme and almost magical inclination with which they reject other forms or sources of human remedy. For this reason the use of medicine (both traditional and 'European') is forbidden in many groups; among the

---

[17] H. W. Turner, *African Independent Church: the Life and Faith of the Church of the Lord (Aladura)*, ii (Oxford, 1967), p. 366.

'Balokole' (Saved Ones, still within their historical churches) it is held to be wrong (sinful) to take up insurance policies or keep dogs at home (since these imply a lack of full trust in the Saviour); many do away with consultation of diviners and doctors, while some even refuse to recognize earthly authorities of the state. As a further demonstration of the power of 'our Saviour', much emphasis is put on revelation (of the Saviour) through dreams and visions, exorcisms, miracles (especially of healing, whether real, attributed or alleged), public confessions and testimonies (concerning the wickedness of man versus the power of 'our Saviour'). Praying is taken as the access to the power of the Saviour (whether God or Jesus or both). In some independent churches, praying sessions by individuals or groups may last several hours. In some the members have to pray up to five times a day, including at such hours as three or four in the morning; fasting adds to the efficacy of prayer; generous giving of their goods and time is an asset in soliciting for help, and so on.

The demonstration of the power of the Saviour is often uppermost in the life and witness of many independent churches. This is summarized well by the first of the seven aims and duties of the 'Apostolic Revelation Society' (Ghana), which is to 'make known the supreme power of God by means of its work, miracles and signs'. Their final aim is to 'destroy fetishism and its wicked practices... by means of signs and miracles'.[18] Thus, the Saviour's power supersedes that of human agents, and the proof of that is signs and miracles. The 'Musama Disco Christo Church' (Ghana) has incorporated into its body of beliefs its invitation: 'Does Christ still heal today? Come and see'; and the church stands for precisely the demonstration of that certainty.[19] The 'Apostolic Revelation Society' (*supra*) observes the 'outdooring of children', whose three benefits are that 'the children should acknowledge God as their Father and Creator from their infancy', 'that they should be under the full care and protection of God', and 'that the parents of the children should be redeemed from the fear of those who can kill the body, the destruction of invisible evil spirits and undue worries'.[20]

Other examples could be cited to illustrate these ideas, but for our purpose we may be content to take note of the summary of the religious concepts in independent churches, that God is held to be 'the living

---

[18] C. G. Baëta, *Prophetism in Ghana* (London, 1962), pp. 159f.
[19] C. G. Baëta, *op. cit.*, p. 157.   [20] C. G. Baëta, *op. cit.*, p. 160.

God, the God of power, the God of miracles, the God of the impossible, the God of our ancestors'.[21] Only at that level is God unquestionably 'our Saviour', and it is immaterial (for many Christians) whether the Saviour is the Father or Jesus Christ. The Saviour is 'the God of the impossible', and the list of these impossibles is inexhaustible when put in the context of redeeming or rescuing needs.

Thus it is the experience of faith in the God of might and power, which mediates acts of redemption and salvation from those forces which work against the physical integrity of the individual and the believing community. Jesus is the human concentration of that divine power which heals the sick, casts out spirits, cleanses from sorcery and witchcraft, renews life, abolishes death, conquers and protects from all evil powers both human and cosmic. In effect the earthly ministry of Jesus, as directed to the physical needs of his audience, now spans two thousand years and becomes alive in African Christians, howbeit through faith in, rather than sight of, the redeemer.

5. CONCLUSION

Although this survey has not concerned itself with a comparative use of the titles 'Saviour' and 'Lord' in African Christianity, it is relevant to point out that, of the two commonest titles for Jesus Christ, 'Saviour' (*Sōtēr*) has far greater meaning than that of 'Lord' (*Kyrios*). *Sōtēr* is personalizable in concrete and demonstrable ways, but that is not the case with *Kyrios*. Therefore African Christians are more attracted by, and interested in, Jesus (or God) as Saviour than as Lord. One can say: 'Jesus saved me from . . .' whereas it is more or less meaningless to say 'Jesus lords me in . . .'. 'Our Saviour is a dynamic, practical and experiential title, whereas in comparison, 'Our Lord' is static, academic and conceptual. Given these two, Saviour has definitive termini which are absent from or unclear in Lord, particularly those of 'salvation from' and 'salvation to'. Saviour is, consequently, a far more common attribute of Jesus and God, among African Christians, than perhaps any other title. This contrasts strongly with the New Testament position in which 'Saviour' is so sparingly used. Did the need for personalizing the work of Christ eventually lead to greater currency of the title 'Saviour' in the post-New Testament history of

[21] D. B. Barrett, *op. cit.*, p. 274.

the church, a need which is not satisfied by the concept of the 'Lordship' of Christ? At any rate African Christians seem to opt more readily for a limited kind of *Sōtēr* christology than *Kyrios* christology, whether or not they understand either or both, and in spite of the theological fact that there can be no effective soteriology without the Lordship of Christ.

Daily and physical concerns of survival seem to have driven African Christians to see and experience 'our Saviour' in the role of a physical rescuer and redeemer. That practical deviation has eclipsed the centrality of sin and the work of atonement as wrought by Christ. This is clearly evident in the independent churches, but we may suspect it to be the same also in mission or historical churches. It is summed up well by Baëta, who writes that:

while such terms as 'sin', 'grace', 'the precious blood of our Lord and Saviour Jesus Christ', and other Christian themes are constantly spoken about, the central preoccupation is and remains how to cope effectively with the ills of worldly life. 'Sin' is really relevant only in so far as it is a potent cause of bodily, mental, and social disorders. The significance of 'the blood of Christ' resides in the fact that, by doing away with sin, it prepares the way for, or itself directly effects, bodily healing... The 'gospel' here may be summed up in the actual words of a very typical separatist church public invitation: 'Bring all your worries of unemployment, poverty, witch troubles, ill-luck, enemy, barrenness, sickness, blindness, lameness, sorrow. Jesus is ready to save all who come to him in belief and faith (Rev. 22: 17; John 6: 37b).'[22]

But this subjection of Christian salvation to physical needs is not confined to independent churches. A veteran missionary reports the same in areas where missionaries were still in control and had preached the orthodox meaning of salvation: 'what the Congolese seeks in the new religion is not a merciful God, but rather a powerful God, who has the power to secure for him happiness on earth. Moreover, he thinks this quite sincerely, for to him salvation is in fact good health, a long life, prosperous offspring, an abundance of possessions, etc. . . . All pagan [one of the missionary offensives!] Africans have understood the preaching of salvation in this way. For them salvation was not a salvation of the soul, but something which made life secure here below,

[22] C. G. Baëta, 'Conflict in Mission: Historical and Separatist Churches', in G. H. Anderson (ed.), *The Theology of the Christian Mission* (London, 1962), pp. 293f.

namely bodily health, happiness in this life, prosperity, success in all undertakings. Misunderstandings of the term "salvation" leave many traces in conversions to Christianity.'[23]

But it must be pointed out that even if the concept of 'our Saviour' is directed first and foremost to physical, present-day situations of life, African Christians have a keen interest in the safety of individual life in the hereafter. Indeed, this is perhaps for them the most significant consequence of accepting the Christian message of salvation. In traditional religion, continuity of life after death is purely mechanical, without any element of 'salvation' to it, and eventually the individual turns into an *it*, thus losing his real personation (rather than personality). But Christian salvation ensures that the safeness received in this physical life is guaranteed even beyond death; the individual survives in his totality, safe and well, protected from all forces that would endanger his wholeness. Thus, African Christians retain in their faith an element of soteriological eschatology, however much it may be a distortion of New Testament eschatology and soteriology. The concept of the kingdom of God, however, is too elusive and abstract; and the same applies to other terms popular in traditional Christian piety, such as 'communion with God', sharing in the 'holiness of God', seeing the 'beatific vision', and so on.

It is clear also that for African Christians 'our Saviour' is a term readily interchangeable between God and Jesus, and sometimes the Holy Spirit. In a saving capacity, Jesus mediates and universalizes the almightiness of God. While in African religion, God is regarded as being able to save or rescue as a last resort, in Christianity the popularization of God as 'Saviour' has meant that in effect the net has been spread far and wide, both in this life and the next, so that 'our Saviour' is able to do all things, to save in all situations, to protect against all enemies, and is available whenever those who believe may call upon him.

One obvious consequence of this interchangeability of usage is that the atoning of Christ's passion is excluded or eclipsed, and the question of sin is minimized. In effect salvation (so understood) is possible without the cross, since this comes about chiefly through the application or availability of God's mighty power to do the impossible. If such be the situation, and the evidence points in that direction, then African

---

[23] E. Andersson, *Churches at the Grass-roots: a study in Congo-Brazzaville* (London, 1968), pp. 148–9.

Christianity may be seriously defective in its (applied) christology. It calls for a thorough re-examination of both the methods and contents of evangelization in Africa, and a deeper appreciation (not necessarily approval) of the traditional African world, whose grip is so strong that it exercises a powerful influence on the manner of understanding and experiencing the Christian message, however that message may be presented to the people.

The concept of the Saviour is probably the most comprehensive in the Christian faith as it has come to, and been received by, African peoples. It stands out above all other aspects of Jesus, even if it is applied also to God the Father and sometimes to the Holy Spirit. But it is more than a concept, it is also a living constant to which final reference is made in the past, the present and the future. In the past as far as the life of Jesus is concerned, where 'miracles' of healing, 'saving', protecting, rescuing, exorcisms, driving out evil spirits, calming the storm, raising the dead, and so on, are sure examples confirming His role as Saviour. In the present in that God and/or Jesus, as 'our Saviour', continues to hear the prayers of the faithful, demonstrates his power in healing, visions, dreams, and so on, particularly in independent churches, many of which claim such miracles and experiences. In the future because if there is a future, he is above it, he will save in whatever situation that future brings, since he is powerful; and people do not fear for that future since their experience of him in the present is an absolute guarantee that he will not fail them.

This figure of the Saviour, whom western scholarship has endeavoured to strip naked by its relentless demythologization exercises, still reaches African hearts and souls only through the shroud of mythological image which does not even distinguish whether he is God or Jesus Christ. The preaching continues to be about Jesus Christ 'our Lord and Saviour'; but the experience is of both God and Jesus as 'our Saviour'. We cannot afford to trim him too thin, otherwise we make him unrecognizable and unheedable for the many whose theology is non-existent but who, nevertheless, experience him in a real saving and redeeming encounter. Perhaps it is only through the myth that he can be so effectively communicated, believed, honoured and hoped for. What inner contents may be found within those mythical wrappings are, and indeed can only be, a private affair in the long run. Consequently, who precisely 'our Saviour' is, can only be answered in the experience of the believer and through the illumination of the Holy Spirit. And in African religion the mythical and mystical is often more valid, more solid, more tenable, than that which is otherwise too explicit and exposed. Indeed, African Christians perhaps experience 'our Saviour' more readily in the capacity of his myth and mystique, than they would if they had a more historical grasp of Jesus and a spiritualized conception of salvation.

27

The moral context of the resurrection faith

DONALD T. ROWLINGSON

Amos N. Wilder has pointed out the tendency in much current thinking to substitute pagan ideas of *apotheosis* for Christian views of *resurrection*, which in effect 'isolates the resurrection of Christ from its moral context and from the whole drama of salvation in which we are involved'.[1] John Knox has stated the historical issue implied here by asserting that 'it was the moral personality of Jesus and the character of his life as these were known and remembered which alone made the death significant and the resurrection possible'.[2] Neither of these scholars has any intention of minimizing the fact that the step across the bridge from the human career of Jesus to the risen Christ is 'neither easy nor automtica';[3] they are intent upon countering a tendency so to emphasize the fact of discontinuity that the fact of continuity is attenuated, at the same time supplying what is called 'the basis of faith' with adequate substance.[4]

With the interests of this volume in view, it is in order to point out the sympathy of Professor Moule with this direction of thought. He has said that the Christian claim was not that just anyone had been raised from the dead, but that 'this superbly good man, Jesus, whom they [the disciples] had known and watched, and by whom they found their own lives at once condemned and inspired . . . had come beyond death absolutely. The content of his life and teaching are, in that sense, highly relevant to the central affirmation of the resurrection'.[5] This is reinforced by any number of indirect statements in the writings of Professor Moule. Typical of these is the view, under the heading of 'the intention of the evangelists', that 'the real core of worship was the experience of the risen Christ within the Christian church through participation in the Spirit', but that the early Christians, fully aware

[1] A. N. Wilder, *Otherworldliness and the New Testament* (New York, 1954), p. 96.
[2] J. Knox, *The Death of Christ* (New York, 1958), p. 132. Cf. *The Church and the Reality of Christ* (New York, 1962), pp. 55ff.
[3] H. Anderson, *Jesus and Christian Origins* (New York, 1964), p. 186.
[4] Cf. G. Ebeling, *The Nature of Faith* (Philadelphia, 1961), pp. 58ff.
[5] 'Is Christ Unique?', in C. F. D. Moule and others, *Faith, Fact and Fantasy* (London, 1964), p. 119.

of the difference between the pre- and post-resurrection situations, made it their aim 'to try to tell faithfully the story of how the former led to the latter'.[6]

It will be recognized that this question of moral context also arises at many points in the current debate among German scholars about the resurrection, as reviewed critically by Hans-Georg Geyer in a volume edited by Professor Moule.[7] The focus of attention in Geyer's essay is not the question of the fact of the resurrection which tends to dominate present discussion, with its concern for problems of empty tomb, appearances, and the like in the resurrection narratives. It is rather what is taken to be the primary issue, namely, the significance which the resurrection had in its original context. The precise point of reference, contextually speaking, differs in the views represented as between the cross (Barth and Bultmann), the words and deeds of Jesus (Marxsen and Ebeling), the apocalyptic expectation of the general resurrection and the final judgement (Pannenberg), or a combination of these (Wilckens and others). Whether emphatically and explicitly or not, the relevance of the moral context question is implied by most of these scholars, Bultmann excepted, as well as by others not treated by Geyer when the question of the 'basis of faith' is in focus.

The purpose of this essay is confined to an examination of the New Testament evidence for the moral context view; more precisely, considering the limits of space, of typical samples of that evidence in order to suggest lines along which the subject may profitably be treated. Before proceeding to that task, however, let us attempt to define precisely what the issue is. Stating it as baldly as Knox does, can we believe that the resurrection faith would have come into being without a profound appreciation of the moral quality of Jesus' life on the part of those who experienced and proclaimed that faith? Or, once again, granting the influence of several contextual factors, was appreciation of the quality of Jesus' character the *one* substantial factor without which the coming into being of the resurrection faith is inconceivable?

A reference to the view of Frederick Herzog may further clarify the question. As he sees it, neither the crucifixion nor the resurrection, taken simply as a historical fact, is self-explanatory. They make sense,

6 *The Phenomenon of the New Testament* (London, 1967), pp. 110f. Cf. also 'Jesus in New Testament Kerygma', in O. Böcher and K. Haacker (ed.), *Verborum Veritas* (Wuppertal, 1970), pp. 15–26.
7 C. F. D. Moule (ed.), *The Significance of the Message of the Resurrection for Faith in Jesus Christ* (Naperville, Ill. and London, 1968), pp. 105–35.

he believes, only as a unity 'interpreted by the reality to which they point'; that is, to God.[8] If we grant this as a reasonable assumption consistent with the New Testament perspective, the question then takes the form of whether a conviction about God's action can really be conceived as arising in the thought of the disciples unless they already had a predisposition to accept such a conclusion because of the impression of moral grandeur which Jesus had made upon them.

This points to the real issue as the New Testament evidence poses it. It is not so much the contrast between apotheosis and resurrection as it is the conflict between a mysterious action of God of a purely formal, even autocratic and coercive, nature and, over against that, one governed by moral values, in this case the moral worthiness of Jesus (implying the moral consistency of God). A large segment of the New Testament evidence can conceivably be interpreted in the former way, such as the idea of Jesus' being 'delivered up according to the definite plan and foreknowledge of God' (Acts 2: 23), the δεῖ of the passion predictions (Mark 8: 31, *al.*), much scriptural apologetic (including 1 Cor. 15: 3–4), and the idea of pre-existence in most of the christological hymns. Explicitly at least, nothing is said in these forms of thought about the moral worthiness of Jesus for the honours bestowed upon him in resurrection/exaltation. The viable question is whether or not there is sufficient evidence to take seriously the moral factor in the New Testament as a whole. Let us proceed to examine the evidence.

Evidence which explicitly relates Jesus' moral worthiness to the resurrection faith is a very small island in a very wide sea. Phil. 2: 8–9 and the letter to the Hebrews stand almost alone in this respect. The familiar facts may be briefly reviewed. Within the framework of so-called 'adoptionist' christological passages, the 'therefore' (διό) of Phil. 2: 9 appears to require some effective relationship in Paul's thought between Jesus' humility and obedience in his human career and his exaltation (resurrection being presupposed), although this dynamic connection appears in the context of an understanding of humility in the form of christological speculation (verses 5–7). Logically, of course, Jesus cannot become 'obedient unto death' without first having relinquished his heavenly status through the kenotic act; but, assuming that, the 'cross' can only refer to a historical event. Whatever exegetical and theological difficulties there may be in this passage, there is no way of avoiding that fact. Other 'adoptionist' references, such as Acts

[8] F. Herzog, *Understanding God* (New York, 1966), p. 63.

2: 36 and Rom. 1: 3, are neutral so far as the moral dimension is concerned. Rom. 1: 3 probably says much more about Jesus being 'designated Son of God' (RSV) on the basis of a prior status (as in John 1: 14 also) than about his adoption at the time of being raised from the dead. The Philippians passage includes this implication, but it goes beyond Rom. 1: 3 to make obedience 'unto death' the (or one) qualification for being 'exalted'.

In the letter to the Hebrews the quality of the earthly life of Jesus is absolutely essential to his preparation and qualifications for heavenly high priesthood, with some affinity between 'crowned with glory and honour because of the suffering of death' (2: 9) and Phil. 2: 9 (cf. also Heb. 2: 10; 5: 8f., *al.*). As in Philippians, resurrection is absorbed into the category of exaltation, and the qualifying idea of pre-existence is also in the picture (Heb. 1: 1ff.). Despite this qualification, since we have two independent ideas which are not fully co-ordinated, these two passages, in part at least, support the moral context view.

The issue really lies with the implications of a series of facts characteristic of the New Testament portraits of Jesus Christ which do not specifically link moral worthiness with resurrection faith, what may be called 'unintentional data'. The first of these is the way in which two images of Jesus, or better, two dimensions of the one person, are consistently held in tension. As Professor Moule has expressed it, having in focus criteria operative in the selection of writings for the canon: 'Any estimate of Jesus which did not acknowledge his historical existence and his real death would be out; so would any which did not acknowledge the resurrection and ... the absolute "transcendence" of Jesus.'[9] In other words, the extremes both of docetism and of ebionism were excluded. Expressed more directly with reference to our precise concern, the 'hallelujah chorus' of christological acclaim which permeates the New Testament portraits, in Gospels and Epistles alike, has as its object not an abstract idea or a mythical figure (despite mythological features), but 'this Jesus' who, mixing our texts, became 'obedient unto death' at a specific time and place in history – 'under Pontius Pilate'.

An examination of what this means for the resurrection appearances is relevant here not only for what they are in themselves, but also for what it implies for other features of the total resurrection tradition. The im-

---

[9] C. F. D. Moule, *The Birth of the New Testament* (New York and London, 1962), pp. 155f.

pression is that, in reacting as they did to (or in) the appearances of Jesus, the disciples, however confused and frightened they may have been, were not reacting as spectators to an official announcement from God without some previous experiential awareness of the intrinsic worth of the one designated. The appearances apparently were confined to those who could meet this condition. That is, there is no evidence that God saw fit to satisfy the request for a 'sign' on the part of Jesus' opponents in the form of appearances to them. If the appearance of the risen Christ to Paul is more ambiguous in this respect, it can still be argued that he was not entirely unprepared for the happening, if not precisely in the same way as Peter. Furthermore, the intensely personal nature of the appearances to Peter and his companions involved a loving and loyal response to one who had proved himself worthy of such a response, being, as it were, an enlightened and intensive continuation of a reaction previously experienced. Whether the resurrection narratives in the Gospels represent early or late tradition, or, more likely, a combination of both, whether or not 'resurrection' is but 'one interpretation among others',[10] this moral facet stands out. If this is not proof, it is at least reasonable inference within the framework of the continuity aspect of the New Testament portraits of Jesus Christ.

The second fact is the united testimony on the part of believers to the moral quality of Jesus, even when the portraits include more formal qualifications for his appointment and exaltation by God. Evidence is abundant, including references to his 'sinlessness' (1 John 3: 5; Heb. 4: 15; 2 Cor. 5: 21), his obedience and faithfulness (e.g., Rom. 5: 18f.; Phil. 2: 8f.; Heb. 2: 9; 5: 8; John 12: 50), his victory in situations of testing (Mark 1: 12–13 par.; 14: 32–42 par. as well as Heb. 4: 15), and much else. So certain is the New Testament of this that, generally speaking, it is taken for granted. The kind of question that arises about the implications of his baptism in the Gospel according to the Hebrews does not bother the canonical evangelists. If anything, the tendency is to shy away from the full implications of Jesus' humanity, that he could sin, as when Paul speaks ambiguously of Jesus' being born 'in the likeness of sinful flesh' (Rom. 8: 2); and the writer of Hebrews, in listing comparatively the qualifications of the High Priest, subtly omits the need of Jesus to make sacrifice for his own sins (5: 1–10).[11]

[10] Cf. W. Marxsen, *The Resurrection of Jesus* (Philadelphia, 1970), pp. 138ff.
[11] Cf. John Knox, *The Humanity and Divinity of Christ* (Cambridge, 1967), pp. 48, 51.

Appeals to Jesus' example for guidance and inspiration are relevant here. A few such 'straws' appear in the Epistles, for example, the one use of ὑπογραμμός in the New Testament (1 Pet. 2: 21) and the picture of Jesus as ἀρχηγός and τελειωτής in Heb. 12: 1–2. Inferences in this respect may well exist in Paul's reference to the directives of 'the Lord' about divorce (1 Cor. 7: 10f.), in his constant attention to the cross, and elsewhere.[12] If Professor Moule's view is correct, and we believe it is, Phil. 2: 5–11 (cf. 2 Cor. 8: 9 also) taken as a whole is an exhortation to follow the example of Jesus.[13]

Of course this emphasis is most evident in the Synoptic Gospels. If concern to set Jesus forth as guide and inspiration to faith does not exhaust the motives of the evangelists, it cannot reasonably be ignored within the total complex of Gospel tradition. Amos Wilder speaks convincingly to this point: 'The Christ-story in the four Gospels safeguarded the new people against intoxication and pride. On the other hand, when the church began to realize the costs of sustaining its way of life in the Empire, the Gospels evoked the needed model.'[14] This fact stands even when we view the Gospels as completely identifying risen Christ and earthly Jesus, as some do.[15] The 'greater works' to be performed by the disciples in John (14: 12), among other things, link the Fourth Gospel with the Synoptics in this respect.

Much is implied with respect to the moral context of the resurrection faith by this emphatic interest of the New Testament in Jesus' character. With this heavy emphasis upon Jesus' moral quality in other respects, it is at least strange, inexplicable in fact, if the resurrection faith itself is the exception to the rule. Logically at least, the resurrection faith can only be considered of vital significance to the degree that it is encompassed within this frame of reference.

As a third fact, the significance of the cross as 'an act of liberation' (Rom. 3: 24, NEB) could have been discussed under previous headings,

---

[12] Cf. D. T. Rowlingson, *The Gospel-Perspective on Jesus Christ* (Philadelphia, 1968), pp. 147–50; V. P. Furnish, 'The Jesus–Paul Debate: From Baur to Bultmann', *BJRL* xlvii (1964–5), pp. 372ff.

[13] Cf. C. F. D. Moule, 'Further Reflections on Philippians 2: 5–11', in W. W. Gasque and R. P. Martin (ed.), *Apostolic History and the Gospel* (Exeter, 1970), pp. 265f.

[14] A. N. Wilder, *The Language of the Gospel* (New York, 1964), p. 78. Cf. also E. Käsemann, 'Sackgassen im Streit um den historischen Jesus', in *Exegetische Versuche und Besinnungen* ii (Göttingen, 1964), pp. 31–68.

[15] Cf. N. Perrin, *Rediscovering the Teaching of Jesus* (New York and London, 1967), p. 26.

but it deserves separate treatment. Except for Phil. 2: 8–9 and Hebrews, as we have observed, the worthiness of Jesus is assumed without direct reference to the resurrection or else the latter is portrayed without specifying the former. This is true of much that Paul has to say about the cross, of references in 1 Peter (2: 21; 3: 18) and Hebrews (12: 1–2), of the worthiness of the Lamb in the Apocalypse (5: 9f.), and the like. We have previously noted that, like much scriptural apologetic, the δεῖ of the Synoptic passion predictions (Mark 8: 31, *al.*) has a certain formal quality without necessarily involving the moral worthiness of the Son of Man. However, a moral factor enters the picture by inference from Daniel 7 when 'one like a Son of man' is taken to mean the remnant which is exalted because of faithfulness in persecution.[16] Furthermore, to the extent that sacrificial ideas are involved in the interpretation of Jesus' death, in the New Testament perspective the prerequisite of the cultic purity of the victim easily becomes transmuted into moral purity (as in 4 Macc. 5: 37; 7: 4). Something of the same thing can be said of the Suffering Servant precedent, although it is infrequently employed in New Testament thought (cf. Mark 10: 45).

With these indicators of much else in the New Testament picture of the cross in view, is it reasonable to interpret them in the light of Phil. 2: 8–9 as containing for the early Christians generally an essential connection between Jesus' moral quality as epitomized in the cross and the resurrection faith? At least it has not been satisfactorily explained how the cross can be viewed as the 'eschatological event' if this factor is omitted.

The last fact concerns the meaning of the whole eschatological background, especially its apocalyptic forms, as a context for determining the significance of the message of the resurrection. Two observations appear to be in order. First, the idea of 'first fruits' in 1 Corinthians (15: 20, 23) says something about the quality of him who is so designated, as well as about the form of the resurrection faith. This is so even if 'Christ' in these verses has something of a collective connotation consistent with the fact that elsewhere 'first fruits' refers to Christians (Rom. 8: 23; 11: 16; Rev. 14: 4). The moral factor enters into this conception of 'first fruits' in the idea of moral judgement which is inherently involved. With all its infinite variety of ideas, the apocalyptic thrust was at its core an answer to the problem of evil in terms of a vindication not simply of God's arbitrary will, but of his justice and his love.

[16] Cf. M. D. Hooker, *The Son of Man in Mark* (London, 1967), pp. 107–14.

This view of God as paradoxically both just and loving in absolute terms permeates the teaching of Jesus, of Paul, and of early Christians in general, and this hardly permits us to think that the early Christian thinkers could have been content with a purely formal conception of predestination with respect to the raising of Jesus from the dead and his victory over death and sin. A scale of values was inherently involved, although, as in John's Gospel and elsewhere, the moral factor may seem to be obscured somewhat by more formal factors of pre-existence and sending from above. In the basic meaning of the eschatological hope, namely, that God was acting redemptively in moral terms, there was the implication that the raising up of Jesus by God said much about Jesus' ethical worthiness as a pre-condition.

The second observation with regard to the apocalyptic context of the resurrection faith concerns the fact that fundamental to it was the conviction of the vindication of 'this Jesus'. If there is confusion as to how precisely 'visitation' or parousia and 'vindication' are related each to the other, there is no doubt that the latter is the primary ingredient of the resurrection faith.[17] As has been indicated, this may conceivably be envisaged as a formality, as the act of God by which he arbitrarily crowns his Messiah-designate just because, while mysterious to finite creatures, that has been his purpose from the beginning. Essentially this means God's vindication without saying very much about Jesus. In the light of much that has previously been said about the moral worth of Jesus as pictured in the New Testament, combined with the view of God's redemptive purpose, it is hard to believe that the early Christians would have been content with a formality of faith with regard to the vindication of Jesus. In order for that conviction to have been fully meaningful the moral element must have had a primary significance.

This concludes our sampling of the relevant evidence. Obviously much is left unsaid, but, for the purpose of this essay, enough has been said to indicate a proper procedure for analysing the question. In addition, taken as a whole, the evidence yields a high degree of probability to the moral context view, even when it is recognized that, within the total complex of early Christian thought on the subject, morally neutral factors are also prominent. With regard to these different dimensions of the subject, the situation was probably analogous to that which Professor Moule has shown to have been the case with regard to *kerygma* and *didache*; that is, rather than being completely sealed off

[17] Cf. J. A. T. Robinson, *Jesus and His Coming* (London, 1957), pp. 39ff.

in air-tight compartments, they interpenetrated in both Gospels and Epistles.[18] Even so, there is a primary, foundational character to be attributed to the moral factor which is not characteristic of the more speculative by-products of efforts on the part of Christians to make the meaning of their experience of Christ intelligible in thought-forms relevant to several different sets of circumstances.[19]

On this premise, while in Paul's thought in Phil. 2: 6–11 kenosis logically precedes crucifixion, actually the former can only be a by-product of a historical event which was of such a nature that it forced speculation about the moral quality of the person involved. The same holds true of Mark's very different solution of the dilemma of the cross, namely, the idea of secret messiahship. Still another example of the priority of the historical, and thus of the moral, factors is the view of John's Gospel held by C. H. Dodd[20] and J. A. T. Robinson in which, to employ the words of the latter, 'the metaphysics came later', in an effort not to detract from the factuality of the event, but to allow it 'to be seen in its ultimate depth and significance'.[21] We may also take note of the idea that the Paraclete in John is patterned on Jesus, Jesus being 'the first Paraclete in his earthly ministry'.[22] These are but indications of a view which appears to be the reasonable meaning of a series of New Testament characteristics relative to the question of the moral context of the resurrection faith.

It is not part of our purpose to deal in any detail with the question of the value of this historical perspective for modern Christian faith. However, it is in order to point out something of the relationship between our selective interest and a quest of the historical Jesus in general within the context of the question of history and faith, or, in terms of the title of Van A. Harvey's very discriminating book on the subject, of *The Historian and the Believer*.[23] We confine our attention to the very practical concern of how the Christian gospel is to be made

[18] C. F. D. Moule, *The Birth of the New Testament*, pp. 130ff.
[19] Cf. C. F. D. Moule, 'The Influence of Circumstances on the Use of Christological Terms', *JTS* n.s. x (1959), pp. 247–63; J. Knox, *The Humanity and Divinity of Christ*, Chapter 1.
[20] C. H. Dodd, *The Interpretation of the Fourth Gospel* (Cambridge, 1953), p. 283.
[21] J. A. T. Robinson, 'The Relation of the Prologue to the Gospel of St John', *NTS* ix (1962–3), pp. 128f.
[22] R. E. Brown, 'The Paraclete in the Fourth Gospel', *NTS* xiii (1966–7), pp. 126f.
[23] Van A. Harvey, *The Historian and the Believer* (New York, 1969), esp. pp. 9–19, 246–89.

credible to empirically-oriented modern people for whom the problem of 'credibility gap' is as pertinent in the religious as in the political arena. In this respect the option which was open to people before the rise of modern Biblical criticism, namely, the mediation of the content of faith through myths of a certain kind ('The Biblical Christ'), is less viable today. If for some this is still an avenue to the truth of faith, however demythologized, for others, as Harvey says, 'the call to faith may be made far more powerful . . . if interpreted in terms of the memory-image of Jesus'.[24]

Certain practical considerations reinforce this view. It appears to be a fact that 'human beings only seem to decide concerning the truth about life in general when they are confronted by a life in particular'.[25] Eduard Schweizer is speaking to this point when he says that 'since man is no computer, but a being of flesh and blood, he needs the manifestation of God's revelation in flesh and blood to continue believing, that is, following Jesus'.[26] This takes realistically our need of inspiration as well as light, and it is also at least a partial answer to the view that it is sufficient to consider Jesus as a symbol of some timeless truth.

Also, since there is a historical component in all knowing, whether recognized or not, every Christian presupposes some historical image of Jesus, be it naïve or sophisticated. If this kind of knowledge is adequately to influence Christian faith today, it would appear that Professor Moule is correct in saying that before we can decide for Jesus we need to discover 'what manner of man he was, how he was related to his antecedents, why he died, and what (so far as it can be indicated) lies behind the conviction that he is alive'.[27] This indicates something of the close relationship between the last of these items, which is the subject of this essay, and other items which inform the quest of the historical Jesus.

This is not to say that it is enough to know Jesus Christ κατὰ σάρκα (2 Cor. 5: 16). It is not to deny an open-endedness to revelation through the Holy Spirit which takes us way beyond a legalistic dependence upon Jesus' earthly image. It is to say that we need the kinds of contributions which Norman Perrin says the historical image can offer to Christian faith today. That is, it can give content to the faith-image of Christ; it can help in the formulation of criteria by

[24] *Ibid.*, p. 281.
[25] *Ibid.*, p. 288.
[26] E. Schweizer, 'Mark's Contribution to the Quest of the Historical Jesus', *NTS* x (1963–4), p. 432.
[27] C. F. D. Moule, *The Phenomenon of the New Testament*, p. 79.

means of which to test the validity of various forms of 'Christian' proclamation; and, under certain conditions, it can open the door to a more direct application of Gospel materials to situations today despite the gap between the first century and our own.[28]

All this, of course, presupposes that it is reasonable to believe that with some measure of success we can reconstruct an authentic historical image of Jesus of Nazareth. The complex problems involved are patent, and they cannot be investigated here. Without minimizing them, however, it is reasonable to believe that a judicious analysis of the memory-impressions in the Gospels by means of historical method, amounting to an 'interpretation of the interpretations', can yield sufficient knowledge to meet the need. The least that can be said is that the risk of historical decision is greater in some areas than in others (for example, with regard to the birth of Jesus as against segments of his teaching and actions and his crucifixion); that on certain fundamental characteristics of Jesus' religious and ethical loyalties and actions there is a high degree of consensus among scholars of varied theological persuasions, including Bultmann to some extent; that we do not need to solve all the historical puzzles in order to have confidence in that much, which is precisely what we most need to know.[29] It is simply avoiding the issue to exaggerate the disagreement among historical scholars on many things. At least, if we consider *Jesus* relevant to Christian faith, we cannot avoid the risk of historical decisions about him, since this is inherent in the venture of faith itself.

Summing up, whether we concentrate on the question of the moral context of the resurrection faith in particular or on that of the historical Jesus in general, whether we approach the New Testament as historian or believer (hopefully as both), we cannot avoid some judgement, explicitly or implicitly, about the 'moral personality' of Jesus and 'the character of his life'. With the problem of the credibility of the Christian gospel in focus, it is difficult to imagine a more important question with reference to the decision of faith. To make such an affirmation is not to say that it alone is important, but only that the both–and nature of the relevant data should be recognized.[30]

---

[28] *Op. cit.*, pp. 242–8.   [29] Cf. V. A. Harvey, *op. cit.*, Chapter 8.

[30] L. E. Keck, *A Future for the Historical Jesus* (Nashville and New York, 1971) appeared too late for assistance in thinking through the subject of this essay. In my judgement, it is an extremely convincing argument for the point of view of this essay with regard both to its specific thesis (cf. pp. 129–31, 187ff., 232ff.) and to the question of the indispensability of the historical Jesus for Christian faith.

Index of Bible References

APOCRYPHA

NEW TESTAMENT